4

MARRIAGE AND FAMILY 95/96

Twenty-First Edition

Editor

Kathleen R. Gilbert
Indiana University

Kathleen Gilbert is an associate professor in the Department of Applied Health Science at Indiana University. She received her B.A. in Sociology and her M.S. in Marriage and Family Relations from Northern Illinois University. Her Ph.D. in Family Studies is from Purdue University. Gilbert's primary areas of interest are loss and grief family context, trauma and the family, family process, minority families. She has published several books articles in these ar

Cover illustration by Mike

7

The Annual Editions Series

Annual Editions is a series of over 65 volumes designed to provide the reader with convenient, low-cost access to a wide range of current, carefully selected articles from some of the most important magazines, newspapers, and journals published today. Annual Editions are updated on an annual basis through a continuous monitoring of over 300 periodical sources. All Annual Editions have a number of features designed to make them particularly useful, including topic guides, annotated tables of contents, unit overviews, and indexes. For the teacher using Annual Editions in the classroom, an Instructor's Resource Guide with test questions is available for each volume.

VOLUMES AVAILABLE

Africa
Aging
American Foreign Policy
American Government
American History, Pre-Civil War
American History, Post-Civil War
Anthropology
Archaeology
Biology
Biopsychology
Business Ethics
Canadian Politics
Child Growth and Development
China
Comparative Politics
Computers in Education
Computers in Business
Computers in Society
Criminal Justice
Developing World
Drugs, Society, and Behavior
Dying, Death, and Bereavement
Early Childhood Education
Economics
Educating Exceptional Children
Education
Educational Psychology
Environment
Geography
Global Issues
Health
Human Development
Human Resources
Human Sexuality
India and South Asia

International Business
Japan and the Pacific Rim
Latin America
Life Management
Macroeconomics
Management
Marketing
Marriage and Family
Mass Media
Microeconomics
Middle East and the Islamic World
Money and Banking
Multicultural Education
Nutrition
Personal Growth and Behavior
Physical Anthropology
Psychology
Public Administration
Race and Ethnic Relations
Russia, the Eurasian Republics, and Central/Eastern Europe
Social Problems
Sociology
State and Local Government
Urban Society
Violence and Terrorism
Western Civilization, Pre-Reformation
Western Civilization, Post-Reformation
Western Europe
World History, Pre-Modern
World History, Modern
World Politics

Cataloging in Publication Data
Annual Editions: Marriage and Family. 1995/96.
     1. Family—United States—Periodicals. 2. Marriage—United States—Periodicals. I. Gilbert, Kathleen, *comp.* II. Title: Marriage and Family.
ISBN 1–56134–363–3   301.42'05   74–84596
HQ 536.A57

Twenty-First Edition

Printed in the United States of America

To the Reader

In publishing ANNUAL EDITIONS we recognize the enormous role played by the magazines, newspapers, and journals of the *public press* in providing current, first-rate educational information in a broad spectrum of interest areas. Within the articles, the best scientists, practitioners, researchers, and commentators draw issues into new perspective as accepted theories and viewpoints are called into account by new events, recent discoveries change old facts, and fresh debate breaks out over important controversies.

Many of the articles resulting from this enormous editorial effort are appropriate for students, researchers, and professionals seeking accurate, current material to help bridge the gap between principles and theories and the real world. These articles, however, become more useful for study when those of lasting value are carefully *collected, organized, indexed,* and *reproduced* in a *low-cost format*, which provides easy and permanent access when the material is needed. That is the role played by *Annual Editions*. Under the direction of each volume's *Editor*, who is an expert in the subject area, and with the guidance of an *Advisory Board*, we seek each year to provide in each ANNUAL EDITION a current, well-balanced, carefully selected collection of the best of the public press for your study and enjoyment. We think you'll find this volume useful, and we hope you'll take a moment to let us know what you think.

The intent of *Annual Editions: Marriage and Family 95/96* is to explore intimate relationships as they are played out in marriage and family. It is also intended to reflect the changing face of the family. The purpose of this anthology is to bring to the reader the latest thoughts and trends in our understanding of the family, to identify current concerns as well as problems and possible solutions, and to present alternative views of family process.

The articles in this volume are taken from professional publications, semiprofessional journals, and popular lay publications aimed at both special populations and a general readership. The selections are carefully reviewed for their currency and accuracy. In some cases, contrasting viewpoints are presented. In others, articles are paired in such a way as to personalize the more impersonal scholarly information. In the current edition, approximately 70 percent of the articles have changed from the previous edition upon updating and responding to reviewers' comments. As the reader, you will note the tremendous range of tone and focus of these articles, from first-person accounts to reports of scientific discoveries or philosophical and theoretical writings. Some are more practical and applications-oriented while others are more technical and research-oriented.

This anthology is organized to cover many of the important aspects of marriage and family. The first unit looks at varied perspectives on the family. The second unit examines the beginning steps of relationship building as individuals go through the process of exploring and establishing connections. In the third unit, the means of finding and maintaining a relationship balance are examined. Unit four is concerned with issues of crises, and the ways in which these crises can act as challenges and opportunities for families and their members. Finally, unit five takes a positive view as it looks at families, now and into the future.

Instructors can use *Annual Editions: Marriage and Family 95/96* as a primary text for introductory marriage and family classes, particularly when they tie the content of the articles to basic information on marriage and family. It can also be used as a supplement to update or emphasize certain aspects of standard marriage and family textbooks. Because of the provocative nature of many of the articles in this anthology, it works quite well as a basis for class discussion about various aspects of marriage and family relationships.

I would like to thank everyone involved in the development of this volume. Special thanks go to Lisa Eckert for her contributions in developing and editing this anthology. I would also like to thank those who sent in article rating forms and comments on the previous edition as well as those who suggested articles to consider for inclusion in this edition. Finally, to all of the students in my Marriage and Family Interactions class who have contributed critiques of articles, I would like to say thanks.

Anyone interested in providing input for future editions of *Annual Editions: Marriage and Family* should complete and return the postpaid article rating form at the end of this book. Your suggestions are much appreciated and contribute to the continuing high quality of this anthology.

Kathleen R. Gilbert
Editor

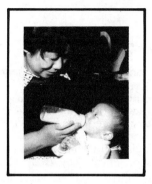

Unit 1

Varied Perspectives on the Family

Six articles explore different views on where our images of family come from and how they are influenced by our life experiences as well as societal and cultural constraints.

The concepts in bold italics are developed in the article. For further expansion please refer to the Topic Guide and the Index.

Unit 2

Exploring and Establishing Relationships

Eight articles address factors that influence the formation of close relationships, both romantic and generative.

The concepts in bold italics are developed in the article. For further expansion please refer to the Topic Guide and the Index.

Unit 3

Finding a Balance: Maintaining Relationships

Fifteen articles consider the complex issues related to keeping a relationship going. From marriage to parent/child relationships and in our sibling relationships and the "grand" alliance, relationship maintenance requires thought and commitment from members.

The concepts in bold italics are developed in the article. For further expansion please refer to the Topic Guide and the Index.

The concepts in bold italics are developed in the article. For further expansion please refer to the Topic Guide and the Index.

Unit 4

Crises – Challenges and Opportunities

A wide variety of crises, normative and catastrophic, are detailed in the fifteen articles. Ranging from broad cultural factors impacting on families to the intimate crises of infidelity, divorce, and death, the articles provide accounts of devastation and hope.

The concepts in bold italics are developed in the article. For further expansion please refer to the Topic Guide and the Index.

The concepts in bold italics are developed in the article. For further expansion please refer to the Topic Guide and the Index.

Unit 5

Families, Now and into the Future

Four articles look at means of establishing and/or maintaining health and healthy relationships in families.

The concepts in bold italics are developed in the article. For further expansion please refer to the Topic Guide and the Index.

Topic Guide

This topic guide suggests how the selections in this book relate to topics of traditional concern to students and professionals involved with the study of marriage and family. It is useful for locating articles that relate to each other for reading and research. The guide is arranged alphabetically according to topic. Articles may, of course, treat topics that do not appear in the topic guide. In turn, entries in the topic guide do not necessarily constitute a comprehensive listing of all the contents of each selection.

TOPIC AREA	TREATED IN:	TOPIC AREA	TREATED IN:
Abortion	25. Single Parents and Damaged Children	**Communication (cont.)**	16. Peer Marriage
Abuse	23. Ten Worst Discipline Mistakes Parents Make . . . and Alternatives		18. Staying Power
	32. Helping Children Cope with Violence		19. But What Do You Mean?
	33. After He Hits Her		20. Saving Relationships
	34. Where Do We Go from Here?		22. When Parents Disagree
Adolescence	4. Children Are Alone		35. Sexual Desire
	10. Choosing Mates—The American Way		41. Lessons from Step-Families
	25. Single Parents and Damaged Children		46. Happy Families: Who Says They All Have to Be Alike?
	44. Sibling Survivors	**Culture**	1. Mything Link
Adoption	13. Adapting to Adoption		5. Ache for Home
Aging	17. Receipts from a Marriage		6. Growing Up in Black and White
	38. Caregiving		18. Staying Power
	39. Long Road Back		26. Family Heart
	45. Trace Your Family Tree		30. Endangered Family
Beliefs	1. Mything Link		32. Helping Children Cope with Violence
	5. Ache for Home		46. Happy Families
	6. Growing Up in Black and White		47. Family Matters
	16. Peer Marriage		48. Rituals for Our Times
	26. Family Heart	**Dating/Mate Selection**	8. Love: The Immutable Longing for Contact
	27. I Don't Sweat the Small Stuff Anymore		9. What Makes Love Last?
	39. Long Road Back		10. Choosing Mates—The American Way
	43. Solace and Immortality	**Divorce**	2. New Crusade for the Old Family
	44. Sibling Survivors		15. What's Happening to American Marriage?
	47. Family Matters		36. Beyond Betrayal
	48. Rituals for Our Times		40. Family Values
Biological Bases	7. Sizing Up the Sexes	**Family Systems**	5. Ache for Home
	8. Love: The Immutable Longing for Contact		14. Family Circle
	37. Sexual Desire		16. Peer Marriage
	45. Trace Your Family Tree		26. Family Heart
Children and Childcare	3. New Family Investing in Human Capital		28. Siblings and Development
	4. Children Are Alone		29. Places Everyone
	6. Growing Up in Black and White		39. Long Road Back
	8. Love: The Immutable Longing for Contact		41. Lessons from Step-Families
	13. Adapting to Adoption		46. Happy Families
	14. Family Circle		47. Family Matters
	16. Peer Marriage		48. Rituals for Our Times
	21. Vanishing Dreams of America's Young Families	**"Family Values" Conflict**	2. New Crusade for the Old Family
	23. Ten Worst Discipline Mistakes Parents Make . . . and Alternatives		3. New Family Investing in Human Capital
	27. Single Parents and Damaged Children		30. Endangered Family
	27. I Don't Sweat the Small Stuff Anymore		31. White Ghetto?
	30. Endangered Family		40. Family Values
	32. Helping Children Cope with Violence		47. Family Matters
	42. Myths and Misconceptions of the Stepmother Identity	**Gender Roles**	7. Sizing Up the Sexes
	43. Solace and Immortality		10. Choosing Mates—The American Way
	44. Sibling Survivors		11. Mating Game
	46. Happy Families		12. Cahl Jooniah
	47. Family Matters		16. Peer Marriage
Communication	7. Sizing Up the Sexes		18. Staying Power
	8. Love: The Immutable Longing for Contact		19. But What Do You Mean?
	11. Mating Game		20. Saving Relationships
			33. After He Hits Her
			34. Where Do We Go from Here?
			37. Myth of the Miserable Working Woman
			42. Myths and Misconceptions of the Stepmother Identity

TOPIC AREA	TREATED IN:	TOPIC AREA	TREATED IN:
Health Concerns	12. Cahl Jooniah 27. I Don't Sweat the Small Stuff Anymore 34. Where Do We Go from Here? 38. Caregiving 39. Long Road Back 45. Trace Your Family Tree	**Poverty**	2. New Crusade for the Old Family 4. Children Are Alone 21. Vanishing Dreams of America's Young Families 30. Endangered Family 31. White Ghetto?
Infidelity	11. Mating Game 35. Sexual Desire 36. Beyond Betrayal	**Pregnancy/ Childbirth**	12. Cahl Jooniah 14. Family Circle
Intimacy/Romantic Love	5. Ache for Home 7. Sizing Up the Sexes 8. Love: The Immutable Longing for Contact 9. What Makes Love Last? 10. Choosing Mates—The American Way 11. Mating Game 12. Cahl Jooniah 15. What's Happening to American Marriage? 16. Peer Marriage 20. Saving Relationships 35. Sexual Desire 36. Beyond Betrayal 40. Family Values 46. Happy Families	**Race/Ethnicity** **Remarriage** **Sex/Sexuality**	4. Children Are Alone 5. Ache for Home 6. Growing Up in Black and White 21. Vanishing Dreams of America's Young Families 30. Endangered Family 31. White Ghetto? 41. Lessons from Step-Families 42. Myths and Misconceptions of the Stepmother Identity 7. Sizing Up the Sexes 11. Mating Game 16. Peer Marriage 20. Saving Relationships 25. Single Parents and Damaged Children 35. Sexual Desire 36. Beyond Betrayal
Laws/Governmental Roles/Policy	2. New Crusade for the Old Family 3. New Family Investing in Human Capital 21. Vanishing Dreams of America's Young Families 25. Single Parents and Damaged Children 31. White Ghetto? 34. Where Do We Go from Here? 40. Family Values	**Siblings** **Single Parent Homes**	28. Siblings and Development 29. Places Everyone 44. Sibling Survivors 3. New Family Investing in Human Capital 24. Of Super Dads and Absent Ones 30. Endangered Family 31. White Ghetto?
Marriage	9. What Makes Love Last? 10. Choosing Mates—The American Way 14. Family Circle 15. What's Happening to American Marriage? 16. Peer Marriage 17. Receipts from a Marriage 36. Beyond Betrayal 37. Myth of the Miserable Working Woman 40. Family Values 41. Lessons from Step-Families 46. Happy Families 47. Family Matters	**Values**	1. Mything Link 5. Ache for Home 6. Growing Up in Black and White 10. Choosing Mates—The American Way 14. Family Circle 15. What's Happening to American Marriage? 16. Peer Marriage 22. When Parents Disagree 25. Single Parents and Damaged Children 26. Family Heart 40. Family Values 44. Sibling Survivors 46. Happy Families 47. Family Matters 48. Rituals for Our Times
Parents/Parenting	6. Growing Up in Black and White 8. Love: The Immutable Longing for Contact 12. Cahl Jooniah 14. Family Circle 16. Peer Marriage 17. Receipts from a Marriage 21. Vanishing Dreams of America's Young Families 22. When Parents Disagree 23. Ten Worst Discipline Mistakes Parents Make . . . and Alternatives 24. Of Super Dads and Absent Ones 25. Single Parents and Damaged Children 26. Family Heart 41. Lessons from Step-Families 42. Myths and Misconceptions of the Stepmother Identity 43. Solace and Immortality 46. Happy Families 47. Family Matters	**Work and Family**	3. New Family Investing in Human Capital 14. Family Circle 16. Peer Marriage 21. Vanishing Dreams of America's Young Families 37. Myth of the Miserable Working Woman

Varied Perspectives on the Family

What is a family? How do you know? How do you know you are doing it right? One's image of family is a powerful combination of personal experience and images to which one is exposed. This image informs decision making and interpersonal interaction throughout one's life and has far-reaching impacts. On an intimate level, it influences individual and family development as well as relationships both within the family and without. On a broader level, it affects social policy and programming.

In many ways, this image can be positive. It can act to clarify one's thinking and facilitate interaction with like-minded individuals. It can also be negative, as it can narrow one's thinking and limit one's ability to see the value of other ways of carrying out the functions of family, simply because these ways are different. In this case, interaction with others can be impeded because of contrasting views. People who have ways of behaving that are different from one's own may be seen as "them" in an "us and them" mentality.

This unit is intended to meet several goals with regard to perspectives on the family: (1) to sensitize the reader to the sources of beliefs about what the family should be and the ways in which family roles should be carried out, (2) to show how different views of the family can influence attitudes toward community responsibility and family policy, (3) to show how views that dominate one's childhood can influence awareness of alternative ways of structuring family life and the individual's sense of self.

The first article, "The Mything Link," asks the reader to consider the mythology of the family and the sources of these myths. The next three articles confront dramatic examples of the changing face of the family. The first two address broad societal responsibilities for these "new" families and their members. The third, "Children Are Alone," looks at what happens if intervention is inadequate or nonexistent. Peggy Orenstein provides a touching look at the lives of two teenaged girls growing up in a demanding world of limited support.

The next two articles look at the ways in which images of family can be restrictive and possibly harmful. In "The Ache for Home," family therapist Monica McGoldrick describes her personal journey toward awareness of culture, gender, class, and race, all of which had been "invisible" to her as she grew up. "Growing Up in Black and White" looks at the societal factors that influence images of self-identity, particularly in young black children. Unless they are countered by images that encourage these children to value themselves, these factors can do serious damage to the self-images of these children.

Looking Ahead: Challenge Questions

What is your image of family? How closely does it match an image of the perfect family? What are the sources of these images?

If you had the power to propose a government program to support today's families, what would it be?

What type of intervention would you propose to help children growing up in troubled families and in a dangerous world?

How would you go about expanding your ideas of what is acceptable in terms of family relationships and family roles? How far do you think you should go in this?

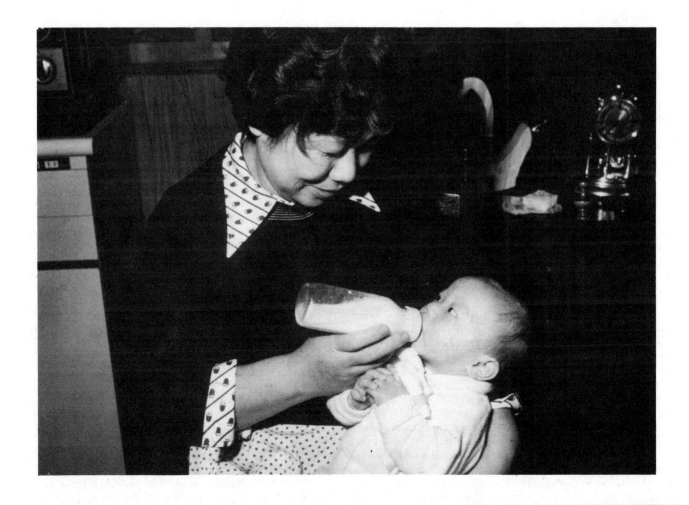

The
Mything
Link

Where does our notion of "the perfect family"
come from? Heaven knows: It incorporates everything
from the Greek gods to the Brady Bunch.

Owen Edwards

The ancient Greeks were onto something, I think, envisioning their gods as one big scrappy family. To those of us hearing their stories more than 2,000 years later, at least, the cast and dynamics seem entirely familiar: Zeus, the all-powerful father, given to fits of temper yet a bit of a bumbler, a compulsive philanderer who endlessly risked the wrath of his wife; Hera, a powerful matriarch ever ready to make things hot for him and his earthly friends; and the brothers—Poseidon, always off somewhere fishing, and lonely Hades—both running branches of the family business and quick to disapprove of Zeus and his brood. Among them were all manner of kids, legitimate and otherwise, real gods and demis, spoiled and neglected, wreaking havoc in a thousand legendary ways. It may be a stretch to picture Zeus coming back from a trip to earth, peeling off his swan suit and calling out, "Hi, honey, I'm home," but it's not so hard to imagine those who listened raptly to Homer's poetry tuned in to "Dallas of the Deities," "Immortalsomething" or "Mt. Olympus 90210." The gods may have been movers and shakers on an unimaginably grand scale, but it was their oh-so-familiar family life that made mere mortals care so passionately about their lofty goings-on.

Imagine someone dropping onto a psychiatrist's couch and saying, "I'll talk about anything except my family." As Ross Perot might say, end of story. Family life is the common thread of human existence, and the meaning of family is central to any search for ourselves. Most of us experience the world first as the small, sheltering universe of our families. Those unlucky enough not to get off to such a start often spend their lives looking for what they imagine to be the equivalent, with unpredictable results (think of the murderous misfits of the Manson family). Even those who ultimately find the universe of the loving family too constricting and break away run the risk of endlessly looking back, reflexively gilding already golden memories. Though we may in the end spend years busily rejecting mom and dad or blaming our siblings for their tormenting ways, few can break entirely free of what can only be called blood yearnings. Because whatever it is or has been in reality, family life remains the great Arcadian dream.

One of the ways we go on dreaming this dream in the face of waking realities is to invent mythical families, or invest real families with a mythical status. These surrogates, be they the Kennedy clan or the Brady Bunch, serve our ritual needs, providing us with family scandals and feuds at no risk of embarrassment to ourselves, and letting us study—at a safe distance—how families ought or ought not to behave. They are loved, and sometimes loathed, with a public passion driven by the implausible notion that somewhere the perfect, wart-free *It's a Wonderful Life* family actually exists, and might, but for an accident of timing, include us.

Whether we know it or not, most of us are looking for dream families most of the time. Some years ago, shortly after arriving on a small island in the Mediterranean, I saw a handsome couple walking with their arms around the shoulders of their beautiful teenage children. Instantly, I decided they were the perfect family; they seemed so intimately knit, and though I had no complaint about my own family, I could never remember either of my parents behaving with such egalitarian intimacy toward me and my brother. When I had dinner with them a few nights later, the French surgeon, his painter wife and their two charming and gift-

 From *Town & Country*, June 1994, pp. 112-113. © 1994 by the Hearst Publishing Corporation. Reprinted by permission.

ed children made my worthy New Jersey kin seem irretrievably flawed by comparison. Only years later, after the couple had divorced and the children had grown up to lead rather neurotic lives in Paris, did I discover that what had seemed enviable substance was in fact mostly style, that a parental arm around a child's shoulder might have looked idyllic to someone raised in a house in which physical shows of affection were rare, but it was not necessarily a more durable bond than a firm fatherly handshake.

More often than not, our mythic families are made up of people we never meet. Why take a chance having our dreams put to the test? We may lament the vast continental dispersions of our real families and enrich long-distance phone companies by trying to reach out and touch them, but the great American tradition of phantom families thrives on the feeling of accessibility—created by television and celebrity magazines—without the likelihood of actual, disappointing contact. Not surprisingly, we seem especially comfortable with families that are entirely invented. Following the lead of Homer, authors have long provided us with literary clans to revere or vilify according to our tastes. Shakespeare, Jane Austen, Evelyn Waugh, William Faulkner, John Updike, Anne Tyler and countless others have profitably played God, gene splicing classic characteristics to produce villain uncles and vixen cousins, wise fathers and feckless sons (or vice versa), darling daughters and mommies dearest, all to our obsessive delight. Whether they live in big houses on the hill or little houses on the prairie, ink-on-paper families—the brilliantly brittle Glass menagerie, Willy Loman and sons, the upright Mr. and Mrs. Bridge and the downright disreputable Snopeses—can evoke feelings as vivid as if they had been coming to Thanksgiving dinner year after year to gossip and complain, reaffirm ties and reembellish lies, and generally doing what frictional, nonfictional families do.

Even more compelling during the past four decades or so are the families who have entered our living rooms, and psyches, across the twilight threshold of the television screen. Like branches newly grafted onto our own family trees, the Waltons and the Cleavers, the lowbrow Bunkers and the highbrow Huxtables, the thirtysomethings and the Golden Girls, even Jetsons or Flintstones or Simpsons, move in and take over like pushy in-laws. Related not by birth but by electrons, we love them until they leave us. (But don't worry—with 500 cable channels threatened, they'll all be back.)

Finally, though, it is those rare real-life families raised to the level of mythology who hold the greatest fascination for us. The gravitational pull on the public of the gods and goddesses whose pleasures and sorrows, scandals and quarrels, true romances and public breakups we know to be as unscripted as our own is so powerful that it may last for generations. Thus, the Greek tragedy of the Kennedys; the shockingly common peccadilloes of the once-dependable Windsors; the tangled fortunes of the Vanderbilts, Whitneys, Pulitzers, et al., turn us all into an infinitely extended family hungry for news of its white knights, black sheep, prodigal sons and dutiful daughters. We no longer care much about Zeus, Hera and their Olympian bratpack—even immortality, it seems, is not forever—but the power of the family, and the need for famous families, will last as long as the human race itself. In the end, what else is there?

The New Crusade for the Old Family

Arlene Skolnick and Stacey Rosencrantz

Arlene Skolnick, a research psychologist at the Institute of Human Development at the University of California (Berkeley), is the author of Embattled Paradise: The American Family in an Age of Uncertainty. *Stacey Rosencrantz is a graduate student in Stanford University's psychology department.*

What is the root cause in America of poverty, crime, drug abuse, gang warfare, urban decay, and failing schools? According to op-ed pundits, Sunday talking heads, radio call-in shows, and politicians in both parties, the answer is the growing number of children being raised by single parents, especially by mothers who never married in the first place. Restore family values and the two-parent family, and America's social problems will be substantially solved.

By the close of the 1992 presidential campaign, the war over family values seemed to fade. Dan Quayle's attack on Murphy Brown's single motherhood stirred more ridicule on late night talk shows than moral panic. The public clearly preferred Bill Clinton's focus on the economy and his more inclusive version of the family theme: "family values" means "valuing families," no matter what their form—traditional, extended, two-parent, one-parent.

Yet Clinton's victory was quickly followed by a new bipartisan crusade to restore the two-parent family by discouraging divorce as well as out-of-wedlock childbearing. The conservative right has for years equated family values with the traditional image of the nuclear family. The new crusade drew people from across the spectrum—Democrats as well as Republicans, conservatives, liberals, and communitarians. Eventually, even President Clinton joined in, remarking that he had reread Quayle's speech and "found a lot of good things in it."

While the new family restorationists do not agree on a program for reducing the number of single-parent families, they generally use a language of moral failure and cultural decline to account for family change. Many want to revive the stigma that used to surround divorce and single motherhood. To change the cultural climate, they call for government and media campaigns like those that have discouraged smoking and drinking. They propose to make divorce harder or slower or even, as the late Christopher Lasch proposed, to outlaw divorce by parents with minor children. And some have also advocated restricting welfare benefits for unmarried mothers or eliminating benefits entirely for mothers who have an additional out-of-wedlock child.

Focusing attention on the needs and problems of families raising children could be enormously positive. But the current crusade draws on the family values scripts of the 1980s, posing the issue in a divisive way (are you against the two-parent family?) and painting critics into an anti-family corner. Restricting legal channels for divorce, cutting off welfare to unmarried mothers, and restoring the old censorious

Despite these strong claims of scientific backing, the research literature is far more complicated than the family restorationists have let on.

attitudes toward single parenthood may harm many children and deepen the very social ills we are trying to remedy.

There's nothing new in blaming social problems on "the breakdown of the family" or in making the "fallen woman" and her bastard child into objects of scorn and pity. Throughout our history, public policies made divorce difficult to obtain and penalized unwed parents and often their children. In the 1960s and 1970s, however, public opinion turned more tolerant and legal systems throughout the West became unwilling to brand some children as "illegitimate" and deprive them of rights due others. Now we are being told that this new tolerance was a mistake.

Most Americans, even those most committed to greater equality between women and men, are deeply uneasy about recent family changes and worried about crime and violence. The new case for the old family owes much of its persuasive power to the authority of social science. "The evidence is in," declares Barbara Dafoe Whitehead, author of a much-discussed article, "Dan Quayle Was Right," which appeared in the April 1993 *Atlantic Monthly*. Divorce and single-parent families, Whitehead argues, are damaging both children and the social fabric. Another family restorationist, Karl Zinsmeister, a fellow at the American Enterprise Institute, refers to "a mountain of evidence" showing that children of divorce end up intellectually, physically, and emotionally scarred for life.

Despite these strong claims of scientific backing, the research literature is far more complicated than the family restorationists have let on. Whitehead says, "The debate about family structure is not simply about the social-scientific evidence. It is also a debate over deeply held and often conflicting values." Unfortunately, the family restorationists' values have colored their reading of the evidence.

Few would deny that the divorce of one's parents is a painful experience and that children blessed with two "good enough" parents generally have an easier time growing up than others. Raising a child from infancy to successful adulthood can be a daunting task even for two people. But to decide what policies would improve children's lives, we need to answer a number of prior questions:

■ Are children who grow up in a one-parent home markedly worse off than those who live with both parents?

■ If such children are so disadvantaged, is the source of their problems family structure or some other factor that may have existed earlier or be associated with it?

■ How effectively can public policies promote a particular form of family and discourage others? Will policies intended to stigmatize and reduce or prevent divorce or single parenthood cause unintended harm to children's well-being? Would positive measures to help single-parent families or reduce the stress that accompanies marital disruption be of more benefit to children?

Finally, is there a direct link, as so many believe, between family structure and what a *Newsweek* writer calls a "nauseating buffet" of social pathologies, especially crime, violence, and drugs? In his Murphy Brown speech, given in the wake of the Los Angeles riots, Quayle argued that it wasn't poverty but a "poverty of values" that had led to family breakdown, which in turn caused the violence. The one sentence about Murphy Brown in the speech—borrowed incidentally from an op-ed by Whitehead—overshadowed the rest of the message. Charles Murray was more successful at linking family values with the fear of crime. In a *Wall Street Journal* article, he warned that because of rising white illegitimacy rates, a "coming white underclass" was going to engulf the rest of society in the kind of anarchy found in the inner cities. But what is the evidence for this incendiary claim? And why do countries with similar trends in family structure not suffer from the social deterioration that plagues us?

The family restorationists do not provide clear answers to these questions. And the answers found in the research literature do not support their extreme statements about the consequences of family structure or some of the drastic policies they propose to change it.

Of course, it's always possible to raise methodological questions about a line of research or to interpret findings in more ways than one. The perfect study, like the perfect crime, is an elusive goal. But some of the family restorationists seem to misunderstand the social science enterprise in ways that seriously undermine their conclusions. For example, they trumpet findings about correlations between family structure and poverty, or lower academic achievement, or behavior problems, as proof of their arguments. Doing so, however, ignores the principle taught in elementary statistics that correlation does not prove causation.

For example, suppose we find that increased ice cream consumption is correlated with increases in drownings. The cause, of course, has nothing to do with ice cream but everything to do with the weather: people swim more and eat more ice cream in the summer. Similarly, single parenthood may be correlated with many problems affecting children, but the causes may lie elsewhere—for example, in economic and emotional problems affecting parents that lead to difficulties raising children and greater chances of divorce. Making it hard for such parents to divorce may no more improve the children's lives than banning ice cream would reduce drowning. Also, causation can and often does go in two directions. Poor women are more likely to have out-of-wedlock babies—this is one of the oldest correlates of poverty—but raising the child may impede them from escaping poverty. In short, finding a correlation between two variables is only a starting point for further analysis.

The social science research itself is also plagued by methodological problems. Most available studies of divorce, for example, are based on well-educated white families; some are based on families who have sought clinical help or become embroiled in legal conflict. Such families may hardly be representative. Comparing one study with one another is notoriously difficult because they use different measures to assess children of different ages after differing periods have elapsed since the divorce. Some studies, such as Judith Wallerstein's widely cited work on the harm of divorce reported in the 1989 book *Second Chances* by Wallerstein and Sandra Blakeslee, use no comparison groups at all.

Others compare divorced families with intact families—both happy and unhappy—when a more appropriate comparison would be with couples that are unhappily married.

In addition, the family restorationists and some researchers lump together children of divorce and children whose parents never married. Yet never-married mothers are generally younger, poorer, and less educated than divorced mothers. And by some measures children living with never-married mothers are worse off than those living in divorced families.

The restorationists paint a far darker and more simplistic picture of the impact of divorce on children than does the research literature. Researchers agree that around the time their parents separate almost all children go through a period of distress. Within two or three years, most have recovered. The great majority of children of divorce do not appear to be impaired in their development. While some children do suffer lasting harm, the family restorationists exaggerate the extent and prevalence of long-term effects. For example, they may state that children of divorce face twice or three times the psychological risk of children in intact families. But the doubling of a risk may mean an increase from 2 to 4 percent, 10 to 20 percent, or from 30 to 60 percent. The effects of divorce tend to be in the smaller range.

In fact, a meta-analysis of divorce findings published in 1991 in the *Psychological Bulletin* reported very small differences between children from divorced and intact families in such measures of well-being as school achievement, psychological adjustment, self concept, and relations with parents and peers. (A "meta-analysis" combines data from separate studies into larger samples to make the findings more reliable.) Further, the more methodologically sophisticated studies—that is, those that controlled for other variables such as as income and parental conflict—reported the smallest differences.

In general, researchers who interview or observe children of divorce report more findings of distress than those who use data from large sample surveys. Yet even in the clinical studies the majority of children develop normally. One point that researchers agree on is that children vary greatly in response to divorce, depending on their circumstances, age, and psychological traits and temperament.

Where differences between children of divorce and those in stable two-parent families show up, they may be due, not to the divorce itself, but to circumstances before, during, and after the legal undoing of the marital bond. Most researchers now view divorce not as a single event but as an unfolding process. The child will usually endure parental conflict, estrangement, and emotional upset, separation from one parent, and economic deprivation. Often divorce means moving away from home, neighborhood, and school. Particular children may go through more or fewer such jolts than others.

Researchers have known for some time that children from intact homes with high conflict between the parents often have similar or even worse problems than children of divorced parents. Recent studies in this country as well as in Australia and Sweden confirm that marital discord between the parents is a major influence on chidren's well-being, whether or not a divorce occurs.

Some of the family restorationists recognize that children in high-conflict families might be better off if their parents divorced than if they stayed together. They want to discourage or limit divorce by parents who are simply bored or unfulfilled. But how should we draw the line between unfulfilling and conflict-ridden marriages? And who should do the drawing?

High-conflict marriages are not necessarily violent or even dramatically quarrelsome like the couple in Edward Albee's *Who's Afraid of Virginia Woolf?*. One major recent study operationally defined a high-conflict family as one in which a spouse said the marriage was "not too happy" or the couple had arguments about five out of nine topics, including money, sex, chores, and in-laws. A number of recent studies do show that even moderate levels of marital dissatisfaction can have a detrimental effect on the quality of parenting.

The most critical factor in a child's well-being in any form of family is a close, nurturant relationship with at least one parent. For most children of divorce, this means the mother. Her ability to function as parent is in turn influenced by her physical and psychological well-being. Depression, anger, or stress can make a mother irritable, inconsistent, and in general less able to cope with her children and their problems, whether or not marital difficulties lead to divorce.

Until recently, the typical study of children of divorce began after the separation took place. However, two important studies—one directed by Jack Block and another by Andrew Cherlin—examined data on children long before their parents divorced. These studies found that child problems usually attributed to the divorce could be seen months and even years earlier. Usually, these results are assumed to reflect the impact of family conflict on children. But in a recent book analyzing divorce trends around world, William J. Goode offers another possibility:

> ... the research not only shows that many of the so-called effects of divorce were present before the marriage, but suggests an even more radical hypothesis: in at least a sizeable number of families the problems that children generate may create parental conflict and thereby increase the likelihood of divorce.

The problems of never-married single mothers and their children set off some of today's hottest buttons—sex, gender, race, and welfare. Dan Quayle's attack on Murphy Brown confused the issue. It is true that more single, educated, middle-class women are having children. The rate nearly tripled in the last decade among women in professional or managerial occupations. But despite this increase, only 8 percent of professional-status women are never-married, Murphy Brown mothers. Out-of-wedlock births continue to be far more prevalent among the less educated, the poor, and racial minorities.

Most people take the correlation between single parenthood and poverty as proof of a causal relation between the two. But the story is more complex. In his book *America's Children*, Donald Hernandez of the Census Bureau shows that if we take into account the income of fathers in divorced and unwed families, the increase in single mothers since 1959 probably accounts for only 2 to 4 percentage points of today's childhood poverty rates. As Kristen Luker has pointed out in these pages ("Dubious Conceptions: The Controversy Over Teen Pregnancy," *TAP*, No. 5, Spring 1991), the assumption that early childbearing causes poverty and school dropouts is backward; these conditions are as much cause as effect.

Elijah Anderson, Linda Burton, William Julius Wilson, and other urban sociologists have shown the causal connections linking economic conditions and racial stigma with out-of-wedlock births and the prevalence of single-mother families in the inner cities. Cut off from the rest of society, with little or no hope of stable, family-supporting jobs, young men prove their manhood through an "oppositional culture" based on machismo and sexual prowess. Young women, with little hope of either a husband or economic independence, drift into early sexual relationships, pregnancy, and childbirth.

Middle-class families have also been shaken by economic change. The family restorationists, however, have little to say about the impact of economic forces on families. In her *Atlantic* article, Whitehead mentions—almost as an afterthought—that the loss of good jobs has deprived high school graduates across the country as well as inner-city young people of the ability to support families. "Improving job opportunities for young men," she writes, "would enhance their ability and presumably their willingness to form lasting marriages." Yet these considerations do not affect the main thrust of her arguments supporting Quayle's contention that the poor suffer from a "poverty of values."

There is no shortage of evidence on the impact of economic hardship on families. The studies of ghetto problems have their counterparts in a spate of recent books about other groups.* Much quantitative research reinforces these analyses. As Glen Elder and others have found, using data

---

* John E. Schwarz and Thomas J. Volgy's *The Forgotten Americans* portrays the fast growing population of working poor, people who "play by the rules" but remain below the poverty line. Lillian Rubin's *Families on the Fault Line* documents the impact on working-class families of the decline of well-paying manufacturing jobs. Katherine Newman's ethnographic studies, *Falling from Grace* and *Declining Fortunes*, document the effects of downward mobility in middle-class families.

from the Great Depression to the 1980s, economic conditions such as unemployment are linked to children's problems through their parent's emotional states. Economic stress often leads to depression and demoralization, which in turn lead to marital conflict and such problems in child-raising as harsh discipline, angry outbursts, and rejection. Child abuse and neglect as well as alcoholism and drug use increase with economic stress.

New research has confirmed earlier findings that poverty and inadequate income are major threats to children's well-being and development. Poverty has a deep impact because it affects not only the parent's psychological functioning but is linked to poor health and nutrition in parents and children, impaired readiness for education, bad housing, the stress of dangerous neighborhoods, and poor schools as well as the stigma of being poor. One recent study comparing black and white children across income levels found that family income and poverty were powerful determinants of children's cognitive development and behavior, controlling for other differences such as family structure and maternal schooling.

Child poverty in the United States, as the family restorationists point out, is higher than it was two decades ago among whites as well as blacks. It is also much higher in the United States than in other Western countries. But it is not an unalterable fact of nature that children born to single mothers have to grow up in poverty. Whereas our policies express disapproval of the parents, the policies of other Western countries support the well-being of the children.

The family structure debate raises larger questions about the changes in family, gender, and sexuality in the past three decades—what to think about them, what language to use in talking about them. The language of moral decay will not suffice. Many of the nation's churches and synagogues are rethinking ancient habits and codes to accommodate new conceptions of women's equality and new versions of morality and responsibility in an age of sexual relationships outside of marriage and between partners of the same gender.

The nation as a whole is long overdue for a serious discussion of the upheaval in

American family life since the 1960s and how to mitigate its social and personal costs, especially to children. The point of reference should not be the lost family of a mythical past conjured up by our nostalgic yearnings but the more realistic vision offered by the rich body of historical scholarship since the 1970s. From the beginning, American families have been diverse, on-the-go, buffeted by social and economic change. The gap between family values and actual behavior has always been wide.

Such a discussion should also reflect an awareness that the family trends we have experienced over the past three decades are not unique. Every other Western country has experienced similar changes in women's roles and family structure. The trends are rooted in the development of the advanced industrial societies. As Andrew Cherlin puts it, "We can no more keep wives at home or slash the divorce rate than we can shut down our cities and send everyone back to the farm."

However, our response to family change has been unique. No other country has experienced anything like the cultural warfare that has made the family one of the most explosive issues in American society. Most other countries, including our cultural sibling Canada, have adapted pragmatically to change and developed policies in support of working parents, single-parent families, and all families raising children. Teenagers in these countries have fewer abortions and out-of-wedlock births, not becase they have less sex, but because sex education and contraceptives are widely available.

Sooner or later, we are going to have to let go of the fantasy that we can restore the family of the 1950s. Given the cultural shocks of the past three decades and the quiet depression we have endured since the mid-1970s, it's little wonder that we have been enveloped by a haze of nostalgia. Yet the family patterns of the 1950s Americans now take as the stand-

ard for judging family normality were actually a deviation from long-term trends. Since the nineteenth century, the age at marriage, divorce rate, and women's labor force participation had been rising. In the 1950s however, the age of marriage declined, the divorce rate leveled off, the proportion of the population married reached a new high, and the American birth rate approached that of India. After the 1950s, the long-term historical trends resumed.

Most of us would not want to reverse all the trends that have helped to transform family life—declining mortality rates, rising educational levels for both men and women, reliable contraception, and greater opportunities for women. Barring a major cataclysm, the changes in family life are now too deeply woven into American lives to be reversed by "just say no" campaigns or even by the kinds of changes in divorce and welfare laws that the restorationists propose.

The task is to buffer children and families from the effects of these trends. Arguing for systematic economic reform in *Mother Jones*, John Judis writes that between the new economic realities and the kinds of broad measures needed to address them, there is "a yawning gulf of politics and ideology into which even the most well-meaning and intelligently conceived policy can tumble." A similar gulf lies between the new realities of American family life and the policies needed to address them.

Yet the potential for ameliorative reform may be greater than it now appears. As E.J. Dionne has pointed out, the debate is more polarized than the public. The 1992 Democratic convention showed how an inclusive pro-family message could be articulated and combined with proposals for economic and social reform. Such a message, recognizing both the diversity of family life and the continuing importance of family, appealed to a broad cross-section of Americans. It continues to make more sense and offer more hope than the punitive and coercive prescriptions of the family restorationists.

THE NEW FAMILY
INVESTING IN HUMAN CAPITAL

DAVID A. HAMBURG

Mr. Hamburg is president of the
Carnegie Corporation of New York.

The dramatic changes in the American family can be highlighted by comparing its structure and function as it was in 1960 with what it had become in 1990. Until 1960 most Americans shared a common set of beliefs about family life. Family should consist of a husband and wife living together with their children. The father should be the head of the family, earn the family's income, and give his name to his wife and children. The mother's main tasks were to support and facilitate her husband's, guide her children's development, look after the home, and set a moral tone for the family. Marriage was an enduring obligation for better or worse. The husband and wife jointly coped with stresses. Sexual activity was to be kept within the marriage, especially for women. As parents, they had an overriding responsibility for the well-being of their children during the early years—until their children entered school, they were almost solely responsible. Even later, it was the parents who had the primary duty of guiding their children's education and discipline. Of course, even in 1960, families recognized the difficulty of converting these ideals into reality. Still, they devoted immense effort to approximating them in practice.

Over the past three decades these ideals, although they are still recognizable, have been drastically modified across all social classes. Women have joined the paid labor force in great numbers stimulated both by economic need and a new belief in their capabilities and right to pursue opportunities. Americans in 1992 are far more likely than in earlier times to postpone marriage. Single-parent families—typically consisting of a mother with no adult male and very often no other adult person present—have become common. Today at least half of all marriages end in divorce. Most adults no longer believe that couples should stay married because divorce might harm their children.

Survey research shows a great decrease in the proportion of women favoring large families, an upsurge in their assertiveness about meeting personal needs, and an attempt by women to balance their needs with those of their children and the men in their lives. A clear and increasing majority of women believe that both husband and wife should be able to work, should have roughly similar opportunities, and should share household responsibilities and the tasks of child rearing. A majority of mothers of preschool children now work outside the home. A growing minority of young married women, often highly educated and career oriented, are choosing not to have any children and have little interest in children's issues—yet one more indication of the dramatic transformation of American families that has been taking place in recent decades.

While the rate of pregnancy among adult women has declined since 1970, that among American adolescents, especially girls under age fifteen, is one of the highest among technically advanced nations. Teenagers account for two-thirds of all out-of-wedlock births. There are 1.3 million children now living with teenage mothers only about half of whom are married. Six million children under the age of five are living with mothers who were adolescents when they gave birth.

Childbearing in adolescence has been a common feature of human history. But traditional societies provided relatively stable employment and had reliable networks of social support and cultural guidance for young parents. For such adolescents to set up a household apart from either family was rare in pre-industrial societies. Even rarer was the single-parent family. Rarest of all was a socially isolated, very young mother largely lacking an effective network of social support.

It is startling to realize that today, whether through their parents' divorce or never having been married, most American children spend part of their childhood in a single-parent family. The increase in the proportion of children living

From *Current*, July/August 1993, pp. 4-12. Originally "The American Family Transformed," from *Society*, January/February 1993, pp. 60-69. © 1993 by Transaction Publishers, Inc. Reprinted by permission.

with just one parent (usually the mother) has strongly affected large numbers of white, black, and Hispanic children. Female-headed families with children are much more likely to be poor than are married-couple families with children, regardless of race. By conservative estimates, one-fifth of young American children are raised in poverty, many by their mothers alone. Black families with children are more likely to be poor than white families with children, regardless of family type.

By the time they reach age sixteen, close to half the children of married parents will have seen their parents divorce. For nearly half of these, it will be five years or more before their mothers remarry. Close to half of all white children whose parents remarry will see the second marriage dissolve during their adolescence. Black women not only marry less often and experience more marital disruption but they also remarry more slowly and less often than do white women. Generally, as compared with other countries, the United States exhibits a pattern of attachments and disruptions in marriage that is certainly stressful for developing children and adolescents.

Divorce and remarriage create a complex set of new relationships, resulting in many different family configurations. About two-thirds of the children in step-families will have full siblings plus either half- or step-siblings. Many children will have multiple sets of grandparents. On the other hand, children of single mothers or mothers who do not remarry will have a more restricted set of active family relationships than children with two parents.

CHILD CARE   In the United States especially, but in many other nations too, mothers of children under three are the fastest-growing segment of the labor market, so child care arrangements at the preschool level are of enormous practical significance. Even though remarriage after a divorce is common, there are still complicated problems of handling child care responsibilities in blended families. For parents who have never been married, the strain is probably greatest. They have all the responsibility as head of household and the least help available. About two-thirds of single mothers with preschool children are employed, most of them full time. No matter how poor they may be, they must find some kind of arrangement for care of their very young children. More often than not, this means a child care center or other home that can take them in.

Child care is thus increasingly moving outside the home, with children's development often placed in the hands of strangers and near-strangers. As late as 1985 only 14 percent of preschool children were cared for in an organized child care facility. This figure has doubled in the last five years. By 1990 half of all children of working parents were either being cared for in a center or in another home. In 1985, 25 percent of working mothers with children under five used a child care facility as the primary form of care, compared with 13 percent in 1977. This transformation was unforeseen, unplanned, and is still poorly understood. With rapid, far-reaching social changes, it is not surprising that public opinion surveys find that many American parents are deeply troubled about raising their children, and two-thirds say they are less willing to make sacrifices for their young than their parents were. Neither they nor the nation's social institutions have had much time to adjust to the new conditions.

HOW PARENTS ARE COPING

Young people moving toward parenthood today face more rapidly changing circumstances and a wider spectrum of life choices than ever before. But choices and decisions as well as transitions can be burdens, even as they offer attractive opportunities and privileges. Young couples today often agonize over decisions taken for granted as recently as a generation ago. Should they get married? If yes, should they wait until one or both have a steady job? What about the fateful decision to have children?

Once married, it is very likely that both husband and wife will be in the paid labor force, and with the advent of the baby, they will have to renegotiate their relationship. How will they divide up the baby-care chores? What sort of parental leaves, if any, will either take? How will they handle the housework? How can they balance work and family life? If the mother takes off from work for a while, when is it sensible to go back, and how can she make the transition in the best interests of the child? Can they afford quality child care? If not, what alternatives are there?

Some studies have been done on the efforts of parents to balance their various interests and responsibilities in new ways. The results show that this is a complicated process that is in its earliest stages. Sociologist Arlie Hochschild of the University of California, the coauthor of *The Second Shift: Working Parents and the Revolution at Home*, has conducted systematic research that illuminates the tension between work and family. She describes the tremendous penalty women pay whether they choose to work at home or to have a paid job. The housewife pays the cost of remaining outside what is today the mainstream of society; the working woman pays the cost in time and energy for family commitments. The evidence clearly indicates that men are sharing very little of the burden of raising children and care of the home. Hence, as Hochschild points out, women are coming home from a paid job to work "a second shift." Most men devote long hours to their jobs. Even if they want to be helpful at home, their institutional settings usually do not make it easy for them to do so.

There is no reason to believe that this phenomenon of the two-parent working family is a transient one. Indeed, a variety of economic and psychological factors reinforce the persistence of the pattern as a financial necessity. The actual and proportionate costs of child raising today are much higher than they were in the 1950s and 1960s. In many families, both husband and wife must have an earned income if the family is to attain or maintain a middle-class standard of living. This is now much harder than it used to be. In the past few decades the shift from a manufacturing to a service-based economy has brought a decline in wages for many people. The industries that have declined in the United States in relation to foreign competition are precisely the ones that historically provided relatively high-earning positions for men, especially those who did not go on to higher education. On the other hand, the new growth in the American economy has been mainly in the sectors that are major employers of women, where the pay is less. One effect of this is that parents have a great deal less leisure time than they used to have and not enough time perhaps for their children.

NEW REALITIES

For all the attractive features of technological progress and economic success, the recent changes have served to attenuate human relationships in the family. Concerns have grown about the effects of the changing family patterns—single-parent families as well as working mothers, and remote fathers—on their availability for intimate, sensitive parenting of young children. The change in the frequency and quality of contact between children and their adult relatives is remarkable.

Not only are mothers home much less, fathers do not seem to spend more time at home to compensate. Only about 5 percent of all American children see a grandparent regularly, a much lower level than in the past. Children spend a huge chunk of time during their years of most rapid growth and development in out-of-home settings or looking after themselves, which often means gazing at the mixture of reality and fantasy presented by television. Adolescents increasingly drift into a separate "teen culture" that is often lacking in adult leadership, mentorship, and support, and is sometimes manifested in violence-prone gangs.

Such attenuation in family relationships is most vividly reflected in rising indicators of adverse outcomes for infants, children, and adolescents. Over the past several decades, the largely unrecognized tragedy of moderately severe child neglect has been accompanied by more visible, flagrant child neglect. This is most

obvious in the growing number of adolescents—even pre-teens—who have babies and then walk away from them. Adolescent mothers are often less responsive to the needs of the infant than are older mothers. They also tend to have more babies in rapid succession than older mothers, placing their infants at greater biological and behavioral risk. Children of adolescent mothers tend to have more cognitive, emotional, behavioral, and health problems at all stages of development than do children of fully adult mothers.

But insidious problems have arisen in a much *POVERTY* wider portion of the society. Not only are more children growing up in poverty than was the case a decade or two ago, but they are increasingly mired in persistent, intractable poverty with no hope of escape. They lack constructive social support networks that would promote their education and health. They have very few models of competence. They are bereft of visible economic opportunity.

The fate of these young people is not merely a tragedy for them, it affects the entire nation. A growing fraction of our potential work force consists of seriously disadvantaged people who will have little if any prospect of acquiring the skills necessary to revitalize the economy. If we cannot bring ourselves to feel compassion for these young people on a personal level, we must at least recognize that our economy and our society will suffer along with them.

As society puts greater emphasis on options, freedom, and new horizons—an accentuation of the longstanding American emphasis on individuality—one side effect clearly is a sharp increase in the divorce rate. Conventional wisdom on this issue had it that if the parents handled the situation with enough sensitivity, the effect of divorce on the children would be minimal. And this certainly can be the case. But practically speaking, divorcing couples find it exceedingly difficult to handle such situations over a long enough period of time and to protect their children from the psychological and economic fallout of divorce.

Studies of divorcing families reveal several recurrent themes. Marital separation commonly involves major emotional distress for children and disruption in the parent-child relationship. Single parents, try as they will, tend to diminish parenting for several years after the break-up. Improvement occurs gradually and is enhanced by the formation of a close, dependable new relationship. Over the years, the non-custodial parent's involvement with the child tends to fade. The effects of marital disruption vary with the age of the children involved. Children aged six to eight react with grief, fear, and intense longing for reconciliation. Those aged nine to twelve tend to be openly angry. They are inclined to reject a stepparent. At both ages, the children's behavior at home and at school often deteriorates. The tranquil passage through middle childhood is altogether disrupted by drastic family changes.

The economic impact of divorce on children is often profound. Most children of divorce end up living with their mother. Since women do not earn as much as men on average, and absent parents frequently fail to provide child support, children growing up in single-parent households headed by women are likely to fall into poverty. In one study of divorce during the 1970s, poverty rates for children rose from 12 percent before divorce to 27 percent after divorce. The 1987 poverty rate among female-headed families with children was 46 percent, compared with 8 percent among married-couple families.

In addition to having fewer financial resources, single parents may be less able to supervise their adolescent children. There is evidence that an adolescent living in a single-parent family and having little parental supervision will be susceptible to delinquent behavior and substance abuse. Of course, some single parents do in fact maintain adequate supervision and overcome many difficulties, but on the average the situation is not conducive to successful child rearing.

FAMILY SUPPORT

While all these remarkable changes of the last three decades were increasingly jeopardizing healthy child development, the nation took little notice. Until a few years ago, political, business, and professional leaders had very little to say about the problems of children and youths. Presidents tended to pass the responsibility to the states and the private sector. State leaders often passed responsibility to the federal government or to the cities. One arcane, but important, manifestation of this neglect has been the low priority given to research and science policy for this field. As a result, the nature of this new generation of problems has been poorly understood, emerging trends have been insufficiently recognized. Authority was substituted for evidence, and ideology for analysis.

All this is now changing. While the government has thus far provided little encouragement or incentive for employers to help parents balance their work and family responsibilities, the debate is growing among decision makers over what measures would strengthen today's families—family leave for new mothers and fathers, job sharing, part-time work, flexible schedules, and the like. Within the scientific and professional communities, a remarkable degree of consensus is emerging concerning conditions that influence child and adolescent development and how parents can cope with the changes within themselves and in the world around them. Much has become known about ways to prevent the damage being done to children.

SUPPORT PROGRAMS

There has been an upsurge in programs. Community organizations, churches, schools, and youth service organizations provide child care, support, and guidance for parents and their young. Successful interventions have taken many forms in programs in many cities. They include home visits, parent-child centers, child and family resource programs, school-based and school-linked services, life-skills training, mentoring, self-help programs, and other supports. These programs have found ways of compensating for a damaging social environment by creating conditions that can build on the strengths and resiliency of those caught in difficult circumstances.

Sadly enough, the emerging consensus and the positive results of some interventions are not widely understood by the general public or, for that matter, by many policymakers in public and private sectors. It is crucial now to have a well-informed, wide-ranging public discussion and to link experts with open-minded policymakers in an ongoing process of formulating constructive policy options. No single approach to families and children can be a panacea; many different approaches are needed to span the years of early childhood, when main growth and development occur, and continuing through middle childhood and adolescence. Social neglect is no answer to the crisis families face.

During their years of growth and development, children need dependable attachment, protection, guidance, stimulation, nurturance, and ways of coping with adversity. Infants, in particular, need caregivers who can promote attachment and thereby form the fundamental basis for decent human relationships throughout the child's life. Similarly, early adolescents need to connect with people who can facilitate the momentous transition to adulthood gradually, with sensitivity and understanding. Despite the radical transformations of recent times, such people are usually within the child's immediate family. If not, they exist in the extended family. But if these caregivers cannot give a child what it needs to thrive, we must make an explicit effort to connect the child with people outside the family who have the attributes and skills, and also the durability, to promote healthy child development.

PRENATAL CARE

Early prenatal care for both parents is fundamental in helping families with children in the crucial formative years. The essential components of prenatal care are medical care, health education, and social support services. Good prenatal care dramatically improves the chances that a woman will bear a healthy baby. Those who do not have access to such services suffer higher rates of infant mortality or may give birth to premature or low-birthweight babies. Yet, one-quarter of all pregnant women in the United States now receive insufficient or no prenatal care.

We can prevent nutritional deficiencies by educating expectant mothers and by providing supplementary nutrition and primary health care. This integrated approach has been demonstrated to work well in the federal Women, Infants, and Children Food Supplementation Program. Through prenatal care, pregnant women can also be informed and provided necessary support and skills to help them stop smoking, minimize alcohol consumption, and avoid drugs if they are to have a healthy baby. The educational component of prenatal care can be expanded beyond pregnancy to include a constructive examination of options for the life course. Such a thrust can lead to job training, formal schooling, or other education likely to improve prospects for the future of the mother and her new family.

A major facilitating factor is the ready availability of a dependable person who can provide social support for health and education through the months of pregnancy and beyond. In one intriguing set of innovations, pregnant girls are connected with "resource mothers." These are women living in the same neighborhood as the adolescent mother. They have assimilated life's experiences in a constructive way, have successfully raised their own children, and have learned a lot that can be useful regarding life skills most relevant for the young mother. They convey what they have learned about the problems facing the young mother and in general provide sympathetic, sustained attention as well as gateways to community resources.

"RESOURCE MOTHERS"

Such examples highlight the value of social support for health and education throughout childhood and adolescence. It is vital that national, state, and local policymakers recognize the importance of prenatal care for all women. They need to understand that it will be much less expensive to society in the long run than is medical care for low birthweight and otherwise unhealthy babies, particularly those born to poor women. Intervention helps two generations at once and can have lifelong significance not only for the children but for their young parents as well.

PREVENTIVE CARE

Well-baby care oriented toward prevention of lifelong damage is vital not only for child health but for building parental competence. Immediately after delivery, the pediatrician assesses the newborn's health and informs the parents. In addition to providing immunizations during infancy, pediatricians also monitor children's growth carefully to detect nutritional problems and treat infectious diseases. Pediatricians nowadays provide well-informed guidance and emotional support to help families attain healthy lifestyles. They foster attachment between mother and baby and help prepare her for coping with unpredictable difficulties with her infant. They answer parents' questions and anticipate questions about growth and development. They provide other vital services, for example, early treatment of ear infections and correction of vision deficits so that hearing and visual impairments do not interfere with learning.

As the infant becomes a toddler, the pediatrician or other primary care provider, in addition to assessing the child's health and growth, can check the child for injuries or signs of neglect and abuse. They can help guide parents in providing safe play areas, dealing with difficult behavior, and easing the child's transition to out-of-home care and preschool. Since pediatricians are often in short supply, particularly in poor city neighborhoods and remote rural areas, it is essential to enlist the aid of pediatric nurse practitioners, home visitors, parent support groups, and primary prevention program directors. Neighborhood health centers have proved to be effective in reaching low-income children with preventive services, but they are not widespread.

More policymakers are seeing the wisdom of such preventive care for children, but greater progress has to be made on the most critical fronts: immunization, low birthweight, child abuse, and health education. Still not widely understood is the fact that the major health hazards for American children no longer stem from disease but from injuries—both accidental or unintentional and intentional. Injuries account for half of all deaths of children and are an increasing source of long-term disability and serious health problems for children and adolescents. Intentional injury and neglect—child abuse—is a very unpleasant subject, but it is slowly being faced as a national problem. Abused children are likely to suffer severe psychological and sexual problems later in life, and all too commonly perpetuate violent behavior in the way they treat their own children. The risk of child mistreatment is increased when parents endure a high level of stress, such as unemployment and social isolation.

Despite the limited amount of research that has been done in this area, preventive efforts have been launched that aim mainly at preventing repeated abuse in families rather than preventing the first incident. These interventions include parent education about child development and parenting behavior, counseling, parent self-help support groups, crisis centers, and protective day care, home visitor programs, and programs to promote stronger early attachment between mother and infant. Such preventive efforts are a good deal less costly than paying for problems of seriously neglected and abused children later on. They deserve vigorous exploration and research.

As child rearing moves beyond the home, the quality of custodial care becomes crucial. The vast majority of responsible parents are eager to ensure that the care their children get will facilitate their healthy development. Just as they want a competent doctor to foster their children's health, so too, they want a capable caregiver. Yet, the more I have probed this issue, the more I have become impressed with how difficult it is to meet this need. There is little precedent for outside-the-home care on such a vast scale as is now emerging in the United States. The crucial factor in quality of care is the nature and behavior of the caregiver. As the demand for child caregivers has surged, those trying to provide it have frantically sought to recruit more child care workers. Even with the best of intentions, this field has been characterized by low pay, low respect, minimal training, minimal supervision, and extremely variable quality. Although most child-care workers try very hard to do a decent job, the plain fact is that many of them do not stay with any one group of children very long. This in itself puts a child's development in jeopardy; it is especially damaging for young children, for whom long-term caretaking relationships are crucial.

At present most professionals recommend that parents defer day care beyond infancy if possible. But in the absence of policies for paid maternity leave, the trend seems to lean increasingly toward day care for infants. Many clinicians and researchers are working to develop effective models and standards of dependable day care that will promote normal, vigorous child development. At present the issue of what constitutes high-quality care and how it can be accomplished in practice is still unresolved. We can learn some lessons from other nations that have addressed this problem seriously. We need a better sense of how powerful institutions might help to fulfill the potential of this extraordinary movement. While there is an emerging consensus on what can be achieved, we do not yet know how to respond to this great challenge.

One of the most important research findings shows that the children who benefit most from child care are those who come from relatively poor families. Perhaps the rich experiences at the center provide such children with opportunities they might be missing at home. Can we extract the essential ingredients and heighten the efficiency of these good effects, so that they may become standard practice?

High-quality child care and preschool education in the mode of Head Start has proven valuable for children age four and now is being offered to those age three. Overall, individuals who have been in good early education programs have better achievement scores in elementary school, are less likely to be classified as needing special education, have higher rates of high school completion and college attendance, and lower pregnancy and crime rates than comparable students who were not in preschool programs.

The lessons of Head Start have wide applicability. Such valuable early stimulation, encouragement, instruction, and health care provided in quality preschool programs (all with substantial family involvement) can be incorporated into a variety of child care settings. Early education should not be seen as a one-time event akin to immunization but as an important component of a constructive series of developmental experiences throughout childhood and adolescence.

PARENTAL COMPETENCE

One of the most important and recurring themes in the research on early intervention is the potential value of teaching young parents to deal effectively with their children. Ideally, such education should begin before the baby is born. Thus, as indicated, a good prenatal care regimen would involve not only obstetrical, nutritional, and other measures that would protect mother and infant throughout pregnancy, labor, and delivery but also some basic preparation for both parents regarding their tasks as parents and their own life course; in the case of poor parents at least, this would include connection with opportunities to develop occupational skills.

Because the first few years of a child's life are a critical period of development, physical, emotional, and psychological, the family's capacity to nurture—or its failure to do so—has the most profound effect on a child's growth. Research findings strongly support the centrality of a loving, dependable relationship for a good start in life. This does not mean that only one person matters to that child or that the biological mother must be that person. Certainly, a baby can form secure attachments with other caregivers and with siblings. But research evidence indicates the great importance of one central caregiver who creates a sustaining, loving relationship with the infant. Expectant or new mothers or other adults in the consistent caregiving role can be taught effective parenting techniques including those that foster attachment.

As their children grow, parents can be helped by programs that promote verbal interaction among family members and the verbal responsiveness of adults to children. Numerous studies confirm that the mother's responsiveness strengthens her child's learning and sense of self-sufficiency and thereby opens doors to development that would otherwise be closed. Parents can also be helped to understand that there is an optimal range for the intensity and variety of stimulation for a child's healthy development. The great challenge is to devise on a broader scale family-centered interventions that will enhance children's cognitive development and emotional resiliency despite the problems of chronic poverty and relative social isolation.

SOCIAL SUPPORTS

As parent education programs spread, it is essential to avoid the extremes of dogmatism on the one hand and vague, wishful, uninformative approaches on the other. We have to look to the scientific and scholarly community as well as experienced practitioners in relevant fields to devise a standard of reference for prospective and actual parents to use.

Studies in a variety of contexts show that social supports for families (that are eroded, disintegrated, or otherwise weakened under circumstances of persistent poverty and social depreciation) can buffer the effects of stressful life transitions for both parents and children. We can no longer take for granted the supportive systems that were built into human experience over millions of years. Even the most successful, capable parents cannot teach their children the wide array of skills needed for today's complex, rapidly changing society. Increasingly, we must consider crucial skills for education and health that have a strong bearing on survival and the quality of life in contemporary American society.

Institutions and organizations beyond the family can provide the social support necessary for strengthening the family and/or offering surrogates for parents, older siblings, or an extended family. Examples of such interventions are in communities across the country, in churches, schools, agencies, and minority-run organizations. They build constructive networks for families that serve parents and attract youngsters in ways that foster their health, their education, and their capacity to be accepted rather than rejected by the mainstream society.

Whereas parent education efforts have historically focused on the child, family support efforts view the entire family as one unit. Their goals are to augment parents' knowledge of a skill in child rearing, to enhance their skills in coping with the child and other family matters, to help families gain access to services and community resources, to facilitate the development of informal support networks among parents, and to organize to counteract dangerous trends in the community. Most of these programs are served by para-professionals who are members of the community, although professionals are also involved.

Social supports for adolescent mothers are particularly vital, especially for those who are poor and socially isolated. Such programs not only teach parenting skills and ensure the provision of health and educational services, they help mothers stay in school and acquire skills for gainful employment. Evaluations of some interventions show that young mothers improve their diets, smoke less, and generally take better care of themselves and their babies than those who do not have such services; they also have fewer children.

FAMILIES WITH ADOLESCENTS

Compared to families with young children, families with adolescents have been neglected. Even for the affluent sector, little work has been done on strengthening support networks for families during the stresses of the great transition from childhood to adulthood. Still less attention has gone into strengthening networks for families who live in poverty or culturally different situations. Although adolescents are moving toward independence, they are still intimately bound up with the family, which is much more important to them than is evident. This is especially true in early adolescence. For that reason, we need to pay attention to the ways in which family relationships can be utilized to help adolescents weather the conditions of contemporary life. This is a difficult time for parents, too. Their own marital relationships, their own coping skills, are often in transition. They may need help in renegotiating family relationships at this time.

Stephen Small has identified for the Carnegie Council on Adolescent Development forty-one programs to help families strengthen their capacity to tackle problems associated with adolescent development. Most of these programs center on curricula developed for this purpose and made available for use by local organizations. Some of the more promising ones are initiated and maintained by voluntary youth-serving organizations such as the Boys Clubs of America, the 4-H Clubs, and the Parent-Teacher Association. One of Small's strongest recommendations is for a network through which parents can obtain social support from other parents—sharing experience, pooling information and coping strategies. A mutual-aid ethic among parents who have a common concern for the well-being of their developing adolescents and yet bring diverse experiences to the encounter can be helpful.

LIFE SKILLS TRAINING

Adolescents have to navigate through a mine field of risks to their healthy education and development. They need attention from adults who can be positive role models, mentors, and sources of accurate information on important topics. They need to understand the biological changes of puberty and the immediate and long-term health consequences of lifestyle choices. They need to learn interpersonal and communication skills, self regulation, decision making, and problem solving. Today there are few guidelines for behavior available to children or even to adults. Many of the messages they receive are conflicting or ambiguous. Clearly, our adolescents need life skills training—the formal teaching of requisite skills for surviving, living with others, and succeeding in a complex society.

Formal education can provide or at least supplement the life skills training that historically was built into the informal processes of family and kin relationships. Successful school programs are typically administered by agencies outside of the schools. Many use some variant of social skills training and use peers in their interventions. Across the nation, most communities have programs outside the schools that offer youngsters recreation or teach them skills. Youth agencies, such as Girls, Inc., serve about 25 million young people annually and thus are in regular contact with almost as many children as are the schools. Their aim is to help teens acquire social skills, develop a constructive personal identity, and build a dependable basis for earned respect. Their strengths are that they are free to experiment, they reach children early, and they typically work in small groups with ten to fifteen young people at a time. Effective programs tend to respond to more than one serious problem or risk factor and try to create incentives for dealing with them that adolescents perceive as relevant to their own lives.

Based on the lessons of experience with all such approaches that work for families and children, it should be possible in the foreseeable future to design interventions that go beyond what has been possible up to now. First, we can use our experience from the programs so far undertaken, ascertain which are the most effective and which need the most attention, and construct informed models for future interventions. With so much at stake, terrible suffering, grievous loss of talent and life, we can surely find ways to make these programs available on a much wider scale.

STRENGTHENING DISADVANTAGED FAMILIES

Democratic societies are being challenged as never before to give all children, regardless of social background, the opportunity to participate in the modern technical world. This means preparing them to qualify for modern employment opportunities; to achieve at least a decent minimum of literacy in science and technology as part of everyone's educational heritage; to make lifelong learning a reality so that people can adjust their knowledge and skills to technical change; and to foster a scientific attitude useful both in general problem solving throughout society and in understanding scientific

aspects of the major issues on which an informed citizenry must decide.

Traditionally, America's technologically educated work force, which has by and large been very efficient by world standards, has come from a small fraction of the white, male, college-educated population. We have skimmed the cream of a very preferred, fortunate group, while blacks, Hispanics, American Indians, and even women have historically been under-represented in the fields that require technical competence. Even if we were not interested in rectifying historical injustices, we must consider that the traditional white male source of scientists and engineers has become inadequate at the very time when more technically trained people are needed. This brings the country to a point where equity intersects with economic vitality, democratic civility, and military security. Because of this intersection, there are now broader and more urgent reasons than ever before to support an unprecedented effort in the education of disadvantaged minority children. What must motivate us is not only decency but also national interest.

In the immediate years ahead, the number of young people in the United States will be smaller than in recent decades. Fewer young people will enter the work force. By the year 2000, about one-third of these young people will be black or Hispanic, the groups now at the bottom of the educational and economic ladder. Already, in the 1990s, racial and ethnic minorities constitute the majority of primary and secondary school students in twenty-three of the twenty-five largest American cities. In another eight years, they will be the majority in fifty-three cities.

While the lives of individual members of minority groups have greatly improved since the 1960s, many of the millions remaining in the inner cities have been relegated to marginal status in our society. They are the poorest and least-educated Americans and are served by the least-adequate health care in the nation. As in past generations, those who can escape severely damaged environments do so, leaving behind those who have come of age on the streets, without stable adult models and constructive support systems and often without parents.

For the majority of American schoolchildren to be excluded from the mainstream of education and worthwhile jobs in the next century would be a personal loss and a tragic waste of human resources that will weaken the country's economic and social foundations. Increasingly, this injustice threatens our democratic foundations as well as the economic vitality of the United States. Plain national interest demands that minority students be educated equally with majority students, particularly in the science-based fields. The country can no longer endure the drain of talent that has been the norm up to now. The entire sequence of developmentally useful interventions must be applied in a concerted effort to poor and disadvantaged communities. There is much that can be achieved if we think of our entire population as a large extended family, tied by history to a shared destiny, and requiring a strong ethic of mutual aid.

WEIGHING COST

The biology of our species makes necessary a huge parental investment in order to achieve the fulfillment of each child's potential. This means far more than an economic investment. It is a continuing, relentless, recurrent demand for investment of time, energy, thought, consideration, and sensitivity. It is an investment in patience, understanding, and coping. It requires persistence, determination, commitment, and resiliency. The awareness of such a large investment, however vaguely formulated, is inhibiting many young people from undertaking childrearing now that the choice is more readily available to them. Others have gone ahead and started families, only to find they are unprepared for the challenge.

If they cannot or will not give their children what they need, then others must do so. But who? In general, parents have responded that they are willing to do a good deal of what is necessary but cannot do all of it. Therefore, we have seen the rise of institutions that provide parent-equivalent functions. We are in mid-passage in this process; no one can say with justifiable confidence what the consequences will be for the generation of children in crisis.

In almost all cases, the expenditures for optimal child and adolescent development are not simply add-ons but can be at least partly achieved by wiser use of existing funds. Huge amounts are already spent for these purposes. Much of this current spending could be greatly improved and redirected by some of the measures suggested here. To replace inadequate interventions would in some cases cost less and in other cases cost more than we are now spending. This sort of analysis must largely be done on a case-by-case, place-by-place basis. What is likely is that the total economic and social costs of present child-relevant activities could be greatly reduced.

We are all paying heavily for the neglect of our children—however inadvertently and regretfully. These costs have many facets: economic inefficiency, loss of productivity, lack of skill, high health care costs, growing prison costs, and a badly ripped social fabric. In one way or another, we pay. The vital investments outlined have to be viewed as the responsibility, not only of the family, but of the entire society—not just the federal government but other levels of government; not just business but labor; not just light-skinned people but dark-skinned ones as well; not just the rich but the middle class and the poor. We are all in this huge leaking boat together. We will all have to pay and reason and care and work together. Our habitual short-term view will not suffice. There are many useful, constructive steps to be taken but no quick fix, no magic bullet, no easy way will do. We will not get rich quick on the backs of our children.

We have to move beyond the easy and pervasive recourse of passing the buck. It is the responsibility of every individual, every institution and organization, of every business, and all levels of government. We cannot lose sight of the fact that wise investment in human capital is the most fundamental and productive investment any society can make. Constructive development of our children is more important than oil or minerals, office buildings or factories, roads or weapons. The central fact is that all of these and much more depend in the long run on the quality of human resources and the decency of human relations. If these deteriorate, all else declines.

CHILDREN ARE
ALONE

Parents can be present and still be missing. A reporter finds that the ultimate test is not race or class, but a child's own strength.

Peggy Orenstein

Peggy Orenstein often writes about issues affecting women and girls. This article is adapted from her book, "Schoolgirls: Young Women, Self Esteem and the Confidence Gap," published by Doubleday.

"Me! Me! Me!" April Welch, a 13-year-old African-American girl, leans forward in her seat, waving her hand frantically in an attempt to catch the attention of her math teacher, who has just asked for the proper way to say "two over five."

"Mrs. Sandoval!" she shouts at the teacher. *"Me!"*

"O.K., April," Mrs. Sandoval says, smiling.

April drops her hand, relieved.

"You can't change it," she announces, indicating the fraction cannot be reduced.

The math teacher's smile tightens almost imperceptibly. "We know that, April," she says. "That wasn't my question."

"Oh," April replies, turning away and rummaging in her backpack for a tube of Chapstick.

The names of the girls, families, teachers and schools in this article are pseudonyms. The Times does not ordinarily employ fictional devices, but for her book, written in collaboration with the American Association of University Women, the author promised to protect the children's identities.

As the class proceeds, April volunteers continuously, each time with the same frenetic urgency. When the teacher takes attendance, April, unasked, informs her of the whereabouts of a student who is cutting class. Later, she offers to take a note to the office and then to pass out math books. But most often, April raises her hand in response to a question that Mrs. Sandoval has posed, although whenever the teacher acknowledges her, April's answers are invariably wrong.

When Mrs. Sandoval asks for the difference between the numbers in a series that begins 26, 24, 22, April's hand flies up.

"They're both in the same range," April says when she's called upon, "but one of them is kind of. . . ."

"Listen to my question, April. What is subtracted to get this number?"

April falls silent, more quiet than she has been all period, and darts her eyes desperately.

Someone stage-whispers, "Two."

She raises two fingers, hesitantly, still not speaking.

Michael, a round-cheeked boy who sits next to April, turns to me. "She's loco in the cabeza," he says.

I have been watching April for several days as she moves from English class to math to science

to social studies. Today, when the bell rings and, like the other seventh graders, she rushes from the classroom, I hurry to catch up. As we fall into step together, I tell her she has me a bit confused. Other students raise their hands when they know an answer. She seems to raise her hand simply because a question has been asked.

April spies a paper clip on the floor, picks it up and begins twisting it open. "I guess," she says, staring at her handiwork, "I guess I raise my hand because I want to be part of the class. I just . . . I just want to talk and feel part of that, you know?"

A friend of April's passes us and April calls out to her, interrupting our conversation. April digs into her backpack again and produces a handwritten invitation to a Halloween party.

"There's going to be music and dancing, and there will be someone to drive everyone home."

The friend studies the invitation. "Is it at your mom's?" she asks.

April shakes her head and fastens her gaze on a spot just to the left of her friend's shoulders. "Uh-uh," she says. "I'm not staying with with her right now."

BECCA HOLBROOK turns to me abruptly. "Do you want to get into my parents' relationship? My mom and my dad?"

"Sure," I say, caught off guard.

We are sitting on the bleachers at the edge of the P.E. field at Weston Middle School, a bucolic suburb that's a good 50 miles from April Welch's math classroom. A group of boys is playing a rowdy game of after-school football and Becca watches them idly, stopping our confidential conversation when they come too near.

Like April, Becca is 13 years old. She is a white girl who sits with her shoulders curved and her head hung slightly forward. Today, like the last few times I've seen her, Becca's eyes are red-rimmed. At first, she says the pinkness is caused by her contact lenses, but later admits it's more often from crying.

"A while ago," Becca says, "my mom came in to my room and she sat on my bed and said, 'Good night, I love you' and that motherly kind of stuff, but she was in tears. It's not like she was bawling or anything, just these tears on her face, and I don't know what's going on. So I say 'O.K., good night, Mom' and she closes the door. The next day, she told me it was 'fear crying.' She told me that she's scared of my dad and that she can't stand sleeping with him anymore. He wants to have sex every night and she doesn't enjoy it at all. She said it's like rape for her every night."

Becca pushes her hair, home-streaked with Sun-In, away from her face, revealing an anxious expression. "She said that if she didn't do it, though, she'd be out of there like the speed of light. So it's like she has to give in to him for, like, an insurance policy or something."

This is not the first time that Becca's mother has confided in her about her embattled marriage. More than once, Becca has told me that she feels older than her friends because of what she knows about "life and relationships and stuff." Given that unique understanding, she believes only she can offer her mother true succor. "When my mom first started telling me these things, I felt suffocated in a way," Becca says now. "But, I realize I'm the only normal thing in her life. I'm the only one who can really comfort her."

She drifts off for a moment as the crowd of football players tromp by us, their game over. "I think sometimes it would be easier for my mom if my parents didn't have kids," she continues when the boys are at a safe distance. "But then, she needs to get things off her chest and so she needs me and I can be there for her. . . . It's like we're two eyes of a hurricane."

I MET APRIL AND BECCA in the spring of 1992, as I began reporting a book about teen-age girls. Beginning the following September, I spent a school year

tracking them and seven of their peers in two Northern California middle schools — one in a middle-class, largely white suburb and the other in a low-income, urban community serving mainly children of color. I sat in on the girls' classes, spent time with them on the playground and at home, talked to parents, teachers and peers. The girls were a diverse lot, within each community as well as between them. They were from single-parent and dual-parent homes; from affluent, working-class and poor families. Some excelled in school; some performed poorly.

At first, April and Becca seemed as different as two girls could be. April, who attends John J. Audubon Middle School, was introduced to me as the kind of girl who slips through the cracks of the educational system: although her teachers say she is bright, she attends classes only sporadically, and her mother, who was a teen-ager when April was born, struggles with an addiction to crack.

Becca is from a two-parent family. Her father is an administrator for the Federal Government. Her mother, herself a teacher, is well read and deeply concerned about teen-age girls' self-esteem. Becca describes herself as a "sensitive" girl. Unlike April, she shies away from participating in class, fearing, she says, that if she makes a mistake, "My self-confidence will be taken away."

In spite of appearances, however, it quickly became clear that Becca and April faced the same predicament: both girls were faltering under the burdens of their mothers' lives and were becoming aware of the limitations of their parents and teachers. Both girls were trying, at home and at school, to make their distress clear. And, as the year unfolded, and their at-

tempts to gain attention continued to go unheeded, both girls were ultimately forced to make critical decisions on their own about how — or even whether — to survive.

INITIALLY, I WAS TOLD that April Welch would be entering eighth grade in the fall, but as it turned out, since she had repeated sixth grade, she was entering seventh and was a year behind her peers. At Audubon, repeating students who attain a C average by the end of the first marking period are promoted to their proper grade, but since retained students are often assigned to the same classes with the same teachers and the same curriculum that failed to inspire them the first time around, that goal is seldom realized. At any rate, the students know that at age 15, no matter how many times they have been left back — and regardless of whether they can read, write or add — district policy is to promote them to high school.

"The first time I was in sixth grade, I hardly came to school at all," April tells me early in the year. "I was enrolled, but I'd just cut. I'd walk into school and walk right back out. I was scared, I guess. I'd just graduated from fifth grade and I thought middle school was a big old step." She shakes her head, as if in disgust toward her former self. "My mother didn't say nothin' 'bout it. She just said it was my life and I'd learn in my own time, and I did. I tried to run from it. I wanted to start over at some other school, but I didn't. I knew I had to face what I did. I came back and started sixth grade again. It was kind of embarrassing, but that's how it had to be. I still haven't caught up, neither. I mean, I have a little, but not how I want to. Not like I was in

elementary school. Back then, I did good. I used to understand better."

Throughout September and October, April held out hope that she could earn the marks that would advance her to eighth grade. By November, however, her grade point average hovered at D-minus, and by the end of the first semester, her teachers had given up on her.

"She's failing," Mrs. Sandoval tells me flatly when I run into her in the school office. "She doesn't come to class anymore. Maybe she comes three times a week, but math is built on structure, on one thing then the next, so unless you're really bright at it . . . sometimes she tries really hard and seems to get it, but she's just falling behind. I offered her after-school help. But if she doesn't come, I can't make her do it."

I ask her how she thinks she could help April.

She answers quickly and her tone becomes curt. "Hey, I got kids of my own," she says. Then her shoulders droop and she sighs. "Look, I know she's on the 'at-risk' list, that they *know* about her. But there are so many kids in the class with so many needs . . . someone like April, when she's not there much, it gets to be out of sight, out of mind."

Later that day, when I ask April's science teacher if I can speak to April in the hall for a few minutes, he seems equally frustrated. "Go ahead," he says. "Keep her the whole period if you want to. At this point, she's just a distraction."

April is a distraction, as would be any student who cannot catch up but will not drop out. Toward the beginning of the second semester, when April jokes too loudly and too often in her art class, the teacher sends her to the counselor's office with a discipline referral slip. On it, he writes in capital letters, underlined several times, "It is my opinion that April should have been staffed out last year"; that is, labeled unmanageable and shipped to another school, where she will become someone else's problem — or someone else's to ignore.

"I know I'm not doing good," April says when I find her wandering in the hall one afternoon. "But I'm not tripping or anything, 'cause I'm still gonna graduate after next year and go to high school."

No one at Audubon can explain how a child reaches seventh grade without being able to add or subtract, particularly a vocal child like April who makes her difficulties quite clear. When, toward the end of March, I question April's counselor, Ms. Peck, about this, she lets out a long, slow breath. Ms. Peck is responsible for "counseling" over 300 students a year. She is a peevish woman with gray skin and sharp features. The first week of school, in an assembly for the entire eighth grade, she announced that the students' fate was already sealed since their high-school applications are based on their *seventh* grade G.P.A.

"It's already done and you can't change it," she told them, effectively extinguishing any motivation for improvement. Today, sitting in her cramped box of an office, Ms. Peck leans across her cluttered desk to pull April's file up on her computer screen. She informs me that April has already racked up between 25 and 30 unexcused absences in every class.

Ms. Peck leans back in her chair. "She's missing an average of two days a week of school," she says. "There's very little we can do if a child is not here. We contact home, but if she doesn't do the work required and she's not here . . . well, there's very little we can do."

Audubon students who are the most vulnerable to leaving school are placed on a special counseling list. Once a month, the counselors, the social worker and other appropriate support staff members convene an "at-risk round table" to discuss what can be done for these children. They request daily progress reports from the teachers (they are rarely provided), meet with parents when possible and evaluate whether students require testing for learning disabilities. April was placed on this list in December and, according to Ms. Peck, her case was discussed shortly thereafter.

"I know we talked about her," Ms. Peck says, "but I don't remember what we said and I don't remember what we were going to do."

I ask Ms. Peck how the school will insure that April receives an adequate education. "I don't know if there's anything that we can do to make a difference for April," she says. "I always say that success in school is a three-legged stool: the parent, the school, the child. If you're missing the parent or the child in that stool, you won't have much chance at success. From what I understand, April goes back and forth between her mother and her aunt; I don't have any idea of what goes on in there, but she doesn't seem to have any parent backing."

Although there are no comprehensive programs at Audubon designed for girls like April, Ms. Peck insinuates that April's home life is solely responsible for her failure. Yet when one of April's aunts calls Ms. Peck and asks to be kept abreast of her niece's progress, the counselor does not offer to meet with her, nor does she invite her to participate in the at-risk round table. Instead, she writes the aunt's phone number on a Post-it that

quickly disappears on her desk. She cannot, Ms. Peck explains, be expected to keep track of every relative who calls when her caseload is so overwhelming.

"I don't have the time," she says. "I don't have the time to do much more than discipline."

A few minutes later, as I am about to leave her office, Ms. Peck makes a final remark, which sounds very much like April herself. "It doesn't matter how well or poorly she does though," she says, grimly. "She'll go on to ninth grade in another year anyway."

IF, AMONG SOME OF her teachers, there is a tacit understanding that April is doomed by her family's circumstances, it is not an understanding that April shares. Ever since she was a toddler living with her grandmother (who died when April was 7), April has been battling fiercely — and largely unassisted — to keep her mother's addiction from defining her. Sitting in the school's litter-strewn back stairwell on a bleak winter day, she discusses that struggle. As she talks, April squirms, fiddling with the ornately braided ponytail she has woven into her hair. Throughout her story, however, her voice remains steady and she speaks with a level of insight that goes untapped in the classroom.

April explains that, after her grandmother died, she became a vagabond, moving back and forth between her mother, who lives in a public housing project with April's 10-year-old brother, and one of her nearby aunts, who seemed more interested in the monthly foster-care check she received from the state than in caring for her niece. Month to month — sometimes night

to night — April was unsure of where she'd lay her head. But it wasn't until the summer after her first sixth-grade year, when her aunt moved in with a boyfriend and her mother succumbed to drug addiction, that April decided she had to find a better life.

"I was living with my mom back then," April says. "She was into the fast life, into drugs and all that. She wasn't at first, but then she took up with her boyfriend and he was, so she started doing it, too. She lost her job and she was just doing crack with her boyfriend all day long. I used to call him, 'Dope Fiend.' "

She breaks into a small, wry smile. "We didn't get along too good," she continues. "He'd yell at me and hit me sometimes. Once I got so mad at him, I took his drugs and crushed 'em up. He tried to slap me and I kicked him and he said he was going to throw me out of the house. That's when I told my mom, 'You gotta choose between us,' but then, I didn't make her choose. I just left. I called the Child Protection Services and they took me, and they took my brother, and they put us in a group home for about four weeks.

"I didn't want to go back with my mom after that, but my brother did. I wouldn't go back to that drug-infested hellhole. I told her that, too, and she cried. So I lived with one of my aunties for a while, until my mom broke up with her boyfriend after he stole some drugs and almost got her killed. My whole family told her to go into rehab then, but ain't nothin' gonna help if you don't want to help yourself. But then, she did.

"I moved back with her now and I stick with her like everything. I watch every move she makes. When she first came back from rehab, she had money and she was going to the store; I followed her where she couldn't see, because I thought she'd buy drugs for sure. But she didn't. So the next time I trusted her, and she came back with food and no drugs, so I think it might be O.K. now. I pray to God it is."

April has been staring intently at an empty candy wrapper as she talks. Now she abruptly turns to face me.

"I would never do drugs," she says passionately. "I saw what it did to my family and I'd never look at it even. But to this day, I tell my mom: 'I don't hate you, I love you, but I hate what you took me through.' I would never, never, take my children through what she took me through. Never. There was people in that house walking around like zombies; there was people with guns threatening to kill people. Once, my mom's boyfriend owed my cousin a thousand dollars for drugs, and when he didn't pay, my cousin put a gun to his head. I used to go in my room and lock the door and cry, and I'd think I should just kill myself it was so bad."

She turns away and stares straight ahead, at the gray light that trickles through the stairwell's frosted windows. "But I learned something, too," she says. "I think I learned to be a positive person. And I learned I would not put myself through that and I would not put my children through that. Not never. I learned all that, so that's O.K."

UNDER THE WEIGHT OF her family burdens, Becca's academic confidence has begun to falter. Like many of the girls I follow at Weston, Becca holds herself to unrealistic standards. (Her mother says Becca's perfectionism sometimes "paralyzes her.") But whereas anxiety drives some of her equally bright peers toward excellence, Becca uses her "sensitivity" as an excuse to shrink from challenge and avoid risk. In sixth grade, Becca was an A student; at the end of seventh grade, she asked to be removed from the advanced math class, and by the middle of eighth grade, her grades in all of her classes were drifting to low C's.

As a quiet girl, Becca has never spoken much in class ("unless I'm really, really sure of an answer and sometimes not even then"), but with her self-esteem flagging, she stops volunteering entirely. She even begins to see her silence as an advantage: as long she's perceived as shy, her teachers won't notice that she has, in truth, disengaged from school.

At the same time, though, Becca complains that teachers make her feel invisible on the few occasions when she does try to participate. After trying, and failing, to get her English teacher's attention one day, Becca observed sadly: "You know how some people have charisma? I have, like, *negative* charisma. I feel like I can be talking and people can be looking right at me and they don't even see me."

In a sense, both Becca and April are invisible. April's inappropriate attempts at garnering adult attention are seen as an unmanageable product of her home life, and so she is shunted aside. Meanwhile, Becca's silence allows her to be overlooked as well. She is not seen as someone in need of counseling or special help because, although her grades have dropped, she is never combustible: she never, for instance, yells in class, fights with other children, conspicuously challenges authority. Becca's is a passive resistance. By opting out rather than acting out, Becca is in many ways the classic female student — quiet, compliant, obedient; as such, she is easily overlooked or seen as "making choices" rather than expressing psychological distress.

"Becca is so quiet," her math teacher admits, "she gets lost in the crowd. I don't like that to happen, but it has happened with her. She doesn't disrupt. She always looks like she's paying attention, but maybe she's not. I don't know."

Says her history teacher: "Maybe she thinks she'll be more cool as a C student. But she doesn't even get it together after she gets the bad grade. I'll say, 'Becca, you have a D, you may fail,' then she doesn't turn in the next homework assignment. But I think of her as someone who's responsible for her own grade and I let her be responsible for that."

Becca has indeed let her grades drop, but not out of laziness. Her disengagement is actually an academic strike, a statement of hopelessness that she willingly acknowledges. "Lately I've been thinking I don't care about anything," she tells me in February. "I don't see why I should care about my grades, you know? It's just a letter. What's the difference. Why do I need to learn anything in these classes." She pauses, weighing the gravity of her statement. "It's not like I really mean that," she says. "I know it's important, but I have to get my anger out."

ELLEN HOLBROOK is a tall, lanky, 44-year-old with sun-roughened skin and, like her daughter, newly blond hair (although hers is professionally tinted). She meets me at the front door of their home, just as Becca did, but where Becca's gaze is circumspect, Ellen's is direct; where Becca draws back, Ellen's handshake is firm. She wears jeans and a black, embroidered blouse; silver earrings coil into lizards just below her lobes, and her red-painted toenails peek out of sling-backed espadrilles.

Ellen teaches special education at a middle school in a neighboring town; she has recently returned to the classroom after 15 years as a reluctant stay-at-home mom, taking care of Becca and Jason, the Holbrooks' 17-year-old, mentally disabled son. She says she took the job in part to try to be a better role model for her daughter.

"Becca and I are kind of on a parallel course," she says, when we've settled into lawn chairs in the Holbrooks' back garden. "We're both learning who we are together. I know the messages I got when I was her age and that's not what I want for her. I want her to be more of an individual, not be defined by her relationship with boys. I try to tell her that responsibility and commitment are important and you have to work on them, but not lose yourself."

Ellen shakes her head and her smile grows rueful. "I said that to her, but I felt like a hypocrite. I mean, I tell you I want her to get the message to be independent, to be strong, but what I tell her is one thing — look at who's the nurturing one in the family, who left off her career to put the family's needs first, who takes care of everything, who's the teacher, who doesn't earn the money."

By making Becca her confidant, Ellen has deepened her daughter's anxiety. Yet she badly wants Becca to rise above her environment; she wants it so badly that she, too, ignores Becca's retreat from her potential, saying that because of Becca's "sensitivity," she "doesn't want to pressure her in school." So several years back, when Becca decided against enrolling in the district's gifted program, saying she didn't want to be seen as a "schoolgirl," Ellen supported that choice.

Last year, when Becca asked to drop advanced math (although her grade was a B), Ellen agreed again, hoping it would boost her daughter's confidence in the subject; it did, temporarily, but by the third quarter of eighth grade, her math grade had slid to a D. More recently, Becca has begun to express anxiety about college (where she would have "the pressure of midterms and stuff and it would be really hard") and Ellen does not question her timidity; instead, she alleviated her daughter's worry by telling her she could delay the option as long as she wants.

"Becca wants to blend in, be part of the crowd," Ellen explains. "She doesn't want to be smart. She's a very sensitive person and if it's easier for her to be average, then that's O.K. with me."

With the adults in her life overlooking her pain, Becca's efforts to gain their attention escalate. Several months after our initial meeting, Ellen tells me that Becca, who is twig thin (and is, in fact, sometimes called Twig by her friends), recently asked her what it means to die of starvation.

"I told her people don't actually die of starvation," Ellen says. "Their organs malfunction. I told her that Karen Carpenter died of a heart attack, not actual starvation. And she thought about that and said, 'Well, maybe I can get my appetite back.' I didn't say anything to her. But I've noticed that sometimes her mirror is out of her closet. She brings it out to look at herself, and she does it a lot. And some days she comes down and says, 'I can't go to school today, I'm too fat.' Then a few minutes later, she'll say, 'O.K., I found something to

wear that hides it, but I've got to lose weight.'"

Echoing Becca's history teacher, Ellen says that, as with academics, developing a body image is Becca's responsibility, so she won't "pick up the rope" and interfere. "I don't say anything," Ellen says. "I see that she doesn't eat for a day or so and then suddenly a whole box of Nutri-Grain bars are gone. Or all the leftover Halloween candy. Or a bag of doughnuts. I know she doesn't binge and purge, but she does have this very erratic way of eating.

"Becca doesn't have an eating disorder, but she's messing with the choices, with the possibilities of it. But I'm not going to give her attention on that topic. I don't want food to be a battleground."

Like Becca's teachers, Ellen plays down her daughter's behavior, although she herself once spoke to me of the perils of misreading girls' passivity. "When boys have problems," she said, "they act out and get in trouble. But with girls, they aren't supposed to get in trouble and often they just turn it in. So you don't hear about the problem until they try to commit suicide."

B Y THE TIME I MEET Tom Holbrook, he has become a mythic, frightening figure. I expect a fierce man and am startled to find a mild-mannered, balding fellow with a goatee wearing jeans, a T-shirt and old deck shoes, who slouches much like his daughter.

Ellen confines her feelings about her husband to a series of journals that Tom has never read, and he seems unconscious of the depths of her anger. He *is* aware, however, of his daughter's increasing moodiness, but he casts about for its source in vain.

"It doesn't make sense," he says, stroking the family cat, which has jumped into his lap. "She's got two parents; we're college-educated; we have all these neat things; she has anything she wants; we don't speak with foreign accents — what's the problem? I think Becca looks for things to get mad about."

Becca has told me that she thinks her father drinks too much and that she's alienated from his as a result. When I mention this to Tom, he seems genuinely shocked. "I don't drink to excess," Tom insists. "I'm never out of control. But maybe Becca sees things she doesn't care for. We've never debated the issue; she's never been negative about it to me."

Tom also briskly dismisses a theory of Ellen's, that his disappointment in his son has placed a wedge in his relationship with Becca. "I didn't expect to live my life through Jason," he says. "It's not like we called him Tom Jr. or anything. When you have kids, you have to accept that all bets are off. That "Father Knows Best" thing is only on TV. I don't know that Becca understands that. We're not perfect — there is no perfect family."

Having rejected other alternatives, Tom attributes his daughter's withdrawal to a natural teen-age phase, carried to an extreme by a pampered child. He considers Becca overwrought and hyperbolic in her emotions, but then he blames himself and Ellen for that: perhaps, he says, their indulgence of her moods encouraged Becca's hypersensitivity. Since it's too late for what he calls "behavior modification," Tom feels the best course of action for him is to steer clear of his daughter, to communicate through Ellen, and to appreciate the rare moments when Becca and he are at ease

in each other's company. In the end, though, he believes that a rift between fathers and daughters is inevitable.

"It's harder to be a father to a daughter than a son," he explains. "I subscribe to that theory that women are from Venus and men are from Mars, and we can't understand certain things about each other because of that. "

F OR MONTHS AFTER April Welch tells me about her mother, Denise, I try to meet her. We talk on the phone nearly a dozen times and she seems eager to discuss April's school progress as well as her own attempt to reconstruct her life. But whenever we choose a time and place to meet, she stands me up. Three times we agree to meet at the school, but she never shows; later we agree to meet at a cafe near her apartment and I wait for two hours; twice we agree to meet at the corner of the housing project where she lives, but even when our talk is scheduled just a few hours after a phone conversation, Denise forgets.

In early spring, I ask April if she'll bring me home with her one day for a sneak attack, but she shakes her head. "I can't do that," she says, her voice thick with pain. "I think . . . I think my Mom might be on drugs again."

By May, I can no longer reach Denise: the family's phone has been disconnected. As her mother becomes increasingly incapacitated, however, April steps in to fill the void, becoming a kind of junior mother. She takes on full responsibility for caring for herself and her younger brother, begging one of her aunts for a few dollars to buy chicken wings and potatoes for dinner, giving the boy her own small portion when his is inadequate and insisting that he attend school even when she does not.

In early June, Denise begins stealing from the small stash of money that April has hidden in her room for emergencies, but April says nothing; she just buys a lock for her door. When, a few days later, Denise breaks the lock and rifles through her daughter's possessions again, stealing a VCR that April had bought for herself before her mother's latest decline, the remainder of her money and some of her clothing, April sits down on her bed and sobs.

"I know my mom," April tells me sadly one afternoon. "I can see what she's doing. She's doing drugs for sure and there's starting to be prostitution, men coming into the house. I don't know what they are doing in there exactly, but I don't want those men coming after me next."

When the year's final grades are reported, April fails every subject except gym. She is still unable to add or construct a simple sentence, but, as predicted, she is promoted to eighth grade anyway. Yet, although the school system has essentially dismissed her, and her mother all but abandoned her, April perseveres.

On a late June night, she lies awake in bed, listening as the sound of her mother trading sex for crack drifts through the wall. She grabs two socks and jams one against each ear to block out the noise. When that doesn't work, she wraps a pillow around her head, the socks still in place. Lying there crying, she realizes once again that the only way she can save herself is to leave home.

"I was thinking, 'I have to do something if I want to do something different in my life or I'll end up doing like my mom's doing,'" she tells me later. "'I'll end up doing prostitution for drugs and

sleeping with all kinds of different guys and having all kinds of kids maybe.' So I prayed to God that night. I decided I'd leave and go with my Auntie Lydia. And if she wouldn't have me, I'd go get a job and pay my own rent somewhere. But I couldn't stay there."

The next morning, April called Child Protective Services and was again placed in a group home. After several days, however, she phoned her great-aunt and uncle, Lydia and George Roberts, who agreed to take her in, at least on a temporary basis. To April, this aunt and uncle are the stuff of fantasy: they both hold stable jobs — Lydia works in the accounting department of a large corporation and George has a job with the city — they go to church every Sunday and the house where they live with their 17-year-old son is clean, calm and safe.

"At first, my husband said this was too much for us, to take April on," Lydia told me when we spoke on the phone shortly after April moved in with her. "We have a child of our own and we're not so young anymore. But somehow, April touched our hearts. The night after she called, my husband woke me up at 2 in the morning and said, 'I don't know why I'm saying this, but if you want to take April in, I'm with you all the way.' I asked him what happened and he said, 'I don't know, I just know you love her.' Well, I don't know about that, but I know she deserves a break. I know that much.

"April has potential. I believe that. She just needs someone to be there for her when she falls to pick her up, push her back out there and tell her she can do it. Someone to be there when she's in need. Someone had to get involved, so I did. I did it because I see a future for

April; I have hope for her. She's very strong. … I still have hope for her mother, too. Denise has come up from the gutter before, gotten a job even. But she's not what concerns me right now. What concerns me is whether April will hold out for the dream, whether she will hold out for all that she hopes for, for all that potential."

THE LAST TIME I SEE April is during a visit to the Roberts' home, a whitewashed row house several miles away from the project where Denise lives. When I ring, April answers the door and immediately apologizes for her appearance. She is wearing purple sweatpants and a ratty T-shirt — what she calls her "kicking around" clothes — and her hair is pulled into a haphazard ponytail.

She leads me to the living room, which is dominated by a large-screen TV, and I sink into an oversize gray sofa. April sits on the floor beside me and leans against a window.

April is noticeably less fidgety than in our previous conversations. And although she says: "I'm hurting. I'm hurting every night about my mom," she is filled with pride in her new life. "With my mother, she let us do what we wanted," she says. "You didn't have to go to school; you could just stay home. You could be out on the street selling drugs — my brother does that. He likes it like that. But I choose not to go down that path. I choose to do good for myself. So I made a change. And it was all me: if I hadn't decided to make that change, there wouldn't never have been no change."

Earlier this year, April told me that she aspired toward a career in cosmetology, but she now says she has a new

goal: "I want to help kids in the situation I was in. I want them to see me and say: 'Dang! April got through high school and college and all, and look at all she went through!'

"You know what I want?" She looks down at my note pad. "I want to write my own book someday. I want to write my *own* book about my experiences so all the kids like me will know they can do better."

As April walks me to the door, I think back to what her counselor said, that there was nothing the school could do for a child who did not want to help herself. If success is, indeed, a three-legged stool, April has, despite profound adult indifference, secured two of those legs on her own. The question is whether she will be provided with the means to shore up the third.

WHEN I FIRST began talking to the girls at the two schools, we agreed that — so they would feel free to speak candidly — I would not discuss our conversations with their parents or teachers. To reassure them further, I explained the journalistic notion of protecting your source, an idea that they met with much enthusiasm. But in the spring, Becca asked me to read her journal and I realized that my promise of confidentiality had to be broken.

Early in the second semester, Becca's two closest friends severed their relationships with her. Although the rift began with an inconsequential spat, one of the girls said she realized she was sick of Becca's "putting herself down." The other said: "You have to reassure her 50 times a day that she's not fat, that she's pretty. She's so sensitive; I know I should be more understanding, but it's kind of a relief not to have to worry about that anymore." As girls will in their middle-school years, they shifted alliances. But when the new cliques were formed, Becca was left alone.

With few emotional reserves to fall back on, Becca panicked. She began spending her lunch periods in the school library so she wouldn't have to be by herself on the schoolyard; when her mother would allow it, she took "mental health days," staying at home in bed. As her social isolation increased, she began confiding in her journal (with an eye toward a reader), trying to sort out her anger with her friends from her own culpability.

"I never really felt that I was that good," she writes in one entry, "It felt like no matter what I did, it wasn't good enough. ... Putting myself down kind of reassured me that I was O.K."; later, she muses, "I lack self-esteem and confidence." But when her anxiety doesn't abate (and her friends don't return), Becca begins to conflate her distress over her parents and friends with her dissatisfaction over her weight: "I need therapy and diet pills *soon*," she writes in March, as if both were needed to affect a true cure.

Then, on March 23, Becca writes: "I downed eight Tylenol P.M. Good. I hope I end up in a coma then die!! ... Why am I suicidal? ... I don't even want Peggy to read this entry. She's an adult and would call a drug or suicide hotline."

I considered myself to be an observer of these girls'

lives, not a participant in them. Yet I felt I couldn't ignore the significance of Becca's gesture. So on my next visit to Weston, I sat Becca down for a talk. That day, she was feeling better and was more interested in discussing some recent prank phone calls she'd made to boys than her journal entries. I told her that her instincts were right: I did have to talk to an adult about what she'd written and we agreed I would talk to her mother. Becca just asked that I not tell anyone at school.

A WEEK LATER, Ellen and I sat on the Holbrooks' front steps — she in her gardening gear, sunglasses covering her eyes — talking about the breach between Becca and her friends. Ellen had tried to intercede, phoning one of the girls to chat "friend to friend," but that didn't seem to patch things up for long. In the meantime, Ellen's own relationship with Becca has grown strained. "Becca's gotten sullen," she says. "Our relationship isn't as intimate or consistent as before. She's been pulling back; sometimes we don't talk at all."

She turns to me, confidentially. "A week ago Monday, I could hardly wake her," she admits. "I came in and her lips were kind of stiff and I thought: 'Oh my God, can I do C.P.R.? How do I revive her? Do I call 911?' I was scared she'd done something. I shook her and she was O.K., but she was sort of stumbling down the stairs, really groggy."

Ellen kept Becca home from school that day and arranged an appointment with the school counselor. She also broke one of her own rules and snooped around her daughter's room while Becca was out. "All I found was Bayer headache formula and that wouldn't account for it. She's being deceptive. She's never been deceptive before." Ellen pauses. "But, she seems O.K. now, and it hasn't come up again, so I let it go."

I tell Ellen what I read in her daughter's journal. She rubs her palms against her thighs; her dark glasses hide her eyes, but her lips and the muscles in her cheeks tighten. "Well," she says and lets out a breath, "I'm not surprised." She pauses. "Oh, dear." Another deep breath. "I guess I'll have to find out what's in her drawers and talk to her about it."

Ellen continues to rub her legs, looking grim. "I guess she's been asking for more help than I've been giving," she says. "Maybe I should've paid attention a long time ago.

"I'd decided already to put her in therapy, but I thought we'd do it this summer, because I didn't have time now. So I guess I have that twinge of mother guilt. I know she needs to get her self-image into some perspective. And she needs to get her thoughts on relationships with boys and men in order." Ellen sits for a moment, staring straight ahead, then says, "Becca really needs a boyfriend, it defines her so much."

I ask if she really thinks that's the solution.

"Well, it has so much to do with her self-image right

now. But I guess, if they broke up. ..." She trails off; the sentence need not be completed.

"I know that, when she goes into therapy, she may get angry with me as well as Tom," Ellen says. "I'm prepared for that. She may get angry at the role model I've been, tolerating what I've been tolerating. But she's experiencing anger now, obviously. I'd like to see it come out in a more healthy way. I'm not sure I'm prepared for what Tom has to deal with, though. I don't know what he'll do with the issues as they come up. But it will be this summer, so we'll see. I think it's going to be, and I apologize to Mr. Shakespeare for this, the summer of our discontent."

Soon after my last conversation with Ellen, I left these girls' lives, uncertain of how their stories will play out. I think of April as I last saw her, standing at the front door of her aunt's apartment full of hope, despite the countless challenges she still faces between now and her high-school graduation. And I think of Becca, too, looking worried and anxious about the summer, and her transition to ninth grade. Becca's obstacles may be less obvious than April's — less a matter of attaining basic literacy or being assured of a roof over her head — but they are no less daunting. Her future also depends on her ability to transcend the model that her parents, for all their good intentions, have set for her: to, like April, choose "not to go down that path" and instead to chart her own.

THE ACHE FOR HOME

Monica McGoldrick

Monica McGoldrick, M.S.W., is the director of the Family Institute of New Jersey. Address: 312 Amboy Ave., Metuchen, NJ 08840.

"The ache for home lives in all of us, the safe place where we can go as we are and not be questioned. It impels mighty ambitions and dangerous capers. We hope that by doing these things, home will find us acceptable, or, failing that, that we will forget our awful yearning for it."

Maya Angelou

"Going Home." What is the meaning of that familiar and evocative phrase? Until recently, I understood it primarily in terms of the ideas of Murray Bowen, family therapy's pioneering theorist, which have so long influenced my thinking and my own family ties. As a therapist, I had always thought that "going home" meant developing a more adult, personal relationship with your parents and your siblings so you could be more fully your grown-up self even when you were with them. In recent years, however, my notions of home have changed.

I turned 50 last July. I now have a 9-year-old son, and, last year, my 80-year-old mother died. Along with my husband, sisters and friends, I am now somewhat startled to find myself a member of the oldest generation.

For me these days, "going home" means not just evoking in memory the house of my childhood, but trying to imagine how to create a safe haven for all of us on this planet. But, I am discovering, it is impossible to think about this larger vision of home, this deeper sense of human connection, without recognizing how the constraints of culture, gender, class and race have kept so many of us from feeling at home in our society in the first place. In fact, so many people are systematically abused, despised, devalued and kept invisible—women, children, people of color, the poor, gays— that for millions of us, "going home" means going to a place where we have never been in the first place. "Home" for too many of us is no safe haven, no home at all.

How can we break through these iron bars of hatred, bigotry, arrogance and invisibility that shut out so many? How can we come to understand the links between our individual stories, secrets and silences, and the ways that the lives of all of us are part of one inextricable pattern, that we all do share a common home? How can we come to realize that, as Susan Griffin says, "our personal stories and the history of the world are all one story"?

Margaret, our maid, was the person I was closest to, emotionally and physically, from the time of my birth until her death while I was in college.

I didn't recognize Margaret's white uniform as a symbol of her status in our family or know that she didn't learn to read until after I did.

UNTIL A VERY FEW YEARS AGO, FOR me, culture, gender, class and race were, to borrow Betty Friedan's famous phrase, issues with "no name." It had never occurred to me that any of them affected the relationships in *my* family, *my* schooling or the communities in which *I* lived. None of these crucial determinants of our life experience was ever mentioned during my childhood, my adolescence, my college or graduate education, or, for that matter, during my family therapy training.

So, even though I spent much of my childhood in what was really an interracial family—my primary caretaker was African American—race was never mentioned. Even though I grew up in a family run by two women who raised three daughters, a family with preferential rules regarding males (a family in which my father was treated like a visiting dignitary), gender was never mentioned. The influence of my Irish background would have been obvious to anyone who could recognize Irish behavior, yet I never thought of myself as Irish. And I grew up in a family in which class was never mentioned, even though we learned implicitly who was above us and below us on the socioeconomic ladder, and we learned rules for behavior that were utterly defined by class hierarchies. In short, we learned to organize our relationships completely according to prescribed, biased and utterly unspoken rules of culture, race, class and gender.

A few years before my mother died, she talked with me about how she had been defined throughout her life—first as a daughter, then as a wife, and finally as a mother:

"I was accustomed to people saying, 'Oh, you're Inspector Cahalane's daughter,'" she told me, "'and then I was accustomed to everybody saying, 'Oh, you're Joseph McGoldrick's wife,' so that I was always somebody's something, just as today I'm Monica's mother. Just once I want to be known as, 'This is Helen McGoldrick. She stands on her own two feet.' But that's never to happen, Monica. So I was always somebody else's something."

My mother's history, her fears and inadequacies, her struggles, continue through me. The pain of always being "somebody's something" is a problem I have to take responsibility for, because during the era in which she lived, she was not able to be all that she could have been. Along with her two sisters and their Barnard classmates in the 1930s, she was part of a privileged and dynamic group of women who, in spite of their education and talents, were raised to submerge their identities in the men and children in their lives. My mother was our nurse, manager, chauffeur, host, and the encourager of our projects. She was a brilliant, courageous and remarkable woman. Yet, for much of her life, I hated her—for her inability to be a "traditional mother," for her foibles and, most of all, for her class pretensions.

In college, when I switched fields from Russian studies to social work, she was embarrassed, because it indicated such a nose dive in class status. She used to introduce me by saying, "This is my daughter Monica, who is doing Psychiatric at Yale." For years, I resented her for what I viewed as bragging and for hiding who we really were by embellishing her stories to impress others. Only now do I feel shame about my anger, because I realize she did it because she was so unsure of her *own* status, and had been made to feel invisible and inadequate all her life. I have come to see it as my business that my mother was not free to be all she could have been. Her invisibility made our lives visible.

I have come to realize that it is not so much our mothers who have let us down, as the yardsticks by which we have measured them. When I speak, you hear, along with the voice of my beloved father, whose love, wisdom and humor I grew up knowing to cherish, the voice of my mother, whose great strengths it took me many years to recognize. And there were many other unsung voices in my family. For one, my Great-Aunt Mamie, only sister of seven brothers and a widowed father, whose family discouraged all suitors, for fear of losing their caretaker. Aunt Mamie took care of her father and brothers until they died or left home. And then she became the Santa Claus for five generations of our family, as well as for her whole court at 90 Saint Marks Place on Staten Island. Yet she lived in poverty for the last years of her life—"on relief," as it was called then—because, not having

the education for work that our society sanctions with remuneration, she could not make ends meet. She taught me a great deal about what you can give others beyond your pocketbook—about humor and generosity of soul, about sacredness that has nothing to do with physical beauty or great accomplishments of the sort that get rewarded in our individualistic, competitive, materialistic society. Her invisibility also made my life visible.

There were other unsung "sheroes" in my family. One of them was my primary caretaker, Margaret Bush, who was descended from slaves in Asheville, North Carolina. She was the person I was closest to, emotionally and physically, from the time of my birth until her death while I was in college. It was to her that I confided my problems—about boyfriends, about teachers, about my mother. After our family moved to the country, like so many African-American domestic workers, she had to live away from her own family much of the time to stay with us. She was always there for me and she loved me unconditionally. I am what she made me. I miss her every day, and she, like my parents, lives in my soul. When I speak, you hear her voice too.

But there is another side to this relationship. Last year, a friend of mine became tearful when I spoke of Margaret. Her own African-American mother, like so many others, had worked in the homes of white families, giving those families love and care that took away from what she had left for her own children. This is the story of racism: black women serving white families at the expense of themselves and their own families. And this is one of the unacknowledged benefits I have received from racism.

I grew up thinking I was innocent— that I had nothing to do with racism and certainly not with slavery. My mother, only a few years ago, told me that I was raised to be so "color blind" that I once tried to describe a black girl in my brownie troop by telling another friend everything about her *except* the color of her skin. My mother had no awareness that this was because I had learned the lessons of racism all too well—I knew you did not refer to skin color. Nor did I recognize the fact of Margaret's white uniform as a symbol of her status within our family. Or the fact that she did not learn how to read until after I did, when she was 50 years old. This, too, reflects the history of slavery, when slaves could be killed for learning to read, as could anyone who taught them. During my childhood, when Margaret learned to read with a local teacher, it was a big secret. I remember I used to go up and spy on her, anxious to discover what she was doing, up there in her room with her teacher, Audrey. How appalling it is now to realize the barriers she had to overcome to get where she did with her life. How incredible that she learned to read from racist books about fair-haired, blue-eyed little *Dick and Jane*, books that invalidated her own experience by leaving it invisible.

I now realize how much I benefited from racism, including the fact that most books were written for me as a white person. I am also coming, slowly and painfully, to realize what it means to carry around, in Peggy MacIntosh's terms, a kind of "invisible knapsack of privilege" that contains special provisions, maps, passports, visas, blank checks and emergency gear. We cannot see this knapsack, but those who don't have one see it all too clearly.

I GREW UP NOT KNOWING I WAS Irish, because my family was trying to "pass" for WASP. Of course, "passing" is what everyone in this country is pressed to do—we are urged to accommodate, to fit the preferred images, to keep invisible the parts of ourselves that do not conform to the dominant culture's values. So growing up, I did not even know that I myself had a cultural background.

It wasn't until the mid-1970s, when my interest in Bowen theory had finally led me to explore my own roots, that I took a trip with my entire family to Ireland. From the moment we landed in Dublin, I had an overwhelming sense of having come home. I seemed to see my relatives everywhere, people using humor, teasing or ridicule to keep others in line or to maintain distance in male-female relationships, failing to talk about vital emotional issues staring them in the face, and expressing anger by giving others the silent treatment. Suddenly, patterns I had taken for granted all my life fit into a larger picture. It wasn't that my family was "crazy"—I was just Irish! It was a transforming experience that has never left me. In some deep way, I still think of Ireland as home.

It was only some years after realizing I was Irish that I first became aware of

gender as an issue in my own life, an awareness that created enormous turmoil in my personal, as well as my professional, life. With regard to my Irishness, I could maintain a certain distance. I could get away from it. But with gender, there was no escape. Wherever I went, the rules for gender inequality still applied. I had a sexist husband who thought he was helping me if he did any chores around the house. But I came to realize that I, too, was sexist, for I felt grateful to him for "helping" me. When I went on a business trip, my husband described me as "abandoning" him and going on vacation. I prepared days ahead for my absence and I would make up for it for days afterward. This was so unlike the treatment of my father when I was a child; he traveled frequently and we did everything we could to make him as welcome as possible on his return.

As I became aware of the unequal nature of my relationship with my husband, I struggled with how to address it—how could I bring up a touchy issue without overloading the circuits? Certainly not when he'd had a hard day or was in a bad mood. But when I would finally decide the time was right, my husband would accuse me of "ruining our relationship." And a part of me would believe this, that it was somehow my fault: If I were only more generous or better at expressing myself, I would have been able to work things out by myself.

In the family therapy field as well, there was no getting away from the pervasive influence of gender and the emotional heat triggered by discussing it. I remember well the first panel on gender at a meeting of the American Family Therapy Academy in 1985. Virginia Goldner, one of the earliest and most articulate voices of feminism in family therapy, pointed out how family therapists had been trained to emphasize generation, but to ignore gender. I marveled at her clarity, the precision and utter truth of what she was saying—how could I not have seen it myself? But afterward, many men disparaged her talk, including one of the leaders in the field, who described her as "Darth Vader." Later, at a national family therapy conference, when the program included—for the first and only time—predominantly female presenters, many men within the organization expressed their outrage and their belief that this shift represented the desire of the women to "kill off" the men.

Over the years, I have been mystified by the reactivity of men to these issues. No matter how carefully we tried to explain that feminism was about equality,

partnership and a new construction of gender relationships and not about women taking over, reasoned conversations were all but impossible. There were threats that men would withdraw from the field if women didn't get off "this kick." Longtime male colleagues came up to me and said, "Monica, you used to be so *nice*. What's happened to you? Why are you so angry at men? Did you hate your father? Are you having trouble with your husband? *I'm* not sexist. I've never mistreated a woman. So why are you blaming me for all this? Why are you saying we have the power? I feel quite powerless. We men have problems too, you know. After all, we're not allowed to feel."

Of course, it is in the nature of patriarchy for men not to experience their power, because in a society that measures everyone hierarchically, there is always

While my father spent the week leading a life apart from the family, my mother always saw herself as defined by her role as wife and mother.

My mother was our nurse, manager, chauffeur, host, and the encourager of our projects. Yet, for much of her life, I hated her.

someone ahead of you or nipping at your heels to take your place. But it often almost seemed impossible for men to envision a way of being with other people that wasn't about winning or losing.

Within the past few years, I began to be confronted with race and racism and now it was *I* who was on the other side of the power imbalance. Immediately, I heard the issues quite differently. Suddenly, I wanted to say to others the same things men had been saying to me: "Why are you so angry? You used to be so nice. Now you're being divisive. I have nothing to do with racism, slavery or segregation. I've never mistreated a person of color. I'm a nice person, not a racist. I would love to change things, but I don't have the power, either. White people have experienced oppression, too—let me tell you about it." I wanted to justify myself, as I had heard men do so often by referring to their good intentions, their own experience of class or ethnic oppression, or their kindness to individual women. And as I heard my own reactivity, I realized that I must be part of the problem. Otherwise, I wouldn't need to be so defensive.

We "right-thinking" liberals react almost viscerally to being called racist. The accusation of racism sounds so damning, conjuring up images of lynchings or the Ku Klux Klan. But when people of color use the term, they often are referring to something much more subtle, the everyday micro-aggressions and insults that we who are white unthinkingly inflict through our ignorance of their history and experience.

Inevitably, when an African American expresses frustration or anger at a family therapy meeting, the white people want to get him or her "feeling okay" in the course of a single conversation. It reminds me of how much I always hated it when men indicated that they hoped each conversation about gender inequality would be the last—women would then feel alright and not be angry anymore. I realize I have taken this attitude myself in conversations about racism, but I now recognize the arrogance of my refusal to see that the pain of racism can't be taken care of so easily. How can we demand that black people's anger and sense of injustice disappear, when the problems that evoke them remain?

To the men who told me they weren't sexist, I used to say, "If you're not actively working on the solution, you're part of the problem." I realize now that unless my own life is about overcoming racism and my invisible knapsack of privilege disappears, I am also a part of the problem—and therefore I am a racist. I must work so that everyone is entitled to those privileges. Then we will all have a home.

Going home—or being unable to do so—is also about class. Until very recently, in my heart, I thought class was a boring, sociological topic, irrelevant to therapy. "I don't know what there is to say about class," I once told a group of students, "except that it's better off not to be poor." Then, one day a few years ago, I got involved in a discussion with some faculty members from the Family Institute of Westchester about the class rules in our families. During the discussion, I remember thinking, then on the way home it hit me—my *whole life* has been organized by class values. The clothes I wear are a class statement, the car I drive, my house, my furniture, the pictures on my walls, the music I listen to, even the language I use to write this article.

The topic of social class was never mentioned in my training—nor is it ever mentioned among family therapists. Everyone knows the class code for the degrees in our field—M.D., Ph.D., Ed.D., D.S.W., M.S.W., M.A. and so forth—yet we don't talk about it. We know, too, the complex hierarchical code for colleges and universities—the Ivy League, the Seven Sisters, Berkeley, Georgetown, Howard, Spellman, Trenton State. This concept of class is exquisitely comprehensive; it governs all social interactions; the rules of class insidiously influence our feelings of otherness, of not being okay.

In one situation or another, the myth of our having a classless society leads to our lying about who we are, whether to hide our WASP roots or the money that would distance us socially in the mental health field, or whether to hide our poverty and working-class origins. Class is about whether you grow up believing the American Dream applies to you, whether you can grow up believing you will ever be able to support yourself through work, whether you can feel protected by society's laws, entitled to society's goods and so forth. Class is also about who is in and who is out, who gets bullied, picked on, excluded, made fun of. While patterns of social exclusion develop most intensely during children's school years, rejection and the concomitant pressure to conform—to "pass"—continue to define us all our lives.

Whatever we cannot acknowledge—the secrets we keep about our own class background, our unspoken feelings about race, or sexual orientation, or gender—carries a cost. Guarding secrets consumes our energy and compromises our relationships. It continues to go unsaid that where you come from *does* matter, that you cannot shed your past and become whatever you want merely through hard work and desire. It goes unsaid that anybody *cannot* become president—not a woman, not an African American, not even a white man if he happens to be gay or Jewish. It goes unsaid that the concept of "liberty and justice for all" was never meant to apply to everyone in this country. We must begin to acknowledge our own beliefs and feelings about class, race and gender, to dare to put our assumptions and prejudices on the table so we can examine them and see what they cost us and what they cost others.

AN EARLY 19TH-CENTURY AMERIcan physician, Samuel Cartwright, described "drapetomania," a mental disorder prevalent among slaves, which was characterized by a single symptom—the uncontrollable urge to escape slavery. This diagnosis turned the desire for liberty into a sickness that was the problem of the slave, not the slave owner or the institution of slavery. Naming is an enormously powerful act. The use of labels to control others continues almost unabated in many sectors of our society, including family therapy. We are much more ready to diagnose the victims of abuse than the abusers. We have numerous acronyms—MPD (multiple personality disorder), PTSD (post-traumatic stress disorder), SCS (survivors of child sexual abuse)—that define the entire life course of those who have experienced trauma. But we omit from our descriptions those who traumatize others, just as we did more than a century ago with slavery. Why, as Ken Hardy and others have asked repeatedly, isn't racism defined as a mental disorder and labeled as psychopathology? Or sexism? Or battering?

Families of color, families of the poor, and immigrant families, whose norms and values are different from those within our naming scheme, remain pathologized as deficient or dysfunctional, or, worse, invisible within our society. They are labeled "dependent," while the dependence of the dominant groups on society is left invisible and they are left to imagine they are autonomous rather than benefiting from schools, health care and legal institutions that silently serve their needs. Many family therapists still are trained without reference to the insidious role that hierarchies related to culture, class, race and gender play in the United States. They are taught concepts of human development, psychopathology, family functioning from the skewed, patriarchal, classist framework of the dominant white groups in our society. They believe that you can learn about "men's issues" and not include issues of African-American men, that you can learn about "couples therapy" or "child sexual abuse" or "the family life cycle" or "dual career families" or "genograms" without including people of color in the discussion.

The problem with naming is not only with the labels we apply to others, but also with the ones we apply to ourselves. A name both includes and excludes. By defining myself as "Irish American," I may be reassured by a sense of belonging to a group, but at a certain point I am also distancing myself from those who are not Irish in ways that may undermine our mutual sense of "home." Focusing on any fixed group identity, whether based on ethnicity or class or race or gender, clarifies some things, but necessarily obscures others. As we try to create a truly multicultural society, enormous challenges face us. We must find ways to appreciate the many levels of our identities, while finding a balance between validating the uniqueness of each of us *and* acknowledging the common humanity we all share.

"All of us are more a hodgepodge of identities, cultural and otherwise, than anything else. So any restrictive characterization inevitably misses much of who we are. This complexity has been captured brilliantly in Louise Erdich and Michael Dorris's novel, *The Crown of Columbus*. With different details, this might be the story of any one of us:

I belong to the lost tribe of mixed bloods, that hodgepodge amalgam of hue and cry that defies easy placement. When the DNA of my various ancestors—Irish and Coeur d'Alene and Spanish and Navajo and God knows what else—combined to form me, the result was not some genteel indecipherable puree that comes from a Cuisinart. You know what they say on the side of the Bisquick box

under instructions for pancakes? "Mix with fork. Leave lumps." That was me. There are advantages to not being this or that. You have a million stories, one for every occasion, and in a way they're all lies and in another way they're all true. When Indians say to me, "What are you? I know exactly what they're asking and answer Coeur d'Alene. I don't add, "Between a quarter and a half," because that's information they don't require, first off—though it may come later if I screw up and they're looking for reasons why. If one of my Dartmouth colleagues wonders, "Where did you study?" I pick the best place, the hardest one to get into, in order to establish that I belong. If a stranger of the street questions where [my daughter] gets her light-brown hair and dark skin, I say the Olde Sodde and let them figure it out. There are times when I control who I'll be, and times when I let other people decide. I'm not all anything, but I'm a little bit of a lot. My roots spread in every direction, and if I water one set of them more often than others, it's because they need it more. . . . I've read anthropological papers written about people like me. We're called marginal, as if we exist anywhere but on the center of the page. We're parked on the bleachers looking into the arena, never the main players, but there are bonuses to peripheral vision. Out beyond the normal bounds, you at least know where you're not. You escape the claustrophobia of belonging, and what you lack in security you gain by realizing—as those insiders never do—that security is an illusion. . . . Caught between two worlds is the way we're often characterized, but I'd put it differently. We are the catch."

THERE ARE TWO COMMON PITFALLS in discussions of diversity. The first is to be so inclusive that the pervasive injustice of racism is trivialized in the rush to embrace the multiplicity of other "isms." The second pitfall is for discussion to get polarized, with the "black/white" issues becoming so predominant that other groups feel their issues have no place or that the discussion turns into an endless argument over which oppression is the worst or most important.

Last year, at a workshop on diversity, several panelists were giving impassioned presentations about the impact of white racism on African Americans. During the break, a gay, white colleague expressed distress that his perceptions about homosexuality were difficult to voice in the context of the presentation. Later, a Latina presenter spoke movingly of how discussions of black/white racism made her feel invisible. A third colleague became upset at some joking about his behavior as a white male. The panel also triggered for him some resentments from his working-class upbringing, but, in the context of this particular discussion, these feelings seemed to him somehow trivial and small-minded. Each of these panelists felt a strong urge to withdraw.

Anyone who has been through a heated public discussion about diversity issues knows how easily it can turn into a divisive contest triggered by the many legacies of oppression found in our society. It is hard for most of us to stay together when our particular "otherness" is not the focus. If we are to keep the conversation going, we have to learn to tolerate ambiguities and hold several different ideas in our minds at the same time. We must realize it is much easier to present ourselves in

My sister Morna's wedding in 1964 took place before the social revolutions of the '60s. My father was still the special man surrounded by all his women.

I grew up in a family with preferential rules regarding males— a family in which my father was treated like a visiting dignitary.

the position of the oppressed than to take responsibility for our role as the oppressor.

One thing is clear to me: in order for people to embrace a multicultural outlook, they first need to feel safe. We must acknowledge the horror of racism to make it safe for people of color to discuss sexism or homophobia in their communities. Similarly, our acknowledgment of homophobia will make it easier for those who are gay or lesbian to acknowledge the racism and classism of their communities.

Making cultural diversity into something more than a catch phrase requires sensitivity, flexibility and the ability to maintain a wider perspective. That means we must take into account the special invisibility of African-American men and the particular way that racism has been directed against them, without ignoring the invisibility of African-American women and the role African-American men play in the oppression of African-American women. While doing this, we must not humiliate or dehumanize white men, even as we must continue to hold them accountable for their privilege, entitlement and lack of awareness of their role in perpetuating the current system.

We must also struggle against the backlash that accompanies profound shifts in deeply held social attitudes. For several years, the family therapy field has been reeling from the reaction to the feminist critique. Many men have withdrawn from professional meetings. Now, as issues of culture and race are beginning to assert themselves, we are witnessing similar efforts to keep these subjects invisible. There is the frequent warning that "We'd

better go slow, or the whites will retreat in droves from our organizations." Or those with the power to employ staff say, "We would love to hire a senior minority family therapist, but we can't find any," without questioning their standards for a senior family therapist. (Most clinicians of color have not defined themselves as family therapists, so we are looking in the wrong places for them.) Or those with the power to plan conferences say, "We did cultural diversity last year. We need something new for this year." Or minorities are pitted against one another, with articles written blaming women for the oppression of poorly paid, minority child-care workers or about how the stereotypes minorities have about one another are stronger than the stereotypes whites have about any of them. Of course, this framework makes invisible the social structure created and held in place by the dominant groups that pits minorities against one another.

We must work actively to overcome the forces that divide us. The forces for segregation are so powerful that, unless we make strong and deliberate efforts to nurture diversity, the status quo will prevail. We cannot assume that racism will disappear just by our being "good people," or by leaving people of color to deal with it. This means that we who are white must confront racism rather than ignore it. We must learn to become uncomfortable in segregated situations and with reading books that pertain only to white people. We must become so uncomfortable that we are moved to do something about it.

But to do what we must do, we need each other. We must consciously divest ourselves of our myths of separateness, our false beliefs that the injustice that traps the

other does not also trap us, that the suffering we experience in our own group or culture or gender, class or race is inherently more serious than the suffering of others. We can no longer tolerate the barriers that have kept us separate for so long. To take pleasure and strength in the particular heritage to which we were born is fine; to buttress our own identities by humiliating or demonizing or rendering invisible those of other heritages is a sure recipe for our own disaster. Isolated in our self-declared tribes, we will surely be defeated by the forces that have traditionally had so much to gain by keeping us divided and encouraging us to blame each other for the social ills of the whole.

Alone, we will be mystified, silenced, invalidated; we will burn out in the struggle. But, together, we can help each other pull down the walls that separate us, demolish the invisible barriers that keep us from the connection that is our human birthright. It will never be easy. We are none of us yet fully formed human beings; in my view, we are all still just half-baked. So we will continue to blurt out racist or sexist or classist or homophobic comments, often without realizing what we are saying. If we are lucky, someone will draw our prejudices to our attention, and, if we have the patience and good grace to listen, to quell our own instinctive self-righteousness and defensiveness, we may learn a little more about our world, about each other and about ourselves. We may then be able to transcend, little by little, the false haven of our prejudice and blindness, to hold ourselves accountable for the fate of each other, and to gradually widen our vision of what we call home until it becomes a safe place for us all.

GROWING UP IN BLACK AND WHITE

For African-American children, learning to love themselves is a tough challenge

Jack E. White

"Mommy, I want to be white."

Imagine my wife's anguish and alarm when our beautiful brown-skinned three-year-old daughter made that declaration. We thought we were doing everything right to develop her self-esteem and positive racial identity. We overloaded her toy box with black dolls. We carefully monitored the racial content of our TV shows and videos, ruling out *Song of the South* and *Dumbo,* two classic Disney movies marred by demeaning black stereotypes. But we saw no harm in *Pinocchio,* which seemed as racially benign as *Sesame Street* or *Barney,* and a good deal more engaging. Yet now our daughter was saying she wanted to be white, to be like the puppet who becomes a real boy in the movie. How had she got that potentially soul-destroying idea and, even more important, what should we do about it?

That episode was an unsettling reminder of the unique burden that haunts black parents in America: helping their children come to terms with being black in a country where the message too often seems to be that being white is better. Developing a healthy self-image would be difficult enough for black children with all the real-life reminders that blacks and whites are still treated differently. But it is made even harder by the seductive racial bias in TV, movies and children's books, which seem to link everything beautiful and alluring with whiteness while often treating blacks as afterthoughts. Growing up in this all pervading world of whiteness can be psychologically exhausting for black children just as they begin to figure out who they are. As a four-year-old boy told his father after another day in the overwhelmingly white environment of his

Connecticut day-care facility, "Dad, I'm tired of being black."

In theory it should now be easier for children to develop a healthy sense of black pride than it was during segregation. In 1947 psychologists Kenneth and Mamie Clark conducted a famous experiment that demonstrated just how much black children had internalized the hatred that society directed at their race. They asked 253 black children to choose between four dolls, two black and two white. The result: two-thirds of the children preferred white dolls.

The conventional wisdom had been that black self-hatred was a by-product of discrimination that would wither away as society became more tolerant. Despite the civil rights movement of the 1960s, the black-is-beautiful movement of the '70s, the proliferation of black characters on television shows during the '80s and the renascent black nationalist movement of the '90s, the prowhite message has not lost its power. In 1985 psychologist Darlene Powell-Hopson updated the Clarks' experiment using black and white Cabbage Patch dolls and got a virtually identical result: 65% of the black children preferred white dolls. "Black is dirty," one youngster explained. Powell-Hopson thinks the result would be the same if the test were repeated today.

Black mental-health workers say the trouble is that virtually all the progress the U.S. has made toward racial fairness has been in one direction. To be accepted by whites, blacks have to become more like them, while many whites have not changed their attitudes at all. Study after study has shown that the majority of whites, for all the commitment to equality they espouse, still consider blacks to be inferior, undesirable and dangerous. "Even though race relations have changed

for the better, people maintain those old stereotypes," says Powell-Hopson. "The same racial dynamics occur in an integrated environment as occurred in segregation; it's just more covert."

Psychiatrists say children as young as two can pick up these damaging messages, often from subtle signals of black inferiority unwittingly embedded in children's books, toys and TV programs designed for the white mainstream. "There are many more positive images about black people in the media than there used to be, but there's still a lot that says that white is more beautiful and powerful than black, that white is good and black is bad," says James P. Comer, a Yale University psychiatrist who collaborated with fellow black psychiatrist Alvin F. Poussaint on *Raising Black Children* (Plume).

The bigotry is not as usually as blatant as it was in Roald Dahl's *Charlie and the Chocolate Factory.* When the book was published in 1964, the New York *Times* called it "a richly inventive and humorous tale." Blacks didn't see anything funny about having the factory staffed by "Oompa-Loompas," pygmy workers imported in shipping cartons from the jungle where they had been living in the trees.

Today white-controlled companies are doing a better job of erasing racially loaded subtexts from children's books and movies. Yet those messages still get through, in part because they are at times so subtle even a specialist like Powell-Hopson misses them. She recently bought a book about a cat for her six-year-old daughter, who has a love of felines. Only when Powell-Hopson got home did she discover that the beautiful white cat in the story turns black when it starts behaving badly. Moreover, when the products are not objectionable, they are sometimes promoted in ways that unintentionally drive home the theme of black inferiority. Powell-Hopson cites a TV ad for dolls that displayed a black version in the background behind the white model "as though it were a second-class citizen."

Sadly, black self-hatred can also begin at home. Even today, says Powell-Hopson, "many of us perpetuate negative messages, showing preference for lighter complexions, saying nappy hair is bad and straight hair is good, calling other black people 'niggers,' that sort of thing." This danger can be greater than the one posed by TV and the other media because children learn so much by simple imitation of the adults they are closest to. Once implanted in a toddler's mind, teachers and psychologists say, such misconceptions can blossom into a full-blown racial identity crisis during adolescence, affecting everything from performance in the classroom to a youngster's susceptibility to crime and drug abuse. But they can be neutralized if parents react properly.

In their book, Comer and Poussaint emphasize a calm and straightforward approach. They point out that even black children from affluent homes in integrated neighborhoods need reassurance about racial issues because from their earliest days they sense that their lives are "viewed cheaply by white society." If, for example, a black little girl says she wishes she had straight blond hair, they advise parents to point out "in a relaxed and unemotional manner . . . that she is black and that most black people have nice curly black hair, and that most white people have straight hair, brown, blond, black. At this age what you convey in your voice and manner will either make it O.K. or make it a problem."

Powell-Hopson, who along with her psychologist husband Derek has written *Different and Wonderful: Raising Black Children in a Race-Conscious Society* (Fireside), takes a more aggressive approach, urging black parents in effect to inoculate their children against negative messages at an early age. For example, the authors suggest that African-American parents whose children display a preference for white dolls or action figures should encourage them to play with a black one by "dressing it in the best clothes, or having it sit next to you, or doing anything you can think of to make your child sense that you prefer that doll." After that, the Hopsons say, the child can be offered a chance to play with the toy, on the condition that "you promise to take the very best care of it. You know it is my favorite." By doing so, the Hopsons claim, "most children will jump at a chance to hold the toy even for a second."

White children are no less vulnerable to racial messages. Their reactions can range from a false sense of superiority over blacks to an identification with sports superstars like Michael Jordan so complete that they want to become black. But if white parents look for guidance from popular child-care manuals, they won't find any. "I haven't included it because I don't feel like an expert in that area," says T. Berry Brazelton, author of *Infants and Mothers* and other child-care books. "I think it's a very, very serious issue that this country hasn't faced up to." Unless it does, the U.S. runs the risk of rearing another generation of white children crippled by the belief that they are better than blacks and black children who agree.

As for my daughter, we're concerned but confident. As Comer says, "In the long run what children learn from their parents is more powerful than anything they get from any other source." When my little girl expressed the wish to be white, my wife put aside her anguish and smilingly replied that she is bright and black and beautiful, a very special child. We'll keep telling her that until we're sure she loves herself as much as we love her.

Exploring and Establishing Relationships

- Emotions and Relating (Articles 7–9)
- Finding a Partner (Articles 10 and 11)
- The Next Generation (Articles 12–14)

What is love? Why do we love? Who do we love? Who should we love? These and other questions enter our minds as we explore the nature of relationship building. By and large, humans are social animals and, as such, we seek out meaningful connections with other humans. Ethological theorists John Bowlby, Mary Ainsworth, and others have proposed that this "drive" toward connection is biologically based and at the core of what it means to be human. However it plays out in childhood and adulthood, the need for connection, to love and be loved, is a powerful force moving us to establish and maintain close relationships.

As they explore various possibilities, people engage in the complex business of relationship building. In this, many processes simultaneously occur: messages are sent and received, and differences are negotiated. Assumptions and expectations may or may not be met. The ultimate goals are closeness and continuity.

How we feel about others and what we see as essential to these relationships play an important role in establishing and maintaining relationships. In this section, we look at factors that underlie the establishment of relationships as well as the beginning stages of relationships.

The first subsection takes a broad look at factors that influence the building of meaningful relationships. The first article, "Sizing Up the Sexes," looks at male-female differences that influence and, unfortunately, sometimes impede relationships between men and women. The next two articles explore the nature of love itself. The first, "Love: The Immutable Longing for Contact," uses attachment theory as the basis for a depiction of the need for a strong connection as a force pushing people toward meaningful relationships. "What Makes Love Last?" considers different ways in which love is played out in long-term relationships.

The second subsection looks at one way in which we establish adult-to-adult relationships in the mate selection process. The first article, "Choosing Mates—The Ameri-

can Way," traces the history of mate selection, contrasting the qualities considered desirable in the past with those considered to be so today. The next essay focuses on the physical and sexual components of "The Mating Game"—factors that, incidentally, have not changed much over the centuries.

In the third subsection, a different way of building family relationships is explored, that of connecting to the next generation through the parent-child bond. The first two articles address different ways to become parents. "Cahl Jooniah," is a lighthearted, yet heartfelt observation of pregnancy through the eyes of a husband anticipating the birth of his child. "Adapting to Adoption: Adopted Kids Generate Scientific Optimism and Clinical Caution" presents a positive counterimage to many of the myths held regarding adoptive children and their families. Finally, "The Family Circle" presents suggestions regarding ways in which new parents can build on family strengths to establish and maintain a positive relationship with their children.

Looking Ahead: Challenge Questions

Do you still find it hard to understand and communicate with members of the opposite sex? What still confuses or frustrates you?

What is your definition of love? How do you "know" you are in love? How do you know you love someone? What does it take for you to believe someone loves you? What can you do when love fades?

What do you look for in a mate? Would you be willing to "settle" for less? Why or why not?

What do you expect of marriage? What type of marital relationship would you see yourself having?

Do you see children as a part of your life? Why or why not? Would you consider adopting? How do children enrich a relationship? What are the drawbacks of having children? If you have children, how will it affect you?

Unit 2

Sizing Up The Sexes

Scientists are discovering that gender differences have as much to do with the biology of the brain as with the way we are raised

CHRISTINE GORMAN

What are little boys made of?
What are little boys made of?
Frogs and snails
And puppy dogs' tails,
That's what little boys are made of.

What are little girls made of?
What are little girls made of?
Sugar and spice
And all that's nice,
That's what little girls are made of.
    —Anonymous

Many scientists rely on elaborately complex and costly equipment to probe the mysteries confronting humankind. Not Melissa Hines. The UCLA behavioral scientist is hoping to solve one of life's oldest riddles with a toybox full of police cars, Lincoln Logs and Barbie dolls. For the past two years, Hines and her colleagues have tried to determine the origins of gender differences by capturing on videotape the squeals of delight, furrows of concentration and myriad decisions that children from 2 1/2 to 8 make while playing. Although both sexes play with all the toys available in Hines' laboratory, her work confirms what most parents (and more than a few aunts, uncles and nursery-school teachers) already know. As a group, the boys favor sports cars, fire trucks and Lincoln Logs, while the girls are drawn more often to dolls and kitchen toys.

But one batch of girls defies expectations and consistently prefers the boy toys. These youngsters have a rare genetic ab-

normality that caused them to produce elevated levels of testosterone, among other hormones, during their embryonic development. On average, they play with the same toys as the boys in the same ways and just as often. Could it be that the high levels of testosterone present in their bodies before birth have left a permanent imprint on their brains, affecting their later behavior? Or did their parents, knowing of their disorder, somehow subtly influence their choices? If the first explanation is true and

biology determines the choice, Hines wonders, "Why would you evolve to want to play with a truck?"

Not so long ago, any career-minded researcher would have hesitated to ask such questions. During the feminist revolution of the 1970s, talk of inborn differences in the behavior of men and women was distinctly unfashionable, even taboo. Men dominated fields like architecture and engineering, it was argued, because of social, not hormonal, pressures. Women did the vast majority

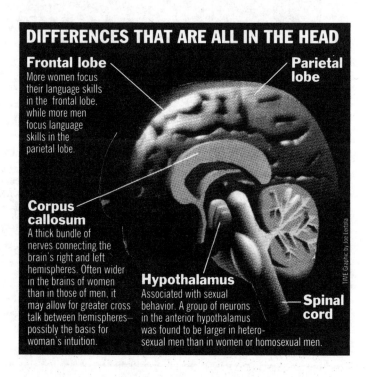

DIFFERENCES THAT ARE ALL IN THE HEAD

Frontal lobe
More women focus their language skills in the frontal lobe, while more men focus language skills in the parietal lobe.

Parietal lobe

Corpus callosum
A thick bundle of nerves connecting the brain's right and left hemispheres. Often wider in the brains of women than in those of men, it may allow for greater cross talk between hemispheres—possibly the basis for woman's intuition.

Hypothalamus
Associated with sexual behavior. A group of neurons in the anterior hypothalamus was found to be larger in heterosexual men than in women or homosexual men.

Spinal cord

TIME Graphic by Joe Lertola

of society's child rearing because few other options were available to them. Once sexism was abolished, so the argument ran, the world would become a perfectly equitable, androgynous place, aside from a few anatomical details.

But biology has a funny way of confounding expectations. Rather than disappear, the evidence for innate sexual differences only began to mount. In medicine, researchers documented that heart disease strikes men at a younger age than it does women and that women have a more moderate physiological response to stress. Researchers found subtle neurological differences between the sexes both in the brain's structure and in its functioning. In addition, another generation of parents discovered that, despite their best efforts to give baseballs to their daughters and sewing kits to their sons, girls still flocked to dollhouses while boys clambered into tree forts. Perhaps nature is more important than nurture after all.

Even professional skeptics have been converted. "When I was younger, I believed that 100% of sex differences were due to the environment," says Jerre Levy, professor of psychology at the University of Chicago. Her own toddler toppled that utopian notion. "My daughter was 15 months old, and I had just dressed her in her teeny little nightie. Some guests arrived, and she came into the room, knowing full well that she looked adorable. She came in with this saucy little walk, cocking her head, blinking her eyes, especially at the men. You never saw such flirtation in your life." After 20 years spent studying the brain, Levy is convinced: "I'm sure there are biologically based differences in our behavior."

Now that it is O.K. to admit the possibility, the search for sexual differences has expanded into nearly every branch of the life sciences. Anthropologists have debunked Margaret Mead's work on the extreme variability of gender roles in New Guinea. Psychologists are untangling the complex interplay between hormones and aggression. But the most provocative, if as yet inconclusive, discoveries of all stem from the pioneering exploration of a tiny 3-lb. universe: the human brain. In fact, some researchers predict that the confirmation of innate differences in behavior could lead to an unprecedented understanding of the mind.

Some of the findings seem merely curious. For example, more men than women are lefthanded, reflecting the dominance of the brain's right hemisphere. By contrast, more women listen equally with both ears while men favor the right one.

Other revelations are bound to provoke more controversy. Psychology tests, for instance, consistently support the notion that men and women perceive the world in subtly different ways. Males excel

EMOTIONS

FEMALE INTUITION: THERE MAY BE SOMETHING TO IT

Do women really possess an ability to read other people's hidden motives and meanings? To some degree, they do. When shown pictures of actors portraying various feelings, women outscore men in identifying the correct emotion. They also surpass men in determining the emotional content of taped conversation in which the words have been garbled. This ability may result from society's emphasis on raising girls to be sensitive. But some researchers speculate that it has arisen to give women greater skill in interpreting the cues of toddlers before they are able to speak.

MALE INSENSITIVITY: IT'S A CULTURAL RELIC

If men seem less adept at deciphering emotions, it is a "trained incompetence," says Harvard psychologist Ronald Levant. Young boys are told to ignore pain and not to cry. Some anthropologists argue that this psychic wound is inflicted to separate boys from their mothers and prepare them for warfare. Many men, says Levant, can recognize their emotions only as a physical buzz or tightness in the throat—a situation that can be reversed, he insists, with training.

at rotating three-dimensional objects in their head. Females prove better at reading emotions of people in photographs. A growing number of scientists believe the discrepancies reflect functional differences in the brains of men and women. If true, then some misunderstandings between the sexes may have more to do with crossed wiring than cross-purposes.

Most of the gender differences that have been uncovered so far are, statistically speaking, quite small. "Even the largest differences in cognitive function are not as large as the difference in male and female height," Hines notes. "You still see a lot of overlap." Otherwise, women could never read maps and men would always be lefthanded. That kind of flexibility within the sexes reveals just how complex a puzzle gender actually is, requiring pieces from biology, sociology and culture.

Ironically, researchers are not entirely sure how or even why humans produce two sexes in the first place. (Why not just one—or even three—as in some species?)

What is clear is that the two sexes originate with two distinct chromosomes. Women bear a double dose of the large X chromosome, while men usually possess a single X and a short, stumpy Y chromosome. In 1990 British scientists reported they had identified a single gene on the Y chromosome that determines maleness. Like some kind of biomolecular Paul Revere, this master gene rouses a host of its compatriots to the complex task of turning a fetus into a boy. Without such a signal, all human embryos would develop into girls. "I have all the genes for being male except this one, and my husband has all the genes for being female," marvels evolutionary psychologist Leda Cosmides, of the University of California at Santa Barbara. "The only difference is which genes got turned on."

Yet even this snippet of DNA is not enough to ensure a masculine result. An elevated level of the hormone testosterone is also required during the pregnancy. Where does it come from? The fetus' own undescended testes. In those rare cases in which the tiny body does not respond to the hormone, a genetically male fetus develops sex organs that look like a clitoris and vagina rather than a penis. Such people look and act female. The majority marry and adopt children.

The influence of the sex hormones extends into the nervous system. Both males and females produce androgens, such as testosterone, and estrogens—although in different amounts. (Men and women who make no testosterone generally lack a libido.) Researchers suspect that an excess of testosterone before birth enables the right hemisphere to dominate the brain, resulting in lefthandedness. Since testosterone levels are higher in boys than in girls, that would explain why more boys are southpaws.

Subtle sex-linked preferences have been detected as early as 52 hours after birth. In studies of 72 newborns, University of Chicago psychologist Martha McClintock and her students found that a toe-fanning reflex was stronger in the left foot for 60% of the males, while all the females favored their right. However, apart from such reflexes in the hands, legs and feet, the team could find no other differences in the babies' responses.

One obvious place to look for gender differences is in the hypothalamus, a lusty little organ perched over the brain stem that, when sufficiently provoked, consumes a person with rage, thirst, hunger or desire. In animals, a region at the front of the organ controls sexual function and is somewhat larger in males than in females. But its size need not remain constant. Studies of tropical fish by Stanford University neurobiologist Russell Fernald reveal that certain cells in this tiny region of the brain swell markedly in an individual male whenever he comes to dominate a school. Unfortunately for the piscine pasha, the cells will also shrink if he loses control of his harem to another male.

Many researchers suspect that, in humans too, sexual preferences are controlled by the hypothalamus. Based on a study of 41 autopsied brains, Simon LeVay of the Salk Institute for Biological Studies announced last summer that he had found a region in the hypothalamus that was on average twice as large in heterosexual men as in either women or homosexual men. LeVay's findings support the idea that varying hormone levels before birth may immutably stamp the developing brain in one erotic direction or another.

These prenatal fluctuations may also steer boys toward more rambunctious behavior than girls. June Reinisch, director of the Kinsey Institute for Research in Sex, Gender and Reproduction at Indiana University, in a pioneering study of eight pairs of brothers and 17 pairs of sisters ages 6 to 18 uncovered a complex interplay between hormones and aggression. As a group, the young males gave more belligerent answers than did the females on a multiple-choice test in which they had to imagine their response to stressful situations. But siblings who had been exposed in utero to synthetic antimiscarriage hormones that mimic testosterone were the most combative of all. The affected boys proved significantly more aggressive than their unaffected brothers, and the drug-exposed girls were much more contentious than their unexposed sisters. Reinisch could not determine, however, whether this childhood aggression would translate into greater ambition or competitiveness in the adult world.

PERCEPTION

HE CAN READ A MAP BLINDFOLDED, BUT CAN HE FIND HIS SOCKS?

It's a classic scene of marital discord on the road. Husband: "Do I turn right?" Wife, madly rotating the map: "I'm not sure where we are." Whether men read maps better is unclear, but they do excel at thinking in three dimensions. This may be due to ancient evolutionary pressures related to hunting, which requires orienting oneself while pursuing prey.

IF LOST IN A FOREST, WOMEN WILL NOTICE THE TREES

Such prehistoric pursuits may have conferred a comparable advantage on women. In experiments in mock offices, women proved 70% better than men at remembering the location of items found on a desktop—perhaps reflecting evolutionary pressure on generations of women who foraged for their food. Foragers must recall complex patterns formed of apparently unconnected items.

While most of the gender differences uncovered so far seem to fall under the purview of the hypothalamus, researchers have begun noting discrepancies in other parts of the brain as well. For the past nine years, neuroscientists have debated whether the corpus callosum, a thick bundle of nerves that allows the right half of the brain to communicate with the left, is

larger in women than in men. If it is, and if size corresponds to function, then the greater crosstalk between the hemispheres might explain enigmatic phenomena like female intuition, which is supposed to accord women greater ability to read emotional clues.

These conjectures about the corpus callosum have been hard to prove because the structure's girth varies dramatically with both age and health. Studies of autopsied material are of little use because brain tissue undergoes such dramatic changes in the hours after death. Neuroanatomist Laura Allen and neuroendocrinologist Roger Gorski of UCLA decided to try to circumvent some of these problems by obtaining brain scans from live, apparently healthy people. In their investigation of 146 subjects, published in April, they confirmed that parts of the corpus callosum were up to 23% wider in women than in men. They also measured thicker connections between the two hemispheres in other parts of women's brains.

Encouraged by the discovery of such structural differences, many researchers have begun looking for dichotomies of function as well. At the Bowman Gray Medical School in Winston-Salem, N.C., Cecile Naylor has determined that men and women enlist widely varying parts of their brain when asked to spell words. By monitoring increases in blood flow, the neuropsychologist found that women use both sides of their head when spelling while men use primarily their left side. Because the area activated on the right side is used in understanding emotions, the women apparently tap a wider range of experience for their task. Intriguingly, the effect

LANGUAGE

IN CHOOSING HER WORDS, A WOMAN REALLY USES HER HEAD

For both sexes, the principal language centers of the brain are usually concentrated in the left hemisphere. But preliminary neurological studies show that women make use of both sides of their brain during even the simplest verbal tasks, like spelling. As a result, a woman's appreciation of everyday speech appears to be enhanced by input from various cerebral regions, including those that control vision and feelings. This greater access to the brain's imagery and depth may help explain why girls often begin speaking earlier than boys, enunciate more clearly as tots and develop a larger vocabulary.

IF JOHNNY CAN'T READ, IS IT BECAUSE HE IS A BOY?

Visit a typical remedial-reading class, and you'll find that the boys outnumber the girls 3 to 1. Stuttering affects four times as many boys as girls. Many researchers have used these and other lopsided ratios to support the argument that males, on average, are less verbally fluent than females. However, the discrepancy could also reflect less effort by teachers or parents to find reading-impaired girls. Whatever the case, boys often catch up with their female peers in high school. In the past few years, boys have even begun outscoring girls on the verbal portion of the Scholastic Aptitude Test.

occurred only with spelling and not during a memory test.

Researchers speculate that the greater communication between the two sides of the brain could impair a woman's performance of certain highly specialized visual-spatial tasks. For example, the ability to tell directions on a map without physically having to rotate it appears stronger in those individuals whose brains restrict the process to the right hemisphere. Any crosstalk between the two sides apparently distracts the brain from its job. Sure enough, several studies have shown that this mental-rotation skill is indeed more tightly focused in men's brains than in women's.

But how did it get to be that way? So far, none of the gender scientists have figured out whether nature or nurture is more important. "Nothing is ever equal, even in the beginning," observes Janice Juraska, a biopsychologist at the University of Illinois at Urbana-Champaign. She points out, for instance, that mother rats lick their male offspring more frequently than they do their daughters. However, Juraska has demonstrated that it is possible to reverse some inequities by manipulating environmental factors. Female rats have fewer nerve connections than males into the hippocampus, a brain region associated with spatial relations and memory. But when Juraska "enriched" the cages of the females with stimulating toys, the females developed more of these neuronal connections. "Hormones do affect things—it's crazy to deny that," says the researcher. "But there's no telling which way sex differences might go if we completely changed the environment." For humans, educational enrichment could perhaps enhance a woman's ability to work in three dimensions and a man's ability to interpret emotions. Says Juraska: "There's nothing about human brains that is so stuck that a different way of doing things couldn't change it enormously."

Nowhere is this complex interaction between nature and nurture more apparent than in the unique human abilities of speaking, reading and writing. No one is born knowing French, for example; it must be learned, changing the brain forever. Even so, language skills are linked to specific cerebral centers. In a remarkable series of experiments, neurosurgeon George Ojemann of the University of Washington has produced scores of detailed maps of people's individual language centers.

First, Ojemann tested his patients' verbal intelligence using a written exam. Then, during neurosurgery—which was performed under a local anesthetic—he asked them to name aloud a series of objects found in a steady stream of black-and-white photos. Periodically, he touched different parts of the brain with an electrode that temporarily blocked the activity of that region. (This does not hurt because the brain has no sense of pain.) By noting when his patients made mistakes, the surgeon was able to determine which sites were essential to naming.

Several complex sexual differences emerged. Men with lower verbal IQs were more likely to have their language skills located toward the back of the brain. In a number of women, regardless of IQ, the naming ability was restricted to the frontal lobe. This disparity could help explain why strokes that affect the rear of the brain seem to be more devastating to men than to women.

Intriguingly, the sexual differences are far less significant in people with higher verbal IQs. Their language skills developed in a more intermediate part of the brain. And yet, no two patterns were ever identical. "That to me is the most important finding," Ojemann says. "Instead of these sites being laid down more or less the same in everyone, they're laid down in subtly different places." Language is scattered randomly across these cerebral centers, he hypothesizes, because the skills evolved so recently.

What no one knows for sure is just how hardwired the brain is. How far and at what stage can the brain's extraordinary flexibility be pushed? Several studies suggest that the junior high years are key. Girls show the same aptitudes for math as boys until about the seventh grade, when more and more girls develop math phobia. Coincidentally, that is the age at which boys start to shine and catch up to girls in reading.

By one account, the gap between men and women for at least some mental skills has actually started to shrink. By looking at 25 years' worth of data from academic tests, Janet Hyde, professor of psychology and women's studies at the University of Wisconsin at Madison, discovered that overall gender differences for verbal and mathematical skills dramatically decreased after 1974. One possible explanation, Hyde notes, is that "Americans have changed their socialization and educational patterns over the past few decades. They are treating males and females with greater similarity."

Even so, women still have not caught up with men on the mental-rotation test. Fascinated by the persistence of that gap, psychologists Irwin Silverman and Marion Eals of York University in Ontario wondered if there were any spatial tasks at which women outperformed men. Looking at it from the point of view of human evolution, Silverman and Eals reasoned that while men may have developed strong spatial skills in response to evolutionary pressures to be successful hunters, women would have needed other types of visual skills to excel as gatherers and foragers of food.

The psychologists therefore designed a test focused on the ability to discern and later recall the location of objects in a complex, random pattern. In series of tests, student volunteers were given a minute to study a drawing that contained such unrelated objects as an elephant, a guitar and a cat. Then Silverman and Eals presented their subjects with a second drawing containing additional objects and told them to cross out those items that had been added and circle any that had moved. Sure enough, the women consistently surpassed the men in giving correct answers.

What made the psychologists really sit up and take notice, however, was the fact that the women scored much better on the mental-rotation test while they were menstruating. Specifically, they improved their scores by 50% to 100% whenever their estrogen levels were at their lowest. It is not clear why this should be. However, Silverman and Eals are trying to find out if women exhibit a similar hormonal effect for any other visual tasks.

Oddly enough, men may possess a similar hormonal response, according to new research reported in November by Doreen Kimura, a psychologist at the University of Western Ontario. In her study of 138 adults, Kimura found that males perform better on mental-rotation tests in the spring, when their testosterone levels are low, rather than in the fall, when they are higher. Men are also subject to a daily cycle, with testosterone levels lowest around 8 p.m. and peaking around 4 a.m. Thus, says June Reinisch of the Kinsey Institute: "When people say women can't be trusted because they cycle every month, my response is that men cycle every day, so they should only be allowed to negotiate peace treaties in the evening."

Far from strengthening stereotypes about who women and men truly are or how they should behave, research into innate sexual differences only underscores humanity's awesome adaptability. "Gender is really a complex business," says Reinisch. "There's no question that hormones have an effect. But what does that have to do with the fact that I like to wear pink ribbons and you like to wear baseball gloves? Probably something, but we don't know what."

Even the concept of what an innate difference represents is changing. The physical and chemical differences between the brains of the two sexes may be malleable and subject to change by experience: certainly an event or act of learning can directly affect the brain's biochemistry and physiology. And so, in the final analysis, it may be impossible to say where nature ends and nurture begins because the two are so intimately linked.

—Reported by
J. Madeleine Nash/Los Angeles

LOVE

The Immutable Longing for Contact

As the child is connected to the parent, to be connected with another person is the only security we ever have in life. In that sense, we never grow up.

Susan Johnson, Ed.D., with Hara Estroff Marano

An illusion. An anesthetic. An irrational compulsion. A neurosis. An emotional storm. An immature ideal. These are the descriptions of love that have long populated the psychological literature. Let us not even consider the obvious fact that they are highly judgmental and dismissive. The question I want to pose is, does any one of them, or even all of them together, come close to capturing the extraordinary experience that for most people is an enormous part of the meaning of life—an experience that fosters well-being and growth?

As a marital therapist, my job is to help people experience love, to move from distance and alienation to contact and caring. But in order to help distressed couples change, I realized early on that I needed a model of what a good relationship is. For too long, the choices have been confined to two. There is the psychodynamic, or psychoanalytic, view, which holds that adult relationships are more or less reflections of childhood relationships—replays of old conflicts. And there is the behaviorist view: Love is a rational exchange in which couples make deals based on their needs, and they succeed to the degree that they master the negotiation process. Love is then either a crazy compulsion or, after couples calm down, a kind of rational friendship where partners make good deals.

I can assure you that if I tried to persuade the couples I see in therapy to leave with an understanding of their childhood or a rational friendship, they would not be satisfied. The truth is that these conventional descriptions do not adequately reflect the process of marital distress or the rekindling of love that I observe as a marital therapist. Possessing insights as to why you have certain sore spots or honing negotiation skills seems to somehow miss the mark. Neither addresses the intense emotional responses that consume distressed couples. As I watch couples, I see that raw emotion, hurt, longing, and fear are the most powerful things in the room. Couples seem to have a desperate need to connect emotionally—and a desperate fear of connecting.

'Couples seem to have a desperate need to connect and a desperate fear of connection.'

There are, of course, many elements to a relationship. It is true that echoes of the past are present in relationships, but this focus does not capture enough of what goes on and ignores the power of present interactions. Couples do also make bargains. But the essence of their connection is not a bargain. It is, rather, a bond.

The bond between two people hinges on two things-their accessibility and responsiveness to each other. The notion that the tie between two people is created through accessibility and responsiveness is an outgrowth of attachment theory. First put forth by the late British psychiatrist John Bowlby 30 years ago and later elaborated both by him and psychologist Mary Ainsworth in America, attachment theory is only now gathering significant momentum. It promises to be one of the most significant psychological ideas put forth in the 20th century. As many researchers are now demonstrating, it is certainly the most viable way of making sense of the mother-infant (and father-infant) bond.

VIEWING LOVE THROUGH A LENS

Over the past decade, a number of psychologists, including myself, have begun to see in attachment theory an understanding of adult relationships. In my experience attachment is the best lens for viewing adult love. When viewed through this lens, love relationships do not seem irrational at all; we do not have to pronounce them mysterious or outside our usual way of being. Nor do we have to shrink them to fit the laws of economic exchange. They make perfect—many would say intuitive—sense. And attachment theory goes a long way toward explaining what goes wrong in relationships and what to do about it.

John Bowlby observed that the need for physical closeness between a mother and child serves evolutionary goals; in a dangerous world, a responsive caregiver ensures survival of the infant. Attachment theory states that our primary motivation in life is to be connected with other people—because it is the only security we ever have. Maintaining closeness is a bona fide survival need.

Through the consistent and reliable responsiveness of a close adult, infants, particularly in the second six months of life, begin to trust that the world is a good place and come to believe they have some value in it. The deep sense of security that develops fosters in the infant enough confidence to begin exploring the surrounding world, making excursions into it, and developing relationships with others—though racing back to mom, being held by her, and perhaps even clinging to her whenever feeling threatened. In secure attachment lie the seeds for self-esteem, initiative, and eventual independence. We explore the world from a secure base.

Thanks to Mary Ainsworth, a large and growing body of research supports attachment theory. She devised a procedure to test human attachment. Called the "strange situation," it allows researchers to observe mothers and children during a carefully calibrated process of separation and reunion. Ainsworth found that whenever children feel threatened or can no longer easily reach their attachment figure, they engage in behavior designed to regain proximity—they call, they protest, they seek, they cry, they reach out. Closeness achieved, they do all they can to maintain it: They hug, they coo, they make eye contact, they cling—and, that all-time pleaser, they smile.

Ainsworth noticed that children differ in their attachment security and their patterns of behavior sort into three basic "attachment styles." Most children are securely attached: They show signs of distress when left with a stranger, seek their mother when she returns, hold her for a short time, then go back to exploring and playing. These infants develop attachment security because they have mothers who are sensitive and responsive to their signals.

On the other hand, she found, 40 percent of kids are insecurely attached. Some are anxious/ambivalent. They show lots of distress separating, and on reunion, they approach and reject their mother. Their mothers usually respond inconsistently to them, sometimes unavailable, other times affectionate. So preoccupied are these infants with their caregiver's availability that they never get to explore their world.

The third group of children have an avoidant attachment style. They do not seem distressed during separation, and they don't even acknowledge their mother during reunion. These infants keep their distress well-hidden; though they appear to dismiss relationships entirely, internally they are in a state of physiological arousal. These children are usually reared by caregivers who rebuff their attempts at close bodily contact.

These responses are not arbitrary but universal. Evolution has seen to that because they serve survival needs. Some researchers are busy identifying the neurobiological systems that underlie attachment behavior and mediate the response to attachment threats. They are finding specific patterns of changes in biochemistry and physiology during experimental separation experiences.

Attachment bonds are particularly durable, and once an infant is attached, separation—or the threat of it—is extremely stressful and anxiety-producing. In the absence of attachment danger, children explore the world around them. But if the accessibility of a caregiver is questionable or threatened, the attachment behavior system shifts into high gear. Facing the loss or unreliability of an attachment figure, infants typically are thrust into panic and they mount an angry protest. Eventually, however, the protest dies down and they succumb to a despair that looks like classic depression.

The implications of attachment theory are extraordinary and extend to the deepest corners of our psyche. Attachment impacts the way we process information, how we see the world, and the nature of our social experience. Our attachment experience influences whether we see ourselves as lovable. Research now shows that we carry attachment styles with us into life, where they serve as predispositions to later behavior in love relationships.

We seek close physical proximity to a partner, and rely on their continuing affections and availability, because it is a survival need. What satisfies the need for attachment in adults is what satisfies the need in the young: Eye contact, touching, stroking, and holding a partner deliver the same security and comfort. When threatened, or fearful, or experiencing loss, we turn to our partner for psychological comfort. Or try to.

The core elements of love are the same for children and adults—the need to feel that somebody is emotionally there for you, that you can make contact with another person who will respond to you, particularly if you are in need. The essence of love is a partner responding to a need, not because it's a good deal—but even when it's not. That allows you to sense the world as home rather than as a dangerous place. In this sense, we never grow up.

It is growing clear that the dynamics of attachment are similar across the life span. Implicit in the anger of a couple who are fighting over everything is the protest of the child who is trying to restore the closeness and responsiveness of a parent. In the grief of adults who have lost a partner is the despair of a child who has lost a parent and experiences helplessness and withdrawal.

THE MUSICALITY OF EMOTION

Attachment theory makes sense of a matter that psychology has just begun to puzzle over—how we come to regulate our emotions. We regulate feelings, specifically negative ones—fear, sadness, anger—through the development of affectional bonds with others, and continuing contact with them. Through

After the Fight

Anger and hostility in marital relationships are usually interpreted by a partner as rejection. They are felt as distancing behaviors, and set off attachment alarms; you respond as if your life is threatened. But hostility itself is often an outgrowth of feelings of fear; your partner is perhaps feeling threatened. It is important to recognize that it may be an attempt to bring you back into contact rather than to control you. In one sense, the appropriate response to hostility may be a hug rather than a return of verbal barrage. But we fight for our life when threatened; we defend ourselves with anything that comes to mind.

It's after the fight that you have a real chance to reprocess the events more accurately, to enlarge the experience to include elements that were left out of the argument while you were trying to win. An attachment lens on relationships encourages us to look at aggression in intimate relationships as a common way of dealing with fear. It also implies there's nothing wrong with dependency needs; it gives us permission to have feelings of wanting to be cared for without feeling weak or judging ourselves as "dependent." After the fight, you need to recapitulate the events with the inclusion of these feelings.

After a fight, in non-distressed relationships, the immediate emotionally reactivity dies down. (The problem in distressed relationships is that it never quite dies down.) When it does die down, if you have a secure base in a relationship, then is the time to talk about fears and attachment concerns.

This creates the opportunity for real closeness. As in: "When I heard you saying that you wanted to go away with your friends for a golfing vacation, I just got scared all to hell. You're saying that you don't need to be with me as much as I need to be with you. I get totally terrified if I think I'm hearing that."

If I have a secure base, I'm much more likely to allow myself to access the feeling that I'm afraid. I'm much more likely to tell my partner I'm afraid. Hopefully, my partner will actually help me with that fear. My fear level will be reduced. My partner's response will help me see myself as lovable, and that exchange also then becomes a positive intimacy experience in the history of the relationship.

This kind of sharing is what adult intimacy is all about. You and your partner find each other as human beings who need comfort, contact, and caring.

---

the lens of attachment we also come to understand that the expression of emotion is the primary communication system in relationships; it's how we adjust closeness and distance. Emotion is the music of the interpersonal dance. And when attachment is threatened—when we feel alienated from a partner or worry about our partner's availability—the music either gets turned way up, into the heavy metal of angry protest, or way down, shut off altogether.

'The expression of emotion is the primary communication system in relationships; it's how we adjust to closeness and distance.'

The lens of attachment sharply illuminates the dangerous distortion personified in a popular icon of Western culture: the John Wayne image of the self-contained man, the man who is never dependent and never needs anyone else. Our need for attachment ensures that we become who we are as individuals because of our connection with other people. Our personality evolves in a context of contact with other people; it doesn't simply arise from within. Our attachment needs make dependence on another person an integral part of being human. Self-sufficiency is a lie.

A PLACE FOR VULNERABILITY

The most basic message of attachment theory is that to be valid adults, we do not need to deny that we are also always, until the end of our life, vulnerable children. A good intimate adult relationship is a safe place where two people can experi-

ence feelings of vulnerability—being scared, feeling overwhelmed by life, being unsure of who they are. It is the place where we can deal with those things, not deny them, control them, or regulate them, the old John Wayne way. Relatedness is a core aspect of our selves.

Yet Western psychology and psychiatry have often labeled feelings of dependency as pathologic and banished them to childhood. Our mistaken beliefs about dependency and self-sufficiency lead us to define strength as the ability to process inner experience and regulate our emotions all by ourselves. Attachment theory suggests that, not only is that not functional, it is impossible. We are social beings not constituted for such physiological and emotional isolation. For those who attempt it, there are enormous costs. A great deal of literature in health and psychology shows that the cost of social isolation is physical and psychological breakdown. Under such conditions, we simply deteriorate.

There is nothing inherently demeaning or diminishing in allowing someone else to comfort you. We need other people to help us process our emotions and deal with the slings and arrows of being alive—especially the slings and arrows. In fact, the essence of making intimate contact is sharing hurts and vulnerability with someone else. You allow someone into a place where you are not defended. You put contact before self-protection. In marital distress the opposite happens, self-protection comes before contact. If you cannot share, then a part of your being is excluded from the relationship.

The couples I see have taught me that it is almost impossible to be accessible, responsive, emotionally engaged with someone if you are not able to experience and express your own vulnerabilities. If you cannot allow yourself to experience and show your vulnerability, you cannot tell others what you need and explicitly ask others to respond to you. But troubled couples naturally want to hide and protect their vulnerability although that usually precludes any satisfying kind of emotional contact.

Like psychoanalytic theory, attachment theory sees early relationships as formative of personality and relationships later on. But unlike Freudian theory, it sees our view of ourselves and relationship styles as subject to revision as we integrate new experiences. This capacity makes growth possible. The past influences the present, but we are not condemned to repeat it.

The attachment system involves attachment behaviors, emotional responses, and internal representations, or models. In our psyches, we create working models of attachment figures, of ourselves, and of relationships. Built from our experience in the world, these internal working models are at the same time cognitive and affective, and they in turn guide how we organize our experience and how we respond to intimate others.

The reason our behavior in relationships is relatively stable is that, although they are susceptible to revision, we carry these internal working models into new social situations. They write the script by which we navigate the social world. Our internal working models of ourselves, our relationship, and our close ones create expectations of support and nurturance—and become the architects of the disappointments we feel. They are the creators of self-fulfilling prophecies.

But the existence of internal models also explains why you can have very different experiences in two different relationships. Essentially, you meet a new potential partner who brings a different behavioral repertoire. This allows you to engage in a different dance of proximity and distance—she is home to receive your phone calls, he doesn't react with veiled hostility when you call him at the office. Being accessible and responsive, your new partner doesn't ignite your anxiety and launch you into attachment panic. What's more, with a different set of internal working models, your new partner appraises your behavior differently and then offers a different response. From such new experience, a tarnished inner vision of relationships or of your sense of self can then begin to change.

A NEW WAY OF CONTACT

That may be what passionate love really is—we find someone who connects with us and alleviates our attachment fears, which opens up a whole new possibility of acceptance and responsiveness. Love is transforming—not just of the world but of the self. We find a whole new way of contacting another human being, and this emotional engagement opens up new possibilities of becoming ourselves. That is the intoxicating thing about the relationship. It modifies how people experience themselves and how they see other people.

From my point of view, attachment theory also redefines the place of sexual behavior. For the past 40 years, we seem to have come to believe that sex is the essence of love relationships. That is not my experience in working with couples. Sex per sex is often but a small part of adult intimacy. Attachment theory tells us that the basic security in life is contact with other people.

We need to be held, to be emotionally connected. I think that the most basic human experience of relatedness is two people—mother and child, father and child, two adults—seeing and holding each other, providing the safety, security, and feeling of human connectedness that for most, in the end, makes life meaningful. Many people use sex as a way to create or substitute for the sense of connection they are needing. I would guess that many a man or woman has engaged in sex just to meet a need for being held.

So perhaps now the mystery of love is becoming clear. We fall in love when an attachment bond is formed. We stay in love by maintaining the bond. We use our repertoire of emotions to signal the need for comfort through contact, the need for a little distance. We help each other process our inner and outer worlds and experience each other's pain, fear, joy.

What, then, goes wrong in couples? As I see it, healthy, normal attachment needs go unmet and attachment fears begin to take over the relationship.

We know that distressed couples settle into rigid interaction patterns. Perhaps the most distressed pattern is that of the disappointed, angry, blaming wife demanding contact from a man who withdraws. Couples can stay stuck in this for years. We know from the research of John Gottman that this is a sure killer of marriages.

But it is only through the lens of attachment that we come to understand what makes such patterns of behavior so devastating. The answer is, they block emotional engagement; they stand in the way of contact and exacerbate attachment fears. As partners hurl anger and contempt at each other or withdraw, emotional engagement becomes more and more difficult. Patterns of attack-defend or attack-withdraw are highly corrosive to a relationship because they preclude a safe way for a couple to emotionally engage each other and create a secure bond.

What couples are really fighting about is rarely the issue they seem to be fighting about—the chores, the kids. It is always about separateness and connectedness, safety and trust, the risk of letting someone in to see the exposed, vulnerable self.

Marital distress, then, is not a product of personality flaws. Nor is anger in relationships irrational. It is often a natural part of a protest that follows the loss of accessibility and responsiveness to a partner. It is an adaptive reaction—anger motivates people to overcome barriers to reunion. Self-defeating as it may be, anger is an attempt to discourage a partner from further distancing.

A COMPELLING EMOTION

But fear is the most compelling emotion in a distressed relationship. Hostility in a partner is usually a sign that the fear level has gone way up—the partner feels threatened. Attachment fears—of being unlovable, abandoned, rejected—are so tied to survival that they elicit strong fight or flee responses. In protecting ourselves, we often undermine ourselves as a secure base for our partner, who becomes alarmed. Our partner then confirms our fears and becomes the enemy, the betrayer.

Such fear sets off an alarm system. It heightens both the anger of those experiencing anxiety in attachment and the dismissal of emotional needs by those given to avoidance.

A NEW FRAME FOR BEHAVIOR

The lens of attachment puts a whole new frame on our behavior in relationships. The angry, blaming wife who continues to pursue with blame, even though she understands this behavior may drive her husband away, is not acting irrationally. Nor do her actions necessarily reflect a lack of communication skill. She is engaged in a desperate intensification of attachment behaviors—hers is an entreaty for contact. She perceives her husband as inaccessible and emotionally unresponsive: a threat that engages the attachment behavioral system. Of course, the defensiveness and conflict make safe contact increasingly less likely, and the cycle of distress escalates. It keeps going because the person never gets the contact and the reassurance that will bring closure and allow the attachment fears to be dealt with.

In working with couples, my colleague Les Greenberg and I have elaborated a therapy, "Emotionally Focused Couples Therapy," that views marital distress in terms of attachment insecurities. It recognizes that relationship problems are created by how individuals react to, cope with, and disown their own attachment needs and those of their spouse. A major goal of therapy is owning and validating needs for contact and security, helping people to expand their emotional range, rather than shut their feelings down or constantly control them. It is not about ventilating feelings, but about allowing people to immerse themselves more deeply in their experience and process elements of it they usually protect against—the desperation and loneliness behind anger, the fear and helplessness behind silent withdrawal.

The most powerful change agent in a distressed relationship seems to be the expression of the tender, more disarming emotions, such as longing, fear, and sadness. It is the most powerful tool to evoke contact and responsiveness from a significant other. If I help couples create contact, couples can then solve their own problems.

Most couples begin by declaring how incredibly angry they are. They have good reason to be angry. As they come to feel more of their anger, not justify or contain it, they usually begin to explore and experience more of what it is about. The experience starts to include elements they don't usually focus on, which they may even [see] as inappropriate. In fact one reason for feeling so angry is that they feel totally helpless and unlovable, which scares them.

Soon one partner begins talking to the other about what happened one second before lashing out—an incredible sense of helplessness, a voice that comes into the head and said, "I'm not going to feel this way. I refuse to feel so helpless and needy. This is unacceptable." And now the experience has been expanded beyond anger and partners start to contact hidden parts of themselves—in the presence of the other.

This is a new and compelling experience for them that enables one partner to turn to the spouse and confide, "Somehow, some part of me has given up the hope of ever feeling cherished, and instead I've become enraged because I am so sure that you could never really hold and love me." This kind of dialogue redefines the relationship as one where a person can be vulnerable and confide what is most terrifying about him or herself or the world. And the partner, with the therapist's help, is there both for comfort and as a validating mirror of those experiences of the self.

BUILDING A SECURE BASE

The relationship is then starting to be a secure base where people can be vulnerable, bring out the neediness or other elements of themselves that frighten them, and ask for their attachment needs to be met. In this safe context, the husband or wife doesn't see the partner as weak but as available—not dangerous. I may hear one say: "That's the part I fell in love with." In a sense, the language of love is the language of vulnerability. While Western psychology focuses on the value of self-sufficiency, in our personal lives we struggle to integrate our needs for contact and care into our adult experience.

Attachment theory is an idea whose time has finally come because it allows us to be whole people. It views behavior gone awry as a well-meaning adaptation to past or present experience. And it views the desire for contact as healthy. Secure attachments promote emotional health and buffer us against life's many stresses. Love then becomes the most powerful arena for healing and for growth, and from this secure base, both men and women can go out and explore, even create, the world.

What Makes Love Last?

Alan AtKisson

Alan AtKisson is a writer, songwriter, and consultant living in Seattle, Washington. He and partner, Denise Benitez, recently celebrated their ninth wedding anniversary by hiking in the North Cascades.

My old friends Karen and Bill, married since 1955, recently celebrated another anniversary. "I wore the same nightgown I wore on our wedding night," confessed Karen to me over the phone. "Just as I have every anniversary for thirty-nine years."

"I wore pajamas on our wedding night," offered Bill. "But last night I didn't wear nothin'." They laughed, and even over three thousand miles of telephone wire I felt the strength of their love for one another.

Long-lasting marriages like Bill's and Karen's are becoming increasingly rare. Not only do more than 50 percent of all first marriages in the United States end in divorce (make that 60 percent for repeat attempts), but fewer people are even bothering to tie the slippery knot in the first place. One fourth of Americans eighteen or older—about 41 million people—have never married at all. In 1970, that figure was only one sixth.

But even while millions of couples march down the aisle only to pass through the therapist's office and into divorce court, a quiet revolution is taking place when it comes to understanding how long-term love really works. Inside the laboratories of the Family Formation Project at the University of Washington in Seattle—affectionately dubbed the Love Lab—research psychologists are putting our most cherished relationship theories under the scientific microscope. What they're discovering is that much of what we regard as conventional wisdom is simply wrong.

"Almost none of our theory and practice [in marital therapy] is founded on empirical scientific research," contends the Love Lab's head, John Gottman, an award-winning research psychologist trained both as a therapist and a mathematician. Indeed, it is this lack of solid research, Gottman believes, that contributes to a discouraging statistic: for 50 percent of married couples who enter therapy, divorce is still the end result.

Gottman believes that, although relationship counseling has helped many people, much of it just doesn't work. Not satisfied with warm and fuzzy ideas about how to "get the love you want," Gottman is scouting for numbers, data, *proof*—and he's finding it.

From *New Age Journal*, September/October 1994, pp. 74-79, 146-148. © 1994 by New Age Publishing, Inc. Reprinted by permission.

...a labora-
...ras, EKGs,
...ed instru-
...gues have
...t happens
...tches them
...He watches
...nd reaffirm
...l expressions
and self-reported emo... heart rhythms
and blood chemistry. He tests urine,
memories, and couples' ability to interpret each other's emotional cues. Then
he pours his data, like so many puzzle
pieces, into a computer. The resulting
picture, he says, is so clear and detailed it's
like "a CAT scan of a living relationship."
[See "Putting Love to the Test," at right.]

What Gottman and his colleagues have
discovered—and summarized for popular audiences in a new book, *Why Marriages Succeed or Fail* (Simon & Schuster)
—is mind-boggling in its very simplicity.
His conclusion: Couples who stay together are . . . well . . . *nice* to each other
more often than not. "[S]atisfied couples," claims Gottman, "maintained a
five-to-one ratio of positive to negative
moments" in their relationship. Couples
heading for divorce, on the other hand,
allow that ratio to slip below one-to-one.

If it ended there, Gottman's research

*Fighting, whether
rare or frequent,
is sometimes the
healthiest thing a
couple can do for their
relationship.*

might remain just an interesting foot-
note. But for him and his colleagues, this
discovery is just the beginning. In fact,
Gottman's novel and methodical approach to marriage research is threatening to turn much of current relationship
therapy on its head. He contends that
many aspects of wedded life often considered critical to long-term success—
how intensely people fight; whether
they face conflict or avoid it; how well
they solve problems; how compatible
they are socially, financially, even sexually

—are less important than people (including therapists) tend to think. In fact,
Gottman believes, none of these things
matter to a marriage's longevity as much
as maintaining that crucial ratio of five
to one.

If it's hard to believe that the longevity
of your relationship depends primarily
on your being five times as nice as you
are nasty to each other, some of Gottman's other conclusions may be even
more surprising. For example:

♥ Wildly explosive relationships that
vacillate between heated arguments and
passionate reconciliations can be as happy—and long-lasting—as those that seem

more emotionally stable. They may even
be more exciting and intimate.

♥ Emotionally inexpressive marriages,
which may seem like repressed volcanoes
destined to explode, are actually very
successful—so long as the couple maintains that five-to-one ratio in what they
do express to each other. In fact, too
much emotional catharsis among such
couples can "scare the hell out of them,"
says Gottman.

♥ Couples who start out complaining
about each other have some of the most
stable marriages over time, while those
who don't fight early on are more likely
to hit the rocky shoals of divorce.

Putting Love to the Test

How the "Love Lab" researchers decode blood, sweat, and tears.

THE STUDIO APARTMENT IS TINY, BUT IT
affords a great view of Seattle's Portage
Bay. The ambiance is that of a dorm room
tastefully furnished in late-'80s Sears,
Roebuck. A cute kitchen table invites you
to the window. A Monet print graces one
wall. Oh, and three video cameras—sus-
pended from the ceiling like single-eyed
bats—follow your every move.

Welcome to the "Love Lab," wherein
Professor John Gottman and a revolving
crew of students and researchers monitor
the emotions, behaviors, and hormones
of married couples. Today, lab coordinator
Jim Coan—a calm, clear-eyed, pony-tailed
young man in Birkenstocks who started
out as a student volunteer three years
ago—is giving me the tour.

The Love Lab is actually two labs. I have
entered through the "Apartment Lab,"
whose weekly routine Coan describes:
A volunteer couple arrives on a Sunday
morning, prepared to spend the day
being intensely observed (for which they
are modestly compensated). Special
microphones record every sound they
make; videotape captures every subtle
gesture. The only true privacy is found in
the bathroom, but even there science has
a presence: A cooler by the toilet has two

little urine collection bottles, today
marked "Bill" and "Jeannie."

At the end of a relaxed day doing
whatever they like (and being watched
doing it), the couple welcomes a house
guest—a psychologist who listens to the
story of how they met, fell in love, and
began building a life together. This "oral
history," which most people greatly enjoy
telling, will later be closely scrutinized:
Gottman and company have learned that
how fondly a couple remembers this story
can predict whether they will stay together or divorce.

Then, after a sleep-over on the Lab's
hide-a-bed (cameras and microphones off)
and a blood sample, a technician takes
the pair out for breakfast, gives them
their check, and sends them on their way.
The videotapes will later be analyzed in
voluminous detail. Every affectionate gesture, sarcastic jab, or angry dispute will be
recorded and categorized using Gottman's "specific affect" emotional coding
system (the lab folks call it SPAFF for
short). At the same time, the couple's
blood and urine will be sent to another
lab and tested for stress hormone levels.
Finally, in four years or so (depending on
the study), the lab will follow up with the

❤ Fighting, whether rare or frequent, is sometimes the healthiest thing a couple can do for their relationship. In fact, blunt anger, appropriately expressed, "seems to immunize marriages against deterioration."

❤ In happy marriages, there are no discernible gender differences in terms of the quantity and quality of emotional expression. In fact, men in happy marriages are more likely to reveal intimate personal information about themselves than women. (When conflict erupts, however, profound gender differences emerge.)

❤ Men who do housework are likely to have happier marriages, greater physical health, even better sex lives than men who don't. (This piece of news alone could cause a run on aprons.)

❤ Women are made physically sick by a relentlessly unresponsive or emotionally contemptuous husband. Gottman's researchers can even tell just how sick: They can predict the number of infectious diseases women in such marriages will suffer over a four-year period.

❤ How warmly you remember the story of your relationship foretells your chances for staying together. In one study that involved taking oral histories from couples about the unfolding of their relationship, psychologists were able to predict—with an astonishing 94 percent accuracy—which couples would be divorced within three years.

THE THREE VARIETIES OF MARRIAGE

In person, Gottman is a fast-talking, restless intellect, clearly in love with his work. Now in his late forties and seven years into a second marriage (to clinical psychologist Julie Schwartz), he seems very satisfied. Yet, in his book, he sheds

---

couple to see if they're still together—and take another look at the data they gathered to see if a predictable pattern can be discerned.

OTHER COUPLES WHO VISIT THE FAMILY Formation Project, as the "Love Lab" is more formally known, merely pass the pleasant apartment on their way to a less cozy destination: the "Fixed Lab." Here they are seated ("fixed") in plain wooden chairs and hooked up with a dizzying array of instruments—EKG electrodes, finger-pulse detectors, and skin galvanometers ("a fancy word for sweat detectors," says Coan). A thick black spring stretched across their chests registers breathing. Their chair itself is a "jiggleometer," recording every fidget and tremor.

A "facilitator" first interviews the pair about what issues cause conflict in their marriage, then gets them talking about the most contentious ones. Video cameras focus on the couple's faces and chests. Computers track the complex streams of data coming in through the sensors and displays them on a color monitor in a rainbow of blips and graphs.

After fifteen minutes of surprisingly "normal" and often emotional conversa-tion, the couple are stopped by the facilitator, who plays back the videotape for them. While watching, each partner rates his or her own emotional state at every moment during the conversation, using a big black dial with a scale running from "extremely negative" through "neutral" to "extremely positive." Then the pair watch the tape again, this time in an attempt to similarly judge their partner's emotional state (with widely varying levels of success).

Later, students trained by Coan will review the tape using a specially designed dial and the SPAFF coding system, to chart the feelings being displayed. It's eerie to see the range of human emotional expression represented on a high-tech instrument panel: disgust, contempt, belligerence, domination, criticism, anger, tension, tense humor ("very popular, that one," Coan tells me), defensiveness, whining, sadness, stonewalling, interest, validation, affection, humor, joy, and positive or negative surprise (students made Gottman aware of the two different kinds). In the middle is a neutral setting for when couples are merely exchanging information without noticeable emotion.

BACK IN THE APARTMENT LAB, COAN SHOWS me videos of couples who have agreed to be involved with the media. Two young parents from Houston discuss the stress around caring for their new baby, and Coan gives me the play-by-play: "He's being very defensive here" or "See that deep sigh? She's feeling sad now" or "Now that was a nice validation."

Coan says that most people seem to enjoy the lab experience—and even get some benefit from it (though it's not meant to be therapeutic). Amazingly, even with sensors attached to their ears and fingers and chests, the couples seem to forget that they're being watched. They giggle and cry and manage to create a genuine closeness while fixed under a physiological microscope.

"It's a real privilege to work here," Coan says thoughtfully. Even in a short visit, I feel it too. The observation of intimacy, both its joy and its pain, is more than just scientific video voyeurism. It's as though the love these couples are trying so devotedly to share with each other seeps out of the box, a gift to the watchers.

— A. A.

the mantle of guru in the first sentence: "My personal life has not been a trail of great wisdom in understanding relationships," he says. "My expertise is in the scientific observation of couples."

Gottman began developing this expertise some twenty years ago, when a troubled couple who came to him for help didn't respond well to conventional therapy. In frustration, Gottman suggested that they try videotaping the sessions. "Both the couple and I were astonished by the vividness and clarity on the tape of the pattern of criticism, contempt, and defensiveness they repeatedly fell into," he recalls. "It shocked them into working harder . . . [and] it gave me my life's work."

Struck by the power of impartial observation, Gottman became fascinated with research. His goal: to systematically describe the differences between happy and unhappy couples, and from those observations develop a scientific theory capable of predicting marital success. This seemed a daunting task, both because "marriage is so subjective" and because "personality theory, in psychology, has been a failure at predicting anything."

The result of Gottman's passion is a veritable mountain of data: tens of thousands of observations involving thousands of couples, gathered by the Love Lab's researchers and stored in its computer data-bases. The geography of that mountain reveals a surprising pattern: Successful marriages come in not one but three different varieties, largely determined by how a couple handles their inevitable disagreements. Gottman calls these three types of stable marriages *validating*, *volatile*, and *conflict-avoiding*.

Validating couples are what most people (including most therapists) have in mind when they think of a "good marriage." Even when these couples don't agree, they "still let their partner know that they consider his or her opinions and emotions valid." They "compromise often and calmly work out their problems to mutual satisfaction as they arise." And when they fight, they know how to listen, acknowledge their differences, and negotiate agreement without screaming at each other. "These couples," Gottman notes, "look and sound a lot like two psychotherapists engaging in a dialogue."

But where modern therapy often goes wrong, says Gottman, is in assuming that this is the only way a marriage can work—and trying to force all couples

Couples who start out complaining about each other have some of the most stable marriages over time.

into the validating mold. While "viewing this style of marriage as the ideal has simplified the careers of marital therapists," it hasn't necessarily helped their clients, he says, who may fall into the other two types of stable pattern.

Volatile couples, in contrast to validating ones, thrive on unfiltered emotional intensity. Their relationships are full of angry growls and passionate sighs, sudden ruptures and romantic reconcilia-

Men who do house-work are likely to have happier marriages, greater physical health, even better sex lives than men who don't.

tions. They may fight bitterly (and even unfairly), and they may seem destined for divorce to anyone watching them squabble. But Gottman's data indicate that this pessimism is often misplaced: These couples will stay together if "for every nasty swipe, there are five caresses." In fact, "the passion and relish with which they fight seems to fuel their positive interactions even more." Such couples are more romantic and affectionate than most—but they are also more vulnerable to a decay in that all-important five-to-one ratio (and at their worst, to violence). Trying to change the style of their relationship not only isn't necessary, Gottman says, it probably won't work.

Nor will conflict-avoiding couples, the third type of stable marriage, necessarily benefit from an increase in their emotional expression, he says. Gottman likens such unions to "the placid waters of a summer lake," where neither partner wants to make waves. They keep the peace and minimize argument by constantly agreeing to disagree. "In these relationships, solving a problem usually means ignoring the difference, one partner agreeing to act more like the other . . . or most often just letting time take its course." The universal five-to-one ratio must still be present for the couple to stay together, but it gets translated into a

Four Keys to a Happy Relationship

DESPITE ALL HIS SOPHISTICATED ANALYSIS of how relationships work (and don't work), researcher John Gottman's advice to the lovelorn and fight-torn is really quite simple.

LEARN TO CALM DOWN.
This will cut down on the flooding response that makes further communication so difficult. "The most brilliant and philosophically subtle therapy in the world will have no impact on a couple not grounded in their own bodies to hear it," he says. Once couples are calm enough, suggests Gottman, they can work on three other basic "keys" to improving their relationship.

LEARN TO SPEAK AND LISTEN NONDEFENSIVELY.
This is tough, Gottman admits, but defensiveness is a very dangerous response, and it needs to be interrupted. One of the most powerful things you can do—in addition to working toward the ideal of listening with empathy and speaking without blame—is to "reintro-

much smaller number of swipes and caresses (which are also less intensely expressed). This restrained style may seem stifling to some, but the couple themselves can experience it as a peaceful contentment.

Things get more complicated when the marriage is "mixed"—when, say, a volatile person marries someone who prefers to minimize conflict. But Gottman suggests that, even in these cases, "it may be possible to borrow from each marital style and create a viable mixed style." The most difficult hurdle faced by couples with incompatible fighting styles lies in confronting that core difference

---

duce praise and admiration into your relationship." A little appreciation goes a long way toward changing the chemistry between people.

VALIDATE YOUR PARTNER.
Validation involves "putting yourself in your partner's shoes and imagining his or her emotional state." Let your partner know that you understand how he or she feels, and why, even if you don't agree. You can also show validation by acknowledging your partner's point of view, accepting appropriate responsibility, and apologizing when you're clearly wrong. If this still seems too much of a stretch, at least let your partner know that you're *trying* to understand, even if you're finding it hard.

PRACTICE, PRACTICE, PRACTICE.
Gottman calls this "overlearning," doing something so many times that it becomes second nature. The goal is to be able to calm yourself down, communicate nondefensively, and validate your partner automatically—even in the heat of an argument.

---

and negotiating which style (or combination of styles) they will use. If they can't resolve that primary conflict, it may be impossible to tip the overall balance of their relational life in the direction of five-to-one.

The important thing here is to find a compatible fighting style—not to stop fighting altogether. Gottman is convinced that the "one" in that ratio is just as important as the "five": "What may lead to temporary misery in a marriage —disagreement and anger—may be healthy for it in the long run." Negativity acts as the predator in the ecosystem of marriage, says Gottman. It's the lion that feeds on the weakest antelopes and makes the herd stronger. Couples who never disagree at all may start out happier than others, but without some conflict to resolve their differences, their marriages may soon veer toward divorce because their "ecosystem" is out of balance.

THE FOUR HORSEMEN
OF THE APOCALYPSE

Even the most stable marriages of any style can fall apart, and Gottman and company have observed an all-too-predictable pattern in their decline and fall. He likens the process to a cascade—a tumble down the rapids—that starts with the arrival of a dangerous quartet of behaviors. So destructive is their effect on marital happiness, in fact, that he calls these behaviors "The Four Horsemen of the Apocalypse."

The first horseman is criticism: "attacking someone's personality or character" rather than making some specific complaint about his or her behavior. The difference between saying, say, "I wish you had taken care of that bill" (a healthy and specific complaint) and "You never get the bills paid on time!" (a generalizing and blaming attack) is very significant to the listener. Criticism often engenders criticism in return and sets the stage for the second horseman: contempt.

"What separates contempt from criticism," explains Gottman, "is the intention to insult and psychologically abuse your partner." Negative thoughts about the other come out in subtle put-downs, hostile jokes, mocking facial expressions, and name-calling ("You are such an idiot

---

around money"). By now the positive qualities that attracted you to this person seem long ago and far away, and instead of trying to build intimacy, you're ushering in the third horseman.

Defensiveness comes on the heels of contempt as a seemingly reasonable response to attack—but it only makes things worse. By denying responsibility, making excuses, whining, tossing back counter-attacks, and other strategies ("How come I'm the one who always pays the bills?!"), you just accelerate your speed down river. Gottman also warns that it's possible to skip straight to the third horseman by being oversensitive about legitimate complaints.

Once stonewalling (the fourth horseman) shows up, things are looking bleak. Stonewallers simply stop communicating, refusing to respond even in self-defense. Of course, all these "horsemen" drop in on couples once in a while. But when a partner habitually shuts down and withdraws, the final rapids of negativity (what Gottman calls the "Distance and Isolation Cascade") can quickly propel the marriage through whirlpools of hopelessness, isolation, and loneliness over the waterfall of divorce. With the arrival of the fourth horseman, one or both partners is thinking negative thoughts about his or her counterpart most of the time, and the couple's minds—as well as their bodies—are in a perpetual state of defensive red alert.

The stress of conflict eventually sends blood pressure, heart rate, and adrenaline into the red zone—a phenomenon Gottman calls *flooding*. "The body of someone who feels flooded," he writes, "is a confused jumble of signals. It may be hard to breathe. . . . Muscles tense up and stay tensed. The heart beats fast, and it may seem to beat harder." Emotionally, the flooded person may feel a range of emotions, from fear to anger to confusion.

The bottom line is that flooding is physically uncomfortable, and stonewalling becomes an attempt to escape that discomfort. When flooding becomes chronic, stonewalling can become chronic, too. Eighty-five percent of the time the stonewaller (among heterosexual couples) is the man. The reason for this gender discrepancy is one of many physiological phenomena that Gottman sees as critical to understanding why mar-

Women are made physically sick by a relentlessly unresponsive or emotionally contemptuous husband. Gottman's researchers can even tell just how sick.

riages go sour, and what people can do to fix them.

Though flooding happens to both men and women, it affects men more quickly, more intensely, and for a longer period of time. "Men tend to have shorter fuses and longer-lasting explosions than women," says Gottman. Numerous observations in the laboratory have shown that it often takes mere criticism to set men off, whereas women require something at least on the level of contempt. The reasons for this are left to speculation. "Probably this difference in wiring had evolutionary survival benefits," Gottman conjectures. An added sensitivity to threats may have kept males alert and ready to repel attacks on their families, he suggests, while women calmed down more quickly so they could soothe the children.

Whatever its origin, this ancient biological difference creates havoc in contemporary male-female relationships, because men are also "more tuned in to the internal physiological environment than women," Gottman reports. (For example, men are better at tapping along with their heartbeat.) Men's bodily sensitivity translates into greater physical discomfort during conflict. In short, arguing hurts. The result: "Men are more likely to withdraw emotionally when their bodies are telling them they're upset." Meanwhile, "when men withdraw, women get upset, and they pursue [the issue]"—which gets men more upset.

Here is where physiology meets sociology. Men, says Gottman, need to rely on physiological cues to know how they're feeling. Women, in contrast, rely on social cues, such as what's happening in the conversation.

In addition, men are trained since early

childhood not to build intimacy with others, while women "are given intense schooling on the subject" from an equally early age. Socially, the genders are almost totally segregated (in terms of their own choices of friendships and playmates) from age seven until early adulthood. Indeed, it would seem that cross-gender relationships are set up to fail. "In fact," Gottman writes, "our upbringing couldn't be a worse training ground for a successful marriage."

Yet the challenge is far from insurmountable, as millions of marriages prove. In fact, Gottman's research reveals that "by and large, in happy marriages there are *no* gender differences in emotional expression!" In these marriages, men are just as likely to share intimate emotions as their partners (indeed they may be more likely to reveal personal information about themselves). However, in unhappy marriages, "all the gender differences we've been talking about

Men's bodily sensitivity translates into greater physical discomfort during conflict. The result: Men are more likely to withdraw emotionally.

emerge"—feeding a vicious cycle that, once established, is hard to break.

Married couples who routinely let the Four Horsemen ransack their living rooms face enormous physical and psychological consequences. Gottman's studies show that chronic flooding and negativity not only make such couples more likely to get sick, they also make it very difficult for couples to change how they relate. When your heart is beating rapidly and your veins are constricting in your arms and legs (another evolutionary stress response), it's hard to think fresh, clear thoughts about how you're communicating. Nor can the brain process new information very well. Instead, a flooded person

relies on "overlearned responses"—old relationship habits that probably just fan the flames.

All this physiological data has enormous implications for relationship therapists as well as their clients. Gottman believes that "most of what you see currently in marital therapy—not all of it, but most of it—is completely misguided."

For example, he thinks it's an exercise in futility when "the therapist says 'Calm down, Bertha. Calm down, Max. Let's take a look at this and analyze it. Let's remember the way we were with our mothers.' Bertha and Max can do it in the office because he's doing it for them. But once they get home, and their heart rates get above 100 beats per minute, whew, forget about it."

Teaching psychological skills such as interpreting nonverbal behavior also misses the mark. "We have evidence that husbands in unhappy marriages are terrible at reading their wives' nonverbal behavior. But they're great at reading other people's nonverbal behavior. In other words, they have the social skills, but they aren't using them." The problem isn't a lack of skill; it's the overwhelming feelings experienced in the cycle of negativity. Chronic flooding short-circuits a couple's basic listening and empathy skills, and it undermines the one thing that can turn back the Four Horsemen: the repair attempt.

HEADING OFF DISASTER

Repair attempts are a kind of "metacommunication"—a way of talking about how you're communicating with each other. "Can we please stay on the subject?" "That was a rude thing to say." "We're not talking about your father!" "I don't think you're listening to me." Such statements, even when delivered in a grouchy or complaining tone, are efforts to interrupt the cycle of criticism, contempt, defensiveness, and stonewalling and to bring the conversation back on track.

"In stable relationships," explains Gottman, "the other person will respond favorably: 'Alright, alright. Finish.' The agreement isn't made very nicely. But it does stop the person. They listen, they accept the repair attempt, and they actually change" the way they're relating.

Repair attempts are "really critical," says Gottman, because "everybody screws up. Everybody gets irritated, defensive, contemptuous. People insult one another," especially their spouses. Repair attempts are a way of saying "we've got to fix this before it slides any deeper into the morass." Even people in bad marriages make repair attempts; the problem is, they get ignored.

Training people to receive repair attempts favorably—even in the middle of a heated argument—is one of the new frontiers in relationship therapy. According to Gottman, "Even when things are going badly, you've got to focus not on the negativity but on the repair attempt. That's what couples do in happy mar-

> *Even people in bad marriages make repair attempts; the problem is, they get ignored.*

riages." He's convinced that such skills can be taught: One colleague has even devised a set of flash cards with a variety of repair attempts on them, ranging from "I know I've been a terrible jerk, but can we take this from the top?" to "I'm really too upset to listen right now." [See Upfront, July/August 1993.] Even in mid-tempest, couples can use the cards to practice giving, and receiving, messages about how they're communicating.

Breaking the Four Horsemen cycle is critical, says Gottman, because "the more time [couples] spend in that negative

perceptual state, the more likely they are to start making long-lasting attributions about this marriage as being negative." Such couples begin rewriting the story of how they met, fell in love, made commitments. Warm memories about how "we were so crazy about each other" get replaced with "I was *crazy* to marry him/her." And once the story of the marriage has been infected with negativity, the motivation to work on its repair declines. Divorce becomes much more likely (and predictable—consider that 94 percent accuracy rate in the oral history study).

Of course, not all relationships can, or should, be saved. Some couples are trapped in violent relationships, which "are in a class by themselves." Others may suffer a fundamental difference in their preferred style—validating, volatile, or conflict-avoidant—that leaves them stuck in chronic flooding. With hard work, some of these marriages can be saved; trying to save others, however, may do more harm than good.

In the end, the hope for repairing even a broken marriage is to be found, as usual, in the courage and effort people are willing to invest in their own growth and change. "The hardest thing to do," says Gottman, "is to get back to the fundamentals that really make you happy." Couples who fail to do this allow the Four Horsemen to carry them far from the fundamentals of affection, humor, appreciation, and respect. Couples who succeed cultivate these qualities like gardeners. They also cultivate an affirming story of their lives together, understanding that that is the soil from which everything else grows.

The work may be a continuous challenge, but the harvest, as my long-mar-

ried friends Bill and Karen would say, is an enormous blessing: the joy in being truly known and loved, and in knowing how to love.

The Lovers' Library

A slew of new books appearing in 1994 address some of the most entrenched problems facing long-term lovers:

■ *Hot Monogamy: Essential Steps to More Passionate, Intimate Lovemaking*, by Patricia Love and Jo Robinson (Dutton, 1994). This is a wonderful guide to enriching your sex life in a host of imaginative ways, and to reducing the shame and anxiety caused by differences in sexual appetite. (Also available as an excellent workshop on cassette from The Sounds True Catalog, 800-333-9185.)

■ *When Opposites Attract: Right Brain/Left Brain Relationships and How to Make Them Work*, by Rebecca Cutter (Dutton, 1994). A very helpful and thorough guide to dealing with the wide range of problems that can stem from fundamental differences in brain wiring.

■ *The Couple's Comfort Book: A Creative Guide for Renewing Passion, Pleasure, and Commitment*, by Jennifer Louden (HarperSanFrancisco, 1994). A highly usable compendium of nurturing and imaginative things to do together, cross-referenced so you can hop around the book and design your own program of relationship rebirth.

Choosing Mates—The American Way

Martin King Whyte

Martin King Whyte is professor of sociology and faculty associate in the Center for Chinese Studies at the University of Michigan. He has published numerous works on family sociology and contemporary Chinese social organization. His is currently involved in a comparative study of mate choice and marital relations in China and the United States. His latest book is Dating, Mating, and Marriage.

As America's divorce rate has been soaring, popular anxieties about marriage have multiplied. Is it still possible to "live happily ever after," and if so, how can this be accomplished? How can you tell whether a partner who leaves you breathless with yearning will, as your spouse, drive you to distraction? Does "living together" prior to marriage provide a realistic assessment of how compatible you and your partner might be as husband and wife? Questions such as these suggest a need to examine our American way of mate choice. How do we go about selecting the person we marry, and is there something wrong with the entire process?

For most twentieth-century Americans choosing a mate is the culmination of a process of dating. Examination of how we go about selecting mates thus requires us to consider the American dating culture. Dating is a curious institution. By definition it is an activity that is supposed to be separate from selecting a spouse. Yet, dating is expected to provide valuable experience that will help in making a "wise" choice of a marital partner. Does this combination work?

How well dating "works" may be considered in a number of senses of this term. Is it easy or difficult to find somebody to go out with? Do dates mostly lead to enjoyable or painful evenings? However, these are not the aspects of dating I wish to consider. The issue here is whether dating works in the sense of providing useful experience that helps pave the way for a successful marriage.

Dating is a relatively new institution. The term, and the various practices associated with it, first emerged around the turn of the century. By the 1920s dating had more or less completely displaced earlier patterns of relations among unmarried Americans. Contrary to popular assumptions, even in colonial times marriages were not arranged in America. Parents were expected to give their approval to their children's nuptial plans, a practice captured in our image of a suitor asking his beloved's father for her hand in marriage. Parental approval, especially among merchants and other prosperous classes, put some constraint on the marriages of the young. For example, through the eighteenth century, children in such families tended to marry in birth order and marriage to cousins was not uncommon. (Both practices had declined sharply by the nineteenth century.) However, parents rarely directly arranged the marriages of their children. America has always exhibited "youth-driven" patterns of courtship. Eligible males and females took the initiative to get to know each other, and the decision to marry was made by them, even if that decision was to some degree contingent on parental approval. (Of course, substantial proportions of later immigrant groups from Southern and Eastern Europe, Asia, and elsewhere brought with them arranged marriage traditions, and contention for control over marriage decisions was often a great source of tension in such families.)

How did young people get to know one another well enough to decide to marry in the era before dating? A set of customs, dominant for the two centuries, preceded the rise of the dating culture. These activities came to be referred to as "calling" and "keeping company." Young people might meet in a variety of ways— through community and church socials, informally in shops or on the street, on boat and train trips, or through introductions from friends or relatives. (America never developed a system of chaperoning young women in public, and foreign observers often commented on the freedom unmarried women had to travel and mix so-

From *Society*, Vol. 29, No. 3, March/April 1992, pp. 71-77. © 1992 by Transaction Publishers, Inc. Reprinted by permission.

cially on their own.) Usually young people would go to church fairs, local dances, and other such activities with family, siblings, or friends, rather than paired off with a partner. Most activities would involve a substantial degree of adult and community supervision. Nonetheless, these gatherings did encourage some pairing off and led to hand holding, moonlit walks home, and other romantic exploration.

By late nineteenth century, a formal pattern of "calling" developed among the upper and middle classes.

As relationships developed beyond the platonic level, the suitor would pay visits to the home of the young woman. By the latter part of the nineteenth century, particularly among the middle and upper classes, this activity assumed a formal pattern referred to as "calling." Males would be invited to call on the female at her home, and they were expected to do so only if invited. (A bold male could, however, request an invitation to call.) Invitations might be extended by the mother of a very young woman, but eventually they would come from the young woman herself. Often a woman would designate certain days on which she would receive callers. She might have several suitors at one time, and thus a number of men might be paying such calls. A man might be told that the woman was not at home to receive him, and he would then be expected to leave his calling card. If this happened repeatedly, he was expected to get the message that his visits were no longer welcome.

Initiative and control in regard to calling were in the hands of women (the eligible female and her mother). Although some variety in suitors was possible, even in initial stages the role of calling in examining potential marriage partners was very clear to all involved. The relatively constrained and supervised nature of calling make it certain that enjoyment cannot have been a primary goal of this activity. (During the initial visits the mother was expected to remain present; in later visits she often hovered in an adjacent room.) If dating is defined as recreational and romantic pairing off between a man and a woman, away from parental supervision and without immediate consideration of marriage, then calling was definitely not dating.

The supervised and controlled nature of calling should not, however, lead us to suppose that propriety and chastity were always maintained until marriage. If the relationship had deepened sufficiently, the couple might progress from calling to "keeping company," a precursor of the twentieth-century custom of "going steady." At this stage, the primary activity would still consist of visits by the suitor to the woman's home. However, now she would only welcome calls from one man, and he would visit her home on a regular basis. Visits late into the evening would increasingly replace afternoon calls. As the relationship became more serious, parents would often leave the couple alone. Nineteenth-century accounts mention parents going off to bed and leaving the young couple on the couch or by the fireplace, there to wrestle with, and not infrequently give in to, sexual temptation.

Even though some women who headed to the altar toward the end of the nineteenth century had lost their virginity prior to marriage, premarital intimacy was less common than during the dating era. (The double standard of the Victorian era made it possible for many more grooms to be non-virgins at marriage than brides. Perhaps 50 percent or more of men had lost their virginity prior to marriage, as opposed to 15 to 20 percent of women, with prostitutes and "fallen women" helping to explain the differential.) What is less often realized is that the formalization of the calling pattern toward the end of the nineteenth century contributed to a decline in premarital sexual intimacy compared to earlier times. America experienced not one but two sexual revolutions—one toward the end of the eighteenth century, at the time of the American Revolution, and the other in the latter part of the twentieth century.

The causes of the first sexual revolution are subject to some debate. An influx of settlers to America who did not share the evangelical puritanism of many early colonists, the expansion of the population into the unsettled (and "unchurched") frontier, the growth of towns, and the individualistic and freedom-loving spirit of the American revolution may have contributed to a retreat from the fairly strict emphasis on premarital chastity of the early colonial period. Historians debate the extent to which the archetypal custom of this first sexual revolution, bundling, (which allowed an unmarried couple to sleep together, although theoretically fully clothed and separated by a "bundling board") was widespread or largely mythical. Whatever the case, other evidence is found in studies of communities, such as those by Daniel Scott Smith and Michael Hindus, which found that the percentage of married couples whose first births were conceived premaritally increased from about 11 percent before 1700 to over 33 percent in the last decades of the eighteenth century.

This first sexual revolution was reversed in the nineteenth century. The reasons for its demise are also not clear. The closing of the frontier, the rise of the middle class, the defensive reactions of that new middle class to new waves of immigrants, the growth of Christian revivalism and reform movements, and the spread of models of propriety from Victorian England (which were in turn influenced by fear of the chaos of the French Revolution)—all these have been suggested as having contributed to a new sexual puritanism in the nineteenth century. According to Smith and Hindus, premarital conceptions decreased once again to about 15 percent of first births between 1841 and 1880.

It was in the latter time period that the customs of calling and keeping company reached their most formal elaboration—calling, in less ritualized forms, can be traced back to the earliest colonial period. Not long after reaching the formal patterns described, calling largely disappeared. In little more than a generation, dating replaced calling as the dominant custom.

Dating involved pairing off of couples in activities not supervised by parents, with pleasure rather than marriage as the primary goal. The rules governing dating were defined by peers rather than by adults. The initiative, and much of the control, shifted from the female to the male. The man asked the woman out, rather than waiting for her invitation to call. The finances and transportation for the date were also his responsibility. The woman was expected to provide, in turn, the pleasure of her company and perhaps some degree of romantic and physical intimacy. By giving or withholding her affection and access to her body, she exercised considerable control over the man and the date as an event. Nonetheless, the absence of parental oversight and the pressure to respond to a man's initiatives placed a woman in a weaker position than she was in the era of calling.

The man might pick up the woman at her home, but parents who tried to dictate whom their daughters dated and what they did on dates generally found such efforts rejected and evaded. Parents of a son might not even know where junior was going or whom he was dating. Dates were conducted mostly in the public arena, and in some cases—such as at sporting events or school dances—adults might be present. But dates often involved activities and venues where no adults were present or where young people predominated— as at private parties or at local dance halls. Or in other cases the presence of adults would have little inhibiting effect, as in the darkened balconies of movie theaters. American youths also developed substantial ingenuity in finding secluded "lovers' lanes" where they could escape the supervision of even peers. (Localities varied in the places used for this purpose and how they were referred to. In locales near bodies of water young people spoke of "watching submarine races;" in the

rural area of upstate New York where I grew up the phrase was "exploring tractor roads.") Community dances and gatherings for all generations and ages practically disappeared in the dating era.

Greater privacy and autonomy of youths promoted romantic and physical experimentation. Not only kissing but petting was increasingly accepted and widespread. Going beyond petting to sexual intercourse, however, involved substantial risks, especially for the female. This was not simply the risk of pregnancy in the pre-pill era. Dating perpetuated the sexual double standard. Men were expected to be the sexual aggressors and to try to achieve as much intimacy as their dates would allow. But women who "went too far" risked harming their reputations and their ability to keep desirable men interested in them for long. Women were expected to set the limits, and they had to walk a careful line between being too unfriendly (and not having males wanting to date them at all) and being too friendly (and being dated for the "wrong reasons").

Rules governing dating were defined by peers rather than adults.

During the initial decades of the dating era, premarital intimacy increased in comparison with the age of calling, but still a majority of women entered marriage as virgins. In a survey in the greater Detroit metropolitan area, I found that of the oldest women interviewed (those who dated and married prior to 1945), about one in four had lost her virginity prior to marriage. (By the 1980s, according to my survey, the figure was closer to 90 percent.) Escape from parental supervision provided by dating weakened, but did not immediately destroy, the restraints on premarital intimacy.

When Americans began dating, they were primarily concerned with enjoyment, rather than with choosing a spouse. Indeed, "playing the field" was the ideal pursued by many. Dates were not suitors or prospects. Seeing different people on successive nights in a hectic round of dating activity earned one popularity among peers. One of the early students and critics of the dating culture, Willard Waller, coined the term "rating and dating complex" to refer to this pattern. After observing dating among students at Pennsylvania State University in the 1930s, Waller charged that concern for impressing friends and gaining status on campus led to superficial thrill-seeking and competition for popularity, and eliminated genuine romance or sincere communication. However, Waller has been accused of both stereotyping and exaggerating the influence of this pattern. Dating was not always so exploitative and superficial as he charged.

Dating was never viewed as an endless stage or an alternative to courtship. Even if dates were initially seen as quite separate from mate selection, they were always viewed as only the first step in a progression that would lead to marriage. By the 1930s, the stage of "going steady" was clearly recognized, entailing a commitment by both partners to date each other exclusively, if only for the moment. A variety of ritual markers emerged to symbolize the increased commitment of this stage and of further steps toward engagement and marriage, such as wearing the partner's high school ring, being lavaliered, and getting pinned.

Growing affluence fueled new industries designed to entertain and fill leisure time.

Going steady was a way-station between casual dating and engagement. Steadies pledged not to date others, and they were likely to become more deeply involved romantically and physically than casual daters. They were not expected explicitly to contemplate marriage, and the majority of women in our Detroit survey had several steady boyfriends before the relationships that led to their marriages. If a couple was of a "suitable age," though, and if the steady relationship lasted more than a few months, the likelihood increased of explicit talk about marriage. Couples would then symbolize their escalated commitment by getting engaged. Dating arose first among middle and upper middle class students in urban areas, and roughly simultaneously at the college and high school levels. The practice then spread to other groups—rural young people, working class youths, to the upper class, and to employed young people. But what triggered the rapid demise of calling and the rise of dating?

One important trend was prolonged school attendance, particularly in public, co-educational high schools and colleges. Schools provided an arena in which females and males could get to know one another informally over many years. Schools also organized athletic, social, and other activities in which adult supervision was minimal. College campuses generally allowed a more total escape from parental supervision than high schools.

Another important influence was growing affluence in America. More and more young people were freed from a need to contribute to the family economy and had more leisure time in which to date. Fewer young people worked under parental supervision, and more

and more fathers worked far from home, leaving mothers as the primary monitors of their children's daily activities. These trends also coincided with a rise in part-time and after-school employment for students, employment that provided pocket money that did not have to be turned over to parents and could be spent on clothing, makeup, movie tickets, and other requirements of the dating culture. Rising affluence also fueled the growth of entire new industries designed to entertain and fill leisure time—movies, popular music recording, ice cream parlors, amusement parks, and so on. Increasingly, young people who wanted to escape from supervision of their parents found a range of venues, many of them catering primarily to youth and to dating activities.

Technology also played a role, and some analysts suggest that one particular invention, the automobile, deserves a lion's share of the credit. Automobiles were not only a means to escape the home and reach a wider range of recreation spots. They also provided a semi-private space with abundant romantic and sexual possibilities. New institutions, such as the drive-in movie theater, arose to take advantage of those possibilities. As decades passed and affluence increased, the borrowed family car was more and more replaced by cars owned by young people, advancing youth autonomy still further.

All this was part of a larger trend: the transformation of America into a mass consumption society. As this happened, people shifted their attention partially from thinking about how to work and earn to pondering how to spend and consume. Marketplace thinking became more and more influential. The image of the individual as *homo economicus* and of modern life typified by the rational application of scientific knowledge to all decisions became pervasive. The new ideological framework undermined previous customs and moral standards and extended to the dating culture.

Dating had several goals. Most obviously and explicitly, dates were expected to lead to pleasure and possibly to romance. It was also important, as Waller and others have observed, in competition for popularity. But a central purpose of dating was to gain valuable learning experience that would be useful later in selecting a spouse. Through dating young people would learn how to relate to the opposite sex. Dating would increase awareness of one's own feelings and understanding of which type of partner was appealing and which not. Through crushes and disappointments, one would learn to judge the character of people. And by dating a variety of partners and by increasingly intimate involvement with some of them, one would learn what sort of person one would be happy with as a marital partner. When it came time to marry one would be in a good position to select "Mr. Right" or "Miss Right." Calling, which limited the possibilities of romantic experimentation, often to only one partner, did not provide an adequate basis for such an informed choice.

What emerged was a "marketplace learning viewpoint." Selecting a spouse is not quite the same as buying a car or breakfast cereal, but the process was seen as analogous. The assumptions involved in shopping around and test driving various cars or buying and tasting Wheaties, Cheerios, and Fruit Loops were transferred to popular thinking about how to select a spouse.

According to this marketplace learning viewpoint, getting married very young and without having acquired much dating experience was risky, in terms of marital happiness. Similarly, marrying your first and only sweetheart was not a good idea. Neither was meeting someone, falling head over heels in love, and marrying, all within the course of a month. While Americans recognized that in some cases such beginnings could lead to good marriages, the rationale of our dating culture was that having had a variety of dating partners and then getting to know one or more serious prospects over a longer period time and on fairly intimate terms were experiences more likely to lead to marital success.

Eventually, this marketplace psychology helped to undermine America's premarital puritanism, and with it the sexual double standard. The way was paved for acceptance of new customs, and particularly for premarital cohabitation. Parents and other moral guardians found it increasingly difficult to argue against the premise that, if sexual enjoyment and compatibility were central to marital happiness, it was important to test that compatibility before marrying. Similarly, if marriage involved not just hearts and flowers, but also dirty laundry and keeping a budget, did it not make sense for a couple to live together prior to marriage to see how they got along on a day-to-day basis? Such arguments on behalf of premarital sex and cohabitation have swept into popular consciousness in the United States, and it is obvious that they are logical corollaries of the marketplace learning viewpoint.

Our dating culture thus is based upon the premise that dating provides valuable experience that will help individuals select mates and achieve happy marriages. But is this premise correct? Does dating really work? What evidence shows that individuals with longer dating experience, dates with more partners, or longer and more intimate acquaintances with the individuals they intend to marry end up with happier marriages?

Surprisingly, social scientists have never systematially addressed this question. Perhaps this is one of those cherished beliefs people would prefer not to examine too closely. When I could find little evidence on the connection between dating and other premarital experiences and marital success in previous studies, I decided to conduct my own inquiry.

Dating was to give valuable experience to help in future mate selection.

My desire to know whether dating experiences affected marriages was the basis for my 1984 survey in the Detroit area. A representative sample of 459 women was interviewed in three counties in the Detroit metropolitan area (a diverse, multi-racial and multi-ethnic area of city and suburbs containing about 4 million people in 1980). The women ranged in ages from 18 to 75, and all had been married at least once. (I was unable to interview their husbands, so unfortunately marriages in this study are viewed only through the eyes of women.) The interviewees had first married over a sixty year span of time, between 1925 and 1984. They were asked to recall a variety of things about their dating and premarital experiences. They were also asked a range of questions about their marital histories and (if currently married) about the positive and negative features of their relations with their husbands. The questionnaire enabled us to test whether premarital experiences of various types were related to marital success, a concept which in turn was measured in several different ways. (Measures of divorce and of both positive and negative qualities in intact marriages were used.)

The conclusions were a surprise. It appears that dating does not work and that the "marketplace learning viewpoint" is misguided. Marrying very young tended to produce unsuccessful marriages. Premarital pregnancy was associated with problems in marriage. However, once the age of marriage is taken into account, none of the other measures—dating variety, length of dating, length of courtship or engagement, or degree of premarital intimacy with the future husband or others—was clearly related to measures of marital success. A few weak tendencies in the results were contrary to predictions drawn from the marketplace learning viewpoint. Women who had dated more partners or who had engaged in premarital sex or cohabited were slightly less likely to have successful marriages. This might be seen as evidence of quite a different logic.

Perhaps there is a "grass is greener" effect. Women who have been led less sheltered and conventional lives prior to marriage may not be as easily satisfied afterward. Several other researchers have found a similar pattern with regard to premarital cohabitation. Individuals who had been living together prior to marriage were significantly less likely to have successful marriages than those who did not.

Individuals who had been living together were less likely to have successful marriages.

In the Detroit survey, these "grass is greener" patterns were not consistent or statistically significant. It was not that women with more dating experience and greater premarital intimacy had less successful marriages; rather, the amount and type of dating experience did not make a clear difference one way or the other.

Women who had married their first sweethearts were just as likely to have enduring and satisfying marriages as women who had married only after considering many alternatives. Similarly, women who had married after only a brief acquaintance were no more (nor less) likely to have a successful marriage than those who knew their husbands-to-be for years. And there was no clear difference between the marriages of women who were virgins at marriage and those who had had a variety of sexual partners and who had lived together with their husbands before the wedding.

Dating obviously does not provide useful learning that promotes marital success. Although our dating culture is based upon an analogy with consumer purchases in the marketplace, it is clear that in real life selecting a spouse is quite different from buying a car or a breakfast cereal. You cannot actively consider several prospects at the same time without getting your neck broken and being deserted by all of them. Even if you find Ms. Right or Mr. Right, you may be told to drop dead. By the time you are ready to marry, this special someone you were involved with earlier may no longer be available, and you may not see anyone on the horizon who comes close to being as desirable. In addition, someone who is well suited at marriage may grow apart from you or find someone else to be with later. Dating experience might facilitate marital success if deciding whom to marry was like deciding what to eat for breakfast (although even in the latter regard tastes change, and toast and black coffee may replace bacon and eggs). But these realms are quite different,

and mate selection looks more like a crap-shoot than a rational choice.

Is there a better way? Traditionalists in some societies would argue that arranged marriages are preferable. However, in addition to the improbability that America's young people will leave this decision to their parents, there is the problem of evidence. The few studies of this topic, including one I have been collaborating on in China, indicate that women who had arranged marriages were less satisfied than women who made the choice themselves. So having Mom and Dad take charge is not the answer. Turning the matter over to computerized matchmaking also does not seem advisable. Despite the growing sophistication of computers, real intelligence seems preferable to artificial intelligence. As the Tin Woodman in *The Wizard of Oz* discovered, to have a brain but no heart is to be missing something important.

Perhaps dating is evolving into new patterns in which premarital experience will contribute to marital success. Critics from Waller onward have claimed that dating promotes artificiality, rather than realistic assessment of compatibility. Some observers suggest that the sort of superficial dating Waller and others wrote about has become less common of late. Dating certainly has changed significantly since the pre-Second World War era. Many of the rigid rules of dating have broken down. The male no longer always takes the initiative; neither does he always pay. The sexual double standard has also weakened substantially, so that increasingly Americans feel that whatever a man can do a woman should be able to do. Some writers even suggest that dating is going out of style, replaced by informal pairing off in larger groups, often without the prearrangement of "asking someone out." Certainly the terminology is changing, with "seeing" and "being with" increasingly preferred to "dating" and "going steady." To many young people the latter terms have the old fashioned ring that "courting" and "suitor" had when I was young.

My daughter and other young adults argue that current styles are more natural and healthier than the dating experienced by my generation and the generation of my parents. Implicit in this argument is the view that, with formal rules and the "rating and dating" complex in decline, it should be possible to use dating (or whatever you call it) to realistically assess compatibility and romantic chemistry. These arguments may seem plausible, but I see no evidence that bears them out. The youngest women we interviewed in the Detroit survey should have experienced these more informal styles of romantic exploration. However, for them dating and premarital intimacy were, if anything, less closely related to marital success than was the case for the older women. The changes in premarital relations do not seem to make experience a better teacher.

While these conclusions are for the most part quite negative, my study leads to two more positive observations. First, marital success is not totally unpredictable. A wide range of features of how couples structure their day-to-day marital relations promote success—sharing in power and decision-making, pooling incomes, enjoying similar leisure time activities, having similar values, having mutual friends and an active social life, and other related qualities. Couples are not "doomed" by their past histories, including their dating histories, and they can increase their mutual happiness through the way they structure their marriages.

Second, there is something else about premarital experience besides dating history that may promote marital success. We have in America not one, but two widely shared, but quite contradictory, theories about how individuals should select a spouse: one based on the marketplace learning viewpoint and another based on love. One viewpoint sees selecting a spouse as a rational process, perhaps even with lists of criteria by which various prospects can be judged. The other, as song writers tell us, is based on the view that love conquers all and that "all you need is love." Love is a matter of the heart (perhaps with some help from the hormonal system) and not the head, and love may blossom unpredictably, on short notice or more gradually. Might it not be the case, then, that those couples who are most deeply in love at the time of their weddings will have the most successful marriages? We have centuries of poetry and novels, as well as love songs, that tell us that this is the case.

In the Detroit study, we did, in fact, ask women how much they had been in love when they first married. And we did find that those who recalled being "head over heels in love" then, had more successful mar-riages. However, there is a major problem with this finding. Since we were asking our interviewees to recall their feelings prior to their weddings—in many cases weddings that took place years or even decades earlier—it is quite possible and even likely that their answers are biased. Perhaps whether or not their marriage worked out influenced these "love reports" from earlier times, rather than having the level of romantic love then explain marital success later. Without either a time machine or funds to interview couples prior to marriage and then follow them up years later, it is impossible to be sure that more intense feelings of love lead to more successful marriages. Still, the evidence available does not question the wisdom of poets and songwriters when it comes to love. Mate selection may not be a total crap-shoot after all, and even if dating does not work, love perhaps does.

READINGS SUGGESTED BY THE AUTHOR:

Bailey, Beth. *From Front Porch to Back Seat.* Baltimore: Johns Hopkins University Press, 1988.

Burgess, Ernest W. and Paul Wallin. *Engagement and Marriage.* Chicago: Lippincott, 1953.

Modell, John. "Dating Becomes the Way of American Youth," in *Essays on the Family and Historical Change,* Leslie P. Moch and Gary Stark (eds.). College Station, Tex.: Texas A&M University Press, 1983.

Rothman, Ellen K. *Hands and Hearts: A History of Courtship.* New York: Basic Books, 1984.

Smith, Daniel S. and Michael Hindus. "Premarital Pregnancy in America, 1640-1971: An Overview and Interpretation," *Journal of Interdisciplinary History,* 4 (1975), 537-570.

Waller, Willard, "Rating and Dating Complex," *American Sociological Review,* (1937), 2:737-739.

Whyte, Martin King. *Dating, Mating, and Marriage.* New York: Aldine de Gruyter, 1990.

THE
Mating
GAME

The sophisticated sexual strategies of modern men and women are shaped by a powerful Stone Age psychology.

It's a dance as old as the human race. At cocktail lounges and church socials, during office coffee breaks and dinner parties—and most blatantly, perhaps, in the personal ads in newspapers and magazines—men and women perform the elaborate ritual of advertisement and assessment that precedes an essential part of nearly every life: mating. More than 90 percent of the world's people marry at some point in their lives, and it is estimated that a similarly large number of people engage in affairs, liaisons, flings or one-night stands. The who, what, when and where of love, sex and romance are a cultural obsession that is reflected in everything from Shakespeare to soap operas and from Tristram and Isolde to 2 Live Crew, fueling archetypes like the coy ingénue, the rakish cad, the trophy bride, Mrs. Robinson, Casanova and lovers both star-crossed and blessed.

It all may seem very modern, but a new group of researchers argues that love, American style, is in fact part of a universal human behavior with roots stretching back to the dawn of humankind. These scientists contend that, in stark contrast to the old image of brute cavemen dragging their mates by the hair to their dens, our ancient ancestors—men and women alike—engaged in a sophisticated mating dance of sexual intrigue, shrewd strategizing and savvy negotiating that has left its stamp on human psychology. People may live in a thoroughly modern world, these researchers say, but within the human skull is a Stone Age mind that was shaped by the mating concerns of our ancient ancestors and continues to have a profound influence on behavior today. Indeed, this ancient psychological legacy

HOW WE CHOOSE

Women are more concerned about whether mates will invest time and resources in a relationship; men care more about a woman's physical attractiveness, which in ancient times reflected her fertility and health.

influences everything from sexual attraction to infidelity and jealousy—and, as remarkable new research reveals, even extends its reach all the way down to the microscopic level of egg and sperm.

These new researchers call themselves evolutionary psychologists. In a host of recent scientific papers and at a major conference last month at the London School of Economics, they are arguing that the key to understanding modern sexual behavior lies not solely in culture, as some anthropologists contend, nor purely in the genes, as some sociobiologists believe. Rather, they argue, understanding human nature is possible only if scientists begin to understand the evolution of the human mind. Just as humans have evolved

specialized biological organs to deal with the intricacies of sex, they say, the mind, too, has evolved customized mental mechanisms for coping with this most fundamental aspect of human existence.

Gender and mind. When it comes to sexuality and mating, evolutionary psychologists say, men and women often are as different psychologically as they are physically. Scientists have long known that people typically choose mates who closely resemble themselves in terms of weight, height, intelligence and even earlobe length. But a survey of more than 10,000 people in 37 cultures on six continents, conducted by University of Michigan psychologist David Buss, reveals that men consistently value physical attractiveness and youth in a mate more than women do; women, equally as consistently, are more concerned than men with a prospective mate's ambition, status and resources. If such preferences were merely arbitrary products of culture, says Buss, one might expect to find at least one society somewhere where men's and women's mating preferences were reversed; the fact that attitudes are uniform across cultures suggests they are a fundamental part of human psychology.

Evolutionary psychologists think many of these mating preferences evolved in response to the different biological challenges faced by men and women in producing children—the definition of success in evolutionary terms. In a seminal paper, evolutionary biologist Robert Trivers of the University of California at Santa Cruz points out that in most mammals, females invest far more time and energy in reproduction and child rearing than do males. Not only must females go through a long gestation and weaning of their offspring, but childbirth itself is relatively dangerous. Males, on the other hand, potentially can get away with a very small biological investment in a child.

Human infants require the greatest amount of care and nurturing of any animal on Earth, and so over the eons women have evolved a psychology that is particularly concerned with a father's ability to help out with this enormous task—with his clout, protection and access to resources. So powerful is this psychological legacy that nowadays women size up a man's finances even when, as a practical matter, they may not have to. A recent study of the mating preferences of a group of medical students, for instance, found that these women, though anticipating financial success, were nevertheless most interested in men whose earning capacity was equal to or greater than their own.

Healthy genes. For men, on the other hand, reproductive success is ultimately dependent on the fertility of their mates. Thus males have evolved a mind-set that homes in on signs of a woman's health and youth, signs that, in the absence of medical records and birth certificates long ago, were primarily visual. Modern man's sense of feminine beauty—clear skin, bright eyes and youthful appearance—is, in effect, the legacy of eons spent diagnosing the health and fertility of potential mates.

This concern with women's reproductive health also helps explain why men value curvaceous figures. An upcoming paper by Devendra Singh of the University of Texas at Austin reveals that people consistently judge a woman's figure not by whether she is slim or fat but by the ratio of waist to hips. The ideal proportion—the hips roughly a third larger than the waist—reflects a hormonal balance that results in women's preferentially storing fat on their hips as opposed to their waists, a condition that correlates with higher fertility and resistance to disease. Western society's modern-day obsession with being slim has not changed this equation. Singh found, for instance, that while the winning Miss America has become 30 percent thinner over the past several decades, her waist-to-hip ratio has remained close to this ancient ideal.

Women also appreciate a fair face and figure, of course. And what they look for in a male's physique can also be explained as an evolved mentality that links good looks with good genes. A number of studies have shown that both men and women rate as most attractive

WHOM WE MARRY

More than 90 percent of all people marry and, they typically choose mates who closely resemble themselves, from weight and height, to intelligence and values, to nose breadth and even earlobe length.

faces that are near the average; this is true in societies as diverse as those of Brazil, Russia and several hunting and gathering tribes. The average face tends to be more symmetrical, and, according to psychologist Steven Gangestad and biologist Randy Thornhill, both of the University of New Mexico, this symmetry may reflect a person's genetic resistance to disease.

People have two versions of each of their genes—one from each parent—within every cell. Sometimes the copies are slightly different, though typically each version works just as effectively. The advantage to having two slightly different copies of the same gene, the researchers argue, is that it is harder for a disease to knock out the function of both copies, and this biological redundancy is reflected in the symmetry in people's bodies, including their faces. Further evidence for a psychological mechanism that links attractiveness with health comes from Buss's worldwide study of mating preferences: In those parts of the world where the incidence of parasites and infectious diseases is highest, both men and women place a greater value on attractive mates.

Some feminists reject the notion that women should alter physical appearance to gain advantage in the mating game. But archaeological finds suggest that the "beauty myth" has been very much a part of the human mating psychology since the times of our ancient ancestors—and that it applies equally to men. Some of the very first signs of human artistry are carved body ornaments that date back more than 30,000 years, and findings of worn nubs of ochre suggest that ancient humans may have used the red and black chalklike

substance as makeup. These artifacts probably served as social signs that, like lipstick or a Rolex watch today, advertised a person's physical appearance and status. In one grave dating back some 20,000 years, a male skeleton was found bedecked with a tunic made from thousands of tiny ivory beads—the Stone Age equivalent of an Armani suit.

Far from being immutable, biological mandates, these evolved mating mechanisms in the mind are flexible, culturally influenced aspects of human psychology that are similar to people's tastes for certain kinds of food. The human sweet tooth is a legacy from a time when the only sweet things in the environment were nutritious ripe fruit and honey, says Buss, whose book "The Evolution of Desire" is due out next year. Today, this ancient taste for sweets is susceptible to modern-day temptation by candy bars and such, though people have the free will to refrain from indulging it. Likewise, the mind's mating mechanisms can be strongly swayed by cultural influences such as religious and moral beliefs.

Playing the field. Both men and women display different mating psychologies when they are just playing around as opposed to searching for a lifelong partner, and these mental mechanisms are also a legacy from ancient times. A new survey by Buss and his colleague David Schmitt found that when women are looking for "short term" mates, their preference for attractive men increases substantially. In a study released last month, Doug Kenrick and Gary Groth of Arizona State University found that while men, too, desire attractive mates when they're playing the field, they will actually settle for a lot less.

Men's diminished concern about beauty in short-term mates reflects the fact that throughout human evolution, men have often pursued a dual mating strategy. The most successful strategy for most men was to find a healthy, fertile, long-term mate. But it also didn't hurt to take advantage of any low-risk opportunity to sire as many kin as possible outside the relationship, just to hedge the evolutionary bet. The result is an evolved psychology that allows a man to be sexually excited by a wide variety of women even while committed to a partner. This predilection shows up in studies of men's and women's sexual fantasies today. A study by Don Symons of the University of California at Santa Barbara and Bruce Ellis of the University of Michigan found that while both men and women actively engage in sexual fantasy, men typically have more fantasies about anonymous partners.

Surveys in the United States show

that at least 30 percent of married women have extramarital affairs, suggesting that, like men, women also harbor a drive for short-term mating. But they have different evolutionary reasons for doing so. Throughout human existence, short-term flings have offered women an opportunity to exchange sex for resources. In Buss and Schmitt's study, women value an "extravagant lifestyle" three times more highly when they are searching for a brief affair than when they are seeking a long-term mate. Women who are secure in a relationship with a committed male might still seek out attractive men to secure healthier genes for their offspring. Outside affairs also allow women to shop for better partners.

Sperm warfare. A woman may engage the sexual interest of several men simultaneously in order to foster a microscopic battle known as sperm competition. Sperm can survive in a woman's reproductive tract for nearly a week, note biologists Robin Baker and Mark Bellis of the University of Manchester, and by mating with more than one man within a short period of time, a woman sets the stage for their sperm to com-

JEALOUS PSYCHE

Men are most disturbed by sexual infidelity in their mates, a result of uncertainty about paternity. Women are more disturbed by emotional infidelity, because they risk losing their mate's time and resources.

pete to sire a child—passing this winning trait on to her male offspring as well. In a confidential survey tracking the sexual behavior and menstrual cycles of more than 2,000 women who

said they had steady mates, Baker and Bellis found that while there was no pattern to when women had sex with their steady partners, having sex on the side peaked at the height of the women's monthly fertility cycles.

Since in ancient times a man paid a dear evolutionary price for being cuckolded, the male psychology produces a physiological counterstrategy for dealing with a woman's infidelity. Studying the sexual behavior of a group of couples, Baker and Bellis found that the more time a couple spend apart, the more sperm the man ejaculates upon their sexual reunion—as much as three times higher than average.

This increase in sperm count is unrelated to when the man last ejaculated through nocturnal emission or masturbation, and Baker and Bellis argue that it is a result of a man's evolved psychological mechanism that bolsters his chances in sperm competition in the event that his mate has been unfaithful during their separation. As was no doubt the case in the times of our ancient ancestors, these concerns are not unfounded: Studies of blood typings show that as many as 1 of every 10 babies born to couples in North America is not the offspring of the mother's husband.

Despite men's efforts at sexual subterfuge, women still have the last word on the fate of a man's sperm in her reproductive tract—thanks to the physiological effects of the female orgasm. In a new study, Baker and Bellis reveal that if a woman experiences an orgasm soon after her mate's, the amount of sperm retained in her reproductive tract is far higher than if she has an earlier orgasm or none at all. Apparently a woman's arousal, fueled by her feelings as well as her mate's solicitous attentions, results in an evolutionary payoff for both.

Cads and dads. Whether people pursue committed relationships or one-night stands depends on their perceptions of what kind of mates are in the surrounding sexual environment. Anthropologist Elizabeth Cashdan of the University of Utah surveyed hundreds of men and women on whether they thought the members of their "pool" of potential mates were in general trustworthy, honest and capable of commitment. She also asked them what kinds of tactics they used to attract mates. Cashdan found that the less committed people thought their potential mates would be, the more they themselves pursued short-term mating tactics. For example, if women considered their world to be full of "cads," they tended to dress more provocatively and to be more promiscuous; if they thought that the world was populated

BEAUTY QUEST

the most attractive men and women are in fact those whose faces are most average, a signal that they are near the genetic average of the population and are perhaps more resistant to disease.

by potential "dads"—that is, committed and nurturing men—they tended to emphasize their chastity and fidelity. Similarly, "cads" tended to emphasize their sexuality and "dads" said they relied more on advertising their resources and desire for long-term commitment.

These perceptions of what to expect from the opposite sex may be influenced by the kind of home life an individual knew as a child. Social scientists have long known that children from homes where the father is chronically absent or abusive tend to mature faster physically and to have sexual relations earlier in life. Psychologist Jay Belsky of Pennsylvania State University argues that this behavior is an evolved psychological mechanism, triggered by early childhood experiences, that enables a child to come of age earlier and leave the distressing situation. This psychological mechanism may also lead to a mating strategy that focuses on short-term affairs.

The green monster. Whether in modern or ancient times, infidelities can breed anger and hurt, and new research suggests subtle differences in male and female jealousy with roots in the ancient past. In one study, for example, Buss asked males and females to imagine that their mates were having sex with someone else or that their mates were engaged in a deep emotional commitment with another person. Monitoring his subjects' heart rates, frowning and stress responses, he found that the stereotypical double standard cuts both ways. Men reacted far more strongly than

EVOLVED FANTASIES

Eroticism and gender

For insights into the subtle differences between men's and women's mating psychologies, one need look no further than the local bookstore. On one rack may be magazines featuring scantily clad women in poses of sexual invitation—a testimony to the ancient legacy of a male psychology that is acutely attuned to visual stimulus and easily aroused by the prospect of anonymous sex. Around the corner is likely to be a staple of women's erotic fantasy: romance novels.

Harlequin Enterprises Ltd., the leading publisher in the field, sells more than 200 million books annually and produces about 70 titles a month. Dedicated romance fans may read several books a week. "Our books give women everything," says Harlequin's Kathleen Abels, "a loving relationship, commitment and having sex with someone they care about." Some romance novels contain scenes steamy enough to make a sailor blush, and studies show that women who read romances typically have more sexual fantasies and engage in sexual intercourse more frequently than nonreaders do.

Sexual caricature. Since sexual fantasy frees people of the complications of love and mating in the real world, argue psychologists Bruce Ellis and Don Symons, it is perhaps not surprising that in erotic materials for both men and women, sexual partners are typically caricatures of the consumer's own evolved mating psychology. In male-oriented erotica, for instance, women are depicted as being lust driven, ever willing and unencumbered by the need for emotional attachment. In romance novels, the male lead in the book is typically tender, emotional and consumed by passion for the heroine, thus ensuring his lifelong fidelity and dependence. In other words, say Ellis and Symons, the romance novel is "an erotic, utopian, female counterfantasy" to male erotica.

Of course, most men also enjoy stories of passion and romance, and women can be as easily aroused as men by sexually explicit films. Indeed, several new entertainment ventures, including the magazine *Future Sex* and a video company, Femme Productions, are creating erotic materials using realistic models in more sensual settings in an attempt to appeal to both sexes. Still, the new research into evolutionary psychology suggests that men and women derive subtly different pleasures from sexual fantasy—something that even writing under a ghost name can't hide. According to Abels, a Harlequin romance is occasionally penned by a man using a female pseudonym, but "our avid readers can always tell."

---

women to the idea that their mates were having sex with other men. But women reacted far more strongly to the thought that their mates were developing strong emotional attachments to someone else.

As with our evolved mating preferences, these triggers for jealousy ultimately stem from men's and women's biology, says Buss. A woman, of course, has no doubt that she is the mother of her children. For a man, however, paternity is never more than conjecture, and so men have evolved psychologies with a heightened concern about a mate's sexual infidelity. Since women make the greater biological investment in offspring, their psychologies are more concerned about a mate's reneging on his commitment, and, therefore, they are more attentive to signs that their mates might be attaching themselves emotionally to other women.

Sexual monopoly. The male preoccupation with monopolizing a woman's sexual reproduction has led to the oppression and abuse of women worldwide, including, at its extremes, confinement, domestic violence and ritual mutilation such as clitoridectomy. Yet the new research into the mating game also reveals that throughout human evolution, women have not passively acquiesced to men's sexual wishes. Rath-

---

DUELING SPERM

If a couple has been apart for some time, the man's sperm count goes up during sex at their reunion—an ancient, evolved strategy against a female's possible infidelities while away.

---

er, they have long employed a host of behavioral and biological tactics to follow their own sexual agenda—behaviors that have a huge impact on men's behavior as well. As Buss points out, if all women suddenly began preferring to have sex with men who walked on their hands, in a very short time half the human race would be upside down.

With its emphasis on how both men and women are active players in the mating game, evolutionary psychology holds out the promise of helping negotiate a truce of sorts in the battle of the sexes—not by declaring a winner but by pointing out that the essence of the mating game is compromise, not victory. The exhortations of radical feminists, dyed-in-the-wool chauvinists and everyone in between are all spices for a sexual stew that has been on a slow boil for millions of years. It is no accident that consistently, the top two mating preferences in Buss's survey—expressed equally by males and females worldwide—were not great looks, fame, youth, wealth or status, but *kindness* and *intelligence*. In the rough-and-tumble of the human mating game, they are love's greatest allies.

WILLIAM F. ALLMAN

Cahl Jooniah

Ian Brown

Lamaze and the degradation of the male soul—
Revelations concerning the passage of wind—The list—
Why women control men's lives

There are twenty-four of us in Lamaze class, twelve pregnant couples in our thirties. In Class One we introduced ourselves and volunteered our impressions of pregnancy. (Lamaze class is nothing if not voluntary.) The guy with the brown hair and the Filofax said, "I've been smoking a lot of dope and I started going to topless bars." For two and a half hours every Thursday night throughout the Lamaze class, he roots in his Filofax. I can't tell if he's trying to schedule his baby into or out of his life. Strung out in a circle, we resemble a fleet of blimps and their mechanics.

Each week the teacher writes out what we'll be covering in class:

Introduction
Names
Due Dates
Discuss Names
Other Children
Other Facts
Self Work

The categories terrify me. Names I can do, but Other Children seems premature, and I become unpleasant if Johanna broaches the subject. She wants to talk about having more; I think we ought to see what one is like. "I'd rather have had none than just one," she says. I didn't know that at the time.

The Lamaze method, the teacher explains, entails psychoprophylaxis, "the prevention of physical pain through psychological means." Which is to say, a form of brainwashing. We'll use formal breathing patterns to "interrupt the fear/pain/tension cycle." The lessons are full of unfamiliar, medieval words: the bloody show, crowning, the almighty fundus. In the instructor's diagrams of the pregnant uterus, the babies are always huge and orange.

The woman to my left hands me a plastic chart the instructor has passed around. The chart consists of ten gradually enlarged holes: this is what will happen to my wife's cervix. The first stage, at one centimeter, is a tiny disk smaller than a dime. Ten centimeters is a dinner plate in some California restaurants. The instructor holds up a rag doll that is attached to a rag placenta by a rag umbilical cord. She asks the men questions. "Coaches," she says, "what do you do in the first phase of labor?"

"Go and play pool," someone says. It is a man, of course. It is impossible for a woman to be flippant during a Lamaze class.

The instructor is a short busty woman with long dark hair. She's a neuropsychiatric nurse with a master's degree in sociology who became a birthing coach because "I had such a wonderful birth experience." She has three children. She is exactly the sort of overeducated walking amnesiac I was afraid would be running the Lamaze class. Her name is Magda. Perfect.

A week later. Actually, I realize, Magda's quite attractive. She makes eye contact.

The women like to catch up on each other's physical news at the beginning of class. They jaw about cramps and gas and bowel movements as if they were discussing stories in the newspaper. The men listen in amazement, gazing upon a new species of talking tomato plant. We are "the coaches"—never men, or husbands, just coaches. I'm certain this is to desexualize us, to make us safe for fatherhood, but I'm wrong. Some teams aren't married, so Magda uses the politically correct term.

Anita, the blabbermouth in class, had a half-hour contraction last night. Every week it's something new with Anita. I know more about her cervix and vagina than I do about my own testicles. "I don't think I'm going to make it to the last class," she says. She describes herself as "an entrepreneur" who makes "vintage baby clothing."

My mood is a car on a slick road, front-heavy and unpredictable. I veer so often between panic and the overwhelming urge to sleep that panic seems familiar. Sometimes I imagine getting up, walking out of the class, throwing my skis in my truck and disappearing for the rest of time. I keep remembering in starts, the way we usually remember bad news, that I am about to make a huge self-sacrifice. It is as if I am willingly throwing myself on an altar to be burned. But when I put my arm around Johanna, I immediately feel calmer. I have no idea why. It never used to happen this fast.

But sometimes, another, even less familiar calm overcomes me: as if finally, in becoming a father, I have a destiny I can't avoid. This idea has been creeping up on me. Marriage, real estate, work, writing, country, friendships: all these I could leave, I presume. But I'll never not be this child's father. Why doesn't that feel like prison? Why does it calm me?

At break, all the men rush out to buy coffee in the vending machines. I tried to memorize the numbers. J2, espresso. J3, coffee with whitener. I still drink coffee at night. I think: I still make unpopular choices. This brainless idea actually passes through my head.

"Who's afraid of the episiotomy?" Magda says. I raise my hand. I am the only person who does. Then I realize this was a question for the women.

But it's true: the episiotomy terrifies me. I see it, vivid and red in my mind, at night in bed. The episiotomy is a surgical incision made in the rear of the vagina to widen the birth canal. This vagina was my private place, and now some person I don't know plans to build an extension onto it. Not that her vagina was ever mine, but she lent it to me, and me alone. Well, not any more. Everything belongs to everybody now. These days when I read the paper, I find myself more sympathetic to capitalists. Suddenly I want to own something.

Wednesday, several packets of stool softeners arrive (by courier, no less) from Celeste, a friend of my wife's. Later Celeste telephones. Apparently the stool softeners were extras left over from her last pregnancy, and hey—why not share them?

"You'll need them," she says. "I can't believe they didn't tell you about that. Don't you have hemorrhoids? No? Well, you'll have them afterward. You'll really need those stool softeners."

Like a lot of ambivalent mothers (name one who isn't), Celeste is routinely driven berserk by her three children. "Having kids turned out to be so much less romantic than I imagined," she once confessed to me in a moment of desperation. But to admit this to anyone else would be to admit that motherhood is something less than the greatest accomplishment mankind can ever know. Having recently promised the next twenty years of her life to proving this proposition true, she can't afford to say it might not be. So she eats her terror and becomes a walking booby trap of resentment. She makes everyone discuss "poopy" for hours. Poopy is as diabolical and intractable a dilemma, apparently, as peace in the Middle East and starvation in Somalia. You may not know much about poopy, or even care much about poopy, but in Celeste's company you don't have any choice: poopy is all. "Having kids is going to totally change your life," she said to me the last time I failed to sidestep the conversation. She bored the words into me, drilling into my brain with the heat of her temper. "Whatever you think, it's going to be different. They're great, but your life is going to be totally different. I mean, totally different."

But Celeste wants to have another baby. Sure. Does Celeste have a vacuum at the center of her being, a terrified hole that keeps collapsing on itself as she tries to find some purpose? From within the hole, having children seems like the easiest way to fill it. Having kids is the thing to do. "Everybody has kids," she says, and it makes me want to yell at her. She thinks her motives are selfless. Not long ago I saw Freddy, her husband, for the first time in a year. He said hello, shook my hand, and

began unstrapping giant cartons of baby clothes from the roof of his Volvo wagon. He carried them over and dumped them, one by one, into my arms. "These are for you," he said.

The longer the baby clothes lay around his house, the longer Celeste would whine about another child.

Every class, Magda repeats everything we've already learned, but I can't remember anything. This is why two and a half hours of information are stretched out over six weeks: Lamaze classes are baby-sitting for adults during the most stressful weeks of their lives.

I'm dissociating like an amoeba. When are we supposed to call the doctor? After two hours of thirty-second contractions that are five minutes apart? Or when the contractions are five minutes long and thirty seconds apart? No one else seems to write anything down. Plus, my minor crush on Magda has now become a major distraction. She is more than attractive. She's a sex goddess.

Johanna, on the other hand, is now quite large. Nevertheless, I experience waves of lust for her whenever I can get near her. She sleeps surrounded by no fewer than five pillows. One supports her leg, another her back, another her breasts. It's like sleeping with a refrigerator wrapped in moving quilts.

Every class kicks off with a game. One night we split up into two groups, "coaches and moms," and make a list of our likes and dislikes about pregnancy.

We separate. The men aren't bashful. They want to talk; they just don't have words for what they're trying to say. It's like listening to chimps.

"I worry that I won't ever read another book," I say.

"Right," someone else joins in. "Plus gaining weight myself."

"One of my dislikes," says the only black man in the group, "is her mood swings."

"No sleep."

"My wife has to stop working."

"Child-care costs, health care."

"I feel like I finally have a destiny I can't avoid," I say. This is my contribution.

"Right, that's the worst."

"I meant it as a positive thing."

"Guys," says the man writing the list down. He's heir to a vast sports fortune. He won't have any goddamn problems affording a kid, the spoiled creep. "We need a few positives."

Silence. "Well," says the fellow with the Filofax, "there's the extra tax deduction."

"Sex is not the greatest," someone says. "I mean, there's desire, but that stomach doesn't exactly make it easy."

"But," says the Filofax man again, ever the optimist, "you get more blow jobs."

"That's true," says a guy who's a talent scout for a record company. "Now you get them whenever you want."

More blow jobs goes on the list. In fact, it is the only positive fact of pregnancy, on which the men are unanimous. After fifteen minutes, the men's list is as follows:

LIKES
A destiny you can't avoid

Can get on first on airplanes
Feeling the baby move
Talking to the baby
Solidifies relationship
Father's Day
Buying toys
Feeling of luck
Teaching
Sharing
Someone to pass things on to
The chance to try to do better than your father
Wife's happiness
Choosing a name
Closer relationship with in-laws and parents
Excitement of family members
Additional tax deduction
Blow jobs
Big breasts
Excitement
Pride

My favorite is "Feeling of luck." But our list of dislikes runs longer:

Destiny you can't avoid
Wife's mood swings
Male weight gain
No time to read
Lack of free time
Unable to sleep through the night
Wife not going back to work
Decisions (child care, health care, pediatricians)
Financial worries
Repetitive questions from wife and others about the pregnancy
Not being able to party with one's wife
Drinking alone
Going to bed early
Worry that baby won't be healthy
Sick of shopping for a crib and baby bumpers
Cost of day care
Competency of day care
Choosing a name
In-laws, parents around more
Hassled to read about pregnancy
Sisters, friends saying "Just wait"
Lack of paternity leave
School decisions
No sex
Cutting back on selfish activities (skiing, vacations)

We break and return to our seats. The women have their own list. This is a conservative crowd: all but one couple are married, and all but two of the twelve women have taken their husbands' names.

LIKES
Feel baby moving
Creativity increases
Energy increases

Ultrasounds
Going to the doctor
Better hair and fingernails
Hearing the heartbeat
Don't have to clean the house
Your husband helps more
More help from strangers, who are nicer
Excitement about having a living baby in you
An excuse to buy clothes
Bigger breasts

The women have many more dislikes, too, most but not all of which are physical:

Breasts too big
Scared of labor pain
Size of body
Clumsiness
Heartburn
Sleeplessness
Leg cramps and back spasms
Can't sleep on stomach
Constant peeing
Nasal congestion
Fear of stretch marks
Fear of death
People asking too many questions
Always feeling warm
Bitchiness, mood swings, crying, depression
Bad maternity clothes
Big ugly underwear
Restricted activities
Shortness of breath
Strangers no longer find you attractive
Limited shoes and clothes
People giving advice
People's expectations of what sex the baby will be
Lack of concentration, spacing out
Acne
No glow, never feeling sexy, lack of desire
Financial worries
Fear of never getting one's body back
Life as you know it is over

"And flatulence," the woman reading the list says. "Not just having a lot of gas, but also the fact that our gas seems to give our husbands tacit permission to fart at will as well around the house." She pauses. "Actually, that was our only unanimous observation."

The men look at one another. The thought speeds across our foreheads: *so, you fart around the house.* Not that pregnancy was required, but now everyone knows. Pregnancy could never be called cerebral.

Listening, I suddenly know what has been left off the guys' list: pregnancy has made me fall in love with my wife again. Is that what am feeling, love? A warmth I am half-ashamed of? Like admitting that I enjoy sitting in the bath? Or, more precisely, like sitting in the bath, replacing the hot water every once in a while, and not getting out, and—this is the part that I think may be love—not telling myself that I should get out of the bath and do some work, not telling myself that I'm losing my self-discipline if I don't, but instead sitting there and saying, *Don't freak, it's okay to sit here in the bath simply because it feels good?* Can somebody please tell me if that's love?

If it is, none of us thought to say so. Maybe we didn't have the words for it. The closest we came was "your relationship is solidified." *Charmant, n'est-ce pas?* Or maybe that's what Peter, the big guy with the moustache, meant when he said "talking." He works as a TV editor at a big network. I smiled when he said it, and he thought I was mocking him. "No, you know;" he said. "I mean, talking in bed and stuff. Just stupid stuff." I knew what he meant.

Before the third class, my mother calls. My mother is seventy-eight and cannot believe I am enrolled in Lamaze class. "Why do you want to be there at the birth?" she says.

I'm not sure I have an answer to this. Once I heard a woman on a TV call-in show say that it made for "kinder men." The best reason I have heard so far, though, was a remark in one of the birth films we have been watching. It was made by an older man in his fifties. "I found out there was more to life than just golf, or fishing, or other things that I just love to do," he said. "I discovered I can generate some of that love right here."

But my old ma is not buying this. "Do you think your father attended these classes? Not on your life. Do you think he watched your birth? Not a chance. I think it would have put him off sex for the rest of his life, gazing up somebody's hoohaw."

This possibility has occurred to me. The sheer thought of a head passing through my wife's vagina—an act, I have read, that some women say is the most erotic sensation of their lives— turns my forehead to rock. The pain! Sex, her vagina, is no longer simply pleasurable; it has consequences, and the consequences will be indelibly indented on my sexual focus. I think this is what my friend Stephen, a three-time father, means when he says, "Stay up at the head. Don't go down and look."

And what will this child look like? Will it have my wife's features or mine? It could be a real nightmare, if it lands my eyes and nose and teeth. And how much will it look like me? How many times did Henderson call me that first year of his daughter's life, hissing into the phone, trying to keep his voice inaudible to his wife (the woman was a German shepherd; she could hear smoke wafting through the air): "I love the kid, but I want her to have a few of my features! I want some Henderson in her!" Strange wild pride of the father.

And what about the baby's appearance right out of the tunnel? How was I going to react to that? It wasn't exactly a limo ride down Birth Avenue, and the journey left its mark, Magda reassured me: stork marks on the face, coneheadedness, cradle cap, enlarged scrotums, molded heads, sucking blisters, crossed eyes, vernex, vaginal discharge, or (truly blessed child!) a slick coating of meconium, high-density amniotic supershit. . . .

Not that it could ever be as bad as it had been for McManus. Poor McManus. He was a Maritimer, a handsome man, with ruddy cheeks and ruddy manner, the great hope of a long line of Prince Edward Islanders. McManus was going all the way with

the Lamaze birth trip, sitting in, coaching his wife. Eighteen hours she was in labor, with McManus running out every eight minutes to phone the clan and broadcast news of any progress all over their tiny island. And finally the great moment occurred, and the fruit of his loins slithered out into the doctor's rough hands, and McManus leaned over to see it, and there beheld—

Jesus Christ! What the hell was it? It was a miniature gorilla! Baby-sized, sure, but covered with thick dark hair, all over its arms and legs and chest and tiny backside and face! "I've given birth to an evolutionary throw-back! " McManus's mind gasped. "My child is King Kong!"

And through the thickening wall of his shock he heard his wife's faint, exhausted voice . . . What's he like, Tommy?"

And McManus, true blue that he was, said "Oh," *we've given birth to the Wolf Child, the brat's a monster,* "he's beautiful." Three days later all the hair fell out. By then someone had told McManus about the common newborn condition known as lanugo.

The women control the tone of the classes, not to mention the moral high ground of the entire subject of birth. This is because pregnancy is submission, because being a mother is a life of sacrifice, because only women can give birth and life, much to their annoyance.

But it's also because labor, as Magda says, is no picnic. We coaches should be direct, verbal, and supportive—not my best side. Direct, verbal, and supportive are in my experience mutually exclusive modes of communication. "Don't take anything she says during labor personally," Magda says.

Magda says the transition between labor and birth will be the worst. The contractions will be ninety seconds long, excruciatingly painful, and only thirty seconds apart.

"How long does that phase last?" someone asks. There's panic in his voice.

Our job as coaches (and therefore as men), Magda says, is to serve our wives: fan them, massage them, remind them (to empty their bladders often, to move about), count their breaths, bring them ice chips. I am the birth butler. The prospect alarms me. I despise servitude. But that is what becoming a father is all about: submitting, obeying, being tamed. I can't find the grace therein, not yet.

I can hear the infant cardio-pulmonary resuscitation class in session in the next room. Downstairs in the lobby of the hospital news crews are camped out, awaiting word on the teenager shot this afternoon in class at the high school a few blocks from our house. This is the world I am bringing a child into, a world of choking and massacre.

But Magda's talking about enemas. Enemas are not required these days, because times have changed, and birth is natural, not to mention a woman's prerogative, and largely sacrosanct. In any event, women in labor are encouraged to pass more than just the child these days.

"I'm going to shit," a woman sitting next to me says to her husband. She thinks she's whispering. "I hope you'll be prepared for that."

He turns his head and looks directly at her. He owns a construction company. He makes his living adapting to unforeseen problems. But tonight I can see raw yellow terror in his eyes. This terror is a question: *And what, exactly, do you want me to do about it?*

I raise my hand, as if I were in grade school. I'm ten years old again, apparently. "Tell me," I say to Magda, "have you read this latest news that Leboyer, who invented the underwater birth, has changed his mind and now says fathers have no business attending birth?" I read it in the newspaper.

Instantly the mood of the women in the room floods against me in a massive tide. I am a traitor and a pariah. It's almost as bad as the class where I asked if people really did eat the placenta to ward off post-partum depression. I read that in the newspaper, too.

"Oh yeah?" Anita says, staring me down. "So where is this guy Leboyer now? Having lunch with Salman Rushdie?" She was fierce.

On break I buy a J3, and sit by myself in the empty classroom. Everyone else is out in the hallway. The door opens, and the CPR instructor walks in from next door. She's a knockout, with red hair and a slim body.

"Can I borrow your strength?" she says. She wants me to carry some mats. Of course. Isn't that what I was made for? I give you my strength, and you give me a little attention.

By now Magda's charts are more alarming:

Thoughts about medication
Fears
Partners' feelings
Types don't want/Types acceptable
Feelings tonight

Feelings tonight. I am trapped inside a Barry Manilow song that is being played over and over again on the oldies station that has enveloped my life.

Tonight we see a film about The Important Job of being a birthing coach. It's mostly wide-angle head-on shots of babies being squeezed out of vaginas. From what I can see, being a labor coach consists of being a physical presence but not getting in the way.

The lights come up, and one of the men, an agent at a major Hollywood agency, can barely speak. For three weeks he has said nothing in class and been more or less unconscious. He always shows up late, and I thought he rather disdained the proceedings. Now he's having a nervous breakdown. His eyes are gaping, he's sucking air like a dying fish. "So," he says, "uh, so, like, how far contracted are we at this point?" *Feelings tonight.*

I visit Dr. Katz, my wife's obstetrician, on one of her appointments. He's younger than I am, a pleasant, capable, goofy guy. He has three partners, all women. A modern guy. The white walls of the waiting room are covered with pictures of babies. Women, bulging upright drumlins, waddle about with their hands on their hips while their husbands speedread back issues of *Time*. Every time I catch the eye of any

nurse, she smiles at me as if I were four years old. This is what happens when you go to the obstetrician: everyone treats you as if you're the baby. Maybe you are. Maybe that's why my wife likes going to the doctor. She gets to be three years old again and spend half an hour with a man who actually knows what he's doing.

Katz shows me the ultrasound picture of the baby. I see my child sketched in gray and white streaks on a video screen. I could be looking at a dozen passing thoughts made real. The baby is now eighteen inches long: I can see its spine, its feet. I am hot and dizzy with excitement, and faint with worry and fear: until now I had no real idea how many things could go wrong. The heartbeat sounds like a toilet flushing again and again very quickly. A squishy heart.

I decide not to visit the doctor's office again. This thing is alive.

On the weekend I have to turn down a game of golf to buy a crib. My resentment is pooling in my shoes. At home afterward I retreat to my study. I open several beers.

I make a list of what I get out of my marriage, and what my wife gets. Under my wife's name I list the baby, love, the fact that she is living where she wants to live. Under my name I list one other word: book. I get to write a book.

My greatest fear is that I have stupidly, thoughtlessly given my time and therefore my life away; made myself, as Bacon wrote in his essay "On Marriage and Children," a "hostage to fortune." Sometimes these thoughts ambush me, and I feel defeated and betrayed, and then, in a crack of fury, I want to break whatever I happen to be holding. These moments pass quickly.

I come to class four drunk. Adrienne, one of the women, is lying on a mat on the floor. Her blood pressure is up on the roof, and she has to spend her days and nights prone. A nightmare.

Another couple, a new pair, are attending this class because it's about Cesarean birth. Their baby, their third, needs an operation on its brain, and so the doctors will be performing a planned Cesarean.

The German guy and his wife have a tiff in class. He's a movie producer. He's counting off her breaths, but she's not following him.

"It's my breathing," she says.

"It's my rhythm," he says. "I'm the coach."

"The coach," Magda says. "Not the boss! Partners!"

Anita's baby is induced this week. During class we take a tour of the hospital and visit her. She's not talking, which is a miracle. She looks empty, and slightly green. Her husband, on the other hand, who barely said a word in five weeks, glows as if he has a 10,000-watt bulb in his head. He can't shut up. He's holding their baby in his arms in the hallway, a small, scowling ball of piss and puke and sleep and yowl. He even cut the cord. Magda considers this "a very positive sign."

"You're in for an amazing experience," he says to me. Blasts of a weird yellow sour smell—what is it, that vapor of babies?— are rising off the kid. But why is he talking so directly to me?

There are other guys standing around. But he's looking straight into my eyes. Have I really seemed so reluctant?

"Before, I thought, ah—me, in the birthing room? I don't think so. But now I see: you have to go through it, and then you understand why. I bawled my head off when the baby came out."

Afterward in class, everyone is amazed. "David seems like a changed man." I would say that's an understatement. I would say David looked like he'd been kidnapped by friendly little blue men.

But we have to rush back to class to see another film. This one's called *Hello Baby* and features three couples from Boston, all of whom are giving birth. All the birth movies we've seen bear marked similarities to pornographic films. The action is about as varied, the characters are even less developed. The sound tracks are comparable, too, heavy on women moaning. We watch them for the same reasons: to focus our imaginations, to cut out external stimuli, to find the source of our desires.

One of the couples in the movie, a lout named Carl (or Cahl, in Bostonese) and his wife, are complete buffoons. Cahl's wife is suffering dull agony; the only place she can bear the pain of labor is in the shower. She can barely tell Cahl to stop fanning her head, and Cahl is not the sort to pick up on things. Cahl is supposed to be soothing her fears and pain and apparently volcanic heartburn. But all Cahl can say is, "Musta bin dat hoagie you ade dis ahftahnoon, huh?" Everyone finds this extremely amusing. And yet when the baby finally fights its way out, and Cahl is leaning over watching, and his lip starts to quiver, and he says, "Ohmigahd, honey, it's Cahl Jooniah, Cahl Jooniah is heah!" and the tears burst from within him—well, I know it sounds idiotic, but all around me, on blue mats in the dark, men and women are crying.

One night toward the end we rehearse labor in class. We have to inflict pain on each other to prove that the Lamaze breathing techniques work. They seem to, which is encouraging. What's even more interesting is how seriously the women try to hurt their husbands. I suppose they don't have the opportunity often.

"If that's as bad as it gets," the guy with the Filofax tells his wife, who's gripping his thigh with all her might, "you have nothing to worry about."

"Okay then," she says, "maybe I'll try gripping a little higher." By now everyone's nervous, even afraid. Everyone, man and woman alike, wants to blame the penis.

We celebrate our last class with a potluck supper and an exchange of phone numbers. We've become a family. I am appalled to find I'm strangely thrilled: I imagine the reunion, and all those babies. At last I will belong to something, I think, even as I tell myself my brain is turning to aspic.

"Let's talk about what this is really going to be like when you go home with your baby," Magda says. "Because sometimes it's like . . ."

Magda stalls. She can't quite find a way to say this bit. For six weeks she has glorified childbirth and family life, but this is harder.

"It's a wonderful life-style change, but sometimes it's hard to get used to. Your relationship definitely changes."

She pauses. She has been saving the worst for last. "You can't come home on Friday and say, Let's go to Palm Springs for the weekend. And the big question here is, Is there sex after birth?"

"No," a woman says instantly.

A few minutes later Magda dims the lights and leads us through a "guided visualization." We lie on the floor in the darkened room on our blue exercise mats, blue the color of a big summer sky. Magda tells us to breathe . . . and to imagine a park . . . where we can relax . . . and where we have three balloons . . . each of which represents our worst fears about birth.

"Let each balloon go," Magda says. "Watch it float up out of sight. Okay, now let the second one go."

My first balloon hasn't disappeared from sight yet. The balloon is my fear that something will be wrong with the baby. I can't stop being afraid.

During the potluck supper, the women pack around Magda like seals and talk about breastfeeding: duration of, when to stop, developmental considerations. "A friend of mine says she stopped when she saw her son lumbering toward her to feed," my wife is saying. "He suddenly reminded her of her husband. She said that was it."

Isn't that just how women understand men? They see us, and if they don't run, they laugh.

The men prefer the perimeter of the room. The German is telling me about the Berlin Wall. He used to live right beside it. He never expected it to fall.

Adapting to Adoption

Adopted kids generate scientific optimism and clinical caution

BRUCE BOWER

Welcome to the adoptive family, where home life takes on a decidedly different look depending on whether it is refracted through the lens of mental health clinicians or behavioral researchers.

For more than 40 years, psychiatrists and others who treat emotional and behavioral problems have noted that adopted children and teenagers make up a disproportionate number of their patients. About 2 percent of children under age 18 in the United States are adopted by unrelated parents, but they make up 5 percent of children in psychotherapy, 10 to 15 percent of youngsters in residential treatment and psychiatric hospitals, and 6 to 9 percent of those identified in schools as suffering from various learning disabilities. An estimated 1 million children in the United States now live with adoptive parents.

Clinicians have focused on the roadblocks to an adoptee's healthy development. According to various mental health workers, adoptive parents and kids often struggle to form strong emotional bonds. The parents tend to ruminate about a child's biological parents; the children begin to realize at age 5 to 7 that one set of parents rejected them and to struggle with a sense of loss and bewilderment about their biological roots. Their self-esteem drops; they cannot seem to make close friends. Adolescent adoptees show a propensity for delinquency, depression, and a confused self-image.

Search movement advocates, who lobby for giving adoptees access to their adoption records so they can seek out their biological parents, take this position further. Adopted people need information about their genetic origins in order to feel whole and secure, they argue; those who lack this knowledge stumble through life feeling isolated and incomplete. Some in the search movement press for the elimination of adoption.

Yet in the past decade, a growing body of research on adoptees who do not receive psychological help indicates that parents usually develop warm and secure relationships with their adopted infants, whose emotional health and self-image throughout the school years equal those of children living with biological parents. Rates of psychological and behavioral problems rise in youngsters adopted after infancy, probably due largely to neglect, abuse, and multiple changes in caretakers before adoption, according to these investigators.

Organizations representing adoptive families consider such findings a refreshing antidote to the clinical emphasis on adoption's inherent problems and to the widespread unease about parents raising children conceived by others, especially children who come from different races or nations.

"This issue is a tangled ball of yarn, and adoption research is only in its infancy," asserts Anu R. Sharma, a psychologist at the Search Institute, a Minneapolis-based organization that studies children and teenagers.

"Useful guidelines for adoptive parents are in short supply, while the adoption process itself has become more diverse," adds Steven L. Nickman, a psychiatrist at Massachusetts General Hospital in Boston. "Adoption is a highly political issue."

Consider interracial adoption. In 1972, the National Association of Black Social Workers branded the adoption of black children by white parents "cultural genocide," a position it still holds. Most adoption agencies try to place children with same-race parents and avoid interracial matches. About 500 black children get adopted by whites annually.

In the case of the approximately 10,000 children adopted annually from abroad by U.S. residents, officials in their countries of origin often confront home-grown pressures to bar this practice.

Some countries allow international adoptions for a short time, then suddenly withhold children from foreigners, as happened in Rumania. South Korea, the major source of babies for international adoption over the past 40 years, plans to phase out such placements by 1996.

On the domestic front, an Illinois Supreme Court judge last month ordered that a 3½-month-old boy be taken from his adoptive parents, who had raised him from the age of 4 days, and given to his biological father, who argued that the adoption had occurred without his knowledge or consent. The adoptive parents plan to appeal the ruling to the U.S. Supreme Court. For now, the boy remains with them.

Still, societies around the world allow, and in some cases encourage, the transfer of children to nonbiological parents. Adoption as either a legal or an informal method of incorporating new members into a family extends back to the earliest centers of civilization, including Rome, Greece, India, China, and Babylonia.

Systematic efforts to understand the emotional adjustment of adopted youngsters have emerged only in the past 25 years. The latest study, conducted by the Search Institute and released in June, finds that teenagers adopted as infants generally have positive self-concepts, warm relationships with their parents, and psychological health comparable to that of nonadopted teens.

"This flies in the face of many clinical reports that adopted teenagers have all sorts of problems," contends Anu Sharma, who participated in the project, directed by institute psychologist Peter L. Benson.

With the help of public and private adoption agencies in Colorado, Illinois, Minnesota, and Wisconsin, the researchers recruited 715 families with teenagers who had been adopted as infants. A total of 1,262 parents, 881 adopted adolescents, and 78 nonadopted siblings completed surveys on psychological and family characteristics.

Most adopted teens regarded their adoption as a fact of life that made little difference in how they viewed themselves; about one-quarter reported that adoption loomed large in their self-views. Adopted girls cited more struggles with identity and self-esteem than adopted boys; however, such sex differences prove difficult to interpret because teenage girls find it easier to express their feelings than teenage boys.

Nearly two-thirds of the adopted youngsters noted an interest in meeting their biological parents, mainly to see what they look like, to tell them "I'm happy," or to find out the reasons for their adoptions. At the same time, only 9 percent reported missing or longing for biological parents.

In addition, adopted adolescents cited emotional attachments to their parents as strong as those of their nonadopted siblings. Close ties to both parents emerged for 54 percent; another 30 percent had a deep bond with one parent; 16 percent reported the lack of a strong attachment to either parent.

Nearly all parents — 95 percent — said they experienced a strong attachment to their adopted child.

Families displayed considerable skill in communication and discipline, as well as a low rate of parental divorce and separation, perhaps partly reflecting a successful preadoption screening process at most agencies. Parents typically maintained a delicate balance in discussing adoption with their children, neither denying its existence nor overplaying it.

On measures of psychological adjustment, nearly three-quarters of the adopted teens showed good mental health. Measures included tobacco, alcohol, and illicit drug use; sexual activity; depression and suicide attempts; delinquent and violent acts; school problems; and bulimia.

A slightly smaller percentage of good mental health—assessed in a similar survey conducted by the Search Institute since 1990—appears in 51,098 teenagers attending public school in the same four states in which the adoptees live, Benson and Sharma assert. Another research team found a slightly higher proportion of good mental health in a national sample of 1,719 teenagers, studied with a battery of clinical scales in 1989, who had not received mental health services or required special academic help.

Reasons for these small differences remain unclear, although Sharma considers similarities in mental health across the three studies more significant.

One-third of the adopted teens had received counseling or psychotherapy, although most of those reported good mental health. Adoptive parents may seek out such services more willingly than other parents, Sharma notes. Also, parents and teachers may assume that adopted adolescents are more prone to emotional problems and refer them for counseling sooner than they do other teens.

The 289 interracially adopted adolescents in the Search Institute survey — most from Korea — displayed psychological health and identity formation comparable to those of adoptees in same-race families.

Adoptees reported much more involvement in churches and in volunteer and community organizations than comparison groups, notes psychologist Matthew K. McGue of the University of Minnesota in Minneapolis, who is participating in further analyses of the data. This may reflect a particular emphasis on such activities by adoptive parents, he says.

Rumination about biological parents tended to occur in adopted teens who showed the most signs of depression or anxiety, McGue adds. "For them, adoption seems to be one more thing to worry about," he holds.

Despite its intriguing glimpse into the lives of adopted teenagers, the Search Institute project contains some important limitations. Half the adoptive families originally contacted for the survey declined to participate, yielding a nonrandom sample; a nonadopted control group given the same survey was not included; and researchers failed to establish how much security teenagers derived from their reported sense of emotional attachment to adoptive parents.

Moreover, the researchers looked only at parents who worked with agencies that provided education and support after the adoption. It remains unclear whether the findings apply to independent adoptions—now the majority of unrelated domestic adoptions.

Several other studies support the positive cast on adoption provided by the Search Institute survey.

In Sweden, psychiatrist Michael Bohman at the University of Umeå directed a longitudinal study of 164 infant adoptees, 208 children raised by biological mothers who had registered them for adoption and then changed their minds, and 203 children placed in foster homes (where many were adopted by age 7).

At age 11, about 20 percent of boys and girls in these three groups exhibited serious emotional and behavioral problems, as rated by their teachers. A much smaller proportion of their classmates got tagged as "problem children."

But at age 15, adopted children rebounded. Teacher ratings of their social, emotional, and academic skills equaled those given their classmates. Youngsters living with biological mothers who reneged on adoption plans and those in foster homes lagged considerably behind the adoptees on these measures.

Infant adoptees continued to do well at ages 18 and 23, but higher rates of alcohol-related problems and criminal behavior, as well as lower scores on intelligence and psychological tests, characterized the other two groups.

Bohman and a colleague describe these findings in The Psychology of Adop-

tion (D. Brodzinsky and M. Schechter, eds., 1990, Oxford University Press).

In the same book, Janet L. Hoopes, a psychologist at Bryn Mawr (Pa.) College, describes a study of 50 adopted and 41 nonadopted teenagers age 15 to 18. All adoptions had occurred by age 2.

Extensive interviews uncovered no differences between the groups on several measures of identity formation, as well as in family and peer relations, school performance, and self-esteem.

The 16 adoptees interested in finding their biological parents showed slightly more difficulty in identity formation, Hoopes says. As a group, "searchers" more often reported unhappy family relationships and perceived themselves as more strikingly mismatched with adoptive parents in physical appearance.

However, adoptees unanimously considered their adoptive parents as among the most significant persons in their lives; none placed his or her biological parents in that category.

A 20-year study of 204 white families with adopted children, most of them black, also documents healthy emotional development. As the youngsters matured, they developed a clear sense of racial identity, says Rita J. Simon, a sociologist at American University in Washington, D.C.

Youngsters in that investigation included 157 interracial adoptees, 42 white adoptees, and 167 biological children of the adopting parents. "Adoptees didn't have worse or different problems than their biological siblings," Simon says.

Around age 11, about one in five adopted children — mainly boys — began stealing money or possessions from family members. But as in the Swedish study, this behavior stopped by age 15 and may have represented a testing of family affection and commitment at a time of increased awareness about the meaning of adoption, Simon contends.

She and Howard Altstein, a social worker at the University of Maryland in Baltimore, describe their project in The Case for Transracial Adoption (1994, American University Press).

Although scientific measures of identity, racial or otherwise, contain much room for improvement, these studies document the overall success of interracial adoptions, holds psychiatrist Ezra E.H. Griffith of Yale University.

Still, political opposition to interracial adoption remains strong, Griffith says. Only Texas forbids a focus on placing children with parents of the same race. Child-welfare workers often hold minority children in foster or institutional care for years rather than place them with white parents. Legislation approved by the U.S. Senate and pending in the House would prohibit delaying or denying adoptions on the basis of race.

Meanwhile, clinicians who treat adoptees and their families agree that this family arrangement generally works well, especially for those adopted as infants. But in their view, the Search Institute survey and related research gloss over the complexities of identity development with which all adoptees must deal. These heighten the risk of psychological problems in late childhood and adolescence.

"As joyous as adoption is, adopted teenagers need to make sense of the more complicated circumstances that led to who they are," contends psychologist Joyce Pavao of The Family Center in Somerville, Mass. "They have to acknowledge and deal with a sense of loss for their biological parents and the issue of physical dissimilarity to adoptive parents and relatives." Pavao regards these as typical concerns and says that clinicians have tended to "pathologize" them.

Serious emotional or identity problems probably occur most often in children adopted after infancy and by parents of a different race, maintains Steven Nickman of Massachusetts General Hospital. Even kids adopted as infants often get little help in grappling with the special brand of grief sparked by the psychological loss of birth parents they never knew, the Boston psychiatrist says.

"Relatively few parents are equipped to help their kids face the depths of sadness that they often feel regarding this loss," Nickman holds.

Psychologist David M. Brodzinsky of Rutgers University in New Brunswick, N.J., estimates that about 25 percent of those adopted as infants develop serious psychological difficulties by adolescence, compared with 15 percent of nonadopted youngsters.

A number of factors play shifting roles in the emotional lives of adopted children, Brodzinsky holds. These include the social stigma attached to adoption (such as teasing by peers and awkward "family tree" assignments at school), feelings of loss about biological parents, traumatic separation from one or more caregivers for older adoptees, and genetic propensities for psychological and behavioral disorders inherited from biological parents.

Children who try to avoid thinking or talking about adoption issues, often in concert with their adoptive parents, most often fall prey to emotional problems and identity confusion, Brodzinsky suggests. He expands on this argument in *Being Adopted: The Lifelong Search for Self* (1992, Doubleday), written with psychiatrist Marshall D. Schechter of the University of Pennsylvania School of Medicine in Philadelphia and science writer Robin Marantz Henig.

Shortcomings in the Search Institute survey render it difficult to interpret, according to Brodzinsky.

"This new study is important because it gets people talking about adoption," he says. "There's still little nonclinical research on adoption."

But more is on the way. A study submitted for publication by Sharma, Benson, and McGue compares 4,682 teenage adoptees recruited from public schools in 35 states with 4,682 nonadopted students matched for sex, age, and race. Overall, adoptees report small, but statistically significant, elevations in legal and illegal drug use, sadness and worry, and aggressive behavior, as well as slightly lower optimism about the future, academic achievement, and parental support and closeness.

Teens adopted as infants display overall psychological adjustment comparable to that of nonadopted controls, Sharma says. Personal and family difficulties increase progressively for those adopted at later ages.

The findings underscore the need to move children quickly out of foster care into adoptive homes, according to the researchers.

Scientists also hope to move quickly toward a better understanding of adoptive families. "These studies are a few chips off a massive block from which we're trying to remove a true representation of adoption," Sharma contends.

In a Family Way

Adoptive parents — including my wife and I, who adopted our 3½-year-old son as an infant in Paraguay — operate amid changing conceptions of family life. The media pounce on sensational adoption-related conflicts, from switched-at-birth Kimberly Mays to switched-at-toddlerhood Baby Jessica (now Anna), but basic transformations in the nature of families and adoption attract less attention.

For much of the past 10,000 years, village-based families chiefly organized production, education, self-defense, health care, and welfare, asserts James Q. Wilson, a political scientist at the University of California, Los Angeles. Parents needed children to work farms and fields and to support them during sickness and old age.

In these societies, adoption not only served the needs of unwanted children and infertile couples, but supplied older children (usually male) to continue a family lineage or to assume specific agricultural or commercial duties.

In today's urban societies, however, families deal mainly with child rearing. Children create a financial burden rather than bolstering the family's fortunes. Rising divorce rates, a greater number of single mothers, and ambiguity about what constitutes a family have followed.

A family now revolves around "a human commitment designed to make possible the rearing of moral and healthy children," writes Wilson in *The Moral Sense* (1993, Free Press).

Or as E. James Lieberman, a psychiatrist at George Washington University School of Medicine in Washington, D.C., puts it: "All good parenting requires adoption. Mental health professionals should emphasize the conscious aspects of parenting in order to enhance the emotional bonding that is not automatic, even in biological families."

U.S. law currently undermines adoption as a valid family form by sealing adoption records and treating the adopted child "as if" he or she were a biological product of the parents, argues Elizabeth Bartholet, a Harvard University law professor and mother of three sons, two adopted and one biological.

Open access to birth records, currently the subject of heated debate, would send the signal that an adoptee's links to biological parents are relevant but not of pivotal importance to personal identity or family relationships, Bartholet contends in *Family Bonds: Adoption and the Politics of Parenting* (1993, Houghton Mifflin).

"Adoption creates a family that in important ways is not 'nuclear,'" Bartholet holds. "Adoptive families might teach us something about the value for families of connection with the larger community." — *B. Bower*

THE FAMILY CIRCLE

When children enter the marriage equation, responsibilities add up fast.

Here are tips to multiply your strength as a couple.

BRUCE A. BALDWIN

Dr. Bruce A. Baldwin is a practicing psychologist and author who heads Direction Dynamics in Wilmington, North Carolina, a consulting service specializing in promoting quality of life. For busy couples, Dr. Baldwin has written Getting Better Together: Living the Good Life with Someone You Love.

In the early years of your marriage, you were an easygoing couple. You could pack up and go to the beach or the mountains for a weekend on an hour's notice. You spent most of your free time together talking, laughing, playing, and creating new adventures. Your life together was simple and emotionally fulfilling.

Then your children were born, and a new phase of your life together began. Your days, already filled with responsibilities, became more hectic as you tried to cope with the demands of raising children. Those spontaneous vacations now take a month of careful planning, if you can get away at all. Between the diaper changes and the demands of your jobs, you try to sandwich in a bit of time for yourselves as a couple.

You enjoyed life as a couple B.C. (Before Children), and although you're now in the middle of the difficult years, you know that there is life A.D. (After Departure). The question is whether you can preserve your relationship in the meantime. If you fail to maintain your closeness during these critical years, you and the children lose.

HOW PROBLEMS DEVELOP

Many couples feel the stresses and strains of parenthood in their marital relationship. It's easy to blame the kids for all the problems, but that's unfair. It's not the kids who create marital problems—it's the husband and wife who allow the demands of parenthood and of life in general to overwhelm them. Here are some basic reasons why the parenting years are so difficult.

Children require attention. It usually takes two decades or more from a child's birth to the day he or she leaves home to begin an independent life. During this time, it's your responsibility as parents to prepare that child for responsible adulthood. Caring for dependent children every day takes tremendous energy.

Children are inherently self-centered. Children focus on personal needs, not the needs of others. As a result, they are not aware of the pressures or emotional turmoil their parents experience.

Children resist socialization. Children have a simple motivational system—they seek pleasure and avoid pain. This motivation flies in the face of your efforts to teach your children responsibility and self-sufficiency. You feel the strain as they resist becoming accountable for their actions.

Children require more care as they age. Some parents naively believe that children need less attention as they grow older. Not so. Only the nature of parental effort changes. Of course, you must help young children dress, eat, and get ready for school. But older children still require supervision, and your continual emotional and psychological energy.

SIGNS OF CHANGE

Over the years, as you respond to the needs of your children, your own values and commitments come into play. As your values and the kids' needs interact, your lifestyle as a couple slowly changes. You may see the signs that the good life you wanted to create together is slipping away. Here are signs that your marriage relationship is suffering.

Stress and conflict increase. Because of emotional neglect and a heavy burden of responsibilities, stress levels typically increase during the parenting years. Tired and overwhelmed, you become chronically tense and, as a consequence, become irritable with one another and the kids.

You take one another for granted. Because you are so busy meeting your many responsibilities, you begin to take your marital relationship for granted. You expend little energy to keep your marriage close and strong. You and your spouse assume that the other will always be there.

Your personal unhappiness deepens. When you neglect one another's emotional needs, you and your spouse slowly become unhappy and disillusioned. A gnawing loneliness often grows. You know you never started out to live this way, but you're not aware how it happened.

A marital crisis develops. As time passes and the marital relationship deteriorates, you develop doubts about your partner and the future of the marriage. You ask yourself whether you can make it or if the relationship is past saving. Sometimes you imagine running away and starting life over—alone.

CORROSIVE PRESSURES

Unless you are aware of what's happening over the years, you lose sight of your sense of self and your life together as a loving couple. You not only lose the ability to take care of yourself physically and emotionally, but also neglect the deeper values required to maintain a strong and fulfilling marriage relationship. Here are several corrosive pressures that, without your vigilance, will chip away at your ability to feel good about yourselves and grow together as a couple.

You've blurred the line between self and selfishness. A major reason you don't feel good these days is that you just don't give much to yourself anymore. You fear that if you are nice to yourself when there's a lot to be done or someone else wants something, you are being selfish. You give to others to avoid the guilt. You get nothing because you can't justify giving to yourself.

To remedy this situation, learn to treat yourself as important. Give yourself small pleasures, and face that irrational guilt instead of running away from it. Giving to yourself will help you feel more well-adjusted and set the stage for giving more to your marital relationship.

You don't respect your physical and emotional limits. Long ago, you and your spouse worked hard, but you also found time to get away from it all. Now you act like Superman and Superwoman. Because of your "limitless" efforts, you both abuse yourselves, and due to your irritability, you abuse your marital relationship as well.

Patch the rift in your relationship by making a commitment to your own health. Improve your eating, sleeping, and exercising habits. Then build in regular time to be together. Do it by learning to say "no" or cutting out a few extra obligations that no longer fulfill you.

Your children's persistent demands control your life. There's a vast difference between caring, healthy giving and giving in to a child's insatiable demands for time and attention. Once you cross this line, you become trapped. Children want more and more as you continue to give and give.

It's up to you to decide where to draw the line. Give your children what they need rather than everything they want. Defining this line clearly to yourself and to them will help you decide when enough is enough. Children who aren't indulged grow up healthier.

You fear that your children will be failures. Today "making it" economically is a much more sophisticated process than it was a single generation ago. Because you feel a responsibility to your children, you provide them with a fantastic array of "enrichment" experiences. While your efforts are laudable, you can carry this so far that it undermines your marital relationship and the stability of your family life.

Build a firm foundation by making family enrichment a high priority. A healthy family life is important to the later emotional security of your children. Set a good example by showing your children how you emotionally nourish yourselves as parents and as a couple.

You've been seduced by materialistic values. Your salary level, neighborhood, social status, even the achievements of your children have become foundations of your self-esteem. As this occurs, you forget deeper values, and you live in a superficial, emotionally unfulfilling manner.

To counteract the threat of materialism, rediscover the basics together. A close marital relationship, good times shared, and leisure activities are all part of healthy living and are more enduring than "things." As you move beyond a materialistic orientation, you can relax in a delightful new way.

You've fallen for the "neighborhood norms" trap. Although you live in close proximity to others in your neighborhood, you're psychologically isolated. Brief and casual contacts with neighbors are the norm. Ironically, while isolated, you've slipped into taking your cues about parenting from what you observe others doing, or you go along with what your kids tell you other parents do.

When it comes to raising your children, think out the issues rather than slipping into neighborhood norms. Talk over basic parenting issues and decisions with your spouse, then coordinate your efforts. Do what makes sense even if it isn't what everyone else is doing.

You've become conditioned to rapid change. These days, nothing seems stable or enduring anymore. You've learned to accept rapid change, and when anything gives you a problem, you shift into "throwaway" mode and get rid of it. Possessions, relationships, communities—all have become replaceable. This destructive social ethic makes it easy to seek something new instead of seeking what is enduring.

It takes work, commitment, time, and energy to make a marriage relationship healthy and strong. The results are worth the effort. Stop taking your couple relationship for granted, and commit yourselves to riding out the storms together and to making your relationship all that it can be.

CREATING CLOSENESS

If you're going to thrive as a couple and be the best parents possible, you must assign your marital relationship primary importance. Your children will benefit, too. Your hopes and your dreams and the part of life that is fun-loving and effervescent have been buried beneath your many responsibilities and obligations for too long. When you learn to focus on yourselves again, you'll become a strong couple as well as good parents.

As a couple, you will be together much longer than the children will be around. Work to keep your marriage strong so you can enjoy one another after the kids are gone. There is life after parenthood, but only if you make it so.

Finding a Balance: Maintaining Relationships

- **Marriage and Other Committed Relationships (Articles 15–20)**
- **Relationships between Parents and Children (Articles 21–27)**
- **Other Family Relationships (Articles 28 and 29)**

"And they lived happily ever after . . ." The romantic image conjured up by this well-known, final line from fairy tales is not reflective of the reality of family life and relationship maintenance. A truism, and yet, the belief that relationships should be easier than they are, that somehow love alone should carry us through, is pervasive. In reality, relationship maintenance takes dedication, hard work, and commitment.

We come into relationships, regardless of their nature, with fantasies about how things "should" be. Spouses, parents, children, siblings, grandparents, and others—all family members—have at least some unrealistic expectations about each other. It is through the negotiation of their lives together that they come to work through these expectations and replace them with other, hopefully more realistic, expectations. By recognizing and acting on their own contribution to the problems in relationships, as well as to their solutions, family members can set and attain realistic family goals. Tolerance and acceptance of differences can facilitate this process, as can competent communication skills of the members. Along the way, family members need to learn new skills and develop new habits of relating to each other. This will not be easy and, try as they may, not everything will be controllable. Factors both inside and outside the family may impede their progress.

Relationships are evolutionary. From its beginnings, the expectations that both parties have of their marriage impacts on their relationship. How best to negotiate their differences is a constant factor in marriages. Adding a child to the family affects the lives of parents in ways that they can only imagine. Feeling under siege, many parents struggle to know the right way to rear their children. These can all combine to make child rearing more difficult than it might otherwise have been. Other family relationships also evolve, and in our nuclear family focused culture, it is possible to forget that family relationships extend beyond those between spouses and parents and children.

The first subsection presents a variety of aspects of marriage and the marital relationship. The first article focuses on the multiple and often competing roles played by today's couples. Work and home are nearly impossible to separate for many of them. They expect to fulfill individual as well as couple needs, which can be a difficult balancing act. Figuring out how they can cope with the expectations and pressures of work, home, and child care and still have time for each other may be the most important way today's couples can prevent the problems and crises that lead to dissatisfaction. There are no easy solutions to these problems. Couples may believe that one possibility is a "Peer Marriage," where couples create a truly egalitarian relationship. The reader will see that there are both positive and negative aspects to such a marriage.

In "Receipts from a Marriage," Margaret Ambry addresses the shifting of spending habits that couples face throughout their marriage.

"Staying Power: Bridging the Gender Gap in the '90s" and "But What Do You Mean?" look at gender differences that may influence relationships between men and women. When we are able to step beyond stereotypes and appreciate differences, the likelihood of success is increased.

Finally, "Saving Relationships: The Power of the Unpredictable" presents a family systems view of relationship process, suggesting ways in which small changes in one aspect of the family can have large impacts elsewhere.

In the next subsection, the parent/child relationship is examined. In "Vanishing Dreams of America's Young Families," Marian Wright Edelman, president of the Children's Defense Fund, depicts the struggle of young families in today's world. She argues that, as a society, we have an obligation to the children of these young families, an obligation we are not yet meeting. The next two articles focus on the day-to-day lives of parents and children. Parents may feel overwhelmed by the task of rearing children, yet alternatives exist and choices can be made that facilitate positive parent/child and spousal relationships. The two essays that follow address radical changes that have been taking place in families and propose possible interventions to support involvement of *both* parents in the lives of their children. "Of Super Dads, and Absent Ones" demonstrates the contradictory pressures on fathers to be involved and *not* to be involved in the lives of their children. There has been a shift in the paternal role, but uncertainty of how to act it out. As a result, men are confused and frustrated. "Single Parents and Damaged Children: The Fruits of the Sexual Revolution," ties many of the American family's (and society's) current woes to the sexual revolution of the 1960s and 1970s and the subsequent rise in teenage out-of-wedlock parenting. The subsection ends with two articles that are case

studies of parents growing through their relationships with their children—in the first, a gay son, and in the second, HIV-positive foster children.

The final subsection expands our focus beyond the nuclear family to other family relationships. Both "Siblings and Development" and "Places Everyone" look at sibling relationships and their impact on children's development and their ability to relate to others. Although raised in the same family, children do not experience identical family influence. Each child goes through a different interactive process in the family and, as a result, they can have radically different family experiences.

Looking Ahead: Challenge Questions

When you think of marriage, what do you picture? What are your expectations of your (future) spouse? What are your expectations of yourself? How much are you willing to give to your marriage? What would you be willing to give up?

How should a husband behave in a marriage? How should a wife? Are they different? Why and why not?

What do you expect parenthood to be like? Have you ever talked with your parents or other parents about their expectations and their experiences? Will you share parenting tasks with your spouse? Would you want to have a child by yourself? Why and why not?

Have you seen differences in the ways in which siblings are treated in families? Why do you think this is so? What is the best way to rear children? Should you focus on equal treatment of children? Why or why not?

AMERICAN MARRIAGE?

Demands for intimacy, emotional support, companionship, and sexual gratification have increased, although there has been a decline in what individuals are willing to sacrifice for a relationship.

Norval D. Glenn

Dr. Glenn is Ashbel Smith Professor of Sociology and Stiles Professor in American Studies, University of Texas at Austin.

OVER THE PAST three decades, there has been a period of substantial changes in the institution of marriage in the U.S. The divorce rate doubled from 1965 to 1975, increased more slowly through the late 1970s, and leveled off in the 1980s, but at such a high level that almost two-thirds of the marriages entered into in recent years are expected to end in divorce or separation. The increase in divorce, a decrease in remarriage after divorce, and a higher average age at first marriage have lowered the proportion of adults who are married. Out-of-wedlock births have increased substantially, so that one-fourth of all births now are to unmarried mothers. The proportion of married women who work outside the home has risen steadily, the increase being especially great among those with pre-school-age children.

Everyone agrees that these changes are important, but different authorities and commentators disagree as to what they mean for the health and future of the institution of marriage. One point of view is that marriage is in serious trouble—that it may disappear or lose its status as the preferred way of life for adult Americans. For example, a recent book is titled *The Retreat from Marriage,* and numerous books and articles refer to a decline or deinstitutionalization of marriage.

An opposing view, held until recently by most social scientific students of marriage, is that recent changes do not indicate decline or decay, but, rather, are adaptive and have kept the institution viable and healthy. These observers point out, for instance, that the increase in divorce has come about because people are rejecting particular marriages, rather than the institution of marriage—that most divorced persons want to remarry, and about three-fourths of them do so. Some of these commentators even view the increase in divorce positively, claiming that it reflects an increased importance people place on having good marriages and a decreased willingness to endure unsatisfactory ones. Divorce and remarriage, according to this view, are mechanisms for replacing poor relationships with better ones and keeping the overall quality of marriages high.

The evidence doesn't support consistently either the most negative or most positive views of what is happening to American marriage. For instance, the notion that it is a moribund or dying institution is inconsistent with the fact that a large percentage of Americans say that having a happy marriage is one of the most important, if not *the* most important, goal in their lives. About two-fifths of the respondents to the 1989 Massachusetts Mutual American Family Values Study indicated this was one of their most important values, and more than 90% said it was one of the most important or very important. Approximately three-fourths of the high school seniors studied by the Monitoring the Future Project at the University of Michigan in recent years have stated they definitely will marry, and the proportion has not declined. When adults are asked what kind of lifestyle they prefer, a very large majority select one involving wedlock, and a substantial minority (more than one-third) choose a traditional marriage in which the husband is the breadwinner and the wife a homemaker.

Even when one takes into account that what people say in response to survey questions may not always reflect accurately what they think and feel, these survey data clearly demonstrate that Americans in general have not given up on matrimony. However, there is even more compelling evidence against the most extremely positive assessments of recent changes. Although having good marriages may be as important to people as ever, or may have become even more important in recent years, my research indicates that the probability of attaining them has declined to a large extent.

Those who argue that marriages in this country in general are doing quite well often cite data showing that a high and rather stable percentage of married persons give positive responses when they are asked

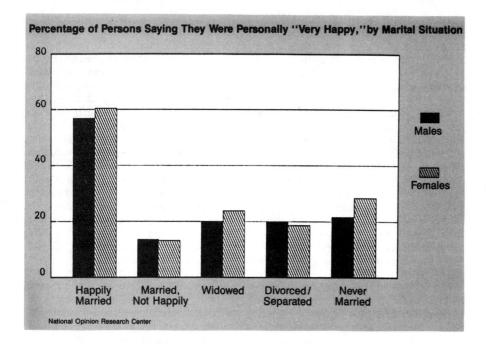

Percentage of Persons Saying They Were Personally "Very Happy," by Marital Situation

National Opinion Research Center

about the quality of their unions. In fact, since the early 1970s, the reported quality of marriages has gone down, though not very much. Most years since 1973, the General Social Survey conducted by the National Opinion Research Center at the University of Chicago has asked people to rate their marriages as very happy, pretty happy, or not too happy. The percentage of those who cited "very happy" fell by five percentage points from 1973-76 to 1988-91, dropping from 68 to 63%.

The indicated over-all happiness quality of American marriages still would be quite high if these ratings were to be taken at their face value, but they should not be interpreted that way. Many people are reluctant to admit to an interviewer—and perhaps even to themselves—that their marriages are less than satisfactory. Therefore, an unknown, but possibly substantial, proportion of the marriages reported to be "very happy" are not of very high quality, whereas virtually all those reported to be less than very happy are seriously deficient.

What is important about the indicated trend in marital quality is not that it has been slightly downward, but that it has not been steeply upward. If, as some commentators have claimed, the increase in divorce resulted only from people becoming less willing to stay in unsatisfactory marriages, the average quality of intact marriages should have climbed in tandem with the divorce rate. The fact that it didn't means that the probability of marriages remaining satisfactory must have declined substantially.

During 1973-76, about 60% of the persons who had first married three-five years earlier were still in their first marriages and

reported them to be "very happy." By 1988-91, it had declined to about 54%. For persons who first married 12-14 years earlier, the decline was greater, from 54 to 38%, while for those who married 20-24 years earlier, it dropped from 50 to 36%. There were declines of around 10 or more percentage points at most other lengths of time since the first marriage.

Those who view recent changes in American marriage positively may not find these data very alarming. To them, what is important is the kind of marriage a person eventually attains, not the success of his or her first union. From this perspective, the percentages of ever-married persons who were in marriages of any order (first, second, or subsequent) that they reported to be "very happy" are even more significant.

The changes from 1973-76 to 1988-91 show a distinct downward trend in the probability of being in a successful marriage. Among persons who have sought marital happiness by marrying at least once, a decreased proportion seem to be experiencing it. This indicates that the increase in divorce and the other changes in marriage during the past three decades have not been solely or primarily a matter of people becoming more willing and able to go from poor marriages to better ones.

Still, one might suspect that there has been one positive aspect of the changes of the past few years—namely, a decreased tendency for people to be in poor marriages. However, the proportion of ever-married persons who were in marriages they reported to be less than "very happy" increased from 1973-76 to 1988-91 at all lengths of time after the first marriage up to 20 years—the changes being in the range

of three to five percentage points. Only among persons who married 20-29 years earlier was there a slight decrease in the percentage of persons in the less satisfactory unions.

Most of the decrease in the probability of being in a very happy marriage resulted from an increase in the probability of being divorced or separated. For instance, at 12-14 years after the first marriage, the percentage divorced or separated at the time of the surveys went from eight to 18%, and at 20-24 years, it rose from eight to 19%.

The most important consequences of the increase in marital failure have been on the offspring. An enormous amount of evidence, from sources varying from in-depth clinical studies to large-scale surveys, indicates moderate to severe short-term negative effects on the well-being and development of most of the children of divorce. Although the causal link is less well-established, there also apparently are some important long-term effects on a substantial minority of those whose parents divorce, including difficulty in making commitments in relationships and an increased probability of various mental health problems. Equally important is evidence for harmful effects from failed parental marriages that do not end in divorce—especially from those unions characterized by high levels of tension and conflict.

The changes in matrimony also have tended to lower the well-being of adults. Although there are exceptions, in general, those who are the happiest and most fulfilled and who function the best are those in successful marriages. On average, the happily married are the happiest, by a large margin, and the less than happily married are the least happy. In other words, to be in a good marriage is the best situation, but a poor marriage is not better than no marriage at all.

The causal relationship between marital situation and well-being is not entirely clear. Happily married individuals may do best partly because those who are the happiest and best-adjusted, for whatever reasons, are more likely than others to marry and to succeed at marriage. However, most researchers who have studied the relationship between marital situation and well-being believe that it primarily is the former that affects the latter. If so, and if the strength of the effects has not diminished markedly in recent years, the decline in the percentage of persons at various stages of adulthood who are happily married has been distinctly detrimental to their welfare.

Why the decline in marital success?

One of the most likely reasons for the decline in marital success is the well-documented increase in what persons expect

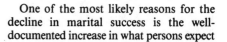

of marriage. The levels of intimacy, emotional support, companionship, and sexual gratification that people believe they should get from marriage have increased, while what they are willing to give very likely has declined. In other words, the motivation for marriage has become more purely hedonistic, or more selfish. This is just one aspect of a general increase in individualism in America and throughout most of the modern world.

Another likely reason is the breakdown in the consensus of what it means to be a husband or wife. Whereas, until recently, the rights and obligations of spouses were prescribed culturally and fairly well understood by just about everyone, they have become a matter for negotiation in individual marriages. This increased flexibility in marital roles, according to its advocates, should have increased the quality of matrimony or at least the quality of the lives of married persons, and for many persons it may have done so. For others, however, it has led to discord and disappointment. The optimistic view is that we eventually will learn to deal more effectively with the new freedom and flexibility in marriage, but that remains to be seen.

Another change that was supposed to have had unambiguously positive effects, but that may not have done so, is the easing of moral, religious, and legal barriers to divorce. The reasoning of those who advocated this was that making it easier for persons to correct marital mistakes—to escape from unsatisfying, stultifying, or dehumanizing marriages—would have positive effects on human welfare. Indeed, if one concentrates only on individual cases, as therapists and marriage counselors do, one readily can see how diminishing the guilt, social disapproval, and legal penalties of divorce has improved the quality of many lives.

However, the changes that resulted in short-term benefits to many individuals may have lessened the probability of marital success and resulted in long-term losses in the well-being of the population as a whole. One spouse's freedom—to leave the marriage, to change the terms of the marital contract—is the other spouse's insecurity. That insecurity tends to inhibit the strong commitment and investment of time, energy, and lost opportunities that are conducive to marital success. The decline in the ideal of marital permanence—one of the most well-documented value changes among Americans in recent decades—also has tended to make persons less willing and able to make the needed commitments to and investments in marriage. To the extent that a person constantly compares the existing marriage with real or imagined alternatives to it, that marriage inevitably will compare unfavorably in some respects. People are hardly aware of needs currently being well-served, but tend to be keenly attuned to them not being well-satisfied. Since attention tends to center on needs not being especially well-met in one's marriage (and there always are some), the grass will tend to look greener on the other side of the marital fence. Therefore, merely contemplating alternatives to one's marriage may engender discontent.

Those authorities who have come to recognize the negative aspects of recent changes in American marriage are dividing into two camps—those who believe that the negative changes are inevitable and irreversible and that the best we can do is to try to lessen their impact, and those who believe that at least some of the changes can be reversed. The pessimists give strong arguments for their position, pointing out, for instance, that the trend to individualism that underlies many of the changes has occurred in most parts of the modern world and may characterize an advanced stage of economic development. Furthermore, the insecurity that inhibits commitment in marriage is likely to be self-perpetuating, as it leads to marital instability, which in turn leads to further insecurity.

There are signs, however, that a reversal in some of the changes already may be occurring. In recent years, there has been a strong reaction against radical individualism among many intellectuals in this country, and attitudinal survey data indicate that a similar reaction may be beginning in the general public. Marriage is just as crucial an institution as ever, and most Americans seem to know that. What has been missing is sufficient awareness of the costs of maintaining the health of the institution. It is to be hoped that Americans will recognize that the loss of personal freedom, renunciation of pleasure seeking, and acceptance of greater responsibility necessary for good marriages will benefit themselves, their children, and the entire society.

PEER MARRIAGE

---

*What does
it take to
create a truly
egalitarian
relationship?*

PEPPER SCHWARTZ

Pepper Schwartz, Ph.D., is a professor of sociology and an author. Address: University of Washington, Seattle, Washington, 98195. Her latest book is Peer Marriage: How Love Between Equals Really Works *(Free Press, 1994).*

WHEN I TOLD PEOPLE THAT I WAS beginning a research study of couples who evenly divided parenting and housework responsibilities, the usual reaction was mock curiosity—how was I going to find the three existing egalitarian couples in the universe? Despite several decades of dissecting the sexism and inequities inherent in traditional marriage, as a society, we have yet to develop a clear picture of how more balanced marital partnerships actually work. Some critics even argue that the practice of true equality in marriage is not much more common today than it was 30 years ago. In fact, authors like Arlie Hochschild have suggested that women's liberation has made prospects for equity worse. The basic theme of her provocative book, *The Second Shift,* is that women now have two jobs—their old, traditional marital roles and their new responsibilities in the work force. A look at the spectacular divorce rates and lower marriage rate for successful women provides further fuel for the argument that equality has just brought wives more, not less, burdens.

All of this figured heavily in my own commitment to exploring the alternative possibilities for marital partnership. Ten years ago this began with *American Couples: Money, Work and Sex*, a study I did with Philip Blumstein that compared more than 6,000 couples—married, cohabitating, gay males and lesbians—looking for, among other things, what aspects of gendered behavior contributed to relationship satisfaction and durability. This study contained within it a small number of egalitarian couples, who fascinated and inspired me. We discussed them rather briefly in the book, but our editor encouraged us to make them the subject of a second study that would examine how couples manage to sustain an egalitarian partnership over time. Unfortunately, my co-author was not able to continue the project and it was not until three years ago that I began the research on what I came to call Peer Marriage. I began looking for couples who had worked out no worse than a 60-40 split on childrearing, housework and control of discretionary funds and who considered themselves to have "equal status or standing in the relationship."

I started out interviewing some of the couples originally studied for *American Couples* and then, using what sociologists call a "snowball sample," I asked those couples if they knew anyone else like themselves that I could interview. After talking to a few couples in a given network, I then would look for a different kind of couple (different class, race, educational background, etc.) in order to extend the range of my sample. I interviewed 57 egalitarian couples, but even after the formal study was over, I kept running into couples that fit my specifications and did 10 more partial interviews.

While initially my design included only Peer Marriages, I also began to interview a lot of couples who others thought to be egalitarian, but who did not meet my criteria. Instead of throwing them out of the sample, I used them as a base of comparison, dividing them into two additional categories: "Traditionals" and "Near Peers." Traditionals were couples in which the man usually had veto power over decision-making (except with the children) and in which the wife felt that she did not have—nor did she want—equal status. The Near Peers were couples who, while they believed in equality, felt derailed from their initial goal of an egalitarian marriage because of the realities of raising children and/or the need or desire to maximize male income. As a result, the husband could not be anywhere near as participatory a father as the couple had initially envisioned. These two groups proved to be a fortuitous addition to the design. It is sometimes hard to understand what peer couples are doing that allows them to fulfill an egalitarian agenda without understanding what keeps other couples from doing the same.

Even though I consider myself to be in a Peer Marriage, I found many surprises among the Peer Couples I studied. Of course, as a researcher, one is never supposed to extrapolate from one's own experience, but it is almost impossible not to unconsciously put one's presuppositions into the hypothesis phase of the research. Clearly, people make their marital bargains for many different reasons, and face different challenges in sustaining them. Here are some of the discoveries I made that I thought might be of use to therapists.

I ASSUMED MOST COUPLES WOULD, like myself, come to egalitarianism out of the women's movement or feminist ideology. Nevertheless, while approximately 40 percent of the women and about 20 percent of the men cited feminism and a desire to be in a non-hierarchical relationship, the majority of couples mentioned other reasons. These included a desire to avoid parental models that they found oppressive in their own upbringing, the *other* partner's strong preference for an egalitarian marriage, some emotional turmoil that had led to their rethinking their relationship, or an intense desire for co-parenting. Women in particular often mentioned their own parents as a negative model. One woman said, "I want a husband who knows how to pack his own suitcase, who puts away his own clothes, who can't tell me to shut up at will . . . My mother may have been happy with this kind of marriage, but I'm still angry at my father for treating my mother like that—and angry at her for letting him." A 25-year-old husband told me, on a different theme, "My main objective in having an equal relationship was not to be the kind of father I had. I want my kids to know me before they are adults. I want them to be able to talk to me. I want them to run to me if they hurt themselves. I want our conversations to be more than me telling them they could do better on a test or that I was disappointed they didn't make the team. I want to be all the things to my kids that my dad was not. I want us to have hugged many, many times and not just on birthdays or their wedding day."

Quite a few men in Peer Marriages said they really had no strong feelings about being in either traditional or egalitarian marriages, but had merely followed their wives' lead. Typical of this group was a

high school basketball coach who said he had had a very traditional first marriage because that was the only arrangement that he and his wife could envision even when it wasn't working. But when he met his current wife, a policewoman who had been single quite a while, her demands for equality seemed perfectly reasonable to him. He just, more or less, fell into line with his future wife's ideas about the relationship. Many of these men told me they had always expected a woman to be the emotional architect of a relationship and were predisposed to let her set the rules.

Most of the couples, however, did have strong ideas about marriage and placed particular emphasis on equity and equality. Even if they didn't start out with a common agenda, most ended up sharing a high degree of conscious purpose. People's particular personal philosophies about marriage mattered less than the fact that their philosophies differentiated their family from a culture that reinforced the general belief that equality is neither possible nor even in the long-term interests of couples. Many people talked about how easy it is to slide into old and familiar roles or follow economic opportunities that started to whittle away at male participation in childrearing. It takes an intense desire to keep a couple on the nontraditional track and a clear sense of purpose to justify the economic sacrifices and daily complications it takes to co-parent. As one wife of 10 years said, "We always try to make sure that we don't start getting traditional. It's so easy to do. But we really want this extraordinary empathy and respect we have. I just know it wouldn't be there if we did this marriage any other way."

I MPORTANT AS RELATIONSHIP IDE-ology is, Peer Marriages depend at least as much on coordinating work with home and childraising responsibilities and not letting a high earner be exempt from daily participation. Previous research had shown me the connection between a husband's and wife's relative income and their likelihood of being egalitarian. So I assumed that most of the couples I interviewed would be working couples, and have relatively similar incomes. This was mostly true, although I was struck by the couples who were exceptions. Four husbands in the study had non-working wives. The men didn't want to dominate those relationships because they felt very strongly that money did not legitimately confer power. For example, one husband had inherited a great deal of money but didn't feel it was

any more his than his wife's. She stayed at home with the children, but he took over in the late afternoon and on weekends. He also was the primary cook and cleaner. In another case, a husband who earned a good deal more than his wife put all the money in a joint account and put investments in her name as well as his. Over time, she had assets equal to his. While these triumphs over income differentials were exceptions, it did make me respect the fact that truly determined couples could overcome being seduced by the power of economic advantage.

However, many Peer Marriages had a significant income differential and husbands and wives had to negotiate a lot just to make sure they didn't fall into the trap of letting the higher earner be the senior decision-maker. Even more tricky, according to many, was not letting work set the emotional and task agenda of the household. The couples needed to keep their eyes on what was the tail and what was the dog so that their relationship was not sidetracked by career opportunities or job pressures. Many Peer Couples had gone through periods in which they realized that they were beginning to have no time for each other, or that one of them was more consistently taking care of the children while the other was consumed with job demands. But what distinguished those couples from more traditional marriages was that they had a competing ideology of economic or career success that guided them when their egalitarianism began to get out of kilter.

One husband, who had an architectural practice designing and building airports, had begun to travel for longer and longer periods of time until it was clear that he was no longer a true co-parent or a full partner in the marriage. After long and painful discussions, he quit his job and opened up a home office so he could spend more time with his wife and children. Both partners realized this would cause some economic privations and, in fact, it took the husband five years to get a modestly successful practice going while the wife struggled to support the family. Without minimizing how tough this period had been, the couple felt they had done the right thing. "After all," the husband said, "we saved our marriage."

This attitude helped explain another surprise in this study. I had presumed that most of the Peer Marriages I would find would be yuppie or post-yuppie couples, mostly young or baby boom professionals who were "having it all." In fact, most of them were solidly middle class: small-business owners, social workers, school-teachers, health professionals (but not

There was an unexpected down side for the couples who did manage to co-parent. I was unprepared for how often Peer Couples mentioned serious conflict over childrearing.

●

doctors). Apparently, people on career fast tracks were less willing to endanger their potential income and opportunities for promotion. There may be childrearing Peer Marriages out there comprised of litigators, investment bankers and brain surgeons—but I didn't find them. The closest I came to finding fast trackers in a Peer Marriage and family were high-earning women who had husbands who were extremely pleased with their partner's success and were willing to be the more primary parent in order to support her career.

When these women negotiated issues with their husbands in front of me, they seemed more sensitive about their husbands' feelings than men of comparable accomplishment with lower earning wives. For example, they did not interrupt as much as high-earning men in traditional marriages, and they seemed to quite consciously not pull rank when I asked them jointly to solve a financial problem. They told me, however, that they consciously had to work at being less controlling than they sometimes thought

they deserved to be. A very successful woman attorney, married to another, significantly-less-prominent attorney, told me that they had some problems because he wasn't used to picking up the slack when she was called away suddenly to represent a Fortune 500 company. She found herself battling her own ambitions in order to be sensitive to his desire for her to let up a bit. As she noted, "We [women] are not prepared to be the major providers and it's easy to want all the privileges and leeway that men have always gotten for the role. But our bargain to raise the kids together and be respectful of one another holds me back from being like every other lawyer who would have this powerful a job. Still, it's hard."

The other fast track exception was very successful men in their second marriages who had sacrificed their first in their climb to the top. Mostly these were men who talked about dependent ex-wives, their unhappiness at paying substantial support and their determination not to repeat the mistakes of their first marriages. One 50-year-old man, who, had traveled constantly in his first marriage raising money for pension funds, told me he was through being the high earner for the company and wanted more family time in the second part of his life. As he put it, "I consciously went looking for someone who I could spend time with, who I had a lot in common with, who would want me to stop having to be the big earner all the time. I don't want to die before I've been a real partner to somebody who can stand on her own two feet . . . and I've been a real father."

When I first realized how often the desire to co-parent led couples into an egalitarian ideology, I thought this might also lead couples to prioritize their parenting responsibilities over their husband-and-wife relationship. But these were not marriages in which husbands and wives called each other "Mom" and "Dad." For the most part, these couples avoided the rigidly territorial approach I saw in Traditional and Near Peer marriages. In both of these types of couples, I observed mothers who were much more absorbed in their children, which both partners regarded as a primarily female responsibility. As a result, women had sole control over decisions about their children's daily life and used the children as a main source of intimacy, affection and unshared secrets. They related stories about things the children told them that "they would never dare tell their father." While quite a few of the mothers talked about how "close" their husbands were with their children, they would also,

usually in the same story, tell me how much closer their children were with them. What surprised me was that while these traditional moms complained about father absence, very few really wanted to change the situation. Most often, it was explained that, while it would be great to have their husband home, they "couldn't afford it." But of course "afford" is a relative term and I sensed that the women really did not want the men interfering with their control over parenting. Or they would have liked more fatherly engagement but definitely not at the cost of loss of income. One young, working Near Peer Couple with four kids was discussing the husband's lesser parenting responsibilities with me when he said, "You know, I could come home early and get the kids by 3:30. I'd like to do that." The wife's response was to straightforwardly insist that with four kids going to private school, his energies were best used paying for their tuitions. She preferred a double shift to a shared one because her financial priorities and her vision of what most profited her children were clear.

But there was an unexpected downside for the couples who did manage to co-parent. I was unprepared for how often Peer Couples mentioned serious conflict over childrearing. Because each partner felt very strongly about the children's upbringing, differences of opinion were not easily resolved. As one peer wife said, "We are both capable of stepping up to the line and staying there screaming at each other." Another husband said, "If you only talked to us about how we deal with disagreements about the kids, you might think we were a deeply conflicted marriage. We're not. But unfortunately, we have very different ideas about discipline and we can get pretty intense with one another and it might look bad. We went to counseling about the kids and this therapist wanted to look at our whole relationship and we had to say, 'You don't get it. This really is the only thing we argue about like this.'"

Peers may, in fact, have more conflict about children than more Traditional partners because unlike Traditional Marriage, there is no territory that is automatically ceded to the other person and conflict cannot be resolved by one person claiming the greater right to have the final word. Still, while a majority of Peer Couples mentioned fights over child-related decisions, there were only a few Peer Marriages where I wondered if these arguments threatened the relationship. In the majority of them, the couples talked about how they ultimately, if not in the heat of battle, followed their usual pattern of talking until agreement was reached. What usually forced them to continue to communicate and reach a joint answer was their pledge to give the other partner equal standing in the relationship. Occasionally, a few people told me, they just couldn't reach a mutually satisfying answer and let their partner "win one" out of trust in his or her good judgement, not because they agreed on a given issue.

The couples that I felt might be in more trouble had recurring disagreements that they were never able to resolve over punishments, educational or religious choices or how much freedom to give kids. Furthermore, in each instance at least one partner said that the other partner's approach was beginning to erode the respect that made their relationship possible. Moreover, this particular kind of conflict was deeply troubling since many of them had organized their marriage around the expectation of being great co-parents. It may be that co-parenting requires that parenting philosophies be similar or grow together. Co-parents may have a particular need for good negotiating and communication skills so that they can resolve their differences without threatening the basis of their relationship.

IN CONTRAST WITH TRADITIONAL or Near Peer Couples, the partners in Peer Marriages, never complained about lack of affection or intimacy in their relationships. What they did mention, that other couples did not, was the problem of becoming so familiar with each other that they felt more like siblings than lovers. Some researchers have theorized that sexual arousal is often caused or intensified by anxiety, fear and tension. Many others have written about how sexual desire depends on "Yin" and "Yang"—mystery and difference. And quite a few women and men I talked to rather guiltily confessed that while they wanted equal partners, all their sexual socialization had been to having sex in a hierarchical relationship: Women had fantasies of being "taken" or mildly dominated; men had learned very early on that they were expected to be the orchestrators of any given sexual encounter and that masculinity required sexual directiveness. For men, sexual arousal was often connected with a strong desire to protect or control.

Peer couples complained that they often forgot to include sex in their daily lives. Unlike Traditional or Near Peers, their sexual frequency did not slow down because of unresolved issues or continuing anger, at least not in any systematic

ways. These couples may start to lose interest in sex even more than the other kinds of marriages because sex is not their main way of getting close. Many Traditional and some Near Peer Couples mentioned that the only time they felt that they got through to each other was in bed. Perhaps the more emotional distance couples feel with one another, the larger the role sexuality plays in helping them feel they still have the capacity for intimacy. Being less dependent on this pathway to intimacy, partners in Peer Marriage may be more willing to tolerate a less satisfactory sexual relationship.

One husband, who worked with his wife in their own advertising firm, even talked about having developed "an incest taboo," which had led to the couple entering therapy. They were such buddies during the daytime, he had trouble treating her as anything else in the evening. The therapist this couple consulted encouraged them to assume new personas in the bedroom. For example, he told them to take turns being the dominant partner, to create scenarios where they created new characters and then behaved as they thought the person they were impersonating would behave. He gave them "homework," such as putting themselves in romantic or sexy environments and allowing themselves to imagine meeting there the first time. The wife was encouraged to dress outrageously for bed every now and then; the husband occasionally to be stereotypically directive. The therapist reminded both partners that their emotional bargain was safe: they loved and respected each other. That meant they could use sex as recreation, release and exploration. They were good pupils and felt they had really learned something for a lifetime.

In another couple, it was the wife who mentioned the problem. Her husband had been the dominant partner in his previous marriage and had enjoyed that role in bed. However, she liked more reciprocity and role-sharing in sex, so he tried to be accommodating. However, early on in the relationship he began treating her, as she put it, "too darn respectfully... it was almost as if we were having politically correct sex... I had to remember that he wasn't my brother and it was okay to be sexually far out with him."

On the other hand, Peer Couples with satisfying sexual relationships often mentioned their equality as a source of sexual strength. These couples felt their emotional security with one another allowed them to be more uninhibited and made sex more likely since both people were responsible for making it happen.

Women with unhappy sexual experiences with sexist men mentioned that for the first time in their lives they could use any sexual position without worrying about any larger meaning in the act. Being on the bottom just meant being on the bottom; it was not about surrendering in more cosmic ways. Being a sex kitten was a role for the evening—and not part of a larger submissive persona.

Many of the Peer Couples I interviewed had terrific sexual lives. The women, especially, felt they had finally met men with whom they could be vulnerable and uninhibited. As one woman said, "I used to be a real market for women's books. I wanted men who fit the stereotype of Clark Gable or Kevin Costner—few words, and when they are delivered, they are real ringers, and there is a lot of eye contact and passion, and that's about as much talking as you get. Maybe it was dating all these guys who were really like that, but even as fantasy objects, I got tired of men who didn't want to explore a feeling or who were only loving when they had a hard-on. I fell in love the first time sharing *Prince of Tides* with the guy I was dating, and fell in love with Eric [her husband] over a discussion of *Eyes on the Prize*. The sexy thing was the conversation and the quality of our mind... I can't imagine anything more boring or ultimately unsexy than a man— and I don't care if he looked like Robert Redford and earned like Donald Trump— who had nothing to say or if he did, didn't get turned on by what I was saying."

Equality brings with it the tools to have a great erotic relationship and also, at the same time, the pitfalls that can lead to sexual boredom. If couples learn that their sexual lives need not be constrained by any preconceived idea of what is "egalitarian sex" or appropriate sexual roles, there is no reason that their equality can't work for them. But couples who cannot separate their nights and days, who cannot transcend their identities in everyday life, may need guidance from a knowledgeable counselor.

WHAT ENABLES COUPLES TO SUS-tain a style of egalitarian relationship in a world that encourages families to link their economic destiny with the male's career and casts women in an auxiliary worker role so that they can take responsibility for everyday childcare and household chores? In Peer Couples, a sense of shared purpose helps guide the couple back to why they are putting up with all the problems that come from putting together a new model of relationship without societal or familial supports.

Peer Couples may start to lose interest in sex even more than couples in other kinds of marriages because sex is not their main way of getting close.

•

Otherwise it is all too easy for mothers to fall in love with their children and assume primary responsibility for their upbringing or for men to allow their careers to sweep them out of the home, away from their children and back into the more familiar territory they have been trained to inhabit. When this begins to happen, a couple's ideology, almost like an organization's mission statement, helps remind them what their central goal is: the marital intimacy that comes from being part of a well-matched, equally empowered, equally participatory team.

But avoiding traditional hierarchy involves a constant struggle to resist the power of money to define each partner's family roles. Peer Couples continually have to evaluate the role of work in their lives and how much it can infringe on parenting and household responsibilities. If one partner earns or starts to earn a lot more money, and the job starts to take up more time, the couple has to face what this means for their relationship—how much it might distort what they have set out to create.

Peer Couples check in with each other an extraordinary amount to keep their relationship on track. They each have to take responsibility for making sure that they are not drifting too far away from reciprocity. Peer Couples manage to maintain equity in small ways that make sure the balance in their marriage is more than an ideology. If one person has been picking up the kids, the other is planning their summer activities and getting their clothes. Or if one partner has been responsible lately for making sure extended family members are contacted, the other person takes it over for a while. If one partner really decides he or she likes to cook, then the other partner takes on some other equally functional and time-consuming job. There's no reason that each partner can't specialize, but both are careful that one of them doesn't take over all the high-prestige, undemanding jobs while the other ends up with the classically stigmatized assignments (like cleaning bathrooms, or whatever is personally loathed by that person).

Besides monitoring jobs and sharing, couples have to monitor their attitude. Is the wife being treated as a subordinate? Does one person carry around the anger so often seen in someone who feels discounted and unappreciated? Is one person's voice considered more important than the other person's? Is the relationship getting distant and is the couple starting to lead parallel lives? Do they put in the time required to be best friends and family collaborators? Are they treating each other in the ways that would support a non-romantic relationship of freely associating friends?

There is nothing "natural" or automatic about keeping Peer Marriages going. There will be role discomfort when newly inhabiting the other gender's world. That is why some research shows that men who start being involved with a child from prenatal classes on show more easy attachment and participation in childrear-ing activities later. While men become comfortable with mothering over time, some need a lot of help. Children will sense who is the primary parent and that will be the person to whom they run, make demands, and from whom they seek daily counsel. One direct way of helping fathers evaluate how they are doing is to help the partners measure how much the children treat them as equally viable sources of comfort and help.

Likewise, being a serious provider is a responsibility some women find absolutely crushing. Most middle-class women were raised to feel that working would be voluntary. After they have made a bargain to do their share of keeping the family economically afloat, they may regret the pressures it puts on them. The old deal of staying at home and being supported can look pretty good after a bad day at the office. But only the exceptional relationship seems to be able to make that traditional provider/mother deal for very long and still sustain a marriage where partners have equal standing in each other's eyes. Couples have to keep reminding themselves how much intimacy, respect and mutual interest they earn in exchange for learning new roles and sustaining the less enjoyable elements of new responsibilities.

Couples who live as peers often attract others like themselves and the building of a supportive community can modify the impact of the lack of support in the larger world. Like-minded others who have made similar decisions help a lot, especially when critical turning points are reached: such as re-evaluating a career track when it becomes painfully clear that it will not accommodate Peer Family life.

This study yielded no single blueprint for successful Peer Marriage. As in all couples, partners in Peer Marriages require a good measure of honesty, a dedication to fair play, flexibility, generosity and maturity. But most of all, they need to remember what they set out to do and why it was important, at least for them. If they can keep their eyes and hearts on the purpose of it all—if we help them do that—more Peer Marriages will endure and provide a model for others exploring the still-unchartered territory of egalitarian relationships.

Receipts from

A Marriage

SUMMARY   Married-couple families are America's largest and most powerful consumer segment. These traditional households experience life as a roller coaster of child-rearing and spending. As married couples advance through various lifestages— from childless couples to new parents, prime-time families, mature families, and empty nesters—their spending waxes, wanes, and shifts in important ways.

Margaret K. Ambry

Margaret K. Ambry is director of consulting services at New Strategist Publications & Consulting in Ithaca, New York.

While single parents and alternative lifestyles get a lot of media attention, business's best customers are still "traditional" families. Married-couple families account for 55 percent of all U.S. households, and seven in ten Americans live in them. Married-couple families also account for 70 percent of total consumer spending. The biggest spenders—married couples with children under 18—comprise just 27 percent of all households, but the number of such households is projected to grow 12 percent during the 1990s.

Blame it on the baby boomlet. There is nothing like a child to change a couple's spending priorities, and baby-boomer par-ents have been making a lot of changes since the mid-1980s. Having a child doesn't mean getting an automatic raise, however. When the average young married couple makes the transition from childless couple to new parents (oldest child under age 6), their total expenditures increase less than 1 percent. Yet their spending patterns shift considerably: they spend more than their childless counterparts on health care, clothing, housing, and food, and much less on alcohol, education, and transportation. They also spend more on cigarettes and less on personal care and entertainment.

As parents and children get older, income and spending increase in nearly every category of household products and services. Married couples who make the transition to prime-time families (oldest child aged 6 to 17) spend 11 percent more overall than new parents. They spend more on virtually all products and services, although they spend less on alcohol and housing.

Mature families are couples with children aged 18 or older at home. They spend 9 percent more than prime-time families, and they generally have the highest incomes. But when children finally leave home, household spending falls by almost 30 percent. Empty-nester couples spend less than mature families on everything except health care and cash contributions.

Our analysis of the 1989-90 Consumer Expenditure Survey (CEX) shows how the birth, growth, and departure of children affect a married couple's spending. It shows that a couple's lifestage is at least as important as their ages in determining consumer behavior.

CHILDLESS COUPLES

Childless couples with a householder aged 25 to 34 have an average annual before-tax income of nearly $46,000. Each year, they spend an average of $34,000, 22 percent more than the average for all American households. The biggest chunk of a childless young couple's budget (32 per-

Parents' Progress

As married couples move through life, their spending patterns change. New parents spend less on alcoholic beverages than young childless couples. As children age, couples spend more on education. When children leave, couples reduce their spending on almost everything.

(percent change in average annual expenditures of married couples by lifestage change and expenditure category)

	childless couples to new parents	new parents to prime-time families	prime-time families to mature families	mature families to empty nesters
TOTAL EXPENDITURES	0.3%	11.0%	8.8%	-29.0%
Food	2.4	29.8	8.6	-33.5
Alcoholic beverages	-33.8	-6.2	17.5	-21.8
Housing	9.5	-5.0	-6.2	-18.8
Apparel and services	10.8	20.4	-0.2	-32.7
Transportation	-10.1	12.6	24.7	-40.1
Health care	49.3	9.2	18.9	28.1
Entertainment	-5.6	25.2	1.8	-34.6
Personal-care products	-7.3	21.7	16.6	-28.6
Reading	-7.4	9.7	4.7	-3.8
Education	-28.9	178.7	101.1	-86.4
Tobacco products	12.4	26.0	25.3	-39.3
Cash contributions*	-32.1	62.8	54.6	5.7
Personal insurance, pensions, Social Security ...	-8.3	6.2	4.3	-41.7
Miscellaneous	-13.3	29.7	5.9	-32.9

Cash contributions include alimony, child support, cash gifts to nonhousehold members, and charitable contributions.

Note: A prime-time family may have both preschool and school-aged children, while a mature family may have both adult children and children aged 0 to 17.

Source: Author's calculations based on 1989-90 Consumer Expenditure Survey data

cent) is devoted to housing. One-fifth of their spending (20 percent) goes directly into dwellings, and another 5 percent is spent on furnishings; both are higher-than-average shares. Yet childless couples spend very little on household operations. With fewer people to care for, their average annual tab for housekeeping supplies—about $400—is less than their liquor bill.

Like other households, childless couples devote the second-largest share of their spending to transportation. Although they spend an average amount on used cars, they spend 72 percent more than the average household on new cars. Spending on new cars drops off once there are young children in the household, then bounces back. It peaks among mature families and young empty nesters.

> **When children finally leave home, household spending falls by almost 30 percent.**

Just 13 percent of a childless couple's spending goes to food, but more than half of those dollars are given to restaurants and carry-out places. In all other lifestages, couples spend the majority of their food dollars on groceries. Childless couples spend an average of $440 a year on alcohol, more than 1 percent of their average annual budget.

Payments to personal insurance, pensions, and Social Security account for nearly 12 percent of a young childless couple's budget, about $4,000 a year. Because most are two-earner households, childless couples spend 70 percent more than average on pensions and Social Security.

Childless couples devote 5 percent of their spending to clothing, a smaller share than other couples. Another 5 percent goes to entertainment, with equal shares devoted to tickets for movies, theater, sports, and other events; TV, radio, and sound equipment; and other entertainment products and services such as sports equipment and boats. Although they have no children, childless couples also spend more than average on pets and toys.

They're young and don't have children to take to the doctor, so childless couples spend 34 percent less than the average household on out-of-pocket health-care expenses. Health care accounts for only about 3 percent of their budgets. They also spend less than average on tobacco products, education, and cash contributions (perhaps because the latter category includes alimony and child support). They spend less than 1 percent of their money on reading materials, although the $190 spent is 22 percent more than average. Young childless couples' trips to the hairdresser, cosmetics, shampoo, and other personal-care products and services take up another 1 percent of their household spending. This share doesn't vary much from lifestage to lifestage.

NEW PARENTS

New parents are couples whose oldest child is under the age of 6. They break down into two groups—younger parents (householders aged 25 to 34) and older new parents (householders aged 35 to 54). Although both types of households average 3.5 people, the older group's average income is just over $15,000 higher. Consequently, older new parents spend more on all major categories of products and services. They also allocate their funds differently than younger new parents do.

Both younger and older new parents devote a larger-than-average share of spending to housing—35 percent and 37 percent, respectively. Younger parents' housing expenditures are boosted by the 4 percent share that goes to household operations, mostly child care. But older parents of preschoolers outspend all other households on child care, mortgage payments, home maintenance, and other household services such as housekeeping, lawn-and-garden work, and household furnishings.

> The average childless couple spends more than 1 percent of their entire budget on alcoholic beverages.

Older new parents also spend more than younger new parents on transportation, although getting around consumes a smaller share of their total spending (15 percent versus 19 percent). Younger new parents outspend their older counterparts on cars, trucks, and other vehicles, while older new parents spend more on operating costs and public transportation.

Because of their higher incomes, older new parents are free to spend more on food and alcohol, although they allocate a smaller share of income to those categories. Food accounts for nearly 14 percent of young new parents' budgets, compared with 12 percent for older new parents. But older parents channel a larger share of funds to personal insurance, pensions, Social Security, entertainment, and cash contributions.

Older new parents outspend younger ones on all other major products and service categories, but the share they spend is similar. For example, both kinds of couples devote about 0.5 percent of their spending to reading materials. But younger couples spend an average amount, while older couples spend 81 percent more than the average household.

PRIME-TIME FAMILIES

Once the oldest child reaches school age, a family's lifestyles and spending patterns shift again. Like Ozzie and Harriet's family, the average household in the prime-time lifestage has two parents and two children, the oldest of whom is aged 6 to 17. Yet householders in this stage range

Doling Out

	ALL HOUSEHOLDS	CHILDLESS COUPLES	N
		25 to 34	25 to 34
NUMBER OF HOUSEHOLDS (in thousands)	96,393	3,020	4,038
AVERAGE INCOME BEFORE TAXES	$31,600	$45,835	$37,846
AVERAGE HOUSEHOLD SIZE	2.6	2.0	3.5
AVERAGE TOTAL EXPENDITURES	$28,090	$34,323	$32,793
FOOD	4,224	4,533	4,492
At home	2,438	2,126	2,826
Away from home	1,787	2,407	1,666
ALCOHOLIC BEVERAGES	289	441	288
HOUSING	8,748	11,119	11,589
Shelter	4,934	7,024	6,279
Owned dwellings	2,902	4,132	4,051
Rented dwellings	1,517	2,390	1,933
Utilities, fuels, public services	1,863	1,746	1,960
Household operations	453	178	1,435
Housekeeping supplies	400	407	495
Household furnishings	1,099	1,763	1,420
APPAREL AND SERVICES	1,600	1,725	1,786
Men and boys	395	449	430
Women and girls	665	658	509
Children younger than age 2	71	38	384
Footwear	207	170	214
Other apparel products and services	262	409	249
TRANSPORTATION	5,154	6,989	6,253
Vehicle purchases	2,209	3,095	2,986
Cars and trucks, new	1,188	2,046	1,430
Cars and trucks, used	999	998	1,533
Gas and motor oil	1,016	1,216	1,149
Other vehicle expenses	1,636	2,286	1,934
Public transportation	293	392	184
HEALTH CARE	1,444	970	1,458
ENTERTAINMENT	1,423	1,867	1,591
Fees and admissions	374	485	290
TV, radios, sound equipment	441	525	484
Pets, toys, playground	263	312	392
Other products and services	345	545	425
PERSONAL-CARE PRODUCTS AND SERVICES	365	427	391
READING	155	189	155
EDUCATION	386	284	192
TOBACCO PRODUCTS	68	226	222
CASH CONTRIBUTIONS	858	791	472
PERSONAL INSURANCE, PENSIONS, SOCIAL SECURITY	2,532	4,026	3,343
MISCELLANEOUS	644	737	562

Cash contributions include alimony, child support, cash gifts to nonhousehold members, and charitable contributions.

in age from 25 to 54, and their average before-tax household income ranges from $35,000 for households with a head aged 25 to 34 to just over $49,000 for households with a head aged 45 to 54. Their total spending ranges from 12 percent above average for prime-time families headed by 25-to-34-year-olds to 49 percent above average for those headed by 45-to-54-year-olds.

Housing accounts for a smaller share of spending for prime-time families than for

Dollars

Older families with children have the highest incomes among married couples, but new parents and mature families spend the most.

(average total income before taxes, average household size, and average annual expenditures by expenditure category and by married-couple lifestage and age of householder)

PARENTS	PRIME-TIME FAMILIES			MATURE FAMILIES			EMPTY NESTERS		
35 to 54	25 to 34	35 to 44	45 to 54	35 to 44	45 to 54	55 to 64	45 to 54	55 to 64	65 and older
1,466	3,952	7,334	2,011	1,857	3,455	1,819	2,796	4,718	7,601
$53,270	$35,251	$47,845	$49,374	$49,214	$51,948	$55,216	$52,736	$38,701	$24,477
3.5	4.3	4.2	3.9	4.5	3.9	3.5	2.0	2.0	2.0
$44,839	$31,500	$41,144	$41,816	$43,149	$45,163	$40,730	$40,778	$31,534	$24,136
5,424	4,993	6,403	6,820	6,634	7,015	6,508	5,252	4,685	3,809
3,350	3,175	3,742	3,724	3,993	3,854	3,830	2,674	2,668	2,399
2,074	1,818	2,661	3,096	2,640	3,160	2,677	2,579	2,017	1,411
371	250	295	271	248	343	407	348	291	192
16,539	9,861	12,518	11,986	11,244	12,052	10,264	12,263	9,034	7,407
9,005	5,397	6,946	6,829	6,176	6,584	5,079	7,179	4,496	3,524
7,003	3,296	5,423	4,604	4,803	4,763	3,848	4,939	3,250	2,335
1,029	1,716	858	1,067	728	683	582	881	390	562
2,366	2,075	2,428	2,513	2,703	2,832	2,674	2,242	2,180	1,959
2,357	760	699	638	322	345	334	301	419	512
637	463	593	596	623	574	687	579	508	482
2,174	1,166	1,852	1,411	1,419	1,717	1,490	1,962	1,432	930
2,490	1,726	2,515	2,815	2,844	2,385	2,119	2,300	1,808	1,108
600	447	704	845	846	721	517	561	457	266
882	679	1,041	1,142	1,202	966	852	1,028	887	511
385	123	53	37	41	65	64	57	39	24
225	240	343	397	315	253	293	215	205	171
399	236	373	393	440	380	393	439	220	137
6,737	6,362	7,366	7,469	9,598	9,655	8,251	7,789	5,585	4,188
2,694	3,104	3,516	3,107	4,300	4,261	3,614	3,518	2,151	1,718
1,441	1,512	1,968	1,790	2,099	2,358	2,089	1,802	1,347	1,078
1,253	1,576	1,504	1,283	2,166	1,868	1,443	1,700	788	640
1,249	1,378	1,414	1,503	1,965	1,886	1,615	1,424	1,194	883
2,387	1,769	2,127	2,468	3,070	3,035	2,607	2,424	1,808	1,307
407	111	309	391	263	473	416	423	432	330
1,862	1,262	1,699	1,794	1,518	1,736	2,123	1,705	2,154	2,824
2,478	1,741	2,486	2,216	2,923	2,358	1,974	2,059	1,765	1,069
541	363	745	621	566	588	566	449	437	428
674	610	680	746	675	644	464	534	402	306
550	401	454	425	360	306	367	407	253	199
713	368	607	424	1,322	820	578	668	673	136
453	372	521	583	562	606	592	462	410	374
281	154	209	208	174	209	216	222	198	180
298	314	633	812	1,125	1,437	1,022	573	99	35
253	353	306	300	401	404	384	321	327	163
921	458	880	1,372	1,197	1,509	1,397	1,721	1,265	1,421
5,734	2,961	4,407	4,333	3,877	4,523	4,472	4,877	3,328	882
997	692	908	837	806	931	1,001	887	585	483

Source: 1989-90 Consumer Expenditure Survey

childless couples or new parents. Prime-time households headed by 45-to-54-year-olds spend just 29 percent of their budget on housing, compared with the 35 to 37 percent allocated by younger householders. With larger households and older children, however, prime-timers devote 16 percent of their budgets to food. They don't allocate more than half of their food budget to restaurants and carry-out food as childless couples do, but they tend to outspend new parents on food away from home.

Transportation claims 18 to 20 percent of a prime-time family's spending. This group outspends new parents on new vehicles, and they drive a lot more. Their tab for gas and oil is 36 percent more than the average household's.

Prime-time families have a lot to protect. That's why they spend 74 percent more than the average household on personal insurance and pensions, allocating 9 to 11 percent of their budgets to this

---

CINCINNATI, OHIO

DEMOGRAM

Tom Parker

Giving birth to twins in America isn't a big deal—it happens about 1,600 times a week. Quadruplet births, on the other hand, only happen four times a week. Quads make the evening news. But what about the 40 mothers a week who give birth to triplets? They get big guts, but what about the glory?

Janet Davis, 25, didn't even think she was pregnant. She went to the doctor for a routine exam. Later, when she gained weight faster than expected, her doctors thought her due date was wrong. So they scheduled a sonogram. "There's a very good reason you're getting so big," said the sonogram technician. "You have three babies in there." Janet, already the mother of two kids, ages 8 and 6, just sat in shock. Her mother said, "Oh, my God! I'm leaving town!" Her husband Pat got the news while at his job moving office furniture. He said he would have fainted if he hadn't been wedged into a phone booth.

That's where the fireworks ended. Janet didn't even discuss the triplets with her doctor until her next appointment a week later. Luckily, she stopped at a garage sale to look at a carseat. When she mentioned needing two more seats, the lady at the sale told her about a woman who lived just up the street with three newborn baby boys. Janet stopped and left a note on the woman's door. That's how she found The Triplet Connection.

The Triplet Connection is a nonprofit information clearinghouse and network for multiple-birth families based in Stockton, California. It was founded by Janet Bleyl, mother of ten, after a particularly difficult triplet pregnancy in 1982. According to Bleyl, the organization now has the largest database of multiple-birth information in the world. "We are in contact with more than 7,000 families of triplets and larger multiple births," she says. "And we currently work with over 1,250 expectant mothers per year."

Bleyl says that because triplets are not very common, most doctors have little experience in the special problems of large multiple pregnancies. And she adds that many doctors lack the nutritional training that is critical for these births. "We've found that the most important factor in large multiple pregnancies is keeping close track of nutrition and weight gain," says Bleyl. "As a rule, a mother hoping to walk out of the hospital with healthy triplets should plan on walking in with a weight gain of 50 to 70 pounds.

"We are also very concerned with the insidious nature of early contractions and preterm labor. In large multiple pregnancies, the uterus becomes so distended that it doesn't behave normally. Unless you take some extraordinary measures, it is often quite difficult to know if you are in premature labor. I had six kids before my triplets, but I didn't know!"

Bleyl's organization relies on two sources: a panel of medical advisors, and what she calls the "fabulous networking abilities of mothers" to help expectant parents and inexperienced physicians.

The Triplet Connection sent Janet Davis a packet of information, a medical questionnaire, an audiotape, and a quarterly newsletter. She says the material helped her check the quality of her doctor's advice. Janet's pregnancy was far from easy. Twice, she went to the hospital with premature contractions. Her doctors sent her home hooked to a Terbutaline pump to help prevent early labor. They kept track of Janet's progress with a fetal monitor hooked to a modem. The identical boys, Andrew, Adam, and Anthony, were delivered at 31 weeks—6 weeks early—by emergency C-section. Pat spent the last hour waiting at the hospital while Janet and her dad sat stuck in Cincinnati traffic.

I met the triplets at age 10 weeks. All three seemed healthy and as hard to tell apart as matching spoons. "Thanks to the good medical care, the boys were in the hospital for less than three weeks," Janet says. "The bill came to $90,000. Luckily, Pat's insurance paid most of it. Since then, Andrew and Anthony have had bouts with viral meningitis, we've moved to a different house, our car died, and our plumbing went out.

"Other than that, my biggest problem is simply getting the babies from one place to the next. Just to get into the doctor's office, I have to call ahead and ask the nurse to watch the parking lot for my arrival. Believe it or not, some mothers have figured out how to nurse triplets. Nursing is one thing, but lifting three babies is a different story. When your babies outnumber your arms, you've got problems."

If life's changes didn't throw us for a few loops, they wouldn't be changes at all. At first, most people respond with their own versions of, "Oh my God! I'm leaving town." But few of us ever really leave. We just gather our wits and do the best we can. And that's what Janet Davis is doing. She's got three bedrooms, one bath, two arms—and she's doing her best to hold seven people together. For more information: The Triplet Connection, P.O. Box 99571, Stockton, CA 95209; telephone (209) 474-0885.

> **Mature families have consistently above-average spending levels for food, transportation, entertainment, personal-care products and services, and education.**

spending category. Clothing and entertainment account for another 5 to 7 percent of their total spending. The amount spent on clothing is highest among prime-timers with householders aged 45 to 54. Households headed by 35-to-44-year-olds spend more on entertainment than others in this lifestage. Prime-time families are also among the biggest spenders on pets and toys.

MATURE FAMILIES

Mature families are couples whose oldest child at home is aged 18 or older. They have consistently above-average spending levels for food, transportation, entertainment, personal-care products and services, and education. Parents in mature families tend to be in their peak earning years, and many adult children also contribute to the family income. Average incomes in this lifestage range from a high of $55,000 for households headed by someone aged 55 to 64 to a low of $49,000 for those headed by someone aged 35 to 44. Mature families also shrink as householders age, from an average of 4.5 persons in families headed by 35-to-44-year-olds to 3.5 persons among those headed by 55-to-64-year-olds.

Compared with families in other lifestages, mature families allocate the smallest share of their budgets (25 to 27 percent) to housing, although they spend more than average on everything except rent, personal services, clothing for children younger than age 2, and household operations. What they save on housing prob-

ably goes to automobiles. Mature families spend 64 to 95 percent more than the average household on vehicles. They also spend above-average amounts on related items such as fuel and maintenance.

Because mature families support ravenous college-age youths, they spend more than other households on food and education. Their expenditures on food are at least 54 percent greater than average, and they allocate 15 to 16 percent of their budgets to food. Education eats up about 3 percent of the average mature family's spending dollar, triple the average amount.

EMPTY NESTERS

Couples' spending doesn't necessarily drop off as soon as the children leave the nest, especially if both spouses are still working. The average before-tax income of empty-nest households headed by people aged 45 to 54 is 67 percent greater than average, and their spending is 45 percent higher than average.

Income and spending do fall off among older couples. But the average income for empty nesters aged 55 to 64 is still 22 percent above the average for all households, and their spending is 12 percent above average. Among empty nesters aged 65 and older, both income and spending are below average (by 23 percent and 14 percent, respectively).

Not surprisingly, empty nesters spend more than younger couples on health care. Young empty nesters spend 18 percent more than average on health care, and their counterparts aged 65 or older spend almost twice as much as the average U.S. household. The share of spending devoted to health care by empty nesters climbs from 4 percent for pre-retirees to 12 percent among the elderly. As empty nesters age and their incomes decline, they also spend higher shares of income on food, personal-care products and services, reading, and cash contributions.

> **Children born to baby boomers will determine household spending for the rest of the decade.**

Young empty nesters spend nearly 60 percent more than the average household on vehicles, while the oldest empty nesters spend 22 percent less than average. Aging empty nesters also spend increasingly smaller budget shares on clothing, education, personal insurance, pensions, and Social Security.

Spending patterns change as children arrive and grow up. Children born to baby boomers during the 1980s and early 1990s will determine the lion's share of household spending for the rest of the decade. As they grow, their family's budget will almost certainly expand. For businesses that have struggled through the recession, this is something to look forward to.

Behind the Numbers This analysis is derived from the Bureau of Labor Statistics' annual Consumer Expenditure Survey (CEX). The unit of analysis in the CEX is a consumer unit, referred to in this article as a household. The analysis is based on a cross-tabulation of age of consumer unit head by composition of consumer unit. In order to obtain a large enough sample, data for the survey years 1989 and 1990 were combined. Because of low frequency counts, spending data could not be tabulated for all types of consumer units for all age groups. The lifestage called childless couples, for example, includes only those headed by someone aged 25 to 34 because there are so few couples headed by a person under age 25. Likewise, most couples aged 35 to 44 have children; the small number who do not are also excluded from the analysis. For more information about the CEX, contact the Bureau of Labor Statistics at (202) 272-5060. Margaret Ambry is co-author of *The Official Guide to American Incomes* and *The Official Guide to Household Spending*, to be published by New Strategist in spring 1993. Some of the data in this article come from these books.

Staying Power

Melinda Blau

Melinda Blau is the author of Families Apart: Ten Keys to Successful Co-Parenting.

Karen Mason*, 40, considers herself lucky. "I have a husband who's a real parent—kissy-huggy with the kids. And three nights a week he cooks dinner so I can be on the swim team."

Yet even this seeming paragon of a modern husband continues to exhibit what she considers to be typically male characteristics. Peter, 40, isn't much of a talker, Karen notes wistfully, and yes, he likes sex whereas she likes romance. And sometimes Karen gets frustrated because her husband just doesn't seem to focus when it comes to the house and children.

When they got married, Karen and Peter were determined not to be bound by traditional gender-role assumptions—that he would bring home the bacon and she would cook it. Peter, a salesman, shared the housework and put in almost equal time with their first child. But then the demands of Peter's work increased, a second child arrived and the couple's time together began to slip away.

Even though Peter is a far cry from his own father, who wasn't home much or "always had his head in the newspaper," some evenings Peter understands how his dad must have felt. "I like to

Couples' names and some identifying details have been changed.

bury myself in the TV," he admits. "I'm exhausted at night." Karen agrees that Peter "is doing his best" but says she's sometimes saddened by what she perceives as their real gender differences.

Many '90s couples are grappling with new ways of being men and women. At the same time that expectations and demands have changed for both, the popular press suggests the battle of the sexes may never end because men and women are irreconcilably different. Books proclaim that *Men Are From Mars, Women Are From Venus,* and personal accounts highlight

Bridging the gender gap in the confusing '90s

the issues on which couples differ: Communication (she wants more talk; he wants more action). Intimacy (she needs to relax to have sex; he needs sex to relax). Division of household labor and child care (she says she does more; he talks about how much he does). Money and careers (she says he doesn't value her job as much as his; he notes that he makes more money).

Yet despite these differences, the fact that men and women can transcend traditional gender roles indicates that many of these distinctions may be more a result of socialization than biology. "Men are not emotionally defective monsters, and women aren't depen-

dent, helpless creatures," says psychologist Susan Johnson at the University of Ottawa in Ontario.

While researchers debate the contributions of nature and nurture to gender differences, family therapists suggest we examine why couples become polarized in the first place. Boston psychologist Kathy McMahon notes that "gender rage," as she calls it, stands for the disappointment couples feel when reality doesn't live up to expectations.

Dr. McMahon offers a typical scenario: Both parents work, and their child gets sick. In a spirit of fairness, they decide to split caretaking, but by the end of the week, they're fighting about who does what around the house. The problem, says McMahon, is that neither has a model for this new behavior—Mom working when a child is sick, Dad staying home—and they can't buck their inner cultural imprinting. When it's time for Mom to go to work, she feels guilty for not living up to her role as mother. And Dad's upset because he's not living up to his role as provider.

Today's couples, say the experts, must acknowledge their unconscious expectations and speak up before gender rage erodes their relationship. "This is not so much about understanding differences," says family therapist Jo-Ann Krestan, "as it is about holding partners equally accountable for the quality of life in a family. Sharing responsibility doesn't mean the husband saying, 'Honey, I'll cook tonight—where's the stove?'"

In essence, men and women usually want the same things from a relationship: closeness, support, respect, fairness, healthy children, a nice home and longevity. But, says California psychologist Lonnie Barbach, co-author of *Going the Distance,* they often differ about how to achieve these things and don't necessarily talk productively with each other about them.

Couples who talk about their needs and feelings fare far better than those who don't. But the longer people stay together, the less time they spend thinking and talking about their relationship, says University of Michigan psychologist Linda Acitelli. Complaining about a spouse's behavior doesn't count. Relationship work, Dr. Acitelli says, is like car maintenance—for safety's sake, you shouldn't wait until the vehicle breaks down.

The process of divvying up both practical *and* emotional responsibilities should be worked out thoughtfully. Some couples allocate chores arbitrarily, according to what has to be done; others earmark assignments based on preference. However it's done, structure—a chart or other means of clarifying who does what—can be helpful.

New York City designer Sara Roark, 41, and her husband, Carl, 42, an architect, drew up a "contract" and even included their four-year-old son, Orin. The major headings represent a bird's-eye view of what it takes to run a house and a family: meals and dishes, laundry, school, shopping, housecleaning, home maintenance, car, mail, finances, medical care, lifestyle decisions and leisure time.

At first the Roarks wanted to keep the assignments objective, but they wound up basing certain responsibilities on each person's skills and availability. "I took over more of the financial things, because it took me less time. My husband is more of a morning person, so he gets Orin ready for school, while I do more of the night things."

To a woman who complains that she's always in charge or that her husband does less than she does, Krestan would say it's her own fault for doing his share. "Sometimes you just have to leave his empty yogurt container on the kitchen counter. Throw it away and you cripple his ability to notice empty yogurt containers in the future."

Indeed, Sara Roark had to redefine "what needs to be done" and to accept the fact that things might not be done the way she'd do them, or when. "It's tough to let go. Sometimes when I come home late, I find that he's given our son crackers and cheese and put him to bed. A lot of women just take over at that point."

Dr. Ron Taffel, a New York City family therapist, concurs: "The biggest complaint I hear from men is, 'She wants me to do it, but when I do, she criticizes me.'" Our society, he explains, puts each member in a no-win situation. "The woman feels responsi-

Arguments over dirty dishes are signs of deeper issues.

ble for how the house looks and how the kids turn out. Society will hold her accountable, so she feels driven to be in charge. And even though the man may want to participate as an equal, he often feels like he has a boss."

Taffel's prescription goes beyond chores: Couples must also reserve time every night for reviewing the day. "One couple began to talk for 15 minutes each night after the kids went to bed about what happened with each other and with their sons. It made them feel more in synch."

While women typically will participate in such sessions, men are generally more resistant. Men tend to focus on what's in front of them, Taffel explains. "When they leave the office, they don't want to talk about work, and when the children finally are in bed, they don't want to talk about them. I try to get them to realize that the more they separate the different aspects of their lives, the more they end up zoning out in front of the TV or walking out on wives who want to talk."

Dave Goodrich, 34, an estate manager in Indianapolis, was happy to share the housework and child care for his two sons. But intimacy was another matter. "When Annie first complained that she was always the one to initiate conversations about our relationship, I was very defensive," he admits. "Guys don't talk about those kinds of things. We had a number of conversations, till

all hours of the night. Now I understand where she's coming from. It's hard sometimes, but I really make an attempt to share the emotional work of our marriage too."

Annie Goodrich, 37, a teacher, realizes that her attitude also made a difference. "In the beginning I would yell and scream, which just pushed him further away. I finally realized that when we had an argument, he needed a cooling-off period before he could talk."

Certainly, it takes perseverance—not

HOW TO CLOSE THE GAP

Get honest before you get angry: Something deeper than dry cleaning is probably bothering you.
Establish systems for sharing chores and child care.
Negotiate the division of labor *and* the division of love.
Don't get locked into your role: Try swapping responsibilities on occasion.
Express your emotional needs and expectations and really listen to your partner.
Review the cultural messages of your childhood to help understand the conflicts inherent in your new roles.
Give each other time to change; don't monitor or criticize.
Accept your differences and applaud each other's strengths.
Protect your intimate time together.

---

the same as nagging—to get some men to talk. More important, it requires the woman to speak honestly about what she needs, not rant about what her spouse is doing wrong. In most relationships, in fact, both partners are usually afraid of intimacy; the fear just looks different on men and women. As Dr. Johnson points out, "To love and to be intimately connected is to be incredibly at risk." A woman may believe she's doing "relationship work" because she starts conversations, but if she doesn't allow herself to be vulnerable and doesn't take responsibility for her own feelings, she may be dodging intimacy by focusing on him. Unexpressed feelings can contaminate a relationship—and obscure the real issues. Arguments over dirty dishes, vacuuming or food shopping or even a partner's infidelity are usually symptoms of deeper problems.

After two children and 14 years of marriage, Dana Berk, 37, finally had to confront why she felt so depressed, so sexually apathetic, so envious of other couples. It had nothing to do with chore wars. "Over the years, without realizing it, Hal and I had both shut down."

Realizing she was attracted to another man was Dana's wake-up call. Rather than act on impulse, she decided to talk to her husband. "It was brutal having to express our bottled-up feelings. I have tremendous gratitude because he was wonderful in terms of being able to face the issues, deal with the pain and support me. We had many talks late into the night. There was anger, but we also cried a lot. I even have a sex drive now, and there's a passion in our relationship that's deeper than we ever had. I think we've really learned how to be there for each other."

Dave and Annie Goodrich learned to be there for each other through a series of crises—beginning with Annie's miscarriage—that made their different styles pale in comparison with their ability to share life's hard knocks. "When we lost the baby, Dave really let go," Annie says. "He knew that we both had to talk about it. When I developed an eating disorder, he was really supportive. Then our youngest was born with a birth defect. Just knowing we can talk about it makes it bearable."

Successful couples constantly and consciously nurture their relationship. "The need to protect intimacy—their time with each other—is central to being together," stresses Taffel, "all the way from having conversations without being interrupted to having weekends together without the kids. When that starts to disappear, it's dangerous; the reservoir dips too low."

Taffel suggests creating rituals. One couple he knows takes a brief walk after dinner. The Roarks try to set aside a portion of every weekend for themselves. The Goodriches try to get away one weekend a month.

Of course, some gender differences will persist: She may not feel as comfortable being away from the kids; he may never be as observant. But such issues don't have to be divisive if you remember to reserve time to be alone together and if you appreciate your common victories instead of bemoaning each other's failings.

"Your partner is probably not going to get it the first time," Dr. Barbach emphasizes. "Acknowledge small changes, even if they're not perfect." Whether your differences are over housework, child care or emotions, she adds, "really value what each of you gives." In some areas, one person probably is more proficient. "If you're better at bringing romance into your relationship, do it."

Last year Karen Mason did just that. On Peter's 40th birthday, she "surprise kidnapped" him for a weekend alone, planning the whole thing meticulously, down to taking his clothes "bit by bit" so she could pack their suitcase. "He was so appreciative," she recalls, "but he admitted that he could never have done it for me. He wouldn't have thought of all the details."

Karen is satisfied, however, because Peter is a loving husband and father who can tolerate that her idea of a great birthday present is to go away *with* the kids. Thus the Masons have reached a workable détente. "As I get older, I realize there are some real differences between men and women," says Karen, "and I'm happier when I accept it."

But What Do You Mean?

Deborah Tannen, Ph.D.

Deborah Tannen is the best-selling author of You Just Don't Understand: Men and Women in Conversation.

Conversation is a ritual. We say things that seem obviously the thing to say, without thinking of the literal meaning of our words, any more than we expect the question "How are you?" to call forth a detailed account of aches and pains.

Unfortunately, women and men often have different ideas about what's appropriate, different ways of speaking. Many of the conversational rituals common among women are designed to take the other person's feelings into account, while many of the conversational rituals common among men are designed to maintain the one-up position, or at least avoid appearing one-down. As a result, when men and women interact—especially at work—it's often women who are at the disadvantage. Because women are not trying to avoid the one-down position, that is unfortunately where they may end up.

Here, the biggest areas of miscommunication.

1. Apologies

Women are often told they apologize too much. The reason they're told to stop doing it is that, to many men, apologizing seems synonymous with

> Men and women really do speak different languages, to praise, thank, apologize, even chat. How to avoid the 7 conversation traps that keep us apart— at work and at home

putting oneself down. But there are many times when "I'm sorry" isn't self-deprecating, or even an apology; it's an automatic way of keeping both speakers on an equal footing. For example, a well-known columnist once interviewed me and gave me her phone number in case I needed to call her back. I misplaced the number and had to go through the newspaper's main switchboard. When our conversation was winding down and we'd both made ending-type remarks, I added, "Oh, I almost forgot—I lost your direct number, can I get it again?" "Oh, I'm sorry," she came back instantly, even though she had done nothing wrong and *I* was the one who'd lost the number. But I understood she wasn't really apologizing; she was just automatically reassuring me she had no intention of denying me her number.

Even when "I'm sorry" *is* an apology, women often assume it will be the first step in a two-step ritual: I say "I'm sorry" and take half the blame, then you take the other half. At work, it might go something like this:

A: When you typed this letter, you missed this phrase I inserted.

This article was originally published in *Redbook,* October 1994, pp. 91-93, 145-147. Adapted from *Talking 9 to 5: How Women's and Men's Conversational Styles Affect Who Gets Heard, Who Gets Credit, and What Gets Done at Work* by Deborah Tannen, Ph.D. © 1994 by Deborah Tannen, Ph.D. Reprinted by permission of William Morrow & Company, Inc.

B: Oh, I'm sorry. I'll fix it.

A: Well, I wrote it so small it was easy to miss.

When both parties share blame, it's a mutual face-saving device. But if one person, usually the woman, utters frequent apologies and the other doesn't, she ends up looking as if she's taking the blame for mishaps that aren't her fault. When she's only partially to blame, she looks entirely in the wrong.

I recently sat in on a meeting at an insurance company where the sole woman, Helen, said "I'm sorry" or "I apologize" repeatedly. At one point she said, "I'm thinking out loud. I apologize." Yet the meeting was intended to be an informal brainstorming session, and *everyone* was thinking out loud.

The reason Helen's apologies stood out was that she was the only person in the room making so many. And the reason I was concerned was that Helen felt the annual bonus she had received was unfair. When I interviewed her colleagues, they said that Helen was one of the best and most productive workers—yet she got one of the smallest bonuses. Although the problem might have been outright sexism, I suspect her speech style, which differs from that of her male colleagues, masks her competence.

Unfortunately, not apologizing can have its price too. Since so many women use ritual apologies, those who don't may be seen as hard-edged. What's important is to be aware of how often you say you're sorry (and why), and to monitor your speech based on the reaction you get.

2. Criticism

A woman who cowrote a report with a male colleague was hurt when she read a rough draft to him and he leapt into a critical response—"Oh, that's too dry! You have to make it snappier!" She herself would have been more likely to say, "That's a really good start. Of course, you'll want to make it a little snappier when you revise."

Whether criticism is given straight or softened is often a matter of convention. In general, women use more softeners. I noticed this difference when talking to an editor about an essay I'd written. While going over changes she wanted to make, she said, "There's one more thing. I know you may not agree with me. The reason I noticed the problem is that your other points are so lucid and elegant." She

went on hedging for several more sentences until I put her out of her misery: "Do you want to cut that part?" I asked—and of course she did. But I appreciated her tentativeness. In contrast, another editor (a man) I once called summarily rejected my idea for an article by barking, "Call me when you have something new to say."

Those who are used to ways of talking that soften the impact of criticism may find it hard to deal with the right-between-the-eyes style. It has its own logic, however, and neither style is intrinsically better. People who prefer criticism given straight are operating on an assumption that feelings aren't involved: "Here's the dope. I know you're good; you can take it."

3. Thank-Yous

A woman manager I know starts meetings by thanking everyone for coming, even though it's clearly their job to do so. Her "thank-you" is simply a ritual.

A novelist received a fax from an assistant in her publisher's office; it contained suggested catalog copy for her book. She immediately faxed him her suggested changes and said, "Thanks for running this by me," even though her contract gave her the right to approve all copy. When she thanked the assistant, she fully expected him to reciprocate: "Thanks for giving me such a quick response." Instead, he said, "You're welcome." Suddenly, rather than an equal exchange of pleasantries, she found herself positioned as the recipient of a favor. This made her feel like responding, "Thanks for nothing!"

Many women use "thanks" as an automatic conversation starter and closer; there's nothing literally to say thank you for. Like many rituals typical of women's conversation, it depends on the goodwill of the other to restore the balance. When the other speaker doesn't reciprocate, a woman may feel like someone on a seesaw whose partner abandoned his end. Instead of balancing in the air, she has plopped to the ground, wondering how she got there.

4. Fighting

Many men expect the discussion of ideas to be a ritual fight—explored through verbal opposition. They state their ideas in the strongest possible terms, thinking that if there are weaknesses someone will point them out,

and by trying to argue against those objections, they will see how well their ideas hold up.

Those who expect their own ideas to be challenged will respond to another's ideas by trying to poke holes and find weak links—as a way of *helping*. The logic is that when you are challenged you will rise to the occasion: Adrenaline makes your mind sharper; you get ideas and insights you would not have thought of without the spur of battle.

But many women take this approach as a personal attack. Worse, they find it impossible to do their best work in such a contentious environment. If you're not used to ritual fighting, you begin to hear criticism of your ideas as soon as they are formed. Rather than making you think more clearly, it makes you doubt what you know. When you state your ideas, you hedge in order to fend off potential attacks. Ironically, this is more likely to *invite* attack because it makes you look weak.

Although you may never enjoy verbal sparring, some women find it helpful to learn how to do it. An engineer who was the only woman among four men in a small company found that as soon as she learned to argue she was accepted and taken seriously. A doctor attending a hospital staff meeting made a similar discovery. She was becoming more and more angry with a male colleague who'd loudly disagreed with a point she'd made. Her better judgment told her to hold her tongue, to avoid making an enemy of this powerful senior colleague. But finally she couldn't hold it in any longer, and she rose to her feet and delivered an impassioned attack on his position. She sat down in a panic, certain she had permanently damaged her relationship with him. To her amazement, he came up to her afterward and said, "That was a great rebuttal. I'm really impressed. Let's go out for a beer after work and hash out our approaches to this problem."

5. Praise

A manager I'll call Lester had been on his new job six months when he heard that the women reporting to him were deeply dissatisfied. When he talked to them about it, their feelings erupted; two said they were on the verge of quitting because he didn't appreciate their work, and they didn't want to wait to be fired. Lester was dumbfounded: He believed they were doing a fine job. Surely, he thought, he had said nothing to give them the impression he didn't like their work. And indeed he hadn't. That was the problem. He had said *nothing*—and the women assumed he was following the adage "If you can't say something nice, don't say anything." He thought he was showing confidence in them by leaving them alone.

Men and women have different habits in regard to giving praise. For

Men expect to fight about ideas, thinking it sharpens their minds. But many women take it as a personal attack.

example, Deirdre and her colleague William both gave presentations at a conference. Afterward, Deirdre told William, "That was a great talk!" He thanked her. Then she asked, "What did you think of mine?" and he gave her a lengthy and detailed critique. She found it uncomfortable to listen to his comments. But she assured herself that he meant well, and that his honesty was a signal that she, too, should be honest when he asked for a critique of his performance. As a matter of fact, she had noticed quite a few ways in which he could have improved his presentation. But she never got a chance to tell him because he never asked—and she felt put down. The worst part was that it seemed she had only herself to blame, since she *had* asked what he thought of her talk.

But had she really asked for his critique? The truth is, when she asked for his opinion, she was expecting a compliment, which she felt was more or less required following anyone's talk. When he responded with criticism, she figured, "Oh, he's playing 'Let's critique each other'—not a game she'd initiated, but one which she was willing to play. Had she realized he was going to criticize her and not ask her to reciprocate, she would never have asked in the first place.

It would be easy to assume that Deirdre was insecure, whether she was fishing for a compliment or soliciting a critique. But she was simply talking automatically, performing one of the many conversational rituals that allow us to get through the day. William may have sincerely misunderstood Deirdre's intention—or may have been unable to

pass up a chance to one-up her when given the opportunity.

6. Complaints

"Troubles talk" can be a way to establish rapport with a colleague. You complain about a problem (which shows that you are just folks) and the other person responds with a similar problem (which puts you on equal footing). But while such commiserating is common among women, men are likely to hear it as a request to *solve* the problem.

One woman told me she would frequently initiate what she thought would be pleasant complaint-airing sessions at work. She'd talk about situations that bothered her just to talk about them, maybe to understand them better. But her male office mate would quickly tell her how she could improve the situation. This left her feeling condescended to and frustrated. She was delighted to see this very impasse in a section in my book *You Just Don't Understand,* and showed it to him. "Oh," he said, "I see the problem. How can we solve it?" Then they both laughed, because it had happened again: He short-circuited the detailed discussion she'd hoped for and cut to the chase of finding a solution.

Sometimes the consequences of complaining are more serious: A man might take a woman's lighthearted griping literally, and she can get a reputation as a chronic malcontent. Furthermore, she may be seen as not up to solving the problems that arise on the job.

7. Jokes

I heard a man call in to a talk show and say, "I've worked for two women and neither one had a sense of humor. You know, when you work with men, there's a lot of joking and teasing." The show's host and the guest (both women) took his comment at face value and assumed the women this man worked for were humorless. The guest said, "Isn't it sad that women

don't feel comfortable enough with authority to see the humor?" The host said, "Maybe when more women are in authority roles, they'll be more comfortable with power." But although the women this man worked for *may* have taken themselves too seriously, it's just as likely that they each had a terrific sense of humor, but maybe the humor wasn't the type he was used to. They may have been like the woman who wrote to me: "When I'm with men, my wit or cleverness seems inappropriate (or lost!) so I don't bother. When I'm with my women friends, however, there's no hold on puns or cracks and my humor is fully appreciated."

The types of humor women and men tend to prefer differ. Research has shown that the most common form of humor among men is razzing, teasing, and mock-hostile attacks, while among women it's self-mocking. Women often mistake men's teasing as genuinely hostile. Men often mistake women's mock self-deprecation as truly putting themselves down.

Women have told me they were taken more seriously when they learned to joke the way the guys did. For example, a teacher who went to a national conference with seven other teachers (mostly women) and a group of administrators (mostly men) was annoyed that the administrators always found reasons to leave boring seminars, while the teachers felt they had to stay and take notes. One evening, when the group met at a bar in the hotel, the principal asked her how one such seminar had turned out. She retorted, "As soon as you left, it got much better." He laughed out loud at her response. The playful insult appealed to the men—but there was a trade-off. The women seemed to back off from her after this. (Perhaps they were put off by her using joking to align herself with the bosses.)

THERE IS NO "RIGHT" WAY TO TALK. When problems arise, the culprit may be style differences—and *all* styles will at times fail with others who don't share or understand them, just as English won't do you much good if you try to speak to someone who knows only French. If you want to get your message across, it's not a question of being "right"; it's a question of using language that's shared—or at least understood.

SAVING RELATIONSHIPS:
THE POWER OF THE UNPREDICTABLE

When one partner silently switches the "rules," both partners can benefit. Welcome to the surprising world systems thinking.

Barry L. Duncan, Psy.D.,
and Joseph W. Rock, Psy.D.

Sharon, 30, and Jeff, 35, have been married for nine years. Since the recent birth of their first child, Sharon has become increasingly aware of Jeff's propensity for giving instructions and pointing out imperfections in her methods of doing things. She knows that he is usually just trying to help.

The first thing Sharon does to address the problem is mention it to Jeff. She explains that when they were first married she needed and appreciated his knowledge and experience but now sometimes feels he is treating her like a child. She asks him to please hold his comments and advice until she asks for them. Jeff agrees to make every effort to treat her like the mature, independent woman she has become.

But before long, Jeff resumes sharing his observations of the way Sharon does things and making suggestions about better ways of doing them. When Sharon points this out to him, he becomes defensive and accuses her of overreacting and not being able to accept constructive criticism.

Sharon continues to make Jeff aware of his now "critical, paternalistic, and sexist nature." She takes every opportunity to point out his need to dominate and keep her in her place. Jeff responds by defensively backing off and withdrawing from conversation in general. When conversa-

tion does occur, he seems more apt to criticize Sharon about her "crazy, feminist" ideas as well as her way of doing almost everything. Their latest interactions seem to be best characterized by an unspoken tension.

Sharon decides to try a different approach. She goes "on strike," discontinuing to do anything Jeff criticizes. When he comments that the spaghetti sauce needs more garlic, she announces she's no longer cooking. When he criticizes how the grass is cut, she blows up in anger, and both Sharon and he say many things that they later regret. Jeff decides not only to stop commenting and suggesting but to stop talking altogether. Now an unspoken hostility hovers over their relationship.

Sharon and Jeff illustrate three ways in which people get stuck in their relationships and sabotage their own attempts to improve them. First Sharon believes she is trying different strategies to improve her relationship when in reality she is trying only slight variations on a single theme: "I will make my dissatisfaction apparent to him, and he will respond with less criticism." People get stuck by trying the same basic approach over and over, even though it might not be obvious to them that they are doing so.

Further, when her first method makes things worse, she tries more of the same. A well-intentioned attempt to resolve a

small difficulty ends up turning it into a serious conflict despite good intentions. Sharon wound up with increased criticism and an overly sensitive, defensive, withdrawn husband.

Third, Sharon recognized the problem but did not succeed in getting Jeff to help solve it. Almost always, one partner notices a joint problem first. That person mentions it to the other and then proceeds to try to solve the problem, while assuming the other person is motivated and cooperative. This can be a faulty assumption even if both people agree on how serious it is or how to solve it.

A widely shared belief is that in order for a relationship to change, both partners have to actively participate in changing it. As family therapists, we disagree. We subscribe to a "systems" approach with couples. In a relationship system, a noticeable change in one person can set in motion a change in the whole system, that is, the couple.

Early in relationships, rules begin to form that grow out of patterns of ways people to relate to each other. Rules can be simple and straightforward—one partner initiates sex, one partner does the dishes; or they can be more subtle—when both partners are angry they don't yell. Sometimes the rules are talked about openly, but typically they are assumed rather than discussed, and those involved

From *Psychology Today,* January/February 1993, pp. 46-51, 86, 95. Adapted from *Overcoming Relationship Impasses* by Barry L. Duncan and Joseph W. Rock. © 1991 by Plenum Publishing Corporation. Reprinted by permission.

may not even be consciously aware of the assumed rules. This non-awareness causes the most difficulty when problems arise.

Rules have their uses; in recurring situations, we don't have to figure out what to do from scratch. But because rules are based on previous experience, they also maintain the status quo. The very qualities that make rules useful day-to-day can render them harmful when a relationship problem needs to be resolved. Rules simplify life by limiting options to an acceptable few. But when we get stuck in solving a problem, we need *more* options, not fewer. The assumed rules we carry into a situation prevent us from exploring potentially helpful options and limit our flexibility. They discourage change—even helpful, necessary change.

Beyond Blame: Systems Thinking

Most theories of human behavior are couched in linear cause-effect terms and offer either historical (unhappy childhood) or physical (bad nerves) explanations for behavior. Both the medical and Freudian perspectives on problem behaviors or emotional stress consider only the individual, apart from his or her relationships.

Systems theory is evolving to explain the complexities of relationships and to help resolve the problems and distress in-

In a relationship, you are not acting completely of your own free will. You are constantly influenced by your partner, and vice versa.

herent in relationships. It offers a refreshing, illness-free lens through which to observe human behavior—the focus of study shifts from what goes on inside a person to what takes place between people.

When two individuals come together in a relationship, something is created that is different from, larger, and more complex than those two individuals apart—a system. The most important feature of such a relationship is communication. Relationships are established, maintained, and changed by communicative interaction among members.

As relationships endure, communication sequences form patterns over time, and it is the patterning over time that is the essence of a couple system. Sometimes the enduring patterns begin to create difficulties for couples, and new patterns are need-

ed. With Jeff and Sharon, the pattern concerning the giving and receiving of advice was at the heart of their relationship problems.

In a system, all elements are mutually dependent. What one person does depends on what the other person does. In the context of a relationship, you are not acting completely of your own free will. You are constantly being influenced by your partner, and vice versa. When Sharon attempted to get less criticism, Jeff responded by criticizing more and pulling away. Each person's actions helped determine what the other did, and each person's actions affected the relationship as a whole.

A marriage, then, is not a static and fixed relationship. No matter how entrenched one's behavior or how strong one's personality, each individual is influenced by the other on an ongoing basis. *Once you recognize your partner's dependence upon your pattern of behavior, you can consciously plan and change your own behavior, thereby influencing your partner and the relationship in a constructive manner.*

Virtually every couple we see in therapy is interested in what, or who, caused their problems; they look for guilt, blame, or responsibility. But influence among people in relationships is reciprocal and mutually dependent, causality is circular. Choosing the point at which the causal chain begins is pointless and arbitrary.

One implication is that the circle can be broken or interrupted at any point, regardless of how the problem started or how long it has existed. If one person in a couple changes behavior noticeably and consistently, the other person's reactions will change, which will change the first person's reactions. In this way, one person can positively impact a troubled relationship; the partner's cooperation is not required.

Does Sharon have a problem with constructive criticism, or does Jeff have a problem with control and sexism? One partner, either partner, can interrupt the causal circle and move the relationship in another direction.

In much the same way that a stone thrown into a pond affects the surface well beyond the small point at which it enters, a small change in a specific area can lead to a positive ripple effect on the entire relationship. When there are many problems in a relationship, people assume that a major overhaul is required. Many times, however, a small adjustment, strategically employed, is all that is needed.

Communication: The Sound of Silence

Communication theory is crucial in systems thinking. Gestures, tone of voice, and facial expressions are important in understanding what someone is saying. Much has been written about body language, addressing what people "say" by their posture. What gets lost is that *all behavior is communicative.* Even silence conveys some message. There is no such thing as *not* communicating.

A spouse who routinely comes home late for dinner without calling may be saying, "Your inconvenience is unimportant compared to what happens at work" or "Your feelings are not a priority to me." The spouse who prepares dinner may not comment to the late spouse. Yet the silence may be a worse indictment than a verbal scolding.

Viewing behavior itself as a powerful means of communication significantly increases your options when verbal com-

What gets lost is that all behavior is communicative. Even silence conveys some message. There is no such thing as *not* communicating.

munication is not working. If, like Sharon, you have tried to fix your relationship problems by talking ad nauseam, then behavioral options may provide a more powerful way.

Communication occurs at different levels, even though most of us focus our attention on only one—the content, or the literal meaning of the words. Most important, but less obvious, is the relationship level. It indicates how the sender of the message is attempting to influence the receiver. It conveys a command or directive concerning the sender's needs and is an implicit attempt to influence the receiver. "My back itches" may mean "Scratch my back." "I had a rough day" may mean "Leave me alone," "I need your support," or "Fix me a drink." Even "I love you" can be an implicit command, depending upon the circumstances. It may mean "Tell me that you love me."

Influence is unavoidable in communication; it is inherent in how we interact. Just as one cannot *not* communicate, one cannot *not* influence when communicating. Implicit directives also define the nature of the relationship. The statement, "The garbage can is overflowing," not only conveys the obvious, but may also contain

Relationship Myths

Myth #1: What people say is very important and has a big impact on what they do.

Words often fall short of accurately depicting someone's intentions and we can't really guess at times what someone else really means. In the long term, behavior is what gives evidence of our true intentions.

Myth #2: People can and should understand and explain their own and others' motives.

Behavior is the result of a tremendous number of interacting influences: biological, psychological, interpersonal, situational. We never get answers to "why," only plausible-sounding guesses. Knowing "why" seldom produces a solution. *Understanding* a behavior pattern and *changing* it are often completely different. Consider *what* is happening now between you and your partner and *how* that pattern can be changed.

Myth #3: In close relationships being completely open and honest is critical if the relationship is to work.

If the person with whom you are communicating is unable or unwilling to respond honestly and openly, honesty and openness may well be a bad idea at times. Being open with someone who will use the information to manipulate you or gain power over you is like playing poker and showing your cards before you bet. An open and honest expression must be interpreted as such by the receiver of the message for it to be truly open and honest. Openness is not the only way, and, in some situations, not the best way.

Myth #4: A good relationship is one in which both people give unselfishly.

Unselfish giving is not a prerequisite for a good relationship. In fact, attempts to do so usually create more problems than they solve. Giving is an important part of any relationship. However, all of us expect something back; it helps to let the other person know what that is. Balance is also important. Rather than expecting to meet all of each other's needs, stay in practice at meeting some of your own. It adds stability to a relationship and reduces the risk of resentment. Complete selfishness certainly does not lend itself to healthy relationships, but it turns out that neither does utter unselfishness.

Myth #5: In any situation there is only one reality or one truth.

Reality is entirely dependent upon who is observing and describing it, especially in complex situations such as interactions in relationships. When two people have very different stories to tell about the same situation, it does not mean that one is lying, although each partner usually believes that about the other. Rather, each is describing reality from his or her frame of reference. A lot of time usually is wasted trying to convince your partner that you are right. This time could be better spent trying to understand the others' point of view and using that understanding to change your own behavior in a way that will help the relationship.

---

the implicit directive, "Take the garbage out." The statement defines the relationship as one in which the sender has the right to comment on the state of garbage and expect the receiver to follow the (implicit) directive.

Implicit commands are largely automatic and occur outside of awareness. As a result, we often address the most important parts of our lives, our relationships, in an extremely haphazard fashion. By becoming aware of the implicit influence in communication we can deliberately use it in improving relationships.

When we think about communication, we usually think of a speaker actively conveying a message and a listener passively receiving it. This, however, is a very inaccurate perception. Listening is an active process. We have to make sense of the speaker's words; we compare their ideas to beliefs and attitudes we hold and to perceptions about the speakers we've already formed. We consider gestures, tone of voice, and facial expressions, and the circumstances. In addition, our needs influence what we hear.

The conclusion is inescapable—the listener helps create meaning. Much of this process tends to be automatic and outside awareness. We're seldom aware of how our beliefs and attitudes affect how we hear, or the ways we interpret nonverbal communication, much less how our own needs affect our perceptions. By paying attention to these factors, however, we can make them conscious, then control them.

The upshot is, we can choose how to interpret a given communication. Words

Words that hurt us before no longer have to have power. We can choose to interpret a message differently from the way the sender intended.

or behaviors that have hurt us before no longer have to have this power. Further, we can choose to interpret a message differently from the way the sender intended. Just because people intend to hurt or manipulate us doesn't mean we have to cooperate by giving their messages the meanings they want us to get.

Often, the listener's understanding of a message is *already* different from the sender's. If a woman believes her husband is stressed out and needs time away, she might suggest he go away for a week. If he interprets this as "She's trying to get rid of me," the whole point of her message is twisted, and caring is perceived as rejection. This may be the most common problem seen in couples: The message sent is not the message received. Finding ways to understand and express your partner's view of a situation can reduce defensiveness and change old, conflictual patterns in a relationship.

Guidelines for Change

The ideas that one person can produce meaningful change in a relationship, and that a small change can and will lead to a ripple of other changes, are not part of conventional wisdom. Nor are the implications that change can occur quickly and that it can happen without the knowledge or cooperation of one member of the couple. But strategies developed from systems concepts do work, even when both partners aren't equally motivated to change. Here, then, are some very practical guidelines for creating change in a troubled relationship where the partners are stuck at an impasse:

•Create confusion. Change the rules by which you've been playing. Be unpredictable. That encourages your partner to find new ways to react.

• Do not be completely honest and open at all times. If your partner tends to manipulate or use power plays, openness just tips your hand and makes you more vulnerable.

• "Give up" power, or "lose" by telling your partner that you agree that he or she is "right," but continue to do whatever you think is best. Allow yourself to give up power verbally, to gain control behaviorally.

• Recognize that words and behaviors are not consistent. People often say one thing but do another. Believe what your partner does, not what he or she says.

• Do things that are truly different, not just variations on a theme. Allow yourself to change 180 degrees in how you approach a problem. That alteration can loosen things up and produce real change in your partner's response.

• Stay off the defensive. If you spend all your time justifying what you are doing, you become reactive and lose track of what you are trying to accomplish. Most people are too busy trying to defend themselves to see other ways of approaching a problem. Relationships are very complex and much creativity is needed.

• If your partner openly resists change, don't push. Finding a different, less confrontational path the change can be much more effective—and less frustrating.

• Go with the flow whenever possible and recognize the disadvantages of change. Things are rarely black and white; consider the advantages of maintaining the problem. This form of creative interpretation directly addresses the ambivalence people have about changing their behavior and aligns with that part of the individual that may be reluctant to change. It helps clarify the feared consequences of change in the hope of motivating the person toward action regarding the problem.

• Start a small, positive ripple of change and let it grow by itself.

• Look at what is going well, instead of what is going wrong with your relationship. It's much easier to build on what is already there than to tear something down and start all over.

Power Disparities in Romantic Relationships

By far, the most common source of problems in a relationship involves the distribution of power. In a good relationship, ideally there is a balance of power. Unfortunately, this ideal is not always real-

ized, and neither party is happy with the unequal power. The powerless, disenfran-

The ideas that one person can produce meaningful change in a relationship, and that a small change will lead to a ripple of other changes, are not part of conventional wisdom.

chised partner feels cheated and resentful, and, whether aware of it or not, usually seeks ways to even the score. The powerful partner gets resentful because he or she has too much responsibility and carries a disproportionate share of the load.

In a relationship with a power disparity, no one wins. Yet the struggle for power underlies virtually every relationship quarrel. There are two common relationship patterns in which power is the key issue.

One involves the dependent partner who needs his partner to do things, but tries to regain the power lost to dependency by criticizing the way those things are done.

IN DEALING WITH A DEPENDENT PARTNER WHO IS RELENTLESSLY CRITICAL:

• Agree in words, but not in action, with criticism.

• Don't explain or defend yourself.

• Interpret your partner's critical message to mean you can stop doing whatever was criticized: "You're right, I am a terrible cook. I'll let you eat prepared frozen food more." Your partner will either stop in his tracks or—even better—refute the criticism himself.

The second power problem is the most common problem we see in troubled relationships. It involves one partner having control in multiple areas—money, decision-making, social life, conversation topics—such that the relationship begins to resemble that of a parent and child, with the powerful partner treating the other like a child. Even when the person in the powerful role, such as a parent, can be very kind and nurturing, the powerless partner can easily feel inferior, helpless, trapped—as well as resentful. Any attempts to speak out against the arrangement will usually sound like the helpless protestations of a child.

IN DEALING WITH A DOMINEERING PARTNER WHO PLAYS A PARENTAL ROLE:

• Do what you want to do—act independently of your partner's expectations.

If criticized, agree you were "wrong" or "misguided," but continue to do what you believe is best.

• Use "constructive payback," in which criticism from your partner is met with your "inadvertent" mistakes and "forgetfulness" (being late, stupid, inefficient) that bother your partner and make your partner's life more difficult. This indirectly expresses your anger and resentment and lets your partner know that he or she can't get away with being abusive.

Communication Problems

Three common communication patterns often make individuals unhappy. The first is lack of communication, in which one partner feels distress concerning the other's unwillingness or inability to talk about things. Unlike most other problems, the roles in this pattern consistently divide along gender lines; most often, the male partner is seen as relatively silent and the female partner distressed about it.

IN DEALING WITH AN UNCOMMUNICATIVE PARTNER:

• Do something that's a noticeable change from your previous strategies. Become less available for conversation and do not try hard to initiate or maintain discussion. Cut it short when it does start. This not only removes but reverses all pressure on the male partner. And it gives the female partner more control. The entire pattern is changing, and the power shifts.

• Interpret silence in a positive way: "We are so close we don't always have to be talking." "I feel good when you're quiet because I know that means everything is all right between us." This negates any power your partner may be expressing through silence.

• Focus less on the relationship and more on satisfying yourself. When you do things for yourself, you need less from others in the way of attention and assurance.

A second common communication problem involves a pattern in which one partner is consistently sad or negative—and verbalizes it—and the other is distressed by the complaints and frustrated in his or her attempts to help. Ordinarily, the complaint has at least some basis in fact—a life circumstance has given the person cause to feel depressed or pessimistic. Unfortunately, most people faced with a chronic complainer become cheerleaders; they assume that encouragement and information of a positive nature will help. But the complainer interprets the cheerleading as lack of understanding. Another losing strategy is ignoring the complaining so that the gates of negativism are never opened. Both strategies wind up intensifying the problem.

IN DEALING WITH A
CHRONIC COMPLAINER:

•Accept, agree, and encourage the complainer's position.

•Encourage complaining rather than trying to avoid it.

•Honestly express any negative opinions you have on the topic being complained about. (Do not express any positive opinions.) Initiate topics of complaint at every opportunity. This gives the complainer the freedom of choice to discuss other issues and positive feelings.

A third communication problem is an accuser-denyer pattern that frequently evolves when one partner accuses the other of lying. Lying may—or may not—actually be involved.

IN DEALING WITH AN ACCUSER:

•Don't explain or defend. This extremely simple solution is effective because the situation doesn't escalate—it's hard to argue with someone who doesn't argue back—and you do not appear guilty by reason of protesting too much. Accusations are often made to get an argument started; if one partner does not go for the bait, the accusation strategy stops working and is eventually dropped.

•Go one step further and reflect the insecurity of the accuser. "You're afraid that I'm having an affair." "You're concerned that you're not attractive to me anymore." "You're feeling insecure about my love for you."

Sex and Jealousy

Key aspects of couples' sex lives have little to do with what happens in bed. Jealousy and trust issues in a relationship are a prime example. Both involve one partner' suspecting that the other isn't being completely loyal or truthful. And in both, the partner who is the object of the jealous feelings or mistrust cannot remove the problem. Many different real or imagined actions can destroy trust, and jealousy certainly isn't the always the result of a real indiscretion. But sometimes it is.

An affair is a very difficult occurrence for a relationship to survive. It is much like surviving the death of a loved one; the relationship as it was before is forever lost. As in coming to grips with a death, the partner who must accept the "loss" needs to grieve, experience, and express the entire range of emotions associated with the affair.

Unfortunately, the partner who had the affair rarely facilitates this grieving process, Rather he or she tries to handle the situation with minimization, avoidance, and indignation, believing that the subject will die if ignored. "It was only sex, not love." "It's over, let's get on with our lives." "It meant nothing to me."

This strategy usually backfires because the other partner, already feeling hurt and angry at the betrayal, now feels dismissed and misunderstood—and brings up the affair even more. Already feeling defensive through guilt, the partner who had the affair gets more defensive ("How long do I have to go on like this?") The mistaken belief that the issue of the affair should be resolved quickly allows this partner to feel wronged, leading greater distance between partners.

IN DEALING WITH A JEALOUS PARTNER:

• Encourage the partner who feels betrayed to express jealous feelings, and listen nondefensively. This allows the affair to be treated as significant; the betrayed partner has no need to emphasize how important and painful an issue it is. And by encouraging discussion of the affair, the agenda of the person who feels betrayed is given priority. This restores some of the lost power and control without necessitating a prolonged power struggle.

•Initiate at every opportunity discussion of actions or situation that provoke jealousy.

•Keep an exceptionally detailed diary of all your daily activities and recite it at length to your partner every day—in a matter-of-fact fashion. This breaks the questioning-defensiveness cycle. The information overload makes it less likely that accusations of giving partial or incomplete data will be made.

Of all the issues that are related to what happens in the bedroom, sexual frequency is the one about which we hear the most complaints. Usually, one partner decides that there is a problem—usually the partner who wants more sex. He or she begins by stating the problem and directly requesting more frequent sex. The verbal response from the partner is usually encouraging ("Okay, let's try to get together more often"), but the behavior frequently remains the same. At this point, the partner who feels deprived pulls out all the stops—adult movies, sexy clothing, candlelight dinners. The partner being pursued feels pressured and backs away further. The pursuer feels unloved and rejected, and may accuse his or her partner of being involved with someone else.

IN DEALING WITH A SEXUALLY
DISINTERESTED PARTNER:

•Remove all pressure to have sex, but increase nonsexual affection.

•Increase the time spent together in mutually enjoyable, nonsexual activities. This helps put sex back in a healthy perspective by focusing on the enjoyable parts of a relationship.

•Become less available for sex, rather than always being ready and eager. This reduces perceived pressure and frees your partner to accept the role of pursuer.

Vanishing Dreams of America's Young Families

The future of today's young parents and their small children is now in great jeopardy. Congress and the President must take immediate steps to ensure that every child has a fair start, a healthy start, and a head start.

MARIAN WRIGHT EDELMAN

Marian Wright Edelman is President of the Children's Defense Fund. This article draws upon her speech of April 14, 1992 delivered to the National Press Club in Washington D.C., and the report, issued jointly by the Children's Defense Fund and Northeastern University's Center for Labor Market Studies, entitled, Vanishing Dreams: The Economic Plight of America's Young Families. *This article and the report on which it is based is under copyright by the Children's Defense Fund, 25 E Street NW, Washington, DC.*

Americans from all walks of life are profoundly anxious—troubled by what they see around them today and even more by what they see ahead. This anxiety, not only about their own futures but also about the nation's future, is manifested in countless ways: in paralyzing economic insecurity; in an emerging politics of rejection, frustration, and rage; in a growing polarization of our society by race and by class; and in an erosion of the sense of responsibility to help the weakest and poorest among us.

But this anxiety about the future is *most* vivid when we watch our own children grow up and try to venture out on their own—struggling to get established as adults in a new job, a new marriage, a new home or a new family.

It's true that young families always have faced an uphill struggle starting out in life. But today's young families have been so battered by economic and social changes over the past two decades that the struggle has taken on a more desperate and often futile quality.

And as parents of my generation watch many of their adult children founder—failing to find steady, decent-paying jobs, unable to support families, shut out of the housing market and often forced to move back home—they know that something has gone terribly wrong. Often they don't know precisely what has happened or why. But they do understand that these young adults and their children may never enjoy the same opportunities or achieve the same standard of living or security that our generation found a couple of decades ago.

Two generations in trouble

Young families with children—those headed by persons under the age of thirty—have been devastated since 1973 by a cycle of falling incomes, increasing family disintegration, and rising poverty. In the process, the foundations for America's young families have been so thoroughly undermined that two complete generations of Americans—today's young parents and their small children—are now in great jeopardy. Figure 1 captures the poverty rates of those two jeopardized generations:

Young families are the crucible for America's future and America's dream. Most children spend at least part of their lives—their youngest and most developmentally vulnerable months and years—in young families. How we treat these families therefore goes a long way toward defining what our nation as a whole will be like twenty, fifty, or even seventy-five years from now.

What has happened to America's young families with children is unprecedented and almost unimaginable.

Figure 1   Poverty Rates of Families With Children,
           By Age of Family Head, 1973, 1979, 1982, 1990

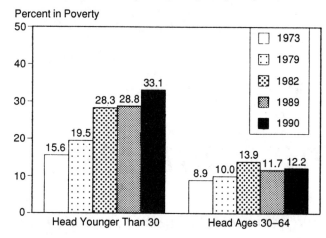

This also is not a story about teenagers. While America's teen pregnancy problem remains tragic and demands an urgent response, only 3 percent of the young families with children we are discussing are headed by teenagers. More than 70 percent are headed by someone aged twenty-five to twenty-nine. The plight of America's young families is overwhelmingly the plight of young adults who are both old enough and eager to assume the responsibilities of parenthood and adulthood, but for whom the road is blocked.

Finally and most importantly, this is *not* simply a story about someone else's children, about minority children or children in single-parent families or children whose parents dropped out of high school.

All young families affected

Huge income losses have affected virtually every group of young families with children: white, black and Latino; married-couple and single-parent; and those headed by high school graduates as well as dropouts. Only young families with children headed by college graduates experienced slight income gains between 1973 and 1990.

In other words, the tragedy facing young families with children has now reached virtually *all* of our young families. One in four *white* children in young families is now poor. One in five children in young *married-couple* families is now poor. And one in three children in families headed by a young *high school graduate* is now poor. Nearly three-fourths of the increase in poverty among young families since 1973 has occurred outside the nation's central cities. And poverty has grown most rapidly among young families with only one child (Figure 2).

There is no refuge from the economic and social shifts that have battered young families with children. We can pretend that they won't reach our children and our grandchildren. We can pretend that those who play by the rules will be O.K.

Adjusted for inflation, the median income of young families with children plunged by one-third between 1973 and 1990 (Table 1). This median income includes income from all sources, and the drop occurred despite the fact that many families sent a second earner into the workforce. As a result, poverty among these young families more than doubled, and by 1990 a shocking 40 percent or four in ten children in young families were poor.

The past two decades have been difficult for many other Americans as well. But older families with children have lost only a little economic ground since 1973, and families without children have enjoyed substantial income gains. By far the greatest share of the nation's economic pain has been focused on the weakest and most vulnerable among us—young families with children.

This is *not* a story about the current recession, although the recession surely is having a crushing impact on young families. Even comparing 1973 to 1989—two good economic years at the end of sustained periods of growth—the median income of young families with children dropped by one-fourth. Then just the first few months of the recession in 1990 sent young families' incomes plummeting to new depths.

Table 1   **Median Incomes of Families With Children By Age of Family Head, 1973–1990**
(in 1990 dollars)*

	1973	1979	1982	1989	1990	Change 1973-1990
All families with children	36,882	36,180	31,819	35,425	34,400	- 6.7%
Family head younger than 30	27,765	25,204	20,378	20,665	18,844	-32.1%
Family head age 30–64	41,068	39,978	35,293	39,525	38,451	- 6.4%
Young families' median income as a share of older families' income	68%	63%	58%	52%	49%	

Note: The money incomes of families for all years prior to 1990 were converted into 1990 dollars via use of the Consumer Price Index for All Urban Consumers (CPI-U). The U.S. Bureau of Labor Statistics has generated an alternative price index for the years preceding 1983 that conforms to the current method of measuring changes in housing costs. This index is known as the CPI-UXI. Use of this price index would reduce the estimated 1973 real income by about 7 percent, thus lowering the estimated decline in the median income of young families between 1973 and 1990 from 32 percent to approximately 25 percent. None of the comparisons of median income between various groups of families are affected by these changes.

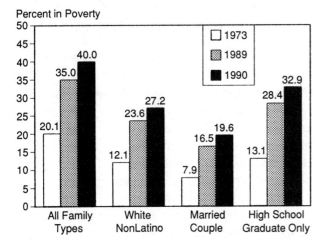

Figure 2   **Poverty Rates
of Children in Young Families,
By Characteristics of the Family Head, 1973, 1989, 1990**

We can pretend, but that will not change the reality—the reality that young families have lost a third of their median income, that two in five American children in young families live in poverty, and that these facts have devastating consequences.

Those consequences include more hunger, more homelessness, more low birthweight births, more infant deaths and more child disability. They also mean more substance abuse, more crime, more violence, more school failure, more teen pregnancy, more racial tension, more envy, more despair and more cynicism—a long-term economic and social disaster for young families and for the country. In virtually every critical area of child development and healthy maturation, family poverty creates huge roadblocks to individual accomplishment, future economic self-sufficiency, and national progress.

Plummeting incomes and soaring poverty and growing gaps based on age and education and race mean more of all these problems, yet many of our leaders seem not to understand why they are occurring. But there is not really a puzzle, when we recognize that the nation has marginalized and pauperized much of two generations of Americans—young parents and young children.

Young families not only lost income in huge amounts, but as the permanence and quality of their jobs deteriorated, they lost fringe benefits like health insurance as well. In the decade of the 1980s the proportion of *employed* heads of young families with children whose employers made health insurance available by paying all or part of the cost dropped by one-fifth. And employers cut back on coverage for dependent spouses and children even more than for workers.

Fewer and fewer young pregnant women have been getting adequate prenatal care because they are poorer and less likely to have adequate insurance or any insur-

ance. And our falling vaccination rates and renewed epidemics of measles and other wholly preventable diseases among preschoolers are being driven by plunging incomes in young families, eroding health insurance coverage, and unraveling government programs.

Falling incomes also have devastated young families in an increasingly expensive housing market. One-third fewer young families with children were homeowners in 1991 than in 1980. Young renter families increasingly are paying astronomical shares of their meager incomes for rent. More and more are doubling up or becoming homeless—in some surveys three-fourths of the homeless parents in this country are under age thirty.

Young families are not only suffering from the hunger, housing, health and other problems that their plummeting incomes have caused. They are suffering as well because they are falling further and further behind the rest of the society—imperiling their attachment to the core work force and to mainstream values and threatening their potential to reacquire the American dream in the decades to come.

In 1973 the income of older families with children was not quite one-and-a-half times that of young families with children. By 1990 it was more than double that of the young families.

Combination of causes

There is no single cause of young families' plight. Instead, they have been pummelled by a combination of profound changes in the American economy; the government's inadequate response to families in trouble; and changes in the composition of young families themselves.

Much of the increase in their poverty is due to economic shifts and to changing government policies that have made it more difficult for young families to obtain adequate incomes. These changes have hurt all young families with children, regardless of their family structure, race or ethnicity, or educational attainment.

Unlike members of earlier generations, young workers today no longer can be confident of finding stable jobs with decent wages, even if they get a high school diploma or spend a couple of years in college. Since 1973, slower growth in U.S. productivity and declines in blue collar employment made some drop in inflation-adjusted median earnings for young workers inevitable. By last year the average wages of *all* nonsupervisory workers (of all ages) in the private sector fell to their lowest level since the Eisenhower Administration.

But the losses have been focused disproportionately on young workers. The median annual earnings of heads of young families with children fell a staggering 44 percent from 1973 to 1990. In other words, in the span of less than a generation this nation nearly *halved* the earnings of young household heads with children (Table 2):

These dramatic earnings losses occurred across-the-board. For example, young white families with children were hit as hard as young Latino families: the median earnings of both groups fell by two-fifths. College graduates as well as high school graduates and dropouts lost big chunks of income. But the drop in median earnings for high school dropouts and for young black family heads has been particularly devastating—in each case more than two-thirds.

Table 2	**Median Annual Earnings of Heads of Young Families With Children, 1973 and 1990** (in 1990 dollars)		
	1973	1990	% Change 1973-1990
All heads of young families with children	22,981	12,832	-44
Married couple	25,907	17,500	-33
Male-headed	18,547	14,000	-25
Female-headed	2,073	1,878	- 9
White, non-Latino	25,024	15,000	-40
Black, non-Latino	13,860	4,030	-71
Latino	15,924	9,000	-44
Other, non-Latino	17,664	12,000	-32
High school dropout	15,014	4,500	-70
High school graduate	23,817	14,000	-41
Some college	26,496	18,000	-32
College graduate	31,795	25,721	-19

The erosion in pay levels (due in part to the declining value of the minimum wage) combined with the growth of temporary or part-time and part-year jobs to put a triple whammy on young workers: far lower annual earnings; less secure employment; and less access to health insurance and other employer-provided benefits.

The huge drop in earnings among America's young workers has not received much attention. In part it has been obscured by the almost Herculean work effort of young parents. Many young married-couple families have tried to compensate for lower wages by sending a second worker into the work force. These second earners have softened (but not eliminated) the economic blow. But the growing number of young parents working longer hours or coping with two jobs has placed young families with children under tremendous stress and generated new offsetting costs, especially for child care. Many families, moreover, have two jobs that together provide less security and less support and less access to health care than one good job did a generation ago. This two-earner strategy is totally unavailable, moreover, to the growing number of single-parent families.

Economic shifts and family changes

Today's young families with children look considerably different from those in the early 1970s. They are more likely to be minority families or single parent families. Both groups are more likely to be paid low wages and to be poor than other families. So poverty among young families and children as a whole also rises.

The growth in young female-headed families with children is in part a reflection of changing values. But the economic hardships associated with falling earnings and persistent joblessness among young adults have contributed significantly to falling marriage rates and the increasing rates of out-of-wedlock childbearing. And the fastest growth in out-of-wedlock childbearing has occurred among women in their twenties, not among teenagers, a growth driven in significant part by the earnings free-fall for young adults.

The capacity to support a family has a powerful impact on the marriage decisions of young people. More than two centuries ago Benjamin Franklin wrote: ''The number of marriages. . .is greater in proportion to the ease and convenience of supporting a family. When families can be easily supported, more persons marry, and earlier in life.''

Increases in poverty among young families with children are *not* the result of young Americans having more children. Indeed, young adults have responded to a tightening economic vise by postponing childbearing and choosing to have fewer children. But these attempts to adapt their behavior have been overwhelmed by the far more rapid pace of economic decline and social disintegration they have encountered.

As a result of these economic and social changes, in 1990 a child in a family headed by a parent under age 30 was:

• twice as likely to be poor as a comparable child in 1973;

• if living with both parents, two and a half times as likely to be poor as in 1973;

• nearly three times more likely to have been born out-of-wedlock than his counterpart two decades ago;

• one-third less likely to be living in a home owned by her family than just a decade ago; and

• three times more likely to see his family pay more than one-half its income for rent.

But despite the devastating suffering these numbers

suggest, children in young families have been given less and less government help over the last two decades. They were getting less to begin with—government programs are particularly stingy when it comes to helping younger adults and young children. And in the 1970s and especially the 1980s young families saw programs that might help them cut rather than strengthened and reconfigured to adapt to new realities. As a result, government programs were less than half as effective in pulling young families out of poverty in 1990 as in 1979.

Hard hit minority families

The changes of the last two decades have had a very profound impact on minority young families, especially those that are black. As Table 2 shows, the median earnings of the heads of young black families with children fell *71 percent* from 1973 to 1990 (from $13,860 to $4,030 in 1990 dollars). Their total family incomes from all sources fell 48 percent. The *median* income of these young black families is now below the federal poverty line for a family of three. In 1973 it was nearly double that poverty line. *Two out of three* children in young black families now are poor.

This crisis for young black families is contributing mightily to the tearing apart of the black community. This society cannot year after year increase the poverty and isolation and hopelessness of black mothers and fathers and children—it can't keep turning the screws tighter and tighter—without appalling consequences. We see those consequences in the emergency rooms and unemployment lines and prisons and homeless shelters and neonatal intensive care wards and morgues of our cities and our suburbs and rural towns. We see it in the omnipresent violence that destroys so many black lives and leaves blacks and whites alike so fearful. More blacks die from firearms each year in this country than died in the century's worth of despicable lynchings that followed the Civil War. More black men die from firearms every six weeks in Detroit than died in the 1967 Detroit ''riot.'' More black and Hispanic men die from firearms in Los Angeles every two weeks than died in the 1965 Watts ''riot.'' [*Editor's note*: This speech was given two weeks before the most recent outbreak of violence in Los Angeles.]

Frankly, though, I would be skeptical that this nation would attack this cataclysm for young black families were it not for the fact that young *white* families are only a step or two behind in the scope of their economic depression and family disintegration. Perhaps the most important story told in this report is the impact of two decades of this Depression for the young on three types of families we often assume are insulated from hard times:

• From 1973 to 1990 the poverty rate for children living in young *white* families more than doubled to *27 percent*.

• From 1973 to 1990 the poverty rate for children in young *married-couple* families went up two-and-a-half times—to *20 percent*.

• And the child poverty rate in young families headed by *high school graduates* went up even faster, to *33 percent*.

In other words, a generation ago white or married-couple young families or those headed by high school graduates were fairly well insulated from poverty. The damage of the last two decades has cut so broadly and deeply that now one in four white children in young families, one in five children in married-couple young families, and one in three children in families headed by young high school graduates is poor.

Private and public response

What response do we see to these problems from private and public leadership? Precious little.

Too much of the business community is wholly untroubled by stripping away from millions of Americans the minimum family-supporting wages, fringe benefits, and job security that could help make our families strong again. The Administration has no higher domestic priority than cutting capital gains taxes for the rich. The Congress and the Administration together persist in keeping defense spending above the levels of the average year in the Cold War—impoverishing our society and the world by arming ourselves not only against real external threats but against weapons-justifying fantasies, while letting the internal enemies of poverty, disintegration, violence, and hopelessness rage unabated. The Congress can't mount the political will to get Head Start—a program universally conceded to be effective and cost-effective—to more than one in three eligible children or to pass the refundable children's tax credit that experts from all parts of the political spectrum think is a minimum first step to tax equity and family economic security.

Finally, far too many of the nation's Governors and state and national legislators have responded to budget crunches and political turmoil by scapegoating the poor—trying to bolster their political fortunes by pummeling the welfare recipients whose assistance gobbles up a grand total of 2 to 3 percent of state budgets.

In hard times in the past our society usually has had escape valves—an inherent balance that gave to the powerless help from one institution when others turned their backs—from the federal government when the states were at their worst, from the courts when Congress and the executive were unresponsive. Now we seem to be in an awful time when every institution is competing to pander to the powerful and further penalize the poor.

A fair start

In response to the economic plight of America's young families, Congress and the President must take three immediate steps in 1992 to ensure that every child has a *fair* start, a *healthy* start, and a *head* start.

A *fair start* means renewed and sustained economic growth and enough jobs at decent wages to restore the pact our nation used to have with young families—that personal sacrifice and hard work will be rewarded with family suppporting jobs. A fair start also means enactment of a refundable children's tax credit to bolster the incomes of families with children, as proposed in recent months in various forms and amounts by the National Commission on Children and key members of Congress from both parties. Such a credit would reduce federal income taxes for middle- and low-income families and help the lowest income families that have no tax liability through a tax refund.

While creating no new bureaucracies, a refundable children's credit would target tax relief and economic support precisely to the group—families with children—that has been hardest hit by declining incomes and rising poverty rates since 1973. The Administration's alternative proposal—to expand the personal exemption for children—is extremely regressive. It gives $310 to a family with two children if their income exceeds about $100,000; $280 if it is over $50,000; $150 if income is between $15,000 and $50,000; and zero if it is under about $15,000.

Finally, a fair start means creation of a child support insurance system to give all single parents the chance to lift their families out of poverty through work, ensuring that all children who are not living with both parents receive a minimally adequate child support payment from the absent parent or the government when it fails to collect from the absent parent.

What we *don't* need in this time of great crisis for young families with children is a negative approach rooted in welfare-bashing and welfare cuts that ends up hurting children. Families on welfare are the victims of the recession, not the cause of it. They are victims of

budget deficits, not the cause of them. But nearly one-fourth of all young families with children are forced to rely upon Aid for Families with Dependent Children (AFDC) to meet their basic needs, and they are extremely vulnerable to misguided attacks on this essential safety net for children.

Our political leaders know these truths. Yet during an election year too many cannot resist the temptation to direct the public's frustration and anger toward the poorest of poor Americans—those families and children who rely upon welfare for basic income support.

There *are* ways we can and must improve welfare. For example, we agree with the Administration that welfare parents often don't have enough financial incentive to work because current welfare rules strip them of virtually all of their earnings when they do work. That is why we opposed the repeal of earnings incentives by President Reagan and the Congress in 1981, and why we think they should be restored now for all welfare families, not just those in a few demonstration counties.

But most of the welfare ''reforms'' now underway in states are little more than crass attempts to slash state budgets without regard to their impact on families with children. Reducing or stopping benefits to newborns when they are the second or third child in a family, as now proposed by several states, is punitive, pointless, and immoral. Only political leaders who are hopelessly out of touch with the realities of poor families' lives could think that an extra $2.50 per day in welfare benefits would cause teen parents to have a second child, or that reducing the added benefit to $1.25/day (as the Governor of Wisconsin and the President now propose for that state) constitutes any serious effort at welfare reform. All they will succeed in doing is taking desperately needed food, clothing and shelter from infants.

It's time for the President, Congress, and more of our Governors to be honest with the American people about the problems facing our economy, our poor families and our children.

The problem is *not* large numbers of welfare parents trying to ''beat the system'' by having more children or moving to another state to get higher benefits. The problem is a set of short-sighted, budget-driven welfare rules that make it virtually impossible for parents to work their way gradually off the welfare rolls and a dearth of stable, family-supporting jobs that would allow them to make it on their own.

In many ways, the welfare problem is the same problem facing all young families with children—the result of sharply falling wages, too few job opportunities for those with little education or training, and too little investment in the skills and supports poor parents need to make it in today's economy. And serious solutions begin with a fair start, a healthy start, and a head start for our young families.

A healthy start, a head start

A *healthy start* means a national health plan to assure insurance coverage for all Americans. Children and pregnant women need basic health care *now*, however. As an immediate step, the president and Congress must extend Medicaid coverage to every low-income child and pregnant woman. And to ensure that this insurance provides real access to essential health services, not merely theoretical coverage, children need universal access to vaccines and increased funding for community health centers, and other public health activities.

A *head start* means full funding of Head Start. A first step in bolstering the productivity of our next generation of workers lies in adequate investments in quality child care and early childhood development. Every dollar invested in good early childhood development programs saves $5.97 in later special education, welfare, crime, and other costs. Yet Head Start still reaches only one in three eligible preschool children.

As recommended by prominent business groups, educators, and a broad range of study commissions that have examined the educational problems of disadvantaged children and youths, the president and Congress should ensure every child a Head Start by 1995 by enacting immediately S. 911, the School Readiness Act, and accelerating the funding increases it provides.

A head start also means passing family preservation legislation that will strengthen and preserve families in crisis so that they can better protect, nurture and support their own children. So many of these young parents want to be better parents, and with intensive family preservation services they can get the help they need.

These are essential first steps. To reach them and go beyond them, we're going to have to make the President and Congress come to recognize that child and family poverty and insecurity are a national disaster that requires our addressing them with a pittance of the zeal and shared commitment we now apply to digging out after a devastating hurricane or earthquake or confronting a crisis abroad.

When Parents Disagree

Two partners, two approaches to discipline—here's how to make it work.

Nancy Samalin with Patricia McCormick

Nancy Samalin is the author of Loving Your Child Is Not Enough *(Penguin) and* Love and Anger: The Parental Dilemma *(Viking).*

Patricia McCormick is an associate editor at Parents *Magazine.*

If you and your spouse have been married long enough to have a child, then you probably already know how to negotiate the finer points of squeezing the toothpaste and finding where to put the dirty socks. You may even successfully manage having a joint checking account with two cash cards.

Enter one small child and that hard-won harmony is threatened. "Honey, you know one soda is the limit," you might tell your child. To which your spouse replies, "Ah, let her have another one." To which your child responds, "Pleease, Mom. Dad says I can." At which point you do something very mature, such as putting your hands on your hips, rolling your eyes, and saying "Fine, then *you* take her to the dentist for the next appointment."

Meanwhile, in the rational part of your brain, there is the voice of an "expert" reminding you that parents should always present a united front when disciplining their children.

All spouses disagree. The key is to respect each other's differences and to fight fair.

As commendable a goal as that may be, it isn't always possible. All spouses disagree; they were brought up in two different households by different parents. When a child comes along, an occasional clash of opinions is inevitable.

A more realistic goal would be to accept the fact that you will have disagreements with your spouse over discipline; you will even, on occasion, fight in front of your children. The key is to respect each other's differences and to fight fair when you fight.

It is 3:00 A.M. Two-year-old Sam is awake—as he has been every night for the past two weeks—crying. Cathy, his mother, wearily throws off the covers and gets up. "Why don't you just let him cry it out?" says Andrew, her husband.

"You know you're just reinforcing this whole crying thing by going in there and rocking him back to sleep every night. I think you're spoiling him," he adds.

"You just don't understand," Cathy replies. "He must be scared or lonely. I think you're too tough on him."

Mr. Softy vs. Mrs. Bad Guy.
Because we are not carbon copies of our mates, we often have different takes on the same situation. If, for instance, your spouse was brought up in a strict home, he or she may be most comfortable with a firm approach to discipline.

If you were raised in a more relaxed environment, you may feel comfortable using an easygoing approach—or the reverse might be true.

The seeds of conflict—planted long ago—are ready to flower with your child's first midnight squall.

The art of compromise.
Instead of trying to present a united front that is sure to crumble, try to accept your differences. When you and your spouse have some time alone, discuss the situations that have put you at odds with each other. You will soon find that one parent has stronger feelings than the other over certain issues—junk food, bedtimes, or homework.

In the interest of harmony, you and your spouse might agree to abide by the wishes of the person whose feelings are stronger. If, for instance, you are strenuously opposed to spanking and your spouse is neutral about it, both parents should agree not to spank. Or, if your spouse wants to take a firm line on junk food, you could agree to go along with his wishes when that issue comes up.

The next step would be for both of you to agree that one parent (usually the one with the stronger feelings) will deal with the child on that issue and the other will stay on the sidelines. And, most important, you should agree to back each other up. This means that you won't intervene when your spouse is carrying out a policy that you may not like but have agreed to abide by.

For example, Cathy might tell Andrew, "I wish I felt as comfortable as you do about letting him cry, because if I did, I'd go back to sleep too. But I can't listen to him cry, so I'm going to get up. I'm not going to try to make you get up, though, because I know that you don't believe in it."

For his part, Andrew might pledge not to interfere or to criticize Cathy. Although this approach will work, it's not always easy; compromise often takes effort and restraint.

The gentle art of compromise works well when you have had a chance to come up with a party line in advance. But it is also an effective policy when a divisive discipline issue crops up without warning. If, for example, your child's request for a second soda triggers a strong reaction in you, you may want to tell your spouse, "I really don't want her to have another soda. I'd like to handle this one."

Hopefully your spouse will oblige and let you manage the situation. It would be even better if he supported you by telling your child, "This is between you and Mommy."

Naturally there will be times when you will feel too angry to handle a disciplinary issue effectively. Such instances would be a good time to say, "I'm too upset about this; will you handle it?" On the other hand, if you are lukewarm about an issue but your spouse is not, you might want to say, "I really don't feel too strongly about this. Why don't you handle it?" or, "You'd probably prefer to handle this since you obviously have strong feelings about it."

You may sometimes find that no matter how accommodating you and your partner try to be, there are situations in which you are still at loggerheads. You may never be able to convince each other of the merits of your different approaches.

Unless disciplining becomes damaging or abusive, resist the urge to lecture or to try to reform each other. (It won't work anyway.) If you really want to win your partner over, try demonstrating your approach. The next time a divisive issue comes up, tell your spouse that you'd like to try to handle it your way, and let him see the results. (No gloating allowed!)

Divide and conquer.

Ann is busily raking leaves while Joe, her husband, is inside paying the bills. Four-year-old Kate makes a beeline across the front yard and dives into Ann's neatly raked pile. "Don't jump in the leaves, Kate," she says.

Ground Rules For Fighting Fair

● Avoid name-calling and sarcasm. Comments such as "How stupid can you be?" and "Oh, great. I married a real genius" are not conducive to compromise or harmony.
● Try not to lapse into angry silences. They don't bring you any closer to a resolution and can be scary for children to observe.
● Try not to use words such as "always" and "never," as in "You always let him have his way" and "You never back me up when I'm disciplining him."
● Try not to "futurize" by saying things such as, "If you keep letting him eat all that junk food, he's going to be the size of a barn."
● Give yourself time to cool off before you approach your spouse about his or disciplinary techniques.
● Reassure your children that your disagreements are not their fault.
—N.S. and P.M.

Children need not be shielded from everyday conflicts. They can learn a lot from how parents resolve disagreements.

"I'm trying to gather them, not scatter them." Kate begs her to change her mind, to no avail.

Kate stomps away into the house. "Dad, can I jump in the leaves?"

Joe, in the middle of adding up a long string of figures, responds without looking up. "Sure," he says absentmindedly. Kate flies out the door and into the pile of leaves.

Her mother, who had just repaired the damage from Kate's first dive into the leaves, yanks her off the ground. "I told you not to jump in the leaves," she says.

"You're so mean! Dad said I could," Kate whines.

There are two rules for family living that can prevent this kind of situation. For children: If one parent says no, it is not acceptable to go to the other one on appeal. The corollary rule for parents: If one parent says no, the other must agree to back him or her up. It is not acceptable to undermine your spouse's decision.

In this example, Joe was an innocent participant in Kate's divide-and-conquer strategy. But children often take advantage of one parent's tendency to say yes when the other has already said no.

Although this strategy can be effective in the short run—Kate got her wish, to jump in the leaves—children need to understand that ultimately it will backfire, that they will get caught when they try to make an end run around one parent. If the child succeeds in igniting fireworks between her parents, the attention is diverted from her misdeed and she has achieved her goal.

To avoid a similar occurrence in the future, Ann might tell Kate, "Daddy and I know that you went behind my back to get him to go along with your wishes, and we don't like it." Joe could add, "When your mother says no, I don't want you to ask me for something that you know she doesn't want you to do." They could then tell Kate that she has to help rake up the scattered leaves.

Another method children use to divide and conquer is to complain to one parent about the other. "Mom was mean to me," so goes the lament. "She made me go to bed when I wasn't tired, and she told me that I couldn't read." How tempting it is to be the nice, understanding parent and come to your poor, "wronged" child's rescue by telling your spouse something along the lines of, "I think you were too hard on Julie. You hurt her feelings." The parents end up pitted against each other, and the spotlight is deflected from whatever Julie did in the first place that prompted Mom to issue such an order.

A more effective and just approach might be to say, "I think you should tell Mom that you're mad at her." If your child says that Mom won't listen, you can encourage her to work out the dispute. "It's between you and your mother—not you and me. I'm sure you can talk to her."

Fight fair.

Ben, three, is in the midst of a full-blown tantrum while the entire extended family, gathered for a family reunion, looks on. "Make him stop," says Paul, his father.

"*You* handle it," replies Jane. "You started it by telling him that he had to take a nap. That was a brilliant move when all of his cousins were going outside to play."

Paul's frown turns into a scowl. "*You're* the expert. *You're* the one reading all the child-rearing books. *You* handle it."

The above scene is understandable; however, it's not good for either the child or the marriage. Although it is very tempting to blame your partner when something goes wrong, this sends kids the message that they are responsible for their parents' disagreements.

What We Fight About

What's there to fight about? Plenty. Here are some common grounds for disagreement between even harmonious couples:

- Junk food
- Bedtimes
- Homework
- Spanking and other punishments
- Mealtime behavior
- Public misbehavior
- Neatness
- Sibling disputes
- Dealing with "the gimmes"
- Allowances
- Chores
- Forgetfulness
- Television

If you feel your temper beginning to rise when your spouse disagrees on how to handle one of these issues, take five. Tell your spouse that you feel strongly about the situation and want to handle it without his or her involvement. Likewise, if your spouse feels strongly and you don't, then step aside. **—N.S. and P.M.**

If you and your spouse can manage to fight fair, your children can learn from such everyday arguments. When they see you argue and then resolve the disagreement, they learn that it is possible to become angry with someone you love and to reconcile your differences.

Fighting about everyday issues is a normal part of home life. Children do not need to be shielded from these conflicts; indeed, they can actually learn a lot from how you and your spouse arrive at an agreeable resolution. But discussions about larger, more divisive issues, such as sex, money, and relatives, are better handled in private. It may also be better to wait and discuss especially difficult situations after the smoke has cleared from the immediate battle.

It takes enormous self-control to hold your tongue when you see your spouse handling a disciplinary matter in a way that bothers you. Later on you can acknowledge how difficult the situation was by saying something like, "I know how frustrating it can be when Julie fights going to bed. I didn't want to interfere, but I don't think threats are the best way to handle this situation. Let's talk about another approach."

If, however, you lose your cool and you and your spouse have a noisy brawl that is witnessed or overheard by your children, you need to reassure them, after you've cooled off, that everything is okay. Tell them that you and your spouse are no longer angry at each other. Reassure them that, yes, it can be frightening to hear their parents lose their temper and fight but that it's okay because they can work things out and make up.

TEN WORST DISCIPLINE MISTAKES PARENTS MAKE . . . AND ALTERNATIVES

James Windell

Bottom Line/Personal interviewed James Windell, a psychotherapist specializing in family problems, and a clinical psychologist for the Oakland County, Michigan, juvenile court's psychological clinic. He is the author of *Discipline: A Sourcebook of 50 Failsafe Techniques for Parents*, Collier Books, 866 Third Ave., New York 10022. $10.

Most good parents realize that there is always much more for them to learn about being good parents.

In a perfect world, parents would all have boundless energy, patience, tolerance, understanding and flexibility. But no one is perfect. So it also helps to have a wide variety of practical skills. *Some alternatives to common mistakes parents make when disciplining their children:*

YELLING

1 Yelling may be an effective way to vent frustration, but most children of "frequent yellers" soon learn to tune it out. *Result:* The behavior does not change and kids grow hostile. *Better:* Stop. Ask yourself how *you* would like being yelled at.

You may have to delay action until your anger is under control. Most children respond better to a calm, reasonable request or command. Save yelling for emergency situations when you really need to get your child's attention: *Look out for that car!*

DEMANDING IMMEDIATE COMPLIANCE

2 People don't respond well to demands to *Do it right now!* because it shows disrespect. Commands to *Come here this in-* stant! or *Stop that this second!* are often ignored and tuned out. *Better:* Make a respectful or firm request…and praise and reward good behavior.

Example: When your child gets ready for bed without a fuss, tell him/her, *You got into your pajamas so nicely, I'm going to read you an* extra *story tonight.*

NAGGING

3 Nagging is often a problem for parents who try to be lenient or permissive. They don't want to get angry but are constantly asking, *Did you clean your room yet?* until they explode. *Better:* Get the child's full attention.

Example: Stand in front of the TV screen rather than calling from another room. Make firm, consistent requests with clear limits.

Helpful: Praise and reward a first-time response. If needed, give a warning…*Lunch is in 20 minutes.* Impose a negative consequence if the task is not completed. *If the garbage is still here, there will be no TV after your homework.*

LECTURING AND ADVICE-GIVING

4 Lecturing is fruitless. People have a limited attention span for monologues that involve no interaction. And lectures often do not address the problem.

Example: Lecturing a child whose homework is chronically late about the value of an education does not address the homework issue.

Better: Ask questions. *What happens when you do your homework? What do you do first? Is there a part that you don't understand?*

Advice is not fruitless, but it is often given when it is not wanted or at the wrong time.

Example: An anxious child who has brought home a poor report card will not be receptive to advice. *Strategy:* Reduce the anxiety. *I see you're upset by this. Let's both think of some ways to help your grades, and we'll talk about it after dinner.*

Other alternatives: Role-playing. *I'll be you, and you'll be your teacher.* Teach a coping strategy. *Would you like to know a good way to handle that?* Learn to use informal opportunities to teach a lesson or make a point.

TAKING ANGER OUT ON KIDS

5 Overreaction and inappropriate anger are extremely common in our high-stress society. *Tip-off:* Similar incidents in the past did not previously provoke the same angry response. *Problem:* You may say things that stick with your kids for a long time. *Effect:* Kids are hurt, confused. *If you overreact:* Offer your kids a heartfelt apology, along with an explanation. *Result:* Kids learn to talk about feelings and understand human fallibility.

Recommended: If you blow up at your kids often, tend to your own needs. Go to the gym—or for a walk—before coming home. Take quiet time, find a support network.

SHAMING AND BELITTLING

6 Parents often don't realize they make remarks that cause their children to feel smaller, inadequate, less intelligent or more insecure.

Examples: Why are you acting like such a baby?...That's the dumbest thing you ever said....If you can't behave, I'm leaving forever.

Better: Monitor your language and be aware how often you say positive, versus negative, things. Make sure you are dealing adequately with your own feelings so they don't spill over onto your kids.

SETTING TRAPS

7 Parents who tend to be punitive and authoritarian often try to catch their children in a lie to prove a point.

Example: You find a note in your child's room that refers to a friend's smoking. A trap-setter says, *Do you or your friends smoke? No? What about this note?* As a result, you have a defensive child who learns to lie, conceal and mistrust parents.

Better: Straightforward, trusting inquiry. *I found this note in your room that*

concerns me. Can we talk about it? Not everything children write is true.

IMPOSING EXCESSIVE GUILT

8 Parents who were raised in dysfunctional families often make the mistake of implying their children are responsible for the circumstances of the parent's life.

Examples: Why do you always upset your father?...I devoted my life to you, and now...If you loved me, you'd do this. The child comes to feel responsible for the problems of the world. *Better:* Examine your own codependent relationships with your parents, spouse and others, with a therapist, support group or counselor.

PHYSICAL PUNISHMENT

9 The purpose of discipline—from *disciple,* a student or follower—is to teach the child to have self-discipline.

This is never accomplished by physical force. *Trap:* Parents who hit or physically punish their children instill hostility and resentment rather than respect. *Outcome:* Usually the behavior is not prevented from recurring, and great damage is done to the parent-child relationship.

Physical punishment tends to repeat in families. If you frequently lose control or routinely hit children as a method of discipline, examine your own childhood. Parents who regularly strike their children in frustration or anger usually lack alternative skills, and often have unrealistic expectations of their children at different ages.

Recommended: Get developmental information on normal child or teen behaviors, and improve parenting skills through many books, magazines, videotapes, support groups, workshops and other widely available resources.

COERCION

10 This is the use of physical force to get the child to do what you want.

Example: Pushing or dragging a frightened child into the doctor's office.

The parent is asserting a need for control rather than responding to the child's feelings. *Result:* The child resists.

Better: Help the child express his feelings: *Is there something scary in the doctor's office?*

Give the child a choice: *Do you want me to hold your hand, or do you want to go in by yourself?* This gives the child a sense of control over the situation, but leaves no question that the child is going into the office.

Of Super Dads, And Absent Ones

Marilyn Gardner

Staff writer of The Christian Science Monitor

CUMBERLAND CENTER, MAINE
At 8:30 every weekday morning, Stephen Harris begins a routine unfamiliar to most men. After his five-year-old son, Ben, leaves for kindergarten and his wife, Alison, heads for her job as editor of a computer magazine in Yarmouth, Mr. Harris settles down to play with 2-1/2-year-old Robin. Two mornings a week he also cares for a neighbor's son.

When Ben returns from school at noon, Harris prepares lunch for the children. Then, after Robin's nap, the afternoon brings what he describes as "more of the same"—playing games, reading stories, and getting together with neighborhood children.

Harris represents a new kind of parent—the full-time father. As the primary care giver, he knows first-hand the rewards a growing number of men are finding in establishing close relationships with their children. So committed is he to these changing roles that he edits and publishes a small bimonthly journal called Full-Time Dads.

"We decided when we first got married that when we had kids, if we could afford it, one of us would stay home," explains Harris, a former photo assistant and restaurant cook. "Alison is more career-oriented than I am."

Two stereotypes dominate media images of modern fatherhood. At one extreme is the new nurturing father—the man who, though usually not as involved as Harris, still plays a far greater role in

Editor's note: This article is the first of a 3-part series. See October 12, 1993 and October 14, 1993, *Christian Science Monitor* issues for Parts 2 and 3.

his children's lives than his own father played in his. He changes diapers. He backpacks babies. He picks up toddlers at the day-care center. Signs of these family-oriented men are everywhere, from the presence of changing tables in airport men's rooms to the proliferation of parenting classes for men.

For all the fanfare given these nurturing fathers, the role is not altogether new. James Levine, director of the Fatherhood Project at the Families and Work Institute in New York, says, "It's actually a return to something that was more prevalent in the 18th century," before the Industrial Revolution.

'DEADBEAT DADS' STEREOTYPE

At the opposite extreme is a darker stereotype—the "deadbeat dad" who often has little involvement, financial or emotional, with his children. Through news coverage of police roundups of delinquent fathers and "10 Most Wanted Dads" lists, these absent fathers have been widely portrayed, not always justly, as uncaring.

The problem of paternal nonsupport cannot be underestimated, of course. As a consequence of divorce, separation, and single parenthood, 15 million American children are growing up in largely fatherless homes. Ten million of those result from divorce and separation. Another five million are out-of-wedlock children, who account for 28 percent of all births.

Modern fathers have been made to seem even more superfluous by reproductive techniques that enable women to become pregnant without men, and by media images of single career women choosing to rear children on their own.

Even so, the number of men actively involved in rearing children continues to grow. Census Bureau data released in September show that fathers now care for 1 in every 5 preschool children while mothers work, up from 1 in 7 three years ago. This reflects what Mr. Levine calls "the beginning of a new stage of awareness about fathers as critical forces and contributors to family life."

For too long, Levine observes, attitudes about fathers have operated on a "deficit model," which holds that men aren't involved with their families and that it isn't possible to get them involved. Now, he says, "There's a major opportunity to get them involved."

Neil Tift, co-founder and director of the Fathers' Resource Center in Minneapolis, a two-year-old nonprofit organization, sums up the shift by saying, "Fathers are moving from being disciplinarians and breadwinners to wanting to be co-parents." That co-parenting begins early. Ninety percent of fathers now attend the births of their children, Mr. Tift notes, compared with only 10 percent in 1975.

Seated in the living room of his Colonial home, Harris, a friendly, easygoing man, reflects on these changing paternal roles as Ben plays with Hot Wheels and Robin scribbles on drawing paper.

"This is a period of transition, both for men individually and the family in general," he says. But, he emphasizes, men's greater involvement does not mean an androgynous approach to parenthood. "Mothers and fathers bring very different things to the family. A man can't be a mother."

Even when fathers want to increase their participation, many find themselves with few mentors. Charlie Kundinger, president of his own home-remodeling company in Minneapolis and the father

MEN FACE DISCRIMINATION AS CARE GIVERS

BOSTON

The long list of double standards that vex society includes a gender bias that assumes a father is the parent to be trusted less.

When Eric Nichols, a professor of human development at the University of Vermont in Burlington, conducts public workshops on fathering, he offers advice to women: "I say to mothers, 'If you want your husband to father, then get out of the way and let him father.' For so long, women have been the primary parents that they find it difficult to let go and let men father. I call it 'gatekeeping.' "

"Let's say Mom has gone out for the evening," Dr. Nichols continues. "What do we call what Dad does? Baby-sitting. Isn't it strange we use this term? We don't say mothers are baby-sitting. Then when Mom comes home, what kind of questions does she ask? 'Did you feed them hot dogs again? Did they have a bath? Did they brush their teeth? Did you put them to bed on time?' If we multiply that situation time and time again, is it any wonder dads don't feel competent?"

To change attitudes in the long run, he says, "We must start with young children." We need to provide young boys and adolescent boys with opportunities to care for children, he says, and to foster their nurturing instincts.

Doing that requires giving children positive images of men as nurturers. Neil Tift, co-founder of the Fathers' Resource Center in Minneapolis, wrote to five large publishers of children's books. "We asked them to send us any books that encourage boys to see themselves as fathers someday," the same way some books encourage girls to be mothers.

Four publishers wrote back that they didn't publish any such books. The fifth publisher never responded.

Mr. Tift points out another double standard: In the United States, a Girl Scout can get a service badge for child care. But Boy Scouts cannot earn such a merit badge. "It's no longer appropriate to limit child-care skill development to girls," he says.

Who is delaying progress? "I don't think either men or women are the bad guys in this," Nichols says. "It's very scary for men and women to make role changes. Even though we say we'd like things to be different, when it really comes down to it, as men and women we cooperate to keep the status quo. We need to look at the ways we do that and keep working for change."

—M. G.

---

of three children in elementary school, echoes the comments of other fathers around the country when he says, "I made up my mind before we had children that I was going to have a heavy involvement. But when I thought about being a father, I didn't know what to do, because I had no model. My mother ran everything. . . . That's not to blame my father. It's just the way it was, because he was working."

Making the transition from "the way it was" to the way it is today, fathers also find little guidance and support from social institutions.

"Many men are very confused about what they're supposed to be doing," Harris observes. "Men are taught to be aggressive. That's exactly the wrong stuff for parenting. Most male role models are sports figures. It's very rare for kids to have this kind of male role model—gentle, nurturing, peaceful."

'I DON'T HAVE TIME'

Tift's organization, the Fathers Resource Center, offers classes for fathers as part of its services. John Andrews of Apple Valley, Minn., who leads one suburban group, hears a recurring theme from the men in his classes, about half of

---

'Men are very confused about what they're supposed to be doing. Men are taught to be aggressive. That's exactly the wrong stuff for parenting.'—Stephen Harris, father and editor

---

whom are married and half divorced. "They say, 'I have to make a living. I have to earn the bucks. I don't have any time for my kids.' They ask, 'How do I spend more time with my children? And how do I play with my children?' "

For some men, spending time with children involves considerable sacrifice, even career changes. Don Spongberg of Everett, Mass., served as a merchant marine for six years, spending five months at a time at sea. "That's the only thing I ever wanted to do, and it's still the only thing I want to do for a living," he says.

But everything changed when his wife was pregnant with their son, Don Jr.,

now two years old. "That's all I could think of at sea," Mr. Spongberg recalls. Back on shipboard after his son's birth, he says he "always wanted to be at home. I realized I was missing being part of his life."

Spongberg left the merchant marines last November and came home. "The money out there is fantastic," he says. "With just a high school education, I knew there was no way I could match the money here." He now drives airport limousines at a much lower salary. "We're just breaking even, just paying the bills," Spongberg says. "We don't have anything. But it's worth it. I get to see him every day. That's what I wanted."

In the eyes of experts and parents, that kind of parental caring is of lifelong value. Gene Thorpe of Boston, the father of an eight-year-old son and a four-year-old daughter, works evenings for Federal Express, giving him time with his children while his wife is at her job. Mr. Thorpe says, "My being a father has been pretty much shaped by the way my father was. He was a two-job man, but he was home for dinner. He was here when I needed to ask him something or show him something. That is what I want to do for my children."

For all the success stories of attentive fathers, no one pretends that the revolution is complete. Robert Griswold, author of "Fatherhood in America," says, "Men talk a better game than they deliver. They talk about being 50–50 dads, but when it gets down to it, they're not. It's in their interest to resist. If you can get somebody to do the less appealing aspects of childrearing, you do. Men don't work as hard within the family, partly because they're privileged economically. They make more money than their wives, and their work culture may be less accommodating than women's."

At the same time, Dr. Griswold and other authorities on fatherhood see heartening signs of progress. "For the first time we're seeing a significant interest on the part of corporations about the needs of working fathers," says Levine of The Fatherhood Project.

Griswold concurs but stops short of total optimism. "The evidence I found from the business community was a cer-tain reluctance to be bold and adopt initiatives that would help," he says.

Chris Stafford of New Brighton, Minn., a father of two, agrees that employers must become key players. "It all hinges on corporate attitudes toward fathers," he says. "If men could feel comfortable meeting family needs and corporate needs simultaneously, they would have a lot more freedom to be the kind of fathers they want to be. . . . It's OK to duck out of the office at 5 p.m. if you have a racquetball game, but not if you have day-care pickup."

Mark Schlemmer of St. Cloud, Minn., a single father of a nine-year-old son, Levi, sees other needed changes. "It's my personal mission to get more men involved in schools," he says. "It's terrible to be in a PTA meeting of 30 women and one man. It just sends the wrong message to children. I love to see men involved with children, because society as a whole has abandoned children."

"Kids need role models of men around them," Mr. Schlemmer continues. "Every time there's a positive interaction with a man and children, it gives children a chance to envision themselves. Boys can say, 'I can do this someday.' That can have a global effect."

Career or family—which comes first? In increasing numbers, fathers now confront the dilemma formerly reserved for working mothers. Schlemmer sums up: "American business doesn't make it easy. Fortune 500 companies have parental leave policies on paper, but the subtext is, 'Don't ask for it. It will play havoc with your advancement.' People have to ask for it anyway. If your career suffers, so be it. Kids don't remember money. Kids don't remember toys. They don't remember big Christmas gifts. They remember time. Any of those other things are irrelevant compared with the time children spend with their fathers."

SINGLE PARENTS AND DAMAGED CHILDREN

The Fruits of the Sexual Revolution

Lloyd Eby and Charles A. Donovan

Lloyd Eby is assistant senior editor of The World & I. *Charles A. Donovan is senior policy consultant at the Family Research Council, Washington, D.C. Research assistance was provided by Diane Falk, Jayne Turconi, and Mark Petersen.*

Vice President Dan Quayle was right. Murphy Brown—the unmarried TV character who became pregnant on the show—was a bad role model for women, legitimizing and glamorizing single motherhood. But Quayle did not go on to raise or discuss the more difficult problems. Should Murphy Brown have had an abortion? Should she have taken more precautions with contraception so she didn't get pregnant? As she was unmarried, was it wrong for her to have sex? Should she have given up the baby for adoption?

The social science evidence now available shows conclusively that children suffer when they grow up in any family situation other than an intact two-parent family formed by their biological father and mother who are married to each other. As recently as 1960, the biological two-parent family was the norm; in that year, about 75 percent of children in the United States lived with both of their biological parents, who had been married only once, to one another. By 1991 this percentage had declined to about 56 percent. Now, if the darker forecasts are accurate, fewer than 50 percent of children can expect to live continuously throughout their childhood in such families.[1]

The costs of this ever-increasing decline in families and family support of children are huge: to the children, to the larger society, and to the nation. An increasing number of our children, largely from single-parent homes, are unable to participate constructively and ethically in our economic, political, and social life, although many children from single-parent families nonetheless do succeed in life. Costs include immense and ever-increasing welfare rolls; remedial and repeated education; anomie, crime, and lawlessness; high and increasing rates of teen suicide; dealing with unemployable people; and the financial, spiritual, and civic costs of all kinds of social pathologies. All these impose very great financial expenditures as well as enormous psychic and civic burdens. Indeed, it may not be too much to say that family breakdown—with its attendant pathologies and their costs—is our country's most serious social and economic problem, threatening to overwhelm us and even threatening our very democracy and the society on which it rests, unless somehow curbed.

When it was published in 1962, Anthony Burgess' *A Clockwork Orange* seemed overwrought in its depiction of the anomie, violence, pathology, and nihilism of some young people. Today, Burgess' fiction appears to have been remarkably prescient; the murders, rapes, thefts, assaults, burnings and lootings, and other crimes and damages committed by feral and often emotionless youths

now surpass his depictions. These developments are very closely linked to the rise in family breakdown and single parenthood.

Today, more than half of all children will live for some period in a single-parent home, either as a result of being born to an unwed mother or as a result of divorce, and the number of such children continues to increase. Some of those children will find themselves having one or more stepparents—even successive series of different stepparents—through the marriage of their previously single parent or parents. But stepfamilies themselves are more prone to divorce, and in general stepparents do not care for or bond as well with children as do biological parents. Increasingly, children are living not with their biological parents but with their grandparents, in foster homes, or in other quasi-family situations. Of course, many children will survive all these troubles and traumas and become fulfilled and productive adults, and many single parents, foster parents, and stepparents cope very well and perform heroically. But those cases increasingly are being overshadowed by the number and severity of other ones. All the children who survive and flourish in these circumstances will do so because they somehow found a way through or around the difficulties, not because of them.

The Murphy Brown character's wealth, prominent social position, education, career success, management skills,

This article first appeared in *The World & I*, July 1993, pp. 405-419. Reprinted by permission of *The World & I*, a publication of the Washington Times Corporation. © 1993.

race, and mature age with its attendant relative emotional stability will protect her and her child from some of the worst consequences of unmarried pregnancy and of growing up with a single parent: poverty, lack of educational opportunity and social standing, and the burdens and chaos resulting from having too much responsibility too young. The same holds for the hundreds of real-life actresses, princesses, and other prominent and successful women who have recently—often publicly and defiantly, sometimes quietly or even secretly—borne children out of wedlock. But even in these cases not all is well; children who grow up in single-parent families invariably suffer. The greatest suffering and deprivation, however—for both mothers and children—comes about from unmarried teenage pregnancy.

PREGNANCY OF UNMARRIED TEENAGERS

Today, the United States has a very high and increasing rate of pregnancies to unmarried teenage girls, a much higher rate than any other country in the developed world. In 1950 there were 56,000 births to unmarried teenage girls aged 15 to 19 years, and the birthrate was 12.6 births per thousand such teenagers. In 1960 there were 87,000 such births, and the rate had climbed to 15.3. Between 1961 and 1962 the rate fell slightly, although the number of such births continued to rise. From that date on, the rate has continued to rise every year, and the rate of increase itself has risen—the problem is accelerating. In 1970 there were 190,000 births to unmarried teenage mothers aged 15 to 19, and the rate of such births was 22.4 per thousand unmarried teenagers. In 1980 the figures were 263,000 births and a rate of 27.6. In 1990—the last year for which reliable statistics are available—the rate was 42.5 and the number of births was nearly 350,000—361,000 if we include those children born to girls under 15.

In 1990, 4,158,212 babies were born in the United States to all women. This means that of all births in 1990, about 8.7 percent—or one out of every twelve—was born to an unmarried teenager between 15 and 19 years of age.[2] One birth in twelve may seem relatively insignificant, but the total is for births to unmarried teenagers of all races, compared to

all births to all women, of whatever age or race, married or unmarried. If the statistics are broken down by race and restricted to unmarried women, a strong trend appears. Of all births to white women of all ages, the percentage of births to unmarried women in 1990 was 20.35 percent. For all births to women of all races, 28.0 percent were to unmarried women. Of all births to black women of all ages,

66.5 percent were to unmarried women.

The figures for nonmarital births to girls age 15 to 19 are even more bracing. For white teens, 56.4 percent of births were nonmarital in 1990; for black teens, 91.97 percent. Overall, 67.1 percent of teen births in 1990 were nonmarital—a mirror image of the situation as recently as 1970, when 70 percent of *all* teen births were to married women.

PRÉCIS

Attitudes changed in America after the post-1950s social-sexual revolution. Unmarried people came to view having sex as normal and right. Avoidance of divorce for the sake of the children gave way to favoring the happiness of adults as individuals. The taboo against birth out of wedlock eventually disappeared. So ever-more children are being born to unmarried women and growing up in single-parent families. The worst consequences—for both children and parent—occur from births to unmarried teenagers.

The costs—financial and nonfinancial—of the decline of families and family support of children are very high: Ever-increasing welfare rolls. Poor mothers who cannot escape poverty for themselves or their children. An increasing number of our children, largely from single-parent homes, who are lost to our economic, political, and social life. All kinds of social pathologies. Can our society and democracy survive these threats?

Previous attempts to deal with the problem have emphasized technological solutions—various forms of contraception, especially the pill and condoms. But teenagers are poor users of contraception. Rates and virulence of sexually transmitted diseases are rising.

What is to be done about all this? Perhaps we should return to teaching and emphasizing abstinence.

If anything, current figures may be worse: More than half the white teens giving birth are unmarried, and among young black mothers fewer than one in ten is married. In short, hardly any births to black teenagers are to married women, and two-thirds of births to all black women are to unmarried women. Each year, one in ten black teenagers will give birth. Nearly half will become unmarried mothers before the end of their teenage years—and many will have more than one child. Another conclusion is that in the United States a large number of children of all races—and the vast majority of black children—are growing up as children of single mothers, that is, as *fatherless* children.

TEENAGE GIRLS AND ABORTION

The figures given above are for live births, not conception rates. To compute conception rates, we need to include the figures for the number of pregnancies terminated through abortion, plus the number of pregnancies that result in miscarriages. The number of miscarriages is unknown but is estimated to be equal to 20 percent of births plus 10 percent of abortions. The number of pregnancies to unmarried teenagers that are terminated through abortion is quite large. Of the 1,590,750 abortions performed in the United States in 1988, 1,314,060, or 82.6 percent, were performed on unmarried women (of all women age 15–44, not just teenagers, and including separated, divorced, and never-married women).[3] Although statistics given by different authorities vary, conservative figures indicate that about 1,033,730 women under 20 became pregnant in 1988, and 40 percent of each age level in that group chose abortion.[4] In any case, we can conclude that a large number of teenage girls are choosing to end their pregnancies through abortion, and that abortion is being used as a last-ditch form of birth control for many teenage girls, establishing a pattern that, after more than two decades of abortion on demand nationwide, is reverberating throughout the cohort of women in their 20s.

Moreover, many counselors and other people concerned with the welfare of teenagers—or, less charitably, with burgeoning welfare rolls—advocate abortion and encourage unmarried pregnant girls to seek abortions.

CAUSES OF TEENAGE PREGNANCY

As Barbara Dafoe Whitehead has noted, a great change in the "social metric" occurred in post-1950s America, from an overarching emphasis on adults sacrificing themselves to achieve child well-being to a concern for adult individual self-fulfillment without regard to whether that is good for children.[5] The attitude that divorce was to be avoided for the sake of the children was exchanged for an attitude that what makes parents happy as individuals is what counts. The ancient taboo against birth out of wedlock was given up. Hugh Hefner's *Playboy* ethic and aesthetic (first issue, December 1953) sanctioned and encouraged young males in their pursuit of unattached sex, and Helen Gurley Brown's *Sex and the Single Girl*, published in 1962, proclaimed loudly that it was not only OK for single women to engage in sex but that they were entitled to it, as an issue of equality. These changes amounted to a great cultural shift, away from the attitude that sex should be restricted to married couples, toward an attitude that proclaimed sex as both good and necessary. The new attitude paid far less attention to marriage, in many cases actually disdaining it. Hollywood and the mass media took up these trends, so that today they are firmly ensconced in American popular culture.

What hardly anyone was willing to see at the time, however, was how children were being affected by these changes. Teenagers—girls especially—became ensnared in a dilemma: Are they adults or children? If they are adults, then they should be able—even encouraged, at least according to one kind of thinking—to participate in all the supposed pleasures of adulthood, including unmarried sex. But if they do engage in sex, then many of the girls will become pregnant. But they are not really adults; they are adolescents, even though their bodies have become sexually mature. The media and the popular culture, however, continually push them toward being sexually active. If the adults who are concerned for their welfare were to claim that it was wrong or misguided for them to be engaging in sex, this would tend to commit those adults to questioning whether the cultural shift is indeed good and beneficial, something very few people who are active in the mass and dominant culture—the universities and the media,

including TV, metropolitan newspapers, movies, the magazines, and so on—have been willing to do, until very recently anyway. Those who do question this cultural shift—for example, Dan Quayle—almost always are attacked as meanspirited, stupid, unrealistic religious bigots who want to "turn back the clock" to some supposed past golden era, as old fogies who are unwilling to accept the facts of contemporary life.

One result is widespread and rising amounts of sexual activity among teenagers at younger and younger ages. In 1982, 30.1 percent of women 15–17 years old reported that they were sexually experienced. By 1988 the figure had risen to 37.5 percent. Among unmarried women 18–19 years old, 59.7 percent reported that they were sexually experienced in 1982, and by 1988, 72 percent of such women reported sexual experience. This increased activity is coupled with a rising rate and number of teenage pregnancies. These changes have occurred across all races and social classes, but the most disruptive and devastating effects have been among those who were the poorest and most vulnerable. For them, the allure of sexual freedom broke the threads of cultural and moral cohesion that were the real safety net between temporary poverty and chronic destitution.

THE COSTS OF UNMARRIED PREGNANCY AND FATHERLESSNESS

Teenage pregnancy has costs to the mothers, to the children, and to the larger society and nation. In 1987, more than $19 billion in public funds was spent for income maintenance, health care, and nutrition for support of families begun by teenagers. Babies born to teenagers have a high risk of being born with low birth weight, and low birth weight requires initial hospital care averaging $20,000 per infant. The total lifetime medical costs for each low birth-weight infant average $400,000. For all adolescents (married and unmarried) giving birth, 46 percent go on welfare within four years, and 73 percent of unmarried teenagers giving birth go on welfare within four years.[6] The costs of welfare are extremely high, especially for state budgets. The total state budget for Michigan in 1992, for example, was about $30 billion, and one-third of this—$10 billion—went to the state's social service (welfare) program. Michigan's plight is similar to that of other states—it has neither the lowest nor the highest such expenditure. Moreover, members of these single-parent–headed, welfare-receiving families are at very high risk of remaining poor and ill educated throughout their lives. When married women go on welfare, they tend to get off welfare within a few years. When unmarried women go on welfare, they tend to remain there permanently. We now have the phenomenon in every state of large numbers of families, made up of unmarried women and their children, being on welfare for three or more generations, with no end in sight.

Has anyone ever heard of a child who is happy because he does not know his father? Being a child of a single mother is a handicap, regardless of the wealth, maturity, or social status of that mother.[7]

Numerous studies of child development have shown that growing up as the child of a single parent is linked with lower levels of academic achievement (having to repeat grades in school or receiving lower marks and class standing); increased levels of depression, stress, and aggression; a decrease in some indicators for physical health; higher incidences of needing the services of mental health professionals; and other emotional and behavioral problems.[8] All these effects are linked with lifetime poverty, poor achievement, susceptibility to suicide, likelihood of committing crimes and being arrested, and other pathologies. One such study, based on data from the 1988 National Health Interview Survey, concludes as follows:

Data ... revealed an excess risk of negative health and performance indicators among children who did not live with both biological parents. These findings are consistent with the hypotheses that children are adversely affected ... by the relative lack of attention, supervision, and opposite-sex role models provided by single parents, regardless of marital status.[9]

THE ATTACK ON FATHERHOOD

While the cultural shift Whitehead describes was occurring, fatherhood was coming under attack. Among other things, these attacks included feminist rhetoric, the claim that fathers are distant and brutal and repressive, based on the observation that some fathers abuse and otherwise mistreat their children and wives, and the observable fact that some children without fa-

thers grow up quite well and become very good and productive adults. "A woman without a man is like a fish without a bicycle," defiantly proclaimed one feminist slogan. But fathers do have a crucial role in rearing children. The small boy with a bicycle wants a father to help him learn to ride it, and both boys and girls usually like their fathers to take them fishing.

Children need two parents, playing into the daily dramas of discipline, self-sacrifice, sincerity, and complementarity. Historically, fathers have given and enforced rules of behavior and provided role models of proper male behavior for both girls and boys. Traditionally, fathers have been very concerned with the sexual virtue of their daughters. Fathers know the attitudes and intentions of teenage boys, having once been teens themselves, and therefore are uniquely able both to guide their daughters and to check out and enforce rules on boyfriends. This does not mean that mothers do not or cannot perform these tasks and roles, but they are handicapped doing it alone. Fathers are vital, and their place cannot be taken by a single mother, however able, resolute, and resourceful she may be. Having fathers as guardians, disciplinarians, and role models is necessary to help teenagers navigate those most difficult experiences and years.

Today, increasing numbers of children, even preteens, are becoming involved in acts of violence and crime, including drug usage and drug dealing, assault, robbery, burglary, theft, carjacking, and shootings and murders, often for seemingly the most trivial of reasons. On the street, a disrespectful look, or an en-

vied pair of sneakers, can provoke a bullet. ("I shot him cause he 'dissed' me.") The costs of this are immense. For all of us—rich and poor, of whatever race—our sense of civic order, safety, and well-being is increasingly threatened, if it has not already collapsed. The monetary

It may not be too much to say that family breakdown—with its attendant pathologies and their costs—is our country's most serious social and economic problem.

price is enormous; public costs include the expenses of law enforcement, prisons, and other expenditures of crime fighting. Private costs include insurance, security systems, repairing the damages, and the forced exodus of people as they flee our cities in an attempt to find a safe area. A majority of the young people who are responsible for these crimes, with their attendant costs, are products of what once was unashamedly acknowledged as "broken homes."

The criminal and other destructive activities of these teenagers tend to make them into poor or unsuitable prospective marriage partners. Female children of single mothers are more likely to engage in early premarital sex, thus leading to increasing rates of unmarried pregnancy at younger and younger ages. Male children of single mothers are less and less able to become responsible fathers and marriage partners. So we can conclude that unmarried parenthood is feeding on itself, contributing to its own rise.

As already stated, women who are single parents tend to be poorer, more prone to being on welfare, less educationally advantaged, less able to handle careers and work, and more beleaguered in every way than their married sisters. These conclusions hold true for the vast majority of cases, even though there are many instances of such women performing notably and heroically. Single mothers are understandably less likely to be able to accumulate any appreciable amount of savings, purchase homes, afford higher education for themselves and their children, or finance a start-up of any business or profession for themselves or their offspring. In fact, if they are on welfare—Aid to Families with Dependent Children (AFDC)—they are forbidden by the rules to have any significant savings. Some economists have gone so far as to suggest that increasing rates of single motherhood point toward the economic demise of a nation. All these effects are especially pronounced and accentuated for women who become mothers as single teenagers. So the cost of teenage pregnancy to all—to the parents, to the children, to the society, and to the nation—is very high and rising.

PREVENTION OF TEENAGE PREGNANCY

It is estimated that 41 percent of unintended pregnancies among teenagers could be avoided if all sexually active teenagers used contraception. But one-fourth of such teenagers use no contraceptive method or an ineffective one. Half of all teenage pregnancies occur within six months of first sexual intercourse, and more than 20 percent of all initial premarital pregnancies occur in the first month after the initiation of sex. But the use of contraception requires planning, and planned initiation of sexual intercourse among teens is rare. Only 17 percent of women and 25 percent of men report having planned their first intercourse. The contraceptives most widely used by teenagers are the pill and condoms.[10]

Nature equips humans with two differing timetables for maturity; physical and sexual maturity comes first, and emotional and psychological maturity appears later. Teenagers, particularly younger ones, are poorly equipped with the ability to foresee the consequences of their acts and plan accordingly. Teens tend to see themselves as invulnerable to risks. Moreover, this is a time of life when peer pressure and media pressure for engaging in sex are especially acute.

There is reliable but anecdotal evidence that, at least for many inner-city and other poor unmarried teenage girls, their pregnancies are not actually unplanned but actively desired. These studies conclude that the girls are not ignorant about contraception; they do not use it because they actually yearn for babies. Their emotional and psychological immaturity, however, does not allow them to know or understand the real consequences of motherhood, especially teenage motherhood. This is the phenomenon

commonly called "babies having babies." Typically, a poor girl who has a baby while unmarried is especially vulnerable to becoming pregnant again while still in her teens.

The primary goal of teenage pregnancy prevention programs since 1970 has been to educate teenagers about the risks of pregnancy and to get them to use contraceptives; this sometimes has been derided as "throwing condoms at the problem." But teenagers typically do not go to see the school nurse or to a health clinic until after they have become sexually active; girls often go for the first time because they think they may be pregnant.

The received approach to the problem of teenage pregnancy has been "technological," in that it has relied on providing teenagers with the technology for avoiding pregnancy, or, once pregnant, with abortions as a technological solution to the pregnancy. But rising rates of teenage pregnancy, abortion, and births to teenage mothers show that these technological solutions have been anything but effective. Advanced as the "realistic " answer to the out-of-wedlock pregnancy problem, these interventions have come athwart the reality of failure statistics. Abortion has reduced the overall adolescent birthrate, but the unmarried adolescent birthrate has gone up dramatically since 1970. Adolescents have become slightly more efficient users of contraception in recent years, but they remain dramatically less so than the adult married population. Moreover, the slight increase in efficiency has been overwhelmed by three factors that are not unrelated to contraceptive availability itself: (a) an increase in the percentage of adolescents in each age cohort having sex; (b) a decrease in the age of the first reported sexual experience; and (c) increases in the frequency of intercourse and the number of sexual partners among adolescents. In this environment, more intense contraceptive use and increased pregnancy rates coexist and may be mutually reinforcing.

All this says nothing about sexually transmitted disease (STD). Increased sexual activity is correlated with rising rates of these diseases in teenagers. Regular, conscientious, and proper use of condoms lowers the incidence of such disease transmission, but we know that teenagers often fail to use them and that, even with conscientious use, condoms sometimes fail. There is no lowering of the risk of sexually transmitted disease through use of oral contraceptives.

This is the fruit of the newfound sexual freedom among adolescents. Not surprisingly, these dismal outcomes are tempting a new generation of advocates to discard freedom when it comes to the latest generation of contraceptive devices.

NORPLANT AND TEENAGE GIRLS

The failure of free-choice use of the pill or condoms to reduce the rates of pregnancy in teenage girls has led to proposals for recommending or requiring Norplant as a contraceptive for teenage girls—particularly for girls who already have a baby. The best technical argument for Norplant is that it removes the diligence factor for those adolescents who receive the implant. Those pregnancies to teenage girls that resulted because they "forgot" to take the pill or because a condom was not readily available will not occur, advocates say, with Norplant. Once inserted in the woman's upper arm, Norplant works automatically, so it would lower the threshold of conscientiousness that adolescents need to practice contraception diligently.

By similar reasoning, however, Norplant will lower adolescent conscientiousness about avoiding sexual encounters on the grounds that pregnancy might result. The conclusion is that, although Norplant arguably would be effective in reducing the number of pregnancies, it may well promote a rise in sexually transmitted diseases.

Norplant advocates recommend continued use of condoms to avert this result, but this raises the diligence problem again. If diligence was not an effective strategy for contraception, will it be so for disease? AIDS infection and syphilis are on the rise, as is antibiotic-resistant gonorrhea. This rise has occurred even in a time when there has been a slight increase in contraceptive efficiency among adolescents. But condom use itself is no guarantee against disease. As one expert notes, "The inescapable fact is that, during one act of intercourse, condoms *may* protect against STD, but for frequent, repeated acts of intercourse over months and years, *they will not*."[11]

Increases also are occurring in other significant venereal diseases, such as chlamydia (which can cause sterility), herpes, and HPV (human papilloma virus). This last is associated with precancerous conditions, from which invasive cancer can develop. So, even if Norplant turns out to reduce the incidence of teenage pregnancy, it may well lead to even more serious problems involving spread of an impressive and growing array of sexually transmissible diseases.

The most recent news on STDs is especially grim. A study released by the Alan Guttmacher Institute on March 21, 1993, reaches the conclusion that 56 million Americans—one in five—are infected with a sexually transmitted viral disease. These diseases can be controlled but not cured. The study estimates that even more Americans are likely to contract an STD during their lifetimes. The greatest effect will be on women and people under the age of 25. According to the study, each year 100,000 to 150,000 women become infertile as a result of STDs. Teenagers and blacks are disproportionately affected by STDs because these people are more likely to be unmarried and thus to have multiple sexual partners. Moreover, teenagers who begin sexual activity earlier are more likely to have more partners. About one in nine women aged 15 to 44 are treated for pelvic inflammatory disease (PID) during their reproductive lifetimes, according to the report, and, if current trends continue, one-half of all women who were 15 in 1970 will have had a PID by the year 2000.[12]

The contraceptive debate of the 1970s occurred in a completely different environment from today's—medically, morally, and socially. Medically, with HIV, the stakes now are significantly higher, even if heterosexual transmission remains relatively uncommon. Morally and socially, the sex education and contraception movements of the 1970s competed against established mores that militated against teen sexual experimentation, but these movements did not compete against an alternative institutional and educational approach, namely abstinence education. Today, the generation that

lived through the '70s is debating the policies of the '90s. Experience of what has happened in this field in the ensuing three decades does not lend much respect or hope for any "magic bullet" approach such as is epitomized by free-choice use of Norplant. In today's debate, advocates of the technological approach embodied in Norplant are battling against advocates of an abstinence-based approach who are armed with texts, studies, and curricula of their own. Veterans of the sexual revolution can be found in both camps, leading to a much more realistic—and interesting—public policy debate, with neither side having a monopoly on scientific opinion.

WHAT IS TO BE DONE?

Patterns of teenage pregnancy, abortion, and out-of-wedlock childbearing, although stabilizing somewhat in the 1980s, continue to worsen. After a trial of two decades, national pregnancy policies have failed to reduce pregnancy rates, have succeeded in lowering birthrates only through a sharp concomitant rise in abortions among adolescents, and have coincided with an unprecedented increase in teenage sexual activity. A generation or more of young people—especially inner-city blacks, but others too, of all races—is being lost to productive adulthood and citizenship and is imposing huge and ever-increasing costs—financial, social, and medical—on the larger society and nation. These costs are so great that they threaten to overwhelm us. Can civil liberties, democracy, civil order, and the rule of law survive these present conditions? For the sake of the next generation of American children, it is time for a generous dose of domestic "new thinking" about one of the nation's most intractable social problems.

If all unmarried women of childbear-

ing age for whom it is not medically contraindicated were forced to use it, Norplant would be one solution, but forced imposition is ethically objectionable as well as impossible in a democratic society. Can voluntary use of this method, or any other contraceptive, significantly lower this rising tide of births to single women, with the enormous and ever-rising attendant costs both to children and the nation? So far, voluntary contraceptive methods have failed to curb this problem. Besides, Norplant does not prevent—and may even exacerbate—the spread of venereal disease. Norplant plus condoms has all the problems of teenagers not being sufficiently diligent to practice effective contraception. Perhaps it is time to abandon technological solutions and return to teaching abstinence on moral grounds. Although it sometimes failed, teaching children to abstain was socially, psychologically, and medically far more effective than any of the methods introduced by the sexual revolution—a revolution that was supposed to offer us freedom but that seems instead to have failed us, threatening our livelihoods, our civil order, and perhaps even our liberty itself.

NOTES

1. Deborah A. Dawson, "Family Structure and Children's Health and Well Being: Data from the 1988 National Health Interview Survey on Child Care," *Journal of Marriage and the Family* 53 (August 1991): 573–84.

2. The National Center for Health Statistics, *Vital Statistics of the United States*, annual and *Monthly Vital Statistics Report*, vol. 41, no. 9 supplement, February 25, 1993.

3. Alan Guttmacher Institute, *Abortion Factbook, 1992.*

4. Cited in Center for Population Options, "Adolescents and Abortion Factsheet," February 1993.

5. Barbara Dafoe Whitehead, "Dan Quayle Was Right," *Atlantic Monthly*, April 1993, 47 ff.

6. David A. Hamburg, M.D., *Today's Children: Creating a Future for a Generation in Crisis* (New York: Random House, Times Books, 1992), 198.

7. Margaret Carlson, "Why Quayle Has Half a Point," *Time*, 1 June 1992, 30, 31.

8. Dawson, 573, 574.

9. Dawson, 580.

10. Cited in Center for Population Options, "Adolescent Contraceptive Use Factsheet," June 1990.

11. Joe S. McIlhaney, M.D., *Sexuality and Sexually Transmitted Diseases* (Grand Rapids, Mich.: Baker Book House, 1990), 36. Emphasis in original.

12. Study by Alan Guttmacher Institute, reported in the *New York Times*, 1 April 1993, A1.

THE FAMILY HEART

Robb Forman Dew

For years I envisioned the passage of time as a sort of steady trudge—not necessarily dreary—just relentless. The minutes accrue imperceptibly into a stretch of history, and you turn around to recognize, with amazement, your own past.

But also, some days have long legs. Now and then an ordinary bit of time takes a yawning scissors step, leaving you to scuttle along behind, scrabbling to cling to ongoing events. I learned this late, when my children were nearly full-grown, because it was exactly such an ordinary moment that enlarged and enlarged upon itself almost three years ago, when my son told me he was gay.

It was spring in New England, a soft day in May, and Stephen was home from his sophomore year at Yale until the first week of June, when he, my husband, Charles, and I would drive to Virginia to see his brother, Jack, graduate from Woodberry Forest School. When the phone rang, Stephen came around the corner from the TV room to answer it, and he stood at the far end of the kitchen, lounging against the long, glass door to chat with Chloe. When I had come downstairs from my study to start dinner, I settled at the table to work the *Jumble* from the morning paper while occasionally tending the chicken I was roasting for dinner.

What happens when a child who is loved more than life itself grows up to be gay? In this moving account, a mother who is also a prizewinning novelist tells how she and her own close-knit family handled the grief, the fear, and—finally—the understanding

I'm not sure why I was suddenly alert to Stephen's end of the phone conversation. My attention was caught, I think, by some tone in his voice, or simply by the realization that his phone calls to or from Chloe were never particularly private; he never took the trouble to take the calls out of earshot of anyone else in the house. Chloe is a beautiful girl, sensuous and angelic-looking at the same time, and she is funny and bright and endearing as well.

It might be that my ear was caught by what I didn't hear: There was no sense of the kind of tension that is inevitably there between two people as attractive and sexual as Chloe and Stephen. And by "sexual," I only mean the kind of magnetism that emanates from some people, especially older adolescents. Chloe and Stephen both possessed it, and, although I couldn't hear Chloe, Stephen's voice was nothing more than friendly. He was completely at ease; there was a certain edginess missing.

Chloe had been at school with Stephen since they were 14, and, in fact, two years earlier Chloe's parents and various of her siblings had settled next to us on the temporary bleachers set up at St. Paul's School in Concord, N.H., to watch Stephen and Chloe's class graduate.

Chloe's mother leaned over to me and said, "Oh, don't you wish this were just their *wedding?*" And I knew exactly what she meant: Their lives seemed perfect and uncomplicated and filled with amazing possibilities in that gorgeous afternoon; perhaps they could go on that way forever. I believe I simply began at that moment to think of Chloe as the probable romantic interest in Stephen's life. There were always friends of Stephen's around, male and female, but, at a certain point, both our sons made it clear that they wouldn't answer questions about their social lives. So, in lieu of any information about Stephen's personal life, I jumped to a conclusion. I made one of many assumptions that parents should learn not to make about their children.

Two years later, though, in the kitchen on that afternoon in May, I only remember suddenly being aware—and being surprised by—the odd lack of interest in Stephen's voice. He was amiable—he is almost always amiable—but he wasn't reluctant to get off the phone.

He hung up and turned away, but I stopped him. "Stephen?" And he paused in the doorway and turned toward me, and I continued, "Have you been involved with anyone at all? I mean romantically?"

For an instant he was surprised, and then he frowned, and I thought he was going to walk away in anger. There was a peculiar feeling of urgency and expectation in the room that I can only recall now; I can't re-create the sensation.

"There's something I've been meaning to tell you," he said finally.

We both fell silent, and then he moved forward a few paces toward me and was backlit by the gauzy light filtering from the screened porch through the glass-paned door. I couldn't read his face because of the shadow, but I know my children in all their moods; I am fairly good at deciphering the nuances of their postures—vulnerable or defensive or joyous. I may well know their very scent. Probably I could find them if I were blindfolded in a room full of people. I remember when they were little boys, and I would suddenly catch sight of one of my sons precariously balanced on a chair, or racing up or down the stairs, and I would experience the sensation of a fall he didn't take. It was a similar sensation I felt watching Stephen standing in the kitchen with his thumbs looped in the waistband of his jeans, his shoulders canted toward me, his head dipped slightly forward in determination. At once I wanted to raise my hands and gesture for him to stop what he was going to say, and I also wanted to urge him on and hear whatever it was. In fact, I sat as still as a stone. I didn't move at all.

"Of course I've been involved with someone since St. Paul's," he said. He wasn't frowning any longer; in fact, he had a slight smile that I knew from years of being connected to him. It was a smile that sought to protect me and Charles from any worry or irritation on his behalf. It's easy for me to classify it now, but looking at him then, in the shadowy room, I only perceived danger.

"I think I might be gay," Stephen said.

In the instant before he spoke I'm convinced I knew what he was going to say, but at the same time I was uncertain that I understood. "Ah...well...you *think* you're gay?"

He looked perplexed, and anxious, too. "No, that's not what I mean. I mean I *am* gay."

This is such a difficult moment to remember, because the two of us had suddenly moved straight ahead into uncharted territory. I got up from the table and hugged him, and he held on to me, too, in a fierce embrace, lowering his chin to the top of my head. I felt lightheaded, and my stomach clenched with dread. I had no idea what to do. "It doesn't make any difference to us," I said. "We love you no matter what."

We moved away from each other, both of us strangely embarrassed and without any rules of etiquette to cover this situation. Stephen seemed lost in his own house; he stood in the kitchen with a tentative air that more than anything in that elongated moment filled me with sorrow. His expression was precisely the curious gaze of assessment he had cast my way 30 minutes after he was born. He looked as though he wasn't at all sure that he could trust me.

I rarely say anything entirely off the cuff. It's almost as if I *see* the words before they come out of my mouth, but I was baffled by what came out of my mouth next in my desperation to alleviate the uneasiness between me and this person I had loved for all his life.

"Well, damn it, Stephen! I wish you'd told me years ago so I wouldn't have been stuck decorating the Christmas tree all by myself every year!" Since my children became teenagers, this has been my recurrent after-Christmas lament—tedious, now, to everyone who knows me, because I'm the only one who cares much if, or how, the Christmas tree is decorated at all.

He was as surprised as I by this peculiar outburst, and he merely looked at me blankly, and then he laughed.

"Yeah. But I didn't think you'd want it decorated all in mauve." And then we both laughed; we were back on sure footing. We had humor between us again, but only fleetingly, because I had brushed off our discomfort with a sophistication and an attempted jauntiness I didn't yet possess, and I have no idea where such glibness came from.

This was one of those events in my life that, as I conjure it up in retrospect, appears to me like a pointillist painting, coming into focus hazily, at first, and slowly gathering the form of a whole experience. "Do you want to tell Dad and Jack?"

"I think it would be better if you told Dad. Do you mind doing that?"

"You know he won't care, Stephen. He loves you."

"I know. But I just think it would be easier."

I don't know if he meant easier on him or easier on his father, and I suspect that it was a little bit of both, but mostly I think he yearned to avoid open embarrassment between the two of them.

"I don't think I should tell Jack yet," he said.

"Well, Stephen...." But he moved back into the other room and sat down in front of the television, although I thought he was as astounded as I was by the revelation of so much truth in the space of, perhaps, five or 10 minutes. An atmosphere of unrelenting honesty is not hospitable, really, to domestic life. It is exhausting, since it bars the possibility of tactfulness or diplomacy.

Charles had dashed home from a history-department meeting and gone upstairs to shower and change clothes before heading back. It seemed imperative that I tell him before he came face-to-face with Stephen, who would assume his father knew, but Charles was obviously in a hurry. He had scarcely noticed that I was standing next to him while he put on his tie in front of the vanity mirror. I put my hand on his arm to draw his attention, and then without taking the time to consider what I was doing, I simply said what I was determined to tell him.

"Listen, Stephen just told me he's gay, and he wanted me to tell you. I know it won't—"

"What? What did you say?" His words fell on top of my own, although he spoke slowly and softly, and he stopped still in the middle of adjusting his tie.

"Stephen is gay. He wants you to know, but...."

He was moving away from me and out of the room as I spoke, and I followed him downstairs. Charles reacted exactly as I had to Stephen's news. In fact, he used almost the same words. "We love you, Stephen. Nothing could ever change that." And he hugged Stephen and held onto him for a long moment. Both of us had the feeling that somehow Stephen was slipping away from us, as though he were being swept off by a strong current, and we wanted desperately to catch hold of him and pull him back to shore.

During several weeks that May, the rooms of my house seemed to me, each one, a foreign country. The three of us ranged around that newly strange place in a paralysis of politeness, afraid that we would blunder into some area of hurtfulness of the other two.

I know now that Charles and I—even in our manner of acceptance—were unwittingly cruel, but either Stephen was so shocked by his act of revelation that he didn't notice, or he took us at our intention. We were doing the best we could with information that filled us with fear and sorrow and confusion.

My husband and I were well brought up; we are excellent products of middle-class Anglo-American behavior. We kept our sorrow to ourselves. I found myself, at one point, standing under the hot water from the shower, cradling my head against the tiled wall and weeping and weeping, struggling with a thought that wouldn't come clear. "It would be easier if he were…." I had no idea how I meant to finish that sentence, nor did I know in what direction it was leading, until finally it occurred to me that I thought it would be easier for Stephen to have discovered he was black than to have realized that he was gay. When I had to admit to myself that I had had that thought—an idea so fraught with my own conveniently repressed knowledge of the hatred and inequity still extant in this country—I stood all alone under the running water and covered my face with my hands in embarrassment.

Stephen must not have known what to do next. Charles and I were relentlessly chipper and incurious over the few days following the day he told us he was gay. We didn't ask any questions at all, apparently less interested than if he had told us he had read a good book, and I don't remember that Charles and I even discussed these new circumstances with each other.

In the evenings we sat with books before us, but we didn't read; it requires reflection. We watched any sports we could find on television. There was no refuge in anything else on TV, because we discovered right away that, in 1991, the most innocent of sitcoms almost invariably had a passive but definite anti-gay agenda. Trotting out a stereotypical gay man—although rarely ever a lesbian—was apparently always good for a laugh. How had we not noticed and been offended by it before? We watched a lot of baseball.

One morning, I awoke to a solid wall of speculation. Had I done this to my son? Most of what I had read about homosexuality dealt with it as a tragic consequence of having a suffocating mother and a weak, indifferent, or absent father. Had I been a suffocating mother? I had meant to be a good mother, the best parent in the world. Was Charles weak, indifferent, or absent? Charles is probably the kindest man I have ever known, and he is

certainly not indifferent to his sons, whom he loves deeply, nor has he been absent—literally or figuratively.

From the upstairs front-hall window, I gazed out at the street, at my neighbors' houses. Standing alone, trying to decipher the future, I don't think that I have ever felt more desolate. I looked out the window and knew that all the people Stephen had counted on for approval—all, of course, but his parents—might now regard him as a threat, an aberration, a stranger, rather than as a much-liked friend, a trusted neighbor, even something of a star in our small sphere. I found that the thought of any disapprobation, any lessening of regard for my own son, filled me with despair and some small, early flicker of ill-defined rage.

If our son were not damaged by the nature of his own sexual orientation, if we were not flawed by virtue of having a son who was gay, then why hadn't I ever heard mention of any other gay child or family of a gay child? If there was no context for homosexuality then it must, indeed, be a terrible and shameful thing. And yet, I knew that there was nothing—nothing—terrible or shameful about Stephen.

Charles and I pretended to an ease with the new status quo that we didn't feel. We had each quickly and independently fashioned a sort of ludicrous etiquette of feigned heartiness, because we couldn't have stood to have Stephen know he had thrown us into a state of grief. His revelation had shattered our expectations of who he was. We pretended that his sudden emergence as a gay man in what we had considered our conventional family was a matter of no consequence, something that had slipped from our minds completely.

The three of us spent several days occupying the rooms in a state of careful good cheer. Charles and I were busy all the time; we never settled very long in one place, and I don't know what Stephen must have thought, but eventually he approached us in the late afternoon when we were sitting on the screened porch in the balmy air.

"Stephen!" Charles said. "Would you like some iced tea? Or a beer?" His

voice was warm, perhaps overly exuberant.

"Yeah. Thanks. I'll get some iced tea. Do you want anything?"

"I'd love some tea, Stephen, if it's not too much trouble," I said, beaming at him. I was so nervous that my mouth went dry. Stephen has my father's family's brown eyes—an orange brown, the iris rimmed with black—and arched brows, and his expression caught my attention that afternoon because it was filled with compassion. I think now that it struck me so forcefully because he was only 19 years old, but his expression held far more empathy than anyone that age usually possesses.

He brought out glasses of tea from the kitchen and sat down, too, not saying anything for a few moments, and then he looked directly at us, still with an expression of gentle tactfulness. He gazed at Charles and me steadily while he spoke, probably afraid we would find some chore to take us off if he didn't say what he wanted us to hear. "Listen, I know this must be really hard for you. I just want you to know how much it means to me to know that it doesn't change the way you feel about me."

"Nothing could ever change the way we feel about you, Stephen," Charles said. "We love you more than you know."

"We do, sweetie," I said.

"I *do* know. But it must be hard for you," he said, "because I know you didn't expect this. I just wanted to tell you that you can ask me anything you want to know. I mean, you must wonder about a lot of things. I don't want to have any secrets…I don't want you to feel uncomfortable around me." This was a terrible admission—a plea—from my own son, and I tried not to let myself start crying. "I'll be glad to answer any questions you want to ask," he said.

All around the porch the lilac bushes were in bud, with just a few blooms among the branches, so that their delicate scent reached us only when a breeze picked up, but I remember the smell of lilacs in conjunction with Stephen's words, and the combination was such a generous offering in the mild weather that it was very nearly heartbreaking.

"I don't sweat the small stuff anymore"

Born HIV-positive, they were three babies nobody wanted. Until one very special family opened up their home and their hearts—and learned a lesson in love in return.

Jan Goodwin

Jan Goodwin, formerly Executive Editor of Ladies' Home Journal, *is the author of* Price of Honor: Muslim Women Lift the Veil of Silence on the Islamic World *(Little, Brown and Company, 1994), which she researched in ten countries.*

The nightly scene at the Godbout home is common to many families across the country: Dad returning home from work, Mom greeting him, the kids pouncing on him and wrestling him to the floor, and then squeals and giggles as the toddlers are tickled, tosed and tumbled. In this suburban New Jersey household even the family bloodhound joins in, and the pet parakeet squawks excitedly on the sidelines. Only the four family cats are too dignified to participate.

An all-American moment? Not quite. Slumped listlessly on the sofa, two-year-old Tom* remains motionless; his large chocolate-brown eyes stare dully at the wall. When a visitor tries to greet him or pick him up, he begins to yowl, his cries quickly turning to piercing screams that seem beyond comfort.

Tom's behavior contrasts sharply with that of his two young sisters. In their pink corduroy pants and matching T-shirts, three-year-old Janice* and twenty-one-month-old Andrea* chase one of the long-suffering cats or the dog, Festus; imitate the sounds of the parakeet; and rush back and forth for hugs and kisses.

Yet, according to the Godbouts, all three of these children started out with the same tragic strikes against them: Janice and Tom's birth mother is a drug addict living on the streets. (Janice's father is unknown; Tom's is in and out

The children's names have been changed to protect their privacy.

Eric Rasmussen

Maureen Godbout cuddles two-year-old Tom,* the sickest of her three foster children

of jail.) As a result of their mother's drug use, both children were born addicted to crack, making the first few months of their lives a nightmare. Andrea's mother was also high when she gave birth, one month early. She abandoned Andrea (her ninth child) almost immediately after her birth.

All this would be a tough enough beginning for any infant. But, say the Godbouts, Janice's, Tom's and Andrea's parents also left them another grim legacy: All three youngsters were born HIV-positive; their parents have AIDS.

For Janice and probably Andrea, though, the future looks bright. They are part of a little-known good-news story about AIDS: Like 70 to 80 percent of children born HIV-positive, Janice has "seroreverted," meaning she no longer tests positive for the virus; doctors believe Andrea will also serorevert.

How is this possible? All babies whose mothers have AIDS will test HIV-positive at birth. That's because infants, who are born with underdeveloped immune systems, receive antibodies (blood cells that fight infections) from their mother. So, if the mother is infected with the AIDS virus, the baby will inherit her HIV antibodies as well, and the HIV test will thus show their presence in the baby's body. Over time, as the infant's own immune system takes over, the inherited antibodies disappear—including, in most cases, the HIV antibodies; this is seroreversion. A child probably has the AIDS virus, experts say, if he does not serorevert by the time he's eighteen months to two years old.

Babies who show antibodies to HIV are tested regularly. Andrea's first two tests were negative, says Maureen Godbout, the children's foster mother. "Janice was in the clear by the age of two years. They are both lucky little girls."

Although Tom has not yet been diagnosed as having the AIDS virus, his health strongly suggests that he has the disease. In his two years of life, Tom has seen more doctors and hospitals, and undergone more tests, than most of us do in our entire lives. Because of chronic upper-respiratory infections, he now takes antibiotics daily. And if any of the last battery of tests he recently underwent proves positive, the Godbouts say, his physicians plan to start him on AZT, the first drug approved as an AIDS treatment.

THE FORGOTTEN CHILDREN
Unfortunately, there are far too many children who start their lives as Tom, Andrea and Janice did. And since the biological parents sometimes die from AIDS before their offspring do, more and more youngsters are becoming orphans. These are children other relatives refuse to take into their homes, children few people consider adopting.

Many HIV babies live full-time in their cribs in a hospital ward. "No one picks them up, plays with them or takes them out," says Maureen, thirty-three, a part-time medical assistant. "That image haunted me after I visited a pediatric HIV hospital ward. It's why we took Janice, Tom and Andrea."

For Bob Godbout, thirty-six, a teacher at a high school for emotionally disturbed adolescents, the reason his family has taken these three African-American children into their home is much more personal. Like most Americans in the early eighties, Bob had barely heard the term AIDS. One evening in 1984, however, the phone rang. "It was a hospital in Georgia telling us my father was terminally ill with AIDS," recalls Bob. By the time he got to the hospital, his fifty-seven-year-old father was already in a coma. He died three weeks later without gaining consciousness.

"I never got to talk to my father," says Bob. "It was the nurses who told me that he was bisexual." Like his mother and sister, Bob was stunned.

In his father's memory, Bob and Maureen made a quilt square, which they took to Washington, D.C. The square is now one of tens of thousands making up the giant AIDS memorial quilt. "But I knew that wasn't enough," says Bob. "I wanted to give my father's death meaning."

The Godbouts first learned about HIV-infected babies who needed homes from the former principal at Bob's school. Terry Zealand, Ph.D., had just founded the AIDS Resource Foundation for Children, which runs three homes for kids with AIDS in New Jersey. "We had no idea such kids existed," said Maureen. "We saw these babies and fell in love."

By becoming foster parents, the Godbouts learned, they could take HIV-infected babies into their home and care for them. The state would still have the ultimate responsibility for the children and would pay the Godbouts for their care; the children's medical bills would be paid by Medicaid.

But before the couple took any action, they gave their two children, Daniel, a sharp twelve-year-old, and shy, ten-year-old Erin, equal votes on the matter. "We've always been very open with our kids," says Maureen, "and this was a major, major decision that was also going to affect their lives, all our lives, in a big way. We wanted our children to still be able to grow up normally and not be ostracized by other people or the kids at school.

"We explained that this child might come into our home and die," says Maureen. "We were honest about every-

home, "we had to be trained in CPR and infectious-disease control," says Maureen, stroking Tom's head as he nestles in her lap. "I spent time in a hospital observing nurses looking after AIDS babies. These kids have to be watched constantly [to monitor whether] they get temperatures during the day, or thrush infections [a yeast infection of the mouth], or if they start to lose their appetite or lose weight. Their heads have to be measured regularly to make sure they are growing properly."

What the couple were not warned about, however, was how to deal with HIV babies who were also born crack-addicted. In July 1990, "the Division of Youth and Family Services [DYFS] just dropped off the first child, Jennifer* [who lived with the family only briefly]," remembers Maureen. "The baby screamed the entire time."

After a week of this, the Godbouts called the DYFS for help. The agency sent out a nurse, who taught Maureen and Bob that crack-addicted infants cannot make eye contact, have difficulty bonding and must not be stimulated. "They told us to tightly swaddle these babies—they feel more secure that way—and to hold them on our chests faced away from us so they didn't make eye contact," says Maureen. "We were

"We saw these babies and fell in love," says Maureen.

thing. They told us they didn't care if the babies were sick; they said we should take them so they could see what it was like to have a real family."

But, while Daniel and Erin were enthusiastic about the idea, the Godbouts' friends and other relatives were very upset. "They asked us, 'How can [you] do this? Aren't you afraid of exposing your own kids, or our kids, to this?' " says Bob, who admits that he and his wife also shared doubts at the beginning, until they educated themselves thoroughly about AIDS.

"Every single person we discussed it with at the beginning tried to talk us out of it," says Maureen. "Some of Bob's family and mine have cut us out of their lives. People who used to visit regularly and invite us to their homes regularly no longer do. It was a testing point in our relationships with people."

OPENING THEIR HOME
The Godbouts applied to be a foster family in the fall of 1988. But before an HIV-positive child could live in their

also told to buy a battery-operated swing. We put Jennifer in it, and for three hours she didn't make a sound. It was the first time she slept properly."

Crack babies frequently have low birth weights and are premature; they may also suffer from mental or physical disabilities. In Tom's case, for example, he doesn't talk yet and prefers to crawl. On the few occasions he does try to walk, he drags one leg behind him. "He's only now learning to eat and gaining weight," says Maureen. "He's still very touch-sensitive; he won't pick things up, for example. And he cannot cope with any irregularities in his life. The moment I take him outside the house, he screams until we return."

Tom currently functions far below his age level. Andrea, on the other hand, is now functioning above her age level. "Once she got through her crack withdrawal, she was fine," says Maureen. And Janice, who is undergoing speech therapy, is now in preschool. "Janice's problems have been emotional," says Bob. "She might have been abused previously;

she was very hostile when she arrived. She threw a lot of temper tantrums, had no socialization skills and had to be taught how to play."

Despite the difference in the toddlers' health, the Godbouts treat all their children the same. Andrea, Janice and Tom receive a great deal of physical affection, and no one thinks twice about picking them up or hugging and kissing them. "Except when changing Tom's diapers, or if dealing with blood, I don't use gloves with these kids," says Maureen. "Everyone who touches HIV-positive children in the outside world wears surgical gloves. It's just so impersonal for them. It also isn't necessary. We know the AIDS virus isn't spread by touch, and we also know it is very fragile and dies quickly outside the human body."

SORROW AND JOY

The Godbouts face many difficulties most families never have to think about. One major problem is finding qualified baby-sitters they can afford. (The DYFS requires that the sitters undergo the same HIV training as foster parents.) Since they can't find a sitter, Maureen and Bob are never able to leave the house together. A night out for a movie or dinner, even sleeping late, is a distant memory. "Because of Tom's problems, we can't just pick him up and take him out with us," says Maureen. "One of us always has to stay home with him." The couple do, however, try to take thirty minutes a day together, "when we just go into the bedroom, close the door and touch base with each other and ask 'How was your day?' " says Maureen. "There have been times when I've thought,

Wow, if I don't get a few minutes to myself, I'll go crazy.

"But, you know, it's a funny thing: Since we've had these kids, I'm able to deal with more," she adds. "I no longer sweat the small stuff. When you are dealing with life and death, it no longer bothers you if the entrance floor was washed today."

How will the Godbouts cope if Tom or another foster child succumbs to AIDS in a few years' time? "We may not have experienced the death of one of these youngsters yet," says Maureen, "but we have experienced loss that was as severe as a death for us." She's referring to Jennifer and Shari,* the first two HIV foster babies who lived with the family. "We fell in love with these little girls; the whole family was head-over-heels," recalls Maureen. "DYFS asked us if we wanted to adopt them. We said yes, and we were so excited when they both seroreverted.

"But once both girls became HIV-negative, we were informed that other relatives would be taking them, and family has more legal rights than foster parents," Maureen says.

Adds Bob, "Maureen, I and the children were emotional wrecks when we lost Jennifer and Shari."

After that experience, the Godbouts seriously considered giving up fostering. "It was Daniel and Erin who changed our minds," says Bob. " 'When's the next baby coming?' they asked us. Erin couldn't stand the idea of babies living in a hospital when we could take them."

The family say they have also had to deal with racism—not only from the public, but from some social workers who don't believe black children should be fostered with white families. "And when I take the babies out shopping with me," says Maureen, "I've had

some strange looks, but only from white people. I've been called white trash. But you learn to ignore the hostility."

Fortunately, the Godbouts have never faced the bigotry experienced by AIDS victims such as Ryan White—the young boy from Kokomo, Indiana, who was barred from school in his own town—during the early days of the AIDS epidemic. Neighbors have not threatened the family or treated the children as lepers. "In fact, ours is the house on the block where the neighborhood kids all congregate, and their parents know about our foster children," says Bob.

The Godbouts themselves have found fostering HIV babies a learning experience. "I've realized that people are *very* easy to love," says Maureen. "And it doesn't matter how sick they are."

Adds Bob, "I've become more open-minded about all sorts of things—biracial couples, gays and other people who are different from what society calls 'normal.' "

Janice, Andrea and Tom have "given more to us than we have ever given to them," says Maureen. "What we're doing may sound like a lot of work, but they're special kids. They've added so much to our lives."

For more information

To find out more about children who are HIV-positive, contact: Pediatric AIDS Foundation, 1311 Colorado Avenue, Santa Monica, CA 90404; 310-395-9051.

For information, or to find out about adopting a child with HIV, contact: The Children with AIDS Project of America, P.O. Box 83131, Phoenix, AZ 85071-3131; 800-866-2437.

Siblings and Development

Judy Dunn

Judy Dunn is Professor of Human Development at the Pennsylvania State University. Address correspondence to Judy Dunn, Center for the Study of Child and Adolescent Development, College of Health and Human Development, Pennsylvania State University, University Park, PA 16802.

The great majority of children—around 80% in the United States and Europe—grow up with siblings. Yet the developmental impact of the experience of growing up in close—often uncomfortably close—contact with another child within the family has until recently been little studied. The attention of investigators concerned with early developmental influences has been focused instead chiefly on parents (usually mothers) or family, often characterized in terms of structure (e.g., single-parent versus two-parent) or background variables (e.g., socioeconomic status), or in broad descriptive terms, such as "enmeshed" or "disorganized."

In the last few years, however, studies of siblings within their families have greatly increased in number,[1] and have challenged our assumptions concerning two quite different issues in developmental science. First, such studies have raised serious questions about how families influence individual development—and suggested some intriguing answers. Second, they have also shed light on the development of social understanding in young children. Here, research on siblings observed at home shows that formal assessments of very young children's abilities in experimental settings may have seriously underestimated the nature of young children's social understanding.

As an introduction to the new perspectives on these two developmental issues, consider the following incident, drawn from an observation of a 30-month-old child with his mother and his 14-month-old sister. Andy was a rather timid and sensitive child, cautious, unconfident, and compliant. His younger sister, Susie, was a striking contrast—assertive, determined, and a handful for her mother, who was nevertheless delighted by her boisterous daughter. In the course of an observation of Andy and his sister, Susie persistently attempted to grab a forbidden object on a high kitchen counter, despite her mother's repeated prohibitions. Finally, she succeeded, and Andy overheard his mother make a warm, affection-

ate comment on Susie's action: "Susie, you *are* a determined little devil!"

Andy, sadly, commented to his mother, "*I'm* not a determined little devil!" His mother replied, laughing, "No! What are you? A poor old boy!"

A NEW PERSPECTIVE ON THE DEVELOPMENT OF INDIVIDUAL DIFFERENCES

This brief incident serves to illustrate some of the key issues emerging from a series of systematic studies of siblings and parents in the United States and Britain,[2] which highlight why we need to study within-family processes to explain the development of individual differences. Three features of these processes, evident in the exchange between Andy and his mother, are important here: the difference between siblings in personality, the difference in their relationships with their parents, and their responses to exchanges between their siblings and parents.

Differences Between Siblings

The striking differences between siblings growing up within the same family—differences in personality, adjustment, and psychopathology—have now been documented in a very wide range of studies,[3,4] and these differences present a major challenge to investigators studying family influence. Why should two children who share 50% of their segregating genes and the same family background turn out to be so different? After all, the family factors assumed to be key in development (e.g., parental mental health, marital quality, social class background) are apparently shared by siblings.

This question of why siblings are so different is not just a matter of interest to fond parents puzzled by their children's differences. It turns out to be key to understanding the development of individual differences more generally. Extensive studies by behavior geneticists have now shown that the sources of environmental influence that make individuals different from one another work *within* rather than *between* families.[3] To understand the salient environmental influences on individual development, we have to be able to explain what makes two children within the same family different from one an-

From *Current Directions in Psychological Science*, Vol. 1, No. 1, February 1992, pp. 6-9. © 1992 by the American Psychological Society. Reprinted by permission of Cambridge University Press.

other. The message from this research is not that family influence is unimportant, but that we need to document those experiences that are specific to each child within a family, and therefore we need to study more than one child per family, with a new perspective on what are the salient influences within the family.

What could the significant processes within the family be—differences in parent-child relationships, differences within the sibling relationship itself, differences in peer relationships outside the family, or chance experiences that affect one sibling and not another? In a series of studies, the relation of each of these to children's developmental outcomes is being explored. A number of different samples have been studied in the United States and in England, including nationally representative samples, and major longitudinal studies have included adoptive and biological samples (enabling us to explore where genetic similarities and differences enter the picture). A wide variety of methods has been employed, including naturalistic observations of the families and interviews with all family members. The results of this body of research are discussed in a recent book;[2] here some illustrative points will be summarized briefly.

Differences Between Siblings' Relationships With Their Parents

It is clear that there are major differences in the affection, attention, and discipline that many siblings experience with their parents—whether the information on these differences comes from parents, children, or observers. The differences in warmth and pride that were evident in the behavior of Andy's mother toward her two children are very common. The extent of such differences and the domains in which they are most marked have now been documented in a range of differing samples of families, as have the variables related to the degree of parental differentiation (e.g., the developmental stages of the children and the mother's personality, educational background, and IQ). An important lesson from both the observational work and the experimental studies is that children are extremely sensitive to such differences.

Sensitivity of Children to Their Siblings' Interaction With Their Parents

From a remarkably early age, children monitor and react to their parents' interaction with their siblings. The example of Andy and Susie is typical: Andy monitors and responds to his mother's exchange with his sister, promptly, and with a self-comparison. A recent study showed that 20% of the conversational turns by secondborn children in one sample were attempts to join the conversation between other people.[5] The salient verbal environment for children is not solely the speech addressed to them, but includes conversations between parents and sibling.

Two lines of evidence from recent developmental work confirm the salience for young children of emotional exchanges between other people: laboratory studies of children witnessing exchanges between others and naturalistic studies of children in their families. A wealth of studies have now documented that children from the end of their first year are interested in the behavior of other family members, and especially in their emotional exchanges. In a series of studies, Zahn-Waxler and her colleagues have documented the development of children's responses to emotional displays between others, and the effects of witnessing such exchanges on play and aggressive behavior.[6,7] Naturalistic observations of siblings at home have shown that children rarely ignore disputes between others, but act promptly to support or punish one of the antagonists, and that the behavior of both firstborn and secondborn children is profoundly affected by their mothers' interactions with the other sibling.[8]

How important are these experiences of differential treatment, developmentally? The first investigations show differential experiences are linked to a range of outcome measures: In terms of adjustment, for example, children who receive less maternal affection and attention than their siblings are likely to be more worried, anxious, or depressed than other children in general. And there is now an accumulation of evidence that differential parental behavior is linked to the quality of the relationship between siblings, with more hostility and conflict found in families with greater differential parental treatment, an association found for preschool children, for siblings in middle childhood, for children with disabled siblings, and for children following divorce.[1]

Other Sources of Differential Experience

Among the other possible sources of differential experience, there is growing evidence that differences in children's experiences within the sibling relationship itself can also be related to adjustment. If instead of focusing on siblings as a dyad, we ask how similarly or differently the two siblings behave toward each other, we find there can be marked differences between the two in the affection or control they show. Whether the information comes from maternal interview, children's own accounts, or observations, the emerging picture is that in only one third of sibling pairs do the two children show very similar degrees of affection toward one another. For hostile behavior there is more reciprocity, but within a pair, the relative differences in negative behavior are correlated with later perceived self-competence, and with conduct problems and anxious or depressed behavior. For example, one study found that the more negative a younger sibling is toward the older, relative to the older's negative behavior, the higher the self-esteem of the younger 3 years later.[2] Of course, these initial findings must be treated with caution until they are replicated, and no causal inferences can be made from such correlational data.

In summary, the focus on siblings and their differential experiences within the family has changed and clarified our picture of what are the salient family influences on individual development. In an important sense children are, it appears, *family members* from early in their second year; they are interested in, responsive to, and influenced by the relationships between their siblings and parents—and this insight brings us to the second developmental arena in which sibling studies have provided illumination, the development of social understanding.

A NEW PERSPECTIVE ON THE DEVELOPMENT OF SOCIAL UNDERSTANDING

Recall the comments made by Andy in the incident with his sister and mother. Andy, in the emotional circumstances of the family exchange, made a self-evaluative comment following his mother's warm remark praising his sister. Yet he was *only* two *and a half*. This is startlingly early for a child to be evaluating himself. At this age, according to the received view of the development of self-reflective powers, based on experimental studies, he should not be able to evaluate himself in this way, or be sensitive to social comparison. Could we be misrepresenting children's sociocognitive abilities by studying them only outside the family? Here, observational studies of siblings at home have proved most illuminating.[8]

A focus on children's disputes, jokes, and cooperative play with their siblings has shown that from 18 months on children understand how to hurt, comfort, and exacerbate their siblings' pain; they understand what is allowed or disapproved in their family world; they differentiate between transgressions of different sorts, and anticipate the response of adults to their own and to other people's misdeeds; they comment on and ask about the causes of others' actions and feelings. Analyses of this growing understanding of emotions, of others' goals, and of social rules have shown that the foundations for the moral virtues of caring, consideration, and kindness are well laid by 3 years, but so too children have by this age a sophisticated grasp of how to use social rules for their own ends. The drive to understand others and the social world is, I have argued,[8] closely linked to the nature of a child's relationships within the family over this period: the emotional power of attachment to parents, of rivalry between siblings, and of the conflict between growing independence and socialization pressure. For a young child whose own goals and interests are often at odds with—and frustrated by—others in the family, it is clearly adaptive to begin to understand those other family members and the social rules of the shared family world. The study of siblings has highlighted why it is important that

social understanding should be high on the developmental agenda.

The subtlety of social understanding that children show in the family context—in contrast to their limited capabilities when faced with more abstract or formal tasks—has considerably changed our view of children's abilities, and why they change. And in addition to delineating the pattern of normative growth of social understanding, sibling studies are beginning to clarify in detail the causes of individual differences in social understanding. These differences are striking: Children vary greatly in their ability to understand the causes and consequences of emotions and to understand what other people are thinking and how this influences their behavior. In the recent burst of productive experimental research on children's understanding of "other minds," there has been little consideration of individual differences: How far such differences are related to verbal intelligence, to the quality of children's relationships, or to other family experiences has not been examined empirically. The study of children with their siblings has enabled us to test predictions concerning the significance of family relationships, parental expressiveness, and children's cognitive ability in accounting for differences in social understanding.[9]

The results highlight the importance—and the independent contribution to the variance—of a number of factors. For example, diffences in family discourse about the social world are important: Children who grew up in families in which feelings and causality were discussed performed better than other children on assessments of social understanding 14 months later. But the quality of children's relationships with their siblings is also key: Children who had experienced frequent cooperative exchanges with their siblings, for example, were more successful than other children on tasks assessing their grasp of the connections between another person's belief and subsequent behavior. Also—most notably—differences in children's social understanding are related to the quality of the relationships between their siblings and their mothers. Children who grew up in families in which they witnessed their mothers being highly attentive, responsive, or controlling to their siblings scored particularly high on social cognition assessments 1 year later.

Thus, the work on social understanding links with the first theme—the processes involved in family influence on individual differences. Examining within-family differential experiences of siblings will enlarge our understanding of the salient processes of family influences on personality and adjustment. Similarly, it is clear that studying children in the complex network of sibling and parental relationships within the family can greatly enhance our knowledge about their understanding of the social world. It is within the daily drama of family life that children's social intelligence is revealed and fostered, and siblings play a central role in that drama.

NOTES

1. F. Boer and J. Dunn, *Sibling Relationships: Developmental and Clinical Issues* (Erlbaum, Hillsdale, NJ, 1992).

2. J. Dunn and R. Plomin, *Separate Lives: Why Siblings Are So Different* (Basic Books, New York, 1990).

3. R. Plomin and D. Daniels, Why are children in the same family so different from each other? *The Behavioral and Brain Sciences, 10,* 1–16 (1987).

4. S. Scarr and S. Grajek, Similarities and differences among siblings, in *Sibling Relationships: Their Nature and Significance Across the Lifespan,* M. E. Lamb and B. Sutton-Smith, Eds. (Erlbaum, Hillsdale, NJ, 1982), pp. 357–386.

5. J. Dunn and M. Shatz, Becoming a conversationalist despite (or because of) having an older sibling, *Child Development, 60,* 399–410 (1989).

6. C. Zahn-Waxler and M. Radke-Yarrow, The development of altruism: Alternative research strategies, in *The Development of Prosocial Behavior,* N. Eisenberg-Berg, Ed. (Academic Press, New York, 1982), pp. 109–137.

7. E. M. Cummings, Coping with background anger, *Child Development, 58,* 976–984 (1987).

8. J. Dunn, *The Beginnings of Social Understanding* (Harvard University Press, Cambridge, MA, 1988).

9. J. Dunn, J. Brown, C. Slomkowski, C. Tesla, and L. Youngblade, Young children's understanding of other people's feelings and beliefs: Individual differences and their antecedents, *Child Development, 62,* 1352–1366 (1991).

PLACES EVERYONE

THE FIRSTBORN IS A PERFECTIONIST, THE MIDDLE CHILD REBELLIOUS, AND THE LAST BORN A CHARMER. DOES BIRTH ORDER PREDICT YOUR PERSONALITY?

Stephen Harrigan

Stephen Harrigan is a novelist and screenwriter who lives in Austin, Texas. His newest novel, Water and Light, *is published by Houghton Mifflin.*

A few months ago, when I was in Los Angeles, I paid a call on my older brother at the gleaming new downtown office building where he works. I gave my name at the reception booth in the lobby, and then ascended the many floors to his corner office in an elevator that glided upward as silently as a spider on a thread.

He was standing there to greet me, dressed in a gray suit, when the doors opened on the 56th floor. As ever, he was three inches taller, and quicker on the draw with his handshake. My older brother's name is Jim, though I have noticed that professionally he goes by the commanding initials J.P. As he led me on a tour of his building, past works of corporate art, through conference rooms and executive dining rooms while I trailed along with my untied shoelace flapping on the marble floor, it occurred to me that even in childhood—when he was Jimmy and I was Stevie—somehow I had already perceived him as J.P.

Decades of adulthood, I realized, had not bred the younger brother out of me. Nor could I expect it to. There is a school of thought—and a cottage industry to go with it—that decrees that birth order is

destiny. We are who we are because of who was there ahead of us when we were born, and who came behind. In my own case, one might argue, the scenario was so predictable it could have been plotted on a graph. "The younger brother of a brother," wrote psychologist Walter To-

The younger brother has lived with an older, taller, smarter, more perfect boy than himself as far back as he can remember.

man, "has lived with an older, taller, smarter, stronger, more perfect boy than himself as far back as he can remember." In order to avoid the hopeless task of competing against Jim, I became in many ways his opposite—a process that is known in psycho-jargon as sibling deidentification. Where he was authoritative, I was cunningly acquiescent. Where he was athletic, I was bookish. Without either of us consciously knowing it, I conceded him the title of standard-bearer, conservator, defender of the realm—then scouted out the terrain and found my own dreamy path.

It is intoxicatingly simple, this idea that our place in the family is the fount of our strengths and failings, our drives and our fears. If we know our place in the family, the birth order gurus suggest in their hyper-friendly self-help books, we know ourselves. If you're one of the 44 percent

of the population who's first or only born, you were the early recipient of the brunt of your parents' attention and expectations. That means you're likely to be hard driving, demanding, doggedly responsible. Oldest children tend to spend more time with adults, so it's natural that they

grow up faster, eager to invest themselves with leadership and grave responsibility. (All seven Mercury astronauts were firstborns.) If you are an only child, you are supposed to be just as much a perfectionist as a firstborn, but intransigent and finicky as well, since you never experienced the tempering trauma of dethronement by a younger sibling.

Middle children, like me, are the hardest to nail down, but in general we are seen as the victims of benign neglect, the ones with the fewest pictures in the family photo album. To cope with that lack of attention, we became rebellious and secretive, relying on friends for the companionship that somehow eluded us within the family. And because we never got our parents all to ourselves, we learned to compromise. By the time we were out of childhood, we were already seasoned diplomats.

Youngest children may smolder with

thwarted ambition (like Joseph in the Old Testament, who dreamed of himself as a sheaf of wheat that suddenly stood upright in a field, commanding obeisance from the lesser sheaves representing his ten brothers), but typically by the time they were born their parents had exhausted their expectations on all the siblings ahead of them, and were content to pamper the youngest without condition. Last borns are described variously as clowns, cutups, and mascots.

Birth order experts are full of breezy observations and prescriptions. They tell us we should marry into relationships that roughly duplicate our old sibling connections. So if we are the youngest brother of sisters we should marry the oldest sister of brothers, or if we are the youngest sister of brothers we should marry the oldest brother of sisters. We are advised that the secret to good parenting is to use birth order to understand the behavior of our own children—the supercharged firstborn, the mediating middle child, the restless last born.

When viewed through the birth order lens, human nature all at once seems marvelously comprehendable. Of *course* Hilary Clinton and Henry Kissinger are firstborns! Of *course* Katie Couric and Richard Simmons are youngest children! Firstborn, second born, last born—thinking of ourselves in these terms, we seem to snap immediately into place.

But is it true? Are the insights we receive from pondering birth order any more authentic than those we find in a daily horoscope, or in the lugubrious responses from a Ouija board?

"What could make more sense?" psychologist Kevin Leman asked one bright morning as we left his Tucson office to go out in search of breakfast. "A theory based on the dynamics between parents and children and between children and their siblings. It's not just that you're number one or number two. It's more complex than that. You have to take the whole family into account. But you *can* use birth order to get a quick handle on people."

Leman is the reigning pooh-bah of birth order, the author of *The Birth Order Book*, which bears the confident subtitle *Why You Are the Way You Are*, as well as *Growing Up Firstborn: The Pressure and Privilege of Being Number One*. His books are found in that vast self-help section of the nineties bookstore devoted to co-dependency, addiction, miscarriage, Cinderella complexes, and books by both sexes on what's wrong with men.

CELEBRATED SIBLINGS

AS A PSYCHOLOGICAL THEORY, birth order may be full of holes. But it's hard to resist guessing someone's place in the family by looking for clues in his or her personality. Here's a chance to put your intuition to the test.

1
WHO CAME FIRST?

Circle the eldest of these famous family members.

A. Dick and Tommy Smothers
B. Jimmy and Billy Carter
C. David and Ricky Nelson
D. Eva and Zsa Zsa Gabor
E. Joan and Jackie Collins
F. Randy and Dennis Quaid
G. Jeff and Beau Bridges
H. Groucho, Harpo, and Chico Marx

BONUS: Who are the two remaining Marx brothers and were they older or younger than the others?

2
SIBLING SAYS:

Match these personalities to their quotes about their kin.

__Yogi Bera __Warren Beatty
__Cher __Meryl Streep
__Diane Keaton __Edward Kennedy
__Joan Rivers __Diane Sawyer
__Charlie Sheen __Candice Bergen

A. "My sister was older by three years, and prettier, and things always seemed easier for her . . . She was vivacious and popular. I was the loner, full of self-doubt and deadly serious in my inch-thick glasses."

B. "It was like having a whole army of mothers around me. While it seemed I could never do anything right with my brothers, I could never do anything wrong with my sisters."

C. "I always wanted to look like [my younger sister], who has blond hair and green eyes . . . We've always been alike in a lot of ways. But we were very different in that she was good in school and I hated it."

D. "During high school I wanted to be a baseball player because nobody else in the family played baseball. [My father acted, and my brother wrestled and played soccer.] So I thought, 'If I could just excel at baseball, they'll think I'm something.'"

E. "I have a younger brother and two younger sisters . . . As a kid, I was always the exhibitionist of the family, constantly trying out for talent contests and school plays and always covering up my supersensitivity by being funny."

F. "Every now and then a reporter who thinks he is Freud asks me if being the youngest is why I made it . . . I almost always say yes—[but] I don't think it had anything to do with it."

G. "I was a rather bossy big sister. I would push my little brothers around—after all, that's what they were there for. When we made home movies, I was always the director. I'd dress my brothers in costumes and order them about."

H. "I get my drive from being the second child and a fat child. My sister was smarter and better than I was in every way. I think what I do embarrasses her terribly because I'm so unladylike."

I. "I was fifteen when my brother was born. He was a child of light, while I was a child of shadows . . . I even forgave him for inheriting my mother's beautiful singing voice."

J. "I don't talk about my sister."

ANSWERS
1. Who Came First? A: Though he portrays the whining younger brother, Tommy is the firstborn. B: Jimmy was the overachieving firstborn and Billy the beer-guzzling baby. C: David was four years older. D: Though both claim to be younger than official records indicate, Zsa Zsa is the elder of the two. E: Joan is Jackie's senior. F: Randy Quaid is older. G: Beau is older by eight years. H: Chico is two years older than Harpo, who is two years older than Groucho. BONUS: Gummo and Zeppo; three and 11 years younger than Groucho.

2. Sibling Says: A: Diane Sawyer B: Edward Kennedy C: Cher D: Charlie Sheen E: Diane Keaton F: Yogi Bera G: Meryl Streep H: Joan Rivers I: Candice Bergen J: Warren Beatty

—*Steven Finch*

Needless to say, Leman's office is not a dark Freudian lair, but a sunny enclave on the second floor of an office strip. Leman himself is as uncomplicated as his book titles suggest. Sandy-haired and clean-shaven, he was wearing jeans the day I met him. (As a last born, he can't stand to wear a suit.)

Leman told me he first heard about birth order when he was a graduate student at the University of Arizona, and the theory had the force of an epiphany. "All I could think about was my family—my firstborn sister who has clear vinyl runners on the carpet and whose children are always color coordinated; my older brother, who bears my father's name; and then me, the baby of the family."

As we approached his car, Leman pointed to his personalized licence plates, which bore the message ZAP ASU. "Now that's a typical thing for a baby of the family to do," he said. "Out here in Tucson, we hate ASU because they're the University of Arizona's rivals. To me it's worth it to pay twenty-five dollars a year to have people pull up and honk.

"Have you ever seen me on TV?" Leman asked as we drove off to the restaurant. "I'm funny. You'll find that most comedians—Steve Martin, Eddie Murphy, Goldie Hawn—are last borns."

Leman has promoted his ideas on most of the major talk shows and in various business seminars, where he advises executives on how to use birth order information as a strategic tool. If you own a car dealership, for example, you'd want to know that a last born might very well be the star of the sales force, but would be a disaster in the general-manager slot, which should go to a firstborn.

"I was on 'Jenny Jones' last week," he said. "Producers love to do this kind of thing: They bring out three siblings and make me guess which one is which. I was in good form that day. I nailed them, which made me feel like Mickey Mantle in 1956. I felt so confident I took a stab at Jenny herself. I guessed that she was a baby girl, since she was overflowing with affection, and I was right."

He turned to me, sized me up for a moment, and said, "I'd say you're the firstborn son with an older sister."

"Actually," I confessed, "second-born son with a younger sister."

"Hmmmm," Leman said.

"MOST OF THIS STUFF on birth order," complains Harold Mosak, a clinical psy-chologist who teaches a course on the subject at the Adler School of Professional Psychology in Chicago, "is just psychological pap that depends on popular notions and misconceptions. People who want to understand themselves rush to this stuff just like they rush to astrology."

Even Alfred Adler, the founding father of birth order theory, believed that the idea could be carried too far.

"There has been some misunderstanding," he wrote in 1918, "of my custom of classification according to position in the family. It is not, of course, the child's number in the order of successive births which influences his character, but the situation into which he is born and the way he interprets it." Adler recognized that classifying people by birth order was overly simplistic. But, in retrospect, his basic observations on the subject still have the sort of ringing self-evidence that is often associated with ideas of genius. He pointed out, for instance, that second-born children often have dreams in which they picture themselves running after trains and riding in bicycle races. "Sometimes this hurry in his dreams is sufficient by itself to allow us to guess that the individual is a second child."

Adler was convinced that his own life was shaped by his birth order. Born in 1870 in Penzing, a suburb of Vienna, he was the second of six children. He was a sickly boy who felt hopelessly overshadowed by his older brother. "One of my earliest recollections," he wrote, "is of sitting on a bench, bandaged up on account of rickets, with my healthy elder brother sitting opposite me. He could run, jump, and move about quite effortlessly, while for me movement of any sort was a strain and an effort." Even when he was an old man, Adler was haunted by the robust power of his older brother. "He is *still* ahead of me!" he lamented near the end of his life.

Adler's resentment of his older brother's authority invested him with a rebellious streak that would leave its stamp on the burgeoning science of psychology. He began his career as a physician, and was keenly interested in the influence of environment on physical and mental health. In 1902, his brilliance brought him to the attention of Sigmund Freud, who was then refining his theories of the unconscious mind and consolidating his position as the high priest of psychoanalysis. Freud was 13 years older than Adler, and in his authoritarian cast of mind a classic firstborn who was used to ruling his younger siblings. ("I am by temperament nothing but a conquistador," he once admitted to a friend.)

Adler was asked to join Freud's famous weekly discussion group that later became known as the Vienna Psychological Society. Over the course of ten years Adler contributed greatly to the insights and even the terminology of Freud's work (the term *inferiority complex*, for instance, was first coined by Adler).

But the firstborn Freud, sensing a rival, began to hound and berate his colleague. Adler, still suffering from his lifelong resentment at being number two, bristled and left the sanctum. "Why should I always do my work under your shadow?" he asked Freud in a parting shot.

Adler took a small group of followers with him and started his own rival mental health dynasty. His ideas were simpler and more pragmatic than Freud's. The hallmark of what he called individual psychology was a conviction that people do not live in a gloomy, deterministic universe, subject to unconscious drives they cannot control. Adler's focus was on getting his patients up and running, showing them what was wrong with their lives and then allowing them to make a choice to either sink into despair or become productive members of society.

Today, Adlerians—such as Kevin Leman—are a distinct minority in a mental health industry still largely influenced by Freudian thought, but it is they who have kept the concept of birth order alive.

Even the Adlerians have found, however, that it's tricky to prove that birth order counts for much. Since Adler's death, various studies *have* turned up some interesting observations. Last borns are more likely to write their autobiographies (what better way to be noticed?). They also are statistically more inclined to alcoholism. It turns out that more firstborns seek psychological counseling. Renowned baseball players have tended to be middle

Last borns are more likely to write their autobiographies. Firstborn girls are overrepresented among striptease artists.

and youngest children (by conditioning, perhaps, they're more drawn to team sports). And firstborn girls are overrepresented among striptease artists.

By and large, though, the idea that birth order is directly related to personality has proven to be as ungraspable as it is enticing. "Birth order influence is a disappointment," says Jules Angst, a psychologist from Zurich. "It doesn't explain a lot."

Angst arrived at this conclusion after surveying, with his colleague Cecile Ernst, 34 years of birth order research, from 1946 to 1980. Ernst and Angst came away unimpressed. In short, birth order didn't consistently predict which sibling is most likely to be an extrovert, feel pain, take risks, lack self-esteem, select certain marriage partners, feel guilt, adopt conservative political views, get frustrated easily, need autonomy, or suffer psychological problems. Only a few of the studies they considered gave even marginal support to the idea that birth order influence is a factor in shaping personality, and most of these, Angst says, were fraught with "methodological fallacies."

"Most serious researchers have stopped talking about birth order," says Toni Falbo, an educational psychologist at the University of Texas in Austin. "If you look at all the factors that lead to a particular outcome in shaping someone's personality, on a good day, birth order might account for one percent."

The big problem with assessing birth order is the almost impossible task of getting a clear focus on what it is that's being studied. A family is a densely woven fabric made up of innumerable threads, some of which are apparent and some of which are not. Even if you could extract that one birth order thread out of the carpet—leaving in place a background of other powerful influences like socioeconomic status, race, class, values, aspirations, disease, death, ancestral history—you would still have a great deal of untangling to do.

Take, as an example, a family with four siblings. The children might have been born one after another at regular intervals, in which case their birth order positions would be fairly clear. But what if they came along in sets of two that were separated by a wide gap of years? Wouldn't the third child be likely to develop the characteris-

tics of a firstborn, and might not the second child share the same last born traits of the fourth child? What if the firstborn was a boy, and all the rest were girls? Wouldn't the oldest girl develop a firstborn personality in relation to her sisters? How would an oldest son turn out if he were haunted by the knowledge of a "phantom" older brother lost to an early death?

The permutations of gender, spacing, and circumstance are so endless and complicating that it hardly seems worthwhile trying to sort through them. For Kevin Leman, however, they're just more spice for the stew.

"Every time another child is born," he says, "the entire environment changes. How parents interact with each child as it enters the family circle determines in great part that child's final destiny.

"Now the reason I guessed that you're a firstborn son with an older sister," he explained to me on the way to the restaurant that morning, "is because you seem to have a nice, easygoing demeanor. Which tells me one of two things: You have sisters above you in the family, or you have a good relationship with your mother. Now one of those things has to be true or you can get out of the car and walk.

"Also," he went on, "you're a reporter. Reporters are almost always firstborns. On my last tour I was interviewed by ninety-two people. Out of the ninety-two, eighty-seven were firstborns. Same thing with pilots. If you want to have fun on the flight home, stick your head into the cockpit and ask, 'How are the firstborns today?' Eighty-eight percent of them are. And librarians! Firstborns are voracious readers. I challenge you to call thirty librarians and find out their birth orders."

Over breakfast, Leman sketched his own history as a last born goofball. He was a poor student and behavior problem in high school, he said, and when he managed to find a college that would take him, he was more or less kicked out in his third semester. Leman was working as a janitor when he met his wife, Sande, who as fate would have it was a firstborn and therefore ideally suited to the task of shaping him up. Leman also credits his wife with helping him find a sustaining belief in God, the ultimate firstborn.

Leman related all this with good humor

and a certain commonsense gravity, which made him seem less superficial than I had expected. But it was clear that his last born traits had prepared him well for the role of pop psychologist. Not only was he gleeful in his disregard for the academics who might consider him a lightweight ("Academia! You want to talk about an unreal world?"), he was also still enough of a showboat to put his birth order knowledge to use as a kind of parlor game.

Just then, for instance, he was trying to guess the birth order of our waiter.

"Okay, Eric," Leman said, glancing at the waiter's name tag. "Give me a description of your mom or dad. Either one."

"Well," Eric said, "my dad is very shy."

"How about little boy Eric? Age five to twelve?"

"Well, I guess some people would have said I was a mama's boy."

"Hmmmm. And when you grew up, did you marry a firstborn, middle child, or baby?"

"Baby. She's the last of four kids."

"So," Leman said. "I bet you're a firstborn son."

Eric smiled. "You got it," he said, and went back to the kitchen.

"What tipped you off?" I asked Leman.

"Two things. First, did you notice the way he came out and wanted our order right away? He was impatient, he didn't want to fool with us. The other thing was *very*. He described his father as 'very shy.' So he probably sees things in black or white—not much gray. That's definitely a firstborn trait."

I went home impressed, willing to overlook Leman's misreading of my own birth order. If the Great Birth Order Theory did not quite bear up under the weight of evidence, it was still tantalizing enough to my imagination to *seem* true. That, surely, is what keeps it alive. Scientific scrutiny may erode the birth order stereotype, but we tend to shore it up again whenever we meet a supercharged eldest child or a last born who is lost in the ozone.

I called 30 librarians. It turned out that only 18 of them were firstborns or only children. As I had come to expect when dealing with the notion that birth order rules our lives, I was neither convinced nor resoundingly disabused. As a middle child, I could see only shades of gray.

Crises - Challenges and Opportunities

- **Family under Siege (Articles 30 and 31)**
- **Family Violence (Articles 32–34)**
- **Sexual Issues and Infidelity (Articles 35 and 36)**
- **The Stress of Family Responsibilities (Articles 37–39)**
- **Divorce and Remarriage (Articles 40–42)**
- **Loss and Bereavement (Articles 43 and 44)**

"Stress is life and life is stress." Sometimes stress in families gives new meaning to this statement. When a crisis occurs in families, many processes occur simultaneously as families and their members adjust and attempt to cope with the stressor and its effects. The experience of a crisis often leads to conflict and reduces the family member's ability to act as resources for each other. Indeed, a stressor can overwhelm the family system and family members may be some of the least effective people in coping with each other's response to a crisis.

Family crisis comes in many forms; they can be more drawn out or the crisis event can be clearly defined. The source of stress can be from outside or inside the family, or it can be a combination of both. It can directly involve all or as few as one family member, but the effects will ripple through the family, affecting all of its members to one degree or another.

In this section, we consider a wide variety of crises. Some result from broad cultural and social forces, others come from more intimate, interpersonal sources. The first subsection is concerned with dramatic changes in the family and the impact of governmental policy and programming on family form and process. Both articles address dramatic changes in families. "Endangered Family" focuses on African American families and "White Ghetto?" addresses the culture of poverty, which is not unique to any single race or ethnic group.

Family violence is the focus of the next subsection. Children can be intentional and unintentional victims of violence in families. "Helping Children Cope with Violence" shows how children growing up in violent surroundings can come away scarred for life. "After He Hits Her" addresses the spousal crisis of domestic violence, and it explores the relationship dynamics involved that can be at the core of a continuing cycle of trauma and pain or help to begin the slow process of change. The final subsection article is an honest "in the trenches" view of

what needs to be done to reduce the incidence of domestic battery of women. Rather than asking why battered women stay in abusive relationships, a better question would be, "Why do men who batter do it, and what can be done to stop them?"

The next subsection focuses on problems in sexuality and sexual relationships. "Sexual Desire" addresses the most significant sexual dysfunction or complaint among couples of the 1990s: that their individual and mutual desire level is out of synch. Then, the final article in the subsection examines infidelity and its aftermath. Frank Pittman recounts the emotional and practical wreckage that results from extramarital sex.

What is the nature of stress that results from caring for others in the family? In the next subsection, the stress (and the rewards) of caregiving are addressed. The first article, "The Myth of the Miserable Working Woman," confronts many of the myths regarding women balancing work and home. Surprisingly, many of the assumptions we have about the overwhelming nature of this balancing act are not found to be true. The next two articles address issues of providing care for a family member with a chronic, debilitating condition—first, from a more scholarly perspective, and second, from a personal perspective.

Divorce and remarriage are the focus of the next section. Changes in marriages, in particular, changes in the ease with which one leaves marriage, and the negative impact on family members, are discussed in "Family Values: The Bargain Breaks." The remaining two articles in the subsection take an optimistic look at stepfamilies. In both, the reader has an opportunity to examine the way our culture has set up stepmothers and families with an impossible evil/angelic dichotomy. Although more complex than traditional families, these articles show that these families are not doomed to failure and unresolved conflict.

The final subsection explores losses that often are not considered when death is discussed. One is not supposed to die young. Yet, these articles address two situations in which young people do die. "Solace and Immortality: Bereaved Parents' Continuing Bond with Their Children" discusses how parents can grieve the loss of their child, not by disconnecting from their child, but by transforming their connection. "Sibling Survivors: How Losing a Brother or Sister to Cancer Can Recast a Child's Destiny" looks at the long-term effects of losing a sibling in one's youth. Such a loss can have a dramatic and long-lasting impact on the surviving sibling.

Looking Ahead: Challenge Questions

What is the future of families living in poverty? If you could develop social programs to help these families, what would these programs contain?

How comfortable do you think you would feel talking with your partner about sex? What hinders you from talking openly?

How would you react if you learned that your spouse had been unfaithful? Under what circumstances would you consider extrarelational sex?

What do you see as your responsibility to your family? What is their responsibility to you? Would you give up anything to care for your parents? What would you expect your children to give up for you?

Do you know anyone who is divorced? How have they been affected? If they have children, how have the children been affected?

Is your family, or that of a friend, a remarried or blended family? If so, how have you, or they, been affected?

Have you ever had anyone close to you die? How did you feel? If you have not, what do you think it would be like? What kind of support did you need?

ENDANGERED FAMILY

*For many African-Americans, marriage and childbearing do not go together.
After decades of denial and blame, a new candor is emerging as
blacks struggle to save their families.*

Late on a sultry summer morning, Dianne Caballero settles onto her porch in the New York suburb of Roosevelt, bemused by the scene playing out across the street. Behind electric clippers, a muscular black man is trimming hedges with the intensity of a barber sculpting a fade; nearby, his wife empties groceries from the car. In most quarters, they might elicit barely a nod. But in this largely black, working-class community, the couple is one of the few intact families on the block. All too common are the five young women who suddenly turn into view, every one of them pushing a baby stroller, not one of them married. Resigned, Caballero says with a sigh, "Where are the men?"

A black child has only one chance in five of growing up with two parents

---

It's a lament she knows too well. Like her mother before her and her daughter after, Caballero, who is black, had a child out of wedlock at 16. Twenty-three years later, even she is astounded at the gulf between motherhood and marriage. When her mother got pregnant in the '50s, she says, she was considered unique. When Caballero had a baby in 1970, no one ostracized her, though it still wasn't something "nice" girls did. But by the time her daughter had a baby seven years ago, it was regarded as "normal." Now, Caballero says regretfully, it's commonplace. "And there doesn't

This article was reported by Farai Chideya, Michele Ingrassia, Vern E. Smith and Pat Wingert. It was written by Michele Ingrassia.

seem to be anything happening to reverse it."

That prospect troubles black leaders and parents alike, those like Caballero, who worries that her granddaughter is destined to be the fourth generation in her family to raise a child without a man. The odds are perilously high:

- For blacks, the institution of marriage has been devastated in the last generation: 2 out of 3 first births to black women under 35 are now out of wedlock. In 1960, the number was 2 out of 5. And it's not likely to improve any time soon. A black child born today has only a 1-in-5 chance of growing up with two parents until the age of 16, according to University of Wisconsin demographer Larry L. Bumpass. The impact, of course, is not only on black families but on all of society. Fatherless homes boost crime rates, lower educational attainment and add dramatically to the welfare rolls.

- Many black leaders rush to portray out-of-wedlock births as solely a problem of an entrenched underclass. It's not. It cuts across economic lines. Among the poor, a staggering 65 percent of never-married black women have children, double the number for whites. But even among the well-to-do, the differences are striking: 22 percent of never-married black women with incomes above $75,000 have children, almost 10 times as many as whites.

Nearly 30 years ago, Daniel Patrick Moynihan, then an assistant secretary of labor, caused a firestorm by declaring that fatherless homes were "the fundamental source of the weakness of the Negro Community." At the time, one quarter of black families were headed by women. Today the situation has only grown worse. A majority of black families with children—62 percent—are now headed by one parent. The result is what

Johns Hopkins University sociologist Andrew Cherlin calls "an almost complete separation of marriage and childbearing among African-Americans."

It was not always so. Before 1950, black and white marriage patterns looked remarkably similar. And while black marriage rates have precipitously dipped since then, the desire to marry remains potent: a NEWSWEEK Poll of single African-American adults showed that 88 percent said that they wanted to get married. But the dream of marriage has been hammered in the last 25 years. The economic dislocations that began in the '70s, when the nation shifted from an industrial to a service base, were particularly devastating to black men, who had migrated north in vast numbers to manufacturing jobs. The civil-rights movement may have ended legal segregation, but it hasn't erased discrimination in the work force and in everyday life. "When men lose their ability to earn bread, their sense of self declines dramatically. They lose rapport with their children," says University of Oklahoma historian Robert Griswold, author of "Fatherhood in America."

Some whites overlooked jobs and discrimination as factors in the breakdown of the black family. Back in the '60s, at the peak of the battle over civil rights, Moynihan infuriated blacks by describing a pattern of "pathology." Understandably, blacks were not willing to tolerate a public discussion that implied they were different—less deserving—than whites. The debate quickly turned bitter and polarized between black and white, liberal and conservative. Emboldened by a cultural sea change during the Reagan-Bush era, conservatives scolded, "It's all your fault." Dismissively, this camp insisted that what blacks need are mainstream American values—read: *white* values. Go to school, get a job, get married, they exhorted, and the family

Steep Rise in Out-of-Wedlock Births

Since the sexual revolution, the rate has shot up for both races. But the numbers are much higher for black women than white women.

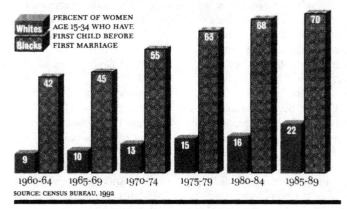

PERCENT OF WOMEN AGE 15-34 WHO HAVE FIRST CHILD BEFORE FIRST MARRIAGE

Whites
Blacks

1960-64	1965-69	1970-74	1975-79	1980-84	1985-89
9 / 42	10 / 45	13 / 55	15 / 63	16 / 68	22 / 70

SOURCE: CENSUS BUREAU, 1992

NEWSWEEK

POLL

WHAT BLACK ADULTS THINK

How important are the following reasons young, unmarried black people today are having children?

(Percent saying very important)

53% They don't understand sex or birth control

48% They won't use birth control or have abortions for personal or religious reasons

38% They want something all their own

37% They want to prove they are adults

35% They are following the examples of older people they know

THE NEWSWEEK POLL, AUGUST 12-15, 1993

will be just fine. Not so, liberals fired back. As neoliberal University of Chicago sociologist William Julius Wilson argued in "The Declining Significance of Race," the breakdown of the African-American family resulted from rising unemployment, not falling values. Liberals have regarded the conservative posture as "blaming the victim," a phrase that, not coincidentally, white psychologist William Ryan coined in a 1965 assessment of Moynihan's study. To this camp, any family structure is good, as long as it's nurturing. "Marriage is important in the black community, just not the most important thing," says Andrew Billingsley, the University of Maryland sociologist who wrote the pioneering "Black Families in White America." "It is not an imperative for black people who can afford it."

Who's right? Both sides are too busy pointing fingers to find out. "We're never going to get to where we need to be if we first have to settle whose fault it is," says writer Nicholas Lemann, whose 1991 book, "The Promised Land," chronicles the great migration of blacks from the rural south to the industrialized North. But if there is any optimism, it is that now, after more than two decades on the defensive and with a Democratic president in the White House for the first time in 12 years, the African-American community is beginning to talk a little more openly about its problems. "Because of all the debate about morality, social programs, individual responsibility, it became very difficult to have an honest discussion," says Angela Glover Blackwell, who heads the Children's Defense Fund's Black Community Crusade for Children. "I'd like to think we've

entered an era where we're willing to accept that there is a dual responsibility" between government and ordinary citizens.

Without question, government must do more to help. But increasingly, African-Americans are unwilling to wait for White America to step in. "During integration," says Virginia Walden, who owns a day-care center in Washington, D.C., "we kept saying that the white people did us wrong, and that they owed us. Well, white people did us wrong, but I tell my children, 'Don't nobody owe you anything. You've got to work for what you get'." In response, many African-American men and women have thrown themselves into a range of grass-roots efforts from volunteer work in their communities to adopting children—stopgap efforts, perhaps, but to many, also cathartic and energizing. In many neighborhoods, the black church has led the awakening. Ministers began chastising themselves for sidestepping some basic moral issues. "We don't use 'family values' as an ax," says Wallace Smith, pastor of Shiloh Baptist Church in Washington. "But if someone is shacked up, we encourage them to get married." Smith is remarkably blunt about his own belief in the importance of a stable marriage. "Dan Quayle," he says, "was right."

At their kitchen tables and in their church basements every day, black families talk to each other, as they always have, about their fears. And part of what worries them is the growing tension between black men and black women, who are quick to blame each other for the massive retreat from marriage. "Black men say black women are 'Sapphires,'

trying to dominate," explains Harvard psychologist Alvin Poussaint, referring to the wife of Kingfish in "Amos 'n' Andy," who epitomized the bitchy, bossy black woman. But Boston anchorwoman Liz Walker believes that many black men mistake self-reliance for highhandedness. "I don't think black women have thrown black men out," says Walker, who sparked a controversy when she became pregnant out of wedlock six years ago, long before TV's Murphy Brown knew what a home pregnancy test was. "I think black women have been abandoned."

More commonly, though, black women feel the fallout of the economic and psychological battering the African-American male has taken in the last generation. Of course black women want love and commitment. But not with a man whose chief qualification for marriage is that he's, well, a man. The remarkable success of Terry McMillan's 1991 novel, "Waiting to Exhale," underscores that passion. The book's main characters are four strong-minded black women who can't seem to find men who measure up. They clearly struck a nerve. "When Terry McMillan wrote that book, the reason it was so popular was because it was *us,*" says Walker, 42. Giddy one night from too much birthday champagne and pepperoni pizza, McMillan's quartet—Robin, Gloria, Bernadine and Savannah—get to the essential question: what's happened to all the men, they ask. Where are they hiding?

4. CRISES—CHALLENGES AND OPPORTUNITIES: Family under Siege

NEWSWEEK
POLL
WHAT BLACK ADULTS THINK

Which one can do most to improve the situation for black families today?

41%	**Black families themselves**
25%	**Churches**
14%	**Community organizations**
14%	**Government**

FOR THIS SPECIAL NEWSWEEK POLL, PRINCETON SURVEY RESEARCH ASSOCIATES INTERVIEWED A NATIONAL SAMPLE OF 600 BLACK ADULTS BY TELEPHONE AUGUST 12-15. THE MARGIN OF ERROR IS +/- 5 PERCENTAGE POINTS. "DON'T KNOW" AND OTHER RESPONSES NOT SHOWN. THE NEWSWEEK POLL © 1993 BY NEWSWEEK, INC.

They're ugly.
Stupid.
In prison.
Unemployed.
Crackheads.
Short.
Liars.
Unreliable.
Irresponsible.
Too possessive . . .
Childish.
Too goddam old and set in their ways.

The litany drives the women to tears. But does marriage really matter? Or is a family headed by a single mother just as good as the nuclear unit? The evidence come down solidly on the side of marriage. By every measure—economic, social, educational—the statistics conclude that two parents living together are better than one. Children of single mothers are significantly more likely to live in poverty than children living with both parents. In 1990, Census figures show, 65 percent of children of black single mothers were poor, compared with only 18 percent of children of black married couples. Educationally, children in one-parent homes are at greater risk across the board—for learning problems, for being left back, for dropping out. Psychiatrist James P. Comer, who teaches at Yale University's Child Study Center, says that the exploding population of African-American children from single-parent homes represents "the education crisis that is going to kill us. The crisis that we're concerned about—that American kids don't achieve as well as European kids and some Asian kids—won't kill us because [American students are] scoring high enough to compete. The one that will kill us is the large number of

bright kids who fall out of the mainstream because their families are not functioning."

Statistics tell only part of the story. Equally important are the intangibles of belonging to an intact family. "Growing up in a married family is where you learn the value of the commitments you make to each other, rather than seeing broken promises," says Roderick Harrison, chief of the Census Bureau's race division. "It deals with the very question of what kind of personal commitments people can take seriously."

Boys in particular need male role models. Without a father, who will help them define what it means to be a man? Fathers do things for their children that mothers often don't. Though there are obviously exceptions, fathers typically encourage independence and a sense of adventure, while mothers are more nurturing and protective. It is men who teach boys how to be fathers. "A woman can only nourish the black male child to a certain point," says Bob Crowder, an Atlanta lawyer and father of four, who helped organize an informal support group for African-American fathers. "And then it takes a man to raise a boy into a man. I mean a real man." Mothers often win the job by default, and struggle to meet the challenge. But sometimes, even a well-intentioned single mother can be smothering, especially if her son is the only man in her life. Down the road a few years, she hears erstwhile daughters-in-law lament how she "ruined" him for every other woman. Like the street-smart New Yorker she is, Bisi Ruckett, who is Dianne Caballero's daughter, says flat out that she can't "rule" her boyfriend. And just as quickly, she concedes she can't compete with his mom. "If he tells her he needs a zillion dollars, she'll get it," says Ruckett, 23.

Without a father for a role model, many boys learn about relationships from their peers on the street. In the inner city in particular, that often means gangs; and the message they're selling is that women are whores and handmaidens, not equals. Having a father does not, of course, guarantee that the lessons a young male learns will be wholesome. But research shows that, with no father, no minister, no boss to help define responsibility, there's nothing to prevent a boy from treating relationships perversely. University of Pennsylvania professor Elijah Anderson, who authored a 1990 study on street life, says that,

among the poor, boys view courting as a "game" in which the object is to perfect a rap that seduces girls. The goal: to add up one's sexual conquests, since that's the measure of "respect."

Often, for a girl, Anderson says, life revolves around the "dream," a variation of the TV soaps in which a man will whisk her away to a life of middle-class bliss—even though everywhere she looks there are only single mothers abandoned by their boyfriends. Not surprisingly, the two sexes often collide. The girl dreams because she must. "It has to do with one's conception of oneself: 'I will prevail'," Anderson says. But the boy tramples that dream because he must—his game is central to his vision of respect. "One of the reasons why, when a woman

---

Wallace Smith, pastor of Washington's Shiloh Church, puts it bluntly: 'Dan Quayle was right.'

---

agrees to have a baby, these men think it's such a victory is that you have to get her to go against all the stuff that says he won't stick around."

For teenage mothers not mature enough to cope, single parenthood is not the route to the dream, but entrapment. They have too many frustrations: the job, the lack of a job, the absence of a man, the feeling of being dependent on others for help, the urge to go out and dance instead of pacing with a crying child. Taken to its extreme, says Poussaint, the results can be abuse or neglect. "They'll see a child as a piece of property or compete with the child—calling them dumb or stupid, damaging their growth and education to maintain superiority," he says. The middle class is not exempt from such pain. Even with all the cushions money could buy—doctors and backup doctors, nannies and backup nannies—Liz Walker says that trying to raise her son, Nicholas, alone was draining. "Certainly, the best situation is to have as many people in charge of a family as possible," says Walker, who is now married to Harry Graham, a 41-year-old corporate-tax lawyer; together, they're raising her son and his two children from a previous marriage. "I can see that now," she adds. "Physically, you *need* it."

Not Just an Underclass Problem

In every economic group, black women are two to six times more likely to have a child before marriage than white women.

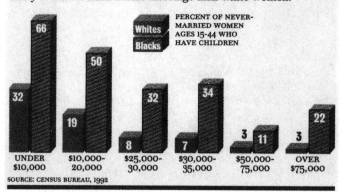

PERCENT OF NEVER-MARRIED WOMEN AGES 15-44 WHO HAVE CHILDREN

Whites
Blacks

UNDER $10,000	$10,000-20,000	$25,000-30,000	$30,000-35,000	$50,000-75,000	OVER $75,000
66	50	32	34	11	22
32	19	8	7	3	3

SOURCE: CENSUS BUREAU, 1992

More and more, black men aren't there to build marriages or to stick around through the hard years of parenting. The question we're too afraid to confront is why. The biggest culprit is an economy that has locked them out of the mainstream through a pattern of bias and a history of glass ceilings. "The economic state of the African-American community is worse in 1993 than it was in 1963," says NAACP head Benjamin Chavis Jr. He could be speaking, just as easily, about the black family, since the two fell in tandem.

A man can't commit to a family without economic security, but for many African-American men, there is none. The seeds of modern economic instability date back to the 1940s, when the first of 6½ million blacks began migrating from the rural South to the urban North as farm mechanization replaced the need for their backs and hands. At first, black men built a solid economic niche by getting factory jobs. But just as the great migration ended in the '70s, the once limitless industrial base began to cave in. And as steel mills and factories swept offshore, the "last hired, first fired" seniority rules disproportionately pushed black men out. During that time, says Billingsley, unemployment for blacks became twice as high as it was for whites, "and it has rarely dropped below that [ratio] since." Unarguably, economic restructuring hit whites as well as blacks, but the new service sector favored those with education—and there were many more educated white men than blacks in the '70s as vast numbers of baby boomers streamed out of the nation's colleges looking for jobs.

Ironically, just as the job market col-

lapsed for black men, it opened for black women, who went to college while black men went to war. Armed with the college degrees that black males didn't have and pushed by the burgeoning women's movement, growing numbers of black women found spots in corporate America. As with white women in the '80s, that bought them greater independence. But the jobs of black women came at the expense of black men. Throughout the workplace, says Yale's Comer, "there was a trade-off. The one black woman was a two-fer: you got a black and a woman." Since then, the gap between white women's income and black women's has disappeared—black women's salaries are the same as whites'.

But the chasm between black and white men has barely moved. In 1969, black men earned 61 cents for every dollar white men earned; by 1989, the number had increased to only 69 cents. And that's for black men who were working; more and more, they found themselves without jobs. During the same time, the number of black men with less than a high-school education who found jobs dropped from two thirds to barely half. And it's likely to worsen: in the last 25 years, the proportion of black men in college has steadily eroded. "America has less use for black men today than it did during slavery," says Eugene Rivers, who helps run computer-training programs as pastor of Boston's Azusa Christian Community.

Though he is scarcely 11, Lugman Kolade dreams of becoming an electrical engineer. But he already wears the grievous pain of a man who feels left out. Lugman is a small, studious, Roman Catholic schooler from Washington,

D.C., who will enter the sixth grade this fall, a superb student who won the archdiocese science fair with a homemade electric meter. Unlike most boys in the Male Youth Project he attended at Shiloh Baptist Church, his parents are married. His mother works for the Department of Public Works; describing what his father does doesn't come easy. "My father used to be a [construction] engineer. He left his job because they weren't treating him right; they would give white men better jobs who did less work. Now he drives an ice-cream truck."

Black men were hurt, too, by the illegal economy. As the legitimate marketplace case them aside, the drug trade took off, enlisting anyone lured by the promise of fast money. Ironically, says Comer, "you had to make a supreme and extra effort to get into the legal system and no effort to get into the illegal system." For many on the fringes, there was no contest. "It overwhelmed the constructive forces in the black mainstream," he says. Disproportionately, too, black men are in prison or dead. While African-Americans represent only 12 percent of the population, they composed 44 percent of the inmates in state prisons and local jails in 1991; and, in 1990, homicide was the leading cause of death for young black men.

The economy explains only one part of what happened. The sexual revolution in the '70s was the second great shift that changed the black family. Although the social tide that erased taboos against unwed motherhood affected all women, whites and blacks took different paths. White women delayed both marriage and childbearing, confident that, down the road, there would be a pool of marriageable men. Not so for black women, who delayed marriage but not children because they were less certain there would be men for them. In what they called a "striking shift," Census officials reported earlier this year that less than 75 percent of black women are likely to ever marry, compared with 90 percent of whites.

More dramatic is the childbearing picture. Between 1960 and 1989, the proportion of young white women giving birth out of wedlock rose from 9 to 22 percent, markedly faster than it did for blacks. The slower rate of increase for blacks was small comfort. Their rate—42 percent—was already so high by 1960 that if it had kept pace with the white race, ti would have topped 100 percent by now. As things stand, it's 70 percent.

Rejecting Marriage

Before 1950, young black women were actually more likely to get married than white women.

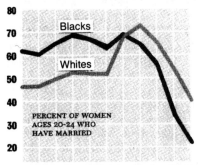

PERCENT OF WOMEN
AGES 20-24 WHO
HAVE MARRIED

SOURCE: ANDREW CHERLIN, "MARRIAGE, DIVORCE, REMARRIAGE",
1992, HARVARD UNIVERSITY PRESS

Traditionally, the extended family has served as a safety net. But the terrible irony of history is that it has also hurt the black family. While intended as a cushion, the network, in effect, enabled more single women to have children. And that helps explain why not only poor black women, but middle- and upper-class blacks as well, have had children out of wedlock at higher rates than white women. Historically, white women have had only themselves to rely on for child rearing, and so marriage became more of an imperative. For blacks, the network of extended kin is a tradition rooted in African customs that emphasize community over marriage. Although historians say that most black children grew up in two-parent households during slavery, as well as in the 19th and early 20th centuries, high rates of poverty, widowhood and urban migration reinforced the need for interdependence that continues today. The oft-repeated African proverb "It takes a whole village to raise a child" echoes back to that.

Now the extended family is breaking down. Yet the black family's expectations for it haven't diminished. Both sides feel the strains. With the soaring number of teenage mothers, grandparents today are getting younger and more likely to be working themselves. A 32-year-old grandmother isn't necessarily eager, or able, to raise a grandchild, especially when that child becomes a teenager and the problems multiply. And, after generations of no fathers, there are no grandfathers, either. What's more, the tradition of a real neighborhood is disappearing. "It used to be that everyone looked out for everyone else," said community activist Claudette Burroughs-White of Greensboro, N.C. "Now I think people are kind of estranged. They don't get involved. It's safer not to." Many families left in the inner city—the ones most in need of support—are increasingly isolated from relatives able to flee to the suburbs. "Not every poor black mother is in a strong kinship network," says Cherlin. "Many are living alone, hiding behind double-locked doors in housing projects."

What's the solution? Nearly 30 years after Lyndon Johnson launched the War on Poverty, experts on the black family return again and again to the same ideas—better education, more jobs, discouraging teen pregnancy, more mentoring programs. But now the question is, who should deliver—government or blacks themselves? Ever since the government started abandoning social programs in the '70s and early '80s, black families have been left on their own to find a way out. Those who would argue against funneling in more government dollars say we tried that, but "nothing works." Lemann, who believes that most of the positive social changes in Black America were sparked by government

intervention, dismisses the conceit that spending on social welfare failed. The War on Poverty, he says "threw out some untested ideas, some of which worked"— like Head Start, the Job Corps and Foster Grandparents—"and some of which didn't." Beyond the all-or-nothing extremes, there is room for solutions. Moynihan believes the nation has been in a collective "denial phase" about the black family for the last 25 years. But he says he's encouraged. "We're beginning to get a useful debate on this."

Will self-help do it? Though few African-American leaders expect what they call "White America" to come to the rescue, they're equally skeptical that the thousands of programs filling church rec rooms and town-hall meeting rooms can, on their own, turn things around. "People who are trying to salvage a lot of the children are burnt out, they think it's like spitting into the ocean," says Poussaint, who doesn't dispute the pessimism. "The problems are overwhelming. It's like treating lung cancer and knowing that people are still smoking."

There aren't many places left to look for answers. When black leaders peak with one voice, it is about the deep crisis of faith and purpose that came with integration: the very promise that African-Americans would be brought into the American mainstream has left many by the wayside. What's the penalty for doing nothing? "We could revert to a caste society," says Moynihan. Others are just as bleak. There are sparks of hope, says Comer, but he warns: "It's getting late, very late." The problems of the black family have been apparent for decades. And so has our collective understanding that we must take them on. What we need to find now is a voice to start the dialogue.

White Ghetto?

Welfare Debate: *Growing numbers of poor white Americans may be forming a new underclass: a generation of young unwed mothers on the public dole. A portrait of inner-city Baltimore.*

Carroll Bogert

Geraldine Anderson is proud that she has never been on welfare. A native of Baltimore, she got pregnant at 15, and her mother forced her to give the baby up for adoption. She raised her subsequent children—Kathy, Jimmy, Kelly, Kim, Diane, Angie and Robert—with a succession of three husbands. The family put cardboard in their shoes to make them last longer, and one time, when her husband suddenly quit his job and disappeared, they ate nothing but potatoes for a week. As soon as the youngest was 3 years old, Anderson started working; for a short period she even worked two full-time jobs, sleeping only a few hours a night. By 6 a.m. she was up and had breakfast ready "We always sat around the table, everybody together," Anderson remembers. "They learned their table manners, too." Anderson, now 52, holds down a secretarial job with a law firm in Wilmington, Dela., and dreams of starting a business making fake-fur coats.

Somehow her children have not embraced the same values of work and thrift. Kathy, Kelly, Kim and Angie are all on welfare. (Diane recently became a beautician and got off the dole. One son is a mechanic, and the other lays carpet and tile.) All the daughters, ranging in age from 26 to 34, have children now—14 altogether—and they're all single mothers, either divorced or separated or never married to the fathers. "I tell 'em to forget about the welfare," says Anderson. "I tell 'em to stop having babies without being married." Her daughters say they intend to do just that, but they seem to find welfare more compelling than their mother's warnings. Angie says that if there were no Aid to Families with Dependent Children, "I never would

have had her," pointing at her second child. Kim was going to abort her second pregnancy, but when she discovered she was carrying twins, "I just didn't have the heart." Still, she says that if welfare weren't an option, she might not have had even her first child.

The contrast between Anderson's dogged work ethic and her daughters' unabashed dependence on AFDC reflects a growing trend in poor white America. Until recently, "the underclass" was a term used mostly to refer to a pattern among poor blacks (pregnant as teenagers, dependent on welfare) that repeated itself over generations. Nearly 30 years ago, Daniel Patrick Moynihan warned of the horrific social consequences of the skyrocketing out-of-wedlock birthrate among blacks. The rate then was about one in four. That's roughly where whites are today—up from 11 percent in 1980, and now social scientists are making equally dire forecasts about "the coming white underclass." Americans know about white rural poverty in places like Appalachia, but they've mostly overlooked its urban counterpart. The state of Maryland, for example, has been unusually successful in preventing teen pregnancy, but the drop in birthrates has been primarily among blacks, to whom scarce resources tend to be directed.

Abolish welfare? Charles Murray, a welfare expert at the American Enterprise Institute, is trying to rectify that by publicizing the idea of a white underclass. He has long argued that, far from easing the plight of poor women and children, welfare worsens it: teenagers think they can support a baby even without a husband or a job or a high-school education. Murray's prescription is simply to abolish welfare. That idea once consigned him to the right-wing fringe;

these days countless moderates are cheering Bill Clinton on in his crusade to "end welfare as we know it"—although few countenance a solution as draconian as Murray's.

Baltimore, with the nation's fourth largest concentration of whites on welfare, is a good spot to examine Murray's arguments. In a white underclass neighborhood west of Baltimore's Pigtown, crack dealers lounge on street corners and addicts stumble through trash-strewn alleys. Young men wander in and out of corner liquor stores, and young women sit on crumbling stoops in the sun, hurling occasional reprimands at their kids. The street feels decayed and forlorn. But it doesn't crackle with the same violence as, say, the black ghetto on Baltimore's east side. Whites below the poverty line are more widely scattered throughout Baltimore than blacks, who can still find it tough to move into a white neighborhood. According to Susan Wiener at the Urban Institute in Washington, D.C., poor black people in Baltimore are seven times more likely to live in a poor neighborhood than poor white people are.

Murray is right that a dramatic change has taken place in poor white families in the last generation. In O'Donnell Heights, where Geraldine's daughters Kim and Angie live, solid blue-collar families were once the community's bedrock. In the mid-1980s the nearby Bethlehem Steel plant began big layoffs of workers, and other local industries shut down. And about the time the jobs began to vanish, so did the stigma against unwed motherhood. Just up the street from Kim and Angie, Ollie Sprouse raised six kids. She was married to Beverley Danbridge Sprouse Sr. for 51 years, until he died this spring. They were on welfare briefly in the 1970s, but not since. Meanwhile,

Sighting a Great White Threat

Mickey Kaus

WHEN CHARLES MURRAY first suggested abolishing welfare in his 1984 book, "Losing Ground," he was demonized by the left and his idea was dismissed as kooky. He's still demonized by the left, but the welfare debate has moved to the right, and Murray's latest concept—"the coming white underclass"—has hit a media nerve. Nowadays, you're likely to turn on your TV and see network correspondents strolling with Murray through fields near his rural home. Murray's theories provide the intellectual basis for an emerging Republican effort to out-tough President Clinton on welfare, cutting off benefits entirely where Clinton would merely impose a two-year time limit.

Does Murray have a hidden agenda? Actually, it's not all that hidden. He is a laissez-faire communitarian who thinks that unless a do-gooding government foolishly interferes, people will naturally form communities that protect themselves by enforcing "norms of safety" and "norms of self-respect" (stigmatizing unwed motherhood, for example). In person, Murray adopts a more-in-sorrow-than-anger tone, as if once you take the "underclass" problem seriously, you must embrace his cut-'em-off prescription. But there are at least three areas where his theories deserve more scrutiny than they have been getting.

Is "the white underclass" an imminent threat? You have the makings of an underclass, Murray argues. "when you have in a community a whole lot of people with kids without fathers." That is what was left in the black ghettos when the black middle class moved out in the '60s and '70s. Today, in many of these ghettos, more than 80 percent of births are illegitimate. But it was race segregation that created the ghettos. Will there be a similar geographic concentration of poor, broken *white* homes? Impoverished whites, after all, tend to be spread throughout the population—only 4 percent live in high-poverty ghettos, according to one study, compared with 26 percent of poor blacks. Although it can't be a good thing that about 22 percent of white births are now illegitimate, 22 percent is still a long way from 80 percent. In an interview with NEWSWEEK, Murray admits he can't name any white underclass neighborhoods "happening now." He is merely predicting that some poor white areas will soon reach a "tipping point."

Is the problem illegitimacy or non-work? "I don't care how many women go to work," Murray has declared. He and his Republican champions like to pooh-pooh the importance of getting single mothers into the labor force. That distinguishes the Murrayites from Clinton, whose welfare plan will stress work. But does Murray really not care about work? He says he's not very concerned about single moms who *do* work—the Murphy Browns. (They would be unaffected by his aid cutoff anyway.) At the same time, he seems quite troubled by the idea that welfare checks might go to two-parent families that *don't* work, where "dad and mom sit around the house." Sounds like work is pretty important after all.

What's the best way to deter illegitimacy? The nub of the underclass problem, black or white, is clearly the *combination* of illegitimacy and non-work. Who has the cure? Here the seeming gulf between the Murray and Clinton plans shrinks even further. Both wind up relying on the need to work as a deterrent to illegitimacy. Murray, by abolishing welfare, would in effect tell prospective unwed mothers that they'd have to support themselves in private-sector jobs. Clinton plans roughly to say the same thing, though he'd offer public jobs as a last resort. Even Murray concedes that a work requirement imposed after two years might have a deterrent effect "if you have an absolute cutoff [of all benefits], so that on the 25th month, every woman who has been on welfare must report to a job site . . . or get nothing." He just doesn't think Clinton will propose anything that rigorous. or that any "mechanisms of government" could make such a requirement stick.

So the debate comes down to the old question of whether, in Murray's words, "the government will screw it up." If the Clintonites are naive about the ability of government, Murray seems equally naive about what would happen in the absence of government. Ending welfare. he says, would "trigger . . . a wide variety of extremely helpful private activities." Perhaps. But what if we abolish welfare and charity doesn't flower? You can be alarmed about illegitimacy, even about a "coming white underclass," and still not think Charles Murray has found the answer.

KAUS *is a senior editor at The New Republic and author of "The End of Equality."*

---

an unmarried welfare mom living nearby has three kids by three different fathers. In the old days, says Mrs. Sprouse, "that would have been a disgrace. People didn't do that . . . How's she going to explain it to those children when they grow up?"

Censorious glare: It isn't easy to put the stigma back into illegitimate birth. The old solution for teen pregnancy, giving the baby up for adoption, has fallen out of favor. Baltimore's Florence Crittenton Mission used to shelter unwed mothers from the censorious glare of polite society while they carried their babies to term. Now called Florence Crittenton Services of Baltimore, Inc., the facility offers drug-treatment programs, parenting classes and therapy for pregnant teens. "Up until 1980, I was still getting a number of adoptions," remembers Crittenton's director, Anne Davis. But none since then. "The need for hiding is no longer there." Geraldine Anderson's mother wouldn't have dreamed of letting her keep her first baby. Nice Catholic girls didn't do that. So Ronnie—whose wife tracked Anderson down nine years ago—was adopted by a middle-class Baltimore family, and grew up an only son. He's the only one of Anderson's children to have graduated from college, and earns a comfortable income as a computer-systems analyst.

At Patterson High School, where kids from O'Donnell Heights go, the school clinic is adorned with posters urging abstinence and warning about teen pregnancy. Studies show that this kind of propaganda works, but it has to start when the kids are very young. Once a girl gets pregnant, the high-school nurses scrupulously avoid suggesting that having a baby will quite possibly ruin their lives. They offer "options counseling" that makes no distinction between keeping the baby, giving it up for adoption or having an abortion. "That's their decision," explains one nurse. "We can't put our values on them."

Her excuse reflects a predictable political deadlock. Liberals think simply distributing condoms will keep teen pregnancy down. Civil libertarians want to keep anything that smacks of moral education—like prayer—out of the public schools. Right-wing moralists, while worrying about illegitimate births, won't face up to some hard truths. All of Charles Murray's logic points to the need to *terminate* teen pregnancies. But virtually nowhere in his writings does he use the dreaded A word; when pressed, in a telephone interview, he sighs deeply and describes himself as "reluctantly pro-choice."

Getting married and getting a job are the twin totems of the welfare debate today. Reformers across the political spectrum want to force welfare moms to do both. But Geraldine Anderson didn't always find her husbands to be reliable providers or protectors. She had three children by a man who, some of the children have charged to p abused her daughters and daughters' kids. He denies an doing, but none of the women argue that the family was better off w he was in the house. And forcing mother to get a job can undermine families, much as it did Geraldine Anderson's. "I was working, and I didn't have much time to watch 'em," Anderson explains. "And we didn't have any money, so we were always living in bad neighborhoods. They got influenced by some bad friends." Even the most persistent, well-intentioned mothers can't always triumph over such influences. So far, at least, the high rhetoric of welfare reform has not yet engaged such messy truths.

White Ghetto?
olice, sexually
even her
wrong-
would
hen

Helping Children Cope With Violence

Lorraine B. Wallach

Lorraine B. Wallach, M.A., is one of the founders of the Erikson Institute in Chicago and is presently a faculty member there. Her recent work includes staff training around issues of children and violence.

Children who grow up in violent communities are at risk for pathological development because growing up in a constant state of apprehension makes it difficult to establish trust, autonomy, and social competence.

Violence is epidemic in the United States today. (The murder rate in this country is the fifth highest in the world.) It is 10 times higher than England's and 25 times that of Spain. For many inner-city children, violence has become a way of life. In a study of more than 1,000 children in Chicago, 74% of them had witnessed a murder, shooting, stabbing, or robbery (Kotulak, 1990; Bell, 1991). Almost half (47%) of these incidents involved friends, family members, classmates, or neighbors. Forty-six percent of the children interviewed reported that they had personally experienced at least one violent crime. These figures are similar to those found in other U.S. urban areas, such as Baltimore (Zinsmeister, 1990), Los Angeles County (Pynoos & Eth, 1985), and New Orleans (Osofsky, Wewers, Hann, Fick, & Richters, 1991).

Children are exposed to several kinds of violence, including child abuse and domestic violence. And there are communities where violence is endemic, where gang bangers, drug dealers, petty crimi-nals, and not-so-petty criminals rule the streets. For children living in these conditions, feelings of being safe and secure do not exist.

Children who are not designated victims of assault can be unintended victims. Shoot-outs between gangs and drive-by shootings result in the wounding, and often killing, of innocent bystanders. In addition, the psychological toll of living under these conditions is immeasurable. The children in these neighborhoods see violence and hear it discussed. They are surrounded by danger and brutality.

Child abuse, other domestic violence, and neighborhood violence can harm development

The effects of this kind of violence on children are widespread and can permeate all areas of development, beginning in infancy and continuing through childhood. The first task a baby faces is the development of trust—trust in the caregiving environment and eventually in himself. Achieving a sense of trust is compromised by growing up in a violent community. Many families find it difficult to provide infants with support, love, and affection in a consistent and predictable manner when they live in a constant state of apprehension—not knowing when they are going to be victims of violence. Toddlers have difficulty developing a sense of autonomy when their families cannot help them explore their environments because their surroundings are filled with danger. Preschoolers, too, are inhibited from going out into the world. Just at the age when they should be expanding their social contacts and finding out about people beyond the family, they are restricted by the dangers lurking outside. Many children living in high-rise housing projects and other dangerous neighborhoods are cooped up inside all day because it is unsafe to go out-of-doors. The situation is even more tragic when children

From *Young Children*, May 1993, pp. 4-11. © 1993 by the National Association for the Education of Young Children. Reprinted by permission.

experience violence within the family. Where can a child find protection when she is victimized within her own home? Although domestic violence occurs in *every* kind of neighborhood, the effects may be even more damaging when compounded by the harmful effects of growing up in *violent* neighborhoods.

Children who grow up under conditions that do not allow them to develop trust in people and in themselves or learn to handle day-to-day problems in socially acceptable ways are at risk for pathological development; they are at risk for resorting to violent behaviors themselves. The anger that is instilled in children when they are mistreated or when they see their mothers or siblings mistreated is likely to be incorporated into their personality structures. Children learn by identifying with the people they love. They also identify with the people who have power and control. When children see and experience abuse and violence as a way of life, when the people who are responsible for them behave without restraint, the children often learn to behave in the same manner.

Another serious problem for children living in chaotic communities is that the protectors and the dangerous people may be one and the same. The police, who are supposed to be protectors, are often seen as dangerous by community members. In his book *There Are No Children Here,* Alex Kotlowitz (1991) describes how a young man who is idolized by his housing project community be-

The young child's protectors and the dangerous people in her life may be one and the same.

It is particularly important for children who come from chaotic environments to have firm but appropriate limits, even though children who feel powerless may try to provoke adults into a battle of wills in an effort to make themselves feel important.

cause he is successful, has graduated from high school, is not caught up in gangs, and is still his own person is mistakenly killed by the police. What do children think when their idol is gunned down by the people who are supposed to protect them?

Children are confused when they cannot tell the good guys from the bad guys. Their teachers and the media tell them that drug dealers are bad and are the cause of the problems in the community, but the children may know

that cousins or friends or even older brothers are dealing. Some people have likened the inner city, especially housing projects, to war zones; but in a war the enemy is more often than not on the outside, and usually everyone knows who he is.

Children growing up with violence face risks other than becoming violent themselves. Children who live with danger develop defenses against their fears, and these defenses can interfere with their development. When children have to defend themselves constantly from outside or inside dangers, their energies are not available for other, less immediately urgent tasks, such as learning to read and write and do arithmetic and learning about geography and history and science. In addition to not having enough energy to devote to schoolwork, there is evidence that specific cognitive functions such as memory and a sense of time can be affected by experiencing trauma (Terr, 1981).

(Boys and girls who are victims of abuse and who see abusive behavior in their families can grow up feeling as if they are responsible for what is happening. Young children cannot always differentiate between what is real and what is part of their inner lives.) The literature on divorce has made clear that many children believe that they have caused the breakup of the family, even though it had nothing to do with them (Wallerstein & Kelly, 1980; Hetherton, Cox, & Cox, 1982). Children who feel guilty about the violence in their families often perceive themselves as being bad and worthless. Feelings of worthlessness can lead children to the idea that they

When children have to defend themselves constantly from inside and outside dangers, there is little energy for schoolwork. There is also evidence that specific cognitive functions such as memory and a sense of time can be affected.

are not capable of learning, which leads, in turn, to a lack of motivation to achieve in school.

(Children who experience trauma may have difficulty seeing themselves in future roles that are meaningful.) Lenore Terr (1983), in her study of the schoolchildren of Chowchilla who were kidnapped in their school bus, found that the views of their future lives were limited and often filled with anticipation of disaster. Children who cannot see a decent future for themselves cannot give their all to the present task of learning and becoming socialized.

Living in unpredictably frightening situations makes children feel as if they have no control over their lives. We know that young children need to feel as if they can direct some parts of their lives,

but children who are victims of violence learn that they have no say in what happens to them. This sense of helplessness interferes with the development of autonomy.

It is difficult for children to keep on growing and maturing when they have been traumatized because an almost universal reaction of children to traumatic occurrences is regression. Children slip back to stages at which they felt more secure. This is particularly true when they have only a tenuous hold on their current status.

What makes some children more resilient than others, and what can we do?

As depressing as all this sounds, however, it does not mean that all children who experience violence are doomed. It is known that some children are more resilient and withstand trauma and stress better than others. If a child has an easy temperament and makes a good fit with his primary caregiver, he or she is more likely to be off to a good start. Some lucky children are born to strong parents who can withstand the ravages of poverty and community violence and still provide some security and hope for their children. Children are shaped not only by their parents' behavior but also by their parents' hopes, expectations, motivations, and view of the future—including their children's future.

It is important to remember that children are malleable, that what happens in the early years is im-

> A kindergarten teacher in a Chicago public school was discussing her dilemma concerning two boys in her classroom. All of the children were at their tables, engaged in drawing, when the teacher noticed these boys crawling under the tables, pretending to have guns. When one of the boys saw the teacher watching them, he reassured her, "Don't worry, we're just playing breaking into an apartment." The teacher questioned whether she should let the play continue or offer a more socially acceptable view of behavior. How should she react? A Head Start teacher in the group said that the boy who was taking the lead in this game had been in her class the year before, and that his family's apartment had been burglarized. The boy had been very frightened and, after that experience, had changed from a confident, outgoing youngster to a quiet and withdrawn child. Here it was a year later, and he was just beginning to play out his experience. He was becoming the aggressor in the play instead of the helpless victim. And he was regaining some of his old confidence.

portant, but that many children can overcome the hurts and fears of earlier times. Many can make use of positive experiences that occur both inside and outside their families. Child care centers, recreation programs, and schools can be resources for children and offer them alternative perceptions of themselves, as well as teaching them skills. One of the things that help determine the resiliency of children is the ability to make relationships and to make use of the people in their environments, people who provide to children what they do not get in their families or who supplement what their families cannot offer.

Child care professionals can help offset the negative effects of violence in the lives of young children by providing that supplement. Although teachers, social workers, and human service personnel cannot cure all of the hurts experienced by children today, they can make a difference.

1. **The first thing they need to do is to make sure that their programs provide opportunities for children to develop meaningful relationships with caring and knowledgeable adults.** Teachers and other staff members can offer each child a chance to form an important relationship with one of them, a relationship within which the child can learn that there are people in the world who can be of help. The best thing to offer children at risk is caring people, people who are available both physically and emotionally.

Some years ago the famous Chicago analyst Franz Alexander (1948) coined the term *corrective emotional experience* to explain the curative power of therapy, and that term best describes what child care professionals can do for children at risk. A corrective emotional experience means having a relationship with another person that touches one's deepest core—not a relationship that

is superficial or intellectual, but one that engages the emotions. It means having a relationship within which a person can redo old patterns and ties. It means feeling safe enough within a relationship to risk making basic changes in one's psychic structure. Children cannot be forced into these kinds of relationships; they can only be offered the opportunities with the hope that they take advantage of them.

Some children attach easily, and it does not take much effort on the part of the adults for these children to form attachments; these are usually the children who have had a good relationship in their past. Other children have not been lucky enough to have had the kind of relationship that makes them want to seek out others and repeat this satisfying experience; these children need more help in forming ties and trusting alliances.

What can adults do to stimulate relationships with children who do not come easily to this task? They can look into themselves and see if they are ready

for this kind of relationship—a relationship that makes demands on their emotions, their energies, and their time. Relationships with children who have inordinate needs and who do not have past experiences in give-and-take partnerships are not 50–50 propositions; adults must meet these children more than halfway.

2. **Child care professionals can organize their schedules and their time with the children so that they provide as much consistency as possible.** Attachment can be encouraged by reducing the number of people a child encounters during the day and by maximizing the amount of meaningful time and activity the child has with one adult. In this way each child is allowed to form an attachment to one person. There are several models—including therapeutic centers, child-life programs, and primary-care nursing—that use relationship as the principal tool in their interventions. Establishing significant relationships with the children who

A nine-year-old boy in a shelter for battered women told a story about his recurring dream. This is what he said: "I dreamed of someone taking me away. He was dressed like a lady, but he had a moustache. I went inside the house. It was dark. The lights were out, and there were people inside having a party. It was ugly. They were eating worms and they asked me to try one. I took one and threw it away. Then I opened the door, and the light came on in there, and I saw there were no more ghosts, and I saw I was sleeping. When I dream like that, I become afraid."

It was obvious that the boy was expressing his fears, but the exact meaning of the details was not evident—not until one of the child care workers who knew the mother reported that the abusive father was bisexual and brought his male sexual partners to the family's apartment. It then became clear that in addition to struggling with feelings about an abusive father, the boy was also frightened and confused about the meaning of his father's behavior and probably about his own sexual identification. In this case the child was able to tell about a disturbing dream through the telling of a story, and the adults were able to understand it with additional information about his family.

have suffered from trauma is the most important thing that can be done, and it is the basis for all of the work that follows. What is this other work?

3. Child care professionals must provide structure and very clear expectations and limits. All children, especially young children, need to know where they stand, but it is particularly important for children who come from chaotic environments to have firm but appropriate limits. It should be noted that they do not take to this kind of structure easily. It is not something they have experienced before, and the newness of it may cause anxiety and tension, just as any new situation does.

Some children see the structure of a new setting as an opportunity to assert themselves and force the adults into power struggles. Children who feel powerless may try to provoke adults into a battle of wills in an effort to make themselves feel important. But even though some of the neediest children may rebel against structure, no matter how benign, it is important to provide it so that the boundaries are clear.

4. Early childhood professionals should offer children many opportunities to express themselves within the confines of a comfortable and consistent schedule, with clear expectations about behavior. Children need to air their emotions; they need to tell their stories. They can do this in several activities that can be a part of any good program for children.

Except for life-sustaining activities, play is, of course, the most universal activity of children

Through play, children learn about the physical and social world. As they play, children develop a map of the world, a map that helps them make sense of the

Josephine, the child of an abused mother, told a story about a girl with red eyes who bit and scratched her mother because she was angry at her and the devil got into her body. The child care worker listened and accepted her story, thereby accepting the child's feelings. In subsequent sessions, after establishing a more trusting relationship with the child, the worker told her a story about the same little girl who told the devil not to bother her and who talked to her mother about how she was going to try harder to be nicer. By using the same characters and theme, she offered the little girl another way of relating to her mother. At the same time, the mother's worker helped her understand her own anger and supported her in trying to alter her behavior toward her daughter.

complexities that define the world today. Play, in the context of a corrective experience, offers children who live with chaos and violence a chance to redraw their world map.

Play provides an avenue for children to express their feelings. Children who are angry or hurt can take their anger out on toys, dolls, and stuffed animals. Children who feel isolated or lonely can find solace in pretending to live in a world with lots of friends. Children who are frightened can seek safety within a game by pretending to be big and strong. In other words, children can play out their own scenarios, changing their real life situations to their own design. They can invent happy endings. They can reverse roles and become the big—instead of the small—people. They can become the aggressors rather than the victims.

Play also allows children to repeat some of the bad things in their lives. Some people think that children want to forget the frightening or horrible things that they have experienced and try to put these events out of their minds. Some people think that children's play reflects only happy experiences; and many times it does. But some children gain strength from repeating situations that were overwhelming to them, as a way of trying to come to terms with the experiences.

Traumatic events have a way of staying with us. Sometimes they are repeated in dreams. Adults may review these events by talking about them with their friends and even with strangers. Adults, through discussion—and children, through play—gain control over trauma by repeating it again and again. Repetition allows the trauma victim to absorb the experience little by little, come to grips with what happened, and learn to accept it or live with it.

Expressive art is very therapeutic

In addition to being given many opportunities for dramatic play, children can benefit from a chance to paint and draw. Just as some children make sad or frightening events into happy occasions in their play, others may draw pictures of happy times, even when they are living in far-from-happy circumstances. They draw pictures of nice houses with flowers and trees and sunshine. Others draw pictures that are, or that represent, disturbing things in their lives. They draw angry or violent pictures and find solace in expressing their feelings through art and conquering their fears by putting them on paper.

Storytelling can bridge to valuable conversation

Storytelling is another way in which children can handle difficult situations and express their inner thoughts. Sharing the telling of stories can be an excellent way to open up communication between adults and children. It can establish rapport between the two and lay the basis for further discussions of a child's difficulties. It is easier for the adult to understand stories than to interpret drawings or play, and the adult is able to engage a child in a conversation about her or his story.

This does not mean that the stories children tell can be accepted verbatim. Just as play and drawing allow children to express themselves symbolically, so do stories offer them a chance to communicate an idea or feeling without acknowledging its closeness to reality. Adults often cannot understand a child's story without having some outside information about the child's life.

If we understand what children are telling us through their stories, we can help them by participating with them in storytelling. Gardner (1971) used this method in his therapy with children. After the child told a story, Gardner told the same story but with a different, healthier ending. Although teachers are not therapists, they can engage children in joint storytelling sessions and offer alternative endings to the stories told by the children.

Collaboration with families is critically important

Direct work with children is invaluable, but if it can be combined with help for parents, its effectiveness can be increased. Young children are best understood in the context of their families and communities. Professionals need to know the facts about a child's life situation, and that information can be gained from the adults who know the child well.

In addition to obtaining information from parents, the most effective help for a child is in collaboration with help for the family. Because the child is entwined with his family for many years, it is important to make changes in his familial relationships, if possible; even small changes can be important.

It is not possible for teachers and other child specialists to also be social workers and parent therapists. The person who makes contact with a child, however, is often in a good position to establish a working alliance with the child's parents. This alliance can then be used to refer parents to community agencies, clinics, churches, or self-help groups for the support, guidance, or therapy that they need. Making a good referral takes skill and patience. It cannot be done quickly, which means that teachers and child care workers must have the time to talk to parents and to make home visits if necessary. They must have time to establish contact with families as an essential part of their work with children who suffer the consequences of violence.

The problems spelled out here are formidable. They will not be easy to solve, but professionals who see children on a daily basis can be an important part of the solution. They cannot cure all of the ills and solve all of the problems that confront children today, but they can offer these children a chance to face and accept their feelings and to see alternative ways of relating to others. If child care professionals can help some—not all, but some—children find alternatives to destructive behavior, be it toward themselves or others, they have helped break the cycle of violence.

References

Alexander, F. (1948). *Fundamentals of psychoanalysis.* New York: W.W. Norton.

Bell, C. (1991). Traumatic stress and children in danger. *Journal of Health Care for the Poor and Underserved, 2*(1), 175–188.

Gardner, R. (1971). *Therapeutic communication with children: The mutual storytelling technique.* New York: Science House.

Hetherton, E.M., Cox, M., & Cox, R. (1982). Effects of divorce on parents and children. In M. Lamb (Ed.), *Non-traditional families.* Hillsdale, NJ: Lawrence Erlbaum.

Kotlowitz, A. (1991). *There are no children here.* New York: Doubleday.

Kotulak, R. (1990, September 28). Study finds inner-city kids live with violence. *Chicago Tribune,* pp. 1, 16.

Osofsky, J., Wewers, S., Hann, D., Fick, A., & Richters, J. (1991). *Chronic community violence: What is happening to our children?* Manuscript submitted for publication.

Pynoos, R., & Eth, S. (1985). Children traumatized by witnessing personal violence: Homicide, rape or suicide behavior. In S. Eth & R. Pynoos (Eds.), *Posttraumatic stress disorder in children* (pp. 19–43). Washington, DC: American Psychiatric Press.

Terr, L. (1981). Forbidden games: Posttraumatic child's play. *Journal of American Academy of Child Psychiatry, 20,* 741–760.

Terr, L. (1983). Chowchilla revisited: The effects of psychic trauma four years after a schoolbus kidnapping. *American Journal of Psychiatry, 140,* 1543–1550.

Wallerstein, J.S., & Kelley, J.B. (1980). *Surviving the breakup: How children and parents cope with divorce.* New York: Basic Books.

Zinsmeister, K. (1990, June). Growing up scared. *The Atlantic Monthly,* pp. 49–66.

After He Hits Her

This study examines the interactional dynamics following woman battering, and specifically addresses the question of whether, as time goes on, male batterers are less likely to offer accounts or aligning actions (i.e., apologies, excuses, justifications, and dismissals) for acts of violence, and whether female victims are less likely to honor the men's accounts. Based on in-depth interviews with 50 white women who had come to a battered women's shelter, the study finds that abusers generally are not likely to stop accounting for their violent behavior but that shelter victims are progressively less likely to honor the accounts. It also is found that, as time goes on, men are more likely to blame their victims for the battering. Similarities and differences between these findings and the research results used to support Walker's (1979, 1984) cycle theory of violence are discussed. Implications for practitioners working with batterers and victims are outlined.

Jane H. Wolf-Smith and Ralph LaRossa

Jane H. Wolf-Smith is an Associate Professor in the Department of Social Sciences, Gainesville College, Gainesville, GA 30503. Ralph LaRossa is a Professor in the Department of Sociology, Georgia State University, Atlanta, GA 30303.

For some time now, researchers and activists in the battered women's movement have realized that "acts of violence" are not discrete acts of physical aggression but are patterns of oppression, occurring over time and including events leading up to as well as following the use of force, itself. Thus, for example, in what may be the most widely cited theory of the pattern or cycle of violence, there is said to be at least three phases—the tension building phase, the acute battering phase, and the loving contrition phase—which ensnare women in a web of punishment and deceit (see Walker, 1979, 1984).

While much has been written about the structural and situational factors which precipitate violence toward women and, as more victims come forward, an all-too-vivid picture of both the range and severity of force in intimate relationships is being acquired, little still is known about

The authors wish to thank the women who participated in the study for their willingness to share their experiences; the staff of the battered women's shelter for their cooperation in arranging the interviews; and Phillip W. Davis and Paula L. Dressel for their comments on earlier versions of this article.

Key Words: cycle theory of violence, family violence, victimization of women.

what happens immediately after the incident—that is, "after he hits her."

Drawing on in-depth interviews with 50 white women who had been abused by their husbands or male companions, and who had come to a battered women's shelter for refuge, this study examines the interactional dynamics following acts of abuse, giving special attention to both the "acts of contrition" (and other verbal strategies) that men use and the kinds of responses that women give to these strategies. The research combines a theoretically informed approach to the concept of contrition with a methodological focus on the sequence of abuse. That is, from the beginning, the intent was to place "acts of contrition" within the class of theoretical concepts variously referred to as "techniques of neutralization" (Sykes & Matza, 1957), "remedial interchanges" (Goffman, 1971), "accounts" (Scott & Lyman, 1968), or "aligning actions" (Stokes & Hewitt, 1976); and, from the beginning, the goal was to examine whether the verbal strategies that batterers used the first time were different from the verbal strategies used later on.

The interest in whether men "repented" in different ways as time went on was sparked by the finding, reported in several previous studies, that men are likely to repent after the first incident of abuse but *increasingly less likely* to repent after subsequent incidents (see Dobash & Dobash, 1984; Ferraro & Johnson, 1983; Walker, 1984). What this means in terms of the cycle theory of violence is that,

after a while, men choose to "delete" the third phase.

If, indeed, abusive men are less contrite as time goes on, this would indicate a shift in their perception of their violent acts. The fact that they would repent for their behavior the first time would indicate some acknowledgment on their part that what they did would be met with disapproval. Their lesser tendency to repent after the 2nd, 10th, or 50th time would indicate that they had begun to "normalize" their violent behavior (i.e., see their violence within the bounds of social acceptability).

The logic here is that deviance and repentance go hand in hand. If individuals feel that they have done something wrong, they often will repent for their apparent misconduct. If, on the other hand, they feel that they are acting correctly, they will not repent. Students, for example, often will talk about why they were late for class, but rarely, if ever, talk about why they were on time (Goffman, 1971; Scott & Lyman, 1968; Stokes & Hewitt, 1976; Sykes & Matza, 1957).

Stopping violence requires an all-out effort to cancel the hitting license. If what happens in abusive relationships is that the license is not only not cancelled but actually renewed and possibly upgraded (i.e., defined as more "normal" than before), battered women and their advocates need to know this. Understanding the part that "acts of contrition" play in the cycle of abuse thus will go a long way toward helping victims of abuse.

From *Family Relations*, Vol. 41, No. 3, July 1992, pp. 324-329. © 1992 by the National Council of Family Relations, 3989 Central Avenue, NE, Suite 550, Minneapolis, MN 55421. Reprinted by permission.

Theoretical Rationale

A Typology of Aligning Actions

From a symbolic interactionist point of view, an act of contrition is *one* example of an *aligning action,* offered in the hope of mending, if only temporarily, a break between socially established norms and misconduct (Stokes & Hewitt, 1976). By offering aligning actions, social actors give neutral or positive meanings to behaviors that are "out of line." If, in turn, the aligning actions are "honored" by the offended party or parties (i.e., if others give the impression that they attach the same neutral or positive meanings to the apparent misconduct), then the aligning actions have the effect of "containing" or "minimizing" what otherwise might have been viewed as a relationship-threatening set of events.

When aligning actions are offered after deviant behavior, they are referred to as *accounts* (Scott & Lyman, 1968). When they are offered before a misdeed—or in the anticipation of a misdeed—they are referred to as *disclaimers* (Hewitt & Stokes, 1975). Given the interest here on what happens "afterward," the focus is on how men account rather than disclaim abusive behavior.

According to Hunter (1984), ex post facto aligning actions generally fall into four categories. Applied to woman battering, what differentiates the four categories is whether or not the batterer (a) makes the case that the violence in question deserves to be viewed as a negative act, and/or (b) says that he is responsible for the violence.

The first category is an apology. An *apology* signifies the batterer's acceptance of both the negative evaluation of the act and responsibility for the act, itself. Regret is also evident in this aligning action: "I know I shouldn't have slapped you. I'm sorry." Apologies are apparently what Walker (1979, 1984) was referring to when she talked about a "loving contrition phase" in her cycle theory of violence.

In [the loving contrition] phase, the batterer constantly behaves in a charming and loving manner. He is usually sorry for his actions in the previous phases, and he conveys contriteness to the battered woman. He begs her forgiveness and promises her that he will never do it again. (Walker, 1979, p. 65)

The batterer may apologize profusely, try to assist his victim, show kindness and remorse, and shower her with gifts and promises. (Walker, 1984, p. 96)

Being contrite or apologizing, however, is not the only account available to abusers. Other "third phase" strategies include the dismissal, the excuse, and the justification.

The *dismissal* is the opposite of an apology. Its intent is to invalidate both responsibility for the act and the negative evaluation of the act: "You pushed me to the limit—besides, you need to know who's boss around here."

Then there is the excuse. When using an *excuse,* the batterer accepts the negative evaluation of the act, but denies responsibility for the act: "That was a lousy thing to do—but I've been under a lot of pressure from my boss."

Finally, there is the justification. With the *justification,* the batterer accepts responsibility for the act but denies its negative evaluation: "I felt I had to do something to keep you from making a stupid decision."

A number of researchers have recognized that efforts on the part of both abusers and victims to account for abusive incidents can include more than apologies or acts of contrition. In one of the earliest studies of violence in the home, Gelles (1974) identified a variety of meanings that abusers gave to their violent acts to "explain" why they were violent—from "She asked for it" (an excuse) to "I tried to knock her to her senses" (a justification). Similarly, Ferraro and Johnson (1983), focusing not on the abusers but on the victims, described how women "rationalized" being abused, saying things like "I asked for it" (an excuse), "He's sick" (also an excuse), and "He didn't injure me" (a justification). Ferraro and Johnson (1983) also demonstrate how these accounts prevented the women from seeking help. Along the same lines, Mills (1985) described the "techniques of neutralization" that battered women use "to help them tolerate violent marriages." Mills (1985) found that one way that women "managed the violence" directed toward them was they used "justifications" (e.g., "compared to others, it seems my problems are small") to "minimiz[e] the significance of their victimization" (p. 109). Finally, Ptacek (1988), in a study of abusive men, discovered that he could classify the bulk of the men's accounts into either excuses or justifications. He also found that the men were more likely to excuse than to justify their behavior.

Drawing on Hunter's (1984) typology and following in the footsteps of Gelles (1974), Ferraro and Johnson (1983), Mills (1985), and Ptacek (1988), this study set out to determine not only whether abusers apologized for hitting their wives but also whether they dismissed,

excused, and justified their violent behavior. Because of the interest, too, in whether men stopped using aligning actions as time went on (and with repeated incidents of abuse), the study also was designed to plot the chronological sequence of accounts.

A Typology of Honoring Stances

One might suppose that a victim has only two choices when her abuser offers to apologize for, or explain, his behavior: she can reject the aligning action or she can honor it. During the preinterview stage of the study, however, it was deduced that there are at least four honoring stances that a victim may take in response to an aligning action (or set of aligning actions). The four stances are: reject, pseudohonor, ambivalently honor, and wholeheartedly honor.

When the victim *rejects* the aligning action, she makes it clear by her verbal and nonverbal behavior that the aligning action is not acceptable, and consequently not effective in smoothing the disruption caused by the abuse.

With *pseudohonor,* the victim pretends to honor the account, with both verbal and nonverbal behavior indicating acceptance, but in self-interaction and in subsequent interaction with others she does not accept the aligning action as legitimate.

When the victim *ambivalently honors* the aligning action, there is some degree of hesitation before she acknowledges its legitimacy. Her honoring stance is characterized by uncertainty, in which she is tempted to honor the account but also doubts its legitimacy.

Finally, a *wholehearted honoring* of the aligning action occurs when the victim, without hesitation, gives it legitimacy. She readily accepts whatever account is issued and fully believes its validity.

The question of whether accounts are rejected has also been the subject of several inquiries. Ferraro and Johnson (1983), for example, talked about the shifts in events and perceptions that lead women to begin to reject their abusers' rationalizations; and Giles-Sims (1983) noted how the women in her study seemed to be willing to "forgive and forget" the first abusive incident but not the most recent. As far as it is known, however, no one has developed a typology of honoring stances like the one described above and applied it to abusive situations. In order to have a clear sense of the interactional dynamics in relationships, it is important to recognize the variety of accounts that men employ *and* the variety of honoring stances that women use in response.

To summarize, the object of this study was to examine the verbal strategies that abusive men use to neutralize or negate their violent actions and the honoring stances that women take to parry these accounts. A central concern of the project from the beginning was whether aligning actions and honoring stances change over time.

Methodology

Sample

The 50 women in the sample were all residents of a battered women's shelter located approximately 50 miles from a major urban area. Hypothesizing that communication patterns after abusive behavior might vary across racial lines, and feeling that an adequate analysis of racial variation would require a much larger sample, the decision was made (due to restrictions on time and other resources) to limit the interviewees to white victims.

The average age of the women in the study was 28 years. While the variation in educational levels was from less than 8 years of education to college graduate, the average number of years completed was 11.5. About one fourth of the women were employed outside the home. Seventy-eight percent were married to their abusers, 20% were cohabiting, and 2% were dating the abuser. The average length of the relationship was 6.5 years. Ninety-eight percent of the sample had children, the average number being 2.4. The average family income for this sample was $17,585.

As reported by the women, the average age of the abusers was 30 years. The average number of years of education completed was 10.7. The majority of the abusers were employed in blue-collar jobs involving manual labor.

Interviews

The interviews were conducted by the first author over a 2-year period, beginning in the fall of 1986 and ending in the fall of 1988. The interviews lasted from 1 to 2 hours, with the average interview lasting an hour and a half. In all but one case the women were interviewed during their stay in the shelter. With the women's consent, the interviews were tape-recorded, and eventually transcribed. The 50 interviews resulted in 1,500 pages of transcripts.

In order to gain an interpretive understanding of the women's point of view, the women were encouraged to talk at length and in-depth about what they thought and how they felt about the abuse in their

relationships. All were asked to report on three separate incidents of abuse—the first, the most recent, and a middle incident. For the middle incident, the victims were asked to select an abusive incident that occurred about halfway between the first and the most recent—one that "stood out" to them for some reason. The women were especially encouraged to talk about what happened *after* an abusive incident, particularly what the batterers did or said. However, the women were not specifically asked whether the batterers apologized, excused, justified, or dismissed their behavior, nor were they specifically asked whether they honored any accounts offered. When the women happened to mention an aligning action, they were asked to repeat, to the best of their recollection, what the batterer said and what he had said and felt in response. Thus, every effort was made *not to solicit* aligning actions or honoring stances.

Analysis

To classify the women's comments into one category or another, the constant comparative method of qualitative analysis was used (Glaser & Strauss, 1967). As the transcripts were read and reviewed, notations were made in the margins about categories suggested by particular sections of the transcript. Often a single passage was coded in two or more categories. Once the entire transcript was reviewed, selected passages were cut from the transcript and placed in the appropriate files. As additional transcripts were reviewed, incidents that were similar to previously noted ones were filed with them. During this time the files themselves were reviewed. Incidents were compared with other incidents within the same category, and common properties were noted. Gradually, particular categories with their own properties began to emerge. It was then possible to compare newly discovered incidents with the properties of the category, rather than with just similar incidents (see also Lofland & Lofland, 1984; Strauss & Corbin, 1990).

Changes in the nature of aligning actions and in the nature honoring stances were examined both cross-sectionally and developmentally. The cross-sectional analysis involved an examination of distributions across the three time periods, looking at the sample as a whole (N = 50). The developmental analysis involved (a) an examination of the patterns of change in aligning actions as reported by 31 (of the 50) women who provided information on aligning actions on at least two of three incidents; and (b) an examination of patterns of change in honoring stances as reported by 23 (of the 50) women who provided information

on honoring stances on at least two of three incidents. The developmental analysis, in other words, is an analysis of change within specific relationships. Sometimes, the women were not specific about when a particular aligning action or honoring stance was used. When this was the case, the women's descriptions of events were classified under a "general" category.

Limitations

There are several limitations to the study which should be considered when interpreting the results. First, the sample was limited to 50 white shelter residents. The experience of white women may be unlike that of other groups, and battered women who come to shelters may be different from other battered women in important ways. A second limitation is that female victims, rather than male batterers, were asked about the batterers' accounts. Essentially, then, the women provided "second-hand" information about the accounts employed. Third, the women were asked about interactions surrounding abusive incidents that had occurred, for most, years earlier. Ability to recall these early incidents of abuse varied from one respondent to the next, with some clearly recalling the first incident and others remembering little about it. Additionally, subsequent events may have altered the victims' perception and interpretation of these earlier incidents. Fourth, the interviewing strategy employed may have resulted in the women's failure to report both aligning actions and honoring stances surrounding abusive incidents. In an attempt to let the victims "tell their story," the women were not specifically asked whether abusers offered accounts for their behavior or, if offered, whether they were honored. Therefore, it is possible that accounts and honoring stances were employed but not reported by the women because the women were not asked about them.

Aligning Actions Following Woman Battering

Altogether, 139 aligning actions were discussed by the 50 victims. Table 1 presents the cross-sectional analysis of these accounts. As can be seen, 68% of all aligning actions issued after the first incident involved an apology only, while 67% after the middle incident and 42% after the last incident involved an apology only.

Here, for example, is how one victim, a 38-year-old mother of two, described how her husband apologized for his abuse:

Yeah, once I kind of calmed down

Table 1.
Aligning Actions Offered by Batterers After the First, Middle, and Last Incidents of Abuse: Cross-Sectional Analysis (N = 139)

	First		Middle		Last		General		Total	
	Percent	Number	Percent	Number	Percent	Number	Percent	Number	Percent	Number
Apology	68	21	67	14	42	13	30	17	47	65
With excuse	26	8	14	3	29	9	5	3	17	23
Excuse	6	2	14	3	16	5	50	28	27	38
Justification	0	0	5	1	3	1	13	7	6	9
With apology	0	0	0	0	6	2	0	0	1	2
With excuse	0	0	0	0	3	1	2	1	1	2
Dismissal	0	0	0	0	0	0	0	0	0	0
Total	100	31	100	21	100	31	100	56	100	139

Note. Percentages may not add up to 100% due to rounding.

and kind of regrouped. I went back in and when I did he was sitting on the chair, sort of mopey looking. And I walked in and I just stood there and he just jumps up and runs over and starts apologizing and hugging and crying and said he never meant to hit me and he'd never do it again.

Noteworthy is the fact that the percentages for the use of the apology (and only the apology) are very similar to the percentages that Walker (1984) reported. In Walker's (1984) study, apologies dropped from 69% after the first incident to 63% after the middle incident and to 42% after the last incident. At first glance, it thus seems that the results of this study are in accord with Walker's. However, when the categories that include the use of an apology (Apology Only, Apology with Excuse, Justification with Apology) are *combined,* a pattern different from the pattern Walker reported is uncovered. Used alone or in combination with other types of aligning actions, apologies were said to have been offered 94% of the time after the first incident, 81% of the time after the middle incident, and 77% of the time after the last incident.

A similar finding emerges in the developmental analysis. Only 32% of the women (i.e., 10 of the 31 women for whom there was enough information to carry out a developmental analysis) reported that their mates continued to use an apology (and only an apology) across the three incidents. However, when the categories that involve the continued use of the apology, (Apology Only, From Apology to Apology with Excuse, From Apology with Excuse to Apology, From Apology to Apology with Justification, From Apology with Excuse to Apology with Justification) are *combined,* it is found that 74% of individual abusers continued to use apologies with repeated incidents of abuse.

Quite often, in other words, men would offer a *mixture* of aligning actions, blending their apologies with other, more "self-preservative" accounts. One woman, for example, a 30-year-old mother of two

reported how her husband used an apology with an excuse:

There was never an "I'm sorry" for what happened. I mean he hugged and kissed me the next day and told me he was sorry but it wasn't like "I'm sorry, sorry," it was just, "Well you shouldn't have asked for that can opener. You shouldn't have been over there talking to those men." And I'm saying, "Well, all I did was ask for a can opener. I wasn't carrying on a conversation with them."

Another victim, a 21-year-old mother of one, echoed a similar theme of mixed accounts:

I had got [the baby] asleep while he was gone and he come in and laid in my lap and said, "Baby, I'm sorry." He said, "I don't believe I did that." He said, "I am sorry." And then in the next breath he said, "But you shouldn't have been up there [at your mother's house]." And then he turned and said, "I'm sorry, but they shouldn't have said that." He'd say he was sorry and then he'd say, "But ..."

Interestingly enough, none of the aligning actions described by the women could be classified as a dismissal. Possibly, batterers will resort to a dismissal rarely and only when they feel that an excuse or justification will not be honored.

Walker's (1984) findings led her to conclude that "over time in a battering relationship ... loving contrite behavior declines" (p. 97). Assuming that by "loving contrite behavior" Walker meant apologetic acts, this study failed to replicate Walker's results; according to the women interviewed for this project, while the singular use of the apology declined over time, the apology in conjunction with other aligning actions continued throughout the battering relationship.

Noteworthy, too, is what the interviews reveal about the use of the excuse. An excuse, again, is an account whereby the batterer admits that the abuse is bad

but denies responsibility. For example, a 2l-year-old mother of three reported:

He'll say things like, "If you wouldn't run your smart mouth, I wouldn't do this." And he'll say stuff like, "I don't want to do it, you make me do it." Sometimes you could just say something wrong and not even think you had bothered anybody and he'd just fuss you out or cuss you out, but he just says, "You don't know when to shut your mouth, you just go on and on." He always blames it on me, it's never his fault.

And a 25-year-old mother of four stated:

Like I'd say, "Why do you hit me all the time?" [He'd say] "Shut up, you don't need to ask. If you'd done what I asked in the first place, you never would have gotten it." So it was always like my fault. I asked him to hit me. In a sense, that's what he was saying. She deliberately did this, you know, so that's why she got it.

In Table 1, it can be seen that 6% of all aligning actions used after the first abusive incident involved the excuse alone, while 14% and 16% after the middle and last incident respectively, involved the excuse alone. Not much of a difference. However, when the categories are *combined,* a clearer picture of change emerges. Collapsing all categories that involve the excuse, either used alone or in combination with other aligning actions (Excuses Only, Apology with Excuse, and Justification with Excuse), it is found that 32% of all aligning actions after the first incident involved the use of an excuse, while 28% and 48% involved the use of an excuse after the middle and last incident, respectively. In other words, excuses, although they may be used in combination with other aligning actions, are most likely to be used after the last incident of abuse.

A somewhat similar pattern regarding the use of the excuse emerged in the developmental analysis. Although apologies were the most common account to be used across the three incidents (see

Table 2.
Honoring Stances Taken by Victims After the First, Middle, and Last Incidents of Abuse: Cross-Sectional Analysis (N = 100)

	First		Middle		Last		General		Total	
	Percent	Number	Percent	Number	Percent	Number	Percent	Number	Percent	Number
Rejection	0	0	0	0	50	13	7	2	15	15
Pseudo	3	1	6	1	42	11	29	8	21	21
Ambivalent	27	8	29	5	4	1	25	7	21	21
Wholehearted	69	20	65	11	4	1	39	11	43	43
Total	100	29	100	17	100	26	100	28	100	100

Note. Percentages may not add up to 100% due to rounding.

Table 1), in 13% of the cases (i.e., 4 of 31), batterers were said to move from an apology to an excuse; and in 23% of the cases (i.e., 7 of 31), batterers were said to move from an apology to an apology with an excuse.

The Honoring of Aligning Actions

Changes in honoring stances were analyzed in the same two ways that changes in the use of aligning actions were analyzed (i.e., cross-sectionally and developmentally). The typology of honoring stances developed prior to the interviews and described earlier (i.e., reject, pseudohonor, ambivalently honor, and wholeheartedly honor) was the coding scheme employed.

Examining the first column in Table 2, it can be seen that 20 of the 29 women who provided information on honoring stances after the first incident wholeheartedly honored the aligning actions offered. A 21-year-old mother of one, for example, said that she genuinely thought her husband's accounts were valid:

I believe he was sorry he did it. He just can't control himself. I believe he does it before he realizes it and sometimes he doesn't even remember doing it the next morning. He'll look at me and say, "I did it again, didn't I?" And I'd say, "Yeah." And he didn't remember doing it. It's just out of his memory. I think in his heart he's really sorry for doing it. He just can't help it.

Eight of the 29 women, however, were unsure, or ambivalent, about what their response should be. A 25-year-old mother of one, for example, talked of the difficulty she had trying to decide whether to honor her husband's accounts:

It was very easy for him. Crying, bawling, and I can't stand to see a man cry and he knows it, too. "I swear I'll never do it again. Things are going to be different, I promise. I won't touch you." Just a bunch of lies. Just totally convincing me and knowing better. Me sitting there telling myself "I know this isn't right."

My second wind [*sic*] was I know this isn't right, but there was something else that won over what I thought was right. My heart would say, "Okay, I'll give him another chance. It might just be true this time." And then there was this other thing inside me saying, "You idiot." I always had like two things fighting inside of me. There was one that knew better and then there was the one that let itself be guided by strings.

These findings, which show that women are likely to wholeheartedly or ambivalently honor their mates' accounts after the first incident of abuse, are consistent with the results of prior research. Giles-Sims (1983), who interviewed 31 battered women who had sought help from a battered women's shelter, asked the women whether they had been willing to "forgive and forget" the first abusive incident. The vast majority—93%—said yes. Most of the women also said that they perceived the first abusive incident as an isolated one, and they did not expect it to happen again.

Looking at the second column in Table 2, it can be seen that 17 incidents of honoring were described after the middle incident of abuse. Of these, 65% were wholehearted honoring, 29% were ambivalent honoring, and 6% were pseudohonoring. There were no rejections. These percentages are similar to those found after the first abusive incident, and illustrate that as the battering progressed, the women were *still* likely to honor the aligning actions.

The real shift in honoring stances occurred after the last incident of abuse. Only a small fraction wholeheartedly or ambivalently honored the aligning actions then. However, 42% of the women who provided information pseudohonored their mate's accounts, and 50% flat out rejected them. Thus, if the categories of pseudohonoring and rejection are *combined,* it can be said that 92% of the women did not honor the account offered, whether or not they conveyed this to the batterer. Here is how one victim, for example, a 24-year-old mother of three, described her use of the pseudohonoring stance:

When he would first apologize to me, I would try to act like I was forgiving him, or he would get mad again. He would like come up and hug me, and I would try to act like I believed him, but I would be thinking, "I just hate you, and I'm leaving you, just wait 'til I can get out of here."

And here is how another, a 35-year-old mother of two, described how she moved to flat out reject her husband's accounts:

He came to the door and he was weeping. I don't mean crying just a little bit, I mean weeping, saying, "Please don't take my kids away, they're the only persons I've got, and I've missed you'all," and all that kind of stuff. And I felt so sorry for him, I just, you know. [He said] "Let me kiss you and hug you ... I am so sorry. It just got out of hand." But I just can't take that anymore. I've heard it too much, I guess.

The developmental analysis again supported the cross-sectional analysis. Eighty-seven percent of the women (i.e., 20 of the 23 for whom there was enough information to carry out a developmental analysis) shifted from honoring stances which more or less accepted the accounts issued by the abusers (wholehearted or ambivalent honoring) to honoring stances which questioned the accounts (pseudohonor or rejection).

These findings, which show that women who come to a shelter are likely to question their mates' accounts, are also consistent with other studies. Giles-Sims (1983) found that only 18% of her sample were willing to "forgive and forget" the last incident of abuse; and Ferraro and Johnson (1983) found that battered women who decide to go to a shelter generally do so only after they have rejected the rationalizations for abuse.

Implications

For counselors, therapists, and social workers who are working with abusive men and/or abused women, this study—like other recent studies on the "phenomenology" of abuse (e.g., Andrews &

Brewin, 1990; Herbert, Silver, & Ellard, 1991)—helps clarify how batterers and victims "give meaning to" and (from their point of view) "cope with" domestic violence.

If one focuses exclusively on the apology, as Walker (1984) did, the findings from this study are very similar to hers. However, if one looks at the full range of accounts that abusers use, the findings differ. According to the women interviewed in this study, the third phase in the cycle of violence is not bypassed with repeated abuse, as Walker (1984) suggested; rather the third phase is *modified* to include other types of accounts. In other words, the "content" of the stage may change, but its "form" (the offering of accounts) remains essentially the same.

This shift in the type of aligning actions is significant because of the message it conveys. In an apology, the abuser accepts responsibility and implies that what he did was wrong. When the abuser moves to the use of the excuse either alone or in combination with other accounts, he is attempting to deny responsibility for his behavior. Something else—stress, financial problems, alcohol or drug abuse, or the victim's behavior—is "causing" the abuse. Not only the batterer but also the victim may be distracted by these excuses, believing that the abuse will stop if the avowed "causes" could be eliminated (e.g., "If I/he would stop drinking, the violence would stop"). Ultimately, however, these accounts serve to perpetuate the abuse because they prevent the abuser from coming to grips with the fact that *he* is responsible for his violent behavior. Ultimately, they enable the abuser to continue *both* his violent behavior *and* his relationship with his victim.

Counselors, therapists, and social workers can help abusers and victims understand how accounts perpetuate domestic violence. Exposing the accounts for what they are—verbal strategies designed to minimize the violence—is the first step in eliminating their use and their power. It is important also for professional helpers to reject the accounts that abusers offer. Honoring apologies, excuses, and justifications leads the batterer to believe that his abusive behavior is acceptable "in some situations" and "under certain conditions." The hitting license must be *cancelled,* not qualified. The repudiation of the battering must be foremost in the practitioner's mind.

All the battered women in this study left their abusive relationships, at least temporarily. The process of getting out of an abusive relationship is a complex one, both emotionally and physically. Many women leave these relationships and return to them, often more than once (Pagelow, 1984). The honoring stance that a woman adopts can help counselors, therapists, and social workers determine whether a woman is emotionally ready to leave. The women in this study sought help from a shelter after the "last" abusive incident, an incident in which 92% (of those reporting a honoring stance) rejected or pseudohonored an account offered by the batterer. These women clearly did not believe that the abuser was sorry, that something or someone else was to blame, or that it would not happen again. Victims who honor accounts, much like the women in Ferraro and Johnson's (1983) study who offered rationalizations for the abuse which they suffered, may still believe that the abuser is sorry, that it will not happen again, and that he will change. Accounts offered by abusers and honored by victims thus serve the same purpose as victim rationalizations—that is, they prevent women from seeking aid.

Finally, it is important to emphasize that while counselors, therapists, and social workers have an obligation to help victims gain insight into their abuse, they also have an obligation to be nonjudgmental of whatever decision a woman makes about her abusive relationship. A number of women in this study talked about the loss of support they experienced from significant others when they made decisions to stay with or return to their abusers. Victims of male battering face difficult choices—choices about what to say to their abusers, choices about whether to stay. Respecting the choices that women make is an integral part of the counseling/therapeutic process. Victims must always know that there are people ready and willing to listen to them and assist them.

REFERENCES

Andrews, B., & Brewin, C. R. (1990). Attributions of blame for marital violence: A study of antecedents and consequences. *Journal of Marriage and the Family,* **52,** 757-767.

Dobash, R. E., & Dobash, R. P. (1984). The nature and antecedent of violent events. *British Journal of Criminology,* **24,** 269-288.

Ferraro, K. J., & Johnson, J. M. (1983). How women experience battering: The process of victimization. *Social Problems,* **30,** 325-339.

Gelles, R. J. (1974). *The violent home: A study of physical aggression between husbands and wives.* Beverly Hills, CA: Sage.

Giles-Sims, J. (1983). *Wife battering: A systems theory approach.* New York: Guilford.

Glaser, B. G., & Strauss, A. (1967). *The discovery of grounded theory.* Chicago: Aldine.

Goffman, E. (1971). *Relations in public: Microstudies of the public order.* New York: Basic Books.

Herbert, T. B., Silver, R. C., & Ellard, J. H. (1991). Coping with an abusive relationship: I. How and why do women stay? *Journal of Marriage and the Family,* **53,** 311-325.

Hewitt, J. P., & Stokes, R. (1975). Disclaimers. *American Sociological Review,* **40,** 1-11.

Hunter, C. H. (1984). Aligning actions: Types and distributions. *Symbolic Interaction,* **7,** 155-174.

Lofland, J., & Lofland, L. H. (1984). *Analyzing social settings: A guide to qualitative research and analysis.* Belmont, CA: Wadsworth.

Mills, T. (1985). The assault on the self: Stages in coping with battering husbands. *Qualitative Sociology,* **8,** 103-123.

Pagelow, M. D. (1984). Family violence. New York: Praeger.

Ptacek, J. (1988). Why do men batter their wives? In K. Yllo & M. Bograd (Eds.), *Feminist perspectives on wife abuse* (pp. 133-157). Newbury Park, CA: Sage.

Scott, M. B., & Lyman, S. M. (1968). Accounts. *American Sociological Review,* **41,** 46-62.

Stokes, R., & Hewitt, J. P. (1976). Aligning actions. *American Sociological Review,* **41,** 838-849.

Strauss, A., & Corbin, J. (1990). *Basics of qualitative research: Grounded theory procedures and techniques.* Newbury Park, CA: Sage.

Sykes, G. M., & Matza, D. (1957). Techniques of neutralization: A theory of delinquency. *American Sociological Review,* **22,** 667-670.

Walker, L. E. (1979). *The battered woman.* New York: Harper & Row.

Walker, L. E. (1984). *The battered woman syndrome.* New York: Springer.

Where Do We Go from Here?

An interview with Ann Jones

Ann Jones is the author of several landmark books on violence against women. "Women Who Kill," "When Love Goes Wrong" (with Susan Schechter), and "Next Time, She'll Be Dead." All contribute to moving the discussion about battery away from women and toward stopping the men who commit the violence. In July [1994], Jones sat down with "Ms." senior editor Gloria Jacobs to explore the current convulsion of soul-searching sweeping the U.S. in the wake of revelations about domestic violence in the O.J. Simpson case.

Gloria Jacobs: In your latest book, *Next Time, She'll Be Dead*, you say that we haven't put an end to violence in the home because society accepts that women are going to be battered, that they serve as an example of "what awaits all women who don't behave."

Ann Jones: We never confront the enormity of this problem. Battery is our greatest health problem, probably worse than breast cancer. It's one of the crimes most frequently committed against women. It's among the crimes most often committed in this country—period. Yet at the present time we have a national debate on health care, of which violence against women is not a part, and a national debate on crime, of which violence against women is not a part. So, if you can't get this issue discussed in the arenas where it is an absolutely central concern, then things aren't going to change. We need to shift the discussion. At the same time, individual women who are still up against this problem have to have a way to evaluate what's happening to

> ### "The thing to remember is that women have a right to live free from bodily harm."

them, and to figure out what to do.

G.J.: I know you don't like the term "domestic violence," but doesn't it acknowledge that the home is not necessarily a safe haven for women?

A.J.: It makes the violence sound domesticated, and it makes it sound like a special category of violence that is somehow different from other kinds—less serious. It's seen as a kind of violence that women volun-

teer for, or inspire, or provoke. I prefer to call it violence against women, because it does include so many other things, like rape and pimping and molestation of children.

G.J.: But do we need to identify the locus of this particular kind of violence? People tend to assume that danger and violence come from outside: the stranger on the street. Is it important to distinguish violence perpetrated, as you say, "by the person who says he loves you"?

A.J.: Yes. But this is the most common kind of violence against women. So when you simply call it violence against women, that in itself redirects our attention. It's not coming out of the bushes, it's coming out of the bedroom. I don't have the answer to how to shift this terminology, but I do think that it gets watered down by being called domestic violence.

The more difficult term is "battered woman," because it suggests a woman who is more or less permanently black and blue and helpless. And of course most women who are abused and controlled by men don't think of themselves as battered women. So, yes, we need some better terms to define what we're talking about. And, in my view, a lot of women are battered who are never hit, because you can, as we know, be subject to control without any physical violence.

I would like to see us start thinking about battered women as resisters, because it's clear to me that women are not battered or emotionally abused or controlled because they're passive and helpless. Often, women get emotionally abused and physically battered because they resist that kind of control. I don't think I've ever met a battered woman who didn't think of herself as a strong woman. Most are doing all the regular things of life—they're keeping their house, they're holding down a job, raising their kids—all while they're living in this terrible situa-

tion. They're doing all the things that put the rest of us under stress, plus they're trying to appease this man to keep him from being violent. So, yes, they're strong. They cope with an incredible amount, and that's the way they think of themselves, and they don't want to—can't—think of themselves as helpless battered women. But at the same time they are being victimized by these tyrannical, abusive men.

G.J.: Will the Violence Against Women Act affect police enforcement?

A.J.: The most important thing about the act is that it conceptualizes battering as a violation of civil rights. Whether it will ensure law enforcement depends upon what jurisdiction you're talking about and who is in charge—it depends on how rigorous a police chief is in monitoring officers and making them conform to public policy.

We still get reports from battered women who say they called the police and nothing happened. But you can also find police departments operating effectively, making arrests, and prosecutors following through.

We pin a lot on police, and say they should make arrests, but the police are quite right in saying that very often when they do, women don't press charges. The real culprit is the prosecutor. If the prosecutor's

> ## "A man beats a woman because he *can* do it. He calls it love and so does everybody else."

office is not going to follow through by prosecuting even without the woman's help—they can use 911 tapes, hospital records, proof of previous battery—why should the police arrest anybody? So we have to insist that the whole system work as a *system*. There are examples, like Duluth and San Diego, where the criminal justice system works as a system—it makes a difference not just in making women safe, but it probably saves the lives of batterers as well. It certainly saves the lives of innocent bystanders, and it certainly makes

---

WHAT ARE BATTERED WOMEN FOR?

The battered women's movement has organized for more than 15 years against "domestic violence," yet the violence continues. Could it be that individual women are to blame after all? Or could it be that battered women play some indispensable part, have some function, some role or social utility we haven't taken into account? Perhaps we should put a different question: What are battered women *for*?

This puts a new light on the problem: battered women are *for battering*. The battered woman is a woman who may be beaten. If you doubt that society views battered women as, by definition, "beatable," then how do you explain the fact that we almost always put responsibility for

woman-beating on the woman? Why else would we probe her psyche to reveal the secret self within, yearning for abuse, if not to set her apart as a *beatable* woman, unlike ourselves? There are millions of these beatable women. Many of them live within "the family," which entitles only the "head" of the family to beat them. Many others live outside "the family"—in which case anyone may beat them. Many live and work in industries that rent or sell beatable women and children—prostitution, for example, and pornography. A few beatable women, like Hedda Nussbaum, become public figures whom everyone can assail.

Battered women are to sexism what the poor are to capitalism—always with us.

They are a source of cheap labor and sexual service to those with the power to buy them, a "problem" for the righteous to lament, a topic to provide employment for academic researchers, a sponge to soak up the surplus violence of men, a conduit to carry off the political energy of other women who must care for them, an exemplum of what awaits all women who don't behave as prescribed, and a pariah group to amplify by contrast our good opinion of ourselves. And for all their social utility, they remain largely, and conveniently, invisible.

—From *Next Time, She'll Be Dead,*
by Ann Jones
(Beacon Press)

the job of the police easier. And it increases public respect for the police, because the police are suddenly doing an effective job.

G.J.: When we jail batterers, don't many come out and batter again?

A.J.: The evidence is that some men really learn a lesson, and they're deterred, while other men have thicker skulls, and these are the guys we should keep locking up.

G.J.: Is there hope for rehabilitation? In *Next Time, She'll Be Dead,* you talk about Duluth, Minnesota, where one activist estimates there is nearly a 60 percent recidivism rate among batterers.

A.J.: Researchers are beginning to examine the batterers. Now they have a theory that batterers suffer from frontal lobe damage. It's the same old crap. Nobody wants to admit that men do this because they like to. Other research claims there are two different kinds of batterers. One is impulsive and gets excited and loses his temper. They say you may be able to retrain some of those guys, using anger management. I don't believe that for a minute. And the other category is the cold, calculating batterer whose heart rate actually drops during an argument. The theory is that these heavy-duty guys are not responsive to therapy.

I think batterers should be given an opportunity to learn to think in a different way, but that's not like mental therapy. They need to be reeducated in terms of their values and their worldview. They need to learn that women are human beings and are not here simply to serve them. Perhaps you can persuade some of them to change their worldview, but until you do that, you can't make those guys stop. And if you can't make them stop, then these are the men who are candidates for three strikes and you're out [the policy of imprisoning people convicted of three felonies to terms from 20 years to life]. These are the people who cause serious damage to one person after another, or to large numbers of people at once.

FACT: Domestic violence causes almost 100,000 days of hospitalization, 30,000 emergency room visits, and 40,000 trips to the doctor every year.

G.J.: What if half of all men are batterers? Is this country ready to lock up many of its "upstanding citizens"?

A.J.: It's possible to look at the whole history of domestic violence in this country as one massive attempt to avoid that very thing. There's a new book out by some academic man who advocates "transcending the punitive response." But we have always transcended the punitive response. Let's face it, that's been our national policy.

In Duluth one in 20 male citizens of the metropolitan area have been through the batterers program at least once. That means that most of them were arrested to begin with. So if you could extrapolate from that nice midwestern community and see that as what might happen in other communities, it's a lot of guys. Some of those men will not re-offend. Others will. And then you have to arrest them and maybe lock them up this time and put them through the program again. You do that two or three times, and each time the punishment gets a little more severe, until either they get it or they get locked up indefinitely. If we were talking about any other crime, it would be clear to people that that's what we have to do. We must make people see this as a real crime and that what happens to women matters.

G.J.: Where do you start in educating boys that women are equal beings?

A.J.: Both boys and girls need to be taught about this. There should be a family violence curriculum in every grade school, starting the earlier the better, because so many children come from homes where violence is going on, and so many are themselves victimized by violence. They should be told that this is not their fault. We should give those kids an opportunity to come forward and say what's happening to them in their homes. That kind of program should be carried on in the high schools, too—there are a lot of high schools now where peer education is going on. In Boston there is a program that's cosponsored by a men's counseling group and a women's group. Educating children and teenagers ought to help.

At the same time you have to look at the scary figures of violence against women in high schools and colleges, and the number of high school and college age boys who say that they get off on intimidating girls and who don't see anything wrong with doing that. [In 1993, for example, the American Association of University Women reported that 66 percent of high school boys admitted to being sexual harassers.]

You can educate young people, but guys also get an education from rock videos, and pornography, and our incredibly violent movies and television, and the constant depiction and identification of sex with violence, the depiction of women in demeaning and abusive situations. So lest they decide to emulate that kind of conduct, there also needs to be strong punishment from the start for kids who are violent.

G.J.: Let's talk about the shelters. What are the strengths and weaknesses of the shelter movement?

A.J.: Shelters were never meant to be permanent. They were always meant to be temporary. Unfortunately we need a lot more of them, because the problem is so great that they're turning away many women. They do save a great many lives. They give many women the breathing space to sort things out and get out, so they've been invaluable. But what they've really done is save the lives of *men.* The rate of women killing men has gone down, and its

FACT: If all women victimized by domestic violence in 1993 joined hands, the line would stretch from New York City to Los Angeles and beyond.

decline began with the advent of battered women's shelters. That's a very clear indication that if you give women a way to get out of these desperate life-and-death situations, they will get out.

But I'd like to see shelters put out of business. I think we ought to be working toward that. Maybe it's the men who should be put out of houses and locked up. The shelters are kind of reverse jails for women.

G.J.: How would we legislate getting the men out of the house so the women could stay there?

A.J.: That has been legislated in many places. Judges are empowered to evict men from the premises. But that means the men have to be arrested and brought to prosecution, and then the judge can evict them, issue stay-away orders, protective orders, and provide for child support.

G.J.: But then the men know where the women are, which would make many women feel like sitting ducks.

A.J.: That requires law enforcement to keep track of the situation and make sure that she's safe, and if she's not, then the guy needs to be locked up for a longer period of time.

G.J.: Often, we hear about women who were killed while they had a valid restraining order against their murderer. What do we need to do to make these orders effective?

A.J.: Again it requires changing the attitudes and procedures of police and prosecutors and judges so that they take the orders seriously. Very often what happens is that a woman gets a restraining order, a man violates it, and the police don't do anything about it. They say, "If he comes back again, let us know." It

should be police policy to seek out and arrest anyone who violates a restraining order, and that should be an unbailable offense, carrying an automatic jail sentence. If a batterer is sent to a reeducation program, it should be in addition to his jail term, not in lieu of it. He should serve real time, because any man who violates a restraining order poses a real danger.

But the attitude now is "Well, gee, we gave her a restraining order, it just made the guy mad. Maybe we shouldn't do that." If you were talking about any other crime you would see how ridiculous that is: "Stole your car? Well, we can't arrest him because he might get mad and steal somebody else's car."

G.J.: This brings up the response we got at *Ms.* to your article about women and guns. Women wrote in, saying: "I'm really frightened. There's someone out there aiming to get me. How can you say I shouldn't have a gun to protect myself? No one else will protect me." What do we tell women who feel the police won't help them?

A.J.: That's a good question. The alternative may be to go underground, and many women do that. Others don't, saying, "He'll find me anyway, and I can't live in that kind of fear." I wouldn't tell a woman in that situation that she shouldn't have a gun if that's what she feels she needs to defend herself. I would tell her to really learn how to use it. But I'm afraid that relying on the gun to save you may not work. I got letters, too, from women who said that they managed to save themselves with a gun, and I think it's a terrible commentary on how we live now. I would suggest that women go underground, but I understand why many women don't.

G.J.: What about this notion of the battered woman syndrome, which says that battered women have been so abused that they're incapable of resistance?

A.J.: I don't think there is a battered woman syndrome. I would call it

post-traumatic stress disorder. What happens is not peculiar to battered women. If you get beaten up enough and if your freedom of movement and autonomy are stripped from you bit by bit, you begin to suffer from post-traumatic stress disorder. The psychiatrist Judith Herman writes in her book *Trauma and Recovery* that there really ought to be a more intense category of post-traumatic stress disorder for battered women, hostages, and prisoners of war, because what happens to them is more prolonged and in many ways worse than a single traumatic event.

But this is not a preexisting condition in women's psychological makeup. People somehow see the battered woman syndrome as a cause of why women get battered—they say, "They have low self-esteem and that's why they get battered." That's nonsense, just nonsense. What happens is often the women resist and the men intensify the violence. If the women get stuck and can't get out of there for one reason or another—usually if they're scared—then they can begin to suffer from post-traumatic stress disorder. It's a consequence of severe and prolonged battery; it's not something women are naturally afflicted with.

G.J.: So what should we teach girls?

A.J.: I think we need to talk about love and romance, what I like to call "true luv," spelled l-u-v, the incredible romantic myth that all girls are subjected to from many sources. The problem is that so much of men's controlling behavior is absolutely synonymous with what is described as signs of love in the "true luv" kinds of literature. All that possessiveness and jealousy and wanting to monopolize your time: "I love you more than anybody ever did, and I want to take care of you," and all that la-di-da stuff—all the stuff that girls are taught to think of as signs of his devotion. We need to tell them: "Hey, those are danger signals. That's the stuff to watch out for."

Girls should be alert, and know that this guy is out to co-opt them.

G.J.: Let's go on to the media. I saw a clipping that said women were reporting that men are saying to them, "I will O.J. you, if you don't watch out." This has become a phrase for abuse and aggression, and the paper put this information in a column of various cute anecdotes rather than taking it seriously.

A.J.: After many highly publicized cases we get reports from local battered women's shelters that men are showing the newspaper headlines to their wives, saying, "Look what happened to her, she didn't do what she should have." That's standard, to use such cases to intimidate women.

And sometimes after a prominent homicide, you find women leaving shelters and going back to their abusers because they feel safer. If they're away from him, they think he'll come after them and kill them.

G.J.: The media often trivialize these stories, talking of "love gone awry."

A.J.: They tend to report the men's point of view. Some of the men who work with batterers have called attention to the fact that the news media and the academics just buy what the batterers tell them. Here's *Time* magazine from the week of July 4 reporting on the relationships that end in murder: it describes a "predictable progression that typically begins either with a steady diet of battery or isolated incidents of violence that can go on for years." You notice it doesn't specify who's doing this steady diet of battering. "Often, the drama is fueled by both parties," all right? "A man wages an assault. The woman retaliates by deliberately trying to provoke his jealousy or anger. He strikes again. And the cycle repeats." Here's a new kind of cycle of violence: he hits her, she provokes him deliberately, and he hits her again, and that's called a cycle. "The two are locked in a sick battle that binds—and reassures—even as it divides." This is hogwash! This is the worst kind of victim-blaming! Where do they get this

---

WORKING FOR CHANGE

In Little Rock, Arkansas, the Women's Watchcare Network (WWN) uses a group of more than 200 volunteers statewide to collect data on violence. Every year, WWN tracks murders of women—especially those related to domestic violence. (It also monitors racist and homophobic violence, incidents of police brutality, and the activities of the Ku Klux Klan and the religious right.) This information is compiled annually in the "Women's Watchcare Log," which is made available to the public. It lists victims' names and ages and the precise nature of the crime when available. Started in 1989, Watchcare is run by the Women's Project of Little Rock, which also publishes a newsletter and holds workshops, conferences, and outreach programs for women in prison.

---

shit? From talking to batterers who say, "I hit her and then she deliberately defied me until I had to hit her again." They would not get this story from a woman.

This is a deliberate misinterpretation of what some women might say; battered women will sometimes say that they knew a beating was coming so they tried to provoke him at a certain time when they thought they could control it. That does happen, but it's a desperate way of trying to cope with the situation. It's not "locked in a sick battle," it's a last-ditch effort to try to maintain some kind of control over a situation that you can't escape from. And some women are so conditioned to think they did something wrong to "cause" an attack that they report it that way. What everyone—like *Time*—forgets is that provocation is not a crime. Battering is.

And the other piece of this is the man who says he beats or murders a woman because he loves her so much. That's what these guys always say. That is not love. Yet reporters accept that language without criticism. They continue to call these cases crimes of passion.

That just has to stop, but again, it's part of the way we bend over backward *not* to look at what's going on. Men are trying to take over the lives of women, trying to control women. A man does that because he *can* do it, it's not that hard to do; it works, it gets him what he wants; nobody stops him. So why shouldn't he do it? And he calls that love, and everybody else calls that love, so there we are.

G.J.: The changes we need are huge. If you had to choose where to start, what would you say?

A.J.: It would be an immense change in the lives of women if we would just grasp the first principle—that women have a right to live free from harm. And keep in mind that bits and pieces of the picture have been changing for the last 20 years. Here and there, some community in this country is now doing a piece of it right. And other communities could copy them. Increasingly, people in one community or one state are starting to say, "Hey, look what's going on in Duluth. Or in San Diego. Or in Quincy, Massachusetts, in the prosecutor's office." So some of it is already happening. For every change we need to make, someone in the country not only already knows how to do it, but *is* doing it successfully.

The main thing is always to remember that women have a right to live free from harm. That's the thing that nobody talks about. We've talked all this time in terms of who the victims are, and how they behave, and how they ought to behave. We've psychologized the problem, as we always do in this country. We've seen it as a matter of personal psychology instead of the material conditions of people's lives.

G.J.: What about researchers who say male violence and aggression are innate, that this is what testosterone does and men just can't help it?

A.J.: Give me a break. There's always going to be some researcher saying biology is everything. Well, if that's what they think, that men can't help

FACT: Of the 35 women on death row in 1993, almost half were there for the murder of an abusive partner.

it, maybe the only answer left is to castrate them all.

G.J.: My last question is about the role of the bystander, the friend, or neighbor. What can we do to help? Should we be calling the police?

A.J.: First, about the police, I wish we could lay to rest this notion that domestic violence calls are so dangerous. The most dangerous calls for police are burglaries, robberies, and drug-related crimes. What probably causes the most trouble for police on these calls is that they don't know whether they're supposed to mediate or arrest or walk the guy around the block. A simple policy of mandatory arrest makes it much safer and easier for them.

The harder question is what the individual should do about it. The first thing to realize is that any woman in a situation of emotional or physical abuse has a much more complicated life than you can possibly understand. And it is very important that, as much as you are able, you let her know that you know or believe that she is being subjected to something that she doesn't have to put up with, that you value her, that you are afraid for her safety, that you stand ready to help her, in whatever way you are actually ready to help her. It's important not to intervene unless you're willing to put your body where your mouth is. You need to do some soul-searching before you take on intervention. And you can say, "I am afraid for my own safety in getting involved, but I

would like to give you this information about a place where you can talk to a counselor," or you can say, "I would like to help you do whatever it is you feel like you can do."

Probably the first thing you ought to do is research exactly what the situation is in your own community. Don't advise the woman to call the police unless you're pretty damn sure what the police are going to do. Don't get her into a situation that might make it worse for her. Do the homework, find out what goes on in your town, get what information you can and offer her that information. Call a shelter hotline or the prosecutor's office, or your state's domestic violence coalition, or NOW. Then realize that she might reject you, tell you it's not happening, get mad at you. The process of getting out of a situation like that sometimes takes a while. Any woman who's in a situation like that is bound to be confused, because it is very confusing to have a person beat you up, and then say he loves you. This is perhaps the single most confusing situation in the world. Offer support, but don't get mad at the woman if she doesn't take you up on it. Every one of us who has interviewed battered women over the years knows that every battered woman says, "Oh, I wish I could thank so-and-so. What they said made such a difference to me, even though I couldn't do anything about it at the time." So you can become part of the process of a woman liberating herself, although you may never know.

G.J.: And should we call the police?

A.J.: Yes, you should. But you should also go to the police yourself and ask what their policy is: Do they practice mandatory arrest? Or tell them you called because you could hear that your neighbor was being beaten up. Ask them exactly what they did about it: Was an arrest

made, and if not, why not? If they tell you she didn't want to press charges, then ask why she should have to press charges. Then you go to the prosecutor and ask what's going on, why they're not pressing charges against violent men, why they're discouraging the police from arresting violent men. And then when the prosecutor says the batterers are not going to get any kind of sentence anyway, then you go to the judge and you say, "What the fuck are you doing here? Why aren't you enforcing the law?" Then you enlist your friends, and you go to the newspapers with it.

And not to be too self-serving about this, but one thing that you can do for someone you suspect is being battered is give them *When Love Goes Wrong* by Susan Schechter and myself. The book shifts the attention from the usual self-help-book question of "Oh, what am I doing wrong, how can I change to make my husband change?" to ask the question "What is he getting out of doing that?" That helps a woman cut through so much confusion. It gives her a tool she can use to evaluate her situation and shift the questions that she's asking herself. Women tell us: "When I started looking at what he was getting out of this, it made it so clear that I changed my own mind about what to do."

The danger with the 12-step programs is they are the equivalent of external victim-blaming. They and the standard self-help books put the responsibility on the woman to change her behavior or character or to love her husband better, and none of that is what the issue is. The issue is always him. It's *his* problem, it's his crime. He's the one who's violating her fundamental rights. He's the one who has to stop and change.

SEXUAL DESIRE

Whether it's dull appetite or ravenous hunger, millions of Americans are unhappy with their intimate lives

She won't look at him. Keeps staring out the window, even though there's nothing to see but the black Minnesota night and a car speeding past, headlights sliding along the glass. "I thought it would just go away," the petite woman says finally, in a small, tired voice. "That it was just a phase I was going through. I would make excuses."

The muffled thuds and shouts of playing children drift from the basement. Her wiry husband, seated on the Early American sofa, is a machinist in his late 30s. She is a homemaker. And all that matters now is that they haven't had sex in eight months. "He'd start a little foreplay. I'd say 'No. Just leave me alone!' "

"Boy, would that put me away," says her husband, his bearded face stony above a red T-shirt. "I was already feeling hurt. I'd roll over and go to sleep."

"Sometimes, every three to four months, I'd force myself," she confesses. "Grit my teeth and get through it."

Neither partner looks at the other, and a hesitant hush hovers over the room. Finally, the husband turns to psychologist Eli Coleman, who runs a sex-therapy clinic in nearby Minneapolis. "There's just one thing I want to know," he says, frowning. "Is this a common situation?"

Common? Try epidemic. The problem under discussion is sexual desire, an instinct that should flow as freely and unself-consciously between two loving humans as the urge for a fine meal or a good night's sleep. This is a story about what happens when desire goes askew. It is a tale of people who typically are articulate, competent and to all appearances quite ordinary, yet they cannot enjoy one of humankind's most basic pleasures. Madonna may be falling out of her bustier on MTV, Prince may be singing the joys of masturbation on FM and the latest sex-and-gore thriller may be packing them in at the Cineplex, but in the bedroom, an estimated 1 in 5 Americans—some 38 million adults—don't want sex at all. As many as 9 million more, meanwhile, suffer almost uncontrollable sexual desire, compulsively masturbating or prowling a surreal landscape of massage parlors and rumpled beds in a frenzied quest for loveless sex.

To be sure, sexual-desire disorders date back a lot further than "The Devil and Miss Jones," or even Don Juan. What's new is that such complaints now constitute the No. 1 problem bringing clients to sex therapists.

Women without orgasms and men who ejaculated prematurely once dominated the practice; now—because of the pioneering research of Dr. William Masters and Virginia Johnson in the 1960s—people with such common conditions seek do-it-yourself solutions. "The simpler cases can go out and get self-help books," says Dr. Constance Moore, head of the Human Sexuality Program at Houston's Baylor College of Medicine. "Today, sex therapists are seeing the more complicated problems."

No one is sure whether the onslaught of Americans seeking help reflects a real rise in desire disorders or whether such problems are simply more visible. In the 1960s, public expectations of sex began to shift in profound ways. Thanks to the birth-control pill, women could for the first time in history separate sex from the fear of pregnancy. Suddenly, it was not only OK for women to enjoy sex—it was *de rigueur*. The 1953 Kinsey report that as many as 29 percent of single women were sexually unresponsive now seemed as old-fashioned as stiff petticoats and white gloves.

At the same time, new cultural messages glorified casual sex. More than 80 percent of women and 90 percent of men now engage in premarital intercourse, compared with 50 percent of women and 80 percent of men in the 1920s. And from seductive Calvin Klein–jeans ads to the estimated 176 monthly sex scenes on prime-time TV, free sex has emerged as the presumptive symbol of the good life. Sexual health has become a right.

And so they come for help: A man who, after pursuing his bride-to-be for months, shuts down sexually on his wedding night in their $200-a-day bridal suite. A school administrator with five boyfriends who sandwiches frenzied appointments for sex between dashes to office and supermarket. They are farmers and salesmen, consultants and lawyers, homemakers and clerks. In the sanitized confines of therapists' offices, they haltingly reveal their secrets—it's hard, after all, to confess even to a best friend that one masturbates five times a day or hasn't slept with one's spouse in a year. Eyes downcast, voices leaden, they evoke the anguish of abusive fathers, of religiously suffocating mothers, of families where sex, if discussed at all, was shameful and dirty and where dad sometimes slipped into bed with the kids.

What unites them is fear. As children, they learned that caring too much for others was risky. As adults, they found they could control their fear by controlling sex. Instead of an intimate and loving act, sex became a tool to manipulate those who might get too close. And while no one can properly distinguish why some people channel childhood anxieties into food or booze while others fasten on sex, it may be that what eating disorders were to the '80s, desire disorders will be in the '90s: the designer disease of the decade, the newest symptom of American loneliness and alienation. "Sex isn't just sex," explains Raul C. Schiavi, head of the Human Sexuality Program at Mount Sinai Medical Center. "It's an avenue to express many more needs: intimacy, support, self-esteem or whatever."

Given that baggage, it's no wonder that the treatments for sex problems are neither identical nor tidy. In the past three years, researchers have discovered that antidepressants like Prozac can markedly improve symptoms in sexual compulsives. But for victims of low desire, the results are sketchier. The quest for an aphrodisiac, of course, is ancient: King Tut gulped licorice root before romancing his queen, and other love potions, from powdered rhinoceros horn to bees' wings, have proved just as disappointing. But for most cases, treatment involves counseling and therapy, beginning with an attempt to define when things went wrong.

WHAT IS NORMAL?

At first it was fun: feverish kisses in his red Chevy, giggly nights of passion in the apartment. But then came marriage, two kids, and suddenly her husband's hands on her flesh felt like tentacles, and the sight of him approaching made her body stiffen with revulsion. Then the disagreements began, hurtful scenes ending with each of them lying wedged against opposite sides of the bed, praying for sleep. "I didn't know what to do— look in the yellow pages?" recalls Karen, 35, a clerk-cashier in suburban Minneapolis. Her husband didn't know, either. "We finally got a phone number from our family doctor," he says. "It was three more months before we called."*

It wasn't so long ago that low sexual desire was considered a good thing—at least in women. Madame Bovary scandalized 19th-century France with her extramarital fling in Gustave Flaubert's novel. And no one ever said that the remote Estella of Dickens's "Great Expectations" had a low-desire problem. Indeed, from Eve's seduction of Adam, women's sexuality outside of procreation was often considered evil, and early Christian thinkers were just as unsparing toward men—a philosophy that found particularly fertile ground in the New World. As recently as 1907, Dr. John Harvey Kellogg developed his popular corn flakes in an unsuccessful effort to curb desire.

Nor were men and women always physically able to enjoy sex. In late 17th-century England, for instance,

*Like many desire disorder victims quoted here, Karen is a client of the University of Minnesota's Program in Human Sexuality. All names and identifications have been changed.

people suffered from long bouts of crippling illness, not to mention bad breath from poor dentistry, running sores, ulcers and skin diseases. Without antibiotics, women endured repeated vaginal and urinary tract infections that made sex painful.

Then came marriage, two children, and suddenly her husband's hands felt like tentacles. His approach made her stiffen with revulsion.

In fact, the idea of "normal" sexual appetite is such a 20th-century artifice that few experts are comfortable defining it. Clinically, hypoactive sexual desire means having sexual urges, fantasies and/or activity less than twice a month. But even that is the loosest of definitions, since if both partners are happy, once a month may be as "proper" as once a day. "I make the diagnosis [of HSD] if there's been a definite change in desire," says sexologist Moore, "and if it's causing the patient some distress." In Karen's case, the distress was acute: Each night she huddled on her side of the bed, tormenting herself with guilt and dread that her marriage was slipping away.

More typically, though, it's the patient's *partner* who is in distress. Consider Tom, 35, a Midwestern advertising executive whose wife has HSD. "I would try to ignore it as long as I could," he says. "Then she'd give in [and have sex]. But she'd lie limp, waiting for me to get it over with. She could have been downtown. I felt terrible afterward, very guilty."

Prodded by their mates, victims of desire disorders often show up for therapy complaining of impotence or lack of orgasm. But in the mid-1970s, therapists began to notice that the real problem was often that, as in Karen's case, they didn't truly *want* to have sex. In her groundbreaking 1979 work, "Disorders of Sexual Desire," Dr. Helen Singer Kaplan found that unlike sexual arousal, desire exists primarily in the mind. As a result, Kaplan concluded, HSD stems not from a lack of ability to perform but from a lack of motivation. Even so, the fact that HSD may be "all in your mind" doesn't make living with it any easier. "The most important part of sex," Kaplan says, "is the emotional, subjective part. Without that, mechanical function is not gratifying."

Therapists have found that HSD appears to be about twice as prevalent in women as in men. While no national samples are available, one 1978 study of 100 nonclinical American couples found that 35 percent of the women reported lack of sexual interest, compared with 16 percent of the men. But despite this gap, the causes of HSD for both men and women are the same, and the problem usually begins with the emotions.

CAUSES OF LOW DESIRE

The memories started coming after two years in therapy: gauzy, not quite distinct, yet so haunting that tears slowly squeezed from her eyes right in front of the therapist. Jeanine was 8 years old, lying in bed in her Wisconsin home, watching the door creak open. Suddenly, her father was silently over her, breathing heavily. She never told anybody. How could she? There were crucifixes in every room of the house, and her father led the family in the rosary nightly during Lent. Her mother once lectured her on how little girls who "touched themselves" must confess to the priest. Years later, after she got married, Jeanine never had an orgasm with her husband, Tom. Later, she shut down altogether. She and Tom last had sex 4 1/2 years ago.

The roots of desire disorders often lie between the "Sesame Street" years and junior high. Some adults, like Jeanine, report having been sexually abused as children; for others, the abuse was more emotional. John Money, who has pioneered treatments for deviate sexuality at Johns Hopkins University, says children raised in homes where sex is viewed as evil and harmless activities like "playing doctor" are cruelly punished are likely to grow up with warped sexual identities. "In girls, often you extinguish the lust completely, so that they can never have an orgasm, and marriage becomes a dreary business where you put up with sex to serve the maternal instinct," says Money. "In boys, sex gets redirected into abnormal channels."

Jeanine was 8 years old, lying in bed, watching the door creak open. Suddenly, her father was silently on her, breathing heavily.

Not surprisingly, women like Jeanine, who learn as children not to trust those closest to them, often have trouble melding passion and intimacy. Although victims of low desire may be drawn to hit-and-run encounters with strangers, when they get close to a partner, it's too dangerous to let themselves go sexually. Many men suffer from Freud's famous "Madonna-whore complex," whereby a man endows his partner with the "Madonna-like" qualities of his mother. "You find a sudden cessation of interest in sex right after the wedding, even on the night the engagement was announced," says Harold Lief, professor emeritus of psychiatry at the University of Pennsylvania. "These men can't lust after someone they love, or vice versa."

Then there are the tangled cases, where the core problem is not so much historical as personal: The husband and wife detest each other. Marital difficulties, say Lief and other therapists, underlie as many as half of desire disorder cases. Often the problem stems from suppressed anger. "If a couple comes into my office," says Kaplan, "and they fight about where they're gonna sit, and the

only question is who's gonna complain about the other more, I know why they're not having sex."

Childbirth, stress and depression can also precipitate low sexual desire. But only in a minority of cases—roughly 15 percent—are the causes medical, such as hormone deficiencies or diseases like diabetes. Some antidepressants and antihypertensives can also squelch desire. The good news is that such problems usually have a medical solution, sparing patients lengthy hours on an analyst's couch. But the story is not so simple for most HSD sufferers.

TREATMENT FOR HSD

"I just can't do this," Karen announced, midway through the first "homework" session. The kids were asleep in the next room, and the suburban Minneapolis woman and her husband, Bruce, lay naked on the bed. For 15 minutes, according to their therapist, Bruce was to gently explore her breasts and genitals, while she told him what felt good. But as she guided his hand across her rigid body, it might have been made of marble: She felt nothing. Devastated she thought: "This is a waste of time. Nothing's going to change." Later, she told Bruce, "I don't want to go back to therapy." He replied: "We have no choice. We've got to go back."

Reversing low desire takes time. "I went into therapy thinking I'd get an instant fix," says Karen, who has seen a psychologist for a year but still has not had intercourse with her husband. Many therapists estimate the cure rate for low desire is 50 percent at best, and can take months or years of therapy. Nor do desire disorders lend themselves to any standard formula. "It's not a cookbook," says Kaplan. "We work out a different program for each."

Take Jeanine, the Wisconsin woman who was abused by her father. At first, her therapist assigned a set of widely used "homework" exercises based on the work of Masters and Johnson. The program aims to demystify the sex act by having couples practice mutual, noncoital "pleasuring" at first. Therapists emphasize that the practice is not strictly mechanical—a loving atmosphere is considered crucial. In Jeanine's case, the exercises helped her experience the first orgasm of her life by masturbating. And while sex with her husband hasn't yet improved, she has begun in therapy to deal with long-suppressed memories of childhood sexual abuse.

It would be a lot simpler, of course, if scientists could somehow find that elusive "sex pill"—a notion that might not be as farfetched as it seems. Researchers know desire is triggered in the brain by the male hormone testosterone, with the help of chemicals like dopamine that act as "messengers" between nerve cells in the brain. In recent years, doctors have begun using testosterone to stimulate desire in menopausal women, as well as in men with low hormone levels. And the pharmaceutical giant Eli Lilly & Co. has had promising preliminary results with drugs that affect dopamine; the results of a full-scale study are due out next year. But for now, drugs hold far more promise for treating people who have too much desire, not too little.

WHEN SEX BECOMES COMPULSIVE

Gary's pattern was always the same: first, the unbearable anxiety, never feeling good enough to handle the latest stress at his architect's job. Then, the familiar response—a furtive scanning of newspaper ads, a drive to a strip show, two straight Scotches to catch a buzz, and finally a massage parlor. He would park about a block away, slip off his wedding ring and dart through the door, where $100 bought a massage, sex and momentary relief. Afterward, he'd sit naked on the edge of the bed, his thoughts roiling in disgust: "I must be sick . . . I can't change." But a few days later, the anxiety would begin again and he'd pore over the ads.

Too *much* sex? For many Americans, especially young men, the notion sounds like an oxymoron. In fact, the downside of sexual compulsiveness has been largely overshadowed throughout history by a romanticized view of the rake, from Casanova to basketball legend Wilt Chamberlain, with his claims of 20,000 affairs. Compulsive sexual behavior is perhaps easiest to define by what it is not: It does not include someone who masturbates occasionally, periodically rents an X-rated video or engages in a limited period of promiscuity following the breakup of a relationship. As best therapists can tell, those prey to CSB alternate between profound anxiety and all-embracing self-loathing.

But these are not perverts in raincoats. Gary, the architect described above, wears a well-cut tweed sports jacket and speaks in measured tones. "I was two different people," he says quietly, seated in a psychologist's office in Minneapolis. "Most people who knew my wife and me would say we were a good couple. But when I was home I wasn't really there. I felt like a dirty person, rotten." Indeed, one hallmark of compulsive sexual behavior is secrecy: Gary's wife didn't find out about his clandestine visits to porn shops and prostitutes until she discovered a phone bill listing multiple calls to a "900" sex line.

After $100 bought a massage, sex and momentary relief, he'd sit naked on the bed, his thoughts roiling in disgust: "I must be sick."

So secret are their escapades that CSB victims have never even been counted, and experts' figures—they estimate roughly 5 percent of the adult American population—are the merest guess. But if the figures are flimsy, the portrait is precise. To the sexual compulsive, sex is not about love or intimacy or even pleasure. It is mainly about relief. "These are highly anxious people who respond to

stress by attempting to 'medicate' their pain through sex," says Eli Coleman, director of the University of Minnesota's Program in Human Sexuality, and a pioneer in treating CSB. Just as the obsessive compulsive washes his hands 100 times in a row, the sexual compulsive turns to a vast erotic menu that might include compulsive masturbation, feverish cruising and anonymous sex, frenzied multiple affairs or insatiable demands within a relationship.

A small proportion of CSB victims cross the criminal divide into hard-core deviations: voyeurism, obscene phone calls, pedophilia, exhibitionism and others. But the majority prefer ordinary sex—taken to an extreme. What they share is an overwhelming sense of powerlessness. Like the alcoholic, the sexual compulsive is so intent on diverting his pain that he often doesn't even *see* a choice. "If I saw a prostitute on the street, that was it," says Jeff, 36, a public-relations executive from St. Paul, Minn. "It was impossible to not do it."

THE CAUSES OF CSB

His parents were strict Catholics who said the rosary every night and sent their 11 kids to parochial school. The messages about sex began early. Once, at age 12, Jeff overheard his 19-year-old sister tell his father. "Sex is fun." His father shouted. "Don't you ever say that!" Jeff's mother didn't even like hugging and protested loudly on the rare occasions that her husband kissed her in front of the children. As for the nuns, Sister Frances told Jeff's third-grade class: "One should never be naked for longer than necessary." The little boy worried that he had condemned his soul to hell by dawdling in the bathroom. "The message was: 'Lord I am not worthy,' " says Jeff, who became hooked as an adult on compulsive phone sex, masturbation and prostitutes. "I took all of it to heart."

Though he has never cheated on his wife, Karl has spent much of his adult life obsessing about sex: fantasizing, masturbating, demanding sex.

Certainly most people survive strict religious upbringing without becoming "Fantasy Hotline" junkies. Yet over and over, as CSB victims have recounted their stories, therapists have seen a disturbing pattern: As children, these men and women learned that sex was anything but a loving, natural experience. Their parents were rarely able to nurture them or allow them to express feelings in healthy ways. In some cases, they simply neglected the kids: Jeff remembers going weeks without a bath and wearing his clothes to bed. Other parents expected their kids to toe some unattainable line of perfection. "My dad yelled at me, taunted me," says Kevin, 32, a professional from the Midwest who started cruising for anonymous sex in public bathrooms at 16. "Sometimes, he would shake me or choke me. He called me Sissie, told me I was worthless, a mess."

In recent years, family therapist Patrick Carnes—author of the 1983 book "Out of the Shadows"—has gained thousands of followers for his claim that CSB is not an anxiety-based disorder but an addiction, much like alcoholism. It is a spiritual disease, he believes, as well as an emotional and physical one, and his plan for recovery involves belief in a higher power. But while the addiction model has spawned four popular nationwide AA-style support groups, many researchers are skeptical, maintaining that it's impossible to be "addicted" to sex since there is no addictive substance involved. Both the chemical and spiritual explanations, they maintain, grossly oversimplify a complex phenomenon. "It's also sex-negative and moralistic," argues Howard Ruppel of the Society for the Scientific Study of Sex. "They confuse normal activity like masturbating with addiction."

TREATMENT OF CSB

Karl is a Wisconsin farmer, a beefy guy of 42 with sharp blue eyes and hands as big as pie plates. "If I went into town here and told them I was a sexual compulsive," he says, "they'd probably shoot me dead." Instead, he went once a week for group therapy. Though he has never cheated on his wife, Karl has spent months obsessing about sex: fantasizing, masturbating, demanding sex two or three times a day. When he eventually sought help, his therapist prescribed the antidepressant Prozac, which immediately "seemed to take the edge off" his craving. The deeper work came in therapy, where Karl found it was safe to talk—even laugh—about his "problem"; no one condemned or ridiculed him, the way his father had. The turning point came when a group member agreed to role-play Karl's dad and Karl shouted back, finally venting his rage at the way his father always put him down. When his dad died, Karl sat by the coffin at the funeral home and told him haltingly that he knew he'd done the best he could. And then he wept.

"It is so inspiring watching people recover—because they *do*," says Minneapolis psychologist Anne J. McBean. "I can see someone in my office who's an utter wreck, depressed, anxious, and I know that two years later, the same person is going to be sitting here saying, 'I can't believe it—I've got my life back.' "

For years, psychiatrists treated sex offenders with antiandrogens, compounds that partly block the action of the male sex hormones. But because such drugs have potential side effects and are not government-approved for treating CSB, therapists considered them unsuitable for widespread use. In 1989, when Judith L. Rapoport published groundbreaking studies on obsessive compulsive disorders, researchers who had been attempting to link sexual compulsivity with OCD got a boost. Rapoport and others found that drugs that affect the brain chemical serotonin seem to help many people reduce their obsessive-compulsive behaviors, such as constant hand washing.

Sexologists like Coleman have applied the same principle to CSB. In small studies and clinical trials, they tested the effects of both lithium carbonate, which is also used to treat manic depression, and Prozac, which enhances serotonin activity in the brain. Both drugs, they found had some success interrupting the compulsive sexual cycle.

But drugs are only half of the answer. By the time CSB victims seek help, they need therapy as well. Typically, sexual compulsives are largely disconnected from the childhood loneliness and shame that drive their behavior. After Karl, the farmer, saw his farm sold at auction a few years ago, he began obsessing about sex constantly—even driving his pickup or feeding the hogs. In fact, one of the first aims of therapy—once medication had relieved his compulsive symptoms—was to bring back for Karl memories of his father's intolerance, so that he could begin to release them. Within two years of entering therapy, Karl was virtually cured.

Ultimately, the problem with treating both extremes of sexual desire is that researchers still struggle with their own ignorance. The most comprehensive national survey of American sexual behavior is still the Kinsey report, completed nearly 40 years ago. Such studies are expensive and inevitably controversial. Just in the past year, for instance, the Bush administration, under pressure from conservatives, has derailed two planned surveys of American sexual practices. Yet in the absence of such research, knowledge about HSD and CSB is based largely on privately funded studies requiring heroic extrapolations from small samples. Key research—studying the areas of the brain that control sexual behavior or the effects of drugs on desire—awaits funding. "We have almost no information about how people form their sexual habits," says psychologist Elizabeth Allgeier, co-author of "Sexual Interactions," a widely used college text. "If we don't know how it develops, we can't change it."

Still, for millions of Americans it is reassuring to know that no one is doomed to a life of torment by sex. At the very least, educating and encouraging adults to have more enlightened sexual attitudes might enable children to grow up with healthier feelings toward sex. Psychologist John Money says that sexually repressive attitudes now force "at least 50 percent of the nation [to] get 57 cents to the dollar on their sex lives." When Americans are less imprisoned by public expectations and a private sense of sexual shame, perhaps more couples will earn their full satisfaction.

The American Academy of Clinical Sexologists (202-462-2122) and the American Association of Sex Educators, Counselors and Therapists (send an SASE with $2 to 435 North Michigan Ave., Suite 1717, Chicago, IL 60611) will provide names of qualified local sex therapists.

Lynn Rosellini

Beyond Betrayal: Life After

INFIDELITY

Frank Pittman III, M.D.

Hour after hour, day after day in my office I see men and women who have been screwing around. They lead secret lives, as they hide themselves from their marriages. They go through wrenching divorces, inflicting pain on their children and their children's children. Or they make desperate, tearful, sweaty efforts at holding on to the shreds of a life they've betrayed. They tell me they have gone through all of this for a quick thrill or a furtive moment of romance. Sometimes they tell me they don't remember making the decision that tore apart their life: "It just happened." Sometimes they don't even know they are being unfaithful. (I tell them: "If you don't know whether what you are doing is an infidelity or not, ask your spouse.") From the outside looking in, it is insane. How could anyone risk everything in life on the turn of a screw? Infidelity was not something people did much in my family, so I always found it strange and noteworthy when people did it in my practice. After almost 30 years of cleaning up the mess after other people's affairs, I wrote a book describing everything about infidelity I'd seen in my practice. The book was *Private Lies: Infidelity and the Betrayal of Intimacy* (Norton). I thought it might help. Even if the tragedy of AIDS and the humiliation of prominent politicians hadn't stopped it, surely people could not continue screwing around after reading about the absurd destructiveness of it. As you know, people have *not* stopped having affairs. But many of them feel the need

to write or call or drop by and talk to me about it. When I wrote *Private Lies,* I thought I knew everything there was to know about infidelity. But I know now that there is even more.

ACCIDENTAL INFIDELITY

All affairs are not alike. The thousands of affairs I've seen seem to fall into four broad categories. Most first affairs are cases of *accidental infidelity,* unintended and uncharacteristic acts of carelessness that really did "just happen." Someone will get drunk, will get caught up in the moment, will just be having a bad day. It can happen to anyone, though some people are more accident prone than others, and some situations are accident zones.

Many a young man has started his career as a philanderer quite accidentally when he is traveling out of town on a new job with a philandering boss who chooses one of a pair of women and expects the young fellow to entertain the other. The most startling dynamic behind accidental infidelity is misplaced politeness, the feeling that it would be rude to turn down a needy friend's sexual advances. In the debonair gallantry of the moment, the brazen discourtesy to the marriage partner is overlooked altogether.

Both men and women can slip up and have accidental affairs, though the most accident-prone are those who drink, those who travel, those who don't get asked much, those who don't feel very tightly married, those whose running buddies

screw around, and those who are afraid to run from a challenge. Most are men.

After an accidental infidelity, there is clearly the sense that one's life and marriage have changed. The choices are:

1. To decide that infidelity was a stupid thing to do, to confess it or not to do so, but to resolve to take better precautions in the future;

2. To decide you wouldn't have done such a thing unless your husband or wife had let you down, put the blame on your mate, and go home and pick your marriage to death;

3. To notice that lightning did not strike you dead, decide this would be a safe and inexpensive hobby to take up, and do it some more;

4. To decide that you would not have done such a thing if you were married to the right person, determine that this was "meant to be," and declare yourself in love with the stranger in the bed.

ROMANTIC INFIDELITY

Surely the craziest and most destructive form of infidelity is the temporary insanity of *falling in love.* You do this, not when you meet somebody wonderful (wonderful people don't screw around with married people) but when you are going through a crisis in your own life, can't continuing living your life, and aren't quite ready for suicide yet. An affair with someone grossly inappropriate—someone decades younger or older, someone dependent or dominating, someone with problems even bigger

Reprinted with permission from *Psychology Today,* May/June 1993, pp. 32-38, 78, 80, 82. © 1993 by Sussex Publishers, Inc.

than your own—is so crazily stimulating that it's like a drug that can lift you out of your depression and enable you to feel things again. Of course, between moments of ecstasy, you are more depressed, increasingly alone and alienated in your life, and increasingly hooked on the affair partner. Ideal romance partners are damsels or "dumsels" in distress, people without a life but with a lot of problems, people with bad reality testing and little concern with understanding reality better.

Romantic affairs lead to a great many divorces, suicides, homicides, heart attacks, and strokes, but not to very many successful remarriages. No matter how many sacrifices you make to keep the love alive, no matter how many sacrifices your family and children make for this crazy relationship, it will gradually burn itself out when there is nothing more to sacrifice to it. Then you must face not only the wreckage of several lives, but the original depression from which the affair was an insane flight into escape.

People are most likely to get into these romantic affairs at the turning points of life: when their parents die or their children grow up; when they suffer health crises or are under pressure to give up an addiction; when they achieve an unexpected level of job success or job failure; or when their first child is born—any situation in which they must face a lot of reality and grow up. The better the marriage, the saner and more sensible the spouse, the more alienated the romantic is likely to feel. Romantic affairs happen in good marriages even more often than in bad ones.

MYTHS OF INFIDELITY

The people who are running from bed to bed creating disasters for themselves and everyone else don't seem to know what they are doing. They just don't get it. But why should they? There is a mythology about infidelity that shows up in the popular press and even in the mental health literature that is guaranteed to mislead people and make dangerous situations even worse. Some of these myths are:

1. Everybody is unfaithful; it is normal, expectable behavior. Mozart, in his comic opera *Cosi Fan Tutti,* insisted that women all do it, but a far more common belief is that men all do it: "Higgamous, hoggamous, woman's monogamous; hoggamous, higgamous, man is polygamous." In Nora Ephron's movie, *Heartburn,* Meryl Streep's husband has left her for another woman. She turns to her father for solace, but he dismisses her complaint as the way of all male flesh: "If you want monogamy, marry a swan."

We don't know how many people are unfaithful; if people will lie to their own husband or wife, they surely aren't going to be honest with poll takers. We can guess that one-half of married men and one-third of married women have dropped their drawers away from home at least once. That's a lot of infidelity.

Still, most people are faithful most of the time. Without the expectation of fidelity, intimacy becomes awkward and marriage adversarial. People who expect their partner to betray them are likely to beat them to the draw, and to make both of them miserable in the meantime.

Most species of birds and animals in which the male serves some useful function other than sperm donation are inherently monogamous. Humans, like other nest builders, are monogamous by nature, but imperfectly so. We can be trained out of it, though even in polygamous and promiscuous cultures people show their true colors when they fall blindly and crazily in love. And we have an escape clause: nature mercifully permits us to survive our mates and mate again. But if we slip up and take a new mate while the old mate is still alive, it is likely to destroy the pair bonding with our previous mate and create great instinctual disorientation—which is part of the tragedy of infidelity.

2. Affairs are good for you; an affair may even revive a dull marriage. Back at the height of the sexual revolution, the *Playboy* philosophy and its *Cosmopolitan* counterpart urged infidelity as a way to keep men manly, women womanly, and marriage vital. Lately, in such books as Annette Lawson's *Adultery* and Dalma Heyn's *The Erotic Silence of the American Wife,* women have been encouraged to act out their sexual fantasies as a blow for equal rights.

It is true that if an affair is blatant enough and if all hell breaks loose, the crisis of infidelity can shake up the most petrified marriage. Of course, any crisis can serve the same detonation function, and burning the house down might be a safer, cheaper, and more readily forgivable attention-getter.

However utopian the theories, the reality is that infidelity, whether it is furtive or blatant, will blow hell out of a marriage. In 30 odd years of practice, I have encountered only a handful of established first marriages that ended in divorce without someone being unfaithful, often with the infidelity kept secret throughout the divorce process and even for years afterwards. Infidelity is the *sine qua non* of divorce.

3. People have affairs because they aren't in love with their marriage partner. People tell me this, and they even remember it this way. But on closer examination it routinely turns out that the marriage was fine before the affair happened, and the decision that they were not in love with their marriage partner was an effort to explain and justify the affair.

Being in love does not protect people from lust. Screwing around on your loved one is not a very loving thing to do, and it may be downright hostile. Every marriage is a thick stew of emotions ranging from lust to disgust, desperate love to homicidal rage. It would be idiotic to reduce such a wonderfully rich emotional diet to a question ("love me?" or "love me not?") so simplistic that it is best asked of the petals of daisies. Nonetheless, people do ask themselves such questions, and they answer them.

Falling out of love is no reason to betray your mate. If people are experiencing a deficiency in their ability to love their partner, it is not clear how something so hateful as betraying him or her would restore it.

4. People have affairs because they are oversexed. Affairs are about secrets. The infidelity is not necessarily in the sex, but in the dishonesty.

Swingers have sex openly, without dishonesty and therefore without betrayal (though with a lot of scary bugs.) More cautious infidels might have chaste but furtive lunches and secret telephone calls with ex-spouses or former affair partners—nothing to sate the sexual tension, but just enough to prevent a marital reconciliation or intimacy in the marriage.

Affairs generally involve sex, at least enough to create a secret that seals the conspiratorial alliance of the affair, and makes the relationship tense, dangerous, and thus exciting. Most affairs consist of a little bad sex and hours on the telephone. I once saw a case in which the couple had attempted sex once 30 years before and had limited the intimacy in their respective marriages while they maintained their sad, secret love with quiet lunches, pondering the crucial question of whether or not he had gotten it all the way in on that immortal autumn evening in 1958.

Every marriage is a thick stew of emotions ranging from lust to disgust.

Both genders seem equally capable of falling into the temporary insanity of romantic affairs, though women are more likely to reframe anything they do as having been done for love. Women in love are far more aware of what they are doing and what the dangers might be. Men in love can be extraordinarily incautious and willing to give up everything. Men in love lose their heads—at least for a while.

MARITAL ARRANGEMENTS

All marriages are imperfect, and probably a disappointment in one way or another, which is a piece of reality, not a license to mess around with the neighbors. There are some marriages that fail to provide a modicum of warmth, sex, sanity, companionship, money. There are awful marriages people can't get all the way into and can't get all the way out of, divorces people won't call off and can't go through, marriages that won't die and won't recover. Often people in such marriages make a *marital arrangement* by calling in marital aides to keep them company while they avoid living their life. Such practical affairs help them keep the marriage steady but

---

In general, monogamous couples have a lot more sex than the people who are screwing around.

5. Affairs are ultimately the fault of the cuckold. Patriarchal custom assumes that when a man screws around it must be because of his wife's aesthetic, sexual, or emotional deficiencies. She failed him in some way. And feminist theory has assured us that if a wife screws around it must be because men are such assholes. Many people believe that screwing around is a normal response to an imperfect marriage and is, by definition, the marriage partner's fault. Friends and relatives, bartenders, therapists, and hairdressers, often reveal their own gender prejudices and distrust of marriage, monogamy, intimacy, and honesty, when they encourage the infidel to put the blame on the cuckold rather than on him- or herself.

One trick for avoiding personal blame and responsibility is to blame the marriage itself (too early, too late, too soon after some event) or some unchangeable characteristic of the partner (too old, too tall, too ethnic, too smart, too experienced, too inexperienced.) This is both a cop-out and a dead end.

One marriage partner can make the other miserable, but can't make the other unfaithful. (The cuckold is usually not even there when the affair is taking place). Civilization and marriage require that people behave appropriately however they feel, and that they take full responsibility for their actions. "My wife drove me to it with her nagging"; "I can't help what I do because of what my father did to me"; "She came on to me and her skirt was very short"; "I must be a sex addict"; et cetera. Baloney! If people really can't control their sexual behavior, they should not be permitted to run around loose.

There is no point in holding the cuckold responsible for the infidel's sexual behavior unless the cuckold has total control over the sexual equipment that has run off the road. Only the driver is responsible.

6. It is best to pretend not to know. There are people who avoid unpleasantness and would rather watch the house burn down than bother anyone by yelling "Fire!" Silence fuels the affair, which can thrive only in secrecy. Adulterous marriages begin their repair only when the secret is out in the open, and the infidel does not need to hide any longer. Of course, it also helps to end the affair.

A corollary is the belief that infidels must deny their affairs interminably and do all that is possible to drive cuckolds to such disorientation that they will doubt their own sanity rather than doubt their partner's fidelity. In actuality, the continued lying and denial is usually the most unforgivable aspect of the infidelity.

One man was in the habit of jogging each evening, but his wife noticed that his running clothes had stopped stinking. Suspicious, she followed him—to his secretary's apartment. She burst in and confronted her husband who was standing naked in the secretary's closet. She demanded: "What are you doing here?" He responded: "You do not see me here. You have gone crazy and are imagining this." She almost believed him, and remains to this day angrier about *that* than about the affair itself. Once an affair is known or even suspected, there is no safety in denial, but there is hope in admission.

I recently treated a woman whose physician husband divorced her 20 years ago after a few years of marriage, telling her that she had an odor that was making him sick, and he had developed an allergy to her. She felt so bad about herself she never remarried.

I suspected there was more to the story, and sent her back to ask him whether he had been unfaithful to her. He confessed that he had been, but had tried to shield her from hurt by convincing her that he had been faithful and true but that she was repulsive. She feels much worse about him now, but much better about herself. She now feels free to date.

7. After an affair, divorce is inevitable. Essentially all first-time divorces occur in the wake of an affair. With therapy though, most adulterous marriages can be saved, and may even be stronger and more intimate than they were before the crisis. I have rarely seen a cuckold go all the way through with a divorce after a first affair that is now over. Of course, each subsequent affair lowers the odds drastically.

It doesn't happen the way it does in the movies. The indignant cuckold does scream and yell and carry on and threaten all manner of awful things—which should not be surprising since his or her life has just been torn asunder. But he or she quickly calms down and begins the effort to salvage the marriage, to pull the errant infidel from the arms of the dreaded affairee.

When a divorce occurs, it is because the infidel can not escape the affair in time or cannot face going back into a marriage in which he or she is now known and understood and can no longer pose as the chaste virgin or white knight spotless and beyond criticism. A recent *New Yorker* cartoon showed a forlorn man at a bar complaining: "My wife understands me."

Appropriate guilt is always helpful, though it must come from inside rather than from a raging, nasty spouse; anger is a lousy seduction technique for anyone except terminal weirdos. Guilt is good for you. Shame, however, makes people run away and hide.

The prognosis after an affair is not grim, and those who have strayed have not lost all their value. The sadder but wiser infidel may be both more careful and more grateful in the future.

distant. They thus encapsulate the marital deficiency, so the infidel can neither establish a life without the problems nor solve them. Affairs can wreck a good marriage, but can help stabilize a bad one.

People who get into marital arrangements are not necessarily the innocent victims of defective relationships. Some set out to keep their marriages defective and distant. I have seen men who have kept the same mistress through several marriages, arranging their marriages to serve some practical purpose while keeping their romance safely encapsulated elsewhere. The men considered it a victory over marriage; the exploited wives were outraged.

I encountered one woman who had long been involved with a married man. She got tired of waiting for him to get a divorce and married someone else. She didn't tell her husband about her affair, and she didn't tell her affairee about her marriage. She somehow thought they would never find out about one another. After a few exhausting and confusing weeks, the men met and confronted her. She cheerfully told them she loved them both and the arrangement seemed the sensible way to have her cake and eat it too. She couldn't understand why both the men felt cheated and deprived by her efforts to sacrifice their lives to satisfy her skittishness about total commitment.

Some of these arrangements can get quite complicated. One woman supported her house-husband and their kids by living as the mistress of an older married man, who spent his afternoons and weekend days with her and his evenings at home with his own children and his sexually boring wife. People averse to conflict might prefer such arrangements to therapy, or any other effort to actually solve the problems of the marriage.

Unhappily married people of either gender can establish marital arrangements to help them through the night. But men are more likely to focus on the practicality of the arrangement and diminish awareness of any threat to the stability of the marriage, while women are more likely to romanticize the arrangement and convince themselves it is leading toward an eventual union with the romantic partner. Networks of couples may spend their lives halfway through someone's divorce, usually with a guilt-ridden man reluctant to completely leave a marriage he has betrayed and even deserted, and a woman, no matter how hard she protests to the contrary, eternally hopeful for a wedding in the future.

Philandering

Philandering is a predominantly male activity. Philanderers take up infidelity as a hobby. Philanderers are likely to have a rigid and concrete concept of gender; they worship masculinity, and while they may be greatly attracted to women, they are mostly interested in having the woman affirm their masculinity. They don't really like women, and they certainly don't want an equal, intimate relationship with a member of the gender they insist is inferior, but far too powerful. They see women as dangerous, since women have the ability to assess a man's worth, to measure him and find him wanting, to determine whether he is man enough.

These men may or may not like sex, but they use it compulsively to affirm their masculinity and overcome both their homophobia and their fear of women. They can be cruel, abusive, and even violent to women who try to get control of them and stop the philandering they consider crucial to their masculinity. Their life is centered around displays of masculinity, however they define it, trying to impress women with their physical strength, competitive victories, seductive skills, mastery of all situations, power, wealth, and, if necessary, violence. Some of them are quite charming and have no trouble finding women eager to be abused by them.

Gay men can philander too, and the dynamics are the same for gay philanderers as for straight ones: the obvious avoidance of female sexual control, but also the preoccupation with masculinity and the use of rampant sexuality for both reassurance and the measurement of manhood. When men have paid such an enormous social and interpersonal price for their preferred sexuality, they are likely to wrap an enormous amount of their identity around their sexuality and express that sexuality extensively.

Philanderers may be the sons of philanderers, or they may have learned their ideas about marriage and gender from their ethnic group or inadvertently from their religion. Somewhere they have gotten the idea that their masculinity is their most valuable attribute and it requires them to protect themselves from coming under female control. These guys may consider themselves quite principled and honorable, and they may follow the rules to the letter in their dealings with other men. But in their world women have no rights.

To men they may seem normal, but women experience them as narcissistic or even sociopathic. They think they are normal, that they are doing what every other real man would do if he weren't such a wimp. The notions of marital fidelity, of gender equality, of honesty and intimacy between husbands and wives seem quite foreign from what they learned growing up. The gender equality of monogamy may not feel compatible to men steeped in patriarchal beliefs in men being gods and women being ribs. Monogamous sexuality is difficult for men who worship Madonnas for their sexlessness and berate Eves for their seductiveness.

Philanderers' sexuality is fueled by anger and fear, and while they may be considered "sex addicts" they are really "gender compulsives," desperately doing whatever they think will make them look and feel most masculine. They put notches on their belts in hopes it will make their penises grow bigger. If they can get a woman to die for them, like opera composer Giacomo Puccini did in real life and in most of his operas, they feel like a real man.

Female Philanderers

There are female philanderers too, and they too are usually the daughters or ex-wives of philanderers. They are angry at men, because they believe all men screw around as their father or ex-husband did. A female philanderer is not likely to stay married for very long, since that would require her to make peace with a man, and as a woman to carry more than her share of the burden of marriage. Marriage grounds people in reality rather than transporting them into fantasy, so marriage is too loving, too demanding, too realistic, and not romantic enough for them.

I hear stories of female philanderers, such as Maria Riva's description of her mother, Marlene Dietrich. They appear to have insatiable sexual appetites but, on closer examination, they don't like sex much, they do like power over men, and underneath the philandering anger, they are plaintively seeking love.

Straying wives are rarely philanderers, but single women who mess around with married men are quite likely to be. Female philanderers prefer to raid other people's marriages, breaking up relationships, doing as much damage as possible, and then dancing off reaffirmed. Like male philanderers, female philanderers put their victims through all of this just to give themselves a sense of gender power.

Spider Woman

There are women who, by nature romantics, don't quite want to escape their own life and die for love. Instead they'd rather have some guy wreck his life for them. These women have been so recently betrayed by unfaithful men that the wound is still raw and they are out for revenge. A woman who angrily pursues married men is a "spider woman"—she requires human sacrifice to restore her sense of power.

When she is sucking the blood from other people's marriages, she feels some relief from the pain of having her own marriage betrayed. She simply requires that a man love her enough to sacrifice his life for her. She may be particularly attracted to happy marriages, clearly envious of the woman whose husband is faithful and loving to her. Sometimes it isn't clear whether she wants to replace the happy wife or just make her miserable.

The women who are least squeamish and most likely to wreak havoc on other people's marriages are victims of some sort of abuse, so angry that they don't feel bound by the usual rules or obligations, so desperate that they cling to any source of security, and so miserable that they don't bother to think a bit of the end of it.

Josephine Hart's novel *Damage,* and the recent Louis Malle film version of it, describe such a woman. She seduces her fiancee's depressed father, and after the fiancee discovers the affair and kills himself, she waltzes off from the wreckage of all the lives. She explains that her father disappeared long ago, her mother had been married four or five times, and her brother committed suicide when she left his bed and began to date other boys. She described herself as damaged, and says, "Damaged people are dangerous. They know they can survive."

Bette was a spider woman. She came to see me only once, with her married affair partner Alvin, a man I had been seeing with his wife Agnes. But I kept up with her through the many people whose lives she touched. Bette's father had run off and left her and her mother when she was just a child, and her stepfather had exposed himself to her. Most recently Bette's man-

All marriages are imperfect, a disappointment in one way or another.

———

ic husband Burt had run off with a stripper, Claudia, and had briefly married her before he crashed and went into a psychiatric hospital.

While Burt was with Claudia, the enraged Bette promptly latched on to Alvin, a laid-back philanderer who had been married to Agnes for decades and had been screwing around casually most of that time. Bette was determined that Alvin was going to divorce Agnes and marry her, desert his children, and raise her now-fatherless kids. The normally cheerful Alvin, who had done a good job for a lifetime of pleasing every woman he met and avoiding getting trapped by any of them, couldn't seem to escape Bette, but he certainly had no desire to leave Agnes. He grew increasingly depressed and suicidal. He felt better after he told the long-suffering Agnes, but he still couldn't move in any direction. Over the next couple of years, Bette and Alvin took turns threatening suicide, while Agnes tended her garden, raised her children, ran her business, and waited for the increasingly disoriented and pathetic Alvin to come to his senses.

Agnes finally became sufficiently alarmed about her husband's deterioration that she decided the only way she could save his life was to divorce him. She did, and Alvin promptly dumped Bette. He could not forgive her for what she had made him do to dear, sweet Agnes. He lost no time in taking up with Darlene, with whom he had been flirting for some time, but who wouldn't go out with a married man. Agnes felt relief, and the comfort of a good settlement, but Bette was once again abandoned and desperate.

She called Alvin hourly, alternately threatening suicide, reciting erotic poetry, and offering to fix him dinner. She phoned bomb threats to Darlene's office. Bette called me to tell me what a sociopathic jerk

Alvin was to betray her with another woman after all she had done in helping him through his divorce. She wrote sisterly notes to Agnes, offering the comfort of friendship to help one another through the awful experience of being betrayed by this terrible man. At no point did Bette consider that she had done anything wrong. She was now, as she had been all her life, a victim of men, who not only use and abuse women, but won't lay down their lives to rescue them on cue.

EMOTIONALLY RETARDED MEN IN LOVE

About the only people more dangerous than philandering men going through life with an open fly and romantic damsels going through life in perennial distress, are emotionally retarded men in love. When such men go through a difficult transition in life, they hunker down and ignore all emotions. Their brain chemistry gets depressed, but they don't know how to feel it as depression. Their loved ones try to keep from bothering them, try to keep things calm and serene—and isolate them further.

An emotionally retarded man may go for a time without feeling pleasure, pain, or anything else, until a strange woman jerks him back into awareness of something intense enough for him to feel it— perhaps sexual fireworks, or the boyish heroics of rescuing her, or perhaps just fascination with her constantly changing moods and never-ending emotional crises.

With her, he can pull out of his depression briefly, but he sinks back even deeper into it when he is not with her. He is getting addicted to her, but he doesn't know that. He only feels the absence of joy and love and life with his serenely cautious wife

Once an affair is known or even suspected, there's no safety in denial but there is hope in admission.

———

and kids, and the awareness of life with this new woman. It doesn't work for him to leave home to be with her, as she too would grow stale and irritating if she were around full time.

What he needs is not a crazier woman to sacrifice his life for, but treatment for his depression. However, since the best home remedies for depression are sex, exercise, joy, and triumph, the dangerous damsel may be providing one or more of them in a big enough dose to make him feel a lot better. He may feel pretty good until he gets the bill, and sees how much of his life and the lives of his loved ones this treatment is costing. Marriages that start this way, stepping over the bodies of loved ones as the giddy couple walks down the aisle, are not likely to last long.

Howard had been faithful to Harriett for 16 years. He had been happy with her. She made him feel loved, which no one else had ever tried to do. Howard devoted himself to doing the right thing. He always did what he was supposed to do and he never complained. In fact he said very little at all.

Howard worked at Harriett's father's store, a stylish and expensive men's clothiers. He had worked there in high school and returned after college. He'd never had another job. He had felt like a son to his father-in-law. But when the old man retired, he bypassed the stalwart, loyal Howard and made his own wastrel son manager.

Howard also took care of his own elderly parents who lived next door. His father died, and left a nice little estate to his mother, who then gave much of it to his younger brother, who had gotten into trouble with gambling and extravagance.

Howard felt betrayed, and sank into a depression. He talked of quitting his job and moving away. Harriett pointed out the impracticality of that for the kids. She reminded him of all the good qualities of his mother and her father.

Howard didn't bring it up again. Instead, he began to talk to Maxine, one of the tailors at the store, a tired middle-aged woman who shared Howard's disillusionment with the world. One day, Maxine called frightened because she smelled gas in her trailer and her third ex-husband had threatened to hurt her. She needed for Howard to come out and see if he could smell anything dangerous. He did, and somehow ended up in bed with Maxine. He felt in love. He knew it was crazy but he couldn't get along without her. He bailed her out of the frequent disasters in her life. They began to plot their getaway, which consumed his attention for months.

Harriett noticed the change in Howard, but thought he was just mourning his father's death. They continued to get along well, sex was as good as ever, and they enjoyed the same things they had always enjoyed. It was a shock to her when he told her he was moving out, that he didn't love her anymore, and that it had nothing whatever to do with Maxine, who would be leaving with him.

Harriett went into a rage and hit him. The children went berserk. The younger daughter cried inconsolably, the older one

Most affairs consist of a little bad sex and a lot of telephoning.

became bulimic, the son quit school and refused to leave his room. I saw the family a few times, but Howard would not turn back. He left with Maxine, and would not return my phone calls. The kids were carrying on so on the telephone, Howard stopped calling them for a few months, not wanting to upset them. Meanwhile he and Maxine, who had left her kids behind as well, borrowed some money from his mother and moved to the coast where they bought into a marina—the only thing they had in common was the pleasure of fishing.

A year later, Harriett and the kids were still in therapy but they were getting along pretty well without him. Harriett was running the clothing store. Howard decided he missed his children and invited them to go fishing with him and Maxine. It surprised him when they still refused to speak to him. He called me and complained to me that his depression was a great deal worse. The marina was doing badly. He and Maxine weren't getting along very well. He missed his children and cried a lot, and she told him his preoccupation with his children was a betrayal of her. He blamed Harriett for fussing at him when she found out about Maxine. He believed she turned the children against him. He couldn't understand why anyone would be mad with him; he couldn't help who he loves and who he doesn't love.

 EN AND WOMEN WHO CHEAT

Howard's failure to understand the complex emotional consequences of his affair is typically male, just as Bette's insistence that her affair partner live up to her romantic fantasies is typically female. Any gender-based generalization is both irritating and inaccurate, but some behaviors are typical. Men tend to attach too little significance to affairs, ignoring their horrifying power to disorient and disrupt lives, while women tend to attach too much significance, assuming that the emotions are so powerful they must be "real" and therefore concrete, permanent, and stable enough to risk a life for.

A man, especially a philandering man, may feel comfortable having sex with a woman if it is clear that he is not in love with her. Even when a man understands that a rule has been broken and he expects consequences of some sort, he routinely underestimates the extent and range and duration of the reactions to his betrayal. Men may agree that the sex is wrong, but may believe that the lying is a noble effort to protect the family. A man may reason that outside sex is wrong because there is a rule against it, without understanding that his lying establishes an adversarial relationship with his mate and is the greater offense. Men are often surprised at the intensity of their betrayed mate's anger, and then even more surprised when she is willing to take him back. Men rarely appreciate the devastating long-range impact of their infidelities, or even their divorces, on their children.

Routinely, a man will tell me that he assured himself that he loved his wife before he hopped into a strange bed, that the women there with him means nothing, that it is just a meaningless roll in the hay. A woman is more likely to tell me that at the sound of the zipper she quickly ascertained that she was not as much in love with her husband as she should have been, and the man there in bed with her was the true love of her life.

A woman seems likely to be less concerned with the letter of the law than with the emotional coherence of her life. It may be okay to screw a man if she "loves" him, whatever the status of his or her marriage, and it is certainly appropriate to lie to a man who believes he has a claim on you, but whom you don't love.

Women may be more concerned with the impact of their affairs on their children than they are with the effect on their mate, whom they have already devalued and discounted in anticipation of the affair. Of course, a woman is likely to feel the children would be in support of her affair, and thus may involve them in relaying her messages, keeping her secrets, and telling her lies. This can be mind-blowingly seductive and confusing to the kids. Sharing the secret of one parent's affair, and hiding it from the other parent, has essentially the same emotional impact as incest.

Some conventional wisdom about gender differences in infidelity is true.

More men than women do have affairs, but it seemed to me that before the AIDS epidemic, the rate for men was dropping (philandering has not been considered cute since the Kennedy's went out of power) and the rate for women was rising (women who assumed that all men were screwing around saw their own screwing around as a blow for equal rights.) In recent years, promiscuity seems suicidal so only the suicidal—that is, the romantics—are on the streets after dark.

Men are able to approach sex more casually than women, a factor not only of the patriarchal double standard but also of the difference between having genitals on the outside and having them on the inside. Getting laid for all the wrong reasons is a lot less dangerous than falling in love with all the wrong people.

Men who get caught screwing around are more likely to be honest about the sex than women. Men will confess the full sexual details, even if they are vague about the emotions. Women on the other hand will confess to total consuming love and suicidal desire to die with some man, while insisting no sex ever took place. I would believe that if I'd ever seen a man describe the affair as so consumingly intense from the waist up and so chaste from the waist down. I assume these women are lying to me about what they know they did or did not do, while I assume that the men really are honest about the genital ups and downs—and honestly confused about the emotional ones.

Women are more likely to discuss their love affairs with their women friends. Philandering men may turn their sex lives into a spectator sport but romantic men tend to keep their love life private from their men friends, and often just withdraw from their friends during the romance.

On the other hand, women are not more romantic than men. Men in love are every bit as foolish and a lot more naive than women in love. They go crazier and risk more. They are far more likely to sacrifice or abandon their children to prove their love to some recent affairee. They are more likely to isolate themselves from everyone except their affair partner, and turn their thinking and feeling over to her, applying her romantic ways of thinking (or not thinking) to the dilemmas of his increasingly chaotic life.

Men are just as forgiving as women of their mates' affairs. They might claim ahead of time that they would never tolerate it, but when push comes to shove, cuckolded men are every bit as likely as cuckolded women to fight like tigers to hold on to a marriage that has been betrayed. Cuckolded men may react violently at first, though cuckolded women do so as well, and I've seen more cases of women who shot and wounded or killed errant husbands. (The shootings occur not when the affair is stopped and confessed, but when it is continued and denied.)

Betrayed men, like betrayed women, hunker down and do whatever they have to do to hold their marriage together. A few men and women go into a rage and refuse to turn back, and then spend a lifetime nursing the narcissistic injury, but that unusual occurrence is no more common for men than for women. Marriage can survive either a husband's infidelity or a wife's, if it is stopped, brought into the open, and dealt with.

I have cleaned up from more affairs than a squad of motel chambermaids. Infidelity is a very messy hobby. It is not an effective way to find a new mate or a new life.

It is not a safe treatment for depression, boredom, imperfect marriage, or inadequate gender splendor. And it certainly does not impress the rest of us. It does not work for women any better than it does for men. It does excite the senses and the imaginations of those who merely hear the tales of lives and deaths for love, who melt at the sound of liebestods or country songs of love gone wrong.

I think I've gotten more from infidelity as an observer than all the participants I've seen. Infidelity is a spectator sport like shark feeding or bull fighting—that is, great for those innocent bystanders who are careful not to get their feet, or whatever, wet. For the greatest enjoyment of infidelity, I recommend you observe from a safe physical and emotional distance and avoid any suicidal impulse to become a participant.

The Myth of the Miserable Working Woman

She's Tired, She's Stressed Out, She's Unhealthy, She Can't Go Full Speed at Work or Home. Right? Wrong.

Rosalind C. Barnett and Caryl Rivers

Rosalind C. Barnett is a psychologist and a senior research associate at the Wellesley College Center for Research on Women. Caryl Rivers is a professor of journalism at Boston University and the author of More Joy Than Rage: Crossing Generations With the New Feminism.

"You Can't Do Everything," announced a 1989 USA Today *headline on a story suggesting that a slower career track for women might be a good idea. "Mommy Career Track Sets Off a Furor," declaimed the* New York Times *on March 8, 1989, reporting that women cost companies more than men. "Pressed for Success, Women Careerists Are Cheating Themselves," sighed a 1989 headline in the* Washington Post, *going on to cite a book about the "unhappy personal lives" of women graduates of the Harvard Business School. "Women Discovering They're at Risk for Heart Attacks," Gannett News Service reported with alarm in 1991. "Can Your Career Hurt Your Kids? Yes, Say Many Experts," blared a* Fortune *cover just last May, adding in a chirpy yet soothing fashion, "But smart parents—and flexible companies—won't let it happen."*

If you believe what you read, working women are in big trouble—stressed out, depressed, sick, risking an early death from heart attacks, and so overcome with problems at home that they make inefficient employees at work.

In fact, just the opposite is true. As a research psychologist whose career has focused on women and a journalist-critic who has studied the behavior of the media, we have extensively surveyed the latest data and research and concluded that the public is being engulfed by a tidal wave of disinformation that has serious consequences for the life and health of every American woman. Since large numbers of women began moving into the work force in the 1970s, scores of studies on their emotional and physical health have painted a very clear picture: Paid employment provides substantial health *benefits* for women. These benefits cut across income and class lines; even women who are working because they have to—not because they want to—share in them.

There is a curious gap, however, between what these studies say and what is generally reported on television, radio, and in newspapers and magazines. The more the research shows work is good for women, the bleaker the media reports seem to become. Whether this bizarre state of affairs is the result of a backlash against women, as *Wall Street Journal* reporter Susan Faludi contends in her new book, *Backlash: The Undeclared War Against American Women,* or of well-meaning ignorance, the effect is the same: Both the shape of national policy and the lives of women are at risk.

Too often, legislation is written and policies are drafted not on the basis of the facts but on the basis of what those in power believe to be the facts. Even the much discussed *Workforce 2000* report, issued by the Department of Labor under the Reagan administration—hardly a hotbed of feminism—admitted that "most current policies were designed for a society in which men worked and women stayed home." If policies are skewed toward solutions that are aimed at reducing women's commitment to work, they will do more than harm women—they will damage companies, managers and the productivity of the American economy.

THE CORONARY THAT WASN'T

One reason the "bad news" about working women jumps to page one is that we're all too willing to believe it. Many adults today grew up at a time when soldiers were returning home from World War II and a way had to be found to get the women who replaced them in industry back into the kitchen. The result was a barrage of propaganda that turned at-home moms into saints and backyard barbecues and station wagons into cultural icons. Many of us still have that outdated postwar map inside our heads, and it leaves us more willing to believe the horror stories than the good news that paid employment is an emotional and medical plus.

In the 19th century it was accepted medical dogma that women should not be educated because the brain and the ovaries could not develop at the same time. Today it's PMS, the wrong math genes or rampaging hormones. Hardly anyone points out the dire predictions that didn't come true.

You may remember the prediction that career women would start having more heart attacks, just like men. But the Framingham Heart Study—a federally funded cardiac project that has been studying 10,000 men and women since 1948—reveals that working women are not having more heart attacks. They're not dying any earlier, either. Not only are women not losing their health advantages; the lifespan gap is actually widening. Only one group of working women suffers more heart attacks than other women: those in low-paying clerical jobs with many demands on them and little control over their work pace, who also have several children and little or no support at home.

As for the recent publicity about women having more problems with heart disease, much of it skims over the important underlying reasons for the increase: namely, that by the time they have a heart attack, women tend to be a good deal older (an average of 67, six years older than the average age for men), and thus frailer, than males who have one. Also, statistics from the National Institutes of Health show that coronary symptoms are treated less aggressively in women—fewer coronary bypasses, for example. In addition, most heart research is done on men, so doctors do not know as much about the causes—and treatment—of heart disease in women. None of these factors have anything to do with work.

But doesn't working put women at greater risk for stress-related illnesses? No. Paid work is actually associated with *reduced* anxiety and depression. In the early 1980s we reported in our book, *Lifeprints* (based on a National Science Foundation–funded study of 300 women), that working women were significantly higher in psychological well-being than those not employed. Working gave them a sense of mastery and control that homemaking didn't provide. More recent studies echo our findings. For example:

• A 1989 report by psychologist Ingrid Waldron and sociologist Jerry Jacobs of Temple University on nationwide surveys of 2,392 white and 892 black women,

conducted from 1977 to 1982, found that women who held both work and family roles reported better physical and mental health than homemakers.
• According to sociologists Elaine Wethington of Cornell University and Ronald Kessler of the University of Michigan, data from three years (1985 to 1988) of a continuing federally funded study of 745 married women in Detroit "clearly suggests that employment benefits women emotionally." Women who increase their participation in the labor force report lower levels of psychological distress; those who lessen their commitment to work suffer from higher distress.
• A University of California at Berkeley study published in 1990 followed 140 women for 22 years. At age 43, those who were homemakers had more chronic conditions than the working women and seemed more disillusioned and frustrated. The working mothers were in good health and seemed to be juggling their roles with success.

In sum, paid work offers women heightened self-esteem and enhanced mental and physical health. It's unemployment that's a major risk factor for depression in women.

DOING IT ALL—AND DOING FINE

This isn't true only for affluent women in good jobs; working-class women share the benefits of work, according to psychologists Sandra Scarr and Deborah Phillips of the University of Virginia and Kathleen McCartney of the University of New Hampshire. In reviewing 80 studies on this subject, they reported that working-class women with children say they would not leave work even if they didn't need the money. Work offers not only income but adult companionship, social contact and a connection with the wider world that they cannot get at home.

Doing it all may be tough, but it doesn't wipe out the health benefits of working.

Looking at survey data from around the world, Scarr and Phillips wrote that the lives of mothers who work are not more stressful than the lives of those who are at home. So what about the second shift we've heard so much about? It certainly exists: In industrialized countries, researchers found, fathers work an average of 50 hours a week on the job and doing household chores; mothers work an average of 80 hours. Wethington and Kessler found that in daily "stress diaries" kept by husbands and wives, the women report more stress than the men do. But they also handle it better. In short, doing it all may be tough, but it doesn't wipe out the health benefits of working.

THE ADVANTAGES FOR FAMILIES

What about the kids? Many working parents feel they want more time with their kids, and they say so. But does maternal employment harm children? In 1989 University of Michigan psychologist Lois Hoffman reviewed 50 years of research and found that the expected negative effects never materialized. Most often, children of employed and unemployed mothers didn't differ on measures of child development. But children of both sexes with working mothers have a less sex-stereotyped view of the world because fathers in two-income families tend to do more child care.

However, when mothers work, the quality of non-parental child care is a legitimate worry. Scarr, Phillips and McCartney say there is "near consensus among developmental psychologists and early-childhood experts that child care per se does not constitute a risk factor in children's lives." What causes problems, they report, is poor-quality care and a troubled family life. The need for good child care in this country has been obvious for some time.

What's more, children in two-job families generally don't lose out on one-to-one time with their parents. New studies, such as S. L. Nock and P. W. Kingston's *Time with Children: The Impact of Couples' Work-Time Commitments,* show that when both parents of preschoolers are working, they spend as much time in direct interaction with their children as families in which only the fathers work. The difference is that working parents spend more time with their kids on weekends. When only the husband works, parents spend more leisure time with each other. There is a cost to two-income families—the couples lose personal time—but the kids don't seem to pay it.

One question we never used to ask is whether having a working mother could be *good* for children. Hoffman, reflecting on the finding that employed women—both blue-collar and professional—register higher life-satisfaction scores than housewives, thinks it can be. She cites studies involving infants and older children, showing that a mother's satisfaction with her employment status relates positively both to "the quality of the mother-child interaction and to various indexes of the child's adjustment and abilities." For example, psychologists J. Guidubaldi and B. K. Nastasi of Kent State University reported in a 1987 paper that a mother's satisfaction with her job was a good predictor of her child's positive adjustment in school.

Again, this isn't true only for women in high-status jobs. In a 1982 study of sources of stress for children in low-income families, psychologists Cynthia Longfellow and Deborah Belle of the Harvard University School of Education found that employed women were generally less depressed than unemployed women. What's more, their children had fewer behavioral problems.

But the real point about working women and children is that work *isn't* the point at all. There are good mothers and not-so-good mothers, and some work and some don't. When a National Academy of Sciences panel reviewed the previous 50 years of research and dozens of studies in 1982, it found no consistent effects on children from a mother's working. Work is only one of many variables, the panel concluded in *Families That Work,* and not the definitive one.

What is the effect of women's working on their marriages? Having a working wife can increase psychological stress for men, especially older men, who grew up in a world where it was not normal for a wife to work. But men's expectations that they will—and must—be the only provider may be changing. Wethington and Kessler found that a wife's employment could be a significant buffer *against* depression for men born after 1945. Still, the picture of men's psychological well-being is very mixed, and class and expectations clearly play a role. Faludi cites polls showing that young blue-collar men are especially angry at women for invading what they see as their turf as breadwinners, even though a woman with such a job could help protect her husband from economic hardship. But in highly educated, dual-career couples, both partners say the wife's career has enhanced the marriage.

THE FIRST SHIFT: WOMEN AT WORK

While women's own health and the well-being of their families aren't harmed by their working, what effect does this dual role have on their job performance? It's assumed that men can compartmentalize work and home lives but women will bring their home worries with them to work, making them distracted and inefficient employees.

Perhaps the most dangerous myth is that the solution is for women to drop back—or drop out.

The only spillover went in the other direction: The women brought their good feelings about their work home with them and left a bad day at home behind when they came to work. In fact, Wethington and Kessler found that it was the *men* who brought the family stresses with them to work. "Women are able to avoid bringing the contagion of home stress into the workplace," the researchers write, "whereas the inability of men to prevent this kind of contagion is pervasive." The researchers speculate that perhaps women get the message early on that they can handle the home front, while men are taking on chores they aren't trained for and didn't expect.

THE PERILS OF PART-TIME

Perhaps the most dangerous myth is that the solution to most problems women suffer is for them to drop back—or drop out. What studies actually show is a significant connection between a reduced commitment to work and increased psychological stress. In their Detroit study, Wethington and Kessler noted that women who went from being full-time employees to full-time housewives reported increased symptoms of distress, such as depression and anxiety attacks; the longer a woman worked and the more committed she was to the job, the greater her risk for psychological distress when she stopped.

What about part-time work, that oft-touted solution for weary women? Women who work fewer than 20 hours per week, it turns out, do not get the mental-health work benefit, probably because they "operate under the fiction that they can retain full responsibility for child care and home maintenance," wrote Wethington and Kessler. The result: Some part-timers wind up more stressed-out than women working full-time. Part-time employment also provides less money, fewer or no benefits and, often, less interesting work and a more arduous road to promotion.

That doesn't mean that a woman shouldn't cut down on her work hours or arrange a more flexible schedule. But it does mean she should be careful about jumping on a poorly designed mommy track that may make her a second-class citizen at work.

Many women think that when they have a baby, the best thing for their mental health would be to stay home. Wrong once more. According to Wethington and Kessler, having a baby does not increase psychological distress for working women—*unless* the birth results in their dropping out of the labor force. This doesn't mean that any woman who stays home to care for a child is going to be a wreck. But leaving the work force means opting out of the benefits of being in it, and women should be aware of that.

As soon as a woman has any kind of difficulty—emotional, family, medical—the knee-jerk reaction is to get her off the job. No such solution is offered to men, despite the very real correlation for men between job stress and heart attacks.

What the myth of the miserable working woman obscures is the need to focus on how the *quality* of a woman's job affects her health. Media stories warn of the alleged dangers of fast-track jobs. But our *Life-prints* study found that married women in high-prestige jobs were highest in mental well-being; another study of life stress in women reported that married career women with children suffered the least from stress. Meanwhile, few media tears are shed for the women most at risk: those in the word-processing room who have no control at work, low pay and little support at home.

Women don't need help getting out of the work force; they need help staying in it. As long as much of the media continues to capitalize on national ignorance, that help will have to come from somewhere else. (Not that an occasional letter to the editor isn't useful.) Men need to recognize that they are not just occasional helpers but vital to the success of the family unit. The corporate culture has to be reshaped so that it doesn't run totally according to patterns set by the white male workaholic. This will be good for men *and* women. The government can guarantee parental leave and affordable, available child care. (It did so in the '40s, when women were needed in the factories.) Given that Congress couldn't even get a bill guaranteeing *unpaid* family leave passed last year, this may take some doing. But hey, this is an election year.

CAREGIVING

CONTINUITIES AND DISCONTINUITIES IN FAMILY MEMBERS' RELATIONSHIPS WITH ALZHEIMER'S PATIENTS*

Thirty families who cared for a family member with Alzheimer's Disease were asked to provide narratives of daily care over one and one-half years. A key finding of the hermeneutic analysis of their narratives was that different family members experience their relationship with the AD patient to be continuous, continuous but transformed, or radically discontinuous with their relationship prior to the disease. Responsiveness to these qualities of family relations by professionals may ease family members' caregiving efforts.

Catherine Chesla, Ida Martinson,
and Marilou Muwaswes**

**Catherine Chesla is an Assistant Professor and Ida Martinson is a Professor in the Department of Family Health Care Nursing, University of California, San Francisco, California, 94143. Marilou Muwaswes is an Associate Clinical Professor, Physiological Nursing, University of California, San Francisco.

The central concern in research on families and Alzheimer's Disease (AD) in the past ten years has been to identify factors that place family members at risk for negative outcomes because of their involvement in AD care (Bowers, 1987; Colerick & George, 1986; Liptzin, Grob, & Eisen, 1988; Ory et al., 1985; Quayhagen & Quayhagen, 1988). This research has identified AD family caregivers to be at risk for poor physical health, mental health, and quality of life, when compared with family members who are not caregivers (Kuhlman, Wilson, Hutchinson, & Wallhagen, 1991). Family burden, resources (including social support), and AD patient characteristics and symptoms im-

*This research was conducted as part of a larger study "Impact of Alzheimer's Disease on the Family and Caregiver," by Ida Martinson, P.I., Catherine Gilliss, Glen Doyle and Marilou Muwaswes, Co-Investigators. The project was funded by Biomedical Research Support Grant, School of Nursing, University of California, San Francisco; Academic Senate Grant, UCSF; NRSA Post-Doctoral Fellowship Grant #1F31 NR06020, National Center for Nursing Research, NIH; Alzheimer's Disease and Related Disorders Association Paine-Knickerbocker Graduate Research Award.

Key Words: Alzheimer's disease, dementia, family caregiving, family relationships, intergenerational relationships.

(*Family Relations*, 1994, 43, 3-9.)

pact negative family outcomes, although factors that place family members most at risk remain to be specified (Baumgarten, 1989). In all of this research, however, AD patients are assumed to be a demand or a drain on family members.

Persons with AD are frequently described as experiencing a loss of self as the disease unfolds (Cohen & Eisdorfer, 1986). Progressive loss of memory, along with personality and behavior changes common to the disease, are thought to overwhelm those with the disease. AD patients are characterized as suffering from a biomedical disorder that severs them from their history and severely restricts their potential in life. The biomedicalization of dementia (Lyman, 1989) has restricted the scope of research to disease progression and biologic processes that give rise to the disease. Research about those who care for demented elders has similarly been restricted by the pervasiveness of the biomedical perspective to the questions about how the disease, in its various stages of progression, impacts family members. Largely unasked, and therefore unanswered, are questions about the lived experience of AD for the person with the disease, the family member's experience of living with and caring for the person with AD, and how qualities of the caregiving environment might influence disease progression (Lyman, 1989).

Research on caregivers of AD patients often progresses from the implicit assumption of particular relations between the ill family member and others in the family. One member in the relationship is assumed to be the passive recipient of care, holding less interpersonal power yet imposing demands and burdens. In a parallel way, the caregiving member is assumed to be an active provider, possessing relatively greater interpersonal power, but at risk of negative outcomes because of the burdens and risks experienced. Recent caregiver research suggests that the quality of relations between ill and other family members is complex, and that factors such as centrality of the relationship, personal qualities of both members, and the degree of reciprocity in the relationship may impact outcomes for both the ill and non-ill family members (Walker, Pratt, & Oppy, 1992; Wright, Clipp, & George, 1993).

One aim of this investigation was to question the assumption of a fixed relation between the family and the person with AD and additionally to specify the range of relations that were apparent in the day-to-day lives of family members living with a person with AD. As part of a larger study aimed at understanding the *experiences* of family members who cared for a person with AD over time, we critically examined family members' self-initiated discussion of relations with

From *Family Relations*, Vol. 43, No. 1, January 1994, pp. 3-9. © 1994 by the National Council of Family Relations, 3989 Central Avenue, NE, Suite 550, Minneapolis, MN 55421. Reprinted by permission.

the person with AD, as well as the content and nature of those relations. Working directly from family members' narratives, we attempted to understand these relations in ways that formal theories, such as exchange or friendship theory, may have missed. We were interested in the whole of the family's experience; what was salient and meaningful for the family members themselves, the difficulties or demands they encountered (Martinson, Chesla, & Muwaswes, 1993) and the skills and practices they developed in living with a person with AD. Through family members' narratives over an 18-month time span, it was evident that relationship issues were paramount to family members in their everyday lives and that qualitatively distinct forms of relations between ill members and other family members were evident.

Relationships Between Caregivers and Family Members with AD

Although little attention has been paid to the positive or sustaining aspects of caring for a family member with AD, detailed studies of the relationship between the AD patient and the family show that: (a) relationships change over time and intimacy declines with time for some but not for all family members (Blieszner & Shifflett, 1990); (b) care of a family member with AD brings both suffering and rewards; and (c) reciprocity in the relationship with a family member with dementia seems to be a key aspect reported by families, but can take many forms (Farran, Keane-Hagarty, Salloway, Kupferer, & Wilken, 1991; Hirschfeld, 1983; Orona, 1990).

Blieszner and Shifflett (1990) produced a sensitive analysis of caregivers' responses to the first 18 months of care after AD had been diagnosed. They found that intimacy between AD patients and family caregivers diminished over the first 18 months of care and that a host of emotional responses was elicited for family caregivers at each point in time. At diagnosis, there was relief at having an understanding of what was happening, but also anger, sadness, and grief. Six months into the disorder, family members focused on the loss of the previously established relationship with the AD patient. One year and six months after diagnosis, caregivers were found to be coping with a dramatically changed but continuing relationship. Coping strategies that predominated were redefining the relationship, working on closure in the relationship, and working on expanding caregiver role responsibilities. These investigators found that, although caregivers on average felt less intimate with the person with AD, some caregivers reported increased intimacy

as the disease progressed (Blieszner & Shifflett, 1989).

Hirschfeld (1983) developed in her grounded theory study a concept of "mutuality" in caregiver, care receiver relations. Mutuality was defined as the caregiver's capacity to find: (a) gratification in the relationship with the impaired person; (b) positive meaning from the caregiving situation; and (c) a sense of reciprocity, even in situations where the elder had severe dementia. The sample of 30 caregivers included both spouses and children of elders with senile brain disease. Most striking was Hirschfeld's finding that the higher the mutuality in the relationship, the less likely the caregiver was to consider institutionalization of the elder.

In a small grounded theory study of family members who cared for a member with AD, Orona (1990) focused on identity loss of the AD patient and its impact on the dyadic relationship over time. Using a social constructionist framework, Orona noted temporality as an important subjective aspect of the caregiving experience. Facets of temporal experience were: (a) the use of memories to maintain the identity of the AD person, (b) the re-enactment of meaningful social interactions with the AD person, and (c) the use of memories as a basis for constructing new images for the future. Caregivers were found to engage in "identity maintenance" via everyday activities with the AD family member, and when reciprocity was lost, these relatives "worked both sides of the relationship," or took on both the caregiver's and the AD patient's social roles, in order to continue some part of the past relating.

In summary, detailed studies that have examined a family member's experience with a relative with dementia over time undermine any standard depiction of the process. Rather, they demonstrate complex variability in issues of intimacy, reciprocity, and management of life tasks given the unbalanced capabilities of well and ill members. Questions remain about the basic nature of these relations and how they evolve over time.

METHOD

This study was designed within a tradition known as hermeneutic phenomenology (Benner & Wrubel, 1989; Packer & Addison, 1989; Van Manen, 1990). The aim of the method is to explain particular and distinct patterns of meaning and action in the lives of those studied, taking into account the context in which they live, their history, and their particular concerns. Rather than trying to characterize a modal or group response, research within this method

provides detailed explanations of varied patterns of human understanding and action. The method is: (a) systematic in its use of practiced modes of questioning the informant about experiences; (b) explicit in its attempt to articulate, through careful interpretation of a text, the meanings embedded in human experience; (c) self-critical and self-corrective in its continual examination of interpretations made on a text; and (d) a shared interpretation that is consensually agreed upon by multiple readers (Van Manen, 1990).

This phenomenological study was part of a multifaceted, longitudinal study of the impact of Alzheimer's Disease on the family and caregiver (Martinson, Gilliss, Doyle, & Muwaswes, 1983). Only the phenomenologic interview data are reported here. Fifteen spouses and fifteen adult-child family members were recruited from support groups and clinics serving AD patients. Semistructured, intensive interviews were conducted at intake and every six months for 18 months. In each interview, family members were asked to reflect on their experiences in the previous 6 months and on changes in the AD patient, family members' feelings, and care arrangements. They were asked to provide narratives of salient, difficult, or memorable episodes of care that had arisen in the past 6 months. Full narratives of the episodes, preceding events, caregivers' emotions, thoughts, and actions throughout the episodes and outcomes were elicited. The interviews, which lasted approximately one hour, were audiotaped and transcribed verbatim.

Hermeneutic interpretation (Packer & Addison, 1989; Van Manen, 1990) of texts from the interviews comprise this paper. The first author, educated in Heideggerian philosophy and hermeneutics, directed the interpretive process and interpreted all texts with the third author. The second author was familiar with all interview texts and provided consensus on summary interpretations.

Interpretation was comprised of two interwoven processes: thematic interpretation and interpretation of exemplars. Three levels of thematic interpretation were used to uncover and isolate themes in a text: (a) the holistic approach, (b) the selective approach, and (c) the detailed or line-by-line approach. In the holistic approach, the whole text was read through and described as a piece in an attempt to capture the fundamental meaning of the text as a whole. In the selective approach, aspects of the text that stood out as essential or revealing of the phenomenon under study were the focus. A line-by-line detailed reading was then completed in which the text was examined for what it revealed about the experience. After completing all three steps, the text was examined in its entirety, in its particular salience, and for fine-grained nuances.

Interpretation of exemplars occurred simultaneously with the search for general themes. Exemplars are narratives of whole incidents of family care elicited from participants in the interviews. All relevant aspects of each exemplar were coded together, including the family member's recollection of what preceded the episode, how the episode unfolded, emotions at the start and throughout the episode, actions considered and taken, direct and indirect clues to what was at stake for the family, and the family member's retrospective reworking of the situation. These episodes, in their complete form, served as examples of particular patterns of action that included a rich description of the situation and responses that evidenced family member's understandings, concerns, and practical involvements with the AD patient.

FINDINGS

Description of Informants

Eighteen of the family members interviewed were female (7 wives and 11 daughters), and twelve were male (8 husbands and 4 sons). The mean age of family members was 57 years. Family members were predominantly Caucasian and from middle socioeconomic strata.

Eight male and 22 female persons with AD entered the study. Their mean age was 74 years (range 59-86) and the mean duration of the illness was 4 years (range 1-11 years). Twenty persons with AD at the start of the study resided in the home of a family member, seven were institutionalized in a nursing or board and care home, and three lived alone. Residence status changed with each data collection period, and at six months 17 AD patients lived in their caregiver's home, 11 lived in institutions, 1 lived alone, and 1 person with AD died. By 18 months, 8 were living in the caregiver's home, 8 were institutionalized, 1 was still living alone, 8 persons with AD had died, and 5 family members had withdrawn from the study.

Severity of the AD patients' illness, as measured by the Mini-Mental Status Exam (Folstein, Folstein, & McHugh, 1975) indicated moderate to severe cognitive dysfunction. Mean scores for AD patients were 9.4 (SD = 6.7) at induction and 6.4 (SD = 8.06) six months later on a 30-point scale, where a score below 24 indicates some cognitive impairment. On a second measure of illness severity, the Older Adults Multifunctional Assessment Questionnaire (Fillenbaum & Smyer, 1981), the AD patients scored significantly lower ($p < .001$) on mea-

sures of physical health and activities of daily living than a comparison group of institutionalized elderly.

Interpretive Findings

Continuity and discontinuity in the relationship between the family member and the person with AD were salient issues in two paradigm cases in an early reading of the narratives. A paradigm case is an outstanding instance of a pattern of narratives that seem to go together, the coherence of which is visible only through the whole reading of a particular case. Continuity and discontinuity in these two cases seemed to set up the kind of care that the family member had with the AD patient. The finding challenged our assumption of what AD relations might be, which most closely resembled a third pattern we eventually observed and labeled *continuous but transformed*. After recognition and identification of three predominant forms of relating through paradigm cases, the texts from the remaining informants were identified as being strongly similar to the aspects of relating evident in these three predominant forms.

One aspect of the experience of living with and caring for a family member with AD is presented in this article: the existential relation that family members had with their spouse or parent with AD as evidenced by their narratives of providing day-to-day care. Three forms of relationship will be presented: (a) a relationship that is maintained as continuous with the relationship between caregiver and AD patient prior to the disease, (b) a relationship that is continuous but is transformed by the disease, and (c) a relationship in which there is radical discontinuity between the present and prior relationship.

Relationship as Continuous

Some family members found possibilities in their relationships to continue to be a wife, daughter, husband or son to the person with AD. Despite the changes in the person with AD, family members continued to define themselves "in relation to" the patient in ways that paralleled their relations prior to the disease. These family members interpreted small gestures or statements made by the AD patient as continuous with past behavior and found remnants of the AD patient's intentions, wishes, likes and dislikes in present behavior. Dramatic losses and changes in the relationship were not denied and there was particular sensitivity in this group to patients' functional and memory losses. Despite realistic assessment and grieving, these family members felt a sense of connection to and continuity with the patient. They watched for, held pre-

cious, and felt comforted by, familiar responses and behaviors by the patient.

One woman exemplifies continuous relating with an AD spouse. She is a 75-year-old woman who had been married to her husband for more than 54 years. The husband had shown signs of AD for the past 10 years and during the course of the study declined from almost complete dementia to death.

This woman's narratives provide evidence that her relationship to her husband is almost unaltered from the life they shared prior to the illness. Despite the AD, she finds access to his person, his intelligence, and his capacity to comfort her. She is distressed that her husband, who never used profanity, now curses her in anger and tries to hit her if he is confused. However, the man with whom she built a life and a family, the person that comprised her world prior to the illness, continues to define her world and focus her daily concerns. She finds comfort that they can share a bed together and feels his presence very strongly in her life. In the first two interviews, when they lived together in their retirement apartment, she noted repeated instances where her husband seemed present and interacted with her in familiar ways:

> Wife: The other morning, for instance, he woke up early and I was just barely awake, and he reached over and held my hand. So you know that is a lot really. He's here. He always has been a very gentle, caring sort of person.

She noted incidents where he commented on her clothes, "I always liked you in that," or tried to comfort her when she became tearful. From an outsider's perspective, his behavior could have been interpreted as random or meaningless, but the woman interprets it as meaningful, coherent, and indicative of his past and present personhood.

This woman's respect for her husband's continuity of person appears in the way she approaches his physical care. She values his lifelong habits and practices and continues them for him now that he cannot carry them out.

> Wife: My son said 'Well you don't have to shave Dad everyday.' I said, 'I know he doesn't have much of a beard but he likes being shaved.' He sometimes sings when I'm shaving him. I remember he always used to clean his finger nails every morning when he was getting ready to go. So why not do that?

In a similar way, this woman relied on past relationship patterns with her husband to comfort *her*. She told of two stressful incidents in which her husband wandered away from her. In both incidents, her husband was found within minutes, but she experienced extreme anxiety and distress, fearing he might be harmed or permanently lost. Both times, she calmed her husband and comforted herself by sitting and talking with him.

> Wife: Well, I talk to him. I just say, 'you know, you really scared me, and you worry me when you wander away like that. I can't keep track of you all the time.' I just talk like you would in general.
>
> Interviewer: And that helps you?
>
> Wife: Yea.
>
> Interviewer: Do you think that sinks in?
>
> Wife: No. It's helpful for me to talk to him. We always talked a lot.

Conversing with her husband re-enacted a 54-year-old ritual in which they sat together and had a glass of wine each night when her husband returned from work. This ritual was time-honored and practiced no matter what was happening with their household of seven children.

One year into the study, the husband had a stroke and had to be placed in a nursing home. While this dramatically changed the nature of her care responsibilities, her relationship with her husband continued largely unchanged. She went to the nursing home for many hours each day to monitor his care and bring him foods he liked. In the final interview, after her husband died, she recounted her sense of continuity with her husband.

> Interviewer: So the Alzheimer's disease didn't take that away from you, that happy feeling of being married to Ron and that relationship you felt with him?
>
> Wife: No, it never did. Never. I would have been happy to bring him home again. . . . I mean, I would have gone on indefinitely. One of the books I read said they usually have Alzheimer's for about 15 years. So I figured that I had about another 7 years to go. He'd come home from the hospital before, so I thought he'd be coming home again, I really did.
>
> Interviewer: So you really felt you had an ongoing relationship with him?
>
> Wife: Yes.

This case demonstrates several aspects of a continuous relationship with an AD family member: (a) the interpretation that the AD patient is still present despite the disease, (b) the interpretation that the person with AD reciprocates in positive ways, and (c) the AD patient continues to define the spouse's or child's world in stable and relatively unchanging ways.

In a similar way, adult children maintained the parent in a place of respect and esteem despite the advance of the disease. Although the parent could not provide advice or support, he or she was still respected and honored by the child as his or her parent. Adult children in this group expressed concern that they "try to maintain her dignity" and "not strip everything away from her."

One daughter's capacity to see her mother in small aspects of the mother's behavior remained present, as in the prior case, throughout the 18-month study. During that time, the mother's physical and mental health declined, she suffered numerous strokes, and the AD progressed to the extent that the mother required placement in a board and care home and eventually a nursing home. Still, the daughter felt an attachment to what she saw in her mother's behavior and appearance that still represented "mother." The daughter continued practices that her mother had maintained throughout her lifetime: coloring her hair red and manicuring her nails. Until the end of the study, the daughter claimed that her relationship with her mother was alive and vibrant.

> Interviewer: So you still very much have that bond with her?
>
> Daughter: Oh yes. I will sit there with her in the evenings. I'll sit on the bed and she's in the wheelchair, and I'll put my arm around her and cuddle with her.
>
> Interviewer: She still likes affection from you?
>
> Daughter: Oh yes. She responds to that. Awhile back when I told her I loved her, I was very richly rewarded because she told me, 'I love you.' That just leveled me. I try to hang on to what's still left of her. She still knows me; she still knows chocolate; she still remembers hymns; she's not gone yet. There's still Mama there.

Relationship is Continuous but Transformed

Another group of family members described the AD patient as fairly lost to them because of AD. These spouses and children saw minimal, residual, and fleeting signs of the AD person's personality and either had doubts about their accessibility or saw them as totally inaccessible. What remained, however, was a strong commitment to the relationship, to maintaining contact with the person that the patient had *become* in the disease. Because of the changes in the AD patient, past relations were mourned, and current relations were on a new footing.

> Interviewer: Is she still the same person to you?
>
> Daughter: No. Oh no! She's a totally different person. She's not Helen anymore. She's not my mom. No. She's just there in body.

These family members found ways to relate to the patient as the symptoms progressed, and continued to adapt their ways of relating as the AD person's capacities became more constricted. For example, one man reported in the first three interviews that his greatest fear was that his wife would no longer recognize him. In the abstract, he feared that her lack of recognition would break the thin continuity that he felt with her. Additionally, he said he was most sustained by his wife's contentment and recognition. Then in the last interview, his wife increasingly did not recognize him. He then found a new way to stay connected to her in her current capacities. He no longer worried that she recognize him but found it essential that she appreciate him and accept his care. Her willingness to eat what he prepared and her cooperation with the caregivers he hired were taken as signs of her acceptance of his care.

Family members who experienced their relationships as transformed lived more in synchrony with the actual decline in the AD patient's functioning than did those family members who experienced continuity in relations with the AD member. Their relationship with the patient evolved and changed with the changes in the disease. They saw their possibilities for relating to the person with AD as being more firmly bounded by the actual symptomatic changes in the person than did those family members who experienced a continuous relationship with the family member with AD.

In the continuous but transformed relationship, reciprocity between the patient and family members was seen as minimally possible and always in doubt. The patient's fleeting smiles or signs of pleasure were noted by family members and brought them satisfaction. What distinguished these family members from those in the continuous relationship category is the fact that small gestures by the AD patient were not interpreted as indications that the patient was still "there" in the same way that those who had continuous relationships interpreted these signs.

> Daughter: I just feel like I've already lost her. She's here but she isn't here. It's probably the most difficult thing.

Spouses found living in this ambiguous relationship difficult because they could no longer relate to their partner as an intimate friend or sexual partner and at the same time they remained married and deeply committed to the spouse. Children also experienced the ambiguity in relations as a dilemma, although the day-to-day impact on their lives was less than for spouses. The children never talked of finding a replacement relationship for that which they had lost, but many of the spouses wished this were possible.

In families where the relationship was transformed, the primary relationship concerns were to provide sensitive care that maintained the dignity of the person and to sustain the AD patient's functional abilities. One spouse, who exemplifies these concerns, demonstrated that to be a good husband to his wife meant providing good care. To this end, he gave up his job in international business and turned his energies entirely to the care of his wife. In his interviews he was exclusively focused on his wife's care requirements and how to sensitively meet them in a way that maintained her current functioning and dignity. He was deeply committed to taking good care of his wife, deeply grieved when there was any evidence that he was not doing a good job, and satisfied when he was successful.

Relationship is Radically Discontinuous

In the third form of relating to a family member with AD, the relationship with the spouse or parent was radically discontinuous with the relationship that existed prior to the illness. These family members found no continuity in the AD patient's personhood and instead found that the AD rendered the patient unrecognizable. They found the behaviors and symptoms of AD to be an affront to the person he or she had been prior to the disease. The relationship these family members experienced was less emotional, less personal and more clinical than that of the first two groups. In their interpretation, the spouse or parent was lost in the disease, and therefore the family member could not continue a truly personal relationship. The concern of these family members for the patient was more objective, abstract, and less tailored to the particular needs of their AD family member.

The coping narratives of these family members focused on caregiving arrangements and problems. When the AD patient gave signs of recognition or pleasure, these family members, like others, were pleased and touched. They did not, however, attempt to elicit such signs and did not interpret such signs as evidence of purposeful, personalized behavior. They diminished the importance of instances of recognition. Instead, there was more of a clinical distancing

and evaluation of the person's disease process.

Emotional distancing was evident in a daughter whose mother had contracted the disease eight years earlier. The daughter described a recent incident where her mother said something that actually seemed to make sense. The daughter was about to take her mother off the commode and the mother said "no" because she needed to stay longer. This moment of possible lucidity in a woman who had not been lucid for 2 years surprised the daughter. But when the interviewer probed about how the incident affected her, she replied:

> Daughter: I don't think it made a difference. I found it interesting that she said 'no' definitely. I thought to myself, how does the correlation go there?

The mother's statement raised for the daughter a clinical question, rather than a relational response. The daughter wondered about how the disease worked, rather than how her mother experienced the disease. Witnessing her mother make sense, and thus have some possibility of making meaningful contact with current reality, made the daughter feel neither closer to nor more distant from her mother. In this daughter's understanding of the situation, the possibility of connecting with her mother simply was not present.

One husband provides some insight about how this emotional break in his relationship with his wife occurred. He recounted that prior to the AD they were "best friends," "did everything together" and in many ways she defined his life. When facing up to her illness, he recognized the only way that he could stay in a relationship with his wife was if he were to "die" himself.

> Husband: I think somehow I'm hardened. If I can say it like that. I've become hardened to a lot of it. It may be by design. Because I had to decide, when I talked about that turning point, whether I was going to live, or whether I was going to sit here and curl up and die because she's got that disease. I don't know if the word's martyr or. . . . Anyway I'm not going to sit around here and let it kill me. I think that's what it was doing.

The dissolution of the relationship with his wife is also evident in this man's hopes and fears for the future. The best possible life he hoped for was: "I would feel good if she died, the sooner the better." He also felt that the worst life for him would be if his wife were to continue to live, and hold him in this "limbo" of being "married, but not married."

Family members who realized radical discontinuities in their relationships

with the AD patient may have had a wide variety of predisposing factors. Perhaps they as a group had more conflicted relations with the person with AD prior to the disease, and thus the disease introduced unsurmountable distance. Perhaps they had difficulty coping with the pervasive losses that one must face as a loved one progresses through AD and distancing was one way of warding off the pain of these losses. We lack the data to thoroughly understand *how* family members came to a discontinuous relationship with the AD patient. What was evident was that these family members found few, if any, possibilities for relating to the person with AD that paralleled their relationship prior to the disease.

Despite the emotional distance that typified the discontinuous relationship, providing good care was a central and focusing concern for family members who experienced this relationship. Proper diet, supervision, safety, and comfort of the AD patient were all raised as issues in the family members' narratives. Providing or arranging care demanded extensive daily effort and time and some of these family members were the primary or sole providers of care. What distinguished the care concerns of this group of families was their relative lack of concern that the care be tailored to the present or past personal needs of the AD patient.

DISCUSSION

In this intensive study of the relationships between family members and AD patients over time, we discovered qualitatively distinct ways that family members interpreted the AD patient's accessibility, capacity to reciprocate affection and concern, and capacity to *relate* as parent or spouse to the family member. For some family members of persons with AD, the loss of self and transformation of the person with AD by the disease were not complete. For these family members, the life and capacities of the person with AD were still a part of their ongoing relationship either fully or in a diminished and transformed way. For other family members, however, the disease covered over the person, overrode their relational possibilities, and care became much more strategic or objectified.

All three forms of relating (continuous, transformed, or discontinuous) presented here were evident in both the children's and spouses' relations with the person with AD. With the exception of continuous relating, both male and female caregivers experienced each form of relating. In our group of informants, there were no male caregivers who demonstrated the continuous form of relating, and wives of persons with AD were the most predominant in this group of caregivers. We acknowledge that the forms of relating that we present may not represent all of the possibilities for how relations between family and the person with AD might evolve. For example, we interviewed only persons who maintained some kind of relationship with the person with AD, whether that relationship was personal or merely organizational. Thus, we have no information on the ways in which family members may sever their relationship with the person with AD.

The severity of illness in the person with AD did not seem to determine the form of relationship that was described by the family member. Moderate to severe Alzheimer's disease was evident in all three forms of relationships when data from both family member ratings and interviewer ratings were considered. The disease itself, and the progression of the disease, was not a clear determinant of what the relationship might be.

Our findings support and further articulate detailed qualitative studies of AD family relationships reported to date. Like Blieszner and Shifflett (1990), we found that closeness between the person with AD and the family members diminished for some but remained strong for others over time, despite sometimes dramatic progression of the dementia and, thus, a decrease in the AD person's "objective" capacities to relate. Orona (1990) reported interactions similar to those we observed in the first two groups of our sample: the reenactment of familiar rituals and the searching for and success at finding familiar behaviors and expressions in the AD patient. She similarly reported the phenomena we observed in the continuous relationships of "working both sides" of the relationship, filling in additional meanings for vague or difficult to interpret behaviors by the person with AD.

Hirschfeld (1983) combined three dimensions of mutuality in a single concept. Considering Hirschfeld's concept of mutuality in light of our own findings, we believe that her three aspects of mutuality might offer greater explanatory power in terms of caregivers' involvements if they are examined independently. In this study, we found that: (a) the caregiver's capacity to find gratification in the *relationship* with the impaired person, (b) *positive* meaning of caregiving, and (c) a sense of *reciprocity* with the care recipient, all aspects of mutuality, did not combine in meaningful ways in our groups of family members who provided care. For example, family members in the continuous group seemed to experience all three dimensions of mutuality in a consistent, coherent fashion. Family members in the con-

tinuous but transformed group also experienced positive meanings from the care situation, questionable reciprocity, and some gratification from the relationship, but here it was a relation acknowledged to be changed by the disease. Finally, family members in the discontinuous group experienced substantial positive meanings from giving care, but found no sense of reciprocity in the caregiving relationship and made almost no mention of relationship gratifications with the AD patient. We believe that Hirschfeld identified important explanatory dimensions in the relationship of family and persons with AD and argue for further refinement of the "mutuality" concept so that each dimension be examined as qualitatively distinct.

Our findings are not in conflict with, but are distinct from, the prevailing themes in the literature on family factors and AD care. This literature has largely ignored the quality of the relationship between the person with AD and the family member who provides care, assuming instead that the former is a passive, uninvolved recipient of care and the latter is burdened by the responsibility for this passive object/person. We wish to argue that the qualitative aspects of the relationship between the AD person and the family members described in this research deserve a more prominent place in research on family processes in relation to AD care. Alongside continuing efforts to identify factors that place the family at risk for negative outcomes, conceptualizations and investigations of family care processes must begin to include an awareness of relationships that may be sustaining and meaningful. As Hirschfeld's research demonstrated a decade ago, the relational qualities may have powerful explanatory power in how families function over time.

CLINICAL IMPLICATIONS

Recognizing that family members who care for a person with AD have distinct relations with that person is vital to their sensitive care and support. Relying on standardized responses to the family situation, or relying on the pervasive literature that emphasizes the losses, burdens, and difficulties in AD care, may lead professionals to overlook the family members' possibilities for hope, satisfaction, and continuity in their relations with and care of the AD patient.

Care for family members who experience their relationship as continuous might explicitly legitimatize their experience of the person as present and encourage their efforts to continue the AD patient's habits and practices. The biomedicalization of dementia (Lyman,

1989) may be so complete that family members feel criticized or isolated because they continue to relate to the person with AD. In recognizing the two-way nature of the family relations, health professionals should give credence to the AD patient as a person with a history and recognize further the AD patient's capacity to carry on in a meaningful way in relationships despite the debilitations of the dementia. Rather than emphasizing the negative changes wrought by the disease, health professionals might learn from family members how the disease makes possible continued exercise of lifelong marital or parental relations. Family members additionally might inform practitioners about authentic commitments to the care of beloved family members that are neither self-sacrificing nor "loving too much." For some, care of the person with AD is the genuine working out and fulfillment of a lifelong relationship; therefore, it is not experienced as burdensome but sustaining and meaningful.

The group of family members who experience a continuous relationship with the person with AD might have the most difficulty, however, with recognizing the true limitations that occur over time in the AD person's abilities. Although all caregivers we observed provided safe and protective environments, some had their choices for care restricted because they believed that the person with AD was capable of doing things that seemed unlikely. Respectful solicitation of what family members perceive as the capabilities of the AD person, and feedback by the professional regarding these perceptions are warranted.

Family members who experienced their relationship with the AD patient as continuous but transformed might similarly benefit from interventions that respect their efforts at continued close relations with the person with AD. These family members, who are more in synchrony with the changes of the disease, are particularly apt to observe firsthand a decline in the AD patient's abilities. Care of these family members may involve helping them find ways to maintain their commitment to closeness, while at the same time being respectful of the AD patient's new restrictions. Providing examples of how other family members have coped with this dilemma, like the spouse who no longer needed his wife's recognition, but merely needed her acceptance of his care, might make these transitions easier.

Work with family members who experience their relationship with the person with AD as discontinuous could focus on helping them find some continuities in the person despite the AD, assisting them with appropriate care arrangements, and showing appreciation for their existential experience of distance from their prior relations with the person with AD. These family members may need help in recognizing that AD dementia does not immediately and totally transform a person, and that she or he may actively contribute to and participate in the life of the family. These family members may also benefit from a frank discussion about how we live in a culture where caring for others is seldom valued, and how the person providing care may be misunderstood as "addicted" to or dependent upon his or her need to care for others (Dreyfus & Rubin, in press). Offering a positive connotation for care of a family member who has AD may make closer relations possible for these families. Both of these interventions, however, must be tempered by attention to the family member's current possibilities in relation to the AD patient. Some family members, because of their background with the AD patient or because of their current social context, cannot tolerate closer emotional proximity to the AD patient, and thus their distance must be honored.

REFERENCES

Baumgarten, M. (1989). The health of persons giving care to the demented elderly: A critical review of the literature. *Journal of Clinical Epidemiology*, 42, 1137-1148.

Benner, P., & Wrubel, J. (1989). *The primacy of caring, stress and coping in health and illness*. Menlo Park, CA: Sage.

Blieszner, R., & Shifflett, P. A. (1989). Affection, communication and commitment in adult-child caregiving for parents with Alzheimer's disease. In J. A. Mancini (Ed.), *Aging parents and adult children* (pp. 231-242). Lexington, MA: Lexington Books.

Blieszner, R., & Shifflett, P. A. (1990). The effects of Alzheimer's disease on close relationships between patients and caregivers. *Family Relations*, 39, 57-62.

Bowers, B. J. (1987). Intergenerational caregiving: Adult caregivers and their aging parents. *Advances in Nursing Science*, 9(2), 20-31.

Cohen, D., & Eisdorfer, C. (1986). *The loss of self*. New York: Norton.

Colerick, E. J., & George, L. K. (1986). Predictors of institutionalization among caregivers of patients with Alzheimer's Disease. *Journal of the American Geriatrics Society*, 34, 493-498.

Dreyfus, H., & Rubin, J. (in press). Kierkegaard on the nihilism of the present age: The case of commitment as addiction. *Synthese*.

Farran, C. J., Keane-Hagerty, E., Salloway, S., Kupferer, S., & Wilken, C.S. (1991). Finding meaning: An alternative paradigm for Alzheimer's Disease family caregivers. *The Gerontologist*, 31, 483-489.

Fillenbaum, G. G., & Smyer, M. A. (1981). The development, validity and reliability of the OARS Multidimensional Functional Assessment Questionnaire. *Journal of Gerontology*, 36, 428-434.

Folstein, M., Folstein, S., & McHugh, P. (1975). Mini-mental state: A practical method for grading the cognitive state of patients for the clinician. *Journal of Psychiatric Research*, 12, 189-198.

Hirschfeld, M. (1983). Homecare versus institutionalization: Family caregiving and senile brain disease. *International Journal of Nursing Studies*, 20, 23-32.

Kuhlman, G. J., Wilson, H. S., Hutchinson, S. A., & Wallhagen, M. (1991). Alzheimer's disease and family caregiving: Critical synthesis of the literature and research agenda. *Nursing Research*, 40, 331-337.

Liptzin, R., Grob, M., & Eisen, S. (1988). Family burden of demented and depressed elderly psychiatric inpatients. *The Gerontologist*, 28, 397-401.

Lyman, K. A. (1989). Bring the social back in: A critique of the biomedicalization of dementia. *The Gerontologist*, 29, 597-605.

Martinson, I. M., Chesla, C., & Muwaswes, M. (1993). Caregiving demands of patients with Alzheimer's Disease. *Journal of Community Health Nursing*, 10, 225-232.

Martinson, I., Gilliss, C. L., Doyle, G., & Muwaswes, M. (1983). *The impact of Alzheimer's Disease on the family and caregiver*. San Francisco: University of California.

Orona, C. J. (1990). Temporality and identity loss due to Alzheimer's Disease. *Social Science in Medicine*, 30, 1247-1256.

Ory, M. G., Williams, T. F., Emr, M., Lebowitz, B., Rabins, P., Salloway, J., Sluss-Radbaugh, T., Wolff, E., & Zarit, S. (1985). Families, informal supports and Alzheimer's Disease. *Research on Aging*, 7, 623-644.

Packer, M. J., & Addison, R. B. (1989). *Entering the circle: Hermeneutic investigation in psychology*. Albany: SUNY Press.

Quayhagen, M. P., & Quayhagen, M. (1988). Alzheimer's stress: Coping with the caregiving role. *The Gerontologist*, 28, 391-396.

Van Manen, M. (1990). *Researching lived experience*. London, Ontario: Althouse.

Walker, A. J., Pratt, C. C., & Oppy, N. C. (1992). Perceived reciprocity in family caregiving. *Family Relations*, 41, 82-85.

Wright, L. K., Clipp, E. C., & George, L. K. (1993). State of the art review: Health consequences of caregiver stress. *Medicine, Exercise, Nutrition & Health*, 2, 181-195.

The Long Road Back
A Daughter Deals With Her
Mother's Stroke

Patricia K. Lynch

Patricia Lynch is a CBS News producer currently working on "Eye to Eye" with Connie Chung and on other projects.

"Good night, darling, I love you," was the last complete sentence I heard my mother say. That was July 17, 1988. Sometime during the next morning, after she dressed and made her bed, a lightning bolt burned into her brain, destroying delicate tissue. That rogue blood clot took away my mother's ability to reason and to understand.

Her best friend found her later standing at the door, incoherent . . . disconnected. "Dementia" is what the doctors called it at the hospital, a psychotic episode. I somehow knew that Violet Lynch, 79, schoolteacher, mother, widow, was gone forever.

There were so many questions I never asked . . . so many things left unsaid. A stranger looked at me now with frightened eyes—pleading eyes, like those of an animal struck by a car. In the seconds that it took for the stroke to obliterate my mother's cognitive skills, our relationship changed irrevocably, from mother-daughter to daughter-child. In this awful role reversal, I became the caregiver to a woman whose first words to me at the hospital were, "Who are you?" My mother. A stranger.

The world *caregiver* is frequently a euphemism for unpaid female relative. A Travelers Insurance Company survey reports that nearly 7 of 10 primary caregivers are women, who spend an average of 16 hours a week providing care. According to the American Association of Retired Persons, 53 percent are daughters who are also employed.

And the elderly population is increasing: According to the census bureau, the number of people over 85 will triple by the year 2030. They are living longer but not better because of debilitating chronic illness and a health-care system that serves them poorly. Those first days she was in the hospital were unforgettable. "What is your mother's Medicare number?" "I don't know." Does she have private insurance?" "I don't know."

The day after my mother's stroke, she seemed to recognize me as someone familiar. Strangely, she also reacted to a photo of my dogs. "My babies," she mumbled, her eyes filling with tears. That night I showed her an old photo of her mother. "Momma . . . Momma," she said, crying.

I had no time to mourn the death of my mother. There was too much to do. I had to learn about Medicare and Medicaid and nursing homes and home care. And bills were coming in . . . from doctors whom I never met . . . "referrals" who were called in by the attending physicians . . . doctors who didn't return phone calls for days and had little to say when they did. One, a psychiatrist my mother had consulted in 1975 after my father and her only sister died, billed me $1,200 for hospital visits—visits to a woman who knew no one but two golden retrievers and a faded picture of her mother.

The hospital stay was a nightmare . . . of "roommates" who left because they could not deal with my mother's agitated behavior . . . of nurses who seldom stopped by . . . and of doctors who dropped by with eager students, and spoke about my mother as if she were a specimen. "See how her eyes do not follow my finger. See how she does not comprehend simple commands." The third day I ordered the medical group to leave the room.

Many of mother's friends stopped visiting. They saw their future in her eyes and were frightened. By the fourth day, my worst fears were realized. "Violet Lynch might improve somewhat, but . . ." My mother, who loved to read and do crossword puzzles and play bridge, would need 24-hour supervision the rest of her life. "I recommend a nursing home," a neurologist advised. A "discharge planner" reminded me of how "lucky" I was that the hospital was keeping her as long as they were—10 days. She also informed me that " 'Mom' is not a good candidate for a nursing home" because she needs "too much care."

I wheeled my mother out of the hospital. She had been given a heavy dose of Haldol, an anti-psychotic drug sometimes given to stroke and Alzheimer's victims. It was July 27, the first day of my vacation. I was very apprehensive because my employer at the time was not known for compassion. To ask for a leave of absence would have been professional suicide.

My mother showed no recognition of her surroundings. She said nothing when we got home and I put her to bed. Then I sat quietly nursing a strong Scotch, wondering what the hell I was going to do.

The next three weeks were a blur: Bathing. Feeding. Cooking. Medicating. Cleaning up mistakes. My mother could never be left alone. I found out the discharge planner was right. Violet was not a "good candidate" for a nursing home. Because of her dementia, no facility I found would accept her in a nonskilled home-care section—where people must be able to take care of their own basic needs.

According to Federal rules at the time, my mother wasn't sick enough for the skilled nursing-care section. After visiting several, I grew to hate the smell of urine and the sight of once-dignified people tied to their chairs, staring at nothing. Medicare didn't cover intermediate facilities. My mother had enough money for a good nursing home...but she didn't fit the requirements. She was put on a waiting list—a year or two for the best places. So I started pursuing home care.

Back then, private agencies wanted $150 just to sit down and talk about my mother's needs. I was told to expect to pay $100 a day excluding carfare and food for a nurse's aide who would feed and bathe my mother and "watch her so she doesn't get into any trouble." Technically, an aide is not supposed to administer medication, but I was told—"off the record"—that most would if I left "specific instructions." Friends began to tell me horror stories—of aides who robbed them blind, of people who never showed up, of abuse. A quick review of our finances revealed that my mother's Social Security and pension couldn't completely pay for home care. My salary and the money she meant for me to inherit would have to make up the difference. Then my luck changed. A friend of mine had a housekeeper whose sister needed a job. Olivia's salary was affordable, and she hit it off with Mother. We began to reduce the dosage of Haldol gradually, and mother became less zombielike. I began to feel I could return to work.

Then, in the middle of one night, I awoke to find my mother standing over my bed...screaming. She was hospitalized for what was described as another psychotic episode. Earlier I had discovered her turning the dial of her TV and looking frantic. She seemed to know that she used to understand what the people on the screen were saying. And now she didn't. The doctors said the "event" was caused by reduced blood supply to the brain. Her prognosis was poor. The glass over her mother's picture was removed, as were all sharp objects—in case she tried to kill herself. Once again she was put on Haldol, which turned her into a robot.

While the doctors tried to find a chemical solution, I spent hours on the phone getting rejections from nursing homes because of my mother's dementia: "too much work."

I called a friend, a Catholic priest, for advice. He gave me names, then asked quietly, "May I pray for your mother?" It was September 6. That night, when I got to the hospital, my mother was coherent for the first time since the "event." "The medicine finally kicked in," a doctor explained. Probably...but I asked Father Ralph to keep praying.

Almost six years have passed. My mother has had two minor "events" since the massive stroke, and she needs a cane to walk. But Violet Lynch, now 85, still lives at home with Olivia. Without her, we could not have made it. I fenced in my mother's yard, and two stray dogs have joined the family. She loves them and her home, which I gradually renovated to meet her needs. (A bathroom downstairs, railings, a heated porch that will be her bedroom when she needs to be downstairs full time.)

My mother lives completely in the present now...without Haldol... and takes only heart and blood-pressure medication. Her doctor is amazed that she made it...and actually has improved. Violet is still aphasic and has trouble remembering words, and she can't read or write, but she understands TV, friendship and love.

Her savings—"my inheritance"— was spent long ago, but we manage. I am happy that my mother is someone I know again. The frightened stranger is gone—I hope forever.

Family Values: The bargain breaks

Marriage is a bargain between men and women. That bargain is increasingly broken by divorce. The sufferers are men, women and children.

ONCE the rock on which society was founded, marriage is being increasingly chiselled away. All over the industrial world, more couples are choosing to live together and even to start a family without marrying. More of those who do marry subsequently divorce. This article examines these trends. It argues that women increasingly see marriage as a bad bargain; but that divorce may not be a better one.

First, the trends. Men and women are **marrying later**. In the 12 countries of the EC the mean age of marriage for women is now just over 25, two years older than in the late 1970s. In the United States by the end of the 1980s, the age of marriage for American women stood at a 20th-century high. To some extent, the decline in marriage has been offset by a rise in **cohabitation**. The prevalence of cohabitation varies enormously. In northern Europe people tend to live together for long periods. In America such partnerships are shorter. In Italy people hardly ever cohabit.

Births out of wedlock are not always births to women living alone. In Sweden more than half of all births are to unwed mothers, but perhaps three-quarters of these are to women living in "consensual unions"—ie, stable partnerships. Such households are also common in Britain, where 30% of all births are out of wedlock, but much rarer in America, where one in four births of all babies (and 60-65% of black babies) is to a single mother.

People enter marriage later; they leave it earlier. By far the highest **divorce** rate in the industrial world is that of the United States. On current rates, about half of all American marriages will be dissolved. In Europe, if present rates continue, two out of every five marriages in Britain, Denmark and Sweden will end in divorce, but only one in ten in some southern European countries. "Even in Japan," says John Ermisch, professor of economics at Glasgow University and au-

thor of a recent book on lone parenthood*, "on present trends one marriage in five will eventually end in divorce."

In many countries the divorce rate picked up in the 1960s and accelerated in the 1970s. In the United States the rate doubled between 1966 and 1976. Now it shows signs of levelling off in several countries, including the United States and Sweden (it has fallen in both), Britain and Holland.

More births out of wedlock and more divorce mean more children spending at least part of their youth in **one-parent families**. In the United States a quarter of all families with children are headed by one parent; in Britain, one in five; in Sweden and Denmark, one family in seven. Divorce is the main reason. In the United States, half of all children are likely to witness the break-up of their parents' marriage; in Britain, a quarter; in Norway, a third.

Breaking up

Does a common cause lie behind these changes in the importance of marriage, and particularly in the increase in divorce? Some see a pervasive cultural change, an erosion of morality that has accompanied the decline of religious belief and the rise of materialism. Others point to changes in the laws which have made divorces easier to obtain. Still others see a link with the rise in women's employment.

A change in attitudes to divorce has certainly taken place. In 1945 and again in 1966, national samples of Americans were asked if they thought the divorce laws in their states were too strict or not strict enough. In both years, the most popular response was "not strict enough". But at some point after 1968, a sharp change in attitudes took place. In 1968 and 1974, a sample of Americans was asked whether divorce should be made easier or more difficult. Between the two sample years, the number replying "easier" rose by 15%, while the num-

ber who said "more difficult" declined by 21%. Since then, the proportion who thought divorce should be more difficult has been increasing once again; by 1989 it accounted for a majority of Americans.

But what people believe and what they do may be quite different. Andrew Cherlin, author of a riveting book† on American marriage, draws attention to a group of young mothers who were interviewed several times between 1962 and 1977. At first, half the women agreed with the sentiment: "When there are children in the family, parents should stay together even if they don't get along." But the women who agreed were almost as likely as those who disagreed to divorce in the following 15 years.

Changes in attitudes may have accompanied or followed the rise in divorce, rather than caused it. The same may well be true of changes in the law, although each time a divorce law is made more permissive, the divorce rate tends to rise a little. But for underlying causes it may be wiser to look at the job market rather than the courts.

Since the end of the second world war, the proportion of women in paid employment has risen dramatically in every industrial country. Increasingly, women now go out to work even while their children are toddlers. Almost two-thirds of all women in the OECD have paid work, and in Sweden the proportion (four out of five) is almost as high as for men.

The expanding employment of women is a theme that runs through many of the changes occurring in the family. Gary Becker, professor of economics at Chicago University and winner of the 1992 Nobel prize for economics, has encouraged people to think of the economic forces that influ-

---

* "Lone Parenthood: an Economic Analysis". National Institute of Economic and Social Research

†"Marriage, Divorce, Remarriage". Harvard University Press

ence people to get married and have children. He believes they are as powerful as the forces that govern decisions to buy a new car or change jobs. The better the opportunities for women to earn, the greater the costs of giving up work to have children, and so the later women are likely to start their families and the fewer children they are likely to have. "Children are cheaper during recessions," Mr Becker observed when he gave his presidential address to the American Economics Association.

Mr Becker was by no means the first to point out that women's employment might affect marriage. Back in 1919 one Arthur W. Calhoun argued that "the fact of women's access to industry must be a prime factor in opening to her the possibility of separation from husband." A number of studies, mainly of American women in the 1970s, have shown that married women with jobs are more likely to divorce or separate than those who stay home.

Mr Ermisch, whose book analyses the economic forces behind the break-up of marriages in Britain, establishes that the more time British women spend in paid work, the more likely their marriage is to end in divorce. Of course, it is unlikely that the mere act of getting a job makes women unhappy in their marriages—although, as Mr Ermisch puts it, "Their employment may provide better opportunities for meeting another partner who compares favourably with their present one." But women with an income may worry less about the poverty that generally comes with divorce; and those in unhappy marriages may see employment as an insurance policy.

Fathers don't do the ironing

Once women earn, one of the oldest advantages of marriage is undermined: economic support. Another, sex, is safely available without marriage, thanks to effective contraception. As a result, couples—or rather, wives—are likely to care more about the other potential benefits of marriage, such as emotional support or help in the home.

The extra emphasis on marriage as an emotional partnership may make it more vulnerable. That men and women expect different things from marriage has been the stuff of good novels for many years, but the differences are now minutely picked over by sociologists. Penny Mansfield, a member of One plus One, a British research group, has been studying a group of 65 London couples who married in 1979. Interviewed in the sixth year of their marriage, each partner was asked to describe a range of social and family relationships, and then to say to whom they felt closest. Several husbands (but no wives) were baffled by the question. "I don't know what you mean, 'feel closest to'," said one. "People of most importance in my life? Who I'd be most worried by if something happened to them?"

The gap between expectation and reality grows wider once children arrive. The sort of partnership advocated by romantic magazines is hugely time-consuming. Finding space for all those candle-lit dinners and meaningful conversations is difficult enough when both partners have jobs; it is harder still when they have children as well. True, husbands—at least in the United States and Britain—boast to sociologists like Miss Mansfield that they play a bigger part in running the house than their fathers did. Sadly, as Kathleen Kiernan, of the Family Policy Studies Centre in London, points out in the latest issue of British Social Attitudes, reality is usually different.

She has looked at couples where both partners are employed, and compared men who disagree with the statement, "A husband's job is to earn money; a wife's job is to look after the home and family", with men who agree. The "egalitarian" men are more likely than the fogeys to share household tasks. But whereas half share the shopping and the evening's washing up, only a third share the cleaning or preparation of the evening meal, and only 12% share the washing and ironing. The proportion of couples who think such tasks should be shared has increased since 1984, but the practice has hardly changed.

Washing up the evening dishes seems to be, she reports, "an idiosyncracy of the British male, or a success story for the British female." Seven out of ten British men do at least some of the washing up, compared with an EC average of four out of ten. Maybe this foible of British husbands explains the extraordinary reluctance of their wives to acquire automatic dishwashers. In 1990 only 12% of British households owned dishwashers; 20% had a home computer and 50% a microwave.

Men seem to be more willing to help with looking after children than with household chores. Miss Mansfield, drawing on British and American research, argues that "men who become involved with their children often do so because their partner is working. They tend to have better relationships with both their children and their wives. Indeed, women seem to find it very sexy when men care for their children. It creates a new bond in the marriage."

But if the husbands do not help much in the home, and the job market beckons, some women may wonder what they gain from being married. The costs of divorce may then seem smaller than the costs of staying in an unsatisfactory marriage. The trouble with that siren song is the evidence that divorce is bad for people: for men, for women and, above all, for children.

Married people tend to be healthier people. At every age, as a recent study of Britain by One plus One records, men and women are more likely to die prematurely if they are single, divorced or widowed than if they are married. These differences partly reflect the lower incomes of those who are not mar-

ried. But whatever adjustments are made, it is clear that people suffer physically from not being married—and, incidentally, men suffer more than women.

Wanting out

As ever, some of the links may run both ways. For example, among both sexes, the divorced are the group most likely to be admitted to mental hospitals. This may simply prove that the unstable make difficult partners. Similarly, in Britain divorced men are the heaviest drinkers. But alcoholics may be less likely to marry and more likely to be thrown out by their partners than those who drink moderately.

Divorce also affects living standards. Men may actually see their disposable incomes rise, especially if they pay little or no child support. Official American figures for 1989 found that 41% of all divorced and separated women living with children under 21 received nothing from their former husbands; the rest received on average just over $3,000 a year.

The predictable upshot is that women and children are poorer. A study of American families who have been interviewed each year since 1968 finds that separated and divorced women suffer an average fall of about 30% in their incomes the year after their marriage breaks up. Worst hurt are middle-class wives who have stayed at home. But 31% of all wives whose incomes were above average when they were married found that their living standards fell by more than half in the first year after their marriages collapsed.

To cope with poverty, divorced mothers go out to work. Their working patterns are different from those of their married sisters. In most countries (but not in Britain), they are more likely to have paid work. Even so, they make up a large and growing proportion of the poor in most industrial countries. It may be a struggle to bring up a family on a single male wage with the free childcare that a stay-at-home wife can provide; it is harder still to raise children on a single female wage, especially if they are young enough to need to be looked after.

Moreover, the poverty does not end when the children grow up. For a women, divorce often means losing pension rights, as well as income; in the next century, some of society's poorest people will be elderly women whose marriages broke up in middle age, especially if they had stayed at home to care for the children. The problem could be particularly severe in Britain, where pension rights are rarely divided at divorce.

Heather Joshi, a British economist, has estimated that the lifetime earnings of a married mother of two may be little over a quarter of those of a similarly qualified married man. Marriage, she points out, is often a bargain: the husband can earn more because the wife gives up employment opportunities to care for the home. The labour market is employing the couple, not the husband alone. Pensions legislation, she argues, should recognise that reality.

Divorce makes men unhealthy and women poor. But it also seems to be worse for children than was once thought. Oddly, the long-term effects of divorce on children is an area where little research has been done, and most of the evidence comes from the United States and Britain. It would be helpful to know whether the effects are the same in, for example, Sweden, where lone parents are less poor and single-parenthood seems to be more socially acceptable.

Children suffer

A dramatic account of the effects of divorce on children has come from work by an American, Judith Wallerstein, who studied 131 children from 60 recently separated families at a counselling centre in Marin County, California. She paints a dismal picture. Ten years after their parents' divorce, the boys were "unhappy and lonely"; they and the girls found it hard to form relationships with the opposite sex. Unfortunately, her study was confined to problem families; and as no control group of children in intact families was monitored, it is impossible to know how many of these young Hamlets would have been miserable anyway.

More convincing than such impressionistic research is the work conducted in America and Britain on surveys of random groups of children as they grow up. In the United States, Sara McLanahan has shown that children who grow up in single-parent families are more likely to drop out of school, marry during their teens, have a child before marrying and experience a breakdown of their own marriages. Some of these consequences—perhaps half, she estimates—are related to the poverty of single-parent families. But the rest do indeed seem to be the other consequences of divorce.

Similar results have been found from surveys of British children born in a single week in 1946 and 1958. One study, by Ms Kiernan, found that girls brought up by lone parents were twice as likely to leave home by the age of 18 as the daughters of intact homes—and three times as likely to be cohabiting by the age of 20 and almost three times as likely to have a birth out of wedlock. Boys seemed to be slightly less affected than girls, but were more likely than their sisters to leave school by the age of 16 if they came from a one-parent family. Martin Richards, a Cambridge psychologist, has looked at the children born in 1958 and concludes that the chance of a child going to university is halved by a parental divorce. All these effects, incidentally, are either weaker or nonexistent when a father has died.

Mr Richards also notices another effect. When their mother remarries, the children of a divorce may no longer be poor. But the other effects of divorce are either unchanged or even strengthened. In particular, girls who live in stepfamilies are much more likely to leave school at 16, to leave home because of friction and to be married by the age of 20 than even girls whose divorced mothers do not remarry. And boys in stepfamilies are particularly likely to leave home early because of a quarrel, and to set up home early. "In surveys," he reports sadly, "teenagers from divorced homes say sensible, cautious things about forming relationships; yet they do exactly the opposite. They seem to have a great need for affection, and when they find a relationship, they jump into it."

Many of these effects may be the result not of the divorce, which is easy to record, but of the thunderous atmosphere of a rocky marriage. An important study of children on both sides of the Atlantic appeared in *Science* in June 1991, by Mr Cherlin, Ms Kiernan and five other authors. It argued that "a substantial portion of what is usually considered the effect of divorce on children is visible before the parents separate." For boys in particular, most of the effects usually ascribed to divorce seem to appear before the parents actually break up.

Ask Mr Cherlin what he thinks today about the effects of divorce, and he responds thus: "Divorce is bad for children, but not for all children equally. It is very bad for a small group of children, and moderately bad for many more. If the marriage is truly filled with conflict, it may be better to have a divorce. But here in the United States, many marriages that could limp along end because people are bored. I'm not sure that children are harmed in such marriages."

lessons from stepfamilies

Yes, they are more complicated. But they're also richer. Stepfamilies turn out to be living laboratories for what it takes to create successful relationships. They have surprising things to tell us all about marriage, gender relations, parenting, and the intricacies of family life.

Virginia Rutter

Virginia Rutter is a freelance writer living in Seattle who reports on family, marital, and sex research, among other things. She has worked as public affairs director at the Johns Hopkins School of Public Health and the American Association for Marriage and Family Therapy. She is currently coordinating a project on collaborative, psychosocial health care.

Here we are, three decades into the divorce revolution, and we still don't quite know what to make of stepfamilies. We loved the Brady Bunch, but that was before we discovered how unreal they were. Now that stepfamilies embrace one of three children and, one way or another, impact the vast majority of Americans, we can't seem to get past seeing them as the spawn of failure, the shadow side of our over-idealized traditional family. When we think of them at all, we see only what they are not—hence their designation as "nontraditional" families, heaped with unwed moms, gay parents, and other permutations that make up the majority of families today. By the year 2000, stepfamilies will outnumber all other family types.

Despite their ambiguous standing, stepfamilies are getting first-class attention from social scientists. Much of what they are discovering is eye-opening. Although, for example, it is widely known that second marriages are less stable than first ones—with a break-up rate of 60 percent, versus 50 percent for first marriages—that statistic paints stepfamilies with too broad a brush; it conceals their very real success. A far more useful, more important fact is that stepfamilies do indeed face instability, but that shakiness occurs early in the re-

marriage—and may ultimately be traced to lack of support from the culture. In denying them the status of "real family," we may be doing much to undermine their chances of success. Nevertheless, once remarriage families make it over the early hurdle, they are even stronger than traditional families.

Let this turnabout truth serve as a metaphor for what is now coming to light about stepfamilies. They are certainly more complex than first-marriage families—but they are also richer. New information about what really goes on, and what goes wrong, in stepfamilies will definitely change the way you think about them. It also promises to change the way you think about *all* families. Among the new findings:

• Contrary to myth, stepfamilies have a high rate of success in raising healthy children. Eighty percent of the kids come out fine.

• These stepkids are resilient, and a movement to study their resilience—not just their problems—promises to help more kids succeed in any kind of family, traditional or otherwise.

• What trips stepkids up has little to do with stepfamilies per se. The biggest source of problems for kids in stepfamilies is parental conflict leftover from the first marriage.

• A detailed understanding of the specific problems stepfamilies encounter now exists, courtesy of longitudinal research—not studies that tap just the first six months of stepfamily adjustment.

• Stepfamilies turn out to be a gender trap—expectations about women's roles and responsibilities are at the root of many problems that develop in stepfamilies.

• After five years, stepfamilies are more stable than first-marriage families, because second marriages are happier than first marriages. Stepfamilies experience most of their troubles in the first two years.

• Stepfamilies are not just make-do households limping along after loss. All members experience real gains, notably the opportunity to thrive under a happier relationship.

• The needs of people in stepfamilies are the needs of people in all families—to be accepted, loved, and cared about; to maintain attachments; to belong to a group and not be a stranger; and to feel some control by maintaining order in their lives. It's just that these needs are made acutely visible—and unavoidable—in stepfamilies.

THE MYTHS AND THE RESEARCH

Despite the prevalence of stepfamilies, myths about them abound. You probably know some of them: There's an Evil Stepmother, mean, manipulative, and jealous. The stepfather is a molester, a sexual suspect—Woody Allen. The ex-wife is victimized, vindictive, interfering—a She-Devil. The ex-husband is withdrawn, inept, the contemporary Absentee Father. And the kids are nuisances intent on ruining their parents' lives; like Maisie in Henry James' story of 19th century post-divorce life, they play the parents and stepparents like billiard balls.

The familiarity of these myths can't be blamed solely on Dan Quayle, nor on nostalgia for the 1950s. Stepfamilies are a challenge. There are attachments that must be maintained through a web of conflicting emotions. There are ambiguities of identity, especially in the first years. Adults entering stepfamilies rightly feel anxious about their performance in multiple roles (spouse, instant parent) and about their acceptance by the kids and by the ex-spouse, who must remain a caring parent to the children. When an ex-spouse's children become someone else's stepchildren and spend time in a "stranger's" home, he or she worries about the children's comfort, their role models—and their loyalty.

Out of this worry are born the mythic stereotypes—and the fear of reliving a bad fairy tale. A stepmother, for example, forced to take on the role of disciplinarian because the children's biological father may lack a clear understanding of his own responsibilities—is set up to be cast as evil.

'Stepfamilies turn out to be a gender trap—expectations about women's roles are at the root of many problems that develop in stepfamilies.'

Still, there is a growing recognition among researchers that for every real pitfall a myth is built on, stepfamilies offer a positive opportunity in return. Researchers and stepfamilies are asking questions about resilience and health, not just pathology. In "The Family In Transition," a special issue of the *Journal of Family Psychology* in June 1993, editors and stepfamily researchers Mavis Hetherington, Ph.D., and James Bray, Ph.D., explained it this way: "Although divorce and remarriage may confront families with stresses and adaptive challenges, they also offer opportunities for personal growth and more harmonious, fulfilling family and personal relationships. Contemporary research is focusing on the diversity of responses to divorce, life in a single-parent household, and remarriage."

It is now clear from detailed research that the adaptation to stepfamily relation-

ships depends on the timing of the transition in the children's lives, the individuals involved, and the unique changes and stresses presented to the group.

THE 80 PERCENT WHO SUCCEED

Take Hetherington's research, considered the definitive, longitudinal study of post-divorce families, conducted at the University of Virginia. She found that children in post-divorce and remarriage families may experience depression, conduct disorders, lower academic performance, and delinquency. Such problems are the result of reductions in parental attention that may immediately follow divorce or remarriage. There are the distractions of starting a new marriage. Such lapses may also be the outgrowth of parental conflict. They may reflect a noncustodial parent's withdrawal from the scene altogether. There's the stress of reductions in resources—typically, the lowered income of divorced mothers—and the disruption of routines, so highly valued by children, when two residences are established.

Hetherington, however, is quick to point to her finding that 80 percent of children of divorce and remarriage do *not* have behavior problems, despite the expectations and challenges, compared to 90 percent of children of first marriage families. Kids whose parents divorce and remarry are not doomed.

This high success rate, Hetherington and others recognize, is a testament to the resilience of children. Further study, she believes, can teach us more about the strengths summoned up in stepfamilies—and how to support them. But that would also contradict the gloom-and-doom scenarios that, though they do not actually describe most stepfamilies, often get trotted out on state occasions.

Needless to say, scientifically researching strength and resilience in stepfamilies, complete with a control group, poses great challenges. Building a scientific model of stepfamilies isn't simply trying to pin down a moving target, it's like trying to pin down many moving targets—up to four sets of kids from previous marriages in as many residences at different times—with none of them on the same radar screen at once.

From the standpoint of the kids, yes, they feel loss going into a stepfamily—it certifies that their original family exists no more. And it takes time to adjust to a new set of people in family roles. But the new arrangement is not just a problem appearing in their lives by default. Elizabeth Carter, M.S.W., director of the Westches-

ter Family Institute, points to specific opportunities a stepfamily affords. Children acquire multiple role models, they get a chance to see their parents happier with other people than they were with each other. They learn how to be flexible.

Because they come into the world with no relationship ties but must forge their own, stepfamilies provide a living laboratory for studying what makes all families successful, insists psychologist Emily Visher, Ph.D., who cofounded the Stepfamily Association of America in 1979 with her husband, psychiatrist John Visher, M.D., after finding herself in a stepfamily and no rules to go by. For their pioneering efforts, the Vishers jointly received a Lifetime Contribution Award from the American Association for Marriage and Family Therapy at its annual meeting last fall.

Addressing an audience packed to the rafters in a mammoth sports arena, Visher

'Stepfamilies provide lessons for all families, because their emotions and problems are common—but they are exposed by an open structure.'

emphasized that "stepfamilies provide lessons for all families, because their emotions and problems are common to all people—but they are exposed by the open structure of stepfamilies." The process of bonding and belonging is made entirely, sometimes painfully, visible.

THE COPARENTING FACTOR

It turns out that it's the parents, not the stepfamily, that make the most difference in the success of stepfamilies.

"Remember, divorce isn't ending the family. It is restructuring it," explains Carter. "Parents and children don't get divorced. Parents and children aren't an optional relationship. One of the biggest issues for stepfamilies is: How can we stay in touch?" The steady, regular involvement of both biological parents in their children's lives come what may is known in the family biz as coparenting.

Today's most familiar stepfamily setup is a mother and her biological children living with a man who is not their birth father, and a noncustodial father in another residence—although the dilemmas of maintaining parenting responsibilities are much more complicated than who lives with whom. The U.S. Bureau of the Census reports that 14 percent of children in stepfamilies live with their biological father, 86 percent live with their biological mother and their stepfather. Whatever the situation, the parents' job is to find a way to stay in touch with each other so that both can remain completely in touch with their children.

Study after study shows that divorce and remarriage do not harm children—parental conflict does. That was the conclusion of research psychologists Robert Emery, Ph.D., of the University of Virginia, and Rex Forehand, Ph.D., of the University of Georgia, in a 1993 review of the divorce research. Sociologist Andrew Cherlin, Ph.D., author of the classic *Divided Families,* reported in *Science* magazine that children with difficulty after divorce started having problems long before divorce took place, as a result of parental conflict.

While divorce forces temporary disruption and a period of adjustment to loss and to new routines, marital conflict produces long-term disturbances. Depression and anger, often acted out in behavior problems, substance abuse, and delinquency, are all especially common among children in families where conflict rages. Following divorce, adversarial coparenting or the withdrawal of one of the parents from his or her (but usually his) role undermines children's healthy development.

The solution, of course, is cooperation of the parents in coparenting following divorce and remarriage. Desirable as it is, cooperative parenting between divorced spouses is rare, attained only in a minority of cases, Hetherington and Bray note.

WHY IS COPARENTING SO DIFFICULT?

Most marriages don't end mutually with friendship—so jealousy and animosity are easily aroused—and ex-spouses aren't two folks practiced at getting along anyway. Yet the ability of exes to get along is a key to the success of a new stepfamily.

Remarriage of one or both ex-spouses only enlarges the challenge of getting along —while possibly increasing tension between the ex-spouses responsible for coparenting. A stepparent who becomes a part of the kids' lives usually has no relationship to the child's other biological parent; if anything there is hostility.

The ideal, says John Visher, is creation of a "parenting coalition" among the parents and stepparents in both households. "From the beginning, the new couple needs to work together in making family decisions." One of the most important is how, and by whom, the children will be disciplined, and on that score the evidence is clear: only a birth parent has the authority to discipline his or her children.

Betty Carter is quick to warn, however, that stepparents cannot interfere with their spouse in parenting. Involved but not interfering? A parenting coalition requires the parents include their new spouses in family decisions. The new spouses, for their part, must support the parenting duties and the coparenting bond between the ex-spouses.

IT TAKES RESPECT

The glue that makes it all happen is respect, the Vishers report. Both parents must require kids and stepparents to treat one another with respect. Only then can bonds between them develop. Despite feelings of jealousy and animosity, first and second spouses must also accord one another respect to accomplish the coparenting tasks the children need to do well.

For their part, the kids also need each of the coparents to refer to the other parent with respect. Children are quick to pick up hints of hostility on either side. For them, hostility becomes an invitation to play the grown-ups off each other, and to imitate unkind behavior.

'Children are quick to pick up hints of hostility on either side. For them, it becomes an open invitation to play the grown-ups off each other.'

When the parents are adversarial, their hostility inhibits children from freely spending time with both parents, and the kids suffer. They lack the one-on-one attention that breeds a sense of self-value. And they are torn in half. All in all, it's a recipe for disappointment and anger.

ANY HELP?

"If you can help parents and stepparents early on to deal with issues of child-rearing appropriately, they have a lot of potential for giving stability to children and exposing them to appropriately happy relationships," says Australian research psychologist Jan Lawton. Lawton is spokesperson for The Stepfamily Project at the University of Queensland, a major government study of behavioral interventions for stepfamilies with troubled children.

What kind of help do stepfamilies need? Information and support. Stepfamily support groups exist across the United States, many of them organized by the Stepfamily Association. The organization responds to about 400 information requests each week from stepfamilies—while 7,000 new stepfamilies are forming weekly.

Stepfamily functioning improves dramatically when participants know which problems are normal, which are temporary, and that it takes time for people to integrate themselves and feel comfortable in a stepfamily. Lawton's study has demonstrated the benefits of practical guidance, and she has found that even a little help goes a long way. "The positive part of this study is that we can help stepfamilies with a very minimal amount of therapy and self-help, aimed at the right areas." The components of the Queensland program are a map of stepfamily problem areas.

•Child-Management Training, for parents and stepparents, to help them focus their attention on the children at a time when there's a tendency to slip a little on monitoring and disciplining the kids. The adults often get overly absorbed in their new romance.

•Partner-Support Training for newly remarried couples, since they don't automatically work together as a team during the first two years, when they are also at high risk for divorce. Such support helps them while their relationship is undergoing trial by fire in the new stepfamily.

•Communication and Problem-Solving Training for the entire new stepfamily helps everyone learn to talk together, understand each other, and learn how to solve problems and reach consensus.

Lawton reports as much as a 60 percent reduction in behavior problems and about 50 percent improvement in child adjustment, self-esteem, and parent/stepparent conflict. While therapy had a slight margin over self-help, persons in both groups outperformed by far the control group that received no help during the study. Those with the most troubled children do best with formal therapy; the rest do fine with self-help. Indeed, programs families could apply at home are especially useful, since stepfamilies involve people already weighed down by multiple demands, and coordinating a formal appointment can be formidable.

The key, Lawton says, is to reach stepfamilies at the beginning when they need basic information about what to expect. Lawton's next project is a prevention study, seeking the most effective ways to help all stepfamilies—not just ones where the children have behavior problems.

MORE HELP: A HAPPY MARRIAGE

If coparenting can be accomplished, children benefit in at least two ways. They feel loved by both biological parents; no child can thrive without affectionate connections. And they gain from being exposed to remarried adults in a successful intimate relationship. Especially when remarriage occurs before the children are teenagers, there is great potential for easy adaptation and smooth development.

A remarriage at adolescence, however, poses added challenges to adjustment and success of the stepfamily, Bray and Hetherington report. It's a critical time of identity formation. Daughters are particularly apt to get into fights with stepmothers. Sexual tension may develop between stepfather and a budding adolescent stepdaughter, manifest in aloofness and what every parent knows as snottiness. Even if the divorce occurred many years before, a parent's remarriage during a child's teen years can revive adjustment difficulties that may have cropped up during the divorce.

Generally, though, a successful second marriage helps to reduce—if not eliminate—kids' problems. Divorced people are generally more compatible with their second partner than their first—even though there is a higher divorce rate among second marriages.

Clinical psychology lore has it that the high divorce rate is because the spouses are making the same mistake again. Divorcing spouses have problems with intimate relationships, not with a particular partner, the

thinking goes, and they are more apt to bail out a second time.

But this view is totally contradicted by those who have closely scrutinized many stepfamilies. The Vishers are among them. So is University of Southern California sociologist Constance Ahrons, Ph.D. They point out that a lot of second divorces are the result not of conventional marital deterioration but of problems in integrating into a household children and adults who are not related to each other.

"The divorce rate among remarried families is high in the first two years—then it slows down," says Lawton. "By about the five-year period, second relationships are more stable than first relationships. I see these couples at very high risk during the first few years, but thereafter offering great benefits to the children."

LOOKING AT THE PROBLEMS

While stepfamilies are doing a lot better than they're generally given credit for, a not insubstantial 20 percent of them—or twice the number of first-marriage families—do have problems with the kids. The research illuminating the specific problems in stepfamilies points to the basic requirements of stepfamilies as the major stumbling blocks. Cooperative coparenting. Equal involvement of both parents after the divorce. Noninterference by stepparents.

'Sexual tension may develop between stepfather and adolescent stepdaughter, and manifest in aloofness and snottiness.'

Support for the coparenting relationship.

Bray's longitudinal study of stepfamilies has tracked mothers, stepfathers, and children, who were around six years old at the time of remarriage, over the next seven years. During the early months of remarriage, behavior problems rise steeply among the children. This is a time when stepfamilies are not yet cohesive—they are not likely to think of themselves as a unit.

Gradually, behavior problems subside over the next two years. By then stepfamilies are just as likely as first-marriage families to have developed useful ways of communicating, rules of behavior, and discipline. They may not consider themselves as cohesive, but objective evaluation finds few practical differences.

In Bray's study, trouble with the children developed when there was a reduction in time and attention from one or both parents, and reduced resources. These parental lapses, Bray notes, arise most often from problems of coparenting, and difficulties of stepparents in supporting the coparenting role.

But even the reduced parental attention does not doom the children. Hetherington observes that the reduced parental attention can also be seen as an opportunity for the children to take on responsibility. The end result is that some children—almost always daughters—wind up more capable and competent.

Others, however, particularly at adolescence, respond to the lapse of parental attention by going off and experimenting with sex or drugs. Younger children may display more conduct problems and depression. Both younger and older kids are at risk for lower academic achievement.

While few distinctions turn up between the ways daughters and sons react to being in a stepfamily, Bray did find increased conflict between stepfathers and stepdaughters at puberty. Hetherington also found difficulties with teenage daughters, and warns that remarriage when a daughter is entering adolescence promises to produce tremendous tension and resentment on the part of the daughter.

Daughters, who have grown close to their mothers and increasingly identify with them at the onset of puberty, will have difficulty with the addition of either a mother's new spouse, who is competition for her, or a father's new spouse—who is competition for her mother. What the girls are feeling is divided loyalty.

DIVIDED LOYALTIES

Stepfamilies are littered with possibilities for loyalty conflicts, say the Vishers. A particularly common one revolves around entry of new stepparent. A mom feels hostile toward her ex-husband's new partner; kids understand that their mom wants them to feel the same way. The same kids are also being asked by their dad to love the new wife, whom he loves. The kids feel torn because their parents are pulling them in opposite ways.

It is an axiom of psychology that when kids feel torn, they erupt in symptoms—like bad behavior or depression. It may be a desperate attempt to draw attention away from the unresolvable conflict between the parents. Whatever the source of divided loyalties, once kids feel them, they develop problems—if not behavior problems or depression, then the symptoms of anxiety. The solution? Back to coparenting. It is up to the adults to rise above jealousy or romanticism and work together for the good of the kids.

The respect they use to make the system operate must include appreciation for the inevitability of ambivalent feelings in the kids. And that, says Emily Visher, is one of the most important lessons from stepfamilies for all families. "The ability of adults to share with children ambivalence over loss and change determines how well they will do in the future. It paves the way for sharing other thoughts. It leads to a sense of mastery of whatever life presents."

> **'Lesson #1:
> The ability of adults to share with kids ambivalence over loss and change determines how well they will do in the future.'**

One of the sizable traps in remarriage is the temptation a new spouse may feel to interfere with the coparenting process, observes William Doherty, Ph.D., family social scientist at the University of Minnesota. The new spouse may feel insecure or jealous of the coparent's continuing attachment to the former spouse. Still, that only succeeds in dividing the loyalty of the biological parent. A weekly conversation with an ex-spouse about the kids might trouble an anxious new spouse—but the communication is essential and the stepparent has the obligation to adjust, just as the parents do, for the good of the kids.

On the other hand, no stepparent should be expected to love, or even like, a partner's kids, nor must demands be placed on kids to love the stepparent. Loyalty just can't be forced. A strong couple relationship is necessary to the success of the stepfamily, but it cannot hinge on whether the stepparent likes the kids, marital therapists agree. After all, a stepfamily essentially brings together strangers.

THE BASIC NEED: ACCEPTANCE

Stepfamilies can't push members into close relationships; still, they may feel the pain of absence of intimacy. Stepfamily life throws into bold relief very fundamental human needs—above all, says John Visher, the need to be a part of something. Entry into a stepfamily puts members in a position of assessing whether they are an insider or an outsider. A new wife belongs to her new husband, and he to her, but she is not a natural part of the husband's children's life. Feeling like an outsider to their relationship may be upsetting to her.

There's no fast solution for the inside/outside dilemma; stepfamilies come with a big catch in their very structure. The relationship between the parents and children predates the new marital relationship. It may even seem to outweigh it. A parent's love for a child must always be unconditional; couple love is not.

Joan Giacomini, a remarried parent and university administrator in Seattle, warns that it is hard for stepmothers to adjust to the fact that they are not number one to their new spouse. "There may be a handful of number ones, but you aren't the only number one," she says.

That gives rise to an all-too-common scenario: a remarried stepparent—often the stepmother—asks, "who is it going to be, me or your kids?" It's a false question—it leads to what Carter calls a "fake fight"—because it erroneously equates parent–child relationships and marital relationships, apples and oranges. Children are dependents; parental obligations to them are always unconditional.

Because the loyalty challenge rests on a mistaken assumption, Carter says, the proper solution is acceptance that relationships between parent and child are qualitatively different from those between spouses. Still, such conflicts can recur from time to time, as life continually presents new situations that assault the loyalties, resources, and time of kids and spouses.

THE ULTIMATE TRAP

Name a stepfamily dilemma and women—biomothers, stepmothers, even stepdaughters—are at the center of the problem. Psychologists know that women are always more likely to express distress wherever troubles exist. But stepfamilies are the ultimate gender trap. Ever-sensitive to interpersonal problems, women sense problems all over the place in stepfamilies.

Traditional male and female roles are troublesome enough, for the marriage and the children, in first-marriage families. But they wreak havoc on stepfamilies, Carter explains; they don't work at all. Indeed, researchers report that there's more equality in the marriage and in the distribution of domestic tasks in stepfamilies. But they still have a lot to learn—or unlearn—about gender roles and domestic life.

"No matter what we say or how feminist you are, everybody knows that women take care of children and men bring in most of the money. This sucks the stepmother into a quagmire of traditional domestic roles; it's not only that somebody makes her do it, she also does it to herself," explains Carter, coauthor of *The Invisible Web: Gender Patterns in Family Relationships*.

"We are raised to believe that we are responsible for everybody. A stepmother sees the children as unhappy and the husband as ineffectual, and she moves in to be helpful. Mavis Hetherington's research shows the consequence of this: a lot of fighting between teenage stepdaughters and stepmothers." Nevertheless, women move toward a problem to work on it—whether it's theirs to work on or not.

Trouble is, explains Carter, "in stepfamilies, everybody has to be in charge of their own children. A biological father has to understand that it is his responsibility to take charge. The stepmother has to back off, let the father do the monitoring and caretaking of the kids—even let him do it wrong. This is very hard to do; it flies in the face of all our gender training."

What's more, a large body of research on depression and marriage demonstrates that women's self-esteem becomes contingent upon relationships going smoothly; it holds in stepfamilies, as well. Women get depressed when stepfamily life goes badly, and they blame themselves.

For all its difficulty, the way parents in stepfamilies devise to take care of their own children contains another lesson for all families. "Stepfamilies demonstrate the importance of one-on-one relationships," says Emily Visher. "Parent–child alone time maintains the security of relationships. It requires conscious planning in all families. The health of all families resides in the quality of the relationships between members."

THE MYTH OF
THE HAPPY FAMILY

If stepfamilies make it out of the gender trap, there's one more to avoid—the myth of the nuclear family. Successful stepfamilies let go of their fantasy of a traditional family life, reports James Bray. They become more realistic, less romantic, and more flexible about family. They can cope with what life deals.

But remarriage often sets up conditions pulling the other way. "There's often a sense of defensiveness," explains Betty Carter. "There's a feeling of 'let's not rock the boat this time. Let's be a happy family immediately so we can prove that this complicated thing—the divorce, the new marriage—was the right move.' People try to achieve an instant family, they don't allow for disgruntlement, fear, anxiety. Now we know it takes about five years for a stepfamily to become fully integrated."

Carter advises stepfamilies to "kiss the nuclear family good-bye. Stepfamilies simply cannot draw a tight circle around the household in the same way that nuclear families do. That always excludes somebody." The stepfamily's task is to keep permeable boundaries around the household, to facilitate coparenting, and to allow children access to the noncustodial parent.

It's a lot like tightrope-walking. "At the very time a stepfamily is trying to achieve its own integration, it has to keep the doors wide open and stay in touch with another household. You are not the lord of all you survey, as in the traditional family myth. You are on the phone regularly with someone about whom you feel, at best, ambivalent."

WHAT TO CALL IT?

Perhaps the most concrete evidence that old-fashioned family ideas don't work for stepfamilies is in the labels stepfamilies prefer for themselves.

Some people reject the label "stepfamily" altogether. Joan Giacomini is one. She is divorced from her grown children's father; he is remarried and has a toddler boy. Joan's husband has grown children from his first marriage, too, but she doesn't want to be referred to as a stepmother, nor does she like the idea of someone being referred to as the "stepmother" of her children.

"In our cases, we don't do any mothering. No one else is mother to my children, and my husband's children have their own mother," she explains. "One of my main goals is to respect their first family, so that they can have their relationships without worry about me." Despite dropping the "step" terminology, Giacomini's various families comprise a successful stepfamily that has respect, shared responsibility, even shared holidays.

Many stepfamilies who start off using step terminology eventually drop it all, reports James Bray. It may be the surest sign of integration. The terms "stepmother" and "stepfather" help clarify roles and remind everybody who belongs to whom, and under what terms, in the transition. Later, though, they don't bother with such names. "Labels connote a struggle for identity that doesn't exist anymore for these groups," says Bray.

For other stepfamilies, such as Ned and Joanna Fox—my mother and her husband—in Charlotte, North Carolina, there is little thought of stepfamily integration.

Nobody considers it a stepfamily, nor is anyone a stepsibling or stepparent. The kids were grown when the divorces and remarriages occurred, and none of the kids seem particularly interested in getting involved with the others. While Joanna's children treat Ned like an uncle, and value his love for Joanna, Ned's children don't warm up to the situation.

The moral of the story: Every stepfamily is different.

Some reject not merely the "stepfamily" label but stepfamily roles as well. In fact, the best way for a new spouse to move into stepparent life, suggests Barry Dym, Ph.D., a family psychologist (and remarried father) in Cambridge, Massachusetts, may be to find a different role than that of stepparent. The term itself may force the relationships into an unrealistic, and even intrusive, parental mold.

Dym suggests that stepmothers might do better modeling themselves after a favorite aunt—involved, but not the mother. My favorite aunt provides acceptance, guidance, honesty, but the obligation on either side is voluntary. If I become a stepmother, I think I'll be an aunt.

The naming issue underscores what stepfamilies have that original families don't always get: there is no monolithic view of what a stepfamily is supposed to be, or even be called. To catalog stepfamily experiences would be to catalog all relationships—there is endless variety, and unlimited routes to success or failure. Unlike traditional families, stepfamilies allow much more room for diversity. And equality. Count that as the ultimate lesson from stepfamilies.

THE MYTHS AND MISCONCEPTIONS OF THE STEPMOTHER IDENTITY

DESCRIPTIONS AND PRESCRIPTIONS FOR

IDENTITY MANAGEMENT*

There are two cross-cultural and trans-historical myths associated with stepmotherhood: the evil stepmother myth and the myth of instant love. The tenacity of these myths has served to stigmatize stepmothers. This paper describes the myths associated with stepmothers, details how these myths affect stepmother life, reveals dilemmas in identity management for stepmothers, and indicates identity management strategies stepmothers might utilize.

Marianne Dainton

Marianne Dainton is a doctoral student at Ohio State University, Department of Communication, 319 Neil Hall, Columbus, OH 43210.

In America there are a multitude of family forms, one of which is the stepfamily. Statistics indicate that currently 16% of all married couples in this country have at least one stepchild (Moorman & Hernandez, 1989). Moreover, current predictions are that 35% to 40% of children born in the 1980s will spend time in a stepparent family before they are young adults (Coleman & Ganong, 1990a).

Although researchers are increasingly turning their attention to the stepfamily form, there are many areas of stepfamily life that have not received adequate attention (Coleman & Ganong, 1990a). One such area is the effect of myths about stepfamily relations on stepfamily members. A focus upon myths is salient to the study of stepfamilies in general, and stepmothers in particular, because of the prevalence of myths concerning step-relations. For example, at least three of the Brothers Grimm's fairy tales—"Hansel and Gretel," "Cinderella," and "Snow White"—revolve

*The author would like to thank Patrick McKenry and Dirk Scheerhorn for editorial comments, and three anonymous reviewers for their valuable suggestions.

Key Words: identity management, myths, stepmothers, stigma.

around the actions of an evil stepmother. These stories may appear innocuous enough, unless of course you happen to be a stepmother or a stepchild. "Fairies do not exist, and witches do not exist, but stepmothers do exist, and therefore certain fairy tales are harmful rather than helpful to large segments of the population" (Visher & Visher, 1979, p. 6).

The myths associated with stepmotherhood may constrain stepmothers' identity management. Identity management refers to efforts on the part of stepmothers to foster preferred perceptions about themselves. Accordingly, this article examines some of the impediments to the identity management strategies enacted by stepmothers. Specifically, throughout the course of this article the myths and misconceptions of stepmotherhood will be identified, the implications of these myths for stepmothers will be discussed, issues of identity will be elaborated, and, finally, some initial steps toward identity management strategies for stepmothers will be detailed.

STEPMOTHER MYTHS

The term *myth* is popularly conceived to be analogous to "falsehood." Indeed, myths often contain false and/or negative information. Scholars, however, define myth as a recurring theme or character type that incorporates infor-

mation about cultural standards (Birenbaum, 1988). Thus, myths represent a way of viewing the world that embodies a culture's beliefs, regardless of whether these beliefs are accurate.

According to Bruner (1960), myths can be characterized by two components. The first component is an externalization, which Bruner describes as a "corpus of images and identities" (p. 280). This externalization provides a cultural explanation of the way the world works. The second component is an internalization. Bruner argues that a myth can only exist to the extent that cultural members internalize personal identities based upon the externalized corpus of ideas propagated by the myth.

Regarding stepmotherhood, there are two generic myths that are simultaneously cross-cultural and transhistorical (Schulman, 1972). The first of the myths is that of the *evil stepmother,* a myth propagated through fiction of all forms. The second myth is that of *instant love,* wherein a stepmother is expected to immediately assimilate into a family and to love the children as if they were her own. Each will be discussed in turn.

Myth #1: The Evil Stepmother

The myth of the evil stepmother has a strong and inveterate legacy; the negative connotations of the term *step* were firmly in place as early as 1400 (Wald,

From *Family Relations,* Vol. 42, No. 1, January 1993, pp. 93-98. © 1993 by the National Council of Family Relations, 3989 Central Avenue, NE, Suite 550, Minneapolis, MN 55421. Reprinted by permission.

1981). Moreover, scholars have identified the existence of evil stepmother folktales in virtually every part of the world. In fact, Smith (1953) identifies 345 versions of the "Cinderella" story alone, revealing the evil stepmother myth as a global phenomenon.

Although evil stepmothers appear in all genres of fiction, the evil stepmother is particularly prevalent in fairy tales (Wald, 1981). In an analysis of fairy tales, one researcher found that the most frequent representations of evil included bears, wolves, giants and ogres, witches, and stepmothers (Sutton-Smith, 1971, cited in Wald, 1981). Thus, fairy tales suggest that stepmothers are the equivalent of wild animals and supernatural beings—entities that children have very little chance of facing in real life—in their wicked treatment of children.

Myth #2: Instant Love

The second myth is instant love (Schulman, 1972; Visher & Visher, 1988; Wald, 1981). This myth is based upon cultural standards about mothering (Visher & Visher, 1988), and the resulting societal expectations about stepmothers' assimilation into the family. Specifically, the myth maintains that remarriage in and of itself creates an instant family, that stepmothers should (and will) automatically love their stepchildren, and that stepchildren will automatically love their stepmother. Further, because of this love, mothering is assumed to come naturally and easily.

In reality, none of the above necessarily happens. Counselors working with stepmothers suggest that many women are surprised and dismayed when they don't feel immediate love for their stepchildren (Lofas & Sova, 1985). Moreover, stepchildren are often afraid, unsure, and uncomfortable with the changes in the family, and may express these feelings by being surly and resentful. As a result, many stepmothers experience a great deal of ambivalence regarding their stepchildren (Ambert, 1986).

The Prevalence of These Myths Today

Despite the increasing number of stepfamilies in America today, the myths identified above show no signs of losing strength. In a series of research efforts, one group of researchers found that the role of stepmother elicited more negative connotations than any other family position (Bryan, Coleman, Ganong, & Bryan, 1986; Ganong & Coleman, 1983). Specifically, stepmothers were perceived as less affectionate, good, fair, kind, loving, happy, and likable, and

more cruel, hateful, unfair, and unloving. More recently, researchers have determined that these negative perceptions still stand, although there is little difference in the perceptions of stepmothers and stepfathers (Fluitt & Paradise, 1991; Ganong, Coleman, & Kennedy, 1990). Similarly, clinicians assert that the myth of instant love has yet to be replaced by more realistic expectations (Visher & Visher, 1988).

Individually, these myths negatively affect the experiences of stepmothers. For example, both clinical and empirical evidence reveals that stepmothers identify the wicked stepmother myth as directly contributing to the stress they experience in adapting to the stepmother role (Duberman, 1973; Hughes, 1991; Visher & Visher, 1979). Further, counselors have identified the unrealistic expectations associated with the myth of instant love as a possible cause of stress for stepmothers in general, and have suggested that such expectations may actively interfere with the family integration that the myth promises (Visher & Visher, 1988).

Ironically, these myths provide external images of the stepmother that are at polar extremes; one myth depicts stepmothers as unrealistically evil, the other as unrealistically loving and competent. Together, these contradictory images may contribute to identity management difficulties, as stepmothers must struggle with internalizing two conflicting sets of ultimately unrealistic expectations. Clearly, taking on the mantle of stepmother includes not only taking on the responsibility of a family, but taking on a host of potential identity management challenges (Hughes, 1991; Visher & Visher, 1979, 1988).

THE CONCEPT OF IDENTITY

Before discussing the identity issues associated with stepmotherhood, some fundamental issues surrounding the concept of identity itself must be addressed. In so doing, some critical distinctions between key terms need to be made. Finally, a framework for understanding identity management must be constructed.

First, *identity* can be defined as an individual's self-concept (McCall & Simmons, 1978). Thus, an individual's identity involves beliefs about whom he or she is, and how he or she should be perceived and treated in social life (Schlenker, 1980). Although our identities are frequently manifested in the roles that we enact, the notion of identity is broader than that of roles. Definitionally, *roles* are expectations held

about the occupant of a social status or a position in a social system, while *identity* is a constellation of all of the roles an individual performs (McCall & Simmons, 1978).

The same distinction can be made between role performance and identity management. A *role performance* (also known as *role enactment*) is the individual's day-to-day behavior associated with a given role (McCall & Simmons, 1978). *Identity management,* on the other hand, is a broader concept; it is an individual's efforts to foster perceptions (usually positive) relevant to his or her self-concept. Similar terms include *self-presentation* (Goffman, 1959) and *impression management* (Schlenker, 1980).

The definitions above imply that an identity is chosen. This is not always the case. McCall and Simmons (1978) assert that individuals do not entirely have discretion in the roles they will enact, and hence in the perceptions others will have of them. For example, most stepmothers do not choose the stepmother persona; it is thrust upon them when they choose to marry a man with children. Identity management for stepmothers, then, is not simply the process of maintaining preferred perceptions, but of preventing unwanted perceptions associated with preconceived evaluations of a given social role.

To clarify, McCall and Simmons argue that each role identity has two elements: the *conventional* and the *idiosyncratic.* The conventional aspect of a role identity consists of social stereotypes. These stereotypes might be captured in myths such as the myths associated with stepmotherhood. The idiosyncratic elements of a role identity, on the other hand, are those characteristics an individual modifies and elaborates within the given role.

IDENTITY DILEMMAS

Generally, identities are inferred by appearance and actions (McCall & Simmons, 1978). In the case of stepmothers, however, the perceptions associated with stepmotherhood are not conveyed by appearance or actions, but are label-bound. Accordingly, stepmothers fulfill the requirements of being a stigmatized group. *Stigmas* are products of definitional processes in which a defining attribute (such as being a stepmother) eclipses other aspects of the stigmatized person, including individual personalities and abilities (Ainlay, Coleman, & Becker, 1986; Stafford & Scott, 1986). Thus stigmas are categorizations that often involve negative affect (Jones et al., 1984).

Goffman (1963) posits that stigmatization is the result of the relationship between a particular attribute and a stereotype about that attribute. "Society establishes the means of categorizing persons and the complement of attributes felt to be ordinary and natural for members of each of these categories" (Goffman, 1963, p. 2). Ironically, the "ordinary and natural" attributes that society has established for stepmothers (through myths) are that they are inherently wicked, yet capable of providing instant love. It is the very fact that stepmothers are characterized in such an extraordinary manner that causes their stigmatization.

Further, Goffman (1963) argues that there are two primary types of stigmas: the *discredited* and the *discreditable*. Discredited individuals are those in which the stigma is immediately apparent (e.g., those with physical deformities). Discreditable individuals are those whose stigma is not known or immediately perceivable. The fact that stepmothers' stigma is not visually apparent would lead one to believe that they have a discreditable stigma. That is, despite fairy tales' depiction of stepmothers as evil hags, real stepmothers look just like real mothers. Their stigma is not immediately apparent.

However, with different audiences stepmothers are sometimes discredited and sometimes discreditable. For example, members of the stepfamily are aware of a woman's stepmother status, so in their eyes she is discredited. In the general public, however, a stepmother remains merely discreditable. This contradiction brings up one of the major problems stepmothers have with identity management; part of the dilemma of managing a stepmother identity is the public/private dichotomy. Stepmothers believe that they are judged based on stepmother myths in both the public and private arenas of social life (Hughes, 1991). Because of this, stepmothers may find themselves with the paradox of having inconsistent identity management strategies become necessary to manage the same identity.

Goffman (1963) has identified two broad classes of identity management strategies. *Corrective practices* are what people do after their preferred identity is threatened. According to Goffman, it is likely that discredited individuals will be forced to engage in corrective strategies. *Preventative strategies,* on the other hand, are behaviors an individual uses to avoid negative perceptions. In general, the discreditable will rely on preventative strategies.

In order to determine which class of strategies to enact, a stepmother must consider a contextual matrix. That is, stepmothers must consider where they are and who their audience is in order to select the appropriate identity management techniques (McCall & Simmons, 1978). This matrix might look like the one in Figure 1.

As the matrix shows, stepmothers face competing concerns when selecting identity strategies: *who* and *where.* Within each of these superordinate categories is a dichotomy. For example, when considering who, a stepmother might be in the company of her family or she may be in the company of some generalized others. When considering *where,* she might be in private (e.g., at home) or in public (e.g., a restaurant).

Taking each quadrant of the grid in turn, the following issues are stressed. First, the upper left quadrant is one in which there is little inconsistency. Here, stepmothers are with their family in private. Given that they are already discredited in this forum (i.e., their stigma is known), it is likely that they will utilize corrective identity management strategies in this case. Such strategies might include assertive techniques described by Jones and Pittman (1980) like *exemplification* (projecting integrity), *self-promotion* (showing competence in mothering), or *ingratiation* (being helpful and positive).

Similarly, there is probably little quandary about strategy selection when in the others/public quadrant; here, the stepmother is discreditable (her stigma is not known). Accordingly, it is likely a stepmother would select what Goffman (1963) describes as preventative strategies, such as *passing* (behaving in a way consistent with a nonstigmatized identity without specifically claiming to be nonstigmatized) or using *disidentifiers* (behaviors deliberately used to indicate a nonstigmatized identity, e.g., saying "my son" instead of "my stepson").

The two remaining quadrants might cause psychological tension between competing identity management options, however. For example, in the family/public quadrant, an initial reaction might be to use preventative strategies. After all, other patrons of a restaurant have little need to know that the normal family seated next to them might in fact be a stepfamily. However, if a stepmother selects such strategies she is neither accomplishing her goal of overcoming negative perceptions within the family, nor is she safe from intentional or unintentional unmasking. The last quadrant, others/private, is liable to involve a very different sort of tension. An example of such a situation is holding a professional gathering at home. Given that the interaction is at home, her stigma is already known among family members who may be present. Therefore, corrective strategies might seem appropriate. However, because she is also with nonintimate others, preventative strategies might be preferred. Here, the tension reflects a pull towards actively managing existing negative stereotypes within the family, and at the same time preventing others from learning of the stigma.

Confounding contextual constraints are the ways in which expectations based upon stepmother myths affect our identity management. That is, people might interpret a stepmother's behavior as negative (even if by objective measures it is not) simply because stepmothers' behaviors are expected to be negative (Coleman & Ganong, 1987a; for a discussion about how this process might work, see Darley & Gross, 1983). A dilemma that stepmothers face, then, is whether they should use corrective strategies at all, since any efforts to actively repair others' perceptions might be interpreted unfavorably. She is stuck in a "damned if you do, damned if you don't" situation.

A final identity management dilemma stepmothers face is related to the

Figure 1. *Matrix for Stepmothers' Identity Management Strategies*

Who

		Family	Others
Where	Private	Corrective	???
	Public	???	Preventative

extent to which they play an active parenting role. That is, in attempting to fulfill the stepparent role, stepmothers are in a double bind. On one hand, they are expected to love the child as if he or she were their own, but on the other hand, they are often sanctioned against adopting a bona fide parental role (Visher & Visher, 1979). Thus, becoming a stepmother requires a careful balancing act, wherein a woman must regulate perceptions of involvement without being perceived as overinvolved or uncaring.

The dilemma described above is complicated by the ambiguity associated with the stepmother role. According to Cherlin (1978), remarriage represents an "incomplete institution" because there are few norms or rules to define expected behavior in stepfamily life. Cherlin posits that this ambiguity causes stress on family members. There is recent evidence for this hypothesis; in a review of the literature, Fine and Schwebel (1991) identified role ambiguity as the core difficulty in stepfamilies.

Role ambiguity involves four types of uncertainty: (a) uncertainty about the scope of one's responsibilities; (b) uncertainty about the particular behaviors needed to fulfill one's responsibilities; (c) uncertainty about whose expectations for role behavior must be met; and (d) uncertainty about the effects of one's actions on the well-being of oneself and others (King & King, 1990). This uncertainty is a function of the difference between stepfamily roles and biological family roles, and the difference between effective stepfamily functioning and effective biological family functioning (Coleman & Ganong, 1987b). There are two primary differences: (a) the degree of clarity about which behavior is appropriate for a given role, and (b) the degree to which the role is either ascribed or achieved (Walker & Messinger, 1979).

IDENTITY MANAGEMENT STRATEGIES

Given the dilemmas of identity management outlined above, the selection of specific strategies may be complex, if not overwhelming, to a stepmother. However, research has provided some preliminary answers as to which strategies stepmothers are likely to use, whether such strategies are likely to work, and which strategies are not often used but might be beneficial given the specific identity problems stepmothers face.

First, because the nature of the stigma of being a stepmother is not immediately apparent to those who don't know a woman's stepmother status, an identi-

ty strategy frequently selected for the general public is one of concealment (e.g., Duberman, 1975; Jones et al., 1984).

> For many women who have chosen to become stepmothers, the realization that they are part of a minority group comes as a bit of a shock. But by masquerading as a natural mother, altering her true identity in order to fit into a society and to be accepted as part of a "normal" family, a stepmother acts like any member of a minority group who is striving to conform. (Morrison, Thompson-Guppy, & Bell, 1986, p. 17)

Concealment is an example of a preventative strategy (Goffman, 1963). Despite the frequency of use of this strategy, however, some counselors have suggested that concealment is ineffective as a long-term solution (Morrison et al., 1986).

A more proactive strategy for public identity management is what Jones et al. (1984) call *confrontation and breaking through*. This strategy involves acknowledging one's stepmother status and working to frame the identity in a constructive and commendable context. Recall McCall and Simmon's (1978) distinction between the conventional and idiosyncratic elements of identity. Based on this distinction, one way to accomplish confrontation and breaking through might be to foster the idiosyncratic elements of the stepmother identity, while simultaneously diminishing the conventional elements. However, due to the strength of the myths of stepmotherhood, such efforts might be construed negatively. As Coleman and Ganong (1987a) noted, people's expectations of negative behavior might lead them to perceive even idiosyncratic elements negatively.

Moving from individual identity management efforts to societal efforts to change the stigma of stepmotherhood, one controversial public strategy that has been suggested is to change the label. If the term *stepfamily* engenders negative reactions, some authors contend we should just change the name to one without such negative connotations (see Coleman & Ganong, 1987a, for a summary of the debate). This can be classified as a corrective strategy. Alternatives to stepfamily include *blended* or *reconstituted family*. What the associated changes in the name of *stepmother* would be is unclear. Other scholars believe that changing the terminology would be confusing (Wald, 1981) or insulting (Lofas & Sova, 1985), or would only add to the mystification (Hughes, 1991).

There have also been some specific strategies identified to overcome the

myths within the stepfamily itself. Based on empirical evidence, Cissna, Cox, and Bochner (1990) assert that an effective way to overcome myths about stepmotherhood involves two steps. First, they claim, the remarried partners must establish the solidarity of the marriage in children's minds. Then, they say, the partners should use this solidarity to establish the credibility of the stepparent as a valid parental authority. Such efforts are clearly corrective in nature, and take into account overly negative expectations due to the evil stepmother myth as well as overly positive expectations due to the myth of instant love.

Taking quite a different approach, Salwen (1990) proposes that stepmothers might remove themselves from the parenting role altogether by insisting that the biological father take on all parenting responsibilities. This does not mean that stepmothers cannot be supportive or nurturing to their stepchildren. However, Salwen argues that by avoiding the parental role, stepmothers simultaneously avoid the negative expectations associated with the role. They are therefore free to work on positive, nonparental relationships with their stepchildren that are not weighted down by preconceived, unfavorable perceptions. Again, such a strategy is an effort to achieve a middle ground between the two myths.

A similar, but perhaps less radical, approach to identity dilemmas within the stepfamily is to focus on alternative role enactment. Furstenberg and Spanier (1984) posit that the stepparent role is ambiguous, as there is no single prescribed role for stepparents (see the section on role ambiguity above). Thus, they should feel free to try on various roles until they find one that fits (see also Walker & Messinger, 1979). Alternative roles a stepmother can don to ease her interactions with stepchildren include *primary mother* (which works only if the biological mother is physically and/or psychologically dead to the child), *other mother,* and *friend* (Draughon, 1975).

Related to alternative roles in managing identity, simply finding a name that a child is comfortable calling the stepmother might assist in the individualization of a stepmother's identity (Visher & Visher, 1988). Very often, a child avoids finding a name for his or her stepmother, referring to her simply as "you" or "she." By insisting on a name, the stepmother moves out of the realm of the group of all stepmothers (a stigmatized group) to personhood (Maglin & Schniedewind, 1989). Possible names include the stepmother's own first name, a mutually agreed upon nickname, or a variation of mother not used for the biological mother (Wald, 1981).

Finally, while not directly related to the problems of stepmothers, Crocker and Lutsky (1986) have identified three strategies for changing cognitions about stigmas. First is the *sociocultural* approach, which emphasizes a change in socialization practices. In the case of stepmothers in particular, this might involve replacing evil stepmother fairy tales with stories with more positive messages. Second is the *motivational* approach. This involves redefining group boundaries to allow the stigmatized persons to become part of the normal population. For example, the category of *mothers* might be expanded to include stepmothers. Lastly, Crocker and Lutsky identify *cognitive* approaches to changing stigmas. This involves proving the stereotype wrong. In global terms this might mean a public relations campaign of sorts for stepmothers. More specifically, however, it might involve allowing a stepmother's positive actions within the stepfamily to prove the myth wrong (i.e., replacing conventional elements of identity with idiosyncratic elements).

IMPLICATIONS FOR RESEARCH

There are several directions for future research. First, Goffman's theoretical differentiation between corrective and preventative identity management strategies needs to be operationalized. Specific research questions might be "What communicative behaviors serve corrective functions?" and "What communicative behaviors serve preventative functions?"

Second, because our knowledge of the identity management strategies stepmothers actually use is quite limited, it would be of interest to identify the specific identity management strategies stepmothers select, when they select them, and why. In addition, future research should strive to fill in the empty squares of the identity matrix detailed by Figure 1. That is, research should focus upon what identity management strategies women select when in a private setting with nonfamily members, and, perhaps more interestingly, what they do when they are with family members in a public situation. Moreover, researchers should ascertain whether the theoretical predictions of strategies that have been identified are correct.

More important than merely identifying what women do, however, is to identify what actually works. A repertoire of strategies is useless unless they actually assist a stepmother in overcoming the negative perceptions associated with stepmotherhood. Thus, critical research questions include: "What spe-

cific identity management strategies work to overcome negative public perceptions?" and "What strategies work to overcome negative perceptions within the family?"

IMPLICATIONS FOR PRACTICE

The issues raised here also have several implications for educators and counselors working with stepfamilies. Most importantly, practitioners can enact two global strategies to ameliorate the identity management difficulties stepmothers face. The first strategy is to assist individual stepmothers in overcoming some of the myths and misconceptions associated with this family role. Ideally, this assistance would take place before the formation of the stepfamily. By presenting future stepmothers—and all stepfamily members—with the reality of stepmother life before the remarriage, the frustrations associated with the myths of the evil stepmother and of instant love might be avoided. A first step in such counseling might be the completion of the Personal Reflections Program (Kaplan & Hennon, 1992).

More realistically, however, this assistance will likely be sought after the identity management difficulties have been encountered. In this case, practitioners might offer some of the strategies described in the previous section on identity management. In addition, referral to organizations proffering support to stepmothers and stepfamilies might be warranted. Finally, preliminary evidence suggests that the use of fiction can assist stepfamilies and stepfamily members in counseling (Coleman & Ganong, 1990b).

The second strategy is to actively work to diffuse these myths and misconceptions on a societal level. This paper points to the need for greater attention to the messages we are sending children about stepmothers. Family life educators and primary school educators might be especially important in normalizing the stepfamily experience (Crosbie-Burnett & Skyles, 1989). Family life educators can assist in debunking the myths by informing the public about the realities of stepmothers and stepfamily life. Similarly, primary school educators might be recruited to assist in this information campaign. Through programs such as the Classroom Guidance Program discussed by Crosbie-Burnett and Pulvino (1990), by selecting texts and children's literature that include normal stepfamilies, and by incorporating stepfamily roles in everyday classroom discussions, grade school teachers might make great

strides in overcoming the evil stepmother myth.

CONCLUSION

The stepmother role is a stressful one that is particularly challenging in terms of identity management. Stepmothers must combat the firmly entrenched myths of the wicked stepmother and of instant love. Despite the fact that the stepfamily form is becoming increasingly more common, empirical and clinical evidence suggests that stepmother myths show little sign of changing (Bryan et al., 1986; Ganong & Coleman, 1983; Fluitt & Paradise, 1991). Thus, identity issues will remain salient for stepmothers for some time to come. Accordingly, researchers and practitioners must incorporate the concept of identity when considering the experiences of stepmothers.

REFERENCES

Ainlay, S. C., Coleman, L. M., & Becker, G. (1986). Stigma reconsidered. In S. C. Ainlay, G. Becker, & L. M. Coleman (Eds.), *The dilemma of difference: A multidisciplinary view of stigma* (pp. 1-13). New York: Plenum Press.

Ambert, A. (1986). Being a stepparent: Live-in and visiting stepchildren. *Journal of Marriage and the Family*, 48, 795-804.

Birenbaum, H. (1988). *Myth and mind.* Lanham, MD: University Press.

Bruner, J. S. (1960). Myth and identity. In H. A. Murray (Ed.), *Myth and mythmaking* (pp. 276-287). Boston: Beacon Press.

Bryan, H., Coleman, M., Ganong, L., & Bryan, L. (1986). Person perception: Family structure as a cue for stereotyping. *Journal of Marriage and the Family*, 48, 169-174.

Cherlin, A. (1978). Remarriage as an incomplete institution. *American Journal of Sociology*, 86, 634-650.

Cissna, K. N., Cox, D. E., & Bochner, A. P. (1990). The dialectic of marital and parental relationships within the stepfamily. *Communication Monographs*, 57, 44-61.

Coleman, M., & Ganong, L. (1987a). The cultural stereotyping of stepfamilies. In K. Pasley & M. Ihinger-Tallman (Eds.), *Remarriage and stepparenting: Current research and theory* (pp. 19-41). New York: Guilford.

Coleman, M., & Ganong, L. (1987b). Marital conflict in stepfamilies: Effects on children. *Youth and Society*, 19, 151-172.

Coleman, M., & Ganong, L. H. (1990a). Remarriage and stepfamily research in the 1980s: Increased interest in an old family form. *Journal of Marriage and the Family*, 52, 925-940.

Coleman, M., & Ganong, L. H. (1990b). The uses of juvenile fiction and self-help books with stepfamilies. *Journal of Counseling and Development*, 68, 327-331.

Crocker, J., & Lutsky, N. (1986). Stigma and the dynamics of social cognition. In S. C. Ainlay, G. Becker, & L. M. Coleman (Eds.), *The dilemma of difference: A multidisciplinary view of stigma* (pp. 95-122). New York: Plenum Press.

Crosbie-Burnett, M., & Pulvino, C. J. (1990). Children in nontraditional families: A classroom guidance program. *School Counselor*, 37, 286-293.

Crosbie-Burnett, M., & Skyles, A. (1989). Stepchildren in schools and colleges: Recommendations for educational policy changes. *Family Relations*, 38, 59-64.

Darley, J., & Gross, P. H. (1983). A hypothesis confirming bias in labeling effects. *Journal of Personality and Social Psychology*, 44, 20-33.

Draughon, M. (1975). Stepmother's model of identification in relation to mourning in the child. *Psychological Reports*, 36, 183-189.

Duberman, L. (1973). Step-kin relationships. *Journal of Marriage and the Family*, 35, 283-292.

Duberman, L. (1975). *The reconstituted family: A study of remarried couples and their children.* Chicago, IL: Nelson-Hall.

Fine, M. A., & Schwebel, A. I. (1991). Stepparent stress: A cognitive perspective. *Journal of Divorce and Remarriage*, 17, 1-15.

Fluitt, M. S., & Paradise, L. V. (1991). The relationship of current family structures to young adults' perceptions of stepparents. *Journal of Divorce and Remarriage*, 15, 159-174.

Furstenberg, F. F., Jr., & Spanier, G. (1984). *Recycling the family: Remarriage after divorce.* Beverly Hills, CA: Sage.

Ganong, L., & Coleman, M. (1983). Stepparent: A pejorative term? *Psychological Reports, 52,* 919-922.

Ganong, L., Coleman, M., & Kennedy, G. (1990). The effects of using alternate labels in denoting stepparent or stepfamily status. *Journal of Social Behavior and Personality, 5,* 453-463.

Goffman, E. (1959). *The presentation of self in everyday life.* New York: Doubleday Anchor.

Goffman, E. (1963). *Stigma: Notes on the management of spoiled identity.* New York: Simon & Schuster.

Hughes, C. (1991). *Stepparents: Wicked or wonderful?* Brookfield, VT: Gower Publishing Co.

Jones, E. E., Farina, A., Hastorf, A. H., Markus, H., Miller, D. T., & Scott, R. A. (1984). *Social stigma: The psychology of of marked relationships.* New York: W. H. Freeman.

Jones, E. E., & Pittman, T. S. (1980). Toward a general theory of strategic self-presentation. In H. Suls (Ed.), *Psychological perspectives on the self.* Hillsdale, NJ: Lawrence Erlbaum Associates.

Kaplan, L., & Hennon, C. B. (1992). Remarriage education: The Personal Reflections Program. *Family Relations, 41,* 127-134.

King, L. A., & King, D. W. (1990). Role conflict and role ambiguity: A critical assessment of construct validity. *Psychological Bulletin, 107,* 48-64.

Lofas, J., & Sova, D. B. (1985). *Stepparenting.* New York: Zebra Books.

Maglin, N. B., & Schniedewind, N. (1989). Women and stepfamilies. Philadelphia: Temple University Press.

McCall, G. J., & Simmons, J. L. (1978). *Identities and interactions* (rev. ed.). New York: The Free Press.

Moorman, J. E., & Hernandez, D. J. (1989). Married-couple families with step, adopted, and biological children. *Demography, 26,* 267-277.

Morrison, K., Thompson-Guppy, A., & Bell, P. (1986). *Stepmothers: Exploring the myth.* Ottawa, Canada: Canadian Council on Social Development.

Salwen, L. V. (1990). The myth of the wicked stepmother. *Women and Therapy, 10,* 117-125.

Schlenker, B. R. (1980). *Impression management: The self-concept, social identity, and interpersonal relations.* Monterey, CA: Brooks/Cole.

Schulman, G. L. (1972). Myths that intrude on the adaptation of the stepfamily. *Social Casework, 53,* 131-139.

Smith, W. C. (1953). *The stepchild.* Chicago, IL: University of Chicago Press.

Stafford, M. C., & Scott, R. R. (1986). Stigma, deviance, and social control: Some conceptual issues. In S. C. Ainlay, G. Becker, & L. M. Coleman (Eds.), *The dilemma of difference: A multidisciplinary view of stigma* (pp. 77-91). New York: Plenum Press.

Visher, E. B., & Visher, J. S. (1979). *Stepfamilies: Myths and realities.* Secaucus, NJ: Citadel.

Visher, E. B., & Visher, J. S. (1988). *Old loyalties, new ties: Therapeutic strategies with stepfamilies.* New York: Brunner/Mazel.

Wald, E. (1981). *The remarried family: Challenge and promise.* New York: Family Services Association of America.

Walker, K. N., & Messinger, L. (1979). Remarriage after divorce: Dissolution and reconstruction of family boundaries. *Family Process, 18,* 185-192.

Solace and Immortality: Bereaved Parents' Continuing Bond With Their Children

Dennis Klass

Webster University, St. Louis, Missouri

How do bereaved parents find solace in the face of irreparable loss? The essay grows out of a 10-year ethnographic study of a chapter of the Compassionate Friends, a self-help group. A recurring pattern is that long-term solace is intertwined with parents' continuing interaction with the inner representation of their dead child. The essay examines the nature of solace, reviews literature on inner representations of the dead, examines ways parents find solace connected with interaction with the inner representation, explores the shared inner representation as a significant element in social support, discusses solace in terms of the psychosocial meaning of immortality, and draws implications for clinicians.

In the sorrow of grief humans need to be consoled. The defining characteristic of solace is the sense of soothing. To console means to alleviate sorrow or distress. Solace is that which brings pleasure, enjoyment, or delight in the face of hopelessness, despair, sadness, and devastation.

This essay looks at consolation within the resolution of the grief of parents whose children have died. It grows out of a long-term ethnographic study of a local chapter of the Compassionate Friends, a self-help group of bereaved parents (Klass, 1988). The 10-year study has resulted in a large body of materials by which to understand parental grief and the interactions within the Compassionate Friends chapter. Materials include: interviews with bereaved parents, writings by members in chapter newsletters, and notes from meetings.

When a child dies, the parent experiences an irreparable loss, for the child is an extension of the parent's self (Benedek, 1959, 1975). While one of the psychological tasks of parenting in modernity is to separate the child from the self so the child can be experienced as a separate being (Elson, 1984), such separation is seldom complete. When a child dies, a part of the self is cut off. Many parents find the metaphor of amputation useful. In a meeting a father said, "It is like I lost my right arm, but I'm learning to live as a one-armed man." A parent who seems to have had experience with amputees wrote in a newsletter article:

> For the amputee, the raw bleeding stump heals and the physical pain does go away. But he lives with the pain in his heart knowing his limb will not grow back. He has to learn to live without it. He rebuilds his life around his loss. We bereaved parents must do the same.

Like amputation, parental bereavement is a permanent condition. The hopes, dreams, and expectations incarnate in the child are now gone.

Bereaved parents do find resolution to their grief in the sense that they learn to live in their new world. They "re-solve" the matters of how to be themselves in a family and community in a way that makes life meaningful. They learn to grow in those parts of themselves which did not die with the child. They learn to invest themselves in other tasks and other relationships. But somewhere inside themselves, they report, there is a sense of loss that cannot be healed. A bereaved father wrote in a newsletter:

> If grief is resolved, why do we still feel a sense of loss on anniversaries and holidays and even when we least expect it? Why do we feel a lump in the throat even 6 years after the loss? It is because healing does not mean forgetting and because moving on with life does not mean that we don't take a part of our lost love with us.

A part of them is missing and their world is forever diminished. It is that part of the self which seeks consolation. How do parents find consolation for their irreparable loss?

THE NATURE OF SOLACE

Horton (1981) finds that the majority of people have a history of solace that they nurture. Most adults can easily identify a solace filled object to which they repair when they need soothing: a memory of a special place or person, a piece of music or art, an imagined more perfect world, a sense of divine presence. Horton finds that solace is necessary for the individual who can live in a society. Psychopathic criminals, he says, have no solace

Address correspondence to the author at Webster University, St. Louis, M0 63119.

From *Death Studies*, Vol. 17, No. 4, July/August 1993, pp. 343-368. © 1993 by Taylor & Frances, Inc., 1101 Vermont Avenue, NW, Suite 200, Washington, DC 20005. All rights reserved. Reprinted by permission.

in their lives. Horton finds that the earliest solace is the transitional object (Winnicott, 1953, 1971) such as a child's security blanket, which helps the child explore new situations and adjust to unfamiliar environments (Passman, 1976; Passman & Weisberg, 1975). Horton says that in adults these objects are no longer transitional, for they are important in the adult's ongoing life. Solace is experienced as blended inner and outer reality. There is a noetic quality in this reality that is self-validating. While the content of solace may have rational characteristics, the truth and comfort of solace are neither provable nor challengeable.

A recurring pattern in Compassionate Friends is that parents find long-term solace in continuing interaction with the inner representation of their dead child. Inner representation can be defined following Fairbairn (1952), as: 1) those aspects of the self that are actualized in interaction with the deceased person, 2) characterizations or thematic memories of the deceased, and 3) emotional states connected with those parts of the self and with those characterizations and memories. Phenomena that indicate interaction with the inner representation of a deceased person are a sense of presence, hallucinations in any of the senses, belief in the person's continuing active influence on thoughts or events, or a conscious incorporation of the characteristics or virtues of the dead into the self.

These phenomena may be experienced in altered states of consciousness. Parents often use phrases like: "It was in a dream, but it was different than other dreams." The phenomena may also be experienced in ordinary states of consciousness and accepted as part of the everyday world. Interaction may be consciously sought or it may seem to come unbidden. Interaction with the inner representation of the dead may be continuous with the self as the characteristics or virtues of the dead are incorporated into the self representation. Or the interaction may seem apart from the self representation as the parent says that having such thoughts and feelings is "just not like me."

The inner representation of the dead child has the character of both outer and inner reality. It is not simply an objective presence, for the meaning of the experience is strongly personal. Neither can it be said to be simply subjective. Many parents in the study argue strongly against reducing the experience to a psychic reality, or as one person said, "Don't tell me that this is just in my head?" Yet, at the same time they are usually able to grant that the meaning of the child's presence is very personal and not generalizable to other people's lives.

The message and meaning of the interaction with the inner representations of dead children are self-evident to the bereaved parent. It does not matter to the parents in the study whether, with the help of the spirits of the dead, parapsychologists can bend spoons. Their children appear, act, speak, and influence. The intense meanings they feel within the bond with their child are quite apart from rational proof or disproof.

Inner representations of the dead are not simply individual phenomena, but they are maintained and reinforced within families and other social systems. The dead child is often a part of the bond within the continuing family and is an integral element of the bond between members of the Compassionate Friends. Parents consciously work to maintain the inner repre-

sentation of the child. Several families do this by including the picture of the dead child on family portraits made after the child's death. Others do it by consciously evoking the memory of the child in significant situations. In the Compassionate Friends (1983), the sense of oneness with other bereaved parents and the sense of oneness within the bonds to the dead child can be seen in the "TCF Credo," which has been adopted by the National Board of TCF and which is recited on special occasions such as holiday memorial services, national, and regional meetings.

> We reach out to each other with love, with understanding and with hope. Our children have died at all ages and from many different causes, but our love for our children unites us. . . . Whatever pain we bring to this gathering of The Compassionate Friends, it is pain we will share just as we share with each other our love for our children.

LITERATURE ON INNER REPRESENTATIONS OF THE DEAD

Extent of the Phenomena

There is ample evidence from research on Western cultures that the inner representation of the deceased continues as an active part of the life of the survivor, even though it has little sanction within the dominant scientific worldview. At present, the inner representation of Elvis Presley plays an active part in many people's lives and within some social systems (Moody, 1987). Lehman, Wortman, and Williams (1987) found that 4 to 7 years after an accidental death 90% of widow(er)s and 96% of bereaved parents said that during the past month memories, thoughts, or mental pictures of the deceased had come to their mind. Kalish and Reynolds (1981) found that 44% of a random sample said they had experienced or felt the presence of someone who had died. The dead appeared and spoke in 73.6% of the experiences, the dead were psychologically felt in 20.3%, and in 6%, there was a sense of touch. Rees (1975) found that 46.7% of the Welsh widows he interviewed had occasional hallucinations for several years. Most common was the sense of the presence (39.2%), followed by visual (14%), auditory (13.3%), and tactile senses (2.7%). Glick, Weiss, and Parkes (1974) found among widows a persistent continuing relationship with the inner representation of the dead husband. They report

> In contrast to most other aspects of the reaction to bereavement, the sense of the persisting presence of the husband did not diminish with time. It seemed to take a few weeks to become established, but thereafter seemed as likely to be reported late in the bereavement as early. (p. 147)

Cross Cultural Differences and Continuities

There are wide cultural variations in what is considered to be the appropriate place of the inner representation of the dead in the family and other social systems. Yamamoto and his colleagues (1969) claim that because Japanese religion (both Shinto and Buddhist) involves ancestor worship, which encourages the mourner to maintain contact to the deceased, mourning is different in Japan than in the West.

There are also some obvious continuities across cultures in the phenomena by which inner representations of the dead are manifest. Matchett (1972) reports three instances of Hopi women having visions of recently deceased people. The mental state he describes is not different from that in bereaved parents.

> The experience to be described is neither truly seance nor truly dream, but appears to represent a mental state with some similarities to both. The apparition is real enough to the beholder to be conversed with, to be described in great visual detail, and even at times to be struggled with physically. However, it is clear to the beholder, even during the experience, that this presence with which he argues and struggles as if it were "real" occurs somewhere outside the usual definition of reality. (p. 185)

Functions of the Inner Representation of the Dead

There have been some studies of how inner representations function in the lives of survivors, though often this aspect is not central to the investigation, or the sample has been very small. Among widows, Silverman (1986) argues that maintaining a changed relationship with the inner representations of the deceased spouses allows the widows to find stability in time. Lopata (1973, 1979) finds what she calls "husband sanctification," which allows the widow to "continue her obligation to the husband to remember him, yet break her ties and re-create herself into a person without a partner" (1979, p. 126). Moss and Moss (1980) claim that the sanctified inner representation of the dead spouse is a factor in the relationship between elderly widows and widowers when they remarry. Goin, Burgoyne, and Goin (1979) find widows, even after remarriage, renew the bond with their dead husband as they decide to have a face-lift operation. Among children whose parent has died, Tessman (1978) finds that children "preserve the relationship psychically and continue to make use of whatever mixture of affection and guidance emanated from the parent" (p. 42). Bushbaum (1987) finds that the inner representation of the dead parent is essential to the child's development. College women, Silverman (1987) finds, reintegrate the dead parent into each new developmental stage.

Inner Representations of the Dead in Contemporary Grief Theory

These experiences of bereaved parents run contrary to most contemporary understandings of the healthy resolution of grief, which hold that the inner representation plays no or only a slight role in the survivor's life after the resolution of grief. The two classic models of grief come from Bowlby and his followers and from the psychoanalytic group. The Bowlby model (Bowlby, 1969, 1973, 1980; Parkes, 1972; Parkes & Weiss, 1983; Raphael, 1983; Worden, 1982) expects that after a period of emotionally searching for the deceased, survivors should let go of the inner representation, and resume normal functioning, albeit in changed social roles. The psychoanalytic model (Volkan, 1981, 1985a, 1985b; Tahka, 1984; Dietrich & Shabad, 1989; Furman, 1974; Jackson, 1957) expects that mourning should detach the ego from the affective bond with the deceased and that the inner representation is transformed into an identification which enriches the ego or self representation.

Models of grief that try to go beyond the Bowlby and psychodynamic models do not find a positive place for the inner representation in the resolution. Brice (1991) in his paradoxical model of parental grief finds that his subjects

> painfully came to see that, while they retained a psychical representation of their child, they had irretrievably lost their child's external presence—something of which their mental images were, alas, a poor copy. (p. 2)

Brice says one of the difficulties that parents have with the experience of presence is that they fear insanity. Although Brice mentions his contact with the Compassionate Friends, he does not seem to have seen that with social validation bereaved parents no longer accept the label of insanity. Sanders (1989) notes that sensing the presence or actually seeing the dead person "brought a sense of comfort," but she understands the experiences to be the "cognitive counterpart of yearning" (p. 70). Thus she is saying that interaction with the inner representation of the dead child is wish fulfillment rather than a positive element in resolution.

The contemporary theoretical difficulties are seen in Rando's (1984) attempt to synthesize the literature for clinicians. She says:

> The single most crucial task in grief is "untying the ties that bind" the griever to the deceased individual. This does not mean that the deceased is forgotten or not loved; rather, it means that the emotional energy that the mourner had invested in the deceased is modified to allow the mourner to turn it towards others for emotional satisfaction. (p. 19)

"Emotional energy" is a problematic concept at best, so the idea of "modified" energy explains very little. Rando gives no way the dead can remain loved and remembered, yet have the emotional energy modified except as "rituals, anniversary celebrations, prayers, commemorations, memorializations, and healthy identification" (p. 78). She does not show the mechanisms by which energy modification takes place. Further, she does not say how rituals, etc. function in the resolution of grief, nor does she give any definition or examples of "healthy identification."

There is a minority voice in the literature that is more congruent with this study. Rubin (1985) finds that breaking bonds with the dead is not the function or measure of successful grief.

> It is in the nature of the relationship of the bereaved to the deceased that is the best determination of whether the mourning has been resolved. . . . The greater the comfort and fluidity with which one can relate to the representations (memories, fantasies, feelings) of the deceased—the more one can refer to "resolution" of the loss. (pp. 231–232)

The Question of Pathology

In many contemporary theories of grief, the widespread continued interaction with the inner representations of dead children seem to be pathological, for beginning with Freud, theorists have understood the purpose of grief as relinquishing the lost object so that new attachments in the present can be formed. Failure to sever the bond has been defined as pathological grief. This is not the venue for a full discussion of the unexamined assumptions and lack of data upon which this definition of pathology is based. The author has discussed the issue previously, especially with regard to Bowlby and his followers

(Klass, 1987), but a few comments can indicate the problems with this view of pathology. The most powerful clinical argument for this definition of pathological grief is the link some researchers have established between depression and the unresolved grief of children for deceased parents. Tennant (1988), however, in a detailed review of this body of research concludes:

> Parental loss has all too readily been accepted as a significant risk factor in adult psychopathology. However a reasonable scrutiny of the empirical findings reveals their fragility. . . . there is no evidence that parental death is a significant risk factor for depression. (p. 1049)

The definition of the healthy resolution of grief as severing bonds with the dead does not stand the test of cross-cultural nor of comparative historical analysis. Stroebe, Gergen, Gergen, and Stroebe (1992) in a historical study show that the definition is an artifact of modernism which values goal directedness, efficiency, and rationality.

> In psychology, modernism has given rise to the machine metaphor of human functionality. When applied to grief, this view suggests that people need to recover from their state of intense emotionality and return to normal functioning and effectiveness as quickly and efficiently as possible. (p. 1206)

Modernism, they note, is a reaction against romanticism in which continuing bonds to the dead were valued and nurtured.

That is not to say that inner representations of dead children, like any significant attachment, do not on occasion become twisted in psychopathology. To understand the etiology of pathology in grief, it is useful to look again at the classic work of Lindemann and Cobb (1979). They do not find causal factors in the processes the bereaved undertake to resolve grief. Rather, Lindemann and Cobb find that persons with a prior history of psychopathology or with a social support system loaded with guilt and conflict are likely to exhibit pathology in their grief. Thus pathology in grief is a function of other pathology.

There have been studies of the destructive possibilities of socially maintained inner representations, though less study of the constructive possibilities. Maintaining the inner representation in the form of "replacement children" can be a heavy burden on the child who is expected to live someone else's life (Cain & Cain, 1964; Johnson, 1984; Legg & Sherick, 1976; Poznanski, 1972). Family systems therapists have focused on the ways in which families can get "stuck" by not publicly mourning losses so the family can reorganize without a "ghost" in the family (Walsh & McGoldrick, 1991). On a more positive note, though on a smaller scale, Rynearson (1987) shows how making the inner representation a party to the social system of psychotherapist and client helps the survivor resolve grief in a healthy way.

> While more investigation should be undertaken, it may be that maintaining the bond with the dead prevents pathology. When relationships to the dead are maintained it makes it less likely that their images will be reincarnated in the form of projections which distort our relationships to other people. . . . A heart that grieves, a heart that communes with the dead in reverie, is immune to falling in love on the rebound. By welcoming the ghosts the bereaved may find themselves to be no longer haunted by them. (Mogenson, 1992, p. 20)

INNER REPRESENTATION AS SOLACE

What forms of relationship to their dead child do parents maintain as solace in their lives? Following, are three common ways among members of the Compassionate Friends: linking objects, religious ideas and devotion, and memory. In the descriptions, both the solace that individuals find and how shared solace-bearing inner representations are a part of the bonds within families and communities will be considered.

Linking Objects

Linking objects are objects connected with the child's life that link the bereaved to the dead; in so doing, they evoke the presence of the dead (Volkan, 1981). Six years after his child's death, a father wrote a birthday letter to him:

> I haven't been able to part with the bicycle cart that I bought for you and your sister a few weeks before you died. It's never used anymore but I keep it in my study at home. . . . I still see your smile as you sat there holding our puppy. . . . Your little wind-up toy, the one of Donald Duck sitting in a shoe, sits on top of the file cabinet in my study. I feel close to you when I'm close to your favorite things.

The sense of smell is particularly intimate. Parents often report that they hold their children's clothes which still have the scent of the child. One mother who miscarried wrote that it is not the usual newborn scent that links her to her child.

> So the flowers I place upon his grave
> Are the only scent I know.
> So when I smell a flower
> My son always comes to mind.

The linking object need not be small toys or fast-fading flowers. A father whose daughter had died five years earlier said:

> It's that old pick-up truck. She used to ride around in it with me. She would lean against me on the seat. It has almost 200,000 miles on it, but I am not going to sell it. By now I probably couldn't get anything for it anyway. I told the boys they could work on it and use it if they got it going. But I'll never sell the truck because I can sit in there and feel my daughter. It's great.

The linking object is a self-validating truth to the parent that, though the child be dead, yet the child lives. One parent had many memories of being at the beach with her child. They would look for sand dollars, which the boy saved. Her memory of those times also include natural mystical experiences (see Hood, 1977) in which her bond with nature and with the child are intertwined. In a newsletter article she wrote that the child "was especially awed by the setting sun and as we walked the beaches, always he would stop and watch the sun go down—I did too! I was so happy with him."

> In February I went to Padre Island and one lonely evening I walked the beach alone—just the sand, the sea, a beautiful setting sun, the screeching gulls, God and me. It was there I begged Him to show me a sign that E. lives—to "please send me a sand dollar." I knew that it was not the season for sand dollars. Even the local people had told me that they had not seen sand dollars since last summer. But I only wanted just one sand dollar—just one! Watching the fading sunset and listening to the roar of the waves, darkness began to fall, so I turned to go back when there by my feet, the waves pushed up one lone sand dollar—a small but perfect sand dollar!
>
> That is exactly the way it happened and I cannot begin to tell you the feelings I had. My prayer had been answered.

The answer to her prayer for a sign that the child still lives is the linking object of the sand dollar. Now that she has had the intense experience of finding the sand dollar, the memory of this experience can be evoked and the memory itself can serve as a linking object.

If the linking object is rich enough, it can serve as an enduring, communally shared symbol. For this to happen, the object must have a cultural meaning by which the parent can connect personal solace to that provided within the social reality. One family in the study found the child's presence at a place in a national park the child had spontaneously called "just like heaven." One couple shared a linking object that has an often unrecognized cultural symbolism. Asked, "Do you ever sense that C. is still around?" the mother answered:

> Every time I see a mourning dove. Mourning doves are magnificent. The day after C. died, Cliff and I were sitting in the den looking out the window and there was a mourning dove on the porch. I didn't know what it was at the time, so I got out my bird book and looked it up. It is m-o-u-r-n-i-n-g dove, not m-o-r-n-i-n-g. It was so ironic because here I'd just lost a daughter and I'm getting out my bird book to look for mourning doves. It was phenomenal that we would see a mourning dove when we were mourning. It's got to mean something, right? So the two of us took this as, "This is C. C. is with the dove." Then, a few days later, there were two doves there. Cliff decided that it was C. telling him that she had a friend with her. It's really fascinating because I'll find myself thinking about her and I'll look around and see the mourning dove. That has become a symbol of C. It was on the year anniversary when we were going to the cemetery and Cliff said, "I wish I could see a mourning dove." So I said, "Come over here, there is usually a mourning dove over here." And I'll be damned if there wasn't a mourning dove on the wire. He said, "That's a sign. Now I can go to the cemetery."

Religious Devotion

Linking objects can have a numinous sense (Otto, 1923) about them, for they function like relics of the saints in which "any personal possession or part of a person's body. . . . can carry the power or saintliness of the person with whom they were once associated and make him or her 'present' once again" (Sullivan, 1987, p. 51). The numinous feeling is clearer in the many people who sense the presence of the child in their religious experience of prayer, ritual, and religious ideation. Religion as used here is the individual's sense of connectedness to that which transcends death (Chidester, 1990). The inner representation of the child is merged with something bigger, but something of which, in the deeper reaches of the psyche, the parent feels a part. Religion can be that provided within an institutionalized framework. One mother wrote a letter to her dead daughters describing the sense of presence at Catholic Mass.

> Every time I attend the sacrifice of the Mass, at the part where our Blessed Lord comes into our hearts, I feel so close to your angelic presence. What a divine experience! The only problem is that it doesn't last long enough. If only the others could share these feelings.

Religion can also be that which is outside of churches or theological doctrine. Parents feel the presence of the child within their bonds with the whole world. On her child's birthday, one mother wrote a letter as if from the child.

> I would have been twenty today, bound by earthly constraints. Do not cry, Mom. I am forever, I am eternal, I am ageless. I am in the blowing wind, the first blades of grass in the spring, the haunting cry of the owl, the shriek of the hawk, the silent soaring of the turkey vulture. I am in the tears of those in mourning, the laughter of little children, the pain of the dying, the hopelessness of the homeless. I am the weightless, floating feeling when you close your eyes at night; I am the heaviness of a broken heart. . . . Like an invisible cocoon I surround you. I am in the moonlight, the sunbeams, the dew at dawn. . . . Do not cry. Remember me with love and laughter and yes, with pain. For I was, I am, and I will always be. Once T., now nameless and free.

The child's presence comes within a sense of the uncanny, a feeling often associated with religious belief and practice (see Dawson, 1989). In a newsletter account, the uncanny appears twice, first as a dream that seems a premonition, and second as an unaccounted-for physical event. A few months before she was murdered, the daughter told her mother of a dream in which she was looking in the window at the family gathered for Christmas.

> On Christmas morning, while we were opening the gifts (which the daughter had made) my husband told me to look out the window. There are two rocking chairs on the porch and one was rocking back and forth. My husband reached over and held my hand, and it was at that moment I remembered what M. had told us about her dream, and I realized then that her dream had become a reality. M. was still with all of us and was indeed content at watching the family she loved so much sharing the joy of Christmas together.

Almost all the parents in the study feel that the child is in heaven. The inner representation of the child as in heaven is held tightly by some parents in the initial shock and disbelief of grief, even before they can develop a sense that they have an active interaction with the child. The separation from the child seems too much to bear for many parents, so even as they feel that their child is nowhere to be found in this world, they retain hope that they will join their child after death. A mother wrote in a newsletter early in her grief, before she had put together an integrated inner representation of the child:

> There's a hole in me. You see, as part of me is missing. I keep looking for my son, and all I find are bits and pieces of him—something he wrote, a picture he took, a book he read, a tape he made, something he drew—but there is an emptiness in me that these bits and pieces cannot fill, that nothing will ever fill. . . . My son is gone and he is not coming back. I will have to go to him and someday I will.

Such a feeling early in the grief often gives way to a more immediate interaction with the inner representation in a way that, while the hope of reunion after the parent's death is retained, there is a sense of a bond with the child in heaven, which is consoling. This is true even with those for whom heaven is not part of their theology. Knapp (1986) found that bereaved parents could not sustain a belief that there is no afterlife for their child. Several people in the study felt the child to be with another significant person who had died. One woman whose father had died 4 years before her child reported:

> It was hard after my father died because I always had this sense that I didn't know where he was. But I was busy with L. because she was so sick all the time. After L. died I was really bothered that I didn't know where she was and that somehow that meant that I didn't know she was safe. That lasted two years. One day I

started crying and I realized I wasn't just crying for L. I was missing my father. And suddenly I just thought, "Daddy is taking care of L. She is OK because she is with him and that's where he is. It is like they are together." That sounds so simple-minded. I don't believe in heaven or afterlife. I think we just live on in memory. But it just feels like I don't have that worry about either of them any more. I know they are together.

Within a social system, sharing a religious sense in the bond with the inner representation of a dead child has a quite common form. Ethnic, racial, or political membership is often infused with religious feelings. Indeed, for many people, God and country feel as one. All peoples encourage a strong bond with the dead hero or martyr. Among the symbols that bind a nation together are the internalized representations of its young who died that the nation could have its land, its freedom, its king, its religion, its form of government, or its economic power. Lincoln's address at Gettysburg offers solace to the parents of those buried there, and at the same time it bonds the citizens to the war dead and to the abstract ideals on which the nation was founded. Such solace can, of course, be used destructively. In some pathological cultural systems or in historical situations in which there has been a regression to what Wilber (1981) calls mythic/membership, blood must be answered by blood. In the name of those fallen for the cause, other people's children may be killed with impunity (Jacoby, 1983). It is difficult to stop a cycle of violence when each side merges the solace of the inner representations of the dead children with a religious feeling of peoplehood and with a drive for revenge which feels as if it has divine sanction.

Memories

Bereaved parents can find solace in memory. Unconflicted and peaceful memory is often at the end of a difficult process of separating self-representation from the inner representation of the child. Memories are at first very painful, for they are reminders of the loss. One mother reflected on the discovery that letting go of the pain did not also mean letting go of the child.

You know, I remember being afraid that someday I would wake up and my feeling of being bonded to K. wouldn't be there. I thought that when the pain left, she would be gone too. But now I find that I hope the memories will come. The times in the hospital are not what I remember. I remember the good times, when she was well. Sometimes I just look at her pictures and remember when we took them. I never know when I will look at the pictures, but I feel better afterwards.

This use of memory as solace seems similar to what Tahka (1984) calls "remembrance formations." He says once the remembrance formation

has been established, its later calling back to mind, reminiscing about it and dismissing it again from the mind, are invariably experienced as activities of the self taking place exclusively on the subject's own conditions. Although it is experienced as a fully differentiated object representation, no illusions of its separate and autonomous existence are involved. In contrast to fantasy objects possessing various wish-fulfilling functions, it includes the awareness that nothing more can be expected from it and therefore, in its fully established forms it has chances for becoming the most realistic of all existing object representations. (p. 18)

A poem in a newsletter makes the point more gracefully.

Memories are the
perennials that
bloom again
after the hard winter grief
begins to
yield to hope.

Memory can be a part of everyday life. The quiet times remembering the dead child have about them a somewhat forbidden quality, but the memory time becomes a personal ritual around which to build a day.

Sometimes I pretend, when no one's around,
that you are still home,
creating your own special sound—
the car, the stereo, singing in the shower.

Such thematic memories, that is memories that catch the essence of the individual child, take the parent out of the present and to a time when the world was better.

I can still envision the surprised, happy look on his face that Christmas when he opened a gift and found a silver vest and pants to wear when he played his bass guitar with his beloved band. . . . I remember when he took me out to eat one Mother's Day, just he and I. . . . how handsome he was in his tux and top hat and how he introduced his date for the prom . . . how proud we all were at his graduation when he gave the welcome address. . . . Wonderful memories are something that no one can take away. Some memories just won't die.

Often it is the emotional states attached to the thematic memories that carry the quality of solace. Writing nearly 20 years after the death of her daughter, a mother reflected on her memory of a beginners' ballet recital.

I can't remember the details of that afternoon. . . . But I remember the feeling, somewhere between laughter and tears. I remember loving that small, beautiful person, my child. I remember my sense of admiration for her, and a fittingly stifled flood of pride. . . . I have forgotten so many things, but I remember the feeling. Always the feeling.

Memory binds family and communities together. In the Compassionate Friends, the members do not remember each other's children as living, for it was the death of the children which brought members to the group. But the solace of memory is important in the group's bond. The group has developed rituals that express the bond with the child as part of the bonds within the community. Such rituals give permission to each parent to hold the inner representation without conflict. A significant portion of national and regional meetings are devoted to ritual activity, such as boards with pictures of the dead children. The holiday candlelight memorial service is the largest gathering of the local chapter. Many of the members, including "alumnae" who no longer attend meetings, bring the child's siblings, grandparents, uncles, aunts, or family friends. The memory of the child is thus included in the holiday and in the family circle. As the children's names are read the parents and those who have come with them rise and light a candle. A liturgy adopted from *Gates of Prayer* (1975), a Jewish prayer book, is a central part of the memorial service.

In the rising of the sun and in its going down,
    We remember them;

In the blowing of the wind and in the chill of winter,
　We remember them;
In the opening of buds and in the warmth of summer,
　We remember them;
In the rustling of leaves and the beauty of autumn,
　We remember them;
In the beginning of the year and when it ends,
　We remember them;
When we are weary and in need of strength,
　We remember them;
When we are lost and sick at heart,
　We remember them;
When we have joys we yearn to share,
　We remember them;
So long as we live, they too shall live, for they are now a part of us as
　We remember them.

SOLACE AND IMMORTALITY

This essay has looked at three ways in which the inner representation of the child is a solace-giving, ongoing part of the parent's inner world and social world: linking objects, religious devotion, and memories. In each of those ways, the child remains immortal, in the sense that the inner representation of the child remains a real, living presence in the parent's inner and social world.

Most psychosocial thinking about immortality is from the self's point of view. Individuals fear annihilation of the self and compensate, as one psychoanalytic scholar finds, by a "regression to the union of the archaic idealized omnipotent figure in the death-transformation passage to the 'new existence' . . . based on symbiosis with the undifferentiated god" (Pollock, 1975, p. 341). The death of a child brings a most difficult grief in this culture because the sense of selfhood involved in parenting is a central part of the being. The bond reaches back to the parent's own infancy and the bond with the parent's own parents and it reaches forward to the hopes for the completion of the self which children represent. The death of the child is the death of a part of the self. But the child is also not the self. The parents must still live in a poorer world. The child's immortality need not be so regressive.

The continuing interaction with the inner representation of the dead child in bereaved parents seems to support Lifton's (1974) idea that the sense of immortality is not compensation or denial and therefore not pathological. Lifton finds that the sense of immortality is "man's symbolization of his ties with both his biological fellows and his history, past and future" (p. 685). The parents' bond with the child already symbolizes the parents' ties to their biological, personal, and cultural history. Bereaved parents often remind each other, "When your parent dies, you lose your past. When your child dies, you lose your future." Solace is for living in that poorer world. The immortal inner representation of the child maintains the bonds to history and future, to biology and culture symbolized by the living child.

Winnicott (1953, 1971) notes that art and religion seem to grow out of the blended inner and outer reality first seen in the child's transitional object. The language of one mother writing in the newsletter shows that she already knew the part of herself where she now feels connected to her child.

I cannot open my eyes to see his smile. I close my eyes and listen to my heart, for it is there that he lives. I must dig deeper inside myself to a place that I ever knew existed to feel the joy this child brought.

In many of his sonnets Shakespeare asks how a dead friend or lover can live on. He seems finally to settle upon the immortality of his own art, for if he can join the reality of the deceased to the "eternal lines" of the poem, the dead person is made immortal (see Hubler, 1952). Thus Shakespeare locates the immortality of the dead in his art much the way bereaved parents locate their dead children in their experience of solace.

And every fair from fair sometime declines,
By chance or nature's changing course untrimm'd;
But thy eternal summer shall not fade
Nor lose possession of that fair thou owest;
Nor shall Death brag thou wander'st in his shade,
When in eternal lines to time thou growest:
So long as men can breath or eyes can see,
So long lives this and this gives life to thee. (Sonnet 18)

For their parents, dead children do not lose possession of that fairness they embodied, nor do they wander only in Death's shade. They have lived just the summer, but their summer does not fade; it remains eternal in a part of the parent's psyche and in the social system where the parent feels most at home. The parents find solace in linking objects that evoke the presence of the dead, in religious ideas and devotion which merge the child with other death-transcending connections of the parent's life, and in memories by which time can drop away and the parent can return to the world when it was a better place. So long lives this in the inner and social world of bereaved parents, this gives life to their children who have died.

Such immortality is not the only immortality available after a child dies. For example, passing of genetic material is a universal form of immortality. Shakespeare recognizes:

But were some child of yours alive at time,
You should live twice; in it and in my rhyme. (Sonnet 17)

Human efforts to create external symbols of immortality feel less sure, and in the end less meaningful, than the immortality bereaved parents find in the solace-filled bond with their child.

Not marble, nor the gilded monuments
Of princes, shall outlive this powerful rhyme;
But you shall shine more bright in these contents
Than unswept stone, besmeared with sluttish time. . . .
So, til the judgement that yourself arise,
You live in this, and dwell in lover's eyes. (Sonnet 60)

The immortal children are present in the same world in which the parent lives, not in another world. Harper (1991) says:

There are persons whom we cannot think of except as being alive. They seem to resist destruction, even when dead. . . . Around them, even remembering them, whether away for a while or permanently, we feel the whole world a more vibrant as well as more interesting place. (p. 89)

In a new life which sometimes feels neither sure nor safe, the immortal child provides a solace-filled reality which feels both inside and outside the self, that does not change, and the truth of which cannot be challenged.

CLINICAL IMPLICATIONS

The resolution of parental grief is adaptation, growth, and change, not recovery of the way they were before the death. Parents now live in a different world with a self that has been changed. The change in the world is that a child, their child, has died. Among the changes in the self is the transformed inner representation of the now-dead child. What, then, is the role of the clinician in grief support groups or counseling? Clinical issues may be 1) stress in everyday life after the death of the child, 2) difficulties in transforming the inner representation of the child, or 3) ensuring that the inner representation of the child is held in as healthy a way as possible.

With parents whom Compassionate Friends describe as "well along in their grief," the nature and mode of the inner representation can be determined with questions like: "Who is C. to you right now?" "How are you still in touch with C.?" "Where is C. for you now?" "What role does C. still play in your life?" Most parents whose grief is well toward resolution can give a rather full answer to these questions and often can discuss problems they are having in managing the relationship with the inner representation of the child. This information enables the clinician to share the client's world in order to deal with whatever issues are at hand. Because some phenomena in the interaction with dead children fall outside socially accepted reality, parents may monitor their answer in terms of the perceived attitude of the questioner.

Bereaved parents who are, as Compassionate Friends describe it, "new in their grief" or "early in their grief," will usually not be able to answer the questions to their own satisfaction; and indeed, many answer the question in terms of absence or of the lack of connection. In this case, the clinician makes the inner representation part of the bond with the client. The clinician gets to know the child through photographs, art work, or stories of the child. It is not unusual for parents to bring linking objects into the consulting room. After the child is established as a social reality and the early issues of grief are navigated, parents begin to discuss the problems of living, the meanings of life, and the meanings of the death partly in terms of the meaning of the child now. Often at this time, the clinician will hear reports of visitations or interchanges with the child, and will begin to hear reports of the solace those interactions bring.

There are two especially difficult clinical situations involving the inner representation of the child. The first is when the inner representation is not shared in the client's natural support networks. There are a variety of reasons the inner representation may not be shared. After miscarriage often family and friends do not regard the fetus as a child, while the parent has already bonded with a whole set of hopes and expectations. When a married couple is a birth-parent and a step-parent, conflict may ensue if the step-parent has not deeply bonded to the child and, thus, does not share the birth-parent's inner representation of the dead child. There are also parents who are unusually isolated from social networks, and parents whose child died in such a socially unacceptable way that the parent is cut off from social support. When the inner representation is not a social reality, it is difficult to use it for solace. In these cases, referral to the Compassionate Friends or other grief support groups is often effective. When referral does not work, the therapist and the client can form the community in which the inner representation can become real.

The second difficult situation is when the inner representation

becomes intertwined in individual or family pathology. In these cases, clinicians can work with individual and family using the same theories and techniques they would use if the bond were with the living child. When the child is maintained as a frozen entity in the family system, the issue is flexibility. As the family can be helped to be more flexible, the inner representation will take a healthier place in the new dynamics. If a parent has so identified with the child that the whole selfhood was dependent on the child, the therapeutic issue is differentiation. When differentiation is achieved, the inner representation will provide solace rather than being a reminder of the parent's unfulfilled narcissistic bond.

In the easiest clinical situation, the clinician is called upon to validate the parents, experiences of interaction with the inner representation of their dead child. The clinician's authority can be used to normalize the experience. Learning that such experiences are normal and common often relieves a great deal of stress and thereby allows the parent to accept the solace being offered by the inner representation of the child.

Bereaved parents in the Compassionate Friends remain in active interaction with the inner representations of their dead children. As clinicians learn to understand how these immortal children take their place in the parents' lives, and how the inner representations give solace in the face of irreparable loss, the clinician can more effectively help parents deal with the stresses in their lives and untangle whatever pathologies present themselves.

REFERENCES

Benedek, T. (1959). Parenthood as a developmental phase. *American Psychoanalytic Association Journal, 7*, 389–417.

Benedek, T. (1975). Discussion of parenthood as a developmental phase. *Journal of the American Psychoanalytic Association, 23*, 154–165.

Bowlby, J. (1969–1980). *Attachment and loss (Vols. 1–3)*. New York: Basic Books.

Brice, C. W. (1991). Paradoxes of maternal mourning. *Psychiatry, 54*, 1–12.

Bushbaum, B. C. (1987). Remembering a parent who has died: A developmental perspective. *The Annual of Psychoanalysis, Vol. XV.* Madison: International Universities Press, pp. 99–112.

Cain, A. C., & Cain, B. S. (1964). On replacing a child. *Journal of the American Academy of Child Psychiatry, 3*, 443–456.

Chidester, D. (1990). *Patterns of transcendence: Religion, death, and dying*. Belmont, CA: Wadsworth.

Compassionate Friends, The, (1983). Oakbrook, IL: Author.

Dietrich, D. R. & Shabad, P. C. (Eds.). (1989). *The problem of loss and mourning: Psychoanalytic perspectives*. Madison: International Universities Press.

Dawson, L. (1989). Otto and Freud on the uncanny and beyond. *Journal of the American Academy of Religion, 58*(2), 283–311.

Elson, M. (1984). Parenthood and the transformations of narcissism. In R. S. Cohen, B. J. Cohler, & S. H. Weissman (Eds.), *Parenthood: A psychodynamic perspective* (pp. 297–314). New York: Guilford.

Fairbairn, W. D. (1952). *An object-relations theory of the personality*. New York: Basic Books.

Furman, E. (1974). *A child's parent dies: Studies in childhood bereavement*. New Haven: Yale University Press.

Gates of prayer: The new union prayer book (1975). New York: Central Conference of American Rabbis; London: Union of Liberal and Progressive Synagogues.

Glick, I. O., Weiss, R. S., & Parkes, C. M. (1974). *The first year of bereavement*. New York: John Wiley & Sons.

Goin, M. K., Burgoyne, R. W., & Goin, J. M. (1979). Timeless attachment to a dead relative. *American Journal of Psychiatry, 136*(7), 988–989.

Harper. R. (1991). *On presence: Variations and reflections.* Philadelphia: Trinity Press International.

Hood, R. (1977). Eliciting mystical states of consciousness in semi-structured nature experiences. *Journal for the Scientific Study of Religion, 16*(2), 155–163.

Horton, P. C. (1981). *Solace, the missing dimension in psychiatry.* Chicago: University of Chicago Press.

Hubler, E. (1952). *The sense of Shakespeare's sonnets.* Princeton, NJ: Princeton University Press.

Jackson, E. N. (1957). *Understanding grief: Its roots, dynamics, and treatment.* New York: Abingdon Press.

Jacoby, S. (1983). *Wild justice, the evolution of revenge.* New York: Harper & Row.

Johnson, S. (1984). Sexual intimacy and replacement children after the death of a child. *Omega: Journal of Death and Dying, 15,* 109–118.

Kalish, R. A. & Reynolds, D. K. (1981). *Death and ethnicity: A psychocultural study.* Farmingdale, NY: Baywood Publishing Company.

Klass, D. (1987). John Bowlby's model of grief and the problem of identification. *Omega: Journal of Death and Dying, 18,* 13–32.

Klass, D. (1988). *Parental grief: Resolution and solace.* New York: Springer.

Knapp, R. (1986). *Beyond endurance: When a child dies.* New York: Schocken.

Legg, C., & Sherick, I. (1976). The replacement child—A developmental tragedy: Some preliminary comments. *Child Psychiatry and Human Development, 70,* 113–126.

Lehman, D. R., Wortman, C. B., & Williams, A. F. (1987). Long-term effects of losing a spouse or child in a motor vehicle crash. *Journal of Personality and Social Psychology, 52,* 218–231.

Lifton, R. J. (1974). On death and the continuity of life: A "new" paradigm. *History of Childhood Quarterly, 1*(4), 681–696.

Lindemann, E., & Cobb, S. (1979). Neuropsychiatric observations after the Coconut Grove fire. In E. Lindemann and E. Lindemann (Eds.), *Beyond grief: Studies in crisis intervention.* New York: Aronson.

Lopata, H. Z. (1973). *Widowhood in an American city.* Cambridge, MA: Schenkman.

Lopata, H. Z. (1979). *Women as widows, support systems.* New York: Elsevier.

Matchett, W. F. (1972). Repeated hallucinatory experiences as a part of the mourning process among Hopi Indian women. *Psychiatry, 35,* 185–194.

Mogenson, G. (1992). *Greeting the angels: An imaginal view of the mourning process.* Amityville, NY: Baywood Publishing Company.

Moody, R. A. (1987). *Elvis after life: Unusual psychic experiences surrounding the death of a superstar.* Atlanta: Peachtree Publishers.

Moss, M. S., & Moss, S. Z. (1980). The image of the deceased spouse in remarriage of elderly widow(er)s. *Journal of Gerontological Social Work, 3*(2), 59–70.

Otto, R. (1923). *The idea of the holy.* Trans. by John W. Harvey. New York: Oxford University Press.

Parkes, C. M. (1972). *Bereavement: Studies in grief in adult life.* New York: International Universities Press.

Parkes, C. M., & Weiss, R. S. (1983). *Recovery from bereavement.* New York: Basic Books.

Passman, R. H. (1976). Arousal reducing properties of attachment objects: Testing the functional limits of the security blanket relative to the mother. *Developmental Psychology, 12,* 468–469.

Passman, R. H., & Weisberg, P. (1975). Mothers and blankets as agents for promoting play and exploration by young children in a novel environment: The effects of social and nonsocial attachment objects. *Developmental Psychology, 11,* 170–177.

Pollock, G. H. (1975). On mourning, immortality, and utopia. *Journal of the American Psychoanalytic Association, 23*(2), 334–362.

Poznanski, E. O. (1972). The 'replacement child': A saga of unresolved parental grief. *Journal of Pediatrics, 81*(6), 1190–1193.

Rando, T. A. (1984). *Grief, dying, and death: Clinical interventions for caregivers.* Champaign, IL: Research Press Company.

Raphael, B. (1983). *The anatony of bereavement.* New York: Basic Books.

Rees, W. D. (1975). The bereaved and their hallucinations. In Bernard Schoenberg et al. (Eds.), *Bereavement: Its psychosocial aspects.* New York: Columbia University Press, pp. 66–71.

Rubin, S. S. (1985). The resolution of bereavement: A clinical focus on the relationship to the deceased. *Psychotherapy, 22*(2), 231–235.

Rynearson, E. K. (1987). Psychotherapy of pathologic grief: Revisions and limitations. *Psychiatric Clinics of North America, 10*(3), 487–499.

Sanders, C. M. (1989). *Grief: The mourning after.* New York: John Wiley and Sons.

Silverman, P. R. (1986). *Widow-to-Widow.* New York: Springer Publishing Company.

Silverman, P. R. (1987). The impact of parental death on college-age women. *Psychiatric Clinics of North America, 10*(3), 387–404.

Stroebe, M., Gergen, M. M., Gergen, K. J., & Stroebe, W. (1992). Broken hearts or broken bonds: Love and death in historical perspective. *American Psychologist, 47*(10), 1205–1212.

Sullivan, L. E. (1987). Death, afterlife, and the soul. *Selections from the encyclopedia of religion,* Mircea Eliade, Editor in Chief. New York: Macmillan.

Tahka, V. (1984). Dealing with object loss. *Scandinavian Psychoanalytic Review, 7,* 13–33.

Tennant, C. (1988). Parental loss in childhood: Its effect in adult life. *Archives of General Psychiatry, 45,* 1045–1049.

Tessman, L. H. (1978). *Children of parting parents.* New York: Jason Aronson.

Volkan, V. D. (1981). *Linking objects and linking phenomena.* New York: International Universities Press.

Volkan, V. D. (1985a). The scope of depressive states. In V. D. Volkan (Ed.), *Depressive states and their treatment* (pp. 1–17). Northvale, NJ: Jason Aronson.

Volkan, V. D. (1985b). Psychotherapy of complicated mourning. In V. D. Volkan (Ed.), *Depressive states and their treatment* (pp. 271–295). Northvale, NJ: Jason Aronson.

Walsh, F. & McGoldrick, M. (Eds.). (1991). *Living beyond loss: Death in the family.* New York: W. W. Norton & Company.

Wilber, K. (1981). *Up from Eden.* Boulder: Shambhala.

Winnicott, D. W. (1953). Transitional objects and transitional phenomena. *International Journal of Psychoanalysis, 34,* 89–97.

Winnicott, D. W. (1971). *Playing and reality.* New York: Basic Books.

Worden, J. W. (1982). *Grief counseling and grief therapy, a handbook for the mental health practitioner.* New York: Springer Publishing Company.

Yamamoto, J., Okonogi, K., Iwasaki, T., & Yoshimura, S. (1969). Mourning in Japan. *American Journal of Psychiatry, 125,* 1661–1665.

Sibling Survivors

How Losing a Brother or Sister to Cancer Can Recast a Child's Destiny

Elizabeth DeVita

> I came to explore the wreck.
> The words are purposes.
> The words are maps.
> I came to see the damage that was done
> and the treasures that prevail.
>
> —From "Diving Into the Wreck" by Adrienne Rich

Like Adrienne Rich, some self-explorers come prepared for the submersion. Others simply fall overboard. And somewhere after the plunge, before being drawn back to the surface, they may decide it's not so bad down there.

I fell overboard on Halloween weekend in October of 1989 at a 4-H camp in Front Royal, Va. I was a camp counselor for siblings of cancer patients. The weekend was an offshoot of an annual camp for children with cancer, and I was in charge of a group of 7-year-olds. It was Saturday. We were all sitting in a grass clearing for a question-and-answer session with a doctor who'd volunteered to come down for the weekend.

"Did I do it?" stammered the boy. He had been silent until then, sitting cross-legged in the cool October grass. Then he got up on his knees.

"Did I do it?" he asked, and for a time the rest of us, campers, and counselors, melted into the grass as the boy summoned himself to face the doctor.

"No," answered the doctor. "You did not cause your sister's cancer by punching her in the arm."

The boy dropped his eyes and sank back on his seat. Slowly and steadily, he began to tug grass from the earth and lay it in a careful pile by his side. Other children raised their hands. Sitting there behind him, watching him pull up the grass, I saw my own hand, minus a dozen years.

Small and white with ragged fingernails, it flipped the radio dial on my mother's maroon Buick. It was summer, 1973, and my bare legs stuck to the seat. My feet didn't reach and my sandals bobbed and swayed with the motion of the car.

We were stopped at the light in Bethesda, waiting to turn into the hospital, when it hit me. My brother Ted was sick because I'd wished it on him. He would probably die. My mother asked me a question and I couldn't look at her. I said, "The maroon glove compartment" instead.

At some point during the course of my brother's eight-year illness, I must have figured out that I hadn't made him sick, but I don't remember that. I hadn't even remembered that moment in the car until the boy at camp got up on his knees and asked for the truth. My brother was 9 when he was diagnosed with aplastic anemia, a disease in which the bone marrow stops producing the immune cells that fight infection. He spent eight years at the Clinical Center at the National Institutes of Health, where my father was chief of the medicine branch. Ted died five months short of his 18th birthday of complications from treatment of his disease. I was 14.

But that morning, as I listened to those children in the clearing, I confronted again the questions that framed my early life.

"Will I get it?" asked a blonde girl just on the edge of teenhood. Probably not, answered the doctor. Her face was impassive.

And in a flash I remembered checking my body in the mornings, looking for the red magic marker X's that told the radiation beams where to shoot. I tugged on my hair to see if chemotherapy was making it fall out, positive that my parents were treating me for cancer in my sleep. They were too scared to tell me, I thought, and I was too scared to ask.

Another thin voice floated out of the crowd. "Is my brother going to die?" The riskiest question so far. The doctor weighed his answer carefully. He said it was possible, but there were many effective treatments now.

There are a lot of us who have lost a sibling—and lost a piece of our childhood and our family.

Many years ago, a 14-year-old boy named David hurt his head in a skating accident and died of a brain hemorrhage. His mother took to her bed, refusing to accept a future without him. Her other son, 7, began writing amusing stories to read at her bedside. An entertainer ever after, James Barrie went on to immortalize his brother by writing "Peter Pan: The Boy Who Never Grew Up."

Surviving siblings know their lives are shaped by the one in the family who never grew up. Sometimes we overcompensate and try to live for two; sometimes we build a protective wall around us so as not to feel the pain. Often we find the missing link in our lives much later on.

From *The Washington Post*, January 19, 1993, pp. 10-14.

Would it help these children to know there are others who are now adults who have asked these same questions?

Andrew Tartler, 47
Licensed social worker, until recently director of one of the American Day Treatment Centers, an outpatient mental health facility in Chevy Chase

Sometimes, the catastrophe opens the door for families to deal with each other more candidly. "People are never more open to change than when they are in a crisis situation, and the family faces no greater crisis than the illness and loss of one of its children," says Tartler.

He grew up in Tampa, Fla., with his parents and a sister two years older and one two years younger. Things were normal in his family, as far as he can remember, until he was about 5. He remembers his mother yelling at his younger sister Susan, telling her to hold her head up straight. She'd taken to holding it to one side.

"I remember wondering why my mother would be so upset with my sister for not holding her head up straight." Then his sister disappeared. "I'm assuming she must have gone to the hospital," he reasons, "but it was never explained to us, and I don't know how much after that she died. We just never saw her again."

To this day, he and his older sister don't know what happened, because it was never spoken of in the house. It was as if she had never existed. If there was a funeral, they were not allowed to go. There were no graveside visits. All pictures of Susan were removed from the house. He and his sister sensed that it was taboo to ask questions, so they kept quiet. When people asked his mother how many children she had, she told them two. "There was always this part of me that wanted to say 'Hey, there is a third kid,' " Tartler says. " 'She's not here right now, but there is a third kid.' "

Sixteen years after her disappearance, when Tartler was 21 and a college student living at home, his mother pulled a box of family treasures out of a closet that included pictures of Susan. It was then he learned that she had died of a brain tumor. "It was real hard for my mother to talk about it," he says. Then she folded the pictures and put them away. "Still," he says, "the important thing was acknowledging that Susan existed. Up until then, she was like the child that never was."

Because he was unaware of his sister's illness, it was the aftermath of her death that affected him the most. His parents started to fight. He began to have nightmares. "The kind of nightmares where terrible creatures, not people necessarily, but more horrible, vicious things would be chasing me and I would wake up screaming."

His father owned and ran a bakery, and for 12 years after Susan's death he worked seven days a week. The rest of the family also became absorbed by the business. His mother went in the morning and worked up front until 7 p.m. or so. Tartler and his sister joined her after school, greasing pans and getting things ready for baking. An uninterrupted dullness took over the

family, a mourning phase that never ended, was never overtly acknowledged.

The only thing that made him feel normal was going to the school playground to play with the neighborhood kids. "I think that's really what saved me."

At college, he found himself reacting to little things with great emotion. During an intramural football game, he flipped one of his fraternity brothers up in the air and landed on his leg. "We thought I had broken it. I got in a fight with another guy, and finally ended up absolutely losing it. I remember walking away from the scene, and I started bawling. It was so unlike me. It was all that pent-up stuff that had been inside of me for years."

Gradually, he began to understand why he reacted like he did. "As I've grown up and matured and come to grips with suppressing all of that in early childhood and early adulthood, I've found healthier ways to examine it and let it out," says Tartler.

Today he freely discusses his emotions. As he talks, he leans back in his office chair, occasionally looking out the enormous window as if he will find the end of his sentence there.

The window ledge and his desk display numerous pictures of his wife and two young boys, ages 3 and 5. "I tell them it's okay to cry if you feel sad." He worries a lot about something happening to them. Every morning when he leaves the house, he kisses them and tells them to be careful. "My younger one says, 'Be careful, Daddy.' " He laughs. "It's crazy that a 3-year-old would be saying something like that."

"It's no accident that he is a social worker. "One of the reasons I've been so successful clinically," he explains, "is because I know pain. I recognize it when I'm in a room with it. I probably know all the tricks about suppressing it on a very intimate level."

For years, he worked with families on a pediatric oncology branch at the National Institutes of Health. Then he became the administrator of The Children's Inn, a residence on the NIH campus for families with a child ill with cancer. During that time, he started an annual weekend for siblings of cancer patients as part of Camp Fantastic, the organization that sponsors a summer camp for kids with cancer.

At one time, he says, his career seemed serendipitous, but no longer. "If you look at my life," he muses, "there is a clear path of the things that I have done to come to grips with this major event that happened when I was 5 years old."

He wants to resolve the issue, at least to get the story straight. "I'd like to sit down with my sister," he says, "and compare her version of the story to mine." And some day, he would like to visit Susan's grave. "I don't think it ever goes away. It's just a part of you."

Stephen Chanock, 36
Senior staff fellow in pediatric oncology at the National Institutes of Health

He graduated from college and was living in France when he found out that his older brother had cancer. "I had already applied to medical school, and a few days after I'd gotten accepted I got a call from my parents saying that my brother was trying to reach me."

His brother told him that the lesion he'd noticed on his leg while playing squash had not gone away and that the doctors said it was cancer. "I was shell-shocked," says Chanock. He and his fiancee were to come back and get married, and by the time they got home to Washington, his brother had already lost all of his hair from the chemotherapy. "It was clearly going to be a difficult road."

During the first year of medical school, he commuted from Boston on weekends to spend time with his brother. A couple of times, his brother came up to visit him. "We spent a lot of time talking, we were very close." he pauses. "He was my closest friend."

Surgery and chemotherapy seemed to keep the cancer at bay for a while, but by the new year it had come back "everywhere." Chanock came back from medical school and took his exams in Washington. His brother lived in what he describes as terrible pain on extensive life support for about six weeks in the intensive care unit before he died in May 1980.

"I can remember what people were wearing when my brother died and the conversation as well as I can remember my wedding day and the birth of my four kids. Those are the days etched in my mind in tremendous detail."

One of the worst parts about the aftermath is "the notion of losing the family unit that had been so close and so happy, and is then shattered. There is the fear that it's going to stay that way. There is the feeling of impending doom, like you're going off to war and don't know if everything will still be there afterward."

His family remains very close, although his brother's death created new tensions. "My parents viewed me as the person who was going to live the dreams and expectations of both kids. It's not like they said I had to go and win an Olympic gold medal, but there was the sense that everything had to go well, needed to go well."

He credits his wife for cutting the pressure. She told him to get on with what he needed to do in his own way. By his fourth year in medical school, he had decided to be a pediatric oncologist, a choice clearly guided by his brother's death. Once he'd made the decision, "the pressures just melted away."

Chanock completed 10 years of training and now treats patients on the same floor where his brother was cared for, working for the physician who had treated him. His brother died in the intensive care unit 500 feet away from his office. "I was able to avoid the ICU until about a month ago," he says. "It hasn't changed much." Flashbacks are common for him there, but he says he has a commitment to his work, a "missionary zeal."

"The day I'm not 100 percent committed to working late or early or on weekends to do whatever I can to get kids better or to help them while they die is the day I walk out of here."

But, he acknowledges that he spends 25 percent of his time with patients, and 75 percent of his time in the lab. "There's my buffer zone, I might feel differently if I was out there on the front line all of the time."

There are other flashbacks of his brother in familiar places: They went to the same school, Sidwell Friends in Washington.

"My brother and I walked the same halls there." Now, two of his children go there. "Not too long ago, I was walking out of the gym and there was this picture on the wall that had been there forever, and I just had this sudden realization that my brother looked at it and now I was looking at it and he wasn't. That started this torrent of memories."

Robert Gallo, 55
Chief of the laboratory of tumor cell biology at the National Institutes of Health and co-discoverer of the AIDS virus

He was 13 when his 6-year-old sister, Judy, was diagnosed with leukemia. His parents told him that Judy had the flu, that she'd have to stay in the hospital for a while. They planned to stay with her, and he was sent to stay with relatives. At first, it didn't seem like a big deal to him. Judy had a habit of following him everywhere, and she was vaguely annoying. "I liked her," he says, "but basically I was always trying to lose her."

As her flu dragged on, "I remember being very resentful. It just went on and on, and it was only the flu. I remember being angry at her for taking my parents away from me, and I remember thinking that they loved her more than they loved me."

When the family went to pick her up at the hospital, he discovered that his sister was sicker than he'd been led to believe. The first reports from the doctors were that Judy was "well." It was then, when she seemed to be out of the woods, that the family told him she had leukemia. She was one of the first patients to be treated with antimetabolites—chemotherapeutic drugs that interfere with cancer cell growth. They brought her into remission. But by the time the family got to the hospital to pick her up, she'd relapsed.

Gallo's strongest memory is the sight of her in the hospital. He expected the sister he'd always known, "a plump, pretty, happy little girl." The sister he saw was pale and emaciated. "Those were the days before supportive care," he explains. "She was bruised, jaundiced, her veins were sunken and there was blood on her teeth. There was blood everywhere."

He remembers standing there shocked, and then she held out her arms to him to be kissed. "I got scared. There were two horrors about it; one was the horrible sadness and second was the horrible physical fear of her. What I remember the most is wanting to get out of there really badly," he recalls. He went home with relatives once again.

One day, his relatives told him to pray hard for Judy. Then they drove him home. It was clear and sunny and his basketball hoop beckoned from the top of his driveway. Underneath it, his parents were pulling luggage out of the car and he started to run to see them, so happy to be home." His uncle stopped him with a hand on his shoulder and said, "Judy's dead."

"I screamed," he remembers, "I broke down. I felt guilty for being angry with her, and I felt guilty for having tried to lose her all of those times."

After that, the family went into constant mourning. There was no music allowed in the house, no more holidays were celebrated. "No Christmas, no Thanksgiving, no Easter."

His father blamed everyone for her death. Normally a cool and reserved man, he spent hours in Judy's room, kissing her belongings and holding her picture to his heart. He went to her grave sometimes twice a day. Gallo had always suspected that Judy was his father's favorite. This proved it.

His father became religious; he began giving money to people on the street, to churches and hospitals. Gallo remembers thinking that his father, a successful businessman, had become foolish. He vowed to be the opposite of him. "My relationship with my father became very estranged after that. He did spoil me rotten, gave me everything I needed, but," he pauses, "he never once hugged me."

His mother and her side of the family were much warmer and more expressive, and he got most of his support from them. But they continued mourning for his sister. When they all got together on the third anniversary of Judy's death, "I remember screaming, 'When are we going to be normal again?' "

It was after Judy's death that he became obsessive about succeeding. His first focus was basketball, but he injured his back playing and turned to schoolwork. By the time he was 17, he knew he wanted to be a hematologist. Looking back, he simply says, "I lost my childhood."

During college and medical school, he was equally driven. By the time he was in college, he'd already had his name published in research papers. After medical school, he went to the National Institutes of Health, where his first assignment was on the pediatric oncology ward. "It was horrible, it was reliving it all over again. Every time I had to go talk to parents, my heart pounded," he recalls. "I hated it."

Since then, all of his work has been in laboratory science. One of his most significant discoveries was isolating a retrovirus that causes leukemia in humans, the disease that killed his sister. But he is leery about drawing associations between her death and his work. "It's too easy," he says.

B ack at camp, the boy in front of me stopped tugging at grass and turned to look me in the eye. "Have you ever seen a Tyrannosaurus Rex?"

I had to admit I'd never seen the dinosaur, but I knew what he was saying to me. Healthy siblings know how to spot safe subjects and treat them accordingly. We know how to make fantasy our reality. It's safer that way.

Soon we were heading back through the tall grass the way we came. My dinosaur friend was relentless. "Why haven't you seen a Tyrannosaurus Rex? I've even seen one," he said. "And I'm only 7."

By the time we reached camp, I had a veritable warehouse of dinosaur lore, most of it made up. This kid had a method. He started simple and then elaborated. "Tyrannosauruses are big," he paused, "One of them ate my neighbor's dog. And his cat. Trees are safe. They don't like vegetables." He cocked his head to the side, pleased with this summation, and ran off after another boy.

I remembered sitting in the waiting room of the 13th floor of the Clinical center, where there were round fake wood tables and swivel chairs. I was sitting there by myself, swiveling and wearing some Mickey Mouse ears someone had given me. A woman with white hair and granny glasses sat herself carefully down in one of the lemon-colored chairs. "Are you a member of the Mickey Mouse club?" I wasn't really sure what the Mickey Mouse club was, except I knew it had been on TV. I answered yes and proceeded to tell her about the singing and dancing we did on the show. I even showed her a few steps. She had white hair and opened her eyes wide when I talked to her. Soon my mother came to collect me and as we waited for the elevator, the woman called out, "You must be very proud of her." My mother smiled politely as we stepped into the elevator.

Back at camp, there was a Halloween party that night. The boy was waiting for me, already dressed in his costume. "I'm a pirate," he said. An eye patch floated in the middle of his forehead; a wrinkled tin-foil sword was jammed in his belt loop. "Have you ever seen a real pirate before?" he asked, giving me another chance. He shook his head when I answered no. "They eat people," he announced. "I saw some land on the beach once and steal five kids, all girls. I didn't see them eat them," he admitted. "But I bet they did." He eyed me levelly. "They wear earrings."

I smiled as the pirate boy yanked on the sleeve of my sweatshirt. "If pirates come here," he said, "I'll protect you, I have a sword."

Parents try to protect healthy siblings by telling them partial truths.

I looked down at him; he'd unwittingly sized up our collective situation. The key to family dynamics when one child gets sick is protection in all forms. There is self-protection by not acknowledging what's going on or by blanking out memories. Parents try to protect healthy siblings by telling them partial truths so as not to frighten them. The kids know what they're doing, and it exacerbates their worries because they resort to the unrefined art of interpretation. They try to cope with their fears on their own, sensing that there is not enough parental concern to go around. And they protect the parents as much as possible from worrying about them, even though their interior life is now filled with fear, guilt, worry and anger.

As I watched this kid dart around, jabbing other kids with his tin-foil sword, I realized that my family had taken part in the same painful pattern. We took the protection game and honed it into an art. I, for instance, protected myself to the point of forgetting, or so it seemed. But these children had brought back a surge of images.

One girl mentioned her brother's bone-marrow transplant, and I had a fleeting vision of walking down a hallway with my family, realizing too late to save myself that they were bringing me for more blood tests to see if I would be an appropriate bone-

marrow donor for my brother. He stayed with me, trying to soothe me as they drew the blood.

Then I saw the bloody patches on the back of his jeans, right above the right hip pocket. My mother could never launder away this evidence of the procedure they used to test my brother's bone marrow. No matter how they bandaged the area, blood would seep through. So he wore his jeans with dark spots hovering over the right hip.

Surviving siblings know their lives are shaped by the one in the family who never grew up. Sometimes we overcompensate and try to live for two; sometimes we build a protective wall around us so as not to feel the pain.

I wasn't sure if I saw myself in these kids or if I just recognized their pain, and their pain brought back the life history that I had killed and buried. The memories were like crocuses peeping through frozen ground.

That Saturday evening, I watched them line their jack-o-lanterns into a circle, fire the candles and turn out the lights to prepare for the evening's ghost stories. My pirate friend, now missing his eye patch and sword, climbed over bodies to the center of the circle.

"It was a dark and stormy night," he began. And I remembered being in the doctor's office a few months before, frozen in terror as a nurse swabbed my arm with alcohol in preparation for drawing blood for a routine test.

"It was a dark dark and stormy night," he continued. And I thought about the boyfriend I had broken up with. To me, closeness meant potential loss.

"It was a dark, dark, dark and stormy night," chanted the boy.

And I thought about how angry I now became when I got sick because I remembered the times my parents had dismissed my colds and flus during my brother's illness.

Dark, dark, dark, but it was making more sense now. There undoubtedly had been a calamitous wreck long ago in my life, and I had effectively covered it up, as surely as oceans swallow foundering ships. But there is nothing to keep me from plumbing the depths of my memory to eye the damage, nothing to keep me from retrieving the treasures.

"The end," cried the boy. The smell of burned pumpkin permeated the room as he crawled back over the sprawled bodies, sat in front of me and carefully leaned himself against my knees.

Families, Now and into the Future

What is the future of the family? Does the family even have a future? These questions and others like them are being asked and many people fear for the future of the family. As articles in previous sections of this volume have shown, the family is a continually evolving institution that will continue to change throughout time. At the same time, there are certain elements of family that appear to be constant. The family is and will remain a powerful influence in the lives of its members. This is because we all begin life in some type of family and this early exposure carries a great deal of weight in forming our social selves, who we are and how we relate to others. From our families, we take our basic genetic makeup while we also learn and are reinforced in health behaviors. In families, we are given our first exposure to values and it is through families that we most actively influence others. Our sense of commitment and obligation begins in family as well as our sense of what we can expect of others.

Much of what has been written about families has been less than hopeful and has focused on ways of avoiding or correcting errors. The articles in this section take an optimistic view of family and its influences on its members. The emphasis is on health, rather than dysfunction.

The first article, "Trace Your Family Tree: Charting Your Relatives' Medical History Can Save Your Life," provides a useful technique for mapping out a family medical history so that one can anticipate and plan health behaviors. The next two articles focus on healthy families and suggest that the statement that "all families are at least a little dysfunctional" might better be stated as "all families are at least a little bit healthy." "Happy Families: Who Says They All Have to Be Alike?" describes the strengths of today's families and provides a glimpse of an assortment of happy, healthy families. "Family Matters" proposes that by looking at families as at least a little bit functional, one can recognize the strengths of the family and build on these. Families are dynamic systems, adapting to meet the needs of their members. Indeed, what may be seen as dysfunctional adaptation in some families may be a functional response to overwhelming social forces in other families. The final article of this volume, "Rituals for Our Times," by family therapists Evan Imber-Black and Janine Roberts, describes the ways in which families use rites and ceremonies to strengthen families. Through examples, the authors provide direction on how the reader might use ritual in his or her own family.

Looking Ahead: Challenge Questions

After having charted your family's medical history, what type of future do you see for yourself? What kinds of changes do you see yourself making in your life?

If it were possible to return to families of an earlier age, would you do it? Why and why not?

What decision have you made about long-term commitments? Is marriage in your future? How about children? Why do you feel that way?

After reading these articles, when you look around at families, what do you think about them? Do you feel hopeful about your future?

What do you think about the state of rituals in your family? What types of rituals can you see yourself building in your family?

Unit 5

TRACE YOUR FAMILY TREE

Charting your relatives' medical history can save your life

RUTH PAPAZIAN

Ruth Papazian, a New York City-based writer specializing in health and medicine, is constructing a family tree for herself and her niece and nephew.

When it comes to health, the apple doesn't fall far fom the family tree: Research suggests that an astonishing number of diseases—from rare to common—have some sort of hereditary link.

That is why constructing a family health tree can offer life-saving glimpses into your future. If you're at risk of inheriting a serious disease, you can get regular checkups to spot early symptoms and increase the chances for a cure. You may also want genetic counseling, to learn the risk of passing a disease on to your children.

Aside from health problems caused by accident or infectious disease, you can assume that most every disease in your family's background has some sort of genetic basis. These can be divided into two classes: *susceptibility diseases,* in which genes don't cause the problem but influence your risk of becoming ill; and *purely genetic diseases,* which people almost invariably develop if they inherit the requisite genes.

Susceptibility diseases typically occur later in life and include major ailments such as heart disease, diabetes (especially the non-insulin-dependent type) and several types of cancer, including breast, lung, colorectal (colon and rectal), prostate, ovarian and skin. The inherited tendency to develop a disease probably results from complex interactions among several genes. Also on the list of disorders with a genetic component: rheumatoid arthritis, allergies, asthma, glaucoma, Alzheimer's disease, osteoporosis, glaucoma and behavioral and emotional problems including schizophrenia, alcoholism and depression. ("Hereditary Risk" lists for several diseases the increased risk faced by someone with an afflicted parent.)

Although genes set the stage for these disorders, the actual illness is usually caused in part by some environmental factor—cigarette smoke in the case of lung cancer, for example, or high-fat diets in heart disease and non-insulin-dependent diabetes, as well as prostate, colorectal and perhaps ovarian cancer. Luckily, people who know that a susceptibility disease lurks in their family tree may be able to control those nongenetic risk factors, or at least be on the alert for early symptoms.

For example, if your mother or sister developed breast cancer before menopause, your lifetime risk would be as

From *American Health*, May 1994, pp. 80-84. © 1994 by Ruth Papazian. Reprinted by permission.

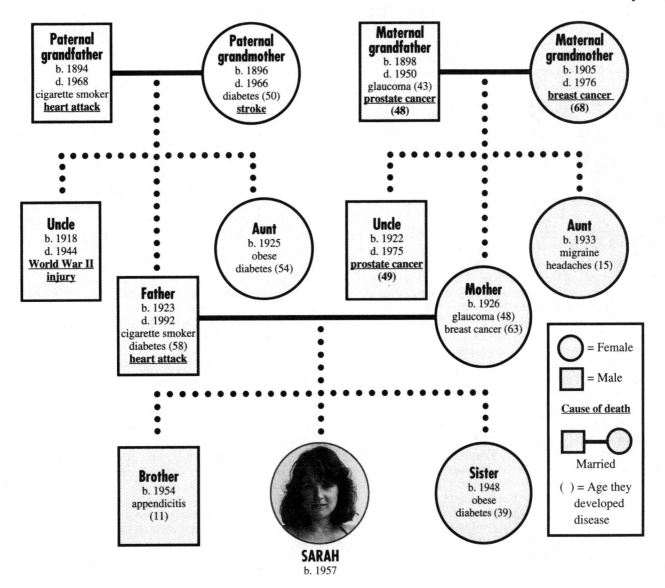

SARAH
b. 1957

Legend:
- ◯ = Female
- ▢ = Male
- **Cause of death**
- ▢—◯ Married
- ( ) = Age they developed disease

Paternal grandfather: b. 1894, d. 1968, cigarette smoker, **heart attack**

Paternal grandmother: b. 1896, d. 1966, diabetes (50), **stroke**

Maternal grandfather: b. 1898, d. 1950, glaucoma (43), **prostate cancer (48)**

Maternal grandmother: b. 1905, d. 1976, **breast cancer (68)**

Uncle: b. 1918, d. 1944, **World War II injury**

Aunt: b. 1925, obese, diabetes (54)

Uncle: b. 1922, d. 1975, **prostate cancer (49)**

Aunt: b. 1933, migraine headaches (15)

Father: b. 1923, d. 1992, cigarette smoker, diabetes (58), **heart attack**

Mother: b. 1926, glaucoma (48), breast cancer (63)

Brother: b. 1954, appendicitis (11)

Sister: b. 1948, obese, diabetes (39)

SARAH'S FAMILY MEDICAL HISTORY

Sarah risks inheriting non-insulin-dependent diabetes from her father's side of the family and breast cancer and glaucoma from her mother's side. But the two fatal heart attacks on her father's side shouldn't cause concern; both occurred relatively late in life and probably stemmed from major risk factors—smoking (her grandfather) and both smoking and diabetes (her father).

Diabetes: Sarah's sister already has it. Sarah and her brother should have their blood sugar monitored regularly; they can help ward off the disease by exercising and adopting a prudent diet.

Glaucoma: Sarah and her two siblings should have yearly eye exams to detect glaucoma at its early stages.

Breast cancer: Sarah and her sister face a higher than normal risk, since their mother and maternal grandmother developed it. Both sisters should have a baseline mammogram between the ages of 30 and 35, and yearly mammograms after 35; her sister should lose weight, since obesity adds to her risk.

Finally, Sarah should alert her brother to the fact that he's at increased risk for *prostate cancer*. His maternal grandfather and uncle both developed it early in life. He needs regular screening: each year, a digital rectal exam, plus a PSA (prostate-specific antigen) test.

225

great as one in three, vs. one in nine for other women. (Early onset of any disease increases the probability that heredity played a role.) A family history of breast cancer means you should get annual mammograms beginning at age 35, plus frequent professional exams.

s for purely genetic diseases, there are more than 4,000—most of them rare—that result from defects in single genes. If you have such a disorder in your family tree, your chance of inheriting it depends on the nature of the gene responsible.

For instance, if one of your parents died of a heart attack before age 60, there's a one-in-five chance that he or she had familial hypercholesterolemia (an inherited extremely high cholesterol level); if so, there's a 50-50 chance you have it too. The gene responsible for familial hypercholesterolemia is "dominant": Inherit a defective version from one parent and you'll get the disease, even if your other parent gave you a normal copy.

Familial hypercholesterolemia, which affects one in every 500 people, can clog arteries and lead to a heart attack at an early age. If you have a family history of heart disease, be sure to get your cholesterol level measured. Once detected, an abnormally high cholesterol level can often be controlled with a lowfat diet and cholesterol-lowering drugs.

Familial adenomatous polyposis, another inherited disorder, afflicts one in 8,000 people and almost always results in intestinal cancer. ("Surviving a Family Curse," below, describes a family coping with this dominant-gene problem.) Other dominant diseases include Huntington's disease (the degenerative nervous-system disorder that killed singer Woody Guthrie), adult polycystic renal disease (a kidney disorder) and Marfan's syndrome (characterized by abnormally long limbs and heart problems). Diseases controlled by a dominant gene rarely skip a generation, so you've probably been spared if neither of your parents had the disease, even if a grandparent did.

Fortunately, most purely hereditary diseases are "recessive": that is, they afflict only those unlucky enough to inherit two copies of a defective gene—one from each parent. The most common of these recessive diseases seem to target certain ethnic groups.

For example, about one in 25 white Americans carries the gene for cystic fibrosis (CF), one of the most common lethal hereditary diseases (for those of northern European descent the risk is somewhat higher). The gene defect in CF results in a thick, sticky mucus in the lungs; the mucus encourages severe respiratory infections that usually prove fatal by age 30.

A CF carrier—with one abnormal and one normal gene—will be healthy. But if someone with the gene marries another carrier, their offspring will have a one-in-four chance of inheriting two defective copies of the gene and being born with CF. Following the discovery in 1989 of the gene that causes CF, a blood test became available that can tell whether a person is a carrier and whether a couple's fetus will develop the disease. ("Family Roots" lists several ethnic groups, the diseases to which they're susceptible, and how common those diseases are.)

Purely hereditary diseases (or disorders) that usually affect only men are called X-linked recessive diseases. The best known are hemophilia, color blindness and Duchenne muscular dystrophy. An X-linked disorder is transmitted from mother to son by a gene on one of her two X chromosomes. Each son has a 50-50 chance of getting the disease, from inheriting just a single copy of the recessive gene.

Mom may be a healthy carrier, since her other X chromosome carries a normal copy of the gene, which masks the defective one. But her son, with his X chromosome paired with a Y from his father, isn't as lucky. A woman should suspect she may be a carrier of an X-linked disorder if the disease has shown up in a male relative.

Virtually every month, researchers identify a gene linked to yet another hereditary disease; these findings are leading to increasing numbers of blood tests to identify people who carry these genes or who are destined to develop the diseases. ("Testing for Risk" lists some of these diseases.) To take advantage of these advances, you must first learn whether you or other family members are at risk.

Surviving a Family Curse

Larry Howard* had considered his family's medical history a curse, but knowing about it probably saved his life.

Larry's mother, three brothers and a sister all had been diagnosed with familial adenomatous polyposis, a disease in which thousands of polyps—tiny wartlike growths—sprout from the lining of the large intestine (colon). People with this condition (about one in 8,000) almost always develop colon cancer from polyps that turn malignant.

Larry's mother and his four affected siblings had to have their colons removed to prevent cancer from taking hold—the treatment reserved for severe cases. But Larry and his other sister, Mary, thought they had been spared.

Since early adolescence, when the polyps generally arise, Larry and Mary had taken part in the Johns Hopkins

University familial polyposis study, undergoing annual sigmoidoscopies (visual examination of the lower third of the colon) and receiving clean bills of health. Ten years ago, when Larry was 32, he was told he didn't need any more checkups, since his risk of having inherited the disease seemed minimal.

Then last year he and Mary were given a new blood test, developed at Johns Hopkins, that identifies the gene that causes familial polyposis. The test determined that Mary did not carry the defective gene, but Larry did. Sure enough, a subsequent exam revealed sprouting polyps.

Larry plans to have his colon removed later this year. His three children have taken the blood test too: One of the three has tested positive.

*Not his real name.

Gathering information about illnesses that run in your family is not as daunting as it may seem—especially if you ask relatives for help. Here is a guide for constructing your medical family tree:

1. Make a list of your first-degree relatives (parents, siblings and children) and second-degree relatives (grandparents, aunts and uncles). Adding more peripheral branches to your tree usually isn't worthwhile: The more distant the relative, the less relevant his medical fate is to you (you and your second cousin, for example, inherit only about 3% of the same genes). A possible exception: when you need more evidence to confirm a pattern involving a serious health problem such as cancer or heart disease.

2. Construct your family tree, using the sample on p. 225 as a guide. Your name and the names of your siblings go on the bottom row. On the row above, put the names of your parents, along with the names of their brothers and sisters. The names of all four grandparents go on the top line. It's customary to put male relatives in squares and female ones in circles and to indicate marriages by connecting relatives with horizontal lines.

3. Record the following information for each relative:
● *Date of birth, date of death and cause of death.* If necessary, you can usually obtain this information from the death certificate. To get a copy, contact the department of vital records in the state where the relative lived. (Be sure to check the family Bible first—birth and death certificates are often tucked inside the covers.)
● *All known illnesses and major surgeries, including the age when they occurred.* This information could be more relevant than the cause of death—if an uncle had a heart attack at age 40 but died 20 years later from an automobile accident, for example. Medical records are the most reliable sources for this information.

Ask relatives who are still living either to give you copies of their medical records or to sign a consent form allowing their doctors to give you this information. To obtain a deceased relative's records, contact the doctor or hospital that treated him; those names should be on the death certificate. You may have to provide a letter of consent from your relative's next of kin, as well as a copy of the death certificate.
● *Lifestyle factors that may have contributed to illness.* For instance, heart disease would be less of a genetic threat if you found that the uncle who suffered the heart attack at age 40 was a chain smoker. Most every family has a self-appointed "historian" who is the repository of family lore. You may be able to learn about relatives' lifestyles by talking to that person.
● *Occupation (optional).* This information may be important if there were job-related factors (such as exposure to toxic chemicals) that may have contributed to illness, miscarriage or birth defects.
● *Unusual physical characteristics.* Prominent features or chronic skin rashes could hint at certain medical conditions or birth defects (but you'll want to corroborate your hunches with medical records or other documents). Again, the family historian may be a good source. Family photo albums can also be revealing: A grandmother's "dowager's hump," for example, probably indicates that she had osteoporosis.

As you research your family medical tree, be prepared for difficulties. Information may be unavailable (some family

TESTING FOR RISK

The genes responsible for more than 300 diseases, most of them rare, can now be identified through blood tests. In some cases, these tests detect the gene itself; in others, they identify DNA "markers" that suggest the gene is present.
● **Cystic fibrosis**
● **Familial hypercholesterolemia**
● **Duchenne muscular dystrophy**
● **Fragile-X syndrome** (the most common inherited form of mental retardation)
● **Huntington's disease**
● **Neurofibromatosis** (a nerve disease characterized by dozens of skin tumors all over the body)
● **Retinoblastoma** (an eye tumor that usually occurs in childhood)
● **Sickle-cell anemia**
● **Tay-Sachs disease**
● **Thalassemia** (a blood disorder that occurs most often in people of Mediterranean descent)
● **Wilms' tumor** (a malignant kidney tumor that usually occurs in childhood)
Source: *Heredity and Your Family's Health,* by Aubrey Milunsky, M.D. (Johns Hopkins University Press, 1992)

FOR MORE HELP

Free pamphlets
● **"Genetic Counseling,"** GC Pamphlet, March of Dimes, 1275 Mamaroneck Ave., White Plains, NY 10605.
● **"Genetic Counseling: Valuable Information for You and Your Family,"** the National Society of Genetic Counselors, 233 Canterbury Dr., Wallingford, PA 19086-6617.
● **"Where to Write for Vital Records,"** Superintendent of Documents, U.S. Government Printing Office, Washington, DC 20402.

Books
● **Heredity and Your Family's Health** by Aubrey Milunsky, M.D. (Johns Hopkins University Press, 1992).
● **How Healthy Is Your Family Tree? A Complete Guide to Creating a Medical and Behavioral Family Tree** by Carol Krause (Collier Books).

Organizations
● **The Hereditary Cancer Institute,** Creighton University School of Medicine, 2500 California Plaza, Omaha, NE 68178.
● **Gilda Radner Familial Ovarian Cancer Registry,** Roswell Park Cancer Institute, Elm and Carlton streets, Buffalo, NY 14263.
● **University of Utah Cardiovascular Genetics Research Clinic,** 410 Chipeta Way, Room 161, Research Park, Salt Lake City, UT 84108.
● **The Hereditary Disease Foundation,** 1427 Seventh St., Suite 2, Santa Monica, CA 90401.

Family Roots

Risk of certain genetic diseases in specific races or ethnic groups.

Racial or ethnic background	Diseases	Carriers	Afflicted
Italian or Greek	Thalassemia	1 in 10	1 in 400
African	Sickle-cell anemia	1 in 12	1 in 650
Caucasian	Cystic fibrosis	1 in 25	1 in 2,500
Eastern or Central European Jewish (Ashkenazic), Cajun American or French Canadian	Tay-Sachs disease*	1 in 30	1 in 3,600
Mediterranean Jewish (Sephardic) or Armenian	Familial Mediterranean fever**	1 in 45	1 in 8,000

*Neurological disorder invariably fatal within the first five years of life.   **Repeated bouts of fever and abdominal pain.
Adapted from *Choices, Not Chances: An Essential Guide to Heredity and Health,* ©1977 by Aubrey Milunsky, M.D.
By permission of Little, Brown and Company.

Hereditary Risk

Estimated risk for some common disorders that are influenced by inherited genes but not directly caused by them. Risks are for people with one parent who had the disease. The risk would be greater if a second parent or a sibling also had the disease.

Disease	General population	One parent with condition
	Lifetime risk	
Alcoholism	5%	10% to 20%
Alzheimer's disease	2% to 5%	19%
Asthma	4%	26%
Cancer, breast	11%	22%*
Cancer, colon	4%	10%
Cancer, ovarian	1%	5%
Cancer, uterine	3%	9%
Diabetes (non-insulin-dependent)	2%	5% to 10%
Duodenal ulcer	10%	30%
Glaucoma	2%	4% to 16%
Manic depression	1%	25%
Migraine	5% to 10%	45%
Schizophrenia	1%	8% to 18%

*The risk may be three times as great as in the general population if the mother was premenopausal when her cancer was diagnosed.
©1992 by Consumers Union. Reprinted by permission from *Consumer Reports on Health.*

members may not cooperate, for example), or it may not exist (as when a child died and no diagnosis was ever made) or it may not be accurate (family legend, for example, may attribute an aunt's pregnancy loss to a miscarriage when in fact she had an abortion).

A little tact goes a long way. Family members may not want to talk about sad events or what they consider to be the family's dirty laundry. A good approach: "My doctor is in-terested in Cousin Bobby's condition because it could affect the children I may have. Can you tell me about his problem so that we can calculate the risks?" Offer to share your completed tree with relatives, along with the opinions of medical or genetic experts you consult.

Now that you've constructed your family tree, here are some tips on interpreting it:

● Your tree's two most important "branches" are your mother and father: Each gave you half your genetic inheritance, so their diseases will be most relevant to you and your siblings.

● The earlier a disease develops, the more likely that heredity played a role in it (except for ailments with obvious non-genetic causes such as infections).

● A disease that strikes two or more relatives at the same age is likely to be strongly influenced by heredity.

● A clustering of cases of the same disease on one side of the tree is more likely to suggest that genes play a strong role in causing it than a similar number of cases scattered on both sides. On the other hand, your risk of inheriting a purely hereditary disease like cystic fibrosis would actually be greater when it's present on both your mother's and father's side.

If you have questions about your family tree, you should show it to your doctor. If the doctor suspects a genetic problem, you will probably be referred to a genetic counselor, who can assess your risk of developing the diseases you're worried about, and of passing them on to a child. A counselor can also tell prospective parents if a fetus can be tested for conditions of concern.

Genetic counselors typically have a master of science degree in genetics and are certified by the American Board of Medical Genetics. Your family doctor, obstetrician or pediatrician can probably refer you to one, or you can contact a major hospital or medical school in your area or your local chapter of the March of Dimes for referrals (for further information, see "For More Help").

Your medical family tree should be a living, growing document. As you and your brothers and sisters get married and have children, keep adding to it: It can contribute to your health today and to the health of future generations.

Happy Families

WHO SAYS THEY ALL HAVE TO BE ALIKE?

Susan Chollar

Susan Chollar writes about science and health for a number of national magazines.

It's Thursday evening in Watsonville, a small agricultural town on California's central coast. Cathy Chavez-Miller is fixing dinner for her "blended" family: her husband, Mike, her stepson, Cliff, and her son from her first marriage, Patrick, who spends half his time with his father. "At times it's been a real challenge," she says, "but we really enjoy each other and wouldn't change the way things are." On the opposite coast, it's nighttime in suburban Washington, and mental health therapist Shelly Costello tucks her five-year-old twins Chelsea and Carly into bed. Worn out after 10 hours in day care followed by a rowdy evening at home with Mom, the kids are soon fast asleep. But Shelly, a single parent, must tackle a sinkful of dirty dishes and a couple of loads of laundry before she can call it a day. Her philosophy concerning our oldest social institution: "I don't believe in the rule that a family has to have two parents living together, but I do believe that people have to be happy. As long as a family is happy, it will be a good place for children to grow up."

American families are not what they were 40 years ago when Father Knew Best and every household was presumed to live *The Life of Riley.* Ozzie and Harriet and the Cleavers have long since given way to Murphy Brown and the *Full House* gang, and the traditional two-parent family sometimes seems like an endangered species.

We all know the statistics: Half of all marriages in the U.S. end in divorce, and nearly a third of our children are born out of wedlock. As a result, four out of 10 kids don't live with both of their biological parents; one in four lives in a single-parent home; and almost one in six families includes at least one stepchild.

Critics such as former Vice President Dan Quayle have blamed these demographic changes for everything from the Los Angeles riots and the growing wave of violence among teenage boys to declining scholastic performance. But while social scientists don't deny that American children and parents face greater challenges than ever before, they increasingly question the assumption that broken homes and single-parent families per se are threatening children. Several recent sophisticated studies suggest that growing up under the same roof with both biological parents is less crucial to a child's psychological health than growing up in a stable home.

"The quality of the individuals and relationships in the household matters more than who the particular actors are," says Dr. Frank Mott, a senior research scientist at the Center for Human Resource Research at Ohio State University in Columbus. "If you have a happy home, you'll probably have well-adjusted children." In other words, the atmosphere of the home counts for more than the type of family who inhabits it—even when it comes to "broken" homes.

In 1980 Dr. Paul Amato, an associate professor of sociology at the University of Nebraska in Lincoln, began charting the progress of 2,000 marriages; over the course of his study, 15% ended in divorce. In 1992 he contacted 500 adult children from those failed marriages and measured their psychological and social adjustment. The offspring of the failed unions tended to fall into two distinct groups: Those from marriages in which there had been little external conflict before the divorce were likelier to have personal problems as young adults than those from overtly troubled marriages.

Amato believes that children from seemingly harmonious homes that break up bear the greater scars because, to them, "the divorce means the loss of a stable home. Although the parents were unhappy with the

THE STRONGEST PREDICTOR OF SUCCESS IS THE LEVEL OF CONFLICT BETWEEN A MOTHER AND HER CHILD: LESS IS BEST.

marriage, from the child's perspective it wasn't really that bad."

For children who had lived in homes where there were arguments and perhaps physical violence, however, divorce often meant an end to discord. Therefore, the adult children from such homes tended to have better psychological health—and even stronger social relationships and marriages—than those from homes in which there had been little external conflict before divorce. "To the children," Amato concludes, "the consequences of divorce depend on the quality of the marriage prior to it." He adds: "It might be better for children to be in a well-functioning divorced single-parent family than a nuclear family marked by high levels of conflict."

Research on families headed by single women also suggests that the quality of a home is more important than its cast of characters. Sociologist David Demo, an associate professor of human development and family studies at the University of Missouri in Columbia, examined the emotional health and academic performance of 742 teens from the four most prevalent types of households: intact two-parent, never married single-parent, divorced single-parent and stepfamily.

When Dr. Demo analyzed all his data, he found that the type of family a child belonged to was a surprisingly weak predictor of the child's well-being and achievement. Although teens who resided with both biological parents tended to do better academically and behaviorally, they did only slightly better than those from never-married single-parent families. The most powerful predictor of the young people's adjustment and academic performance was the level of conflict between mother and child: Less is best.

"Dan Quayle argues that families headed by never-married mothers are inherently harmful to children," says Demo, "but the data don't show that. In fact, the never-married [single-parent] family offers a type of continuity that can parallel that of intact two-parent families." He summarizes his research this way: "Families are diverse by race, class, structure and well-being. Some are in trouble, some are doing very well. And some are somewhere in-between."

If some divorces—but not all—cause problems, so do some stepfami-

lies. Dr. Louise Silverstein, a family therapist and an assistant professor of psychology at Yeshiva University in New York City, observes that research shows relationships are often more difficult in stepfamilies, particularly for girls who find themselves living under the same roof with their mother's new husband. Boys who accompany their mother to a new household seem to fare better, presumably because there is less sexual tension in their relationship with a same-sex stepparent.

Children who deal with strife that continues between parents *after* divorce also often suffer. Silverstein illustrates with a case history: The parents of three-year-old Sean separated in a tangle of bitterness and anger when his mother, Mary Ann, was six months into a second pregnancy her husband, Tom, opposed. When Tom reacted by embarking on an affair with Mary Ann's closest friend, their conflict escalated into screaming matches and even physical violence that showed no sign of abating months after their marriage dissolved. "They were completely out of control," says Silverstein. Unfortunately Sean was his parents' real victim: Over eight months, his once normal behavior deteriorated into frequent tantrums and a severe case of separation anxiety.

Researchers who found that children from broken homes generally don't do as well as those whose parents stayed together may have misinterpreted the causes. Nearly half of single-parent families live in poverty, for example, compared with only 8% of married families. Almost 12 million households are headed by women, whose economic status is slashed by at least a third following divorce; never-married mothers are among the poorest members of our society. In many single-parent homes, low income—not divorce—causes children to live in high-crime neighborhoods and to have more health and academic problems.

Sociologist Nicholas Zill is vice president of the Westat research corporation in Rockville, Md., which explores social issues for the federal government, among other clients. "If you are the classic Murphy Brown type with all the advantages, and you decide to have a child out of marriage," he says, "your child is not nec-

essarily at risk. But if you're a teenager with little education or money, that can be a recipe for disaster."

Assessing the effects of growing up in a household headed by a single woman is clearly not a simple matter. Ohio State's Mott analyzed data about 1,714 youngsters aged five to eight from various socioeconomic backgrounds, to see if a father's absence from the home caused academic and/or behavioral problems. He discovered that those from fatherless homes indeed scored lower on math and reading achievement tests. But additional probing revealed that the children's mothers scored lower on aptitude tests than the married mothers; they also tended to be poorer and were more likely to have dropped out of school. When he compared children in the sample from similar socioeconomic backgrounds, he found that they performed equally well, regardless of a father's presence.

When it came to behavior, the absence of a father didn't correlate with any particular problems among black children. But fatherless white children had significantly more behavioral difficulties than peers who had fathers, even when income and education levels were similar. White girls and white boys from fatherless homes were less sociable and less independent than white children from homes with fathers. In addition, white boys from fatherless homes were also more prone to hyperactivity, peer conflict, anxiety and depression.

Mott offers several suggestions for these race- and gender-based differences. Girls may be less vulnerable than boys in the absence of a father, he says, because they're closer to their mothers. And black children are part of a culture in which single parenting is not only more prevalent but also more accepted. While nearly half of the fatherless black households in Mott's study had never had a paternal presence, 94% of similar white homes had; many more white children had "lost" their fathers due to divorce or other family disruption. "From a child's perspective," says Mott, "never having had a father in the home may be better, at least in a psychological sense, than having had one who left." Along with more accepting attitudes toward families without fathers, many

The '50s: Not So Happy Days

The 1950s are often portrayed as a simple time when fresh-faced children flourished in nuclear families, men ruled their castles with wisdom and benevolence, and women relished their roles as ever-nurturing wives and mothers. Not so, says Stephanie Coontz, a family historian at The Evergreen State College in Olympia, Wash. "The reality of these families was far more painful and complex than the situation-comedy reruns or the expurgated memories of the nostalgic would suggest," she writes in *The Way We Never Were: American Families and the Nostalgia Trap* (Basic Books, 1992, $27). "Contrary to popular opinion, *Leave It to Beaver* was not a documentary." A quarter of Americans, a third of U.S. children and nearly two-thirds of the elderly were desperately poor, making do without food stamps or housing programs. Half of two-parent black families lived in poverty, and 40% of black women with small children had to work outside the home.

Even for families who came closer to the Cleaver mold, life was often not as simple or happy as it appeared. A quarter to a third of '50s marriages eventually ended in divorce. Many who described their unions as "happy" in national polls nonetheless admitted many dissatisfactions with their mates and day-to-day lives. Child and spouse abuse was common, though largely unacknowledged.

For women in particular, the '50s were not what they seemed to be on *Ozzie and Harriet*. (In his new book, *The Fifties*, author David Halberstam argues that the real-life Nelsons—dominated by autocratic, workaholic Ozzie, who stole "the childhood of both his sons and used it for commercial purposes"—were in fact a dysfunctional family.) "It was a period where women felt tremendously trapped,"

says Coontz. "There were not many permissible alternatives to baking brownies, experimenting with new canned soups and getting rid of stains around the collar." In some states, husbands had legal control over family finances. In 1954, an article in *Esquire* magazine labeled working wives a "menace." Feminist values and lack of interest in childbearing were considered abnormal, if not pathological. Some women unwilling or unable to fulfill their expected domestic roles were subjected to electro-shock or confinement to psychiatric institutions. Throughout the '50s, the press reported a growing wave of frustration and resentment among full-time homemakers, whose use of tranquilizers and alcohol skyrocketed.

To those who point to the '50s as an era of conservative sexual values, look again, says Coontz. Birth rates among teenagers reached numbers since unequaled. The percentage of pregnant white brides more than doubled, and the number of babies born out of wedlock and put up for adoption rose 80% between 1944 and 1955. "What we now think of as 1950s sexual morality," writes Coontz, "depended not so much on stricter sexual control as on intensification of the sexual double standard."

Although Coontz's research shines light on the weaknesses of American families from earlier historical periods as well, she denies that family bashing is her goal. "To say that no easy answers are to be found in the past is not to close off further discussion of family problems, but to open it up," she says. "Only when we have a realistic idea of how families have and have not worked in the past can we make informed decisions about how to support families in the present or improve their future prospects."

with boys and girls raised by gay parents also tends to refute the conventional wisdom. After reviewing studies of the children of lesbian mothers, Dr. Charlotte Patterson, an associate professor of psychology at the University of Virginia in Charlottesville, concluded in the October 1992 issue of *Child Development* that there was no evidence that these children's development had been compromised in any significant respect. "Children don't need a father to develop normally," says Silverstein, "and future research on children raised by gay fathers will probably show that they don't need a mother either. What children need are affectionate, nurturing adults—regardless of their gender or biological relationship—who love them."

Considering the very real challenges of growing up in a nontraditional home, family researchers are quick to acknowledge the advantages that the *right kind* of traditional family can confer. If the worst scenario is a family marked by hostility and conflict, "the best situation," says Nebraska's Amato, "is to grow up in a family where there are two adults who get along well and love the child. Two parents can supervise a child better, provide more practical help, discipline and guidance, and serve as effective role models."

What is most promising about the new research, says Missouri's Demo, "is the suggestion that a lot of these changes in traditional family structure are not harmful to children. But what is disturbing is that the studies point out that negative and disruptive events in children's lives do have important effects on their well-being. Those are the real problems—and those are the patterns that are increasing in our society."

One point on which family experts agree is that we should spend our energy on securing a happy future for our children rather than waxing nostalgic about the past. "It is important to look at the realities of how families are actually functioning," says Westat's Zill, "rather than labeling some as inevitably bad and others as inevitably good." Adds Amato: "All of these types of families are here to stay. And by and large, all of them can work quite well. We need to concern ourselves with making sure that each of them works as well as it can."

black communities offer single parents more extended-family support.

This extra help can make the difference between success and failure in families of any color, says Yeshiva's Silverstein, offering another case history as an example: Alice, now a well-adjusted, young white adult, was raised in a household consisting of her mother, grandmother and aunt; the mother was the breadwinner, while

the grandmother created a warm, nurturing atmosphere. "The additional adults also acted as an emotional safety net for Alice," Silverstein says. "If she had a fight with her mother, there was always her grandmother or aunt to comfort her. And their presence meant she didn't have to experience her mother's anger or disappointment so intensely."

The newest research conducted

FAMILY MATTERS

WE HAVE HEARD A GREAT DEAL ABOUT THE DYSFUNCTIONAL FAMILY AND THE ALTERNATIVE FAMILY. HERE'S A DEFENSE OF THE FUNCTIONAL FAMILY.

Lance Morrow

I come from a large family. We were eleven children in all, out of four marriages—six brothers and sisters, two half brothers, one half sister, two stepbrothers. The age range among us is wide. The oldest, my brother Hugh, was born toward the end of the Great Depression, and the youngest, my half sister Carolyn, arrived around the time of the Cuban missile crisis. My brother Michael, who promised to be the best of us, died of cancer when he was 17.

"The reason grandparents and grandchildren get along so well is that they have a common enemy." Attributed to Sam Levenson

We were—are—complicated, I suppose, as families always are. Being so numerous, and as distinctly unlike one another as the brothers Karamazov (though infinitely more cheerful), we could populate a small branch of sociology, or a 19th-century novel—but with 20th-century themes. The Sixties, for example arrived like a traveling circus at my father's big house in Bronxville, New York, and recruited some of the children away for a time. They almost need not have left, since the Bronxville house ran like a commune anyway, a counterculture Brady Bunch, although on its bad days it felt like an orphanage.

Most of the things that happen to families happened to ours: dysfunction (to use the therapy cant of the Nineties), happy marriages, a bitter divorce, widowhood and widowerhood, dogs and cats and parakeets and neurotics, success and catastrophe, dramas of banishment and prodigals' return, silences that lasted for years, sweet reconciliations. There were follies by the grown-ups and follies by the children, and, through the years, that almost

involuntary steadfastness, the complex, aching, binding love that is the real biological energy of families.

"When I was a boy of fourteen, my father was so ignorant I could hardly stand to have the old man around. But when I got to be twenty-one, I was astonished at how much he had learned in seven years." Mark Twain

There was also a lot of fun. Morrows are a multitude to begin with, and the fact that so many Morrows are talented mimics (of famous people, of ethnic types and of one another) could sometimes seem to double or triple our numbers—funny and fugitive identities flying through the air. A family reunion in Baltimore, which for many years brought together my father's seven surviving brothers and sisters and *their* dozens of children and grandchildren, and assorted other cousins and kinsmen, was a dear, Morrow-populous occasion. My father's brothers and sisters the children of my grandfather Dr. Hugh Morrow and grandmother, Marjorie—all looked amazingly alike, with the same distinctive high foreheads and Morrow nose, a thin, noble, slightly curving Roman variety. All the eight brothers and sisters, standing together in Baltimore, smiling on my Uncle Rowland's grand green lawn in early June, looked hilariously like a Dr. Seuss drawing of the same outlandish creature eight times repeated and perched like birds on a limb: a remarkable effect. (Dr. Seuss—that is, Theodor Geisel—died the same day my father did, in 1991, a fact that carried a small, surreal private meaning for me, because of my mental picture of the happy Morrows arrayed on that Seuss branch.)

Tolstoy was surely wrong when he wrote that all happy families are the same, and all unhappy families are unhappy in different ways. In the first place, there are rarely such things as happy families and unhappy families. A family by definition is both happy and unhappy. Of all social forms, the family is truest to life. In fact, it *is* life. Besides, Tolstoy (whose own home life tended toward the wretched) was insulting happy families. If any formula applies, it goes the other way around from the way he concocted it: A happy family is the ingenious one, the novelty, the original. A happy family represents a sort of artistic creation. Unhappy families from the House of Atreus to the House of Menendez—have a certain miserable sameness: depression and compulsion and violence soaking in an unwholesome marinade.

In any case, the family is what we all start out with, the cards the genes have dealt us. It is the place where we acquire first memories, the beginnings of love and politics, the first lessons about the world. The family is everybody's particular origin myth—those demigods above us (miraculous in their love, apocalyptic in their displeasure), that home, that universe are all the incubator that we come out of. The family is, to some extent, our fate.

The family is so basic, such an extension of self, that sometimes it becomes overwhelming; people spend years trying to establish a separate identity. One night in the late Seventies, I received an unexpected call from a girlfriend from college days. I had not heard from her in years. She brought me up to date: She had rebelled against her oppressively all-controlling parents and their highly social world, and had not seen them in several years. (She had been an only child and their only reason for being, their obsession: I understood why she wanted to get away. But I almost wept for the pain they must have felt when she walked out and slammed the door.)

She had married a man of a different race.

And do you have children? I asked.

"We have chosen not to reproduce ourselves," she replied stiffly.

WHAT IS THE FAMILY?

A sociologist produced this bloodless—and fleshless—definition, as if he were talking about a compact piece of machinery: "[The family is] a small kinship-structure group with the key function of the nurturant socialization on the newborn."

No. The meaning of family is never abstract, because it is precisely particular lives arranged in clusters, even in bouquets. It represents an extravagantly organic and even floral human story form—never linear, rarely predictable—that elaborates itself through time, performing soap operas, comedies, tragedies, follies. The individual is the atom; the family is the molecule, the building block, the structure of energy. One of the fascinations of family is that it makes generalization difficult.

"Grownups never understand anything for themselves, and it is tiresome for children to be always and forever explaining things to them." Antoine de Saint-Exupéry, The Little Prince

I think of families sometimes in terms of music—a tone of the cello, for example, rich and deep, which I associate with some poignancy of family love, with an undertone of forgiveness, and of the passage of time, and of eventual loss. But more often it seems to me that the family genius is essentially narrative and dramatic. From families flows an endless stream of stories. They bubble up from an abundant underground source. Without the family, tabloids would go bankrupt. Literature would fall back upon adventures and love affairs that end before they become serious (what would be the point?). Shakespeare and the Bible would virtually shut down (no Lear and his daughters, no Hamlet and his father, no Ruth in the alien corn, no Abraham prepared to sacrifice Isaac—no Adam and Eve for that matter).

For all the family's fierce vitality, sociologists have been debating for a generation the question of whether or not it will survive. I consider this an absurd speculation. Nevertheless: In America's 95.7 million households, there are now 3.3 million couples living together without marrying—six times more than in 1970. Of the remaining couples, 50 percent of their marriages will end in divorce. Sixty percent of today's children at some point live in single-parent households; 30 percent live in single-family homes for most of their first eighteen years.

The family's prestige has declined—or grown problematic—anyway. In the Sixties, it had become intensely political, so much so that by the Nineties, "family values" had become a campaign issue—a cry of protest against pornography, AIDS, drugs and all the other centrifugal forces. Heterosexuals get unmarried while homosexuals fight for the right to marry and "have" children. Is that a compensatory expansion of the family's franchise, as the gay-rights movement might have it, or is it yet another symptom of the forces threatening the family, as some conservatives would have it?

"The family is one of nature's masterpieces." George Santayana, The Life of Reason

Americans traditionally cherish an official piety about the family—a Norman Rockwell vision of wholesomeness that was converted to video back in the early Flintstones age of television. Americans of the baby boom began absorbing the images and values of mass electronic families like the Nelsons, the Andersons, the Cleavers, the Petries, the Brady bunch—family idealizations that visited weekly for half an hour (with commercial interruptions) and left behind, after a period of years, a sort of residual ghost universe of functional and sentimentalized families. Off this TV product, American actuality has played in a curious mental intermingling of corny sitcom and on-rushing real life. The dissonance between the two universes helped to produce the indignant protests of the Sixties and still (thanks to the metaphysics of reruns, which make the ideal video families timeless) causes a poignant confusion in the minds of children. How tidy were the plot resolutions after half an hour, the denouement mellow and edifying. How symmetrical was the Brady Bunch—males, females, complementary, complete. How untidy was the reality of things.

Of late, of course, that ghost universe of television has lost some of its idealization. During the 1992 Presidential campaign, when the issue of Murphy Brown's out-of-wedlock sitcom child became an issue, President Bush announced that he would like "to make American families a lot more like the Waltons and a lot less like the Simpsons."If the baby boomers grew up with an idealized family in the back of their minds, the young today see a very slightly rawer and more knowing version, which also gives a curious and alarming prominence to a quality some Americans think is ascendant in their country: sheer stupidity. Beavis and Butthead make a sort of virtue of it.

The family ranks high in the American hierarchy of values. But the idealized American self-image is difficult to reconcile with the dreary and sometimes violent life on the ground.

The dysfunctional family, of course, has become something of a cliche. Everyone knows what a dysfunctional family looks like. I have sometimes wondered what we would mean if we spoke of the "functional" family. Does such a thing exist? Of course it does, we think instinctively, and have in mind its general shape and certain soft-edged qualities: love, security, stability . . .

Consciously or unconsciously, most Americans thinking of the functional family—often visualizing it as a sort of nostalgic memory, the way they might think of the American small town—have in mind some model of the much-maligned bourgeois family: that is, the sturdy, freestanding model with responsible mother and father and two or three children deemed fully worthy of being raised well.

And yet the drift of American history in the last two generations has worked to subvert and discredit that model. In the first place, the word "bourgeois" carries a certain amount of unpleasant connotation acquired from Marxist polemic and then echoed by Sixties leftism—a concoction of theories (Adorno and Marcuse and R. D. Laing and Wilhelm Reich as absorbed by the countercul-

ture) that combined with strains of feminism and distilled itself into an attitude of repugnance for "bourgeois domesticity." The critic George Steiner referred to "the Sundays and suet of the bourgeois life form." The home in some circles became a kind of prison; and the family was seen as a patriarchal, authoritarian arrangement designed to repress women and children and preserve the domineering prerogatives of the male.

"Home is the place where, when you have to go there, they have to take you in."
Robert Frost, The Death of the Hired Man

We've all had these arguments in the last twenty or twenty-five years—abstract yet urgent arguments, because they address difficult, intimate choices: Does the functional family require both mother and father? Living together in the same house with the children? (In other words: Should we keep the marriage together for the sake of the children?) Or can it remain functional, though in a different way, if we are divorced? Or when both parents are away at work? That last question became even more difficult, in some ways, than the divorce question. How many hours a week of day care will begin to subvert the functionality of the family?

The family, God knows, is an institution with a tremendous amount of guilt swirling about in it anyway—and the issues reflected by these questions quadruples the guilt. But those issues seem simple compared to others: What if both parents belong to the same sex, are gay and "married?" What if a single woman is artificially inseminated with the sperm of a donor she does not know? What if a couple, unable to conceive a child, hire a woman to conceive a baby, using the husband's sperm, and bear the child to term?

These are all familiar cases now, of course. It is almost hard to remember when they would have seemed somewhat sinister, in a futuristic way. And beyond these questions lies an entire world being opened up by biotechnical tinkering, by gene altering. If you want to be futuristically sinister, think of what the family might become if cloning were to seem a more reliable way to reproduce than sex.

In recent years, as baby boomers have married and had children and grown older, they have tended to embrace, *faute de mieux*, the bourgeois family. Well, everyone rediscovers the wheel eventually. Rousseau (a grotesquely irresponsible family man, by the way) pronounced that "the earliest of all societies, and the only natural one, is the family."

Some version of the bourgeois family is obviously here to stay. A part of the legitimacy that it seemed to lose during the last generation is being regained among immigrant groups for whom the bourgeois values—hard work, honesty, reliability, a focus on the next generation—are still powerful drives. A spirit of entrepreneurial democratic capitalism also implicitly encourages variations on the bourgeois family approach. Among many Asian immigrants, Confucianism, with its respect for elders and for family cohesion, functions in somewhat the same way that the Protestant work ethic did for earlier generations arriving from Europe.

Does the family have a future? One somewhat visionary strain suggests that the family, in an ever more mobile age of information and genetic engineering, will evolve out of existence, or evolve toward social forms we will eventually not recognize as the old traditional family.

The sociologist Christopher Lasch has touched on the darker theme: At the end of the 20th century, too many parts of the United States—even the suburbs—have become terrible places to raise children. "To see the modern world from the point of view of a parent," Lasch said, "is to see it in the worst possible light."

"Heredity is something a father usually boasts about, until his son starts acting like a damn fool." Ring Lardner

---

A generation or two ago, it was fashionable for the young to say they would not get married and start a family because they could not bear to bring children into a world shadowed by the threat of nuclear war, or by neo-Malthusian-style extinctions such as overpopulation and planetary famine. The end of the cold war presumably ended the nuclear problem, at least for the moment. But there are other apocalypses available closer at hand: drugs, guns, AIDS, poverty.

It becomes clearer every day what happens to societies in which families disintegrate. Unless those societies find some substitute—and few of them do, gangs being a sad, violent alternative form of love and acceptance—then the young men turn feral and prey upon one another, the economy disintegrates, the children grow up dodging bullets, and the downward spiral produces a result that is already visible in every major city in America. In Freudian terms, the superego comes down like a detonated building and what remains is a violent, id-ridden maelstrom.

Curiously, however, the new plagues may have the effect of making the traditional family stronger than ever. As the outer world becomes more dangerous, it is likely that people will draw close in upon home and family. They may begin to erect moral fortifications reminiscent of old small-town values, even of a certain repressive mentality. The balance may tip away from license toward a sort of puritanical realism enforced by economic troubles and physical threats.

But my suspicion is that most of what goes on in a family, the important part, is unaffected by outside ideas. Families have their own powerful inner dynamics. Families are complicated organisms, with so many variables at work in them (genes, temperament, tradition, environment, luck and 10,000 other imponderables) that ideology is just one more strand of influence. The real life of families—their enduring power—is something of a secret, individual and inarticulate.

The analysts working with chaos theory in the last few years suggest that reality is almost infinitely asymmetric and nonlinear. These scientists could probably come closer than anyone else to explaining the family's jagged, ever-shifting, asymmetric coherences—the harmony of accidents, the exuberances, the inner resources of family blood. I know that when I think of chaos theory, my own difficult, sprawling family clicks, somewhat weirdly, into place, and becomes almost comprehensible to me.

Rituals

FOR OUR TIMES

**Evan Imber-Black
and Janine Roberts**

*Evan Imber-Black is the director of the
Family and Group Studies program of the
Department of Psychiatry at Albert Einstein
College of Medicine. Janine Roberts is the
director of the Family Therapy program of
the School of Education at the University of
Massachusetts.*

• • • • • • • • •

**How today's
families are
developing
innovative rites
and ceremonies
to ease difficult
transitions, heal
relationships, and
celebrate life.**

• • • • • • • • •

E VERY FOURTH OF JULY, PAUL
and Linda Hoffman pack their
three children and their dog
into the station wagon and
drive 250 miles to Paul's sister's
home, where all of the Hoffmans gather.
The event is fairly unpleasant. The
women spend the day cooking, which
Linda resents, while the men watch sports,
an activity Paul doesn't care for. The
young cousins spend most of the day
fighting with one another. In the evening,
Grandpa Hoffman sets off fireworks, but
no one really pays attention. On the fifth
of July, Paul and Linda drive home, wearily vowing that this is the last year they will
spend their holiday this way.

The following June, however, when
Paul and Linda dare mention that they are
thinking about doing something different
for Independence Day, Paul's sister calls
and tells them how upset their parents will
be if the couple and their children don't
come this year. Alternate plans fall by the
wayside, and on the Fourth of July into
the car they go.

Does this story sound at all familiar to
you? Because of experiences like the Hoffmans', in which celebrations are static and
meaningless, many of us have minimized
the practice of rituals in our lives. One

woman we know who grew up in a family
whose rituals were particularly confining
put it this way: "I don't want any rituals in
my life. Rituals are like being in prison!"

Yet in these times of rapid and dramatic
change in the family—with more children
being raised by single parents, more mothers working outside the home, fewer
extended families living in close proximity
—rituals can provide us with a crucial
sense of personal identity as well as family
connection. Despite the changing status

of the family, membership within a family
group is still the primary way that most
people identify themselves. Rituals that
both borrow from the past and are
reshaped by relationship needs of the present highlight for us continuity as well as
change. A family in which ritual is minimized may have little sense of itself
through time. Everything simply blends
into everything else.

As family therapists who have been
working with and teaching the use of rituals since the late '70s, we have encountered
an increasing number of people who are
longing to revitalize the rituals in their lives.
They just don't know how. Rituals surround
us and offer opportunities to make meaning from the familiar and the mysterious
at the same time. Built around common
symbols and symbolic actions such as
birthday cakes and blowing out candles,
or exchanging rings and wedding vows,
many parts of rituals are well known to us.

A ritual can be as simple as the one that
sixty-two-year-old Eveline Miller practices
when she needs to sort things through.
She goes to her grandmother's rocking
chair, sits, and rocks. When she was a
child and needed comfort, this was where
she used to go to lay her head upon her
grandmother's lap. Her grandmother
would stroke her hair and say, "This too
will pass." Now, as Eveline rocks and
thinks, she repeats those words to help
calm herself and provide perspective.

Rituals also can be more elaborate and
creative, such as one that Jed and his wife,
Isabel, a couple in their early twenties,
designed for Jed's brother. Several months
after Jed married Isabel, his mother died
suddenly, leaving Jed's nineteen-year-old

brother, Brian, orphaned. Brian came to live with Jed and Isabel. The young couple thus found themselves not only newlyweds but also new "parents." One day Brian told them, "You know, I feel like I don't have a security blanket. My friends at school, other people in my classes—most of them have at least one parent still alive. Their parents can help them if they're having trouble in school, or if they need a place to stay, or can't find a job. And I don't have that security blanket because both of my parents are dead."

What Brian had said seemed so important to him that Jed and Isabel talked about it between themselves and eventually came up with an idea: They would make Brian a quilt—a security blanket. Jed's sister had an old nurse's uniform of their mother's that they could use for material. An older brother had a Marine camouflage shirt of their father's. They found some other old fabric among their mother's things. Then, as they began to cut the material into squares, they realized that they would need help sewing them together into a quilt. Jed thought of his maternal grandmother, who had sewn a number of quilts for other family members.

The siblings and the grandmother began gathering in secret to sew the quilt and share memories of Brian's parents and their earlier life. And when the family gathered to celebrate the grandmother's eightieth birthday, Brian was given the quilt—a blanket that symbolized both the ability of Jed and Isabel to "parent" in creative ways and the new network of contact that had been built between the siblings and their grandmother. Together, these family members had proved to be Brian's "security blanket."

The symbols and symbolic actions of rituals embrace meaning that cannot always be easily expressed in words. Eveline Miller's rocking chair, for example, was much more than a place to sit; it evoked safety, reassurance, and the memory of her grandmother. Brian's quilt was not just a cover; it represented the interconnected people in his life—from the past and the present—whom he could carry with him into the future. The textures, smells, and sounds of ritual symbols—an heirloom rocking chair, a family-made quilt—can be powerful activators of sensory memory. Family members may recall scenes and stories of previous times when similar rituals were enacted or some of the same people were together. Rituals connect us with our past, define our present life, and show us a path to our future.

FAMILY RITUALS TAKE A VARIETY OF FORMS. There are daily practices, such as the reading of a child's bedtime story or the sharing of a mealtime. There are holiday traditions, some celebrated with the community at large (seasonal events such as the solstice, religious events such as Passover, national events such as the Fourth of July) and others exclusive to a particular family (birthdays, anniversaries, reunions). Then there are life-cycle rituals, which mark the major transitions of life.

All human beings throughout the world and throughout time are born, and all die. All of us experience emerging sexuality. And most create sustained adult relationships to form new family units and new generations. Such changes are enormously complicated, involving both beginnings and endings; holding and expressing both pain and joy. They may shape and give voice to profoundly conflicting beliefs about our personal existence and our relationships. It's little wonder that every culture in the world has created rituals to celebrate and guide our way through these life-cycle passages.

The truly magical quality of rituals is embedded in their capacity not only to announce a change but to actually create the change. Given that volumes have been written advising people how to change, and that people spend countless hours in therapy, often agonizing over their inability to make needed changes, it is easy to see why rituals exist in all cultures, to ease our passage from one stage of life to another. Using familiar symbols, actions, and words, rituals make change manageable and safe. Simply knowing which rituals lie ahead during a day, a year, or a lifetime stills our anxiety. Change is *enacted* through rituals and not simply talked about—couples don't change from being single to being married by talking about marriage, but rather by participating in a wedding ceremony. Teens don't graduate from high school when a teacher says "you're finished now"; they attend proms, picnics, and the graduation ceremony itself.

As families have changed, life-cycle events have changed too, and there are many crucial transitions for which there are no familiar and accepted rituals in our culture. Changes that often go unmarked include divorce, the end of a nonmarried relationship, adoption, forming a committed homosexual relationship, leaving home, pregnancy loss, and menopause. Since life-cycle rituals enable us to begin to rework our sense of self and our relationships as required by life's changes, the lack of such rituals can make change more difficult.

Rituals tend to put us in touch with the profound circle of life and death, so it is not surprising that healing moments emerge spontaneously during these celebrations. If you keep that in mind when changes are occurring in your life or in the lives of those close to you, you can plan a ritual to specifically generate healing.

• • • • • • • • •

A family in which ritual is minimized may have little sense of itself through time.

• • • • • • • • •

Healing a Broken Relationship

The crisis of shattered trust and broken promises can lead to genuine atonement, forgiveness, reconciliation, and relationship renewal or, alternatively, to chronic resentment, bitterness, parting, and isolation. Since rituals are able to hold and express powerful contradictory feelings, such as love and hate, anger and connectedness, they enhance the possibility of relationship healing.

For Sondra and Alex Cutter, ritual provided a way to bury that past. The Cutters had spent seven of their twelve years of marriage in bitter arguments about a brief affair Alex had had just before their fifth anniversary. Sondra didn't want to leave her marriage, but she felt unable to let go of the past. Alex, in turn, had become extremely defensive about his behavior and was unable to genuinely show Sondra that he was sorry. In couple's therapy, Sondra and Alex were asked to bring two sets of symbols of the affair. The first set of symbols was to represent what the affair meant to each of them at the time it occurred. The second set was to symbolize what the affair had come to mean in their current life together. As a symbol of her feelings at the time of the affair, Sondra brought a torn wedding photograph to show that the affair meant a break in their vows. Sondra was surprised by Alex's symbol: an old picture of his father, who had had many affairs. "I thought this was just what husbands did," said Alex. "I thought this was what made you a man, but I found out quickly that this didn't work for me and for what I wanted my marriage to be. Then we couldn't get past it." Sondra had never heard Alex speak about the affair in this way. Her belief that the affair meant he didn't love her and that he loved another woman began to shift for the first time in seven years.

As a symbol of what the affair meant currently, Alex brought the wheel of a hamster cage, remarking, "We just go round and round and round and get nowhere." Sondra brought a bottle of bitters, and said, "This is what I've turned into!" After a long conversation engendered by their symbols, Sondra said quietly, "This is the first time in seven years that we've talked about this without yelling and screaming." When the therapist asked if they were ready to let go of the past, both agreed that they were. They decided to revisit a favorite spot from early in their relationship and to bury these symbols there. During the ceremony, Alex cried and for the first time asked Sondra to forgive him, which she readily did. They followed this with a celebration of their anniversary, which they had stopped celebrating seven years earlier.

This healing ritual was created as part of couple's therapy, but you don't need the help of a therapist to create rituals to effect healing. Common to all healing rituals is a dimension of time—time for holding on and time for letting go. Selecting symbols to express painful issues generally allows for a new kind of conversa-

tion to emerge. Taking some joint action together, such as symbolically burying the past, can impart a new possibility of collaboration. Creating a ritual together can help you to rediscover the playful parts of your relationship, such as the couple who "put an affair on ice," placing symbols in their deep freezer and agreeing that they could only fight about the affair after they had thawed these symbols out!

A Ceremony for Grieving

There is no life that is lived without loss. We all experience the death of people we love and care for deeply. When healing rituals have not occurred, or have been insufficient to complete the grief process, a person can remain stuck in the past or unable to move forward in meaningful ways. Even the unhealed losses of previous generations may emerge as debilitating symptoms in the present. When this happens, new rituals can be created to address the need for healing.

Joanie and Jeralynn Thompson were identical twins who had a close and loving

Rituals shape our relationships and give us a basis for a healthy society. Simply having a family meal together helps establish a stronger sense of self.
(UN photo/John Isaac)

relationship. They went away to the same college and planned to graduate together. During their junior year, however, Jeralynn developed leukemia. She died within the year. Before her death, Jeralynn talked with Joanie about how important it was that Joanie continue college and graduate. Joanie did go back to school after her sister's funeral, but she found it impossible to study. At the urging of friends, she took a year off in order to be with her family and begin to deal with the terrible loss of her sister. But a year turned into two years, two years into three. Finally, her family insisted that she go back to college. Joanie returned to school and finished all of her courses, but remained unable to do her senior thesis. She didn't graduate that June. "I don't know how I can graduate without Jeralynn," she told her mother. "It'll mean that she's really gone." Once her mother began to understand what was stopping Joanie from finishing, she talked with her daughter about how they might honor Jeralynn's life while still celebrating Joanie's entering adulthood with her college graduation. After developing a plan with her mother, Joanie finished her thesis in time to graduate the following December.

Joanie and her mother planned a special ceremony to be held two nights before graduation. They invited extended family and close friends, asking them to bring symbols of Jeralynn and to speak about her openly. During a very moving ceremony, many people spoke about what they thought Jeralynn would have wished for Joanie. One aunt made a video that showed places the two sisters had both loved, and after showing it told Joanie, "These places still belong to you." Joanie's father brought photographs of several pets the twins had raised, carefully pointing out the individual contributions each twin had made to these animals. Then, in a five-minute talk, he highlighted the strengths and gifts of each young woman and gave Joanie permission to be her own person. People grieved the loss of Jeralynn openly and then embraced Joanie for finishing school and going on in life.

Several months later, settled in a new job as a teacher, Joanie talked about this ceremony and her graduation: "They all helped me to graduate. If we hadn't had our memorial first, I know all I would have been wondering about on graduation day was what my family was feeling about Jeralynn's death. Instead, all of it was out in the open. We could be sad together and then we could be happy together on my graduation day. They call graduation a

Rituals connect us with our past, define our present life, and show us a path to our future.

commencement, an ending that's really a beginning, and that's what mine was. I miss my sister terribly—I'll always miss her—but my family and friends helped me take the next step in my life, and Jeralynn's spirit was right there with me."

Celebrating Recovery from Illness
Sometimes very important changes take place but remain unacknowledged. This may be because the changes are difficult to talk about, because they bring up the pain of how things used to be, or because no one had thought about how to mark the change. In our experience, recovery from medical or psychiatric illness is an aspect of change that is seldom marked by a ritual. Families, relationships, and the individual's own identity remain stuck with the illness label, and behavior among family members and friends remains as it was when the person was ill.

Adolescents who have recovered from cancer or adults who are now healthy after heart surgery often maintain an "illness identity," and others treat them accordingly. A ritual can declare in action that a person has moved from illness to health. Such a ritual might include a ceremony of throwing away no-longer-needed medicines or medical equipment, burning or burying symbols of a long hospital stay, or writing a document declaring new life and health.

After recovering from breast cancer,

Gerry Sims had a T-shirt made that read HEALTHY WOMAN! She wore this T-shirt to a family dinner and announced to everyone that they were to stop treating her as a patient, and that, in particular, she wanted people to argue with her as they had before she became ill. Then she handed out T-shirts to her husband and children that read HUSBAND OF A HEALTHY WOMAN, CHILD OF A HEALTHY WOMAN, and TEENAGER OF A HEALTHY WOMAN. Everyone put on his or her T-shirt and for the first time spontaneously began to talk about what they had been through together during Gerry's year-long illness. They cried out loud to each other. Following this, Gerry's teen-age daughter picked a fight with her, just as Gerry had hoped!

A Rite of Passage
Like many life-cycle passages, a child leaving home is an event that carries deeply mixed feelings, including a sense of joy and accomplishment, fear regarding what lies ahead, sadness over the loss of relationships in their present form, and curious anticipation about what life will look like next. This life-cycle passage of leaving home may be even more difficult when the leaving is unanticipated or when the child has grown up with a handicap. Creating a leaving-home ritual whose symbols and symbolic actions speak to the many contradictory issues can ease this passage for everyone in the family.

Jennifer Cooper-Smith was born with some severe disabilities that affected her capacity to read, write, and speak. During her childhood she took the handicap in stride despite the cruel teasing of other children and despite coming from a family where high academic achievement was the norm. Through it all she taught her family a lot about perseverance in the face of enormous struggles and about building on strengths rather than focusing on weaknesses.

When Jennifer reached nineteen, since her disabilities would preclude her going to college, it was clear that high school graduation was to be her rite of passage. The family wanted to create a ritual that would both honor all that she had accomplished and send her forth into the adult world with confidence.

Jennifer wanted a party at a Chinese restaurant with her favorite festive food. Her mother and stepfather invited people who were important to Jennifer—extended family who lived far away, friends who had supported her, special teachers and co-workers from her part-time job. The invitation included a secret request for special items—poems, letters, photos, stories, drawings, and so on—to help make a "becoming an adult woman" album for Jenni. During the weeks before the party, her mom worked secretly to construct the album, which began at the time Jennifer joined the family as an adopted infant and included sections that marked significant stages of her development. Although the handicaps had sometimes made it difficult for both Jennifer and those around her to notice her growth and changes, this album recorded them for all to see.

When Jennifer arrived at the party, the album was waiting for her as a special symbol of her development. What she still didn't know, though, was that the album was open-ended, and a new section, "Becoming an Adult Woman," was about to be added during the party. After dinner, when people were invited to give their presentations to Jennifer, a moving and unexpected ceremony unfolded. Person after person spoke about how they experienced Jenni and what she meant to them,

and they gave her their own special brand of advice about living.

Her grandma Dena gave Jenni a photograph of Dena's late husband—Jenni's grandfather—down on his knees proposing marriage. She spoke about enduring love and her wish that Jenni would have this in her life. Her aunt Meryle Sue read an original poem, "Portrait of Jenni," and then spoke through tears about what this day would have meant to Jenni's grandfather and how proud he would have been of her. Her cousin Stacey wrote a poem that captured who Jenni was to her and offered words about Jenni's future. Advice about men and what to beware of was given by Jenni's step-grandfather and received with much laughter. Photographs of strong women in history were presented.

Person after person spoke with grace and love and special stories about Jennifer's strengths. Her mother watched as Jennifer took in all that she was to people and the sometimes unknown impact that her own courage had had on family and friends. And then all who gathered wit-

nessed the emergence of Jennifer, the adult woman, as she rose from her seat and spoke unhaltingly and with no trace of her usual shyness, thanking each person in turn for what they had given her in life, and talking about the loss of her grandfather and her wish that he could be with her today. She ended with all that she anticipated next in her life.

The weeks and months following this ritual were perhaps even more remarkable than the ceremony itself. Her family experienced a changed Jennifer, a Jennifer who moved from adolescence to young womanhood—starting a full-time job, auditing a community college course, traveling by herself, making new friends, and relating on a previously unseen level.

As all of these examples illustrate, rituals ease our passage through life. They shape our relationships, help to heal our losses, express our deepest beliefs, and celebrate our existence. They announce change and create change. The power of rituals belongs to all of us.

Credits/ Acknowledgments

Cover design by Charles Vitelli

1. Varied Perspectives on the Family
Facing overview—United Nations photo by Jan Corash.

2. Exploring and Establishing Relationships
Facing overview—Digital Stock photo.

3. Finding a Balance
Facing overview—Photo courtesy of Sandra Nicholas.

4. Crises—Challenges and Opportunities
Facing overview—Photo by EPA Documerica. 151—Photo by Subjects & Predicates.

5. Families, Now and Into the Future
Facing overview—Photo courtesy of Leslie Holmes Lawlor.

ANNUAL EDITIONS ARTICLE REVIEW FORM

■ NAME: _____ DATE: _____

■ TITLE AND NUMBER OF ARTICLE: _____

■ BRIEFLY STATE THE MAIN IDEA OF THIS ARTICLE: _____

_____

_____

_____

_____

■ LIST THREE IMPORTANT FACTS THAT THE AUTHOR USES TO SUPPORT THE MAIN IDEA:

_____

_____

_____

_____

_____

■ WHAT INFORMATION OR IDEAS DISCUSSED IN THIS ARTICLE ARE ALSO DISCUSSED IN YOUR
TEXTBOOK OR OTHER READING YOU HAVE DONE? LIST THE TEXTBOOK CHAPTERS AND PAGE
NUMBERS:

_____

_____

_____

_____

_____

_____

■ LIST ANY EXAMPLES OF BIAS OR FAULTY REASONING THAT YOU FOUND IN THE ARTICLE:

_____

_____

_____

_____

■ LIST ANY NEW TERMS/CONCEPTS THAT WERE DISCUSSED IN THE ARTICLE AND WRITE A
SHORT DEFINITION:

_____

_____

_____

_____

*Your instructor may require you to use this Annual Editions Article Review Form in any number of ways:
for articles that are assigned, for extra credit, as a tool to assist in developing assigned papers, or simply
for your own reference. Even if it is not required, we encourage you to photocopy and use this page;
you'll find that reflecting on the articles will greatly enhance the information from your text.

ANNUAL EDITIONS: MARRIAGE AND FAMILY 95/96
Article Rating Form

Here is an opportunity for you to have direct input into the next revision of this volume. We would like you to rate each of the 48 articles listed below, using the following scale:

1. **Excellent: should definitely be retained**
2. **Above average: should probably be retained**
3. **Below average: should probably be deleted**
4. **Poor: should definitely be deleted**

Your ratings will play a vital part in the next revision. So please mail this prepaid form to us just as soon as you complete it.
Thanks for your help!

Annual Editions revisions depend on two major opinion sources: one is our Advisory Board, listed in the front of this volume, which works with us in scanning the thousands of articles published in the public press each year; the other is you—the person actually using the book. Please help us and the users of the next edition by completing the prepaid article rating form on this page and returning it to us. Thank you.

Rating	Article	Rating	Article
	1. The Mything Link		27. "I Don't Sweat the Small Stuff Anymore"
	2. The New Crusade for the Old Family		28. Siblings and Development
	3. The New Family: Investing in Human Capital		29. Places Everyone
	4. Children Are Alone		30. Endangered Family
	5. The Ache for Home		31. White Ghetto?
	6. Growing Up in Black and White		32. Helping Children Cope with Violence
	7. Sizing Up the Sexes		33. After He Hits Her
	8. Love: The Immutable Longing for Contact		34. Where Do We Go from Here? An Interview with Ann Jones
	9. What Makes Love Last?		35. Sexual Desire
	10. Choosing Mates—The American Way		36. Beyond Betrayal: Life after Infidelity
	11. The Mating Game		37. The Myth of the Miserable Working Woman
	12. Cahl Jooniah		38. Caregiving: Continuities and Discontinuities in Family Members' Relationships with Alzheimer's Patients
	13. Adapting to Adoption: Adopted Kids Generate Scientific Optimism and Clinical Caution		39. The Long Road Back: A Daughter Deals with Her Mother's Stroke
	14. The Family Circle		40. Family Values: The Bargain Breaks
	15. What's Happening to American Marriage?		41. Lessons from Step-Families
	16. Peer Marriage		42. The Myths and Misconceptions of the Stepmother Identity
	17. Receipts from a Marriage		43. Solace and Immortality: Bereaved Parents' Continuing Bond with Their Children
	18. Staying Power: Bridging the Gender Gap in the Confusing '90s		44. Sibling Survivors: How Losing a Brother or Sister to Cancer Can Recast a Child's Destiny
	19. But What Do You Mean?		45. Trace Your Family Tree: Charting Your Relatives' Medical History Can Save Your Life
	20. Saving Relationships: The Power of the Unpredictable		
	21. Vanishing Dreams of America's Young Families		46. Happy Families: Who Says They All Have to Be Alike?
	22. When Parents Disagree		47. Family Matters
	23. Ten Worst Discipline Mistakes Parents Make . . . and Alternatives		48. Rituals for Our Times
	24. Of Super Dads, and Absent Ones		
	25. Single Parents and Damaged Children: The Fruits of the Sexual Revolution		
	26. The Family Heart		

(Continued on next page)

ABOUT YOU

Name_____ Date_____

Are you a teacher? ☐ Or student? ☐

Your School Name _____

Department _____

Address _____

City _____ State _____ Zip _____

School Telephone # _____

YOUR COMMENTS ARE IMPORTANT TO US!

Please fill in the following information:

For which course did you use this book? _____

Did you use a text with this Annual Edition? ☐ yes ☐ no

The title of the text? _____

What are your general reactions to the Annual Editions concept?

Have you read any particular articles recently that you think should be included in the next edition?

Are there any articles you feel should be replaced in the next edition? Why?

Are there other areas that you feel would utilize an Annual Edition?

May we contact you for editorial input?

May we quote you from above?

ANNUAL EDITIONS: MARRIAGE AND FAMILY 95/96

BUSINESS REPLY MAIL

First Class   Permit No. 84   Guilford, CT

Postage will be paid by addressee

The Dushkin Publishing Group, Inc.
Sluice Dock
DPG **Guilford, Connecticut 06437**

No Postage
Necessary
if Mailed
in the
United States